PORTUGUESE
LITERATURE

Oxford University Press
London   Edinburgh   Glasgow   Copenhagen
New York   Toronto   Melbourne   Cape Town
Bombay   Calcutta   Madras   Shanghai
Humphrey Milford Publisher to the UNIVERSITY

PORTUGUESE LITERATURE

BY

AUBREY F. G. BELL

OXFORD
AT THE CLARENDON PRESS
1922

PRINTED IN ENGLAND.

TO THE TRUE PORTUGAL OF THE FUTURE

La letteratura, dalla quale sola potrebbe aver sodo principio la rigenerazione della nostra patria.

GIACOMO LEOPARDI.

THIS book was ready in October 1916, but the war delayed its publication. A few alterations have now been made in order to bring it up to date. It is needless to say how welcome will be further suggestions, especially for the bibliography. Only by such help can a book of this kind become useful, since its object is not to expatiate upon schools and theories but to give with as much accuracy as possible the main facts concerning the work and life of each individual author.

AUBREY F. G. BELL.

S. João do Estoril,
Portugal.
July 1921

CONTENTS

Introduction

PAGE

Portuguese literature in the nineteenth and twentieth centuries — D. Carolina Michaëlis de Vasconcellos — Dr. Theophilo Braga — Portuguese prose — Portuguese writers in Spanish and Latin — Character of the Portuguese — Special qualities of their literature — Splendid achievement — Lack of criticism and proportion but not of talent 13

I. 1185–1325.

[i. e. from the accession of Sancho I to the death of Dinis.]

§ 1. *The Cossantes* 22

Earliest poems — Their indigenous character and peculiar form — Their origin — Galicia in the Middle Ages — The pilgrimages — Dance-poems — Themes of the *cossantes* — Their relation to the poetry imported from Provence — Writers of *cossantes* : Nuno Fernandez Torneol — Joan Zorro — Pero Meogo — Pay Gomez Chariño — Airas Nunez' *pastorela* — The *cantigas de vilãos* — Songs of women — Persistence of the *cossante* to modern times — *Cossantes* and *cantigas de amor.*

§ 2. *The Cancioneiros* 37

Cancioneiro da Ajuda — *Cancioneiro da Vaticana* — *Cancioneiro Colocci-Brancuti* — Relations of Portugal with Spain, with France, with other countries — The Galician language — Its extension — Alfonso X — The *Cantigas de Santa Maria* — Poetry at the Court of Afonso III — Provençal poetry in Portugal — Monotony and technical skill of the Portuguese poets — *Cantigas de amigo* — Satiric poems — Joan de Guilhade — Pero Garcia de Burgos — Pero da Ponte — Joan Airas — Fernan Garcia Esgaravunha — Airas Nunez — King Dinis.

II. 1325–1521.

[i. e. from the accession of Sancho IV to the death of Manuel I.]

§ 1. *Early Prose* 58

Comparatively late development of prose — Spanish influence in the second period of Portuguese literature — King Dinis' translation

CONTENTS

of the *Cronica Geral* — *Regra de S. Bento* — Translations from the Bible — Sacred legends — Aesop's Fables — Chronicles — *Livros de Linhagens* — The Breton cycle — The Quest of the Holy Grail — *Livro de Josep ab Arimatia* — *Estorea de Vespeseano* — *Amadis de Gaula* — Problem of its origin — Early allusions — Vasco de Lobeira — Probable introduction of *Amadis* into the Peninsula through Portugal.

§ 2. **Epic and Later Galician Poets** . . . 72

Dearth of epics — Apocryphal poems — Afonso Giraldez — *Romances* — Their connexion with Spain — Survival of Galician lyrics — Macias — Juan Rodriguez de la Cámara — Fernam Casquicio — Vasco Perez de Camões — Gonçalo Rodriguez, Archdeacon of Toro — Garci Ferrandez de Gerena — Alfonso Alvarez de Villasandino — *Cantigas de escarnho* — The Constable D. Pedro.

§ 3. **The Chroniclers** 81

Fernam Lopez — *Cronica do Condestabre* — Zurara — Ruy de Pina — *Cronica do Infante Santo*. Other prose: King João I — King Duarte — Pedro, Duke of Coimbra — Letters of Lopo de Almeida — *Boosco Delleytoso* — *Corte Imperial* — *Flos Sanctorum* — *Vita Christi* — *Espelho de Christina* — *Espelho de Perfeiçam*.

§ 4. **The Cancioneiro Geral** 96

The break in Portuguese poetry — Its revival — Garcia de Resende — *Cancioneiro Geral* — Its shallow themes — More serious poems — Alvaro de Brito — The *Coudel Môr* — D. João de Meneses — D. João Manuel — Fernam da Silveira — Nuno Pereira — Diogo Brandam — Luis Anriquez — Rodriguez de Sá — The Conde de Vimioso — Duarte de Brito — Spanish influence.

III. The Sixteenth Century [1502-80].

§ 1. **Gil Vicente** 106

The sixteenth century — Gil Vicente's first play (1502) — The year and place of his birth — His life — Poet and goldsmith — His *autos* — Types sketched in his *farsas* — Devotional plays, comedies and tragicomedies — Origin of the drama in Portugal — Enzina's influence on Vicente — French influence — Other Spanish writers — Traditional satire — Number of Vicente's plays — Their character and that of their author — His patriotism and serious purpose — His achievement and influence in Spain and Portugal.

§ 2. **Lyric and Bucolic Poets** 132

Bernardim Ribeiro — Cristovam Falcão — Sá de Miranda — D. Manuel de Portugal — Diogo Bernardez — Frei Agostinho da Cruz

— Antonio Ferreira — Andrade Caminha — Sá de Meneses — Falcão de Resende — Jorge de Montemôr — Fernam Alvarez do Oriente — — Faria e Sousa — Francisco Rodriguez Lobo.

§ 3. *The Drama* 156
Gil Vicente's successors — Anonymous plays — Afonso Alvarez — Antonio Ribeiro Chiado — Balthasar Diaz — Anrique Lopez — Jorge Pinto — Antonio Prestes — Jeronimo Ribeiro Soarez — Simão Machado — Francisco Vaz — Gil Vicente de Almeida — Frei Antonio da Estrella — Classical drama : Sá de Miranda — Antonio Ferreira — Camões — Jorge Ferreira de Vasconcellos.

§ 4. *Luis de Camões* 174
Family of Camões — His birth and education — In North Africa — In India — Return to Portugal — Last years and death — Camões as epic and lyric poet — The *Lusiads* — Its critics — His greatness — Influence on the language — His *Parnasso* — Camões and Petrarca — Later epic poets — Corte Real — Pereira Brandão — Francisco de Andrade.

§ 5. *The Historians* 190
Historians of India — Alvaro Velho — Lopez de Castanheda — Barros — Couto — Corrêa — Bras de Albuquerque — Antonio Galvam — Special narratives — Gaspar Fructuoso — Frei Bernardo de Brito — Francisco de Andrade — Osorio — Bernardo da Cruz — Jeronimo de Mendoça — Miguel de Moura — Duarte Nunez de Leam — Damião de Goes — André de Resende — Manuel Severim de Faria — Faria e Sousa.

§ 6. *Quinhentista Prose* 217
Vivid prose — *Historia Tragico-Maritima*. Travels : Duarte Barbosa — Francisco Alvarez — Gaspar da Cruz — Frei João dos Santos — Tenreiro — Mestre Afonso — Frei Gaspar de S. Bernardino — Manuel Godinho — Fernam Mendez Pinto — Garcia da Orta — Pedro Nunez — Duarte Pacheco — D. João de Castro — Afonso de Albuquerque — Soropita — Rodriguez Silveira — Fernandez Ferreira — Francisco de Hollanda — Gonçalo Fernandez Trancoso — Francisco de Moraes.

§ 7. *Religious and Mystic Writers* . . . 235
Mysticism — Frei Heitor Pinto — Arraez — Frei Thomé de Jesus — Frei Luis de Sousa — Lucena — Preachers : Paiva de Andrade — Fernandez Galvão — Feo — Luz — Calvo — Veiga — Ceita — Lisboa — Almeida — Alvarez — Samuel Usque — Frei Antonio das Chagas — Manuel Bernardes.

CONTENTS

IV. 1580–1706.
[i.e. from the accession of Philip II of Spain to the death of Pedro II.]

The Seiscentistas 251

Culteranismo — D. Francisco Manuel de Mello — *Fenix Renascida* — Soror Violante do Ceo — Child Rolim de Moura — Veiga Tagarro — Galhegos — The epic : Pereira de Castro — Bras Garcia de Mascarenhas — Sá de Meneses — Sousa de Macedo — Mousinho de Quevedo — The Academies — Martim Afonso de Miranda — Leitão de Andrade — The Love Letters — *Arte de Furtar* — Ribeiro de Macedo — Freire de Andrade — Antonio Vieira.

V. 1706–1816.
[i.e. from the accession of João V to the death of Maria I.]

The Eighteenth Century 270

The Arcadias — Corrêa Garção — Quita — Diniz da Cruz e Silva — Filinto Elysio — Tolentino — The Marquesa de Alorna — Bocage — Xavier de Mattos — Gonzaga — Costa — Brazilian epics — Macedo — The Drama : Figueiredo — Antonio José da Silva — Nicolau Dias — The Academy of Sciences — Scholars and critics — Theodoro de Almeida — Letters.

VI. 1816–1910.
[i.e. from the accession of João VI to the fall of the Monarchy.]

§ 1. *The Romantic School* 287

Portugal at the opening of the century — Almeida Garrett — Herculano — Historical novelists — Rebello da Silva — Camillo Castello Branco — Poetry : Castilho — Mendes Leal — Soares de Passos — Gomes de Amorim — Xavier de Novaes — Thomaz Ribeiro — Bulhão Pato.

§ 2. *The Reaction and After* 304

The Coimbra School — History : Oliveira Martins — Pinheiro Chagas — Research and criticism — The Drama : Ennes — Azevedo — D. João da Camara — Marcellino Mesquita — Snr. Lopes de Mendonça — Snr. Julio Dantas — The Novel : Julio Diniz — Eça de Queiroz — J. L. Pinto — Snr. Luiz de Magalhães — Snr. Magalhães Lima — Bento Moreno — Snr. Silva Gayo — Snr. Malheiro Dias — Abel Botelho — Ramalho Ortigão — Snr. Teixeira Gomes — Snr. Antero de Figueiredo — D. Maria Amalia Vaz de Carvalho — The Conde de Sabugosa — The *Conto* : Machado — The Conde

CONTENTS

de Ficalho — Fialho de Almeida — D. João da Camara — Trindade Coelho — Snr. Julio Brandão — Poetry : Quental — João de Deus — Guilherme Braga — A. da Conceição — G. de Azevedo — João Penha — Cesario Verde — Gonçalves Crespo — Snr. Guerra Junqueiro — Gomes Leal — Snr. Teixeira de Pascoaes — Antonio Nobre — Colonel Christovam Ayres — Joaquim de Araujo — Antonio Feijó — Snr. Eugenio de Castro — Snr. Corrêa de Oliveira — Snr. Afonso Lopes Vieira.

APPENDIX

§ 1. *Literature of the People* . . . 338

Unwritten literature — Traditional themes — *Flores e Branca Flor* — Bandarra — The Holy Cobbler — Primaeval elements — Connexion of song and dance — Modern *cantigas* — Links with ancient poetry — Cradle-songs — *Alvoradas* — *Fados* — Proverbs — Folktales.

§ 2. *The Galician Revival* 347

Xogos Froraes of 1861 — Añon — Posada — Camino — Rosalía de Castro — Lamas Carvajal — Sr. Bárcia Caballero — Losada — Eduardo Pondal — Curros Enriquez — Martelo Pauman — Pereira — Garcia Ferreiro — Núñez González — Nun de Allariz — Sr. Rodríguez González — Sr. López Abente — Sr. Noriega Varela — Sr. Cabanillas — Sr. Rey Soto — *Cancionero Popular Gallego* — Prose — Pérez Placer — D. Francisca Herrera.

INTRODUCTION

PORTUGUESE literature may be said to belong largely to the nineteenth and twentieth centuries. Europe can boast of no fresher and more charming early lyrics than those which slept forgotten [1] in the Vatican Library until the late Professor Ernesto Monaci published *Il Canzoniere Portoghese* in 1875. And, to take a few more instances out of many, the poems of King Alfonso X, of extraordinary interest alike to historian and literary critic, first appeared in 1889; the plays of Gil Vicente were almost unknown before the Hamburg (1834) edition, based on the Göttingen copy of that of 1562; Sá de Miranda only received a definitive edition in 1885; the *Cancioneiro Geral* became accessible in the middle of the nineteenth century, when the three volumes of the Stuttgart edition were published; the exquisite verses [1] of Sá de Meneses, which haunted Portuguese poetry for a century,[2] then sank into oblivion till they were discovered by Dr. Sousa Viterbo in the Torre do Tombo.[3] The abundant literature of popular *quadras, fados, romances, contos* has only begun to be collected in the last fifty years.

In prose, the most important *Leal Conselheiro* [4] of King Duarte

[1] A few Portuguese sixteenth-century writers in touch with Italy may have known of their existence. But they were neglected as *rusticas musas*. The references to King Dinis as a poet by Antonio Ferreira and once in the *Cancioneiro Geral* do not of course imply that his poems were known and read. André de Resende seems to have been more interested in tracing an ancestor, Vasco Martinez de Resende, than in the poets among whom this ancestor figured (see C. Michaëlis de Vasconcellos, *Randglosse* XV in *Ztft. für rom. Phil.*, xxv. 683).

[2] *Illud vero poemation quod vulgo circumfertur de Lessa . . . nunc vero cum plurimum illud appetant . . .* (Soares, *Theatrum*). Cf. F. Rodriguez Lobo, *Primavera*, ed. 1722, pp. 240, 356, 469; Eloy de Sá de Sottomayor, *Ribeiras do Mondego*, f. 27 v., 28 v., 120–1, 186; *Canc. Geral* of A. F. Barata (1836–1910), p. 235; Jeronimo Bahia, *Ao Mondego* (*Fenix Ren.*, ii. 377–9). Cf. Brito, *Mon. Lus.* I. ii. 2 : *O rio Leça celebre pelas rimas de nosso famoso poeta*.

[3] The documents of the Torre do Tombo are now in the able keeping of Dr. Pedro de Azevedo and Snr. Antonio Baião.

[4] Even its title was inaccurately given, as *O Fiel Conselheiro* (Bernardo de Brito), *De Fideli Consiliario* (N. Antonio, *Bib. Vetus*, ii. 241), *Del Buen Consejero* (Faria e Sousa); correctly by Duarte Nunez de Leam. A *Conselheiro Fiel* by Frei Manuel Guilherme (1658–1734) appeared in 1727.

was rediscovered in the Paris Bibliothèque Nationale and first printed in 1842, and Zurara's *Cronica da Guiné*, lost even in the days of Damião de Goes,[1] similarly in 1841; Corrêa's *Lendas da India* remained in manuscript till 1858; so notable a book as King João I's *Livro da Montaria* appears only in the twentieth century, in an edition by Dr. Esteves Pereira, and the first trustworthy text of a part of Fernam Lopez was published by Snr. Braamcamp Freire in 1915; D. Francisco Manuel de Mello, who at the end of his second *Epanaphora* wrote ' Se por ventura tambem despois de meus dias acontece que algum vindouro honre ao meu nome quanto eu procuro eternizar e engrandecer o dos passados ', had to wait two and a half centuries before this debt was paid by Mr. Edgar Prestage.[2] Even now no really complete history of Portuguese literature exists, but the first systematic work on the subject was written by Friedrich Bouterwek in 1804. Other histories have since appeared, and during the last half-century the ceaseless, ingenious, and enthusiastic studies of Dr. Theophilo Braga have sifted Portuguese literature, chiefly the poetry, in all directions, and a flood of light has been thrown on it by the works of D. Carolina Michaëlis de Vasconcellos. Perhaps, therefore, one may be forgiven for having been tempted to render some account of this ' new ' literature which continues to be so strangely neglected in England and other countries.[3] Yet a quarter of a century hence would perhaps offer better conditions, and a summary written at the present time cannot hope to be complete or definitive. Every year new studies and editions appear, new researches and alluring theories and discoveries are made. The Lisbon Academy of Sciences during its long and honourable

---

[1] *De que não ha noticia* (Goes, *Cronica de D. João*, cap. 6).

[2] *D. Francisco Manuel de Mello. Esboço biographico.* Coimbra, 1914, an admirably clear and very important work, in which much light from new documents is thrown on Mello's life.

[3] It would be interesting to know how many English-speaking persons have ever heard of the great men and writers that were King Dinis, Fernam Lopez, Bernardim Ribeiro, Diogo Bernardez, Heitor Pinto, Frei Thomé de Jesus, Ferreira de Vasconcellos, Frei Luis de Sousa, Antonio Vieira, Manuel Bernardes. Their neglect has been largely due to the absence of good or easily available texts; there is still nothing to correspond to the Spanish *Biblioteca de Autores Españoles* or the many more modern Spanish collections. But is not even Camões still ' an abused stranger ', as Mickle called him in 1776?

INTRODUCTION

history[1] has rarely if ever rendered greater services—' essential services' as Southey called them in 1803—to Portuguese literature. A short history of that literature must, apart from unavoidable errors and omissions, do less than justice to many writers. In appropriating the words of Damião de Goes, 'Haud ignari plurima esse a nobis omissa quibus Hispania ornatur et celebrari possit,' one may hope that MR. EDGAR PRESTAGE, who has studied Portuguese literature for a quarter of a century,[2] and whose ever-ready help and advice are here gratefully acknowledged, will eventually write a mellower history in several volumes and give their full due both to the classics and to contemporary authors and critics.

No one can study Portuguese literature without becoming deeply indebted to D. CAROLINA WILHELMA MICHAËLIS DE VASCONCELLOS. Her concise history, contributed to Groeber's *Grundriss* (1894), necessarily forms the basis of subsequent studies, but indeed her work is as vast as it is scholarly and accurate, and the student finds himself constantly relying on her guidance. Even if he occasionally disagrees, he cannot fail to give her point of view the deepest attention and respect. Born in 1851, the daughter of Professor Gustav Michaëlis, she has lived in Portugal during the last forty years and is the wife of the celebrated art critic, Dr. Joaquim de Vasconcellos (born in 1849). Her edition of the *Cancioneiro da Ajuda* (1904) is a masterpiece of historical reconstruction and literary criticism, and her influence on Portuguese literature generally is as wide as her encouragement and assistance of younger scholars are generous.[3] *Femina*, as was said of the Princess Maria, *undequaque spectatissima et doctissima*.

Most of the works of DR. THEOPHILO BRAGA are of too provisional a nature to be of permanent value, but a summary, *Edade Medieval* (1909), *Renascença* (1914), *Os Seiscentistas* (1916), *Os*

---

[1] See F. de Figueiredo, *O que é a Academia das Sciencias de Lisboa* (1779-1915) in *Revista da Historia*, vol. iv, 1915.
[2] His valuable study on Zurara, which has not been superseded by any later work on the subject, is dated 1896.
[3] She has, indeed, laid the Portuguese people under an obligation which it will not easily redeem. That no formal recognition has been bestowed in England on her work (as in another field on that of Dr. José Leite de Vasconcellos, of Snr. Braamcamp Freire, and of the late Dr. Francisco Adolpho Coelho) is a striking example of our insularity.

Arcades (1918), gives his latest views. The best detailed criticism of the literature of the nineteenth century is that of DR. FIDELINO DE FIGUEIREDO, Member of the Academy of Sciences and Editor of the *Revista de Historia* : *Historia da Litteratura Romantica Portuguesa* (1913) and *Historia da Litteratura Realista* (1914).

The only completely methodical history of Portuguese literature in existence is the brief manual by the learned ex-Rector of Coimbra University, DR. JOAQUIM MENDES DOS REMEDIOS : *História da Literatura Portuguêsa* (5th ed., Coimbra, 1921), since it contains that rarity in Portuguese literature : an index.[1] Dr. Figueiredo published a short essay in its general bibliography in 1914 (*Bibliographia portuguesa de critica litteraria*), largely increased in a new (1920) edition, but otherwise little has been done in this respect (apart from a few special authors). The bibliography attached to the present book[2] follows—*longo intervallo* —the lines of PROFESSOR JAMES FITZMAURICE-KELLY's *Bibliographie de l'Histoire de la Littérature Espagnole* (Paris, 1913). After its proved excellence it would, indeed, have been folly to adopt any other method.

It has been thought advisable to add a list of works on popular poetry, folk-lore, &c. (since in no country are the popular and the written literatures more intimately connected), and of those concerning the Portuguese language. Unless energetic and persistent measures are taken to protect this language it will be hopeless to look for a great Portuguese literature in the future. Yet with the gradually developing prosperity of Portugal and her colonies such expectations are not unfounded. A new poet may arise indigenous as Gil Vicente and technically proficient as Camões. And in prose, if it is not allowed to sink into a mere verbiage of gallicisms, great writers may place Portuguese on a level with and indeed above the other Romance languages. The possibilities are so vast, the quarry ready to their hand so rich— the works of Manuel Bernardes, Antonio Vieira, Jorge Ferreira de Vasconcellos, Luis de Sousa, João de Lucena, Heitor Pinto, Arraez ; an immense mass of sermons (*milhões de sermonarios*),

---

[1] It does not include living writers. Its dates must be received with caution.
[2] It has been found necessary to publish the bibliography separately.

INTRODUCTION

most of them in excellent Portuguese, as those of Ceita, Veiga, Feo, Luz, in which, as in a large number of political tracts, notably those of Macedo, intense conviction has given a glow and concision to the language; old *constituições, ordenações*, and *foros*[1]; technical treatises,[2] folk-lore, popular phrases,[3] proverbs. But unless a scholarly use of Portuguese be more generally imposed no masterpieces will be produced. The same holds good of Brazilian literature, which, although, or perhaps because, it has provided material for a history in two portly volumes (Sylvio Romero, *Historia da Litteratura Brazileira*, 2nd ed., 1902-3), is here, with few exceptions, omitted.

A supplementary chapter on modern Galician literature has been added, for although the language from which Portuguese parted only after the fourteenth century is now quite independent,[4] modern Galician is not more different from modern Portuguese than is the language of the *Cancioneiros* with which Portuguese literature opens. The Portuguese have always shown a strong aptitude for acquiring foreign languages, and the individual's gain has been the literature's loss. Jorge de Montemôr, who

con su Diana
Enriqueció la lengua castellana,

was not by any means the only Portuguese who wrote exclusively in Spanish, and others chose Latin. The reason usually given in either case was that Portuguese was less widely read.[5] It was

---

[1] e. g. King Sancho II's *Foros da Guarda*, printed, from a 1305 manuscript, in vol. v (1824) of the *Collecção de Ineditos*, or the *Foros de Santarem* (1385). The *Livro Vermelho do Senhor D. Affonso V*, printed in the *Collecção de Livros Ineditos*, vol. iii (1793), is also full of interest.

[2] e. g. the fourteenth-century *Livro de Cetreria* of PERO MENINO; MESTRE GIRALDO'S *Tratado das Enfermidades das Aves de Caça* and *Livro d'Alveitaria*; the *Arte da Cavallaria de gineta e estardiota* (1678) by ANTONIO GALVAM DE ANDRADE (1613?-89); *Correcçam de abusos introduzidos contra o verdadeiro methodo da medicina* (2 pts., 1668-80) by the Carmelite FREI MANUEL DE AZEVEDO (†1672); *Agricultura das Vinhas* (1711) by Vicente Alarte (i. e. SILVESTRE GOMEZ DE MORAES (1643-1723)); *Compendio de Botanica* (2 vols., 1788) by FELIX DE AVELLAR BROTERO (1744-1828).

[3] Many will be found in *Portugalia* and the *Revista Lusitana*.

[4] In the beginning of the sixteenth century Galician is already despised in Portugal, and became more so as Portuguese grew more latinized. Cf. Gil Vicente, ii. 509: *Pera que he falar galego Senão craro e despachado?*; Chiado, *Auto das Regateiras*: *Eu não te falo galego.*

[5] *Por ser lingua mais jêral* (Vera, *Lovvores*), *mais universal* (Sousa de

18   INTRODUCTION

a short-sighted view, for the more works of importance that were written in Portuguese the larger would naturally become the number of those who read them. While Portuguese literature may be taken to be the literature written in the Portuguese language, in a sense it must also include the Latin and Spanish works of Portuguese authors. Of the former, one collection alone, the *Corpus Illustrium Poetarum Lusitanorum qui latine scripserunt* (Lisbonae, 1745), consists of eight volumes, and Domingo Garcia Peres' *Catálogo Razonado* (Madrid, 1890) contains over 600 names of Portuguese authors who wrote in Spanish.

Portuguese names present a difficulty, for often they are as lengthy as that which was the pride of Dona Iria in Ennes' *O Saltimbanco*. The course here adopted is to relegate the full name to the index and to print in the text only the form by which the writer is generally known.[1]

The Portuguese, a proud and passionate people with a certain love of magnificence and adventure, an Athenian receptivity,[2] an

Macedo). *Os grandes ingenios não se contentão de ter por espera de seu applauso a hũa só parte do mundo* (D. Francisco de Portugal). Cf. Osorio, writing in Latin, *De Rebus*, p. 4, and Pedro Nunez' reason for translating his *Libro de Algebra* into Spanish : *he mais comum*, and the advice given to Luis Marinho de Azevedo to write in Spanish or Latin as *mais geral* (*Primeira Parte da Fundação, Antiguidades e Grandezas da mvi insigne cidade de Lisboa. Prologo*). Faria e Sousa condemns the practice of writing Spanish *glosas* to a Portuguese *mote*, and declares that he himself wrote in Spanish *con gran pesar mio*. Frei Antonio da Purificaçam considered that had he written his *Cronica* in Latin or Spanish *fora digno de grande nota*, in this following Frei Bernardo de Brito, who indignantly rejected the exhortation to use Latin or Spanish (*Mon. Lus.* i, *Prologo*), although he wrote under Spanish rule. Bernarda Ferreira de Lacerda wrote in Spanish *por ser idioma claro y casi comun*. Simão Machado explains why he wrote *Alfea* in Spanish as follows (f. 72 v.) : *Vendo quam mal aceitais As obras dos naturais Fiz esta em lingoa estrangeira Por ver se desta maneira Como a eles nos tratais*.

[1] Portuguese spelling is a vexed and vexing question, complicated by the positive dislike of the Portuguese for uniformity (the same word may be found spelt in two ways on the same page both in modern and ancient books ; the same person will spell his name Manoel and Manuel). In proper names their owners' spelling has been retained, although no one now writes Prince Henry the Navigator's name as he wrote it : Anrique. Thus Mello (modern Melo) ; Nunez (13th c.), Nunes (19th c.) ; Bernardez (16th c.), Bernardes (17th–18th c.). The late Dr. Gonçalves Vianna himself adopted the form Gonçalvez Viana. In quoting ancient Portuguese texts the only alteration made has been occasionally to replace *y* and *u* by *i* and *v*.

[2] *Este desejo* (*de sempre ver e ouvir cousas nouas*) *he moor que nas outras nações na gente Lusitana*. André de Burgos, *Ao prudente leitor* (*Relaçam*, Evora, 1557). It is displayed in their fondness for foreign customs, for the Spanish language, for India to the neglect of Portugal, the description of

INTRODUCTION

extensive sea-board and vague land-frontiers, naturally came under foreign influences. Many and various causes made their country cosmopolitan from the beginning. It is customary to divide Portuguese literature into the Provençal (13th c.), Spanish (14th and 15th c.), Italian (16th c.), Spanish and Italian (17th c.), French and English (18th c.), French and German (19th c.) Schools. The question may therefore be asked, especially by those who confuse influence with imitation, as though it precluded originality: What has Portuguese literature of its own? In the first place, the Celtic satire and mystic lyrism of the Galicians is developed and always present in Portuguese literature. Secondly, the genius for story-telling, displayed by Fernam Lopez, grew by reason of the great Portuguese discoveries in Africa and Asia to an epic grandeur both in verse and prose. Thirdly, the absence of great cities, the pleasant climate, and fertile soil produced a peculiarly realistic and natural bucolic poetry. And in prose, besides masterpieces of history and travel—a rich and fascinating literature of the East and of the sea—a fervent religious faith, as in Spain, with a more constant mysticism than in Spain, led to very high achievement. Had one to choose between the loss of the works of Homer, or Dante, or Shakespeare, and that of the whole of Portuguese literature, the whole of Portuguese literature must go, but that is not to say that the loss would not be very grievous. Indeed, those who despise Portuguese literature despise it in ignorance,[1] affecting to believe, with Edgar Quinet, that it has but one poet and a single book; those who are acquainted with it—with the early lyrics, with the quaintly alluring eclogues of Ribeiro and Sá de Miranda, with the works of Fernam Lopez, described by Robert Southey as 'the best chronicler of any age or nation', *naïf, exact, touchant et philosophe*[2]; of Gil Vicente, almost as far above his contemporary Juan del Enzina as Shakespeare is above Vicente; of Bernardim Ribeiro, whose *Menina e moça* is the earliest and best of those pastoral romances which led Don Quixote to contemplate a quieter

---

epic deeds rather than of ordinary life, high-flown language as opposed to the common speech (*da praça*), &c. Antonio Prestes calls the Portuguese *estranho no natural, natural no estranjeiro*.

[1] In Spain it has had fervent admirers, notably Gracián. More recently Juan Valera spoke of it as *riquísima*, and Menéndez y Pelayo explored this wealth. [2] F. Denis, *Résumé* (1826), p. xx.

sequel to his first adventures; of Camões, 'not only the greatest lyric poet of his country, but one of the greatest lyric poets of all time'[1]; with Fernam Mendez Pinto's travels, 'as diverting a book of the kind as ever I read'[2]; or Corrêa's *Lendas*, Frei Thomé de Jesus' *Trabalhos*, or the incomparable prose of Manuel Bernardes—know that, extraordinary as were Portugal's achievements in discovery and conquest, her literature is not unworthy of those achievements. Unhappily the Portuguese, with a notorious carelessness,[3] have in the past set the example of neglecting their literature, and even to-day scarcely seem to realize their great possessions and still greater possibilities in the realm of prose.[4] The excessive number of writers, the excessive production of each individual writer, and the *desleixo* by which innumerable books and manuscripts of exceptional interest have perished, are all traceable to the same source: the lack of criticism. A nation of poets, essentially lyrical,[5] with no dramatic genius but capable of writing charmingly and naturally without apparent effort, needed and needs a severely classical education and stern critics, to remind them that an epic is not rhymed history nor blank verse mangled prose, that in bucolic poetry the half is greater than the whole, and to bid them abandon abstractions for the

---

[1] Wilhelm Storck, *Luis de Camoens' Sämmtliche Werke*, Bd. I (1880).
[2] Dorothy Osborne to Sir William Temple.
[3] For a good instance of this *descuido portugues* see Manuel Pereira de Novaes, *Anacrisis Historial* (a history of the city of Oporto in Spanish), vol. i (1912), *Preámbulo*, p. xvii. It is lamented by the editors of the *Cancioneiro Geral* (1516) and *Fenix Renascida* (1716).
[4] Portuguese literature begins for most Portuguese with Camões and Barros, and its most charming and original part thus escapes them. Cf. F. Dias Gomes, *Obras Poeticas* (1799), p. 143: Camões 'without whom there would have been no Portuguese poetry'; and ibid., p. 310: Barros 'prepared the beautiful style for our epic writers'. Faria e Sousa's homely phrase as to the effect of Camões on preceding poets (*echólos todos a rodar*) was unfortunately true.
[5] Much of their finest prose is of lyrical character, personal, fervent, mystic. As to philosophy proper the greatest if not the only Portuguese philosopher, Spinoza, a Portuguese Jew, left Portugal as a child, and Francisco Sanchez (c. 1550–c. 1620), although probably born at Braga, not at *a soberba* Tuy, lived in France and wrote in Latin. He tells us that he in 1574 finished his celebrated treatise *Quod nihil scitur*, published at Lyon in 1581, in which, at a time of great intolerance, he revived and gave acute and curious expression to the old theory that nothing can be known. To modern philosophy Dr. Leonardo Coimbra (born in 1883) has contributed a notable but somewhat abstruse work entitled *O Criacionismo* (Porto, 1912).

concrete and particular and crystallize the vague flow of their talent. But in Portugal, outside the circle of writers themselves, a reading public has hitherto hardly existed, and in the close atmosphere resulting the sense of proportion was inevitably lost, even as a stone and a feather will fall with equal speed in a vacuum. The criticism has been mainly personal,[1] contesting the originality or truthfulness of a writer, without considering the literary merits of his work. To deprecate such criticism became a commonplace of the preface, while numerous passages in writers of the sixteenth century show that they feared their countrymen's scepticism, expressed in the proverb *De longas vias mui longas mentiras*, which occurs as early as the thirteenth century.[2] The fear of slovenly or prolix composition was not present in the same degree. But these are defects that may be remedied partly by individual critics, partly by the increasing number of readers. Meanwhile this little book may perhaps serve to corroborate the poet Falcão de Resende's words:

Engenhos nascem bons na Lusitania
E ha copia delles.[3]

[1] Or political, or anticlerical, or anything except literary. The critics seem to have forgotten that an *auto-da-fé* does not necessarily make its victim a good poet, and that even a priest may have literary talent. A few literary critics, as Dias in the eighteenth, Guilherme Moniz Barreto in the nineteenth century, are only exceptions to the rule. It has been the weakness of Portuguese criticism, more lenient than the gods and booksellers of ancient Rome, to suffer *mediocres* gladly.

[2] *C. da Vat.* 979 (cf. Jorge Ferreira, *Eufrosina*, v. 5: *como dizia o Galego: de longas vias longas mentiras*).

[3] *Poesias, Sat.* 2. The remark of Garrett still holds good: *Em Portugal ha mais talento e menos cultivação que em paiz nenhum da Europa.*

I
1185–1325

§ 1
The Cossantes

UNDER the Moorish dominion we know that poetry was widely cultivated in the Iberian Peninsula, by high and low. At Silves in Algarve ' almost every peasant could improvise '.[1] But the early Galician-Portuguese poetry has no relation with that of the Moors, despite certain characteristics which may seem to point to an Oriental origin. The indigenous poems of Galicia and Portugal, of which thirteenth-century examples have survived, are so remarkable, so unlike those of any other country, that they deserve to be studied apart from the Provençal imitations by the side of which they developed. Half buried in the *Cancioneiros*, themselves only recently discovered, these exquisite and in some ways astonishingly modern lyrics are even now not very widely known and escape the attention of many who go far afield in search of true poetry. The earliest poem dated (1189) by D. Carolina Michaëlis de Vasconcellos, in which Pay Soarez de Taveiroos, a nobleman of Galicia or North Portugal, addresses Maria Paez Ribeira, the lovely mistress of King Sancho I, *mia sennor branca e vermelha*, does not belong to these lyrics[2]; but the second earliest (1199), attributed to King SANCHO I (1185–1211) himself, is one of them (C. C. B. 348). This unique form of lyric requires a distinctive name, and if we adopt that used by the Marqués de Santillana's father, Diego Furtado de Mendoza († 1404), we shall have a word well suited to convey an idea of their striking character.[3] His Spanish poem written in parallel

---

[1] Kazwînî ap. Reinhart Dozy, *Spanish Islam*, trans. F. G. Stokes, London, 1913, p. 663.
[2] C. A. 38. It is a *cantiga de meestria*, of two verses, each of eight octosyllabic lines (*abbaccde bfbaccde*).
[3] Although neither English nor Portuguese, it is a name for these poems, of lines *pariter plangentes*, less clumsy than *parallelistic songs* adopted by

distichs, *A aquel arbol*, is called a *cossante*.[1] In an age when all that seemed most Spanish, the *Poema del Cid*, for instance, or the *Libro de Buen Amor*, has been proved to derive in part from French sources, it is peculiarly pleasant to find a whole series of early poems which have their roots firmly planted in the soil of the Peninsula. The indigenous character of the *cossantes* is now well established, thanks chiefly to the skilful and untiring researches of D. Carolina Michaëlis de Vasconcellos.[2] They are wild but deliciously scented single flowers which now reappear in all their freshness as though they had not lain pressed and dead for centuries in the library of the Vatican. One of the earliest is quoted by Airas Nunez (C. V. 454) and completed in *Grundriss*, p. 150 :

1. Solo ramo verde frolido
   Vodas fazen a meu amigo,
   E choran olhos d'amor.

2. Solo verde frolido ramo [3]
   Vodas fazen a meu amado,
   E choran olhos d'amor.

What first strikes one in this is its Oriental immobility. The second distich adds nothing to the sense of the first, merely intensifying it by repetition. Neither the poetry of the *trouvères* of the North of France nor that of the Provençal *troubadours* presents any parallel. The scanty Basque literature contains

Professor Henry R. Lang (who also uses the words *serranas*—but see C. D. L., p. cxxxviii, note 2 ; Dr. Theophilo Braga had called them *serranilhas*—and *Verkettungslieder*), *Parallelstrophenlieder* (D. Carolina Michaëlis de Vasconcellos), *cantigas parallelisticas* (D. Carolina Michaëlis de Vasconcellos and Snr. J. J. Nunes), *chansons à répétitions* (M. Alfred Jeanroy). *Cantos dualisticos, cantos de danza prima*, and *bailadas encadeadas* have also been proposed.

[1] Perhaps = rhyme (*consoante*), but more probably it is derived from *cosso*, an enclosed place, which would be used for dancing : cf. Cristobal de Castillejo, *Madre, un caballero Que estaba en este cosso* (*bailia*). In the *Relacion de los fechos del mui magnifico é mas virtuoso señor el señor Don Miguel Lucas [de Iranzo] mui digno Condestable de Castilla*, p. 446 (A.D. 1470), occurs the following passage : *Y despues de danzar cantaron un gran rato de cosante* (*Memorial Histórico Español*, tom. viii, Madrid, 1855). Rodrigo Cota, in the *Diálogo entre el Amor y un Viejo*, has *danças y corsantes*, and Antón de Montoro (el Ropero) asks *un portugues que vido vestido de muchos colores* if he is a *cantador de corsante* (v.l. *cosante*) (*Canc. General*, ed. Bibliófi. Esp., ii. 270, no. 1018).

[2] In the *Grundriss* (1894), *Randglossen* (1896-1905), and especially vol. ii of the *Cancioneiro da Ajuda* (1904).

[3] Or *Solo ramo verde granado* : the green branch in (red) flower.

nothing in this kind. But it is unnecessary to go for a parallel to China.[1] None more remarkable will be found than those contained in the books of that religion which came from the East and imposed its forms if not its spirit on the pagans of the Peninsula. Verses 8, 9 of Psalm 118 are very nearly a *cossante* but have no refrain. The resemblance in Psalm 136, verses 17, 18, is still more marked :

> To him which smote great kings,
> For his mercy endureth for ever,
> And slew famous kings,
> For his mercy endureth for ever.

The relations between Church and people were very close if not always very friendly. The peasants maintained their ancient customs, and their pagan jollity kept overflowing into the churches to the scandal of the authorities. Innumerable ordinances later sought to check their delight in witchcraft and mummeries, feasts and funerals (the delight in the latter is still evident in Galicia as in Ireland and Wales). Men slept, ate, drank, danced, sang profane songs, and acted plays and parodies in the churches and pilgrimage shrines. The Church strove to turn their midsummer and May-day celebrations into Christian festivals, but the change was rather nominal than real. But if the priests and bishops remained spiritually, like modern politicians, shepherds without sheep, the religious services, the hymns,[2] the processions evidently affected the people. Especially was this the case in Galicia, since the great saint Santiago, who farther south (as later in India) rode into battle on a snow-white

---

[1] Translations of Chinese poems resembling the *cossantes* are given by Dr. Theophilo Braga, C. V. B., *Introd.*, p. ci, and Professor H. R. Lang, C. D. L., *Introd.*, p. cxlii. A Provençal poem with resemblance to a *cossante* is printed in Bartsch, p. 62 : *Li tensz est bels, les vinnesz sont flories.*

[2] Any one who has heard peasants at a *Stabat* singing the hymn

> Stabat Mater dolorosa
> *Jussa crussa larimosa*
> *Du penebat* Filius

realizes that the words for them have no meaning, but that they will long remember tune and rhythm. Compare, for the form, the Latin hymn to the Virgin by the Breton poet Adam de Saint Victor (†1177) :

> Salve Verbi sacra parens,
> Flos de spinis spinis carens,
> Flos spineti gloria.

steed before the Christians, gave a more peaceful prosperity to the North-west. Pilgrims from all countries in the Middle Ages came to worship at his shrine at Santiago de Compostela. They came a motley company singing on the road,[1] criminals taking this opportunity to escape from justice, tradesmen and players, jugglers and poets making a livelihood out of the gathering throngs, as well as devout pilgrims who had 'left alle gamys' for their soul's good, *des pèlerins qui vont chantant et des jongleurs*. Thus the eyes of the whole province of Galicia as the eyes of Europe were directed towards the Church of Santiago in Jakobsland. The inhabitants of Galicia would naturally view their heaven-sent celebrity with pride and rejoice in the material gain. They would watch with eager interest the pilgrims passing along the *camino francés* or from the coast to Santiago, and would themselves flock to see and swell the crowds at the religious services. When we remember the frequent parodies of religious services in the Middle Ages and that the Galicians did not lag behind others in the art of mimicry,[2] we can well imagine that the Latin hymns sung in church or procession might easily form the germ of the profane *cossante*. A further characteristic of the *cossante* is that the *i*-sound of the first distich is followed by an *a*-sound in the second (*ricercando ora il grave, ora l'acuto*) and this too may be traced to a religious source, two answering choirs of singers, treble and bass.[3] It is clear at least that these alter-

---

[1] Cf. Luis José Velázquez, *Orígenes de la Poesía Castellana* (Málaga, 1754) ap. C. M. (1889), i. 168 : *las cantares y canciones devotas de los peregrinos que iban en romería a visitar la iglesia de Compostela mantuvieron en Galicia el gusto de la poesía en tiempos bárbaros*. A Latin hymn composed in the twelfth century by Aimeric Picaud is printed in *Recuerdos de un Viaje á Santiago de Galicia* por el P. Fidel Fita y D. Aureliano Fernández-Guerra (Madrid, 1880), p. 45 : *Jacobi Gallecia Opem rogat piam Glebe cujus gloria Dat insignem viam Ut precum frequentia Cantet melodiam. Herru Sanctiagu! Grot Sanctiagu! Eultreja esuseja! Deus, adjuva nos!*

[2] Cf. Simão de Vasconcellos, *Cronica da Companhia de Jesu do Estado do Brazil* (1549-62), 2nd ed. (1865), Bk. I, § 22 : *chegamos a huma praça* [in Santiago de Compostela] *onde vimos hum ajuntamento de mulheres Gallegas com grande risada e galhofa ; e querendo o irmão meu companheiro pedir-lhe esmola vio que estavão todas ouvindo a huma que feita pregadora arremedava, como por zombaria, o sermão que eu tinha pregado.*

[3] One has but to watch a Rogation procession passing through the fields in the Basque country (which until recently preserved customs of immemorial eld and still calls the Feast of Corpus Christi, introduced by Pope Urban IV in 1262, ' the New Feast—*Festa Berria*.') to realize the singularly impressive

nating sounds are echoes of music : one almost hears the clash of the *adufe* in the *louçana* (answering to *garrida*) or *ramo* (*pinho*). The words of these poems were, indeed, always accompanied by the *son* (= music). But if born in the Church, the *cossante* suffered a transformation when it went out into the world. The rhythm of many of the songs in the *Cancioneiros* is so obtrusive that they seem to dance out of the printed page. One would like to think that in the ears of the peasants the sound of the wheel mingled with the echo of a hymn and its refrain as they met at what was, even then, no doubt, a favourite gathering-place—the mill[1]—and thus a lyric poem became a dance-song. The *cossante Solo ramo* would thus proceed, sung by ' the dancers dancing in tune ' :

> (Verses 3 and 4) Vodas fazen a meu amigo (amado)
> Porque mentiu o desmentido (perjurado)
> E choran olhos d'amor,

the first line of the third distich repeating the second line of the first (and in the same way the first line of the fifth the second line of the third), in *leixa-pren* (*laisser prendre*) corresponding evidently to the movements of the dance.[2] The love-lorn maidens danced together, the men forming a circle to look on. St. Augustine considered the dance to be a circle of which the Devil was the centre ; in real life the Devil was often replaced by a tree (or by a *mayo*). The refrain was a notable feature of the *cossante* in all its phases as it went, a *bailada* (dance-song) from the *terreiro*, to become a *serranilha* on the hills, or at pilgrimage shrines a *cantiga de romaria*,[3] or a *barcarola* (boat-song) or *alvorada* (dawn-

effect of the singing, first the girls' treble Ave Ave Ave Maria, Ave Ave Ave Maria, then the answering bass of the men far behind, Ave Ave Ave Maria, Ave Ave Ave Maria (with the slow ringing of the church bell for a refrain like the *contemplando* and *tan callando* in the *Coplas de Manrique*).

[1] Cf. Gil Vicente, *Tambor em cada moinho*. It is a curious coincidence that the word *citola* (the *jogral's* fiddle) = mill-clapper. Cf. also *moinante* in Galicia = *pícaro*.

[2] Cf. the *leixapren* and refrain of the *cantiga* danced and sung at the end of Gil Vicente's *Romagem de Aggravados* (*Por Maio era, por Maio*). The parallelism and *leixapren* are present also in religious poems by Alfonso X : C. M. 160, 250, 260. Snr. J. J. Nunes has noted that in modern peasant dances, accompanied with song, the dancers sometimes pause while the refrain is sung.

[3] C. V. contains many striking pilgrimage songs, sometimes wrongly called

song). A marked and thoroughly popular characteristic of the *cossante* is its wistful sadness,[1] the *soidade* which is already mentioned more than once in the *Cancioneiros*,[2] and, born in Galicia, continued in Portugal, combined with a more garish tone under the hotter sun of the South. Thus we have the melancholy Celtic temperament, absorbed in Nature, acting on the forms suggested by an alien religion till they become vague cries to the sea, to the deer of the hills, the flower of the pine. The themes are as simple and monotonous—the monotony of snowdrops or daffodils—as the form in which they are sung. A girl in the gloom of the pine-trees mourning for her lover, the birds in the cool of the morning singing of love, the deer troubling the water of a mountain-stream, the boats at anchor, or bearing away *meus amores*, or gliding up the river *a sabor*. The *amiga* lingers at the fountain, she goes to wash clothes or to bathe her hair in the stream, she meets her lover and dances at the pilgrim shrine, she waits for him under the hazel-trees, she implores the waves for news of him, she watches for the boats *pelo mar viir*. The language is native to the soil, far more so, at least, than in the *cantigas de amor* and *cantigas de amigo* written under foreign influence. Their French or Provençal words and learned forms [3] are replaced in the *cossante* by forms Galician or Spanish. Despite its striking appearance to us now among *sirventes senes sal* in the *Cancioneiro Colocci-Brancuti*, it must be confessed that the early *cossante* of King Sancho has a somewhat meagre, vinegar aspect, and the *genre* could hardly have developed so successfully in the next half-century had it not been fixed in the country-side, ever ready to the hand of the poet in search of fresh inspiration. It is possible to exaggerate the effect of war on the life of the peasant. Portugal in the twelfth century was only gradually and by constant conflict winning its territory and independence. It had no fixed capital and Court at which the Provençal poets

cantigas de ledino. The word probably originated in a printer's error (*de ledino* for *dele dino*) in a line of *Chrisfal* : *cantou canto de ledino*.

[1] Cf. the wailing refrains of C. V. 415, 417 ; and, for the *form*, compare *e de mi, louçana !* with *¡ ay de mi, Alfama !* In the *sense* of the two refrains lies all the difference between the poetry of Portugal and Spain.

[2] C. C. B. 135 (= C. A. 389) ; C. V. 119, 181, 220, 527, 758, 964.

[3] *Endurar, besonha, greu, gracir, cousir, escarnir, toste, entendedor, veiro* (*varius*, Fr. *vair*, C. M. 213 has *egua veira*), *genta* (*genser, gensor*).

might gather. But while king and nobles and the members of the religious and military orders were engaged with the |Moors to the exclusion of the Muses, so that they had no opportunity to introduce the new measures, the peasants in Galicia and Minho no doubt went on tilling the soil and singing their primitive songs. In the thirteenth century Provençal poetry flourished in Portugal, but so monotonously that it failed to kill the older lyrics, and they reacted on the imported poetry. In the trite conventions with which the latter became clothed the *cossante* had a new opportunity of life. *Trobadores* wearied by their own monotony, *jograes* wishing to please a patron with a *novidade*, had recourse to the *cossante*. The *jogral* wandering from house to house and town to town necessarily came into close touch with the peasants. Talented men among them, prompted by patrons of good taste, no doubt exercised the third requisite of a good *jogral (doair' e uoz e aprenderdes ben,* C. C. B. 388)—a good memory—not only in learning his patron's verses to recite at other houses but in remembering the songs that he caught in passing from the lips of the peasants, songs of village mirth and dance, of workers in the fields and shepherds on the hills. These, developed and adorned according to his talent, he would introduce to the Court among his *motz recreamens e prazers*. When Joan de Guilhade in the middle of the thirteenth century complained that *os trobadores ja van para mal* (C. V. 370), he might almost be referring to the fact that the stereotyped poems of the Portuguese *trobadores* could no longer compete with the fresh charm of the *cossante*. Alfonso X reproached Pero da Ponte for not singing like a Provençal but, rather, like Bernaldo de Bonaval (first half 13th c.). King Dinis in the second half of the century viewed the *cossante* with such favour that he wrote or collected some of the most curious and delightful that we possess. But although King Dinis set his name to a handful of the finest *cossantes*, most of the *cossante*-writers belonged to an earlier period and were men of humble birth. Of NUNO FERNANDEZ TORNEOL[1] (first half 13th c.), poet and soldier, besides conventional *cantigas de amor* we have eight simple *cossantes* of which the *alvorada* (C. V. 242), the *barcarola* (C. V. 246), and C. V. 245 with its dance rhythm are

[1] C. V. 242–51, 979; C. C. B. 159–71 (= C. A. 70–81, 402).

especially beautiful. PEDR' ANEZ SOLAZ[1] (early 13th c.) wrote a *cossante* (C. V. 415) celebrated for its refrain, *lelia doura, leli leli par deus leli*, in which some have seen a vestige of Basque (*il* = dead). Of MEENDINHO (first half 13th c.) we have only one poem, a *cantiga de romaria* (C. V. 438), but its beauty has brought him fame;[2] and another *jogral*, FERNAND' ESGUIO[3] (second half 13th c.), is remembered in the same way chiefly for C. V. 902 : *Vayamos, irmana*. Bernaldo de Bonaval, one of the earliest Galician poets, and the *jograes* Pero de Veer, Joan Servando, Airas Carpancho,[4] Martin de Ginzo,[5] Lopo and Lourenço, composed some charming pilgrimage songs in the second third of the thirteenth century. This was a popular theme, but the two poets who seem to have felt most keenly the attraction of the popular poetry and to have cultivated it most successfully are JOAN ZORRO (fl. 1250) and PERO MEOGO (fl. 1250). The *cossantes* of Zorro, one of the most talented of all these singers, tell of Lisbon and the king's ships and the sea. In this series of *barcarolas* (C. V. 751-60) and in his delightful *bailada* (C. V. 761)[6] he evidently sought his inspiration in popular sources, as with equal felicity a little later did Pero Meogo,[7] whose *cossantes* (C. V. 789-97), each with its biblical reference to the deer of the hills (*cervos do monte*), are as singular as they are beautiful. MARTIN CODAX at about the same time was singing graceful songs of the *ondas do mar* of Vigo (C. V. 884-90). But the real poet of the sea was the Admiral of Castille, PAY GOMEZ CHARIÑO[8] (†1295). He belonged to an ancient family of Galicia, was

[1] C. V. 414-16, 824-5 ; C. A. 281.
[2] Meen di nho in the C. V. M. index. Thus he is scarcely even a name.
[3] Or Esquio (? = *esquilo*, 'squirrel').
[4] Or Corpancho (Broade) or Campancho (Broadacre) ; but the word *carpancho* (= basket) exists in the region of Santander (*La Montaña*). There is a modern Peruvian poet Manuel Nicolás Corpancho (1830-63).
[5] This is the most probable form of his name, although modern critics have presented him with various others.
[6] M. Alfred Jeanroy (*Les Origines*, 2ᵉ ed., 1904, p. 320) compares with this *bailada* the fragments *Tuit cil qui sunt enamourat Vignent dançar, li autre non* and *N'en nostre compaignie ne soit nus S'il n'est amans*, but even if there was direct imitation here, which is doubtful, that would not affect the indigenous character of the *cossantes*.
[7] Or, according to D. C. Michaëlis de Vasconcellos, Moogo (from *monachus*). *Meogo* (= *meio*) occurs in C. M. 65 and 161, *moogo* (= monk) in C. M. 75 and 149.
[8] C. V. 392-402, 424-30, 1158-9 ; C. A. 246-56. Chariño is buried at Pontevedra, in the Franciscan convent which he founded.

prominent at the Courts of Alfonso X (between whose character and the sea he draws an elaborate parallel in C. A. 256) and of his son Sancho IV, played an important part in the troubled history of the time, and fought by land and sea in Andalucía, at Jaen in 1246 and Seville in 1247. On the lips of his *amiga* he places a touching *cantiga de amigo* (C. V. 424 : she expresses her relief that her *amigo* has ceased to be *almirante do mar*; no longer will she listen in sadness to the wind, now her heart may sleep and not tremble at the coming of a messenger) and the two sea *cossantes* C. V. 401, with its plaining refrain :

> E van-se as frores d'aqui ben con meus amores,
> idas son as frores d'aqui ben con meus amores,

—one can imagine it sung as a chanty [1]—and C. V. 429, in which she prays Santiago to bring him safely home : ' Now in this hour Over the sea He is coming to me, Love is in flower.' Beauty of expression and a loyal sincerity are conspicuous in his poems, as well as a certain individuality and vigour. He escaped the perils of the sea, the *mui gran coita do mar* (C. A. 251), but to fall by the hand of an assassin on shore. His sea lyrics are only excelled by the enchanting melody of the poem (C. V. 488) of his contemporary and fellow-countryman ROY FERNANDEZ (second half 13th c.), who was apparently a professor at Salamanca University, Canon of Santiago, and Chaplain to Alfonso the Learned. Of the later poets ESTEVAM COELHO, perhaps father of one of the assassins of Inés (†1355), wrote a *cossante* of haunting beauty (C. V. 321) :

> Sedia la fremosa, seu sirgo torcendo,
> Sa voz manselinha fremoso dizendo
> Cantigas d'amigo,

and D. AFONSO SANCHEZ (*c.* 1285–1329) in C. V. 368 (*Dizia la fremosinha—Ay Deus val*) proved that he had inherited part of his father King Dinis' genius and instinct for popular poetry. King Dinis, having thrown wide his palace doors to these thyme-scented lyrics, would turn again to the now musty chamber of Provençal song (C. V. 123) :

> Quer'eu en maneira de provençal
> Fazer agora un cantar d'amor.

[1] Cf. the modern *Ai lé lé lé, marinheiro vira á ré* or *Ai lé lé lé Ribamar e S. José.*

The *cossantes* had become so familiar that Airas Nunez, of Santiago, could string them together, as it were, by the head, without troubling himself to give more than the first lines, precisely as Gil Vicente treated *romances* three centuries later. The reader or listener would easily complete them. His *pastorela* (C. V. 454) would be an ordinary imitation of a *pastourelle* of the *trouvères* [1] were it not for the five *cossante* fragments inserted. Riding along a stream he hears a solitary shepherdess singing and stays to listen. First she sang *Solo ramo verde frolido*,[2] then—as if to prove that she is a shepherdess of Arcady, not of real life—

> Ay, estorniño do avelanedo,
> Cantades vos e moir'eu e peno,
> D'amores ei mal,

an impassioned cry of the heart only comparable with

> Thine earth now springs, mine fadeth :
> Thy thorn without, my thorn my heart invadeth ;

or that wonderful line of a wonderful poem :

> Illa cantat, nos tacemus : quando ver venit meum ? [3]

Next she sang the first lines of a *cossante* by Nuno Fernandez Torneol (C. V. 245) with its dance refrain *E pousarei solo avelanal*. The refrain is identical in C. V. 245 and C. V. 454, but the distich has variations which seem to imply that Airas Nunez was not quoting Fernandez, rather that both drew from a popular source. The fourth *cossante* we also have complete, a lovely *barcarola* by Joan Zorro (C. V. 757) :

> Pela ribeira do rio (alto)
> Cantando ia la dona virgo (d'algo)
> D'amor :
> Venhan as barcas pelo rio
> A sabor.[4]

---

[1] For later reminiscences of the *pastorela* see C. Michaëlis de Vasconcellos, *João Lourenço da Cunha, a 'Flor de Altura' e a cantiga Ay Donas por quê em tristura?* (*Separata da Revista Lusitana*, vol. xix) Porto (1916), pp. 14-15.
[2] See *supra*, p. 23.
[3] A modern Portuguese quatrain runs
> Passarinho que cantaes
> Nesse raminho de flores,
> Cantae vos, chorarei eu :
> Assim faz quem tem amores.
[4] By the margin of a river Went a maiden singing, ever Of love sang she :

Lastly she (or he), as he rides on his way, sings:

> Quen amores ha
> Como dormira,
> Ai bela fror!

i. e. *este cantar* which is familiar in the *villancico* (*Por una gentil floresta*) by the Marqués de Santillana (1398–1458):

> La niña que amores ha
> ¿Sola cómo dormirá?

Very few, if any, of the *cossantes* were anonymous, which only means that modern folk-lore was unknown; it was not the fashion to collect songs from the lips of the people without ulterior purpose. A variety known as *cantiga de vilãos* existed, but it was deliberately composed by the *trobadores* and *jograes*.[1] A specimen is given in C. V. 1043:

> Ó pee d'hũa torre
> Baila corpo piolo,[2]
> Vedes o cós, ay cavaleiro.

No drawing-room lyric, evidently: more likely to be sung in taverns; composed perhaps by a knight like him of C. V. 965, whose songs were not *fremosos e rimados*. Like the Provençal poet Guilherme Figueira who *mout se fetz grazir ... als ostes et als taverniers*, this knight's songs pleased 'tailors, furriers and millers'; they had not the good taste of the tailor's wife in Gil Vicente who sings the beautiful *cantiga*

> Donde vindes filha
> Branca e colorida?

The *cantiga de vilãos* was no such simple popular lyric, but rather a drinkers' song, picaresquely allusive, sung by a *jogral* who *non fo hom que saubes caber entre 'ls baros ni entre la bona gen* but sang *vilmen et en gens bassas, entre gens bassas per pauc d'aver* (Riquier), *cantares de que la gente baja e de servil condicion se alegra* (Santillana). The *cossante*, on the contrary, came straight from field and hill into palace and song-book. Probably Up the stream the boats came gliding Gracefully. All along the river-bent The fair maiden singing went Of love's dream: Fair to see the boats came gliding Up the stream.   [1] *Poetica* (C. C. B., p. 3, ll. 50–1).

[2] It probably does not rhyme (*e morre* or *corre*) purposely. D. Carolina Michaëlis de Vasconcellos proposes *gracioso* or *friolo* (*A Saudade Portuguesa*, Porto, 1914, pp. 84, 140).

many of them were composed, as they were sung, and sung dancing, by the women. The women of Galicia have always been noted for their poetical and musical talent. We read of the *choreas psallentium mulierum*, like Miriam, the sister of Moses, at Santiago in 1116,[1] and there is a cloud of similar witnesses. But whether any of the *cossantes* that we have in the *Cancioneiros* is strictly of the people or not, their traditional indigenous character is no longer doubtful. It would surely be a most astounding fact had the Galician-Portuguese Court poets, who in their *cantigas de amor* reduced Provençal poetry to a colourless insipidity, succeeded so much better with the *cossantes* that; while the originals from which they copied have vanished, the imitations stand out in the Portuguese *Cancioneiros* like crimson poppies among corn. It is remarkable, too, that of the three kinds of poem in the old *Cancioneiros*, satire, love song, and *cossante*, the first two remain in the *Cancioneiro de Resende* (1516), but the third has totally disappeared. The explanation is that as Court and people drew apart and the literary influence of Castille grew, the poems based on songs of the people were no longer in favour. But they continued, like the Guadiana, underground, and D. Carolina Michaëlis de Vasconcellos has traced their occasional reappearances in poets of popular leanings, like Gil Vicente and Cristobal de Castillejo, from the thirteenth century to the present day,[2] while Dr. Leite de Vasconcellos has discovered whole *cossantes* sung by peasants at their work in the fields in the nineteenth century.[3] Dance or action always accompanies the *cossante* as it does in the *danza prima* of Asturias (to the words *Ay un galan d'esta villa, ay un galan d'esta casa*).[4] If it

[1] *España Sagrada*, xx. 211.
[2] C. A. M. V. ii. 928–36. Almeida Garrett had written in a general sense: *os vestigios d'essa poesia indigena ainda duram* (*Revista Univ. Lisbonense*, vol. v (1846), p. 843).
[3] At Rebordainhos, in Tras-os-Montes, e. g. *Na ribeirinha ribeira Naquella ribeira Anda lá um peixinho vivo* (*bravo*) *Naquella ribeira*. Other examples of the *i–a* sequence are *amigo* (*amado*), *cosido* (*assado*), *villa* (*praça*), *ermida* (*oraga*), *linda* (*clara*), *Abril* (*Natal*), *ceitil* (*real*). See J. Leite de Vasconcellos, *Annuario para o estudo das tradições populares portuguezas* (Porto, 1882), pp. 19–24. Cf. the modern Asturian song with its refrain *¡ Ay Juana cuerpo garrido, ay Juana cuerpo galano !*
[4] Francisco Alvarez, *Verd. Inf.*, p. 125, speaks of *cantigas de bailhos e de terreiro* (dance-songs).

be objected that the songs printed by Dr. Leite de Vasconcellos are rude specimens by the side of a poem like *Ay flores, ay flores do verde pinho*, it should be remembered that the *quadra* (or perhaps one should say distich without refrain) has now replaced the *cossante* on the lips of the people, and that among these quatrains something of the old *cossante's* charm and melancholy is still found. D. Carolina Michaëlis de Vasconcellos and others have remarked that these *quadras* pass from mouth to mouth and are perfected in the process, smoothed and polished like a stone by the sea, and this may well have been true of the earlier *cossantes*.[1] The *jogral* who hastened to his patron with a lovely new poem was but reaping the inspiration of a succession of anonymous singers, an inspiration quickened by competition in antiphonies of song at many a pilgrimage. One singer would give a distich of a *cossante*, as to-day a *quadra*, another would take it up and return it with variations. The *cossante* did not always preserve its simple form, or, rather, the more complicated poems renewed themselves in its popularity. We find it as a *bailada* (C. V. 761), *balleta* (cf. C. A. 123 : *Se vos eu amo mais que outra ren*), as *cantiga de amor* (C. A. 360 or 361, C. V. 657-60), *cantiga de maldizer* (C. V. 1026-7), or satirical *alba* (C. V. 1049). But these hybrid forms are not the true *cossante*, which is always marked by dignity, restraint, simple grace, close communion with Nature, delicacy of thought, and a haunting felicity of expression. The *cossante* written by King Sancho seems to indicate a natural development of the indigenous poetry. In its form it owed nothing to the poetry of Provence or North France, but its progress was perhaps quickened, and at least its perfection preserved, by the systematic cultivation of poetry introduced from abroad at a time when no middle class separated Court and peasant. The tantalizing fragments that survive in Gil Vicente's plays show all too plainly what marvels of popular song might flower and die unknown. In spirit the original grave religious character of the *cossante* may in some measure have affected the new poetry. To this

[1] Cf. Barros, *Dial. em lovvor da nossa ling.*, 1785 ed., p. 226: *Pois as cantigas compostas do povo, sem cabeça, sem pees, sem nome ou verbo que se entenda, quem cuidas que as traz e leva da terra ? Quem as faz serem tratadas e recebidas do comum consintimento ? O tempo.*

in part may be ascribed the monotony, the absence of particular descriptions in the *cantigas de amor*. In religious hymns obviously reverence would not permit the Virgin to be described in greater detail than, for example, Gil Vicente's vague *branca e colorada*, and the reverence might be transferred unconsciously to poems addressed to an earthly *dona*. (Only in the extravagant devotional mannerisms (*gongorismo ao divino*) of the seventeenth century could Soror Violante do Ceo describe Christ as a *galan de ojos verdes.*) *Dona genser qu'ieu no sai dir* or *la genser que sia* says Arnaut de Marueil at the end of the thirteenth century. The Portuguese poet would make an end there: his lady is fairest among women, fairer than he can say. He would never go on to describe her grey eyes and snowy brow: *huelhs vairs* and *fron pus blanc que lis.* But introduced into alien and artificial forms, like mountain gentians in a garden, the monotony can no longer please. In the *cantigas de amor* the iteration becomes a tedious sluggishness of thought, whereas in the *cossantes* it is part of the music of the poem.

C. A. = Cancioneiro da Ajuda.
C. A. M. V. = Cancioneiro da Ajuda. Ed. Carolina Michaëlis de Vasconcellos. 2 vols. Halle, 1904.
C. A. S. = Fragmentos de hum Cancioneiro Inedito que se acha na Livraria do Real Collegio dos Nobres de Lisboa. Impresso á custa de Carlos Stuart, Socio da Academia Real de Lisboa. Paris, 1823.
C. A. V. = Trovas e Cantares de um Codice do xiv Seculo. Ed. Francisco Adolpho de Varnhagen. Madrid, 1849.
C. V. = Cancioneiro da Vaticana.
C. V. M. = Il Canzoniere Portoghese della Biblioteca Vaticana. Ed. Ernesto Monaci. Halle, 1875.
C. V. B. = Cancioneiro Portuguez da Vaticana. Ed. Theophilo Braga. Lisboa, 1878.
C. T. A. = Cancioneirinho das Trovas Antigas colligidas de um grande Cancioneiro da Bibliotheca do Vaticano. Ed. F. A. de Varnhagen. Vienna (1870), 2nd ed. 1872.
C. A. P. = Cantichi Antichi Portoghesi tratti dal Codice Vaticano 4803 con traduzione e note, a cura di Ernesto Monaci. Imola, 1873.
C. L. = Cantos de Ledino tratti dal grande Canzoniere portoghese della Biblioteca Vaticana. Ed. E. Monaci. Halle, 1875.
C. D. M. = Cancioneiro d' El Rei D. Diniz, pela primeira vez impresso sobre o manuscripto da Vaticana. Ed. Caetano Lopes de Moura. Paris, 1847.
C. D. L. = Das Liederbuch des Königs Denis von Portugal. Ed. Henry R. Lang. Halle, 1894.
C. C. B. = Il Canzoniere Portoghese Colocci-Brancuti. Ed. Enrico Molteni. Halle, 1880.
C. M. = Cantigas de Santa Maria de Don Alfonso el Sabio. 2 vols. Madrid, 1889.
C. G. C. = Cancioneiro Gallego-Castelhano. Ed. H. R. Lang. Vol. i. New York, London, 1902.
C. M. B. = Cancionero Musical de los Siglos xv y xvi. Transcrito y comentado por Francisco Asenjo Barbieri. Madrid (1890).
C. B. = Cancionero de Juan Alfonso de Baena. Madrid, 1851.
C. G. = Cancionero General (1511).
C. R. = Cancioneiro de Resende. Lisboa, 1516 (= Cancioneiro Geral).

§ 2.

The Cancioneiros

IF, besides the *Cancioneiros da Vaticana, Colocci-Brancuti*, and *da Ajuda*, we include King Alfonso X's *Cantigas de Santa Maria* (C. M.) we have over 2,000 poems, by some 200 poets. Of these the *Cancioneiro da Ajuda* (C. A.) contains 310. Preserved in the Lisbon *Collegio dos Nobres* and later in the Royal Library of Ajuda at Lisbon, it was first published in an edition of twenty-five copies by Charles Stuart (afterwards Lord Stuart of Rothesay), British Minister at Lisbon (C. A. S.). Another edition, by Varnhagen, appeared in 1849 (C. A. V.), and the splendid definitive edition by D. Carolina Michaëlis de Vasconcellos in 1904 (C. A. M. V.). C. A. M. V. contains 467 poems, in part reproduced from C. V. M. and C. C. B. The third volume, of notes, is still unpublished.

Of the *Cancioneiro* preserved as Codex Vaticanus 4803, and now commonly known as *Cancioneiro da Vaticana* (C. V.), fragments were published soon after its rediscovery: viz. that portion attributed to King Dinis, edited by Moura in 1847 (C. D. M.). This part received a critical edition at the hands of Professor H. R. Lang in 1892; 2nd ed., with introduction, Halle, 1894 (C. D. L.). A few more crumbs were given to the world by Varnhagen in 1870, 2nd ed. 1872 (C. T. A.), and in 1873 (C. A. P.) and 1875 (C. L.) by Ernesto Monaci, who printed his diplomatic edition of the complete text (1,205 poems) in the latter year (C. V. M.), and with it an index of a still larger *Cancioneiro* (it has 1,675 entries) compiled by Angelo Colocci in the sixteenth century and discovered by Monaci in the Vatican Library (codex 3217). Dr. Theophilo Braga's critical edition appeared in 1878 (C. V. B.).

In this very year a large *Cancioneiro* (355 ff.), corresponding nearly but not precisely to the Colocci index, was discovered in the library of the Conte Paolo Antonio Brancuti (C. C. B.

For convenience' sake C. C. B. also = the fragment published by Enrico Gasi Molteni), and the 442 of its poems, lacking in C. V. (but nearly half of which are in C. A.), were published in diplomatic edition by Enrico Molteni in 1880 (C. C. B.). All these (C. A., C. V., and C. C. B.) were in all probability derived from the *Cancioneiro* compiled by the Conde de Barcellos. When his father, King Dinis, died, silence fell upon the poets. The new king, Afonso IV, showed no sign of continuing to collect the smaller *Cancioneiros* kept by nobles and men of humbler position, a custom inaugurated by his grandfather, Afonso III (if the *Livro de Trovas del Rei D. Afonso* in King Duarte's library was his), continued by King Dinis (*Livro de Trovas del Rei D. Dinis*), and perhaps revived by King Duarte a century later (*Livro de Trovas del Rei*). It was thus a time suitable for a 'definitive edition', and Count Pedro, who was the last of the *Cancioneiro* poets and who was more collector than poet, probably took the existing *Cancioneiros* (of Afonso III and Dinis) and added a third part consisting of later poems. Besides the chronological order there was a division by subject into *cantigas de amor, cantigas de amigo*, and *cantigas d'escarnho e de maldizer* (Santillana's *cantigas, serranas e dezires,* or *cantigas serranas*, the Archpriest of Hita's *cantares serranos e dezires*). C. V. is divided into these three kinds; in the older and incomplete C. A. 304 of the 310 poems are *cantigas de amor*. Eleven years after the death of King Duarte the Marqués de Santillana wrote (1449) to the Constable of Portugal, D. Pedro, describing the Galician-Portuguese *Cancioneiro— un grant volume*—which he had seen in his boyhood in the possession of D. Mencia de Cisneros. (This may have been the actual manuscript compiled by D. Pedro, Conde de Barcellos and bequeathed by him in 1350 to Alfonso XI of Castille and Leon—a few days *after* Alfonso XI's death. Or it may have been a copy of the *Cancioneiro* of D. Pedro or the *Cancioneiro* of Afonso III or of Dinis.) It is significant that in this very important letter it is a foreigner informing a Portuguese. Under the predominating influence first of Spain then of the Renaissance, the old Portuguese poems, even if they were known to exist, excited no interest in Portugal. They were *musas rusticas, musas in illo tempore rudes et incultas.*[1] With this disdain the *Cancioneiro* became a real will-o'-the-wisp. Even as late as the nineteenth century one disappeared mysteriously from a sale, another emerged momentarily (see C. T. A.) from the shelves of a Spanish grandee only to fall back into the unknown. In the sixteenth century the evidence as to its being known is contradictory. Duarte Nunez de Leam in 1585 says of King Dinis that *extant hodie eius carmina*. Antonio de Vasconcellos in 1621 declares that time has carried them away: *obliviosa praeripuit vetustas*.

A few vague allusions (as that of Sá de Miranda concerning the echoes of Provençal song) were all that was vouchsafed in Portugal to the *Cancioneiro*, although prominent Portuguese men of letters—as Sá de Miranda, André de Resende, Damião de Goes—travelled in Italy and met there Cardinal Pietro Bembo (1470–1547), who had probably owned the *Cancioneiros* (copies by an Italian hand of a Portuguese original) acquired by Angelo Colocci; yet at this very time Colocci (†1549) was eagerly indexing and annotating the *Cancioneiros* in Rome. It is this Portuguese neglect and indifference to the things of Portugal which explains the survival of the *cossantes* only in Rome while the more solemn and less indigenous poems of the *Cancioneiro da Ajuda* remained in the land of their birth. A fuller account of the Portuguese *Cancioneiros*, with the fascinating and complicated question of their descent and inter-relations, will be found in the *Grundriss* (pp. 199–202) and D. Carolina Michaëlis de Vasconcellos' edition of the *Cancioneiro da Ajuda* (vol. ii, pp. 180–288).[2]

When the poetry of the troubadours flourished in Provence Portugal was scarcely a nation. The first Provençal poet, Guilhaume, Comte de Poitou (1087–1127), precedes by nearly a century Sancho I (1154–1211), second King of Portugal, who wrote poems and married the Princess Dulce of Aragon; and the Gascon Marcabrun, the first foreign poet to refer to Portugal, in his poems *Al prim comens del ivernaill* and *Emperaire per mi*

---

[1] Antonio de Vasconcellos, *Anacephalaeoses, id est Svmma Capita Actorum Regum Lusitaniae* (Antverpiae, 1621), p. 79.
[2] See also C. V. B., pp. xcv-vi.

mezeis, in the middle of the twelfth century, spoke not of her poetry but of her warrior deeds : *la valor de Portegal*. Gavaudan similarly refers at the end of the twelfth century to the Galicians and Portuguese among other (Castille, &c.) barriers against the ' black dogs ' (the Moors). It was in Spain that the Portuguese had opportunity of meeting Provençal poets. The Peninsula in the thirteenth century was, like Greece of old, divided into little States and Courts, each harbouring exiles and refugees from neighbouring States. Civil strife or the death of a king in Portugal would scatter abroad a certain number of noblemen on the losing side, who would thus come into contact with the troubadours as Provençal poetry spread to the Courts of Catalonia and Aragon, Navarre, Castille and Leon. The first King of Portugal, although a prince of the House of Burgundy, held his kingdom in fief to Leon, and all the early kings were in close touch with Leon and Castille. Fernando III, King of Castille and Leon (St. Ferdinand), was a devoted lover of poetry, and his son Alfonso X gathered at his *cort sen erguelh e sen vilania* a galaxy of talented troubadours, Provençal and Galician. Portugal came into more direct touch with France in other ways, but the influence might have been almost exclusively that of the *trouvères* of the North had not the more generous enthusiasm of Provence penetrated across the frontier into Spain. Trade was fairly active in the thirteenth century between Portugal and England, North France and Flanders. Many of the members of the religious orders—as the Cluny Benedictines—who occupied the territory of the Moors in Portugal were Frenchmen. With foreign colonists the new towns were systematically peopled. The number of French pilgrims was such that the road to Santiago became known as the ' French Road '. The Crusades also brought men of many languages to Portugal.[1] The Court by descent and dynastic intermarriage was cosmopolitan; but indeed the life of the whole Peninsula was cosmopolitan to an extent which tallies ill with the idea of the Middle Ages as a period of isolation and darkness. The Portuguese had already begun to show their

[1] An English Crusader writing from Lisbon speaks of *inter hos tot linguarum populos* (*Crucesignati Anglici Epistola de Expugnatione Olisiponis*, A.D. 1147).

fondness for *novedades*. Yet it was they who imposed their, the Galician, language. As the Marqués de Santillana observed and the *Cancioneiros* prove, lyric poets throughout the Peninsula used Galician.[1] Probably the oldest surviving instance of this language in verse by a foreigner is to be found (ten lines) in a *descort* (*descordo*) written by Raimbaud de Vaqueiras (1158-1217) at the Court of Bonifazio II of Montferrat towards the end of the twelfth century. We cannot doubt that the character and conditions of the north-west of the Peninsula had permitted a thread of lyric poetry to continue there ever since Silius Italicus had heard the youth of Galicia wailing (*ululantem*) their native songs, and that both language and literature had the opportunity to develop earlier there than in the rest of Spain. The tide of Moorish victory only gradually ebbed southward, and the warriors in the sterner country of Castile, with its fiery sun and battles and epics, would look back to the green country of Galicia as the idyllic land of song, a refuge where sons of kings and nobles could spend their minority in comparative peace. When from the ninth century Galicia became a second Holy Land its attractions and central character were immeasurably increased. Pilgrims thither from every country would return to their native land with some words of the language, and those acquainted with Provençal might note the similarity and the musical softness of Galician.[2] It is not certain that the eldest of the ten children of San Fernando, ALFONSO X (1221?-84), *el Sabio*, King of Castile and Leon, Lord of Galicia, and brother-in-law of our Edward I, passed his boyhood in Galicia. But when he was compiling a volume of poems referring to many parts of the world besides Spain, to Canterbury and Rome, Paris and Alexandria, Lisbon, Cologne, Cesarea, Constantinople, he would naturally choose Galician not only, or indeed chiefly, because it was the more graceful and pliant medium for lyric verse but because it was the most widely known, and, like French, *plus commune à toutes*

---

[1] *Colección de Poesías Castellanas* (1779), vol. i, p. lvii. The important passages of Santillana's letter have been so often quoted that the reader may be referred to them, e. g. in the *Grundriss*, p. 168.

[2] Milá y Fontanals (*De los Trobadores*, p. 522) lays much stress on the resemblance between Galician and Provençal.

gens.[1] He had no delicate ear for its music and made such poor use of its pliancy that it often becomes as hard as the hardest Castilian in his hands. His songs of miracles offer a striking contrast to contemporary Portuguese lyrics in the same language. Their jingles are only possible as a *descort* in the Portuguese *Cancioneiros*. At the same time he would be influenced in his choice of language by his knowledge of Galicia as the traditional home of the lyric, of the encouraging patronage extended to Galician poets by his son-in-law Afonso III, of the Santiago school of poets, and of the promising future before the Galician language in the hands of the conquering Portuguese. *Multas et perpulchras composuit cantilenas*, says Gil de Zamora, and likens him to David. But when we remember the prodigious services rendered by Alfonso X to Castilian prose, the first question that arises is whether he was indeed the author of the 450 poems in Galician[2] that we possess under his name. Of these poems 426, or, cancelling repetitions, 420, are of a religious character, written, with one or two exceptions, in honour of the Virgin : *Cantigas de Santa Maria*. Many of these poems themselves provide an answer to the question : they record his illnesses and enterprises and his *trobar* in such a way that they could only have been written by himself : he is the *entendedor* of Santa Maria (C. M. 130), he exhorts other *trobadores* to sing her praises (C. M. 260), he himself is resolved to sing of no other *dona* (C. M. 10 : *dou ao demo os otros amores*) ; and his attractive and ingenuous pride in these poems accords ill with an alien authorship. When he lay sick at Vitoria and was like to die it was only when the *Livro das Cantigas* was placed on his body that he recovered (C. M. 209), and he directed that they should be preserved in the church in which he was buried. There is little reason to doubt that he was the author, in a strictly limited sense, of the majority of the poems, although not of all.

[1] It must be remembered that in the early thirteenth century (1213) the range of the Galician-Portuguese lyric already extended to Navarre (C. V. 937).
[2] Guiraut Riquier and Nat de Mons placed Provençal poems on his lips, which may be taken as an indication that he also wrote in Provençal. As proof that he wrote poems in Castilian we have a single *cantiga* of eight lines (C. C. B. 363 : *Señora por amor dios*). The other poem of the *Cancioneiros* in Castilian (with traces of Galician) is by the victor of Salado, Alfonso XI (1312-50), King of Castille and Leon : *En un tiempo cogi flores* (C. V. 209).

Various phrases seem to imply a double method. C. M. 219 says: 'I will have that miracle placed among the others'; C. M. 295: 'I ordered it to be written.' On the other hand, C. M. 47 is 'a fair miracle of which I made my song'; C. M. 84 'a great miracle of which I made a song'; of 106 'I know well that I will make a goodly song'; of 64 'I made verses and tune'; for 188 'I made a good tune and verses because it caught my fancy'; for 307 'according to the words I made the tune'; of 347 'I made a new song with a tune that was my own and not another's'. The inference seems to be that, the personal poems and the *loas* apart, if a miracle especially attracted the king he took it in hand; otherwise he might leave it to one of the *joglares*, and he would perhaps revise it and be its author to the extent that the Portuguese *jograes* were authors of the early *cossantes*. We know that he had at his Court a veritable factory of verse. The vignettes[1] to these *Cantigas* show him surrounded by scribes, pen and parchment in hand, by *joglares* and *joglaresas*. Poets thronged to his Court and he was in communication with others in foreign lands. Some of the miracles might come to him in verse, the work of a friendly poet or of a sacred *jogral* such as Pierres de Siglar, whom C. M. 8 shows reciting his poems from church to church: *en todalas eigreias da Uirgen que non a par un seu lais senpre dizia*,[2] and this would account for the variety of metre and treatment. Of raw material for his art there was never a scarcity, nor was the idea of turning it into verse original. In France Gautier de Coincy (1177–1236) had already written his *Miracles de la Sainte Vierge* in verse, and the Spanish poet Gonzalo de Berceo (1180–1247) had composed the *Milagros de Nuestra Sennora*. But there was no need for direct imitation. If the starry sky were parchment and the ocean ink, the miracles

---

[1] Their antiquarian interest was recognized over three centuries ago. Cf. Argote de Molina, *Nobleza de Andalvzia* (Seuilla, 1588), f. 151 v.: *es un libro de mucha curiosidad assi por la poesia como por los trages de aquella edad q̃ se veen en sus pinturas*.
[2] Some of King Alfonso's *Cantigas* were recited in the same way. C. M. 172 implies this in the lines:
Et d'esto cantar fezemos
Que cantassen os iograres
And of this we made a song for the *joglares* to sing).

could not all be written down, says King Alfonso (C. M. 110). Churches and rival shrines preserved an unfailing store for collectors. Gautier de Coincy spoke of *tant miracles*, a *grant livre* of them, and King Alfonso chooses one from among 300 in a book (C. M. 33), finds one written in an ancient book (265) written among many others (258), in a book among many others (284), and refers to a book full of them at Soissons. The miracles were recorded more systematically in France, and the books of Soissons and Rocamadour (*Liber Miraculorum S. Mariae de Rupe Amatoris*) provided the king with many subjects, as did also Vincent de Beauvais' *Speculum Historiale*, of which he possessed a copy. But the sources in the Peninsula were very copious, as, for instance, the Book of the Miracles of Santiago, of which a copy, in Latin, exists in the Paris Bibliothèque Nationale. Of other miracles the king had had personal experience, or they were recent and came to him by word of mouth. Thus he often does not profess to invent his subject: he merely translates it into verse and sometimes appraises it as he does so. It is ' a marvellous great miracle ' (C. M. 257), ' very beautiful ' (82), ' one in which I have great belief ' (241), ' one almost incredible ', *mui cruu de creer* (242), or ' famous ' (195), ' known throughout Spain' (191). Many of these miracles occurred to the peasants and unlettered: then as now the humbler the subject the greater the miracle. Accordingly we find the king in his poems dealing not with the conventional shepherdesses of the *pastorelas* but with lowly folk of real life, peasants, gleaners, sailors, fishermen, beggars, pilgrims, nuns; and it is one of the king's titles to be considered a true poet that he takes an evident pleasure in these themes and retains their graphic, artless presentment. The collection abounds in charming glimpses of the life of the people. Indeed, in many of the poems there is more of the people than of King Alfonso,[1] and he sings diligently of the misdeeds of clerics and usurers, of the incompetence of doctors, and of massacres of Jews. He seems to have followed the originals very closely, and evident traces

[1] Their popular origin is borne out by the music. See H. Collet et L. Villalba, *Contribution à l'étude des Cantigas* (1911). Cf. also P. Meyer, *Types de quelques chansons de Gautier de Coinci* (*Romania*, vol. xvii (1888), pp. 429-37): *paroles pieuses à des mélodies profanes*.

of their language remain, French, English, and perhaps Provençal. The poems are often of considerable length, sometimes twenty or thirty verses, and as a rule the last line of each verse must rhyme with the refrain. The attention thus necessarily bestowed upon the rhymes sometimes mars the pathos of the subject, and the reader is reminded that he has to do with a skilful, eager, and industrious craftsman but not with a great original poet. In the remarkable *Ben vennas Mayo* and in many of his other poems materialism and poetical ecstasy go hand in hand. Yet in several of the more beautiful legends the poet proves himself equal to his theme. Some of these legends are still famous, that of the Virgin taking the place of the nun (C. M. 55 and 94), of the knight and the pitcher (155), of the stone miraculously warded from the statue of the Virgin and Child (136 and 294), of the monk's mystic ecstasy at the *lais* of the bird in the convent garden (103). Others had probably an equal celebrity in the Middle Ages, as that of the captive miraculously brought from Africa and awaking free in Spain at dawn (325),[1] of the painter with whom the Devil was wroth for always painting him so ugly (74), or of the peasant whose vineyard alone was saved from the hail (161). Every tenth poem (the collection was intended originally to consist of one hundred) interrupts the narratives of miracles by a purely lyrical *cantiga de loor*, and some of these, written with the fervour with which the king always sang *as graças muy granadas* of the *Madre de Deus Manuel*, are of great simplicity and beauty. The king had not always written thus, and of his profane poems we possess thirty [2] (since no one who has read the lively essay by Cesare de Lollis will doubt that C. V. 61–79 and C. C. B. 359–72 (=467–78) were written by Alfonso X). The most important of these are historical, and invoke curses on

[1] Padre Nobrega came upon a crowd of *pobres pedintes peregrinos* at Santiago feasting merrily and having *grandes contendas entre si* as to which of them was cleverest at taking people in. The trick of one of them was to declare that, being captive in Turkey, *encommendando-me muito á Senhora... achei-me ao outro dia ao romper da alva em terra de Christãos* (Simão de Vasconcellos, *Cronica*, Lib. I, § 22). Cf. Jeronymo de Mendoça, *Jornada de Africa*, 1904 ed., ii. 34, and Frei Luis de Sousa, *Hist. de S. Domingos*, 1. i. 5.

[2] i. e. besides the Spanish *cantiga* (C. C. B. 363), C. C. B. 359, which belongs to the *Cantigas de Santa Maria*, and C. C. B. 372, which consists of a single line.

false or recalcitrant knights, *non ven al mayo!* C. V. 74 is a battle-scene description so swift and impetuous that we must go to the *Poema del Cid* for a parallel. And indeed some of the old spirit peeps out from the *Cantigas de Santa Maria*, as when he prays to be delivered from false friends or praises the Virgin for giving his enemies ' what they deserved '.

From the return and enthronement of Afonso III imitation of French and Provençal poetry was in full swing in Portugal. The long sojourn of the prince in France, accompanied by several noblemen who figure in the *Cancioneiros* (as Rui Gomez de Briteiros and D. Joan de Aboim), had an important bearing on the development of Portuguese poetry. He came back determined to act the part of an enlightened patron of letters; he encouraged the immigration of men of learning from France and maintained three *jograes* permanently in his palace.[1] Princes and nobles as *trobadores* for their own pastime, the *segreis*,[2] knights who went from Court to Court and received payment for the recital of their own verses, the *jograes*, belonging to a lower station, who recited the poems of their patrons the *trobadores*, all vied in imitation of the love songs of Provence. In general, i. e. in the structure of their poems, the resemblance is close and clear enough. The decasyllabic love song in three or four stanzas with an *envoi*, the satirical *sirventes*, the *tenson* (*jocs-partits*) in which two poets contended in dialogue, the *descort* in which the discordant sounds expressed the poet's distress and grief, the *balada* of Provence, the *ballette* and *pastourelle* of North France, were all faithfully reproduced.

If, on the other hand, we look for imitations in detail it is perhaps natural that we should find them less frequently.[3]

[1] *El Rei aia tres jograes en sa casa e non mais.*
[2] Riquier's *segriers per totas cortz* (King Alfonso X (C. M. 194) speaks of a *jograr andando pelas cortes*). See also C. V. 556. The word probably has no connexion with *seguir* (to follow). Possibly it was used originally to differentiate singers of profane songs, *cantigas profanas e seculares*. Frei João Alvarez in his *Cronica do Infante Santo* has ' obras ecclesiasticas e *segrãaes* ' ; King Duarte counted among *os pecados da boca* ' cantar cantigas *sagraaes* '. The *Cancioneiros* show that the *segrel* was far less common than the *jogral* in the thirteenth century. For *segre* (= *saeculum*) see *infra*, p. 93, n. 2.
[3] For instances see H. R. Lang, *The Relations of the Earliest Portuguese Lyric School with the Troubadours and Trouvères* (*Modern Language Notes* (April, 1895), pp. 207–31), and C. D. L., pp. xlviii et seq.

THE CANCIONEIROS 47

The conventional character of the Portuguese poems would sufficiently account for this, and moreover their models were probably more often heard than read, so that reproduction of the actual thought or words would be difficult. When Airas Nunez in a poem of striking beauty, which is almost a sonnet (C. V. 456), wrote the lines:

> Que muito m'eu pago d'este verão
> Por estes ramos et por estas flores
> Et polas aves que cantan d'amores,

he need not have read Peire de Bussinac's lines:

> Quan lo dous temps d'Abril
> Fa 'ls arbres secs fulhar
> E 'ls auzels mutz cantar
> Quascun en son lati,

in order to know that birds sing and trees grow green in spring. And generally it is not easy to say whether an apparent echo is a direct imitation or merely a stereotyped phrase. The Portuguese *trobadores* introduced little of the true spirit of the Provençal *troubadours*—that had passed to Palestine and to the Lady of Tripoli. In their *cantigas de amor* is no sign of action—unless it be to die of love; no thought of Nature. Jaufre Rudel (1140–70), that prince of lovers, had 'gone to school to the meadows' and might sing in his *maint bons vers* of *la flor aiglentina* or of *flors d'albespis,* but in the Portuguese *cantigas* nothing relieves the conventional dullness and excessive monotony (which likewise marked the Provençal school of poets in Sicily). Composed for the most part in iambic decasyllables they describe continually the poet's *coita d'amor, grave d'endurar*, his grief at parting, his loss of sleep, his pleasure in dying for his *fremosa sennor*. She is described merely as beautiful, or, at most, as

Tan mansa e tan fremosa e de bon sen (C. C. B. 206).

Fremosa e mansa e d'outro ben comprida (C. C. B. 278).

Vocabulary and thought are spectre-thin. Indeed, it was part of the convention to sing vaguely. *Eu ben falarei de sa fremosura,* says one poet [1] (C. C. B. 337)—he will sing of her

[1] This poet, Fernam Gonçalvez de Seabra or Fernant Gonzalez de Sanabria (C. V. 338; C. C. B. 330–7; C. A. 210–21, 445–7), apparently obtained some

beauty, but not in such a way that the curious who *non o poden adevinhar* should guess his secret. As to allusions to Nature, perhaps the climate, with less marked divisions than in Provence, furnished less incentive to sing of spring and the earth's renewal or to imitate Guiraut de Bornelh in going to school all the winter (*l'ivern estava a escola a aprender*) and singing only with the return of spring. King Dinis, perhaps in reference to that troubadour, declares that his love is independent of the seasons and more sincere than that of the singers of Provence:

> Proençaes soen mui ben trobar
> E dizen eles que é con amor,
> Mais os que troban no tempo da frol
> E non en outro sei eu ben que non
> An tan gran coita ... (C. V. 127)

and even as he wrote the words he was unconsciously imitating the thought of the Provençal poet Gace Brulé, who had spoken of *les faus amoureus d'esté*. The exceeding similarity of the *cantigas de amor* did raise doubts as to the sincerity of all this dying of love (cf. C. V. 353 and C. V. 988) and as to whether a poem was a *cantar novo* or an article at second hand (C. V. 819). Yet the poets evidently had talent and poetic feeling; indeed, their skill in versification contrasts remarkably with their entire absence of thought or individuality. They appear to revel in monotony of ideas and pride themselves on the icy smoothness of their verse. All their originality consisted in the introduction of technical devices, such as the repetition at intervals of certain words (*dobre*), or of different tenses of the same verb (*mordobre*, as C. V. 681), to carry on the poem without stop from beginning to end by means of 'for', 'but', &c., at the beginning of each verse (*cantigas de atafiinda*,[1] as C. V. 130,

fame by his mystification, unless the object of his devotion was as high-placed as the Portuguese princess for love of whom, according to legend, D. Joan Soarez de Paiva died in Galicia. The latter wrote in the first years of the thirteenth century (C. V. 937, *Randglosse* xi). They are the only two Galician-Portuguese poets—besides King Dinis—mentioned in Santillana's letter.

[1] *Poetica*, ll. 126, 130. Much of the information of this *Poetica* (printed in C. C. B.) may be gleaned from the *Cancioneiros*, but it shows how carefully the different kinds of poem were distinguished. There were apparently special names for poems to trick and deceive: *de logr' e d'arteiro*, and for

C. A. 205), to begin and end each verse with the same line (*canção redonda*, as C. V. 685), to repeat the last line of one verse as the first line of the next (*leixapren*), to use the same word at the end of each line (as *vi* in C. A. 7). The poet who addressed *cantigas de amor* to his lady also provided her with poems for her to sing, *cantigas de amigo* in complicated form, or as the simpler *cossante*, which the *cantigas de amigo* include. These are poems with more life and action, often in dialogue. Perhaps the *dona* herself, wearied by the monotonous *cantigas de amor*, had pointed to the songs of the peasant women, and the form of these *cantigas de amigo* was a compromise between the Provençal *cantiga de meestria* and the popular *cantiga de refran*. The peasant woman composed her own songs, and the poet places his song on the lips of his love: thus we find her describing herself as beautiful, *eu velida*; *eu fremosa*; *trist' e fremosa*; *fremosa e de mui bon prez*; *o meu bon semelhar*. Poetical shepherdesses sing these *cantigas de amigo*; the fair *dona* sings them as she sits spinning (C. V. 321). The old *Poetica* (ll. 2-12) distinguishes between the *cantigas de amor*, in which the *amigo* speaks first, and the *cantigas de amigo*, in which the first to speak is the *amiga*. Both were artificial forms, but the latter are clearly more popular in theme (the *amiga* waiting and wailing for her lover), and in treatment sometimes convey a real intensity of feeling.[1] The favourite subject of the *cantiga de amigo* is that the cruel mother prevents the lovers from meeting. The daughter is kept in the house: *a manda muito guardar* (C. V. 535). She reproaches and entreats her mother, who answers her as choir to choir; she bewails her lot to her friends, or to her sister. She is dying of love and begs her mother to tell her lover. Her mother and lover are reconciled. Her lover is false and fails to meet her at the trysted hour. She waits for him in vain, and her mother comforts her in her

---

festive laughter poems: *de risadelha* (or *refestela* ?) = *de riso e mote*. Santillana's *mansobre* is, it seems, a misprint for *mordobre*. It occurs again in the *Requesta de Ferrant Manuel contra Alfonso Alvarez* (*Canc. de Baena*, 1860 ed., i. 253):

        Sin lai, sin deslai, sin cor, sin descor,
        Sin dobre, mansobre, sensilla o menor,
        Sin encadenado, dexar o prender.

[1] e.g. C. V. 300: *Por Deus, se ora, se ora chegasse Con el mui leda seria.*

distress. She pines and dies of love while her *amigo* is away serving the king in battle or *en cas' del rei*.

The third section of the *Cancioneiro da Vaticana* does not sin by monotony. We may divide Pope's line, since if the *cantigas de amor* are 'correctly cold' many of the satiric poems are 'regularly low'. In these verses, containing violent invective and abuse (*cantigas de maldizer*) or more covert sarcasm and ridicule (*cantigas d'escarnho*), the themes are often scandalous, the language ribald and unseemly. They were written with great zest, although without the fiery indignation of the Provençal and Catalan *sirventeses*. They are concerned with persons: the haughty *trobador* may take a *jogral* to task for writing verses that do not rhyme or scan, but even then it is a personal matter and he rebukes his insolence for daring to raise his thoughts to *altas donas* in song. Some of these poems should never have been written or printed, but many of them give a lively idea of the society of that time. They laugh merrily or venomously at the poverty-stricken knight with nothing to eat; at the knight who set his dogs on those who called near dinner-time; the *jogral* who knows as much of poetry as an ass of reading; the poet who pretended to have gone as a pilgrim to the Holy Land but never went beyond Montpellier; the physician (Mestre Nicolas) whose books were more for show than for use (*E sab' os cadernos ben cantar quen* [1] *non sabe por elles leer*, C. V. 1116); the Galician unjustifiably proud of his poetical talent (*non o sabia ben*, C. V. 914); the *jogral* who gave up poetry—shaved off his beard and cut his hair short about his ears—in order to take holy orders, in hope of a fat living, but was disappointed; the *jogral* who played badly and sang worse; the poet who was the cause of good poetry in others; the gentleman who spent most of his income on clothes and wore gilt shoes winter and summer. We read of the excellent capon, kid, and pork provided by the king for dinner; of the fair *malmaridada*, married or rather sold by her parents; of the impoverished lady, one of those for whom later Nun' Alvarez provided; of the poet pining in exile not of love but hunger; of the lame lawyer, the unjust

---

[1] *q'coi* (C. V. M.), *qual cór* (C. V. B.). D. Carolina Michaëlis de Vasconcellos proposes *quiça* (cf. C. V. 1006, 1. 8).

judge, the *parvenu villão*, the knighted tailor, the seers and diviners (*veedeiros, agoreiros, divinhos*). These *cantigas d'escarnho e de maldizer* were a powerful instrument of satire from which there was no escape. A hapless *infançon*, slovenly in his ways, drew down upon himself the wit of D. Lopo Diaz, who in a series of eleven songs (C. V. 945-55) ridiculed him and his creaking saddle till at Christmas he was fain to call a truce. But the implacable D. Lopo forthwith indited a new song: 'I won't deny that I agreed to a truce about the saddle, but—it didn't include the mare ',[1] and so no doubt continued till *pascoa florida* or *la trinité*. But the majority of these verses are not so innocently merry. Many of the poets of the *Cancioneiros* wrote in all three kinds : *cantigas de amor, de amigo*, and *de maldizer*. Of JOAN DE GUILHADE[2] (fl. 1250) we have over fifty poems.[3] He imitated both French and Provençal models, and, having learnt lightness of touch from them, would appear to have contented himself with writing *cantigas de amigo* (besides *cantigas de amor* and *escarnho*) without having recourse to the *cossante*. There is life and poetical feeling as well as facility of technique in his poems.

PERO GARCIA DE BURGOS (fl. 1250) is, with Joan de Guilhade, one of the more voluminous writers of the *Cancioneiros*. He shows himself capable of deep feeling in his love songs, but speaks with two voices, descending to sad depths in his poems of invective. His contemporary, the *segrel* PERO DA PONTE, is also an accomplished poet of love, in the even flow of his verse far more accomplished than Pero Garcia, and in his satirical poems wittier and, as a rule, more moderate. He placed his poetical gift at the service of kings to sing their praises for hire, and celebrated San Fernando's conquest of Seville in 1248 ; Seville, of which, he says, ' none can adequately tell the praises '. To satire almost exclusively the powerful courtier of King Dinis' reign, STEVAM GUARDA, devoted his not inconsiderable talent, and the *segrel* PEDR' AMIGO DE SEVILHA (fl. 1250) shone in the same kind with a great variety of metre as well as in

---
[1] *Aqueste cantar da egoa que non andou na tregoa* (C. V. 956).
[2] Or D. Joan Garcia de Guilhade. See C. A. M. V. ii. 407-15.
[3] C. V. 28-38, 343-61, 1097-1110 ; C. A. 235-9 ; C. C. B. 373-6.

numerous *cantigas de amigo*. MARTIN SOAREZ (first half 13th c.), born at Riba de Lima, and considered the best *trobador* of his time (by those who could not appreciate the charm of the indigenous poetry), wrote no *cossante* nor *cantiga de amigo*, and in his satirical poems displayed a contemptuous insolence —towards those whom he regarded as his inferiors in lineage or talent—which places him in no attractive light. A notable poet at the Courts of Spain and Portugal was JOAN AIRAS of Santiago de Compostela (fl. 1250), of whom we have over twenty *cantigas de amor* and fifty *cantigas de amigo*. Contemporary criticism apparently viewed their quantity with disfavour,[1] for he complains that *Dizen que meus cantares non valen ren porque tan muitos son* (C. V. 533). But if his poems lack the variety of those of King Dinis, which they almost rival in number, they are nevertheless marked not only by harmony but by many a touch of real life. Of most of the other singers we have far fewer poems. Like Meendinho and Estevam Coelho, PERO VYVYÃES (first half 13th c.) is known chiefly for a single song : his *bailada* (C. V. 336). By D. JOAN SOAREZ COELHO (*c.* 1210–80) there are two *cossantes* (C. V. 291, 292) and numerous other poems. He was prominent at the Court of Afonso III (1248–79) and in the conquest of Algarve, as was also D. JOAN DE ABOIM (*c.* 1215–87), whose poems are less numerous but include a dozen *cantigas de amigo* and a *pastorela* (C. V. 278 : *Cavalgava noutro dia per hun caminho frances*), and FERNAN GARCIA ESGARAVUNHA,[2] whose *cantigas de amor* show characteristic life and vigour, and a good command of metre. There is an engaging grace and spirit in the *cantigas de amigo* written in dancing rhythm by FERNAN RODRIGUEZ DE CALHEIROS (fl. in or before 1250), who preceded those soldier poets ; deep feeling and melancholy in the *cantigas de amor* of D. JOAN LOPEZ DE ULHOA, their contemporary. Neither of these, however, possessed the poetical genius and versatility of the priest of Santiago, AIRAS NUNEZ (second half

---

[1] A large number of *cantigas* by the same hand would emphasize the monotony of the kind and provide an unwelcome mirror for contemporary bards. Of Roy Queimado (fl. 1250) other love-lorn poets said that he was always dying of love—in verse.

[2] Soares de Brito in his *Theatrum* mentions 'Ferdinandus Garcia Esparavanha, optimus poeta.' (= *bom trovador*).

13th c.)—the name appears in a marginal note to one of King Alfonso's *Cantigas de Santa Maria* (C. M. 223 in the manuscript j. b. 2)—whose poems show a perfect mastery of rhythm and a true instinct for beauty. He wrote a *pastorela* in the manner of the *trouvères*, and combined it with some of the most exquisite specimens of the indigenous poetry.[1] The fact that one of these was by Joan Zorro makes it probable that Nunez' celebrated *bailada* (C. V. 462) is but a development of Zorro's (C. V. 761), unless both drew from a common popular source. Another of his poems (C. V. 468) reads like an anticipatory slice out of Juan Ruiz' *Libro de Buen Amor*. Great importance has been attached to another (C. V. 466) as a remnant of a *cantar de gesta*, but D. Carolina Michaëlis de Vasconcellos has shown that it was written to commemorate a contemporary event, probably in 1289.[2] More than any other poet of the *Cancioneiros*, with the exception, perhaps, of King Dinis, Nunez anticipated that *doce estylo*, the introduction of which cost Sá de Miranda so many perplexities.

The *Cancioneiros* contain poems by high and low, prince and, one would fain say, peasant, noble *trobador* and humble *jogral*, soldiers and civilians, priests and laymen, singers of Galicia, Portugal, and Spain, but more especially of Galicia and North Portugal. As in the case of C. V. 466, the interest of many of the poems is historical : C. V. 1088, for instance, written by a partisan of the dethroned King Sancho II ; or C. V. 1080, a *gesta de maldizer* of fifty-six lines in three rhymes, with the exclamation *Eoy !* at the change of the rhyme, which was written by D. Afonso Lopez de Bayan (*c.* 1220–80), clearly in imitation of the *Chanson de Roland*.[3] Almost equally prominent, though not from any historical associations, is the curiously modern C. A. 429 (= C. C. B. 314) among the *cantigas de amor*. It tells of a girl forced against her will to enter a convent, and who says to her lover : ' My dress may be religious, but God shall not have my heart.' (For the metre, cf. C. V. 342.) Its author was the *fidalgo*

---
[1] See p. 31.
[2] See *Randglosse* xii. An incidental interest belongs to this poem of eighteen dodecasyllabic lines from the fact that in C. V. B. it is printed in thirty-six lines, as a proof of the early predominance of the *redondilha*.
[3] Cf. the Provençal passage in Milá y Fontanals, *De los Trobadores*, p. 62.

D. Rodrig' Eanez de Vasconcellos, one of the pre-Dionysian poets. But indeed no further proofs are needed to show that, even had King Dinis never existed, the contents of the early Portuguese *Cancioneiros* would have been remarkable for their variety and beauty. When Alfonso X died his grandson Dinis (1261–1325)[1] had sat for five years on the throne of Portugal. Plentifully educated by a Frenchman, Ayméric d'Ébrard, afterwards Bishop of Coimbra, married to a foreign princess, Isabel of Aragon (the Queen-Saint of Portugal), profoundly impressed, no doubt, by the world-fame of Alfonso X, to whom he was sent on a diplomatic mission when not yet in his teens, he became nevertheless one of the most national of kings. If he imitated Alfonso X in his love of literature, he showed himself a far abler and firmer sovereign, being more like a rock than like the sea, to which the poet compared Alfonso. Farsighted in the conception of his plans and vigorous in their execution, the *Rei Lavrador*, whom Dante mentions, though not by name: *quel di Portogallo* (*Paradiso* xix), fostered agriculture, increased his navy, planted pine-forests, fortified his towns, built castles and convents and churches, and legislated for the safety of the roads and for the general welfare and security of his people. Among his great and abiding services to his country was the foundation of the first Portuguese University in the year 1290, and in the same spirit he ordered the translation of many notable books from the Spanish, Latin, and Arabic into Portuguese prose, including the celebrated works of the Learned King, so that it is truer of prose than of poetry to say that he inaugurated a golden age.[2] Had he written no line of verse his name must have been for ever honoured in Portugal as the real founder of that imperishable glory which was fulfilled two centuries later. But he also excelled as a poet, *d'amor trobador*. It had no doubt been part of his education to write conventionally in the Provençal manner, but his skill in versification, remarkable even in an age in which Portuguese poetry had attained exceptional proficiency in technique, would have

[1] He thus overlapped Dante's life by four years at either end.
[2] T. A. Craveiro, *Compendio* (1833), cap. 5: *D. Diniz trouxe a idade de ouro a Portugal.*

THE CANCIONEIROS 55

availed him, or at least us, little had he not also possessed an instinct for popular themes, perhaps directly encouraged by Alfonso X. The *Declaratio* placed by Guiraut Riquier of Narbonne on the lips of that king in 1275 marked the coming asphyxia of Provençal poetry, for it showed the tendency to take the *jogral* [1] away from tavern and open air and to cut off his poetry from the life of the people. It was owing to the personal encouragement of Dinis that the waning star of both Provençal and indigenous poetry continued to shine in Portugal for another half-century. The grandson of Alfonso X was the last hope of the *trobadores* and *jograes* of the Peninsula. From Leon and Castille and Aragon they came to reap an aftermath of song and *panos* at his Court, and after his death remained silent or unpaid (C. V. 708). The poems of King Dinis are not only more numerous but far more various than those of any other *trobador*, with the exception of Alfonso X, and it may perhaps be doubted whether they are all the work of his own hand. In poetry's old age he might well wish to collect specimens of various kinds for his *Livro de Trovas*. But many of the 138 poems [2] that we possess under his name are undoubtedly his, and display a characteristic force and sincerity as well as true poetic delicacy and power. Among them are some colourless *cantigas de amor* and others more individual in tone, *pastorelas* (C. V. 102, 137, 150), *cantigas de amigo* (more Provençal than Portuguese in their spirit of vigorous reproach are C. V. 186 : *Amigo fals' e desleal*, and C. V. 198 : *Ai fals' amigo e sen lealdade*), a jingle worthy of the *Cantigas de Santa Maria* (C. V. 136), a poem in 8.8.4.8 metre (C. V. 131), *atafiindas* (e. g. C. V. 130), a *mordobre* in *querer* (C. V. 113, *Quix ben, amigos, e quer' e querrei Ũa molher que me quis e quer mal E querrá*), and *cossantes* of an unmistakably popular flavour : *Ay flores, ay flores do verde pino* (C. V. 171), two *albas* (C. V. 170, 172), C. V. 168, 169, with their refrains *louçana* and *ai madre, moiro d'amor*, C. V. 173 with its

---

[1] A late echo of the early (Alfonso X) legislation against the *jogral* is to be found in King Duarte's *Leal Conselheiro*, cap. 70 : *Dos Pecados da Obra*. These include *dar aos jograaees*. Nunez de Leam translates *joglar* as *truão* (1606).

[2] C. V. 80–208 (= C. D. L. 1–75, 77–128, 76) and C. C. B. 406–15 (= C. D. L. 129–38). C. V. 116 = C. V. 174.

quaint charm: *Vede-la frol do pinho*—*Valha Deus*, and the *bailada-cossante* (C. V. 195: *Mia madre velida, Voum' a la bailia Do amor*). If the king wrote these *cossantes* he must be reckoned not only as a musical and skilful versifier but as a great poet. And certainly, at least, his *graciosas e dulces palavras* well earned him the reputation of being not only the best king but the best poet of his time in the Peninsula.

It would seem that, unlike his grandfather, who had begun with profane and ended with religious verse, King Dinis, no doubt at his grandfather's bidding, who would be delighted to find a disciple (*Dized', ai trobadores, A Sennor das Sennores Por que a non loades ?*), began writing songs in honour of the Virgin and sent them to the Castilian king. His book of *Louvores da Virgem Nossa Senhora* is said to have been seen in the Escorial Library and in the Lisbon Torre do Tombo, and it is impossible altogether to set aside the statements of Duarte Nunez de Leam [1] and Antonio de Sousa de Macedo, who says that he read religious poems by King Dinis at the Escorial.[2] On the other hand, it must be remembered that it was the common opinion that King Dinis had been the first to write Portuguese poetry, and the temptation to attribute ancient poems to him would be strong. The possibility of confusion with the *Livro de Cantigas* of Alfonso X (to which his grandson may well have contributed poems)[3] is also obvious. But the statement of Sousa de Macedo, who was no passing traveller in a hurry, and who had wide experience of books and libraries,[4] is very precise. No trace or

[1] *Cronica del Rei D. Diniz*, 1677 ed., f. 113 v.
[2] *Mandou hum livro delles escrito por sua mão a seu avò . . . o qual eu vi na livraria do Real Convento do Escurial, em folha de papel grosso, de marca pequena, volume de tres ou quatro dedos de alto, de letra grande, latina, bem legivel, e o que ly era de Louvores a Nossa Senhora, e outras cousas ao divino* (*Eva e Ave*, 1676 ed., pp. 128–9). This interesting passage is not included in those quoted in C.A.M.V. ii. 112–17; it is obviously the source of no. 17. It does not imply that the poems were exclusively religious. Can the book three or four fingers in height have been the *Canc. da Ajuda* (460 millimètres) from which a section of sacred poems may have been torn ? If so the letters *Rey Dõ Denis* (C. A. M. V. i. 141) would explain the attribution to King Dinis.
[3] The language of C. M. and the Portuguese *Cancioneiros* was of course the same. Identical phrases occur.
[4] He twice visited Oxford, he says, in order to see the library, which he describes—*hũa das grandes cousas do mundo* (*Eva e Ave*, 1676 ed., p. 156). At the Escorial he also examined an original manuscript of St. Augustine (ibid., p. 150).

memory of the existence of this manuscript exists, however, at the Escorial Library, nor is to be found in the *Catálogo de los Manuscritos existentes antes del incendio de 1671*. The subjects of King Diniz' ten[1] satirical poems are trivial, but he had too much force of character to descend to such vilenesses as were common among *profaçadores*. (His concise definition of a bore: *falou muit' e mal* (C. C. B. 411) is worthy of Afonso de Albuquerque.) Of his illegitimate sons, besides D. Afonso Sanchez, D. Pedro, Conde de Barcellos, long had a reputation as a poet almost equal to that of his father, owing to the association of his name with the *Cancioneiro*; but of his ten poems six (C. V. 1037–42) are satirical, and the four *cantigas de amor* (C. V. 210–13) are perhaps the heaviest and most prosaic in the collection. It was as a prose-writer and editor of the *Livro de Linhagens* that he worthily carried on the literary tradition of King Dinis.

[1] C. C. B. 406–15.

II

1325–1521

§ 1

Early Prose

WITH prose a new period opens, since, although there are Portuguese documents of the late twelfth century[1] and the Latin chrysalis was in an advanced stage of development even earlier, prose as a literary instrument does not begin before the fourteenth century or the end of the thirteenth at the earliest. The fragments of an early *Poetica*[2] clearly show how slow and awkward were still the movements of prose at a time when poetry had attained an exceedingly graceful expression. The next two centuries redressed the balance in the favour of prose. The victory of Aljubarrota (1385) made it possible to carry on the national work begun by King Dinis—the preparation of Portugal's resources for a high destiny. In this constructive process literature was not forgotten, and indeed its deliberate encouragement, as though it were an industry or a pine-forest, may account for the fact that it consisted mainly of prose—chronicles, numerous translations from Latin, Spanish, and other languages, works of religious or practical import. The first kings of the dynasty of Avis, who rendered noble service to Portuguese literature, were not poets, and in the second half of the fifteenth century Spanish influence, checked at Aljubarrota, succeeded by peaceful penetration in recovering all and more than all that it had lost, till it became common to hear lyrics of Boscan sung in the streets of Lisbon,[3] and uncommon for a Portuguese poet to versify in his mother tongue.[4] Prose

---

[1] Portuguese is then *uma lingua coherente, clara, um instrumento perfeito para a expressão do pensamento, cuja maior plasticidade dependerá apenas da cultura litteraria*, F. Adolpho Coelho, *A Lingua Portugueza* (1881), p. 87.

[2] See *supra*, p. 48.

[3] See p. 160.

[4] Cf. for the seventeenth century Galhegos' preface and *Mon. Lusit.*

EARLY PROSE

was more national. King Dinis had encouraged translation into Portuguese, and among other works his grandfather King Alfonso the Learned's *Cronica General* was translated by his order. The only edition that we have, *Historia Geral de Hespanha* (1863), is cut short in the reign of King Ramiro (cap. ccii, p. 192). The first 'O' of the preface in the manuscript contains the king in purple robe and crown of gold, pen in hand, with a book before him. The style is primitive, often a succession of short sentences beginning with 'And'.[1] In the convents brief lives of saints, portions of the Bible, prayers and regulations were written in Portuguese. Thus we have thirteenth- or fourteenth-century fragments of the rules of S. Bento, *Fragmentos de uma versão antiga da regra de S. Bento*, with its traces of a Latin original (e. g. *os desprezintes Deos = contemnentes Deum*); the *Actos dos Apostolos*, written in the middle of the fifteenth century by Frei Bernardo de Alcobaça and Frei Nicolao Vieira, that is, copied by them from an older manuscript; the eloquent prayers (*Libro de Horas*) translated by another Alcobaça monk, Frei João Claro (†1520?); the *Historias abreviadas do Testamento Velho*, printed from a manuscript of the fourteenth century, or of the thirteenth retouched in the fourteenth. The translation is close; the style foreshadows that of the *Leal Conselheiro*. The importance of these and other fragmentary versions of the Bible, in which there can rarely be a doubt as to the meaning of the words, is obvious. Extracts from the *Vida de Eufrosina* and the *Vida de Maria Egipcia*, published in 1882 by Jules Cornu from the manuscripts formerly in the Monastery of Alcobaça, now in the Torre do Tombo, show that they were written in vigorous if primitive prose (14th c.). *A Lenda dos Santos Barlaam e Josaphat* is perhaps a little later (end of the fourteenth or beginning of the fifteenth century). The *Visão de Tundalo*, of which the Latin original, *Visio Tundali*, was written by Frei Marcos not long after the date of the vision (1140),

---

V. xvi. 3: *achandose neste reino poucos que escrevão versos e não seja na lingua estranjeira de Castilla.*

[1] e.g. *E matou a grande serpente dallagoa de lerne que auja sete cabeças. E perseguio as pias filhas de finees que lhe aujã odio e o queriã desherdar. E foy cõ jaasson o que adusse o velloso dourado da ylha de colcos. E destroyu troya,* &c.

exists in two Portuguese versions, probably both of the fifteenth century (Monastery of Alcobaça). The *Vida de Santo Aleixo* also exists in two codices belonging to the middle and beginning of the fifteenth century, and Dr. Esteves Pereira, who published the latter, considers that the variants point to an earlier manuscript of the beginning of the fourteenth or end of the thirteenth century. To about the same period (14th–15th c.) belong the *Lenda de Santo Eloy*, the *Vida de Santo Amaro*, the *Vida de Santa Pelagia*, and many similar short devout treatises and legends which concern literature less than the development of the Portuguese language. Both literature and philology are interested in the early fifteenth-century work printed by Dr. Leite de Vasconcellos from the manuscript in the Vienna *Hofbibliothek* : *O Livro de Esopo*, which consists not of direct translations [1] from *Exopo greguo* of Antioch but of *estorias ffremosas de animalias*, told in the manner of Aesop, half a century before William Caxton and Robert Henryson, with great naturalness, vigour, and brevity.

The earliest entry of the *Cronica Breve do Archivo Nacional* is dated 1391, and both it and the *Cronicas Breves e memorias avulsas de Santa Cruz de Coimbra* are laconic annals of the first kings of Portugal, a few lines covering a whole reign. The *Livro da Noa de Santa Cruz de Coimbra* is an extract from the *Livro das Heras* of the same convent, and is, as the latter title indicates, a similar simple chronicle of events by years.[2] It begins in Latin, then Latin and Portuguese entries alternate till 1405. From 1406 to the end (1444) they are exclusively Portuguese. The *Cronica da Ordem dos Frades Menores* (1209–85) is a fifteenth-century Portuguese translation of a fourteenth-century Latin chronicle, and has been carefully edited by Dr. J. J. Nunes from the manuscript in the Lisbon Biblioteca Nacional; the *Vida de D. Tello* (15th c.), and the *Vida de S. Isabel*, the Queen-consort of King Dinis (earlier 15th c.), are 'historical' biographies

[1] Cf. *Por este enxemplo este doutor nos mostra,* or *este poeta nos dá ensinamento,* &c. The Fables of Aesop were translated into Portuguese prose by Manuel Mendez, a schoolmaster at Lagos (Algarve) : *Vida e Fabulas do Insigne Fabulador Grego Esopo.* Evora, 1603.

[2] e.g. of an earthquake: *Era de mil e quatrocentos e quatro desoito dias do mez de Junho tremeo a terra ao serão muy rijamente e foi por espaço que disserom o Pater tres vezes.*

EARLY PROSE

which contain more legend and less history than the *Cronica da Fundaçam do Moesteiro de S. Vicente de Lixboa* (*Cronica dos Vicentes*), a fifteenth-century version from a Latin original, *Indiculum*, of the eleventh century. There is far more life if equal brevity in the *Cronica da Conquista do Algarve* (*Coronica de como Dom Payo Correa . . . tomou este reino de Algarve aos Moros*)—a rapid, vivid sketch which reads almost like a chapter out of Fernam Lopez. Here at last was some one with will and power to make the dry bones live.[1] But meanwhile history of another kind had been written from a very early date. As a first rough catalogue of names the *livros de linhagens*, books of descent, as they were called by their compilers,[2] go back farther than the chronicles or religious prose, but so far as concerns their claim to literary form they belong like those to the fourteenth century. Of the four that have come down to us the *Livro Velho* is a jejune family register (11th–14th c.); the second is a mere fragment of the same kind. The manuscript of the third (*O Nobiliario do Collegio dos Nobres*) was bound up with the *Cancioneiro da Ajuda*, and together with the fourth, *O Nobiliario do Conde D. Pedro*, represents the lost original of the *Livro de Linhagens* of D. PEDRO, CONDE DE BARCELLOS (1289–1354). The *Nobiliario do Conde* has been shown by Alexandre Herculano, who printed it from the manuscript in the Torre do Tombo, to be the work of various authors extending over more than a century (13th–14th), the Conde de Barcellos being but one of them. It was in fact compiled like a modern peerage,[3] and was not intended to be final, new entries being added as time made them necessary, so that the passage *diz o Conde D. Pedro em seu livro* is as natural as the mention of Innocencio da Silva in a later volume of his great dictionary. But it was this son of King Dinis who with infinite diligence searched for documents far and wide, had recourse to the writings of King Alfonso X and others, and spared no pains to give the work

---

[1] The *Cronica Troyana*, edited in 1900 by the Spanish scholar and patient investigator D. Andrés Martínez Salazar, is a fourteenth-century Galician version of Benoît de Saint-More's *Roman de Troie*.

[2] The name *Nobiliario* is one of the erudite words which in the sixteenth century, here as in so many other cases, ousted the indigenous.

[3] Its object was *por saberem os homens fidalgos de Portugal de qual linhagem vem e de quaes coutos, honras, mosteiros e igreias som naturaes*.

an historical as well as a genealogical character. His researches (*Ouue de catar*, he says, *por gram trabalho por muitas terras escripturas que fallauam das linhagees*) set an excellent example to Fernam Lopez. Certainly the *Livro de Linhagens* is a vast catalogue of names, with at most a brief note after the name, as ' he was a good priest ' or ' a very good poet ' ; but it also gives succinct stories of the Kings of the Earth from Adam, including Priam, Alexander, Julius Caesar, and the early kings of Portugal, and it contains rare but charming intervals, green oases of legend and anecdote, such as the tale of King Lear with its happy ending, or the account of King Ramiro going to see his wife, who was a captive of the Moors.[1] Count Pedro, by his humanity and his generous conception of what a genealogy should be, really made the book his own. It was naturally consulted by the early chroniclers, its worth was recognized by the ablest author of the *Monarchia Lusitana*,[2] and recently, in the skilful hands of D. Carolina Michaëlis de Vasconcellos, it has rendered invaluable service in reconstructing the lives of the thirteenth-century poets.[3]

The *Livro de Linhagens* refers not only to King Lear but to Merlin, King Arthur, Lancelot, and the Isle of Avalon. Many other allusions, both earlier and later, to the Breton cycle, the *matière de Bretagne*, are to be found in early Portuguese literature : to the lovers Tristan and Iseult, to the *cantares de Cornoalha*,[4] to the chivalry of the Knights of the Round Table. In the fourteenth century many in Portugal were baptized with the name of Lancelot, Tristan, and Percival; and Nun' Alvarez (1360–1431) chose Galahad for his model, and came as near realizing his ideal as may be given to mortal man. In Gil Vicente's time the name Percival had already descended to the sphere of the peasants : as Passival (i. 11) in 1502

---

[1] His successful wile is similar to the stratagem in *Macbeth* : *e pois que a nave entrou pela foz cobrio-a de panos verdes em tal guisa que cuidassem que eram ramos, ca entonce o Douro era cuberto de hũa parte e da outra darvores.*

[2] *A escritura de maior utilidade que temos em Espanha* (Frei Francisco Brandão, *Mon. Lus.* V. xvii. 5).

[3] i. e. the copy printed in *Portug. Mon. Hist.* from the only existing manuscript (= the copy by Gaspar Alvarez de Lousada Machado (1554–1634) in the Lisbon Torre do Tombo).

[4] The ' songs of Cornwall ' are mentioned in C. V. 1007. Cf. 1140.

(*Auto Pastoril Castelhano*) and Pessival (i. 117) in 1534 (*Auto de Mofina Mendes*).

The early Portuguese *Cancioneiros* contain many references to this cycle, and the *Cancioneiro Colocci-Brancuti* opens with five celebrated songs,[1] imitations of Breton *lais*, with rubrics explaining their subjects, and mentioning King Arthur and Tristan, Iseult, Cornwall, Maraot of Ireland, and Lancelot. Whether they were incorporated in the *Cancioneiro* from a Portuguese *Tristam* earlier than the Spanish version (1343 ?), or, as is more probable, directly from the Old-French *Historia Tristani*, their presence here is a sufficient witness to the Portuguese fondness for such themes. It was but natural that a Celtic people living by the sea, delighting in vague legends and in foreign novelties, should have felt drawn towards these misty tales of love and wandering adventure, which carried them west as far as Cornwall and Ireland, and also East, through the search for the Holy Grail. It was natural that they should undergo their influence earlier and more strongly than their more direct and more national neighbours the Castilians, whose clear, definite descriptions in the twelfth-century *Poema del Cid* would send those legends drifting back to the dim regions of their birth. (Even to-day connexion with and sympathy for Ireland is far commoner in Galicia than in any other part of Spain.) Unhappily, most of the early Portuguese versions of the Breton legends have been lost. King Duarte in his library possessed *Merlim, O Livro de Tristam*, and *O Livro de Galaaz*. The probability that these were written in Portuguese, not in Spanish, is increased by the survival of *A Historia dos Cavalleiros da Mesa Redonda e da Demanda do Santo Graall*, as yet only partially published from the manuscript (2594) in the Vienna *Hofbibliothek*. It was written probably in the fourteenth century, perhaps at the end of the thirteenth, although the Vienna manuscript is more recent and belongs to the fifteenth century, in which the work was referred to by the poet Rodriguez de la Cámara.[2] It is a Portuguese version of the story of the Holy Grail, and, although not a

---

[1] See C. Michaëlis de Vasconcellos, *Cancioneiro da Ajuda*, ii. 479–525. They are called *lais, layx* (C. C. B. 7, 8).

[2] *En la grand demanda de Santo Greal Se lee*. *Gral* is still a common Portuguese word (= *almofariz*, a mortar).

continuous translation, was evidently written with the French original (doubtfully ascribed to Robert de Boron,[1] author of a different work on the same subject) constantly in view. Traces of French remain in its prose.[2] This was clearly part of a larger work,[3] perhaps of a whole cycle of works dealing with the search for the Holy Grail. The only others that we have in print are the *Estorea de Vespeseano* and the *Livro de Josep ab Arimatia*, the manuscript of which was discovered in the nineteenth century in the Torre do Tombo. This, in the same way as the *Demanda do Santo Graall*, is a later (16th c.) copy of a thirteenth–fourteenth-century Portuguese translation or adaptation from the French, and retains in its language signs of French origin. The incunable *Estorea de Vespeseano* (Lixboa, 1496) is a work in twenty-nine short chapters, which only incidentally[4] refers to the Holy Grail, but recounts vividly the event mentioned in the *Demanda*[5]: the destruction of Jerusalem by Vespasian and Titus. It was also known formerly as *Destroyçam de Jerusalem*.[6] It is an anonymous translation, made in the middle of the fifteenth century, not from the French *Destruction de Jérusalem*, but from the Spanish *Estoria del noble Vespesiano* (c. 1485 and 1499). Dr. Esteves Pereira believes that the 1499 Spanish edition is a retranslation from the Portuguese text originally translated from the Spanish.

Tennyson's revival of the Arthurian legend in England evoked no corresponding interest in Portugal in the nineteenth century, and the primitive and touching story as published in 1887 has left Sir Percival in the very middle of an adventure for over a generation. The descent of the Amadis romances from the noble ideal of chivalry of King Arthur's Court is obvious, but their exact pedigree, the date and nationality of the first ancestor of the Amadis who is still with us, has been the subject of some little contention.

[1] ruberte de borem is mentioned, 1887 ed., p. 44.
[2] Not to speak of *certas, onta, febre* (= *faible*), *a voso sciente*, which may be found in other Portuguese works of the fifteenth century, *san* (p. 136 *ad fin.*) apparently = Fr. *s'en*.
[3] Cf. *asi como o conto a ja deuisado* (1887 ed., p. 7).
[4] 1905 ed., p. 95.
[5] 1887 ed., p. 43: *despois uespesiom os eyxerdou e os destruio*.
[6] 1905 ed., pp. 17, 23, 106.

Amadis de Gaula has indeed been doubly fortunate. The successor of Lancelot, Galahad, and Tristan as a fearless and loyal knight, he early won his way in the Peninsula; he was spared by the priest and barber in the *Don Quixote* scrutiny, and now when Vives' 'pestiferous books',[1] those 'serious follies', are no longer read widely, he has received a new span of immortality as a corpse of Patroclus between the contending critics. The problem of the date and authorship has become more fascinating than the book. Champions for Spain and Portugal come forward armed for the fight: Braunfels, Gayangos, Baist are met by Theophilo Braga, Carolina Michäelis de Vasconcellos, Marcelino Menéndez y Pelayo, while Dr. Henry Thomas holds the scales. The ground is thick with their arrows. And beneath them all lies the simple ingenuous story as retold by Garci Rodriguez de Montalvo in or immediately after 1492 and published in 1508, still worth reading for its freshness and for its clear good style, which Braunfels, following up the praise in Juan de Valdés' *Diálogo de la Lengua* (*c.* 1535), declared could not be a translation.[2] The argument, conclusive in the case of the masterpiece of prose that is *Palmeirim*

[1] *De Institutione Christianae Feminae*, Bk. I, cap. 5 : 'Tum et de pestiferis libris cuiusmodi sunt in Hispania [= the whole Peninsula], Amadisius, Splandianus, Florisandus, Tirantus, Tristanus, quarum ineptiarum nullus est finis ; quotidie prodeunt novae : Caelistina laena, nequitiarum parens, carcer amorum : in Gallia Lancilotus a Lacu, Paris et Vienna, Ponthus et Sydonia, Petrus Provincialis et Magelona, Melusina, domina inexorabilis : in hac Belgica Florius et Albus Flos, Leonella et Cana morus, Curias et Floreta, Pyramus et Thisbe ' (*Ioannis Ludovici Vivis Valentini Opera Omnia*, 7 vols., Valentiae Edetanorum, 1782–8, iv. 87). A Portuguese *Tristan* may have existed, a Portuguese original of *Tirant lo Blanch* less probably, although Pedro Juan Martorell, who began it in the Valencian or Lemosin *a ii de Giner de lany 1460*, declares that he had not only translated it from English into Portuguese but (*mas encara*) from Portuguese into Valencian. He dedicated it to the *molt illustre Princep* Ferdinand of Portugal. Very probably the fame and origin of *Amadis* accounted for this 'English' original, as mythical as the Hungarian origin of *Las Sergas de Esplandian*, and for its alleged translation into Portuguese.

[2] Braunfels, *Versuch*: 'Montalvo hätte, um einer Uebersetzung den Ruhm des mustergiltigen Styls und des reinsten Kastilianisch zu verschaffen, ein Geist ersten Rangs sein müssen, was er nicht war.' Montalvo was probably not the real author even of the fourth book. The words (in this *Prólogo* of his *Amadis*), *que hasta aqui no es memoria de ninguno ser visto*, refer not to the fourth book but to Montalvo's *Sergas de Esplandian*, which is conveniently replaced by dots in T. Braga, *Questões* (1881), p. 99, and *Hist. da Litt. Port.*, i (1909), p. 313, and which the priest in *Don Quixote* properly consigned to the flames.

de Inglaterra, loses its force here, since Montalvo himself tells us that he corrected the work from old originals. Naturally we are curious to know what these *antiguos originales* were, but the question did not arise in the fourteenth and fifteenth centuries: readers did not then concern themselves greatly with the origin and authorship of a book; they were content to enjoy it. Evidently *Amadis* was enjoyed both in Spain and Portugal. It is mentioned in the middle of the fourteenth century in the Spanish translation, by Johan Garcia de Castrogeriz, of Egidio Colonna's *De regimine principum*, at the very time, that is, when the Spanish poet and chronicler, Pero López de Ayala (1332–1407), was reading *Amadis* in his youth.[1] Half a century later, in the last quarter of the fourteenth century, a poem by Pero Ferrus in the *Cancionero de Baena* refers to *Amadis* as written in three books. This is one of the most definite early references to *Amadis*, but of course reference to the book by a Spaniard does not necessarily imply that it was written in Spanish, and indeed some of the vaguer allusions may refer to a French or Anglo-French original. The most frequent Spanish references occur in the *Cancionero de Baena*, which was compiled in the middle of the fifteenth century, at a period, that is, which the last Galician lyrics written in Spain connected with the time when all eyes were turned to Portuguese as the universal language of Peninsular lyrics. Because the Portuguese language was used throughout Spain in lyric poetry, it is sometimes argued as if the Portuguese had no prose, could only sing. (The more real division was not between verse and prose but between the Portuguese lyrical love literature and the Spanish epic battle literature, and the early romances of chivalry, although written in prose, belong essentially to the former.) The prose rubrics of the Portuguese *Cancioneiros* and the *Poetica* of the *Cancioneiro Colocci-Brancuti* are sufficient to dispel this delusion. Whether this *Poetica* be contemporary (13th c.) of the lyrics or later (14th c.), it offers a striking contrast between the clumsiness of its prose and the smooth perfection of the poetry for which

---

[1] His connexion with Portugal was not voluntary. It was probably when he was a prisoner after the battle of Aljubarrota (1385) that he wrote the *Rimado de Palacio*, in which (st. 162) *Amadis* is mentioned.

it theorizes. Miguel Leite Ferreira's statement (1598) that *Amadis* is contemporary with the lyrics is therefore remarkable. He says that the archaic (time of King Dinis) language of the two sonnets—*Bom Vasco de Lobeira* and *Vinha Amor pelo campo trebelhando*—written by his father, Antonio Ferreira (1528–69), is the same as that in which Vasco de Lobeira wrote *Amadis of Gaul*. We know that King Dinis encouraged not only lyric poetry but also translations into Portuguese prose, but all the early Portuguese prose works are assigned to the fourteenth, not the thirteenth century. One of the earliest, the *Demanda do Santo Graall*, the language of which bears a close relation to that of the *Cancioneiros*, still belongs to the fourteenth century. Probably the later development of prose misled Leite Ferreira into making fourteenth-century prose contemporary with thirteenth-century verse. The Infante whom he here on the strength of the passage in Montalvo's *Amadis* identifies with the son of King Dinis, not with the earlier Prince Afonso (*c.* 1265–1312), may as Infante have expressed dislike of a certain incident (the treatment of Briolanja) in the already well-known story, and his preference would be borne in mind when the Portuguese version was written in his reign (1325–57). If the first Peninsular version of *Amadis* was composed in Portuguese in the middle of the fourteenth century, it may have been eagerly read as a novelty by López de Ayala. In the fourteenth century most Spaniards read, a few wrote[1] Portuguese lyrics; and there seems to be no reason why we should rigorously confine them to the reading of verse, to the exclusion of Portuguese prose. There is no means of deciding with certainty whether López de Ayala and Ferrus read *Amadis* in Spanish or in Portuguese, but there are inherent probabilities in favour of Portuguese. No one without a thesis to support would deny that, generally, the cycle of the Round Table, to which *Amadis* is so closely related, was more congenial to the Portuguese than to the Spanish temperament, that the geographical position of Portugal facilitated its introduction, and that, in the particular case of *Amadis*, the style and subject of the work, certainly of the first three

---

[1] For the later writers of Galician (second half 14th c.) see Professor Lang's *Cancioneiro Gallego-Castelhano* (1902).

books, are Portuguese rather than Spanish. Melancholy incidents, sentimental phrases and tears occur on nearly every page. Some critics even discern traces of Portuguese in the language.[1]

But if we admit that *Amadis* was written *c.* 1350, who was its author? It is noteworthy that while in Spanish it had been attributed to many persons, in Portugal tradition has persistently hovered round the name of Lobeira. Unfortunately the Lobeira authorship has given far more trouble than that of prince, Jew, or saint in Spain. Zurara, basing his statement on an earlier fifteenth-century authority, in a perfectly genuine passage of his *Cronica do Conde D. Pedro de Meneses*,[2] written in the middle of the fifteenth century, ascribes *Amadis* to Vasco de Lobeira. In the next century Dr. João de Barros [3] (not the historian) and Leite Ferreira agree with Zurara.[4] There was no reason why they should say Vasco rather than Pedro or João. According to Nunez de Leam, Vasco de Lobeira was knighted on the field of Aljubarrota (1385), according to Fernam Lopez he was already a knight in 1383.[5] If he was not a young but an old knight at

---

[1] *Lua* (glove), *cedo*, &c., of course occur in early Spanish prose. *Soledad* certainly occurs in the first three books more frequently than in other Spanish prose. The Portuguese atmosphere is altogether absent in *Las Sergas*.

[2] Cap. 63 : *o Livro d' Amadis, como quer que soomente este fosse feito a prazer de hum homem que se chamava Vasco Lobeira em tempo d' El Rey Dom Fernando, sendo todalas cousas do dito Liuro fingidas do Autor.*

[3] *Libro das Antiguidades* (1549), f. 32 v. : *E daqui [do Porto] foi natural uasco lobeira q̃ fez os prim*^(ros) *4 libros de amadis, obra certo muj subtil e graciosa e aprouada de todos os gallantes, mas comos [so] estas couzas se secão em nossas mãos os Castelhanos lhe mudarão a linguoagem e atribuirão a obra assi* [so]. This passage is, however, absent in the earliest manuscript. The spelling *couzas* implies a late date for its introduction.

[4] So did Faria e Sousa, but he, too, had his Lobeira doubts, and after noting that Vasco de Lobeira was knighted by King João I says : ' si ya no es que era otro del mismo nombre. Pero la Escritura de Amadis se tiene por del tiempo deste Rey don Iuan ' (*Fuente de Aganipe* (Madrid, 1646), § 10). The obvious sympathy of the author for the *escudero viejo* who is knighted in *Amadis* (ii. 13, 14) amidst the laughter of the Court ladies is perhaps significant.

[5] *Cronica de D. Fernando*, cap. 177. The year of his death, given as 1403, is quite uncertain. Soares de Brito in the *Theatrum* forms no independent opinion : ' Vascus de Lobeyra inter Lusitanos Scriptores enumeratur a Faria. . . . Floruit tempore Fernandi Regis.' Antonio Sousa de Macedo, in *Flores de España*, also follows Faria : Vasco de Lobeira *fué el primero que con gentil habilidad escribió libros de caballerías*. Nicolás Antonio (1617-84), *Bib. Nov.*, 1688 ed., ii. 322, says that Vasco de Lobeira *vulgo inter cives suos existimari solet auctor celeberrimi inter famosa scripti* Historia de Amadis de

Aljubarrota, it is just possible that he wrote the book thirty-five years earlier, in the same way that the historian Barros wrote *Clarimundo* in his youth.

If he lived on through the reigns of Pedro I (1357–67) and Fernando (1376–83), and acquired new distinction in battle in the reign of the latter, this might account for Zurara's assertion that he wrote *Amadis* in the reign of Fernando. But the chief obstacle to the authorship of Vasco is the existence in the *Cancioneiro Colocci-Brancuti* (Nos. 230 and 232 A) of a song by Joan de Lobeira, *Leonoreta, fin roseta,* which reappears with slight variations in Montalvo's *Amadis* (Lib. II, cap. xi : *este villancico*). It would seem then that Joan, not Vasco, wrote *Amadis*. Joan de Lobeira,[1] or Joan Pirez Lobeira, flourished in the second half of the thirteenth century, and so we have *Amadis* dating not only from the reign of King Dinis but from the first half of his reign. But does the existence of the poem entail that of a prose romance ? The early mention of Tristan, e.g. by Alfonso X, does not necessarily imply the existence of a thirteenth-century Peninsular *Tristan* in prose. May we not accept the poem, written in the stirring metre, dear to men of action, used by Alfonso X (C. M. 300), as merely a proof of the popularity of the story, fondness for an episode perhaps treated in greater detail in the Anglo-French original than in Montalvo's version ? Certainly it is in the highest degree improbable that a Spaniard, writing at the end of the fifteenth century, should extract a poem from the Portuguese *Cancioneiros* and insert it in his prose ; but the improbability disappears if in the middle of the fourteenth century a Portuguese (Vasco de Lobeira), perhaps drawn to the story by the poem of his ancestor, incorporated it in his romance. The late Antonio Thomaz Pires in 1904 discovered at Elvas the will of a João de Lobeira, *mercador*, who died

---

Gaula . . . *cuius laudes nos inter Anonymos curiose collegimus. Ostendere autem Lusitanos Amadisium hunc Lusitane loquentem, uti Castellani Castellanum ostendunt, ius et aequum esset in dubia re ne verbis tantum agerent.* The challenge in the last sentence is of interest, as coming in date between the two statements (by Leite Ferreira and the Conde da Ericeira) asserting the existence of the Portuguese text.

[1] There was a Canon of Santiago of this name in 1295, and he may have come to the Portuguese Court on business concerning certain privileges of the Chapter which King Dinis confirmed in 1324.

there in 1386, and in Dr. Theophilo Braga's latest opinion [1] there were three Portuguese versions of *Amadis*: that of the father, this João de Lobeira, written in the time of King Dinis (a long-lived race these Lobeiras!), that of the son,[2] Vasco, and a third by Pedro de Lobeira in the first half of the fifteenth century. The threefold authorship of this family heirloom is even more *cruu de creer* than the theory that a single Lobeira—Vasco—wrote it in the middle of the fourteenth century. A certain note of disapproval of *Amadis* as fabulous, shared by Portuguese and Spanish writers,[3] perhaps indicates a fairly late date: its irresponsible fiction would be less excusable if it was written in an age which was beginning to attach serious importance to *nobiliarios* and 'true' chronicles. Moreover, if the Portuguese adaptation of an Anglo-French legend had been even remotely as developed as the form in which we now have it, the Infante Afonso must have seen at once that the faithfulness of Amadis was absolutely essential to the story. But especially the fact that the Portuguese *Cancioneiros*, familiar with Tristan and the *matière de Bretagne*, are silent on the subject of *Amadis* is significant.

In Gottfried Baist's argument, based on a rigid division between early lyric poetry (as Portuguese) and early prose (as Spanish), the Leonoreta lyric, far from being a stumbling-block, is actually a sign of the Spanish origin of *Amadis*: as a fragment (14th c.) of a prose *Tristan* exists in Spanish, and five Portuguese Tristan *lais* figure in the *Cancioneiro Colocci-Brancuti*, so the Leonoreta poem belongs to a Spanish *Amadis* in prose. But although the priority and relations of early Portuguese and Spanish prose works are intricate and have not yet been thoroughly studied, it is clear that in many cases versions have been more carefully preserved in conservative Spain, while the Portuguese through neglect, fire, and earthquake have perished, and also that the natural tendency and development of prose, in view of

[1] *Hist. da Litt. Port.* i (1909).
[2] In the document the only son mentioned is named Gonçalo.
[3] Zurara, loc. cit., *cousas fingidas*; López de Ayala, *mentiras probadas*. According to D. Francisco de Portugal (*Arte de Galantería*, p. 146) such lies could only be written in Spanish (*en la Portuguesa no se podía mentir tanto*). Portugal was writing in Spanish.

EARLY PROSE

the growing power of Castille and the greater pliancy of the Portuguese, was from Portuguese to Spanish, not from Spanish to Portuguese. And in one instance at least we have an early Portuguese prose work of the first importance, the *Demanda do Santo Graall*, which with its gallicisms can by no stretch of imagination be accounted a version from the Spanish. It is plainly legitimate to hold that the story of Amadis was first reduced to book form in the Peninsula in precisely the same way as was the story of Galahad, i.e. as a fourteenth-century Portuguese adaptation with the French text in view. Nicholas d'Herberay des Essarts, we know, claimed to have discovered fragments of *Amadis en langage picard*, Jorge Cardoso (1606–69) declared that Pero Lobeira translated *Amadis* from the French,[1] and Bernardo Tasso, whose *Amadigi* appeared in 1560, believed (*non è dubbio*) *Amadis* to be derived *da qualche istoria di Bretagna*. Nor would the Portuguese, for all their familiarity with the story and topography of the Breton cycle, be likely to compose original works dealing with Vindilisora (Windsor) or Bristoya (Bristol). Unhappily, however deep may be our conviction (a conviction which stands in no need of antedating Hebrew versions of the 1508 *Amadis*) that the Peninsular *Amadis* was originally Portuguese, it has now ceased to belong to Portuguese literature; another instance, if we may beg the question, of the gravitation to Spain. The Portuguese text, of which a copy, according to Leite Ferreira, existed in the library of the Duques de Aveiro in the sixteenth century (1598), and, according to the Conde da Ericeira, in the library of the Condes de Vimieiro in the seventeenth (1686), is still missing, as it was in 1726.

[1] *Agiologio Lusitano*, i (1652), p. 410 : *E por seu mandado* [of the Infante Pedro, son of João I] *trasladou de Frances em a nossa lingua Pero Lobeiro* [so], *Tabalião d'Eluas, o liuro de Amadis*.

§ 2

Epic and Later Galician Poetry

SOME of the poems of the early *Cancioneiros*, as we have seen, have an historical character, but they are all written from a personal point of view. Portuguese history, with its heroic achievements such as the conquest of Algarve, seems to have begun just too late to be the subject of great anonymous epics, or rather the temperament of the Portuguese people eschewed them. Of five poems, long believed to be the earliest examples of Portuguese verse but no longer accepted by any sane critic as genuine, only one belongs to epic poetry. This *Poema da Cava* or *da Perda de Espanha* was an infant prodigy indeed, since it was supposed to have been written (in *oitavas*) in the eighth century. With a discretion passing that of Horace it kept itself from the world not for nine but nine hundred years, and was first published in Leitão de Andrada's *Miscellanea* (1629)[1]: *O rouço da Cava imprio de tal sanha*, &c.

Of the four other spurious poems, two[2] were alleged to be love letters of Egas Moniz Coelho, a cousin of the celebrated Egas Moniz Coelho of the twelfth century; another, published by Bernardo de Brito,[3] *Tinherabos nam tinherabos*, has a real charm as gibberish. Fascination, of a different kind, attaches also to the fifth :

No figueiral figueiredo,   no figueiral entrei :
Tres niñas encontrara,   tres niñas encontrei,

for if this poem is not genuine, and the fact that it was first published by Brito[4] at once lays it open to grave suspicion, it is nevertheless undoubtedly based on popular tradition of a yearly

[1] 1867 ed., p. 333.   [2] Ibid., pp. 304–7.
[3] *Cronica de Cister*, Bk. VI, cap. 1, 1602 ed., f. 372. It has been several times reprinted : cf. J. F. Barreto, *Ortografia* (1671), p. 23 ; Bellermann, *Die alten Liederbücher*, p. 5 ; *Grundriss*, p. 163.
[4] *Monarchia Lusitana*, 1609 ed., ii. 296 (also in *Miscellanea*, 1867 ed., pp. 25–6 ; Bellermann, pp. 3–4).

tribute of maidens to the Moors such as the Greeks paid to the Minotaur, and must be the echo of some Algarvian song. Its simple repetitions have a haunting rhythm, but they are perhaps a little too emphatic. The impression is that its author had been struck by the repetitions in songs heard on the lips of the people, perhaps crooned to him in his infancy (cf. *Miscellanea*, p. 25: *sendo eu muito menino*), and worked them up in this poem. One early epic poem Portugal undoubtedly possessed, the *Poema da Batalha do Salado*, by AFONSO GIRALDEZ, who himself probably took part in the battle (1340). The subject of the poem is the same as that of the Spanish *Poema de Alfonso Onceno*, but whether its treatment was similar we cannot say, as only forty lines of the Galician-Portuguese poem survive. Since the authorship of the Spanish poem is doubtful and its rhymes run more naturally in Galician than in Spanish, the theory has arisen, among others, that Rodrigo Yannez, whose name perhaps denotes a connexion with Galicia, merely translated the poem of Afonso Giraldez. But against this it is argued that Yannez or Eanez was a Galician or wrote Galician lyrics (there are several poets of that name in the *Cancioneiro da Vaticana*), and when called upon to compose an epic—for Spain a late epic—chose Castilian, the traditional language of such poetry, and in executing his design found that his enthusiasm had outrun his knowledge of Castilian.[1] It is not strange if so brilliant a victory inspired two poets independently with its theme. It is perhaps more extraordinary that both should have chosen a metre (8 + 8) which has called for remark as showing the *romance* through the *cantar de gesta*.[2] Frei Antonio Brandão, indeed, called the Portuguese poem a *romance*, a type of poem which did not exist in the fourteenth century. Since the battle was fought in Spain it would be considered in Brandão's day a proper subject for a *romance*, but would be noticeable as being written in Galician. Castilian was throughout the Peninsula regarded as the fitting medium for the *romance*, as for its father the epic, just as, a century earlier, Galician was the universal

---

[1] See *Grundriss*, p. 205. D. Ramón Menéndez Pidal supports the suggestion of Leonese authorship (*Revista de Filología Española*, I. i (1914), pp. 90–2).
[2] See J. Fitzmaurice-Kelly, *Littérature Espagnole*, 1913 ed., p. 64.

language of the lyric.[1] Portuguese poets, if they wrote a *romance*, would usually do so in Spanish. The best-known instance is Gil Vicente's fine poem (*muy sentido y galan* as the 1720 editor says) of *D. Duardos e Flerida*, which only belongs to Portuguese literature through the excellent ' translation of the Cavalheiro de Oliveira ', among whose papers Garrett professed to have found it. Portugal possessed no epic *cantares de gesta* of her own, had not therefore the stuff out of which the *romances* were formed, and the birth of the *romance* coincided with the predominance of Spanish influence in Spain. It is therefore surprising to find in Portugal a large number of *romances* unconnected with Spain, the explanation being that, having accepted with characteristic enthusiasm the new thing imported from abroad, the Portuguese turned to congenial themes, of love, religion, and adventure. Had the *romances* been elaborated in the same way as in Spain, we might have expected a large number of anonymous Portuguese *romances* dealing with the Breton cycle, and indeed with early Portuguese history, so rich in heroic incidents. The fact that this is not the case and the number of *romances* collected in Tras-os-Montes alike point to their Spanish origin, while their frequency in the Azores denotes how popular they became later in Portugal. In the sixteenth century their Spanish character was recognized. The poor *escudeiro* in *Eufrosina* is bidden go to Spain to gloss *romances*, and in the seventeenth century, as a passage in Mello's *Fidalgo Aprendiz* well shows, they were better liked if written in Spanish. The partiality for Spanish applied to poetry of other kinds, and Manuel de Galhegos says (1635) that it is a bold venture to publish poetry in Portuguese.[2] But it did not as a rule extend to popular poetry. It is therefore noteworthy that the nurse in Gil Vicente sings *romances* in Spanish.[3] Dr. Theophilo Braga, who considers Spanish influence on the *romances* in

---

[1] Cf. Rodriguez Lobo, *Primavera* (1722 ed.), p. 369 : *tinhão os nossos guardadores por muyto difficultoso fazeremse em a lingoa Portugueza, porque a tem por menos engraçada para os romances.* Sousa de Macedo says that *Romance he poesia propria de Hespanha*, but Hespanha here means Spain and Portugal and he instances Góngora and Rodriguez Lobo (*Eva e Ave*, 1676 ed., p. 130).

[2] See *infra*, p. 258.

[3] *Obras*, 1834 ed., ii. 27.

EPIC AND LATER GALICIAN POETRY 75

Portugal to have been 'late and insignificant',[1] is obliged, in order to support his argument, to quote not Portuguese but Spanish *romances*.[2] Nor is it a happy contention that Portuguese *romances* were not printed owing to *desleixo*, since the publication of Spanish *romances* at Lisbon cannot be attributed merely to a craze for things foreign. More persuasive is the theory, developed by D. Carolina Michaëlis de Vasconcellos,[3] that many *romances* in Spanish were the work of Portuguese poets, especially those related to the Breton cycle, such as *Ferido está Don Tristan*, those concerned with the sea, and those of a soft lyrical character, as *Fonte Frida* and *La Bella Malmaridada*. However that may be, the fact that *romances* appear on the lips of the people in Gil Vicente, that is, before the publication of the *romanceros*, indicates how rapidly their popularity spread,[4] and accounts for their numerous progeny in Portugal, collected in the nineteenth century. True historical *romances* the Portuguese did not possess, unless we are to consider that certain lines which occur in Vicente's parody of *Yo me estaba allá en Coimbra*, in Garcia de Resende's *Trovas*, and elsewhere, are echoes of a Portuguese *romance* on the death of Inés de Castro.[5] But that is not to say that they did not possess *romances*, and many of these might be almost as old as their Spanish models, although not derived directly from *cantares de gesta*. These Portuguese *romances* or *xacaras* (in the Azores *estorias* and *aravias*) often differ from the Spanish in a certain vagueness of outline and sentimental tone. They are frequently of considerable length. Many of them are undoubtedly of popular origin and have a large number of variants in different parts of the country. If

[1] *Hist. da Litt. Port.*, ii (1914), pp. 267-87.   [2] Ibid., pp. 280-5.
[3] *Estudos sobre o Romanceiro Peninsular. Romances velhos de Portugal*, Madrid, 1907-9.
[4] Lucena (*Vida*, Bk. III, cap. 3) speaks of *romances velhos em que elles* [the natives of India] *como nos, por ser o ordinario cantar da gente, guardam o successo das memorias e cousas antigas*. The expression *romance velho* in the sixteenth century may mean a *romance* that has gone out of fashion. Cf. Vicente, *Os Almocreves*: *Hei os de todos grosar Ainda que sejam velhos*. *Antigo* may similarly mean 'antiquated' rather than ancient. Barros, *Grammatica*, 1785 ed., p. 163, mentions *rimances antigos*. D. Carolina Michaëlis de Vasconcellos considers that the *romances* came from Spain to Portugal at the latest in the third quarter and perhaps in the first half of the fifteenth century.
[5] See *Estudos sobre o Rom. Penins.* (the lines are *Polos campos do Mondego Cavaleiros vi somar*).

there are none to compare with *Fonte Frida* or *Conde Arnaldos* (which belong to Castilian literature, whatever the nationality of their authors), they nevertheless, with a total lack of concentration, present many natural scenes and incidents of affecting pathos and an attractive simplicity. One of the best and most characteristically Portuguese is *A Nau Catharineta*, and others almost equally famous are *Santa Iria, Conde Nillo*, and *Brancaflor e Flores*. The second edition of Dr. Theophilo Braga's *Romanceiro* runs to nearly two thousand pages. The first two volumes contain over 150 *romances* (together with numerous variants). Of these 5 belong to the Carolingian, 8 to the Arthurian cycle, 63 are *romances sacros* or *ao divino*, 11 treat of the cruel husband or unfaithful wife. In the third volume are reprinted *romances* composed by well-known Portuguese authors of the sixteenth and seventeenth centuries. It must be admitted that Spain generously repaid to Portugal the loan of the Galician language for lyrical composition—although in each case it was the lender's literature that profited (especially if some of the most beautiful Spanish *romances* were the work of Galician or Portuguese poets). But even after the birth of the *romance* Spain continued to cultivate the Galician lyric, until the second half of the fifteenth century. The last instance is supposed to be a Galician poem by Gomez Manrique (1412–91), uncle of the author of *Recuerde el alma dormida*, No. 65 in the *Cancioneiro Gallego-Castelhano*. This collection, published by Professor Lang at the suggestion of D. Carolina Michaëlis de Vasconcellos, contains the meagre crop of Portuguese verse of the transition period from 1350 to 1450, meagre in quality and quantity. One name dominates the period. The love and tragic fate of MACIAS (second half 14th c.), *o Namorado, idolo de los amantes*, gave him a renown similar to but far exceeding that of D. Joan Soarez de Paiva in the preceding century. As the ideal lover he is met with at every turn in the Portuguese poetry of the fifteenth century,[1] and later became the subject of Lope de Vega's *Porfiar hasta morir* (1638). Of his story we know definitely nothing, but some lines in one of his poems, *En meu*

---

[1] In later Portuguese his name was often written Mansias. So Moraes transforms Mlle de Macy's name into Mansi.

cor tenno ta lança and *Aquesta lança . . . me ferio*, would appear to have inspired the famous legend which dates from the end of the fifteenth century. Imprisoned at Arjonilla in Andalucía for paying court to his *sennora*, he continued to address her in song and was killed by the lance that her infuriated husband hurled through the prison window. In an older version, that of the Constable D. Pedro in his *Satira de felice e infelice vida*, he saved the lady of his heart from drowning, and afterwards, as he lingered where she had stood, was struck down by the jealous husband. According to Argote de Molina,[1] both he and the husband served in the household of D. Enrique de Villena (1385-1434), who was perhaps only six when Macias died. Most of the twenty poems ascribed to Macias that survive are written in Galician, and of many, as *Loado sejas amor*,[2] the authorship is doubtful. Clearly his fame would act as a strong magnet to poems of uncertain origin. The matter is of the less importance in that these poems, however love-sick, have but little literary merit. If the Galician JUAN RODRIGUEZ DE LA CÁMARA, a native, like Macias, of Padron, was the real author of the *romance* of *Conde Arnaldos* (which is improbable), he was a far greater poet than his friend. Both the lyrics and the prose of his *El Sieruo libre de Amor* are in Castilian. Of the other two fourteenth-century Galician poets mentioned by Santillana, FERNAM CASQUICIO and VASCO PEREZ DE CAMÕES (†1386?),[3] no poems have survived. The latter, a knight well known at the Court of King Ferdinand and an ancestor of Luis de Camões, played a leading part in the troubles preceding the battle of Aljubarrota. He had come to Portugal from Galicia, and his name appears frequently in the pages of Fernam Lopez (where it is written Caamoões) till the year 1386. In the middle of the sixteenth century he is mentioned by Sá de Miranda's brother-in-law as a Court poet corresponding to Juan de Mena in Spain. But there were other poets whose verse was probably not inferior

---

[1] *Nobleza de Andaluzia* (1588), ii, f. 272 v.
[2] This and two other Macias poems (*Ai que mal aconsellado* and *Crueldad e trocamento*) are in C. G. C. (Nos. 33, 38, 41) ascribed to Alfonso Alvarez de Villasandino.
[3] The *Cancionero de Baena* contains poems addressed to Vasco *Lopez* de Camões, *un cavallero de Galizia*, and an answering poem by him.

to that of Perez de Camões and Casquicio. Besides Macias the *Cancioneiro Gallego-Castelhano* contains the names of sixteen writers whose poems may not attain high distinction but prove that the Galician lyric continued to be cultivated by poets in the fourteenth and first half of the fifteenth century in Castille and Leon, Aragon and Catalonia. The Archdeacon of Toro, Gonçalo Rodriguez (fl. 1385),[1] was one of a group of such poets; a man with a keen zest of living and capable of vigorous verse, in which he took a characteristic delight (*a minna boa arte de lindo cantar*). In his farewell poem *A Deus Amor, a Deus el Rei*, which Cervantes perhaps remembered, he bids good-bye to the *trobadores con quen trobei*, and in a quaint humorous testament he mentions a number of friends and relatives, two of whom, at least, his cousin Pedro de Valcacer or Valcarcel and Lope de Porto Carreiro, also wrote verse. In the last of the sixteen stanzas (*abbacca*) of this *testamento* the Archdeacon appoints his namesake Gonçalo Rodriguez de Sousa and Fernan Rodriguez to be his executors. He may have been alive in 1402, for a Doctor Gonçalo Rodriguez, Archdeacon of Almazan, is mentioned as one of the witnesses to the oath taken by the city of Burgos to the Infante María in that year.[2] In that case he must have been transferred to Almazan, some 150 miles farther up the Duero. More chequered was the career of Garci Ferrandez de Gerena (*c.* 1340–*c.* 1400). Having married one of King Juan I's dancing girls (*una juglara*) in the belief that she was rich, he repented when he found *que non tenia nada*. He next became a hermit near Gerena, and, this not proving more congenial than married poverty, he embarked ostensibly for the Holy Land, but in fact landed at Malaga with his wife and children. At Granada he turned Moor, satirized the Christian faith, and deserted his wife for her sister. After such proven inconstancy we may perhaps doubt the sincerity of his repentance when he returned to Christianity and Castille at the end

[1] For the name of this hitherto anonymous poet see *The Modern Language Review* (July 1917), pp. 357–8.
[2] Gil Gonzalez Davila, *Historia de la Vida y Hechos del Rey Don Henriqve Tercero*, &c. (Madrid, 1638), p. 173. The name was a common one. The Spanish translator of Pero Menino's *Livro de Cetreria*, Gonçalo Rodriguez de Escobar, may have been a relation. There was also a fourteenth-century poet called Ruiz de Toro.

of the fourteenth century. But for all his weakness and folly he seems not to have sunk utterly out of the reach of finer feelings; he sang various episodes of his life, e.g. when he went to his hermitage (*puso se beato*), in lyrics of some charm, and addressed the nightingale in a dialogue, as did his contemporary, ALFONSO ALVAREZ DE VILLASANDINO (*c.* 1345–*c.* 1428). This Castilian Court poet, born at Villasandino near Burgos and possessed of property at Illescas, was of a sleeker and more subservient mind than Garci Ferrandez and prospered accordingly, *en onra e en ben e en alto estado*. He wrote to order and was considered the 'crown and king of all the *poetas e trovadores* who had ever existed in the whole of Spain'. This extravagant claim of his admirers need not prevent us from recognizing that there is often real feeling and music in his poems, of which the *Cancionero de Baena* has preserved over twenty. He writes in varying metres with unfailing ease and harmony, rarely sinks into mere verbal dexterity, and well deserves to be considered the best of these later Galician poets. Side by side with the lyric the *cantiga d'escarnho* continued to flourish. Alfonso Alvarez (C. G. C. 48) upbraids Garci Ferrandez for renouncing the Christian faith and leaguing himself with the Devil (*gannaste privança do demo mayor*); Pero Velez de Guevara (†1420), uncle of the Marqués de Santillana, addresses a satiric poem to an old maid, and an anonymous poet in a vigorous *sirventes* attacks degenerate Castille, *cativa, mezela Castela*, perhaps, as Professor Lang thinks, immediately after the Portuguese victories of Trancoso, Aljubarrota, and Valverde in 1385. Five fragmentary poems belong to the Infante D. PEDRO (1429–66), Constable of Portugal. There are, besides his three short Portuguese poems in the *Cancioneiro de Resende*, only forty-one lines in all, for while Galician, already separated from her twin sister of Portugal, went to sleep—a sleep of nearly four centuries—in these last accents of her muse preserved in the *Cancionero de Baena*, the Infante Pedro turned definitely to the new forms of lyric appearing in Castille. As a transition poet he may be mentioned here before his father D. Pedro, Duke of Coimbra, since his prose works, which would naturally place him with his father and with D. Duarte, his uncle, belong, together with most of his poetry (*prosas* and *metros*) to Spanish literature. By stress of circumstance rather than any set purpose he inaugurated the fashion of writing in Castilian, a fashion so eagerly taken up by his fellow-countrymen during the next two centuries. After the tragic death of his father at Alfarrobeira (1449) he escaped from Portugal, of which his sister Isabel was queen,[1] spent the next seven years as an exile in Castille, and after returning to his native land died an exile, but now as King of Aragon (1464–6). His life of thirty-seven years was thus as full of wandering adventure as that of any troubadour of old. To him Santillana addressed his celebrated letter on the development of poetry, and his own influence on Portuguese literature was important, for he introduced not only a new style of poetry, including *oitavas de arte maior*, but the habit of classical allusion and allegory. His first work, *Satira de felice e infelice vida*, was written in Portuguese before he was twenty, but re-written by himself in Castilian, the only form in which it has survived. This firstfruit of his studies was dedicated to his sister, Queen Isabel, whose death (1455) he mourned in his *Tragedia de la Insigne Reyna Doña Isabel* (1457), a work of deep feeling and some literary merit, first published by D. Carolina Michaëlis de Vasconcellos 444 years after Queen Isabel's death. His longest and most important poem, in 125 octaves, *Coplas del menosprecio e contempto de las cosas fermosas del mundo* (1455), reflects the misfortunes of his life and the high philosophy they had brought him. Under a false attribution to his father, the Duke of Coimbra [2] (his Portuguese poems were also wrongly ascribed to King Peter I of Portugal, through confusion with the later King Peter, of Aragon), it was incorporated in the *Cancioneiro de Resende*, which appeared half a century after the Constable's death.

[1] Another sister, D. PHILIPPA DE LENCASTRE (1437–97), lived in retirement in the convent of Odivellas near Lisbon, and as a dedicatory poem to her translation of the Gospels wrote the simple, impressive lines beginning
Non vos sirvo, non vos amo,
Mas desejo vos amar.

[2] Cf. Ribeiro dos Santos, *Obras* (MS.), vol. xix, f. 205 : *A frente de todos os Poetas deste Seculo apparece como hum Ds [Deus] da Poezia o Infante D. Pedro, filho do Snr. Rey D. João I.* In reality he was not gifted with greater poetical talent than his brothers.

§ 3
The Chroniclers

THE father of Portuguese history, FERNAM LOPEZ (*c.* 1380–*c.* 1460), had grown up with the generation that succeeded Aljubarrota, and from his earliest years imbibed the national enthusiasm of the time. He had himself seen Nun' Alvarez as a young man and the heroes who had fought in a hundred fights to free their country from a foreign yoke, and he had listened to many a tale of Lisbon's sufferings during the great siege.[1] Since 1418, at latest, he was employed in the Lisbon Torre do Tombo (the State Archives), for in that year he was appointed keeper of the documents (*escrituras*) there. Sixteen years later, King Duarte, who as prince encouraged him to collect materials for the work,[2] entrusted him with the task of writing the chronicles of the Kings of Portugal (*poer em caronycas as estorias dos reys*), and at the same time (March 19, 1434 [3]) assigned him a salary of 14,000 *réis*. His work at the Torre do Tombo covered a period of over thirty years. He won and kept the confidence of three kings, was secretary to João I (*escrivam dos livros*) and to the Infante Fernando (*escrivam da puridade*), whose will exists in Lopez' handwriting.[4] His son Martinho accompanied the Infante to Africa as doctor, and died (1443) in prison soon after the prince. The last document signed by Lopez as official is dated 1451; in July 1452 he seems to have resigned his position at least temporarily, and on June 6, 1454, he was definitely superseded by Zurara as being 'so old and

[1] Lopez himself was probably of humble birth. It appears from a document presented by Dr. Pedro de Azevedo at a meeting of the *Sociedade Portuguesa de Estudos Historicos* in July 1916 that his wife's niece was married to a shoemaker.
[2] Zurara, *Cron. D. Joam*, cap. 2.
[3] i.e. eighty-nine years before the first English translation of Froissart was published. Needless to say, no English translation of Lopez exists.
[4] A facsimile of a page of this lengthy document is given in Snr. Braamcamp Freire's excellent edition of the *Primeira Parte da Crónica de D. Joam I* (1915).

weak that he cannot well fulfil the duties of his post'. That he lived for at least five years more we know from the existence of a document (July 3, 1459) referring to the pretensions of an illegitimate son of Martinho which Fernam Lopez rejected.[1] Of the chronicles of the first ten Kings of Portugal written by Lopez[2] only three survive: the *Cronica del Rei Dom Joam de boa memoria*, *Cronica del Rei Dom Fernando*, and *Cronica del Rei Dom Pedro*. The latter is but a brief sketch, and lacks the unity which the subject-matter gives to the other two. His chronicles of the seven earlier kings disappeared in the revised versions of subsequent historians. Although they no doubt incorporated large slices of his work with little alteration, the freshness and the style are gone, the good oak hidden beneath coats of paint. It was a proceeding the more deplorable in that Lopez had been at great pains to discover and record the truth, 'the naked truth'.[3] His successor, Zurara, represents him as 'a notable person', 'a man of some learning and great authority';[4] he travelled through the whole of Portugal to collect information and spent much time in visiting churches and convents in search of papers and inscriptions, while King Duarte had documents brought from Spain for his use. Whatever sources he utilized, Latin, Spanish, or Portuguese, he stamped his work with his own individuality. He himself frequently refers to previous historians, and often expresses his disapproval of their methods.[5] He seems to have drawn largely from a Latin work of a certain Dr. Cristoforus. Keenly alive to the dignity and responsibilities

[1] See A. Braamcamp Freire, ibid., pp. xl–xlii.
[2] *Fez todas as chronicas dos Reis té seu tempo, começando do Conde dom Henrique, como prova Damião de Goes* (Gaspar Estaço, *Varias Antigvidades de Portugal* (1625), cap. 21, § 1); cf. Goes, *Cron. de D. Manuel*, iv. 38.
[3] *Nosso desejo foi em esta obra escrever verdade—nuamente—a nua verdade* (*Cr. D. Joam, Prologo*).
[4] Zurara, *Cr. D. Joam*, cap. 2. Cf. Lopez' preface to his *Cr. D. Joam*: *Oo com quamto cuidado e diligemçia vimos grandes vollumes de livros, de desvairadas linguageẽs e terras; e isso meesmo pubricas escprituras de muitos cartarios e outros logares nas quaaes depois de longas vegilias e grandes trabalhos mais çertidom aver nom podemos da contheuda em esta obra* (1915 ed., p. 2).
[5] Usually he does this without naming the offender, but he refutes the *razões* of Martim Afonso de Mello, a person well known at the Court of King João I and author of a technical book on the art of war, *Da Guerra* (see Zurara, *Cr. D. Joam*, cap. 99). Mello refused the governorship of captured Ceuta in 1415. A work on a similar subject, *Tratado da Milicia*, is ascribed to Zurara's friend and patron, King Afonso V (Barbosa Machado, i. 19).

of history, he was anxious that his work should be well ordered and philosophical.[1] He has been called the Portuguese Froissart, but he combines with Froissart's picturesqueness moral philosophy, enthusiasm, and high principles, is in fact a Froissart with something of Montaigne added, and easily excels Giovanni Villani or Pero López de Ayala. The latter must descend from the pedestal given him by Menéndez y Pelayo,[2] since he only occasionally rises to the height of Fernam Lopez, as in the account of the murder of the Infante Fradique, which Lopez copies very closely (although abbreviating it as really foreign to his history), evidently appreciating such dramatic touches as the sentence which describes how, as the murdered man advanced through the palace, ever fewer went in his company. By the side of the laborious prose and precocious wisdom of King Duarte this child of genius seems to give free rein to his pen, but it is his greatness and his title to rank above all contemporary chroniclers, not only of Portugal but of Europe, that he could combine this spontaneity with the scruples of an accurate historian, and be at once careful and impetuous, or, as Goes calls him, copious and discreet. He assigns speeches of considerable length to the principal actors, but they contain not mere rhetoric[3] but arguments such as might well have been used; and the frequent shorter sayings of humbler persons, often anonymous and as illuminating as *graffiti*, have the stamp of truth and bring the scenes most clearly before us. Indeed, every sentence is living; his unfailing qualities are rapidity and directness. Sometimes the sound of galloping horses or the loud murmur of a throng of men is in his pages. He ever and anon rivets the reader's—the listener's—attention by some captivating phrase, by his quaintly expressed wisdom, by his personal keenness and delight in the ' marvellous deeds of God ' (*maravilhas que Deos faz*) or in the actions of his heroes (*Oo que fremosa cousa era de veer !*). His chronicles are not only a succession of imperishably

[1] *Cr. del Rei D. Fern.*, cap. 2 : *a ordenança de nossa obra* ; *Cr. D. Joam*, 1915 ed., p. 51 : *Certo he que quaaesquer estorias muito melhor se entemdem e nembram se som perfeitamente e bem hordenadas* ; *Cr. del Rei D. Fern.*, cap. 139 : *guardando a regra do philosopho* [of cause and effect].
[2] *Antología*, iv, p. xx : *Nada hay semejante en las literaturas extranjeras antes de fin del siglo xv*. The words apply more accurately to Fernam Lopez.
[3] *Leixados os compostos e afeitados razoamentos* (*Cr. D. Joam, Prologo*).

vivid scenes—King Pedro dancing through his capital by night, the escape of Diogo Lopez, the punishment of D. Inés' murderers, the siege of Lisbon, the murder of D. Maria Tellez —but describe fully and with skilful care the character of the actors, pleasure-loving King Ferdinand, cunning, audacious, and accomplished Queen Lianor Tellez, wise and noble Queen Philippa, even morose Juan I, and principally the popular Mestre d'Avis and his great Constable, Nun' Alvarez Pereira. And the Portuguese people is delineated both collectively and as individuals, in its generous enthusiasm, unreasoning impetuosity, and atrocious anger. That Lopez paid attention to his style is proved by his modest disclaimer bidding the reader expect no *fremosura e afeitamento das pallavras*, but merely the facts *breve e sãamente contados, em bom e claro estilo*. His style is always clear and natural, the serviceable handmaid of his subject, admirably assuming the colour and sound of the events described, and his longest sentences are never obscure. He wrote his history on a generous scale, for in the rapidity of his descriptions this inimitable story-teller preserved his leisure. His last chronicle ended with the expedition to Ceuta (1415). The kernel of that chronicle had been the illustrious deeds and character of Nun' Alvarez, also described in the hitherto anonymous *Coronica do condestabre de purtugal*, of which the earliest edition is dated 1526. Large tracts of this chronicle are included, with alterations, in Lopez' Chronicles of King Fernando and King João I. Dr. Esteves Pereira and Snr. Braamcamp Freire have now independently come to the conclusion that it is the work of Lopez, clearly an earlier work[1] written shortly after the death of Nun' Alvarez (1431), i. e. before he concluded the *Cronica de D. Fernando*[2] and wrote the *Cronica de D. Joam*, at which he was working in 1443.[3] We are forced to accept this view, although of course it is no argument to say that the conscientious and scrupulous Fernam Lopez could not be a plagiarist since it was the duty of the official chronicler of the day to incorporate the best work of other historians. Lopez'

---

[1] The references in cap. 76 and 80 to events of 1451 and 1461 are evidently later additions.
[2] Cf. *Cr. do Cond.*, cap. 14 and 15, with *Cr. del Rei Fern.*, cap. 166.
[3] A. Braamcamp Freire, *Cr. de D. Joam* (1915), *Introdução*, p. xxi.

authorship is borne out by two passages which at a first glance seem to refute it. In chapter 55 of the *Cronica de D. Joam* (1915 ed., p. 120) he introduces the version given in the *Cronica do Condestabre* (cap. 22) with the words ' now here some say ' (*ora aqui dizem algũs*), and then cites *huũ outro estoriador, cujo fallamento nos pareçe mais rrazoado*, i.e. he now rejects the version (of *algũs*) which he had adopted in his earlier work. In chapter 152 (1915 ed., p. 281) he similarly quotes what *dizem aqui algũs* and then the version of *huũ outro compillador destes feitos, de cujos garfos per mais largo estillo exertamos nesta obra segundo que compre, rrecomta isto per esta maneira*, a manner which is not that of the *Cronica do Condestabre*. But indeed the style of the two works is conclusive. A single age does not produce two Fernam Lopez any more than it produces two Montaignes or two Malorys. Those who read the continuation of the *Cronica de D. Joam* (i.e. the *Cronica da Tomada de Ceuta*, completed in 1450) by GOMEZ EANEZ DE ZURARA (*c.* 1410–74) find themselves in a very different atmosphere. We are told[1] that this soldier, turned historian, acquired his learning late in life, and he parades it like a new toy. Aristotle, Avicenna, and all the Scriptures are in his preface; Job, Ovid, Hercules, and Xenophon, a motley company, mourn the death of Queen Philippa (cap. 44). Sermons extend over whole chapters, although, as he is careful to state, the exact words of the preachers could not be given.[2] Philosophy had been graciously woven into Lopez' narrative, but here it stands in solid icebergs interrupting the story. And if he wishes to say that memory often fails in old age he must quote St. Jerome; a date occupies half a page, being calculated in nine or ten eras;[3]

[1] By Matheus de Pisano (whom some have considered the son of Christine de Pisan). He wrote in Latin: *De Bello Septensi* (*Ined. de Hist. Port.*, vol. i, 1790), Portuguese tr. Roberto Correia Pinto: *Livro da Guerra de Ceuta* (1916).
[2] *Não seja porem algum de tam simples conhecimento que presuma que este é o teor proprio*, &c. (cap. 95).
[3] But he can also be picturesque in expressing time (like Lopez, who for ' early morning ' says, ' at the time when people were coming from Mass '), e.g. *Cr. D. Joam*, cap. 102 *ad fin.*: Ceuta had been captured so swiftly that ' many had left the corn of their fields stored in their granaries and returned in time for the vintage '. The whole description of the expedition against Ceuta and the attack and sack of the city are extremely clear.

and the style is sometimes similarly inflated, so that 'next morning' becomes 'When Night was bringing the end of its obscurity and the Sun began to strike the Oriental horizon' (cap. 92). He also delights in elaborate metaphors.[1] But it must not be thought that Zurara is all froth and morals: in between his purple patches and erudite allusions he tells his story directly and vividly, and, what is more, he has his enthusiasm and his hero. Nun' Alvarez has faded into the background, but in his place appears the intense and fervent spirit of Prince Henry the Navigator. His partiality for Prince Henry appears in the *Cronica de D. Joam*, and in his *Cronica do Descobrimento e Conquista da Guiné* it is still more evident.[2] In this chronicle, written at the request of King Afonso V and finished in the king's library in February 1453, he made use of a lost *Historia das Conquistas dos Portugueses* by Afonso Cerveira, and profited by much that he had heard from the Infantes Pedro and Henrique and other makers of history. For Zurara was a sincere and painstaking historian,[3] and when the king bade him record the deeds of the Meneses in Africa (the *Cronica do Conde D. Pedro de Meneses* was completed in 1463, and the *Cronica dos Feitos de D. Duarte de Meneses* about five years later) he was not content with the 'recollections of courtiers', but set out for Africa (August 1467) and spent a whole year there gathering material at first hand. An affectionate letter[4]

---

[1] Cf. Goes, *Cr. D. Manuel*: *escrevia com razoamentos prolixos e cheos de metaforicas figuras que no estilo historico não tem lugar*; *Cr. do Princ. D. Joam*, cap. 17: *com a superflua abundancia e copia de palavras poeticas e metaforicas que usou em todalas cousas que screveo*. His style is less involved than is often said. Some of his sentences may contain as many as 500 words and yet be perfectly plain and straightforward, whereas Mallarmé could be obscure in five words.

[2] Cf. cap. 2: *Oo tu principe pouco menos que devinal!* and *Tua gloria, teus louvores, tua fama enchem assi as minhas orelhas e ocupam a minha vista que nom sei a qual parte acuda primeiro*. This chronicle has the same plethora of learned quotations. Chapter 1 quotes St. Thomas, Solomon, Tully, the Book of Esther, and introduces Afonso V, King Duarte, the French duke Jean de Lançon, the Cid, Nun' Alvarez, Moses, Fabricius, Joshua, and King Ramiro.

[3] He re-wrote the *Cronica do Conde D. Pedro de Meneses* twice. João de Barros, who was inclined to slight earlier and contemporary historians, acknowledges his great debt to Zurara. Damião de Goes regards him less favourably.

[4] November 22, 1467 (*Coll. Liv. Ined.* iii. 3–5). There is also an affectionate letter from King Pedro of Aragon to Zurara, dated June 11, 1466, or 1460.

from King Afonso to the historian in his voluntary exile shows the pleasant relations existing between the liberal king and his grateful librarian. He praises him as well learned in the *arte oratoria*,[1] and for undertaking of his own free will a journey which was imposed on others as a punishment, and promises to look after the interests of his sister while he is away. Zurara was a Knight of the Order of Christ, with a *comenda* near Santarem, owned other property, and suffered himself to be adopted by a wealthy furrier's widow, an unusual proceeding for a person in his station. But if, as this indicates, he had a love of riches (satisfied by the king's generosity and this fortunate adoption), this in no way interfered with his work of collecting and verifying evidence nor affects the truth of his chronicles. He had proposed to write that of Afonso V, but the king, wisely considering that his reign was not yet over, refused his consent,[2] and this chronicle was reserved for the pen of RUY DE PINA (c. 1440–1523?).[3] Herculano's 'crow in peacock's feathers' has been somewhat harshly treated by modern critics. Not he but the taste and fashion of his time was to blame if he laid desecrating hands on the invaluable chronicles of Fernam Lopez, and thus became the 'author' of the chronicles of the six kings, Sancho I to Afonso IV. The mischief is irreparable, but it is well at least that these chronicles should have been dealt

[1] Zurara, on the other hand, with feigned diffidence represents himself as 'a poor scholar', 'a man almost entirely ignorant and without any knowledge', and if he has any learning it is but the crumbs from King Afonso's table (*Cr. D. Pedro*, cap. 2). He can rise to real eloquence, as in the beginning of cap. 25 of the *Cr. da Guiné*: *Oo tu cellestrial padre, que com tua poderosa mão, sem movimento de tu devynal essencia, governas toda a infinda companhya da tua sancta cidade*, &c., or sober down into a Tacitean phrase such as that of cap. 26, describing the fate of natives of Africa brought to Portugal: *morriam, empero xrãdos* (they died, but Christians). He has a misleading trick of saying 'The author says—*diz o autor*', meaning himself.

[2] *Nunca me em ello quis leixar obrar segundo meu desejo* (*Cr. D. Pedro*, cap. 1).

[3] His son Fernam de Pina became *Cronista Môr* in 1523. The immediate successor of Zurara as *Cronista Môr* was VASCO FERNANDEZ DE LUCENA, whose life must have coincided almost exactly with the sixteenth century. He represented King Duarte at the Council of Basel in 1435, and according to Barbosa Machado, who calls him *um dos varões mais famosos da sua idade assim na profundidade da litteratura como na eloquencia da frase*, he was still living in 1499. Unfortunately none of his works have survived. His manuscript translation of Cicero's *De Senectute* and other works were destroyed in the Lisbon earthquake (1755).

with by Ruy de Pina, and not, for instance, by the uncritical
DUARTE GALVÃO (*c.* 1445–1517), the friend of Afonso de
Albuquerque, who died in the Arabian Sea when on his way as
Ambassador to Ethiopia, and who as *Cronista Môr* revised the
Cronica de D. Afonso Henriquez (1727). Ruy de Pina has
further been attacked because the people no longer figures, and
the king figures too prominently, in the chronicles for which
he was more directly responsible : *Cronica de D. Duarte, Cronica
de D. Afonso V*, and *Cronica de D. João II*. That is to
censure him for faithfully recording the changed times and not
writing as if he were his own grandfather. Pina was no flatterer,
but the chronicle of João II inevitably centred round the king,
and, in spite of its excellence and of the moving incident of
Prince Afonso's death, is less attractive than those which are
a record of freer, jollier times. Born at Guarda, of a family
originally Aragonese, Pina served as secretary on an embassy to
Castille in 1482 and on two subsequent occasions, and in the
same capacity in a special mission to the Vatican in 1484. He
became secretary (*escrivão da nossa camara*) to King João II,
and succeeded Lucena as *Cronista Môr* in 1497. Both King
João II and King Manuel showed their appreciation of his
services, and Barros lent authority to a foolish story that Afonso
de Albuquerque sent him rubies and diamonds from India as
a reminder, in Corrêa's phrase, to *glorificar as cousas de Afonso
de Albuquerque*. Ruy de Pina in his chronicles of King Duarte
and Afonso V used material collected by Fernam Lopez and
Zurara, and he in turn left material for the reign of King Manuel
of which Damião de Goes availed himself, while his *Cronica
de D. João II* was laid under contribution by Garcia de Resende.
It may be doubted whether the *Cronica de D. Afonso V* contains
much that is not Ruy de Pina's own. It was poetical justice
that the interest of the story should be transferred from the
Infante Henrique to the Infante Pedro.[1] His death and that of
the Conde de Abranches at Alfarrobeira are told with the most
impressive simplicity, which produces a far greater effect than

[1] Much later, in the first third of the seventeenth century, GASPAR DIAZ
DE LANDIM wrote a *copiosa relação* from a point of view unfavourable to
D. Pedro and dedicated it to the Duke of Braganza : *O Infante D. Pedro,
Chronica Inedita*, 3 vols. (1893–4).

the long *exclamação* that follows. Lacking Lopez' genius, but possessed of an excellent plain style, which only becomes flowery on occasion, and on his guard against what he calls the *vicio e avorrecimento da proluxidade*, Pina relates his story straightforwardly, almost in the form of annals. He does not attempt to eke out his matter with rhetoric and has chapters of under fifty words. The *Cronica de D. Afonso V* effectively contrasts the characters of the weak and chivalrous Afonso, who is praised as man but not as king, and the vigorous practical João II, and has an inimitable scene of the meeting of the former and Louis XI at Tours in 1476. The glow of Fernam Lopez is absent, but Pina none the less deserves to be accounted an able and impartial historian.

To the fifteenth century belongs the *Cronica do Infante Santo*. It is impossible to read unmoved the clear and unaffected story of the sufferings and death (1437–43), as a captive of Fez, of this the most saintly of the sons of King João I and Queen Philippa. It was written at the bidding of his brother, Prince Henry the Navigator, with the skill born of a fervent devotion, by FREI JOÃO ALVAREZ, an eyewitness [1] of D. Fernando's misfortunes and one of the few of his companions to survive (till 1470 or later). A curious indication of the writer's accuracy in detail is the correct spelling of a Basque name,[2] of the meaning of which he was probably ignorant.

The founder of the dynasty of Avis, KING JOÃO I (1365–1433), found time in his busy reign of forty-eight years to encourage literature, ardently assisted no doubt by English Queen Philippa, and was himself an author. His keen practical spirit turned to Portuguese prose, and while as a poet he confined himself to a few prayers and psalms, in prose he caused to be translated the Hours of the Virgin and the greater part of the New Testament, as well as foreign works such as John Gower's

---

[1] *Tudo o contheudo no siguiente trautado eu o uy e ouuy* (1911 ed., p. 2).
[2] 1911 ed., p. 117 : Ichoa (= Blind). The fact that no other name is given shows that then as now Basques were known by their nicknames. The same name figures in ' Pierre Loti's ' *Ramuntcho* (1897) : Itchoua. In the sixteenth century Martim Ichoa and João de Ychoa appear among the *moradores* of King Manuel's household (1518). The substantive *ichó* (= *armadilha*), derived from *ostiolum*, is used by Diogo Fernandez Ferreira (*Arte da Caça*) and Garcia de Resende (*Cron. João II*).

Confessio Amantis (c. 1383), and himself wrote a long treatise on the chase. This *Livro da Montaria*, which has little but the title in common with Alfonso XI's *Libro de Montería*, lay unpublished for four centuries, but is now available in a scholarly edition by Dr. Esteves Pereira from the manuscript in the Lisbon Biblioteca Nacional. Valuable and interesting in itself, this book is of great significance in Portuguese literature by reason of the impulse thus given to Portuguese prose. It is impossible as yet to estimate the full value of the prose works that followed: many are lost, others remain in manuscript, as the *Orto do Sposo* by Frei Hermenegildo de Tancos, or the *Livro das Aves*. But with King João's son and successor Portuguese prose came into its kingdom.

Punctilious and affectionate, gifted with many virtues and graces, the half-English KING DUARTE (1391–1438), *o Eloquente*, shared the high ideals of all the sons of João I. Liable to fits of melancholy, and of less active disposition than his brothers Henrique and Pedro, he proved himself not less gallant in action than they at the taking of Ceuta in 1415, and had even earlier been entrusted by his father with affairs of State. His scruples as philosopher- or rather student-king during his unhappy reign of five years may have hampered his decisions, but his love of truth made the saying *palavra de rei* proverbial. The corroding cares of State prevented him from giving all the time he would have wished to literary studies, but he was a methodical collector of books [1] and papers written by himself and others, and his great work, *Leal Conselheiro* (c. 1430), consisted of such a collection on moral philosophy and practical conduct, addressed to his wife, Queen Lianor. It contains 102 chapters, often stray papers, sometimes translated from other authors.[2] Besides a detailed consideration of virtues and vices which are treated with an Aristotelian precision, and always with preference for the

[1] The extremely interesting list of his important library has been published in *Provas Genealogicas*, i. 544, in the 1842 ed. of *Leal Conselheiro*, and edited by Dr. T. Braga in *Historia da Univ. de Coimbra*, i. 209. It contained *O Acypreste de Fysa* (= the Archpriest of Hita) and *O Amante*, i.e. the translation by Robert Payne, Canon of Lisbon, of Gower's *Confessio Amantis*.

[2] p. 9, *Fiz tralladar em el alguus capitullos doutros livros*: the *Vita Christi*, St. Thomas Aquinas, Diogo Afonso Mangancha on Prudence, Cicero, *De Officiis*, St. Gregory.

Portuguese as opposed to the latinized word, it has chapters on the art of translation, food, chapel services, and other subjects.[1] The book reveals a character of rare charm, combining humility with a clear instinct for what was right, humanity with common sense. His literary genius was akin to that of his father; he scarcely possessed poetical talent, although he translated in verse the Latin hymn *Juste Judex*, and possessed in his library a *Livro das Trovas del Rei*, in all probability a collection of the poems of others. Wit and originality he also lacked. But as a prose-writer he ranks among the greatest Portuguese authors, and in style was indeed something of an innovator, using words with an exactness and scrupulous nicety hitherto unknown in Portugal. He gave the matter long and serious consideration, and the directness of his style corresponds to his sincerity of thought. His clear, concise sentences and careful choice of words show a true artist of unerring instinct in prose.[2] King Duarte wished to be read as Sainte-Beuve recommended that one should read the *Caractères* of La Bruyère: *peu et souvent (pouco . . . tornando algũas vezes)*. The first part of the precept has been followed, but unhappily for Portuguese prose the second has been neglected. In his youth the king was noted for his horsemanship, and his *Livro da Ensinança de bem cavalgar toda sella* is a practical treatise based on his personal experience (*nom screvo do que ouvi*, as he says) begun when he was prince, laid aside after his accession, and left unfinished at his death. It is remarkable, like the *Leal Conselheiro*, for the excellence of its style and the manly, thoughtful character of its author. But for his premature death, King Duarte might have done for Portuguese prose what Alfonso X and Don Juan Manuel had done for Castilian. An excellent translator himself, he encouraged translations into Portuguese, in Portugal and Spain; the Bishop of Burgos, Don Alonso de Cartagena, translated Cicero for him,

---

[1] It contains papers written at various times (between 1428 and 1438). The date 1435 occurs p. 474. Cf. p. 169, King João I (†1433), *cuja alma Deos aja*.

[2] His modern editor, José Ignacio Roquette (1801–70), comments (p. 37) on the passage *he bem de lavrar e criarem* as a great grammatical *discordancia* and *erro*, but it is by no means certain that King Duarte did not omit one of the personal infinitives deliberately, for the sake of euphony, as the *-mente* is omitted in the case of two or more adverbs.

and the Dean of Santiago Aristotle. More active than King Duarte, more literary than his younger brother Prince Henry the Navigator (1394-1460), D. PEDRO (1392-1449), created Duke of Coimbra after the capture of Ceuta in 1415, became almost a legendary figure owing to his extensive travels (1424-8) —*andou as sete partes do mundo*—and his equally exaggerated reputation as a poet, through confusion with his son the Constable. Regent from 1438 to 1448, he resigned when the young king, his nephew and son-in-law, Afonso V, came of age. His enemies succeeded in effecting his banishment from Court. Civil strife followed, and D. Pedro fell in a preliminary skirmish at Alfarrobeira in May 1449. Had he been granted a peaceful old age he would probably occupy a more important place in Portuguese literature. Apart from the historical value of his letters, his chief claim to be remembered literarily consists in the translations from the Latin, principally from Cicero, undertaken under his supervision or by himself personally, as the *De Officiis*, which was dedicated to King Duarte and is still unpublished. The *Trauctado da Uirtuosa Benfeyturia* was originally a translation by the prince of Seneca's *De Beneficiis*. Except the dedication to King Duarte (between 1430 and 1433), the work as it stands in six books is properly not D. Pedro's, since he had not leisure for the corrections and additions which he wished to make, and accordingly handed over his translation and the original to his confessor, Frei João Verba, who made the necessary alterations,[1] and expanded the book from a literal translation to a paraphrase of the *De Beneficiis*. The reader who does not bear this in mind might be startled to find references in a work of Seneca's to St. Thomas, Nun' Alvarez, the noble knight Abraham, or the virtuous knight Cid Ruy Diaz. The work lacks King Duarte's gift of style which set the *Leal Conselheiro* high above contemporary prose.

LOPO DE ALMEIDA, created first Count of Abrantes in 1472,[2]

---

[1] *Corregendo e acrecentando o que entendeo ser compridoiro acabou o liuro adeante scripto.*

[2] Damião de Goes (*Cr. do Pr. D. Joam*, cap. 88) says 1476. His father Diogo Fernandez was *Reposteiro Môr* at the Court of King Duarte, and his mother a half-sister of the Archbishop of Braga. One of his sons was the famous and unfortunate Viceroy of India (1505-9), D. Francisco de Almeida.

accompanied D. Lianor, daughter of King Duarte, on her marriage to the Emperor Frederick III in 1451. In four letters written to King Afonso V from Italy (February to May 1452) he displays a keen eye for colour and much directness in description, so that the Emperor bargaining miserly over the price of damask or the two wealthy Italian dukes so sorrily horsed (*em sima de senhos rocins magros*) remain in the memory, and the letters are more original than most of the Portuguese prose of the century.

One of the most important early prose works is the *Boosco Delleytoso* (1515). It consists of 153 short chapters,[1] and is dedicated (on the verso of the frontispiece portraying the 'delightful wood') to Queen Lianor, widow of King João II. It is a homily in praise of the hermit's life of solitude and against worldly joys and traffics, and is marked by a pleasant quaintness, an intense and excellent style, a fervent humanity and love of Nature. The hermit's independent and healthy life [2] is contrasted with that of the merchant in cities.[3] In chapter 1 the repentant sinner is introduced in 'a very thick wood of very fair trees in which many birds sang very sweetly' near 'a very fair field full of many herbs and scented flowers'—*frolles de boo odor*. He prays to be delivered from this darkness of death, and a very fair youth appears 'clothed in clothes of gleaming fire and his face shone as the sun when it rises in the season of great heat'. His 'glorious guide', *grorioso guyador*, leads him to a *dona sabedor* and to *dom francisco solitario*, who in a *fremoso fallamento* praises the solitary life and condemns those who are puffed up with the conceit of learning, in itself 'a very fair

---

[1] Seventy-four black-letter double column folios, unnumbered, of fifty lines each. The colophon runs: *Acabouse do* [so] *emprimir este lyuro chamado boosco delleytoso solitario p. Hermã de cãpos bombardeiro del Rey nosso Sêhor cõ graça & preuilegio de sua alteza em ha muy nobrem* [so] *& sempre leal çidad* [so] *de lixboa cõ muy grande dilligencia. Ano da encarnaçã de nosso Saluador & Redentor jhesu xpo. De mil & quinientos & quinze a vinte quatro de Mayo* (*Bib. Nacional de Lisboa*, Res. 176 A [lacking f. 1]). Nicolás Antonio thus refers to the work (*Bib. Nova*, ii. 402) : *Anonymus, Lusitanus, scripsit & nuncupavit Serenissimae Eleonorae Reginae Ioanis II Portugalliae Regis Coniugi librum ita inscriptum. Bosco deleitoso. Olisipone 1515.*

[2] He can do *ho que lhe praz*; at sunrise he goes up *alguũ outeiro de boo & saaom aar* far from the *delleytaçoões do mundo, arroydo do segre* and os *auollimentos & trasfegos das çidades.*

[3] The *malauẽturado negociador que q̃r seer rico tostemẽte.*

thing'. He tells of the lives of saintly hermits; St. Bernard, St. Thomas Aquinas, Dom Seneca, Dom Cicero, *a mui comfortosa donzella*, and others exhort the sinner to leave the world, and he ends by relating his frequent raptures until his soul is carried to the *terra perduravil*. In its main subject, praise of the solitary life, the book recalls the title of the treatise ascribed to D. Philippa de Lencastre: *Tratado da Vida Solitaria*, a translation or adaptation from the Latin of Laurentius Justinianus.[1] The latter's *De Vita Solitaria* is, however, quite different from the *Boosco deleytoso*, which was probably composed before the birth of D. Philippa (1437).

Another remarkable early work is the anonymous *Corte Imperial* (14th or early 15th c.), the language of which often bears traces of a Latin original.[2] Many of its sentences are veritable *dobres* and *mordobres* in prose,[3] and to a superficial reader will have little meaning; but in fact this mystic treatise is closely reasoned. It may have some connexion with similar works by Juda Levi, Ramon Lull, and Don Juan Manuel. In a *corte* or parliament the Church Militant, in the person of a ' glorious Catholic Queen ' argues with Gentile, Moor, and Jew on the nature of God and the Trinity. The Gentiles and Moors gradually accept her doctrines, but the Jewish rabbis prove more contumacious. Saints and angels and all the company of heaven discourse sweet music in the intervals of the discussion. One of the best known of the many other important translations of this time was the *Flos Sanctorum* (1513),[4] which begins [5] with extracts from the Gospels and has a savour of the Bible about its prose. There were many later versions of the Gospel story, as *A Paxã de Jesu Christo Nosso Deos e Senhor*, &c. (1551);

[1] See *Grundriss*, p. 249, and *Divi Lavrentii Ivstiniani Protopatriarchae Veneti opera Omnia* (Coloniae, 1616), pp. 728–70 : *De Vita Solitaria*.

[2] Cf. 1910 ed., pp. 1, 4. The writer claims to be only a compiler : *começo este livro nom como autor e achador das cousas em elle contheudas mas como simprez aiuntador dellas em huũ vellume*. It has been attributed to the Infante D. Pedro and to João I.

[3] e.g. p. 85 : *Ca per entender entende o entendedor e per entender é entendido o entendido e o entendedor entende que elle mesmo é Deos.*

[4] The title is simply *Ho Flos Sctõrȝ em lingoajẽ p̃orgue*ˢ. The colophon says that it *se chama ystorea lombarda pero comuũmente se chama flos sanctorum*.

[5] *Aqui se começa ha payxam do eterno Principe christo Jhesu nosso Senhor & saluador segundo os sanctos quatro euangelistas.*

Tratado en que se comprende breue e deuotamente a Vida, Paixão e Resurreição, &c. (1553); *Traatado em q̃ se contẽ a paixam de xp̃o*, &c. (1589?). But the earliest and most splendid, an incunable of which Portugal has reason to be proud on account of its beautiful print, is the *Vita Christi* (Lixboa, 1495), translated *em lingoa materna e portugues linguagem* from the original of Ludolph von Sachsen by the Cistercian monk Frei Bernardo de Alcobaça († 1478?), at the bidding of Queen Isabel, sister of the Constable D. Pedro, in the middle of the fifteenth century (1445).

Another notable translation for the same queen is the *Espelho de Christina* (1518),[1] from the French of Christine de Pisan: *Livre des trois vertus pour l'enseignement des princesses* (1497). The Portuguese manuscript, translated from the French manuscript nearly half a century before the latter appeared in print,[2] was published at the bidding of Queen Lianor (wife of João II), who so keenly encouraged Portuguese art, language, and literature. Her squire Valentim Fernandez' version of Marco Polo, *Marco Paulo*, was published at Lisbon in 1502. The *Espelho de Prefeyçam* (1533) was translated from the Latin by the Canons of Santa Cruz, Coimbra, and edited by Bras de Barros (*c*. 1500–59), Bishop of Leiria and cousin of the historian João de Barros. A Portuguese version of a scriptural work entitled *Sacramental*, originally written in Spanish by Clemente Sanchez de Vercial, was published apparently in 1488 (it would thus be one of the earliest books printed in Portugal), and was reprinted at Lisbon in 1502.

[1] The only known copy exists in the Biblioteca Nacional, Lisbon. The colophon (in Spanish) gives the alternative title (*das tres virtudes*). The French original was also called *Trésor de la Cité des Dames*.
[2] See J. Leite de Vasconcellos, *Lições de Philologia Portuguesa*, p. 137.

§ 4

The Cancioneiro Geral

THE silence that falls on Portuguese poetry after the early *Cancioneiros* lasts for over a century, scarcely interrupted by the twilight murmurings of the later Galician poets, and is only broken for us by the publication of the *Cancioneiro Geral* five years before the death of King Manuel. The native *trovas* had no doubt continued to be written by many poets in a country where poetry is scarcely rarer than prose, far commoner than good prose. But no one had cared to preserve them in a collection corresponding to the *Cancionero de Baena* in Spain. When Portuguese poetry again emerges into the clear light of day Spanish influence is in full swing and behind it looms that of Italian poetry, the natural continuation of one side of the *Cancioneiro da Vaticana*. No Spanish poet now writes in Portuguese, many Portuguese in Spanish. Popular poetry and royal troubadours have alike disappeared, leaving a narrow circle of Court rhymesters. It is to one of these that we owe the collection which embraces the poetry of the day, from the middle of the fifteenth century to the actual year of publication, 1516. Stout, good-natured GARCIA DE RESENDE (*c.* 1470–1536), a favourite alike with king and courtiers, often the butt of the Court poets' wit—he is a tunny, a barrel, a wineskin, a melon in August—belonged to an old family which in the sixteenth century distinguished itself in literature. Born at Evora and brought up in the palace as page and then as secretary of King João II, he had every opportunity of observing the events which he so graphically describes in his *Vida de Dom João II* (1545).[1] Talented and many-sided, Resende continued in high favour during the succeeding reigns: in 1498 as secretary he accompanied King Manuel to Castille and Aragon, and in 1514 was chosen for the much coveted post

[1] The book has as many titles as editions, that of 1545 being *Lyuro das Obras de Garcia de Resêde que trata da vida e grãdissimas virtudes*, &c.

THE CANCIONEIRO GERAL

of secretary to Tristão da Cunha's mission to Rome with wonderful presents for Pope Leo X. Resende not only drew and wrote verses but was a musician and an accomplished singer : *de tudo intende* laughed his friend Gil Vicente. Perhaps it only required the stress of adversity to inspire to greatness this blunted, prosperous courtier—*fidalgo da casa del Rei*. He was not a great poet, although he excelled the Court poets of the fifteenth century. As historian he has been unjustly condemned. If in his Chronicle of João II he made use of Ruy de Pina's manuscript chronicle, first published in 1792, it must be remembered that it was customary for the official historians to regard their predecessors as existing mainly for purposes of plagiarism. Herculano called Resende's chronicle a poor bundle of anecdotes,[1] and no doubt Resende was not a Herculano nor a Fernam Lopez but a more limited Court chronicler. He is none the less delightful because he deals not in tendencies and abstractions but in concrete details and persons, Court persons. With an artist's eye for the picturesque he makes his readers see the event described, and his chronicle is throughout singularly vivid and dramatic. He is certainly an attractive writer, and perhaps he is also instructive. The incident, for instance, of the Duke of Braganza being kept waiting while a scaffold of the latest Paris pattern is being erected for his execution (1483), which a grander historian might have omitted, is possibly not without its significance and shows *francesismo* in action four centuries before Eça de Queiroz. Besides various minor works in prose Resende composed, not without misgiving,[2] a long survey of the events of his day in some 300 *decimas* : *Miscellania e Variedade de Historias*, which throws curious and valuable light on the times. His literary work was prompted by a real desire to serve his country. His delicate appreciation of the past appears in his remarkable and charming verses on the death of Inés de Castro; and wishing in so far as lay in his power to remedy the Portuguese neglect which had allowed so many poems and records and *gentilezas* to perish, he collected what he could of past and present poets and published

[1] *Historiadores Portugueses* in *Opusculos* (1907), ii. 27. The author of the *Theatrum* has a similar verdict : *Scripsit Chronicam Ioannis II ut quidem potuit sed longe impar regis et rerum magnitudinis.*
[2] *Sem letras e sem saber*, he says modestly, *me fui nisto meter.*

them in one great volume which he dedicated to the Infante João:
Cancioneiro Geral (1516), often known as the *Cancioneiro de
Resende* to distinguish it from the Spanish *Cancionero General*
(1511). Resende wrote to the poets of his acquaintance requesting
them in verse to send him their poems, and they sent him answers,
also in verse, accompanying their poems.[1] The receipt of these
he would acknowledge as editor, promising, still in verse, to have
them printed. Politeness no doubt induced him to include more
than his judgement warranted, for his own poems are superior
to those of most of his contemporaries. A large number of the
Cancioneiro's poems—some 1,000 poems by between 100 and 200
poets—should scarcely have been included, for, however well
they might answer their purpose as occasional verse, they were
not intended as a possession for ever, and massed together produce an effect of dull and endless triviality. These love poems
can indeed be as monotonous, the satiric poems as coarse, licen-
tious, and irreverent, as those of the *Cancioneiro da Vaticana*.
One of the poets, D. João Manuel, like King Alfonso X of old,
does beseech his colleagues to cease singing of Cupid and Macias
and turn to religious subjects. But it was not Garcia de Resende's
purpose to include religious verse. Poems recording great deeds
and occasions he would gladly have printed in larger number, but,
as he (among others) complained in his preface, it was characteristic of the Portuguese not to record their deeds in literary form.
Satiric verses he included in plenty, satire being one of the
recognized functions of the poet's art: *per trouas sam castigados*.[2]
But if we turn to the poems of his collection we are amazed by
the pettiness of the subjects, and our amazement grows when
we remember that this was the period in the world's whole
history most calculated to awe and inspire men's minds with the
thought of vast new horizons. While Columbus was discovering
America, Bartholomeu Diaz rounding the Cape of Good Hope,

[1] Or he would seek to obtain them through a friend as in the case of *o Cancioneiro do abade frei Martinho* of Alcobaça. It is improbable that Resende,
who valued friendship above good poetry, altered the manuscripts he received,
in spite of Francisco de Sousa's permission : *as quaes podeys enmendar*.

[2] *Prologo*. 'Had you forgotten that *trovas* are still written in Portugal ?'
asks Nuno Pereira of one of his victims ; and of a dress it is said that it
would be *certo de leuar Trouas de riso e mote*. Cf. the phrase *dar causa a
trovadores*.

Vasco da Gama sailing to India, or Afonso de Albuquerque making desperate appeals for men and money to enable him to maintain his brilliant conquests, the Court poets were versifying on an incorrectly addressed letter, a lock of hair, a dingy head-dress, a very lean and aged mule, the sad fate of a lady marrying away from the Court in Beira, a quarrel between a tenor and soprano, a courtier's velvet cap or hat of blue silk, a button more or less on a coat, the length of spurs, fashions in sleeves: themes, as José Agostinho de Macedo might say, ' prodigiously frivolous '. When news reached Lisbon of the tragic death of D. Francisco de Almeida and of the defeat of Afonso de Albuquerque [1] and the Marshal D. Fernando de Coutinho before Calicut, with the death of the latter, Bras da Costa wrote to Garcia de Resende that at this rate he would prefer to have no pepper, and Resende answered that for his part he certainly had no intention of embarking. But, as a rule, such events received not even so trivial a comment, and no doubt the poets felt that the verse which served to pass the time at the *serões* was inadequate to any great occasion. But the *trovador segundo as trovas de aquelle tempo* [2] had little idea of what subjects were suitable or unsuitable to poetry. A typical instance of the themes in which they delighted is an event which seems to have produced a greater impression than the discovery of new worlds: the return from Castille of a gentleman of the Portuguese Court wearing a large velvet cap. For over 300 lines of verse this cap is bandied to and fro by the witty poets. It must weigh four hundredweight, says one. Another advises him to lock it up *em arcaaz* until he can turn it into a doublet; another bids him sell it in the Jews' quarter. Small wonder, chimes in a fourth, that no galleys come now with velvet from Venice.[3] ' I would not wear it at a *serão*, not for a million,' says another. 'A Samson could not wear it all one summer,' is the comment of a sixth. Another remarks that he would rather read Lucan (or Lucian)

---

[1] Or Albuquerque would be mentioned in a game of *Porque's* (why's) common among the *praguentos da India*: *Porque Afonso d'Albuquerque Dá pareas a el rey de Fez?*
[2] Zurara, *Cr. de D. Joam*, cap. 29.
[3] The *Cancioneiro* contains many references to Venice. The *pimenta de Veneza* mentioned in one of the poems must have sounded strange to Portuguese readers in 1516.

(*antes leria por luçam*) in the heat of the day than wear it.
' He will need a cart to bring it to the *serão*,' says yet another.
The wit, it will be seen, is not brilliant, although it may have
effectively nipped this budding Castilian fashion and enlivened
an evening. But there were duller contests. For score on score of
pages the rival merits of sighing and of loving in silence are discussed by poet after poet (*O Cuidar e Sospirar*). Such a subject
once started tended to accumulate verses like a snowball. But
the *Cancioneiro* also contains poems on serious topics, although
they are rarer, as well as delicate, airy nothings (*sutiles nadas*)
like Vimioso's *vilancetes*.[1] There are two poems on the death of
King João II, there is Luis Anriquez' lamentation on the death of
the Infante Afonso (1491), that of Luis de Azevedo on the death
of the Infante Pedro, Duke of Coimbra, at Alfarrobeira, and a
few poets, like Resende himself, stand out from the rest. Besides
the elaborate Spanish poem by that noble prince the Constable
D. Pedro we have several long poems dealing with high matters
of the soul or the State. The sixty-one interesting stanzas by
the querulous, satirical, intolerant ALVARO DE BRITO PESTANA
treat of the condition of the city of Lisbon and the decay of
morals. The correspondent of Gomez Manrique and contemporary of his nephew Jorge, in the metre of whose famous *Coplas*
he wrote, he was present at the battle of Alfarrobeira. His
trovas on the death of Prince Afonso, with the recurrent *choremos
perda tamanha*, are wooden and artificial and his sixteen alliterative verses scarcely belong to literature, but at least he chose
themes which were not concerned with passing Court fashions.
The few simple lines written as he lay dying show him at his
best.[2] His friend and distant relative FERNAM DA SILVEIRA,
o Coudel Môr, is concerned with more mundane matters. A man
of noble birth and high character, he was held in great honour
by Afonso V and João II. The latter, a keen judge of men, had
implicit confidence in the justice of this upright magistrate, who

---

[1] e. g. *Meu bem, sem vos ver Se vivo um dia, Viver nam queria. Caland'
e sofrendo Meu mal sem medida, Mil mortes na vida Sinto nam vos vendo,
E pois que vivendo Moiro toda via, Viver nam queria.*

[2] *La t'arreda Satanas, Cristo Jesu a ti chamo, A ti amo, Tu Senhor me
salvarás. O sinal da cruz espante Minha torpe tentaçam, Com devaçam
Espero dir adiante.*

was also a soldier, a poet, and a finished courtier. He deals with affairs of State, writes an account in *trovas* of six syllables of the *Cortes* held by the king at Montemôr in 1477 and a short poem on the appointment of various bishops in 1485. Or he sends a poem to his nephew Garcia de Mello with detailed instructions as to how he should dress and behave at Court. His *trovas* are thoroughly Portuguese, vigorous, concise, and picturesque. He is less at home in the *trovas de poesia* (i. e. *de arte mayor*) written on a journey from Evora to Thomar, but he could skilfully turn a short love poem, and for a wager of capons for Easter (with Alvaro de Brito) wrote a stanza containing as many rhymes as it has words. In fine he belonged to his age, but his poetry bears the impress of his strong character and his love of Portuguese ways. On the other hand, the younger brother of the Conde de Cantanhede, D. JOÃO DE MENESES (†1514), wrote indifferently in Portuguese or Spanish. He fought for many years in Africa, although his slight love poems, fluent and harmonious, give no sign of a life of action, and died in the expedition against Azamor.[1] Another soldier, courtier, and poet marked out by birth and ability was D. JOÃO MANUEL (*c.* 1460–99), son of the Bishop of Guarda. Legitimized in 1475 and brought up at Court with the prince Manuel, he continued to be a favourite after the latter's accession, became Lord High Chamberlain, and was sent to the Court of Castille in 1499 to arrange the marriage of the king with the daughter of Ferdinand and Isabella. In Spanish octaves he had written a lament on the death of Prince Afonso, which both in feeling and technique excels the verses of Alvaro de Brito on the same subject. Towards the end of his poem he introduces the saying of St. Augustine that ' our soul exists not where it lives but where it loves ', which in the following century was quoted by two writers so different as Ferreira de Vasconcellos and Frei Heitor Pinto and soon became a commonplace. In other works he shows a high seriousness, sometimes a sententious strain, combined with a very real poetical talent. His death during his mission to Castille was a loss for the Court and for Portuguese poetry. By another writer, FERNAM DA SILVEIRA (†1489), we have

---

[1] One of his poems has the heading: *Outro vilançete seu estãdo em Azamor antes q̃ se fynasse.*

but a few poems, the principal of which is a lament for his own death, in the metre of Manrique, which he places on the lips of various ladies of the Court. His death was tragic, for, having succeeded his father as secretary to King João II, he took part in the ill-fated conspiracy of the Duke of Viseu. After lying hidden in the house of a friend he fled in disguise to Castille and thence to France, but, although he thus succeeded in prolonging his life for five years, the king's justice relentlessly pursued and he was stabbed to death at Avignon. A favourite of João II, especially before his accession, was NUNO PEREIRA (fl. 1485), *homem galante, cortesão e bom trovador*, who married the daughter of the *Coudel Môr* and valiantly sustained the part of *Cuidar* against his relative Jorge da Silveira's *Sospirar* in the great literary tournament of the courtiers. Later, after serving as Governor (*Alcaide*) of the town of Portel, he retired to live in the country, and presents a happy picture of himself in the midst of harvesters and pruners. He finds, he says, more pleasure in his vines, in the chase, in digging and watering his garden, than in being a favourite at Court. He had not always thought thus, for when the lady he was courting married a rival he could devise no worse fate for her than to bid her go and die among the chestnut groves of Beira. He had, indeed, made a name for himself by his courtly satire, which he turned to good use in ridiculing those who came back from Castille with a supercilious disdain for everything Portuguese. It is pleasant to find him bidding them not speak their ' insipid Castilian ' in his presence. DIOGO BRANDAM (†1530) of Oporto wrote an elaborate poem in octaves on the death of King João II. He also used the octosyllabic metre with breaks of single lines (*quebrados*) of four syllables, so familiar in Gil Vicente's plays, and in his *Fingimento de Amores* (27 verses of 8 octosyllabic lines), under Spanish-Italian influence, he touches a richer, more generous vein of poetry : the poet-lover descends into the region of Proserpine, the dominion of Pluto, and sees the torments of Love's followers. His *vilancete* to the Virgin is in the same metre with the difference that the verses have seven lines only (*abbaacc*). The spirit of Jorge de Manrique is absent from the stanzas written in the metre of his *Coplas* by LUIS ANRIQUEZ on the fatal accident which ended the life of Prince Afonso in his teens. His lamentation on the death of King João II is written in octaves, as that of Diogo Brandam, which they resemble. Both poets invoke Death: *Ó morte que matas quem é prosperado* (Brandam); *Ó morte que matas sem tempo e sazam* (Anriquez). Other historical poems by Anriquez in the same metre are the verses written on the occasion of the transference of the remains of João II and thirty-five stanzas addressed to James, Duke of Braganza, when he left Lisbon with his fleet to attack Azamor in 1513. If we turn from these somewhat heavy pieces to Anriquez' other poems we find a hymn in praise of the Virgin, written more in the manner of Alfonso X, and various love *cantigas*. The nephew of D. João de Meneses, Joam rroiz de saa, that is, JOAM RODRIGUEZ DE SÁ E MENESES (1465 ?-1576), studied in Italy as a disciple of Angelo Poliziano (†1594) and died a centenarian. He wrote a poem in *decimas* describing the arms of the noble families of Portugal, and translated into *trovas* three long letters from the Latin which by their spirit of *saudade* appealed to Portuguese taste: Penelope to Ulysses, Laodamia to Protesilaus, and Dido to Aeneas. He was also versed in the Greek language, and for his noble character and courtly ways as well as for his learning and poetical talent was venerated by the younger generation into which he lived: Antonio Ferreira salutes him as the 'ancient sire of the muses of this land'. The 'most discreet' D. FRANCISCO DE PORTUGAL, first Conde de Vimioso (†1549), although he did not live to be a centenarian, also survived most of the poets of João II's reign and died towards the end of that of João III. Son of the Bishop of Evora and great-grandson of the first Duke of Braganza, he was created a count by King Manuel in 1515, and was equally renowned as soldier, statesman, courtier, and poet, 'wise and prudent in peace and war'. His *Sentenças* (1605), over one hundred of which are rhymed quatrains, were published by his grandson D. Anrique de Portugal. Some of these moral sayings have considerable subtlety, and they reveal a fine character and insight into the character of others.[1] Most of his poems, in Spanish and Portuguese,

---

[1] e.g. *A culpa de quem se ama doe mais & perdoase mais asinha, Nam pede louvor quem o merece, Da fee nace a rezam da fee*, &c.

preserved in the *Cancioneiro* are brief *cantigas* which prove him to have been a skilful versifier and a typical Court poet. On the other hand, a feeling for Nature, a constant command of metre, and a certain passionate sadness mark out an earlier poet, DUARTE DE BRITO (fl. 1490), the friend of D. João de Meneses, from most of the other writers in Resende's song-book. The *redondilha* in his hands is no wooden toy but a living, moving instrument. His most celebrated poem, *em que conta o que a ele & a outro lhaconteçeo com huũ rrousinol & muitas outras cousas que vio*, is written after the fashion of Diogo Brandam's *Fingimento de Amores* and Garci Sanchez de Badajoz' *Infierno de Amor*, in imitation of the Marqués de Santillana's *El Infierno de los Enamorados*; but there is real feeling in these eighty verses of eleven lines (of which the eighth and eleventh are of four, the rest of eight syllables). The Italian influence, working through Spanish, was already present in Portuguese poetry in the fifteenth century, although Brito writes exclusively in *redondilhas*, as indeed does the introducer of the new style, Sá de Miranda, in the few and short poems which he contributed to the *Cancioneiro* immediately before its publication. Duarte de Brito did not condescend to those artificial devices which give us in this *Cancioneiro* a poem of sixty lines all ending in *dos*, alliterative stanzas, and other verbal tricks. The real business of the *serões*, so far as poetry was concerned, was *ouvir e glosar motes*. These *glosas* and the similar *cantigas* and *esparsas*, short poems of fixed form, often written with skill and spontaneous charm, were merely one of the necessary accomplishments of a courtier. Such a view of poetry could scarcely give rise to great poets, and these versifiers indeed styled themselves *trovadores*, reserving the name of poet for those who wrote, often but clumsily, in *versos de arte mayor, de muita poesia*. But, worse still, the poets of the *Cancioneiro* were often scarcely Portuguese.[1] Many wrote in Spanish, and Spanish influence is to be found at every turn: that of Juan de Mena, Gomez and Jorge Manrique, Rodriguez de la Cámara, Macias, Santillana. Unlike Macias, who is but a name, Santillana

[1] D. Carolina Michaëlis de Vasconcellos goes so far as to call the Portuguese *Cancioneiro Geral* a mere supplement or second part of the Spanish *Cancionero General* (*Estudos sobre o Romanceiro*, p. 303).

is not mentioned, but his influence is constantly felt. On the other hand, King Dinis, unexpectedly introduced once as a poet by Pedro Homem (fl. 1490)—*invoco el rei dom Denis Da licença Daretusa*—is nowhere imitated. By method, subject, and foreign imitation, this Court poetry was thus inevitably artificial and uninspired. Perhaps in the whole *Cancioneiro* the only poem marked by authentic fire is that of the obscure FRANCISCO DE SOUSA—the few lines beginning *Ó montes erguidos, Deixai-vos cair*. The contributions of Sá de Miranda, as those of three other famous poets, give no sign of the coming greatness of the contributor. The names of the other three are Bernardim Ribeiro, Cristovam Falcão, and the prince of all these poets, here the humblest of Cinderellas, Gil Vicente.

III
The Sixteenth Century [1502-80]
§ 1
Gil Vicente

IN Portugal a splendid dawn ushered in the sixteenth century. The discovery of the sea route to India, while it gave an impulse to science and literature, also increased religious fervour, since the Portuguese who contended against the Moors in India were but carrying on the work of their ancestors five centuries earlier in Portugal. Old-fashioned Portugal thus only gradually welcomed the Renaissance and stood firm against the Reformation. But in the reign of João III (1521-57) the University of Coimbra came to be one of the best-known universities in Europe. André de Gouvêa (†1548), whom Montaigne called 'sans comparaison le plus grand principal de France',[1] and Diogo de Teive returned from the Collège de Sainte-Barbe to inaugurate its studies, and many of its chairs were offered to distinguished Portuguese and foreign scholars, such as Ayres Barbosa (†1540) and George Buchanan (1506-82), as well as to Portuguese humanists such as Antonio de Gouvêa and Achilles Estaço (†1581). Nicholas Cleynarts or Nicolaus Clenardus (1493 or 1494-1542), Professor of Greek and Hebrew at Louvain, came to Portugal from Salamanca as tutor to the Infante Henrique in 1533, and from Portugal wrote some of his wittiest letters.[2] He found Coimbra a second Athens, and few great Portuguese writers of the century had not spent some years there or at the University before it was transferred to Coimbra from Lisbon in 1537. King João III and especially his son, the young prince João (1537-54), Cardinal Henrique (1512-80), and the many-sided Infante Luis (1506-55), *favorecedor de toda habilidad*, himself a poet of no mean order [3]

---
[1] *Essais*, I. xxv.
[2] *Nicolai Clenardi Epistolarum libri duo.* Antuerpiae, 1561.
[3] Several fine sonnets have been ascribed to him (cf. *Fenix Renascida*, iii. 252, *Horas breves*, and, with more reason, iii. 253, *Á redea solta corre o pensamento*), as was also Gil Vicente's *Dom Duardos* and a manuscript *Tratado dos modos, proporções e medidas*.

and pupil of Pedro Nunez, eagerly patronized letters; the household of the accomplished Infanta Maria (1521-77) became the 'home of the Muses'[1]; learned Luisa Sigea (†1560), of French origin, but born at Toledo and brought up in Portugal, wrote a Latin poem in praise of *Syntra*; her sister Angela, Joana Vaz, and Publia Hortensia de Castro were likewise noted for their learning, and D. Lianor de Noronha (1488-1563), daughter of Fernando, Marques de Villareal, did good service to Portuguese prose by her encouragement of translations. But Portuguese literature lost something by its latinization, and it is pleasant to turn back half a century to a time when it was humbler and more national. The 'very prosperous' Manuel I, Lord of the Ocean,[2] Lord of the East,[3] had been seven years king, Vasco da Gama had returned triumphantly from Calicut (1497-9), Cabral had discovered Brazil for Portugal (1500), Afonso de Albuquerque (†1515) stood on the threshold of his career of conquests and glory, the Portuguese Empire was advancing from North Africa to China,[4] the gold and spices were beginning to arrive in plenty from the East, and hope of honour and riches was drawing nobleman and peasant to Lisbon, when GIL VICENTE (*c.* 1465-1536?) introduced the drama into his

dear, dear land,
Dear for its reputation through the world.

Dressed as a herdsman on the night of June 7, 1502, he congratulated the queen on the birth of the Infante, later King João III (born during the night of June 6), in a Spanish monologue of 114 lines. This speech gives promise of two qualities apparent in his later work: extreme naturalness (the embarrassed peasant wonders open-mouthed at the grand palace and his thoughts turn at once to his village) and love of Nature (mountain and meadow are aflower for joy of the new prince born). But,

---

[1] Duarte Nunez de Leam, *Descripção*, 2ª ed. (1785), cap. 80: *Da habilidade das molheres portuguesas para as letras e artes liberaes*. Severim de Faria speaks of her *sancto desejo de saber*. The author of *Dos priuilegios & praerogatiuas q̃ ho genero femenino tem* (1557) says (p. 9): *se pode estranhar esta hidade na qual as molheres não se aplicam aas letras e sciencias como faziam as antigas Romanas e Gregas.*
[2] Gil Vicente, *Obras* (1834), ii. 414. [3] Ibid. iii. 350.
[4] Cf. João Rodriguez de Sá e Meneses in the *Cancioneiro Geral*: *De Çeita atee os Chijs*.

it may reasonably be asked, where is the drama? It consists principally in the *vaqueiro*, who is restless as one of the wicked in a Basque *pastorale*. He rushes into the queen's chamber, has a look at its luxuries, turns to address the queen, declares that he is in a hurry and must be going, leaps in gladness, and finally introduces some thirty courtiers in herdsman's dress who offer gifts of milk, eggs, cheese, and honey. There is little in this simple piece—the *Visitaçam*, or *Monologo do Vaqueiro*—to foreshadow the sovereign genius,[1] the Plautus, the Shakespeare[2] of Portugal that was Gil Vicente. His life is wrapped in obscurity, and the known existence of half a dozen contemporary Gil Vicentes makes research a risky operation. There was a page (1475) and an *escudeiro* (1482) of King João II, an official at Santarem, a Santarem carpenter (†1500), there was a Gil Vicente in India in 1512,[3] and a Gil Vicente goldsmith at Lisbon. We know that the poet spoke of himself as near death (*visinho da morte*) in 1531, although apparently in good health. This would seem to place his birth a few years before 1470.[4] Unfortunately the *Auto da Festa*, in which he says that he is over sixty, is undated. As, however, it was written before the *Templo de Apolo* (1526) we may place it probably about 1525. We are thus brought back to about the same date (*c.* 1465). Almost certainly he was not of exalted parentage.[5] Indeed, he would appear to have been slighted for his humble birth, and sarcastically spoke

[1] M. Menéndez y Pelayo, *Antología*, vol. vii, p. clxiii.
[2] A. Herculano, *Historia da Inquisição*, 3ª ed. (1879), i. 238. Cf. Camillo Castello Branco, *A Viuva do Enforcado, ad init*. No one of course thinks of comparing Gil Vicente with Shakespeare, but one may perhaps say that he resembles what Shakespeare might have been had he been born in the fifteenth century. The shipwreck in the *Triunfo do Inverno* recalls the opening scene of *The Tempest*, as the mad friar recalls poor Tom, and the magnificent fidalgo Falstaff. In the *Farsa de Inés Pereira* Inés, without being a shrew, is tamed by her husband, who says:

Se eu digo : Esto é novello
Vos aveis de confirmalo.

[3] In 1513 Afonso de Albuquerque writes of 'the son of Gil Vicente' in India.
[4] It is customary in Portugal to fix the date of his birth in 1470 owing to the statement of the judge in the *Floresta de Enganos* (1536) that he—the judge—was already sixty-six. It is a method which might lead to comical results if further pressed in the case of Vicente or other dramatists. Was Mello seventy-three when he wrote the *Fidalgo Aprendiz* ?
[5] 'A gentleman of good family' (Ticknor) ; *hijo de ilustres padres* (Barrera y Leirado); *na qualidade nobilissimo* (Pedro de Poyares).

of himself as the son of a pack-saddler and born at Pederneira (Estremadura).[1] He may have been the son of Luis Vicente or of Martim Vicente, 'said to have been a silversmith of Guimarães' (Minho).[2] The frequent mention of the province of Beira is, however, noticeable in his plays. If it were only that his peasants use words such as *nega, nego*, which according to the grammarian Fernam d'Oliveira were peculiar to Beira (in 1536),[3] it might pass for a dramatic device, since Oliveira remarks that old-fashioned words will not be out of place if we assign them to an old man of Beira or a peasant.[4] Indeed, the grammarian seems to have had Gil Vicente especially in view (he mentions him in another connexion) since three of the six words that he notes—*abem, acajuso, algorrem*—occur in three successive lines of the *Barca do Purgatorio*, and another, *samicas*, is as great a favourite with Vicente as at first was *soncas*,[5] derived from Enzina. But it is impossible to explain all the references to Beira by the supposition that *beirão* is equivalent to rustic and Beira to Boeotia, for Beira and the Serra da Estrella intrude constantly and indeed pervade his work. He shows personal knowledge of the country between Manteigas and Fundão, and we may suspect that it was in order to connect 'Portuguese Fame desired of all nations' with Beira 'our province' rather than with rusticity that he makes her keep ducks as a *mocinha da Beira*. We do not know when Vicente came to Lisbon, nor whether, as José de Cabedo de Vasconcellos, another (17th c.) genealogist, would have us believe, he became

---

[1] iii. 275. Pederneira is mentioned again in ii. 390 and iii. 205.
[2] The authority is Cristovam Alão de Moraes in his manuscript *Pedatura Lusitana* (1667) (No. 441 in the Public Library of Oporto). This genealogist, says Castello Branco, *era ás vezes ignorante e outras vezes mal intencionado*. He does not say that Martim Vicente exercised his alleged profession of silversmith at Guimarães, or that Gil was born there. What more probable than for Guimarães, proud of its poetical traditions, to invent a silversmith father for the famous poet-goldsmith ? Pedro de Poyares, *Tractado em louvor da villa de Barcellos* (1672), says that Gil Vicente, *em tempo de D. João o terceiro poeta celebre, foi natural de Barcellos e andam algumas cousas suas impressas*.
[3] *Grammatica*, ed. 1871, p. 118.
[4] Ibid., p. 81. See J. Leite de Vasconcellos, *Gil Vicente e a Linguagem Popular*, 1902. Feo, *Trattados Quadragesimais* (1619), f. 10, mentions the *somsonete de pronunciação* of the *ratinhos*.
[5] *Soncas* occurs no less than seven times in the brief *Auto Pastoril Castelhano*. It occurs twice in the first twenty-eight lines of one of Enzina's eclogues (*Cancionero de todas las obras* (Çaragoça, 1516), f. lxxviii, and again f. lxxviii verso and lxxx).

THE SIXTEENTH CENTURY

the tutor (*mestre de rhetorica*) of King Manuel, then Duke of Beja. Of his life at Lisbon our information is almost as meagre. We know, of course, that he accompanied the Court to Evora, Coimbra, Thomar, Almeirim, and other towns to set up and act in his plays, that besides acting in his plays he wrote songs for them and music for the songs. We know that he received considerable gifts in money and in kind both from King Manuel and from João III, in whose reign he complains of being penniless and neglected. Some hold that he married his first wife, Branca Bezerra, in 1512, that he owned the *Quinta do Mosteiro* near Torres Vedras (a supposition no longer tenable), that the name of his second wife was Melicia Rodriguez, but we have no certainty as to this, nor as to the number of his children. The accomplished Paula became musician and lady-in-waiting to the Infanta Maria before the death of her father, whom she helped—runs the legend—in the composition of his plays,[1] as she helped her brother Luis in editing them in 1562. From a document concerning another brother, Belchior, we know that Gil Vicente (*seu pae que Deus haja*) died before April 16, 1540. There is some reason to believe that he died in the year of his last play (1536) or early in 1537. From his assertion that the mere collection of his works was a great burden to his old age[2] we might judge him to have been very old, but he may have been worn out with labour in many fields and his health had not always been good. He suffered from fever and plague, which brought him to death's door in 1525, and he had grown stout with advancing age. An incident at Santarem on the occasion of the great earthquake of 1531, so vividly described by Garcia de Resende, shows him in a very attractive light, for by his personal prestige and eloquent words he succeeded in restraining the monks and quieting the half-maddened populace, and thus saved the 'new Christians' from ill-treatment or massacre.

[1] A. dos Reis, *Enthusiasmus Poeticus* (*Corpus Ill. Poet. Lus.*, tom. viii, pp. 18–19): *Quem iuvisse ferunt velut olim Polla maritum*. Manuel Tavares, *Portugal illustrado pelo sexo feminino* (1734), calls her a *discretissima mulher*.

[2] *Com muita pena de minha velhice*. Ruy de Pina calls a man *mui velho* whose father (King João I) would have been but ninety-one in that year (*Cr. de Afonso V*, cap. 105). Cf. Jorge Ferreira, *Ulysippo*, iii. 3: *velho se pode chamar pois vai aos cincoenta anos*.

We know a little more about him if we identify him with Gil Vicente, the goldsmith of Queen Lianor (1458–1525), sister of King Manuel and widow of King João II, whose most famous work is the beautiful Belem monstrance, wrought of the first tribute of gold from the East (from Quiloa or Kilwa).[1] The probabilities in favour of identity are so convincing that we are bound to assume it unless an insuperable obstacle presents itself. Our faith in manuscript documents and genealogies is not increased by the fact that one investigator, the Visconde Sanches de Baena (1822–1909), emerges with the triumphant conclusion that the two Gil Vicentes were uncle and nephew, while another, Dr. Theophilo Braga, declares that they are cousins. Perhaps we may be permitted to believe in neither and to restore Gil Vicente to himself. For indeed this was a singular instance of cousinly love. The goldsmith wrote verses; the poet takes a remarkable interest in the goldsmith's art.[2] The goldsmith is appointed inspector (*vedor*) of all works in gold and silver at the convent of Thomar, the Lisbon Hospital of All Saints, and Belem. The poet is particularly fond of referring to Thomar,[3] and in its convent in 1523 staged his *Farsa de Inés Pereira* (who lived at Thomar with her first husband), while at the Hospital of All Saints was played the *Barca do Purgatorio* in 1518. The goldsmith was in the service of the widow of João II, Queen Lianor, who mentions two of his chalices in her will; the poet at the request of the same Queen Lianor wrote verses, probably in 1509, in a poetical contest about a gold chain and was encouraged by her to write his early plays.[4] The goldsmith was *Mestre da*

---

[1] See Barros, *Asia*, I. vi. 7. Beckford has glowing praise for 'this gold custodium of exquisite workmanship': 'Nothing could be more beautiful as a specimen of elaborate Gothic sculpture than this complicated enamelled mass of flying buttresses and fretted pinnacles' (*Italy, with Sketches of Spain and Portugal*, Paris, 1834).

[2] Reference to gold, jewels, sapphires, pearls, rubies is frequent in his plays. The goldsmith in the *Farsa dos Almocreves* uses the technical word *bastiães* which occurs in the *Livro Vermelho* of Afonso V: *E porque alguns Ouriueses tem ora feita algũa prata dourada e de bastiães*. It occurs, however, in the *Cancioneiro Geral* (*galantes bastiães*), in Resende's *Miscellania* (*bestiães*), and other writers.

[3] Cf. i. 127, 130; ii. 391, 488; iii. 151, 379.

[4] An unfortunate interpolation by the 1834 editors in the rubric of the *Auto da Sibila Cassandra* was largely responsible for the belief that his patroness was not Queen Lianor but King Manuel's mother D. Beatriz.

Balança from 1513 to 1517; the poet goes out of his way to refer to *os da Moeda*, familiarly but not as one of them, in 1521. He henceforth devoted himself more ardently to the literary side of his genius, speaks of himself as Gil Vicente who writes *autos* for the king, and with an occasional sigh[1] that he can no longer afford to stage his plays as splendidly as of old (in King Manuel's reign) produces them with increasing frequency. 'Had Gil Vicente been a goldsmith and a goldsmith of such skill,' said the late Marcelino Menéndez y Pelayo (1856–1912), 'it would have been impossible for him to leave no trace of it in his dramatic works and for all the contemporary writers who speak of him to have kept complete silence as to his artistic talent.'[2] But his work is essentially that of an artist (Menéndez y Pelayo himself well calls him an *alma de artista*)[3] : involuntarily one likens his sketches to some rough terra-cotta figure of Tanagra or sculpture in early Gothic, and his lyrics are clear-cut gems, a thing very rare in Portuguese literature. Intensely Portuguese in his lyrism and his satire, he is almost un-Portuguese in the extreme plasticity of his genius. Concrete, definite images spring from his brain in contrast to the vaguer effusions of most Portuguese poets. And if Queen Lianor's goldsmith, like the troubadour *ourives* Elias Cairel, or, to come to the fifteenth century, like Diogo Fernandez and Afonso Valente of the *Cancioneiro de Resende*,[4] set himself to write verses, this would call for no comment. Every one wrote verses. Had a celebrated poet—say the Gil Vicente of 1520—wrought the *custodia* his contemporaries might have recorded the fact, but Gil Vicente was not a famous

Yet the rubric of the *Auto dos Quatro Tempos* says clearly that *a sobredita senhora* is King Manuel's sister.

[1] *Mas ja não auto bofé Como os autos que fazia Quando elle tinha com que* (*Auto Pastoril Portugues*, i. 129).

[2] *Antologia*, vii, p. clxvi. It should be said that Dr. Theophilo Braga, the late General Brito Rebello, and the late Dr. F. A. Coelho agree with Menéndez y Pelayo. Dr. Theophilo Braga even declares that he can prove an alibi. D. Carolina Michaëlis de Vasconcellos opposed identity in 1894, and has not definitely expressed herself in its favour since. On the other hand, Snr. Braamcamp Freire is a convinced supporter of identifying poet and goldsmith. [3] *Antologia*, vii, p. clxxvi.

[4] And later Jeronimo Corrêa († 1660) at Lisbon, author of *Daphne e Apollo* (Lisboa, 1624) and other prosaic verses, Xavier de Novaes (1820–69) at Oporto, and others. Perhaps the gold-beater of Seville, Lope de Rueda (1510 ?–65), whose *pasos* are akin to Vicente's *farsas*, was fired by his example and success.

GIL VICENTE

poet when the *custodia* was begun in 1503. Stress was therefore naturally laid on the plays of Gil Vicente the goldsmith, not on the art of Gil Vicente the poet. The historian Barros refers in 1540 to Gil Vicente *comico*,[1] and since 1517 he had certainly been more *comico* than *ourives*. But the *comico* who was dramatist and lyric poet, musician, actor, preacher in prose and verse, may also have been a goldsmith. His versatility was that of Damião de Goes a little later or of his own contemporary Garcia de Resende, with genius added. The fact that the official document in which *Gil Vicente lavrador da Rainha Lianor* is appointed to his post in the Lisbon *Casa da Moeda* (Feb. 4, 1513 [2]) has above it a contemporary note *Gil Vte trouador mestre da balãça* should in itself be conclusive evidence that the poet was the goldsmith of the queen. This modest but intimate position at Court accords well with what we know of the poet and with the production of his plays. The offerings at the end of the *Visitaçam* seem to have suggested to Queen Lianor the idea of its repetition on Christmas morning, but Gil Vicente, considering its matter inappropriate, wrote a new play with parts for six shepherds. This *Auto Pastoril Castelhano* is four times as long as the *Visitaçam*. The shepherds pass the time in dance and song, games, riddles, and various conversation (the dowry of the bride of one of them is catalogued in the manner of Enzina [3] and the Archpriest of Hita). To them the Angels announce the birth of the Redeemer, and they go to sing and dance before *aquel garzon*. The principal part, that of the mystic shepherd Gil Terron, ' inclined to the life contemplative ', well read (*letrudo*) in the Bible, with some knowledge of metaphysics and perhaps of the *Corte Imperial*, devoted to Nature and the *sierras benditas*, was evidently played by Gil Vicente himself. A fortnight later, for the Day of Kings, he had ready the *Auto dos Reis Magos* (1503), again at the request of Queen Lianor, who had ' been very pleased ' with what Vicente himself called a *pobre cousa*. This brief interval of time limited the length of the new play. Its action is as slight. A shepherd enters who has lost his way to Bethlehem. He meets

---

[1] *Dialogo em lovvor de nossa linguagem*, 1785 ed., p. 222.
[2] Registers of the Chancellery of King Manuel (vol. xlii, f. 20 v.) in the Torre do Tombo, Lisbon.   [3] Cf. *Cancionero*, f. lxxxvi v.

another shepherd and then a hermit, whom they ply with irreverent problems. To them enters a knight of Araby, and finally the three kings, singing a *vilancete*. The *Auto da Sibila Cassandra* has been assigned to the same year, but is probably a later play (1513 ?). Nearly twice as long as the *Auto Pastoril Castelhano*, it combines the ordinary scenic display—*todo o apparato*—of a Christmas *representação* with a presentment of the early prophecies now to be fulfilled, and introduces Solomon, Isaiah, Abraham, and Moses, who describes the creation of the world. The play includes a profane theme, since Cassandra in her mystic aversion from marriage realistically portrays the sad life of married women in Portugal. Although Cassandra appears as a shepherdess and her aunt Peresica as a peasant, they speak a purer, more flowing Castilian than the *toscos, rusticos pastores* of the preceding *autos*, and the play is remarkable for the beauty of its lyrics—*Dicen que me case yo*, *Sañosa está la niña*, *Muy graciosa es la doncella*, and *A la guerra*. For the Corpus Christi procession of 1504 was provided, at short notice from Queen Lianor, the *Auto de S. Martinho*. The subject of this piece, merely ten dodecasyllabic *oitavas* followed by a solemn *prosa*, is that of El Greco's marvellous picture—St. Martin dividing his cloak with a beggar, whom Vicente treats with characteristic sympathy and insight:

¿Criante rocío, qué te hice yo [1]
Que las hiervecitas floreces por Mayo
Y sobre mis carnes no echas un sayo?

The *Auto dos Quatro Tempos*, of uncertain date, acted before the Court in the Lisbon palace of Alcaçova on Christmas morning in or after 1511, opens with a mystic ode on the Nativity and a *vilancete* (*A ti dino de adorar*) and proceeds rapidly with snatches of song in a splendid rivalry between the four seasons. The praises of Spring are sung with a delightful freshness, as are Winter's rages, while Summer in a straw hat appears sallow and fever-stricken. Jupiter comes with countless classical allusions and David with much Latin, and they all worship together

---

[1] An effective instance of a line shortened by emotion. The long pause on *tardas* in *Oo morte que tardas, quien te detien?* is equally impressive, but the 1562 ed. has *de quien* and Vicente may have written *Oo morte que tardas, di ¿ quien te detien?*

the new-born King. Very different is the *Auto da Alma*, written for Queen Lianor and acted in King Manuel's Lisbon palace of Ribeira on the night of Good Friday, 1518 (Snr. Braamcamp Freire's plausible suggestion in place of the commonly accepted 1508). It represents the eternal strife between the soul and sin. The soul, slowly journeying in the company of its guardian angel, is alternately tempted by Satan with the delights of the world, with fine dresses and jewels, and exhorted by the Angel, till it arrives at the Church, the Innkeeper of Souls, and confesses its guilt, imploring protection (*Ach neige, du schmerzenreiche!*). Then, while Satan in a restless fury of disappointment makes a last effort to secure his victim, the ransomed soul is fortified with celestial fare served by St. Augustine and other *doutores*. The whole theme, to which the language rises fully adequate, is treated with great delicacy and with a mystic fervour.

In 1505 King Manuel and his Court in his Lisbon palace had witnessed the first of those *farsas* in which Gil Vicente has sketched for all time Portuguese life in the first third of the sixteenth century. It rapidly became popular and went from hand to hand as a *folha volante*, receiving from the people the name of *Quem tem farelos?* i.e. the first three words of the play. The plots of the twelve *farsas* written from 1505 to 1531 are so slight that only one calls for detailed notice, the *Farsa de Inés Pereira*[1] (1523), which in its carefully defined characters and developed story more closely resembles a modern comedy. It tells how the hapless Inés, having rejected a plain suitor for a more romantic lover, a poor but deceptive *escudeiro* presented to her by two Jewish marriage agents, learns by bitter experience the truth of the old proverb that 'an ass that carries me is better than a horse that throws me'. But the types and persons in all these farces are etched with so much realism and humour that they bite into the memory and rank with the living malicious sketches of *Lazarillo de Tormes*. Who can forget the famished *escudeiro* Aires Rosado with his book of songs (*cancioneiro*) and

---

[1] *Auto de Inés Pereira* in the 1562 ed. So *Auto dos Almocreves*. It will, however, be convenient to call them *farsas*, since *auto* is a more general term applicable to all the plays.

guitar, continuing to sing beneath the window of his love while the curses of her mother fall thick as snowflakes on his head,[1] or the lady of his affections, vain and idle Isabel, or his servant (*moço*) Apariço who draws so cruel a picture of his master, or that other penniless *escudeiro* who considers himself ' the very palace ' and calls up his *moço* Fernando at midnight to light the lamp and hold the inkstand while he writes down his latest verses ?[2] Equally well sketched is the splendid poverty-plagued *fidalgo* who walks abroad accompanied by six pages, but cannot pay his chaplain or his goldsmith; his ill-used, servile, ambitious chaplain[3]; the witch Genebra Pereira mixing the hanged man's ear, the heart of a black cat, and other grim ingredients : *Alguidar, alguidar, que feito foste ao luar*[4]; the household of the Jewish tailor who delights in songs of battles-at-a-distance and is filled with pride when the *Regedor* salutes him in the street[5]; M. Diafoirus' lineal ancestors Mestres Anrique, Felipe, Fernando, and Torres[6]; the sporting priest[7]; the unfaithful wife of the Portuguese who has embarked for India with Tristão da Cunha ; the vainglorious, grandiloquent Spaniard who takes the opportunity to pay his court to her.[8] They are all drawn from life with a master hand, even the more insignificant figures, the girl keeping ducks, the *moços*, the gipsy horse-dealers,[9] the old man amorous,[10] the carriers faring leisurely along with their mules, the braggart who disables six of his fourteen imaginary opponents, the Frenchman and Italian with their stock phrases *Par ma foi, la belle France, tutti quanti*,[11] the wily and impudent

---

[1] *Quem tem farelos ?*
[2] *O Juiz da Beira*, a continuation suggested by the success of the *Farsa de Inés Pereira* and acted at Almeirim in 1525.
[3] *Farsa dos Almocreves* (or *do Fidalgo Pobre*) acted at Coimbra (1525). It is curious to compare the sterner type of chaplain denounced in *Don Quixote*. [4] *Auto das Fadas* (1511).
[5] *Auto da Lusitania* (1532) acted in honour of the birth of Prince Manuel (1531). [6] *Farsa dos Fisicos* (1512).
[7] *O Clerigo da Beira* (1529 ?). [8] *Auto dá India* (1509).
[9] *Farsa das Ciganas* (or, in the 1562 edition, *Auto de hũas ciganas*), a very slight sketch acted in a *seram* before the king at Evora (1521).
[10] *O Velho da Horta* (1513).
[11] *Auto da Fama* (Lisbon). Its date has been given as 1510, but internal evidence shows that it is later, probably 1515 or 1516 (although perhaps prior to the knowledge of Albuquerque's death in India (December 16, 1515) since so splendid a paean in honour of the Portuguese victories would be out of place afterwards).

negro, the poor *ratinho*[1] Gonçalo, who loses his hare and capons and his clothes as well, the page of peasant birth ambitious to become a *cavaleiro fidalgo*, the roguish and pretentious palace pages. Side by side with these farces Vicente continued to write religious *autos* as well as comedies and tragicomedies. The difference between these various pieces is less of kind than of the occasion on which they were produced, the *obras de devação* on Christmas morning or other solemn day,[2] the *farsas de folgar*, *comedias*, &c., at the evening parties—those famous *serões* of King Manuel's reign to which the courtiers thronged at dusk, and which Sá de Miranda remembered with regret.[3] All provide us with realistic sketches since the background is filled with the common people, the real hero of Gil Vicente's plays as it is of Fernam Lopez' chronicles. Thus the *Auto da Mofina Mendes* (Christmas, 1534), besides its heavenly *gloria* with the Virgin, Gabriel, Prudence, Poverty, Humility, and Faith, has a very life-like peasant scene in which Mofina Mendes, personifying Misfortune, represents a Portuguese version of *Pierrette et son pot au lait*. The *Auto Pastoril Portugues* (Christmas, 1523) is a similar scene of peasant life, relating the cross-currents of the shepherds' loves and the finding of an image of the Virgin on the hills. The *Auto da Feira*, acted before King João at Lisbon in 1527, is a more elaborate Christmas play. Mercury, Time, Rome, and the Devil attend a fair, and this furnishes opportunity for a vigorous attack upon the Church of Rome, with her indulgences for others and her self-indulgence, who has not the kings of the Earth but herself to blame if she is rushing on ruin, ruin that will be inevitable unless she mends her ways. But to the fair also come the peasants Denis and Amancio, as dissatisfied with their wives as their wives are dissatisfied with them (their conversation is most voluble and natural), and market-girls, basket on head, come down singing from the hills. Another

---

[1] = labourer from Beira. He figures in comedy as the slow-witted (or malicious) clod-hopper, to the delight of an urban audience.
[2] In the palace (at Lisbon, Almeirim, Evora) or in convents (Enxobregas, Thomar, Odivellas), once (as part of a procession) in a church (*Auto de S. Martinho*).
[3]   Os momos, os serões de Portugal
      Tam fallados no mundo, onde são idos,
      E as graças temperadas do seu sal?

Christmas play, the *Auto da Fé*, was acted in the royal chapel at Almeirim in 1510, and consists of a simple conversation between Faith and two shepherds. The *Breve Summario da Historia de Deos*[1] (1527) and the *Auto da Cananea* (written for the Abbess of Odivellas in 1534) are both based on the Bible; the former, which contains the *vilancete* sung by Abel (*Adorae montanhas*), outlines the story of the Fall, of Job, and of the New Testament to the Crucifixion, sometimes in passages of great beauty. The latter develops the episode of the woman of Canaan (Matt. xv. 21–8). The great trilogy of *Barcas*, which ranks among Vicente's most important works, is of earlier date. The first part, *Auto da Barca do Inferno*, was acted before Queen Maria *pera consolação* as she lay on her death-bed in 1517, the second, *Auto da Barca do Purgatorio*, at Christmas of the following year in Lisbon, and the *Auto da Barca da Gloria* at Almeirim in 1519. The plot, again, is of the simplest: the Devil, combining the parts of Charon and Rhadamanthus, ferryman and judge, invites Death's victims to show cause why they should not enter his boat; and the interest is in the light thus thrown upon the earthly behaviour of nobleman, judge, advocate, usurer, fool, love-lorn friar, the cheating market-woman, the cobbler who throve by deceiving the people, the peasant who skimped his tithes, the little shepherdess who had seen God 'often and often', of Count, King,[2] and Emperor, Bishop, Cardinal, and Pope. The first part ends with a noble invocation to the knights who had died fighting in Africa, and the second begins with the mystic jewelled *romance*: *Remando vam remadores*.

The comedies and tragicomedies vary greatly. The *Comedia de Rubena* (1521) is, like *A Winter's Tale*, quite without unity of

---

[1] This play is written in lines of 10, 11, or 12 syllables with a break of a line of 5 or 6 syllables after every four lines. Most of Gil Vicente's plays are in octosyllabic *redondilhas* with or without breaks of a line of four syllables, as in the poems of Duarte de Brito and others in the *Cancioneiro Geral*. Lightness, grace, and ease mark this metre in Vicente's hands.

[2] This splendour-loving king bears an unmistakable resemblance to King Manuel, before whom the play was acted, but in no other instance does Vicente allow his satire to touch the king or royal family: *cumpre attentar como poemos as mãos* (*Cortes de Jupiter*).

GIL VICENTE

time or place (for this primitive humanist, although he might mention Plato, did not 'reverence the Stagirite'), but is divided into three acts (called scenes) as in a modern play. Cismena, like Perdita born in the first scene, is conveyed by fairies to Crete, where she is wooed and won by the Prince of Syria. The *Comedia do Viuvo* (1514) is much more compact and has a delicate charm. Don Rosvel, a prince in disguise, serves in the house of a widower at Burgos for love of his daughters. (He is in love with both, but his brother in search of him arrives and marries the second.) On the other hand, the *Comedia sobre a divisa da cidade de Coimbra*, acted before King João III in his ever-loyal city of Coimbra in 1527, is a lengthy, far-fetched explanation of the city's arms, and the *Floresta de Enganos* (played before the king at Evora in 1536) is a succession of scenes of pure farce—the deceit practised upon a merchant, the ludicrous predicament to which love reduced the grave old judge who had taken his degree in Paris—with a more serious theme, a Portuguese version of the story of Psyche and Eros. Of the 'tragicomedies' two, *Dom Duardos* (1525?) and *Amadis de Gaula* (1533), dramatize romances of chivalry: *Primaleon*, that '*dulce & aplacible historia* translated from the Greek',[1] and *Amadis*.[2] The work is done with skill, for Vicente succeeds here as always in being natural, and in this twilight atmosphere of garden flowers and romance keeps his realism.[3] Both plays contain passages of great lyrical beauty, and *Dom Duardos* ends with the *romance* beginning *Pelo mes era de Abril*. Thus in his latter age he successfully adapted himself to pastures new. In his letter dedicating *Dom Duardos* to King João III he wrote: 'Since, excellent Prince and most powerful King, the comedies, farces and moralities which I wrote for (*en servicio de*) the Queen your Aunt were low figures[4] in

---

[1] 1598 ed. (colophon). The date of the first edition is 1512.

[2] Montalvo's *Amadis* clearly. Vicente, who invariably suits his language to his subject, would have written in Portuguese had the text before him been Portuguese. If Montalvo's *Amadis* became fashionable in Portugal this was characteristic of the Portuguese, who would welcome foreign books while they despised and neglected their own.

[3] When Flerida meets D. Duardos disguised as a gardener she supposes that his ordinary fare is garlic.

[4] For the words *quanto en caso de amores* the Censorship is evidently responsible.

which there was no fitting rhetoric to satisfy the delicate spirit of your Highness, I realized that I must crowd more sail on to my poor bark.' For us the words have a tinge of irony, and however much some readers may admire the hushed rapture of these idyllic scenes we miss the merry author of the *farsas*, and gladly turn to the *Romagem de Aggravados* (1533) in which Vicente proves that his hand had lost none of its cunning. 'This tragicomedy is a satire' says the rubric, and it introduces us to the inimitable Frei Paço, the mincing courtier-priest with gloves, gilt sword, and velvet cap (one of Sá de Miranda's *clerigos perfumados*), to the discontented peasant who brings his son to be made a priest, the talkative fish-wives, the hypocrite Frei Narciso scheming to be made a bishop, and awkward Giralda, the peasant Aparicianes' daughter, whom Frei Paço instructs so competently in Court manners. This long play was written for a special occasion, the birth of the Infante Felipe. Gil Vicente for many years, as poet laureate, had celebrated great events at Court. When the Duke of Braganza was about to leave with the expedition against Azamor in 1513 he wrote the eloquent *Exhortaçam da Guerra*, which is introduced by a necromancer priest and ends with a rousing call to war (*soiça*) :

> Avante avante, senhores,
> Pois que com grandes favores
> Todo o ceo vos favorece;
> El Rey de Fez esmorece
> E Marrocos dá clamores.

When King Manuel's daughter, the princess Beatrice, married the Duke of Savoy in 1521 Vicente wrote the *Cortes de Jupiter*, in which the Providence of God bids Jupiter, King of the Elements, speed her on her voyage, and the courtiers and inhabitants of Lisbon accompany her ship, swimming, to the mouth of the Tagus. The *Fragoa de Amor* (1525) was written on the occasion of the betrothal of King João and Queen Catherina (who replaced Queen Lianor as Vicente's protector and patron). Into the forge, to the sound of singing, goes a negro, and then Justice in the form of a bent old woman who is forced to disgorge all her bribes and reappears upright and fair. A similar play, *Nao de Amor* (1527), in which courtiers caulk a miniature ship on the stage, was played before their Majesties in Lisbon two years later. The *Templo de Apolo* (1526) was acted when another daughter of King Manuel left Lisbon to become the wife of the Emperor Charles V. The author introduces the play and excuses its deficiencies on the plea that he has been seriously ill with fever. He then relates the dream of fair women—*las hermosas que son muertas*—that he had seen in his sickness. Apollo then enters, and after declaring that he would have made the world otherwise mounts the pulpit and preaches a mock sermon. The world, Fame, Victory, come to his temple and bear witness to the greatness of the Emperor Charles V. A Portuguese peasant also comes and has more difficulty in obtaining admittance. The author called the play an *obra doliente*, and it was propped up by a passage from the earlier *Auto da Festa* (1525 ?), edited by the Conde de Sabugosa from the unique copy in his possession. Its figures are Truth, two gipsies, a fool, and seven peasants. Their speech is markedly *beirão* and the old woman closely resembles the *velha* of the tragicomedy *Triunfo do Inverno*, written to celebrate the birth of Princess Isabel in 1529, as the *Auto da Lusitania* celebrated that of Prince Manuel in 1532 and the *Tragicomedia Pastoril da Serra da Estrella* that of Princess Maria in 1527. The latter is a wholehearted play of the Serra with a *cossante*, a *baile de terreiro* and *chacota*, and continual fragments of song : one of the most Portuguese of Vicente's plays. The *Triunfo do Inverno* contains some most effective scenes and a bewildering wealth of lyrics : before one is finished another has begun, and the whole long play goes forward at a gallop. The first triumph of Winter is on the hills, the Serra da Estrella (*serra nevada*) ; the second, on the sea, affords a telling satire against the pilots on India-bound ships. The pilot here begins by stating that the storm will be nothing, then he says that he is not to blame for Winter's conduct, finally he falls to imploring the Virgin and St. George and St. Nicholas ; and but for his incompeténce the ship might have been lying safe at Cochin. The second part of the tragicomedy is the Triumph of Spring in the Serra de Sintra. Spring enters in a lyrical profusion singing

> Del rosal vengo, mi madre,
> Vengo del rosale,

breaks off into *Afuera, afuera nublados*, and resumes his song:

A riberas de aquel rio
Viera estar rosal florido,
Vengo del rosale.

Enough has perhaps been said to suggest the variety of these plays, the glow of colour that pervades them, and to show how far their author, although his genius was never fully realized in his *autos*, had travelled from the first glimmerings of the drama in Portugal and from his first model, Enzina. Rudiments of dramatic art existed in the Middle Ages in the ceremonies provided by an essentially dramatic Church and in the mummeries and mimicking *jograes* that delighted the people. Bonamis and his companion furnished some kind of extremely primitive play (*arremedillum*) for King Sancho I, and they were probably only the most successful of hundreds of wandering mimics and players. Mimicry and scenic display[1] were the principal ingredients of the *momos* in which Rui de Sousa excelled[2] and the *entremeses* for which Portugal was famous: they scarcely belonged to literature, although they might include a song and prose *breve* such as the Conde do Vimioso's, printed in the *Cancioneiro Geral*. Religious processions and Christmas, Epiphany, Passion, or Easter scenes[3] gave further scope for dramatic display, as also popular ceremonies such as that in which 'Emperors' and 'Kings'—figures similar, no doubt, to those still to be seen in Spanish processions (e. g. at Valencia)—were carried in triumph to the churches, accompanied by *jograes* who invaded the pulpit and preached profane sermons containing 'many iniquities and abominations', even while mass was in progress. The popular tendencies darkly suggested in the *Constituições* are manifest in Vicente's plays—the Christmas *representações*, the preaching of burlesque sermons, parodies of the mass, profane litanies, parodies and paraphrases of the Lord's Prayer. Like the *Clercs de la Bazoche* in France, he represents the drama

[1] Cf. Zurara, *Cronica de D. João I*, 1899 ed., i. 116: *Alli houve momos de tão desvairadas maneiras que a vista delles fazia mui grande prazer.*
[2] *Cancioneiro Geral*, 1910 ed., i. 326.
[3] The Portuguese in the East in the sixteenth century maintained these customs. We read of Christmas *autos* in India and a *representaçam dos Reis* in Ethiopia. Cf. the Good Friday *centurios* in Barros, II. i. 5.

breaking its ecclesiastical fetters. It was, however, from Spain that the idea of his *autos* first came to him, as the direct imitations of Juan del Enzina (1469?–1529?) in Vicente's early pieces and the explicit statement of Garcia de Resende in his *Miscellania* prove : he speaks of the *representações* of very eloquent style and new devices invented in Portugal by Gil Vicente, and adds the qualifying clause that credit for the invention of the *pastoril* belongs to Enzina. But the wine of Vicente's genius soon burst the old bottles, and when his plays ceased to be confined to the *pastoril* he naturally turned elsewhere for suggestion. He himself towards the end of his life called his religious plays *moralidades*, and the real name of the play popularly known as the *Farsa da Mofina Mendes* was *Os Mysterios da Virgem*.[1] The introduction of Lucifer as *Maioral do Inferno* and Belial as his *meirinho*[2] may have been derived from French *mystères* ; the conception of his *Barcas* certainly owed more to the *Danse macabre* (probably through the Spanish fifteenth-century *Danza de la Muerte*) than to Dante. The burlesque *testamento* of Maria Parda[3] is one of a long list of such wills (of which an example is the mule's testament in the *Cancioneiro Geral*),[4] but in some of its expressions appears to be copied from the *Testament de Pathelin*. His knowledge of French was perhaps more fluent than accurate, like his Latin which, albeit copious, did not claim to be ' pure Tully '. But there are many references to France in his plays, as there are in the *Cancioneiro Geral*, and, although the *enselada* from France with which the *Auto da Fé* ends (i. 75) and the French song (i. 92) *Ay de la noble ville de Paris*[5] were no doubt some fashionable courtier's latest acquisition, Vicente in literary

[1] i. 103. The word was of course not new in the Peninsula. Cf. the thirteenth (?)-century *El Misterio de los Reyes Magos*.
[2] *Breve Summario da Historia de Deos* (i. 309).
[3] In the *Pranto de Maria Parda* ' because she saw so few branches on the taverns in the streets of Lisbon and wine so dear and she could not live without it '.
[4] *Do macho rruço de Luys Freyre estando pera morrer*. See also Dr. H. R. Lang, C. G. C., pp. 174–8, note on the will of the Archdeacon of Toro ; and the extract from a manuscript *testamento burlesco* in J. Leite de Vasconcellos, *De Campolide a Melrose* (1915).
[5] As neither of them is printed in his plays we cannot say whether they were two or one and the same, or whether the French of his song was more intelligible than the version preserved in Barbieri's *Cancionero Musical* (No. 429).

matters probably shared the curiosity of the Court as to what was going on beyond the frontiers of Portugal. The great majority of his songs are, however, plainly indigenous. His knowledge of Italian certainly enabled him to read Italian plays and poems. We know that he was a great reader—he mentions ' the written works that I have seen, in verse and prose, rich in style and matter'. In Spanish he did not confine himself to Enzina. He read romances of chivalry, imitated the *romances* with supreme success, mentions Diego de San Pedro's *La Carcel de Amor*, had read the *autos* of Lucas Fernandez, the *comedias* of Bartolomé de Torres Naharro probably, and without doubt the Archpriest of Hita's *Libro de Buen Amor*, possessed by King Duarte, and the *Celestina*. Indeed, for some time past barriers between the two literatures had scarcely existed and Vicente enriched both. Celestina would have spoken many proverbs had she foreseen that he would allow two men (*judeos casamenteiros*) to take the bread out of her mouth, but he copies her in his Brigida Vaz, Branca Gil, the formidable Anna Diaz, and the *beata alcoviteira* of the *Comedia de Rubena*, although he may also have had in mind the *moller mui vil* of King Alfonso X's *Cantigas de Santa Maria* (No. 64), with the spirit of which—their fondness for popular types and satire—Vicente had more in common than with the *Cancioneiro Geral*, compiled by his friend Resende. With this collection he was naturally familiar, and must have heard many of its songs before it was published in 1516. A line here and there in Vicente seems to be an echo of the *Cancioneiro*,[1] although the fact that it mentions some of his types (as in the *Arrenegos*[2] of Gregorio Afonso) merely means that he drew from the life around him. His satire of doctors and priests, although essentially popular and mediaeval—both are present in the *Cantigas de Santa Maria*—was also due to his personal observation: that is to say, he gave realistic expression to a satire of which the motive was literary (since satire directed against priests had long been one of the chief resources of comic

---

[1] For instance, the following lines and phrases of the *Cancioneiro Geral*: Hirmee a tierras estrañas, Oo morte porque tardais, Vos soes o mesmo paço, E outras cousas que calo, O eco pelos vales. The Portuguese fifteenth-century poet by whom he was most influenced was probably Duarte de Brito.

[2] They were published separately in the following century: Lisboa, 1649.

writers in France, Italy, Spain, and Portugal).[1] The type of the poor *fidalgo* or famishing *escudeiro* on which Vicente dwells so fondly—we have the latter as Aires Rosado in *Quem tem farelos?* and anonymous in the *Farsa de Inés Pereira* and *O Juiz da Beira*[2] —is another instance of literary tradition combined with observation at first hand. Of the priest-satire Vicente was the last free exponent in Portugal. That of the poor gentleman was even older and survived him. It dates from Roman times. The *amethystinatus* of Spanish Martial[3] reappears in the *Cancioneiro da Vaticana*, in the Archpriest of Hita's Don Furon, in the *lindos fidalgos que viven lazerados* of Alfonso Alvarez de Villasandino, in the *Cancioneiro Geral*, and just before Vicente's death is wittily described, as the *raphanophagus purpuratus*, by Clenardus,[4] and less urbanely in *Lazarillo de Tormes*. With no Inquisition to crush him he continued to starve in literature—for instance, in the anonymous later sixteenth-century play *Auto do Escudeiro Surdo* he and his *moço* come on the scene in thoroughly Vicentian guise : *a vossa fome de pam . . . meio tostão gasto quinze dias ha*[5]— as he starves in the real life of the Peninsula to-day.[6] In a sense Gil Vicente no doubt borrowed widely; he was no sorcerer to make bricks without straw, and straw, like poets, is not manufactured : it has to be gathered in. But the *homens de bom saber* who, as we know from the rubric to the *Farsa de Inés Pereira*, doubted his originality must have been very superficial as well as envious critics, for the bricks were essentially his own. Indeed,

---

[1] Many writers note the large number of priests. The north of Portugal is *chea de muitos sacerdotes* says Dr. João de Barros in his *Libro de Antiguidades*, &c., a book full of curious information collected by the author when he was a magistrate (*ouvidor*) at Braga, and written in 1549. [A different work, *Compendio e Summario de Antiguidades*, &c., variously attributed to Ruy de Pina and to Mestre Antonio, surgeon to King João II, appeared in 1606.] Gil Vicente was never in India, otherwise he would certainly have borne witness to the devotion and courage of monks and priests in the East and on the dangerous voyages to and from India.
[2] The anonymity may have been intentional, to emphasize the fact that there was no personal allusion to any of the poor *escudeiros* who thronged the capital and Court.
[3] *Ep.* ii. 57.   [4] Letter from Evora, March 26, 1535.
[5] In the same play reappears Vicente's Spaniard : *Castelhano muy fanfarrão*.
[6] According to the *Arte de Furtar*, decimas and sonnets were written on the subject of a poor *fidalgo* who was in the habit of sending his *moço* to two shoemakers for a shoe on trial from each, since they would not trust him with a pair.

every page of his *autos* is hall-marked as his, *ca non alheo*, and he could say with King Alfonso X:

> Mais se o m'eu melhoro faço ben
> E non sõo por aquesto ladron.

Besides the *Auto da Festa* we have 42 plays [1]: 12 *farsas*, 16 *obras de devaçam*, 4 *comedias*, 10 *tragicomedias*. Some of them were staged with much pomp and *grande aparato de musica* in the spacious times of King Manuel, but they lose little in being merely read. They contain a few scenes of dramatic insight and power, a few touches of real comedy, but above all we value them for their types and characters, the insight they afford us into man and that particular period of man's history, and for the lyrics and lyrical passages, fragments of heaven-born poetry thrown out tantalizingly at random as the dramatist passes rapidly, carelessly on. We do not possess all Vicente's plays. A farce which in a poem to the Conde de Vimioso (? 1525) he says that he had in hand, *A Caça dos Segredos*, was perhaps never finished, or perhaps it was produced seven years later as the *Auto da Lusitania* (1532). Others were probably lost as *folhas volantes* before the edition of 1562 could collect them. Three at least, the *Auto da Aderencia do Paço*, *Auto da Vida do Paço*, and *Jubileu de Amor* or *Amores*, were suppressed.[2] The latter, in Spanish and Portuguese, was probably the cause of the loss of the two other plays, for, having ventured far away from the natural piety of Portugal, it was acted in Brussels on December 21, 1531, in the house of the Portuguese Ambassador, D. Pedro de Mascarenhas, and in the mind of the Nuncio, Cardinal Aleandro, who was among those invited, this 'manifest satire against Rome' caused such commotion that, as he wrote, he 'seemed to be in mid-Saxony listening to Luther[3] or in the horrors of the sack of Rome'.[4] Yet in

---

[1] If the *Dialogo da Resurreiçam* be counted separately we have forty-four in all.

[2] Index of 1551. See C. Michaëlis de Vasconcellos, *Notas Vicentinas*, i (1912), p. 31. But here again the *Auto da Vida do Paço* might be the *Romagem de Aggravados*.

[3] Cf. Barros, prefatory letter to *Ropica Pnefma* (May 25, 1531): *falam tam solto como se estivessem em Alemanha nas rixas de Luthero*.

[4] *Notas Vicentinas*, p. 21, where the letter is given in the original Italian and in Portuguese. The Legate had lent a cardinal's hat for the occasion, little realizing that it was to be worn by one of the actors in such a play (a witness to the realism with which Vicente's plays were staged).

1533 impenitent, the incorrigible Vicente is pillorying the Court priest, Frei Paço. The fact is that in Portugal no one could suspect the sheep-dog, who had for so long and so mordantly kept watch over the Court flock, of turning wolf and encouraging the *seitas* and *cismas* against which Alvaro de Brito had already inveighed. He was himself deeply, mystically religious and perhaps cared the less for creeds and dogmas. His mystic philosophy appears as early as 1502. Yet they do him a poor service who represent him as a profound theologian, a great philosopher, an authoritative philologist. His plays show us a man lovable and human, tolerant of opinions, intolerant of abuses,[1] a man of many gifts, with a passionate devotion to his country. We have only to turn to the ringing *Exhortaçam da Guerra* or the *Auto da Fama*. The whole of the latter is written in a glow of pride and patriotism at Portugal's vast, increasing empire and the victories of Albuquerque:

> Ormuz, Quiloa, Mombaça,
> Sofala, Cochim, Melinde.

Clearly the words to him are a sweet music.[2] From one point of view Gil Vicente's position exactly tallied with Herculano's description of the *bobo*. He was a Court jester, expected to render the idle courtiers *muy ledos*. To this purpose he was compelled to saddle his plays with passages which for us have lost their savour and significance but almost every line of which must have elicited a smile or a shout of laughter at the *serões*. We may instance *O Clerigo da Beira*, which ends with the signs and planets under which various courtiers were born, the *Tragicomedia da divisa da cidade de Coimbra*, with the origins of various noble

[1] His tolerant spirit, expressed in his letter to the King in 1531, was remarkable in an age not very remote from the day when Duarte de Brito wrote to Anton de Montoro (*c*. 1405–80) that he would have been burnt had he written in Portugal the blasphemous lines addressed to Queen Isabella of Spain:
> Si no pariera Sanctana
> hasta ser nacida vos,
> de vos el hijo de Dios,
> rescibiera carne humana.

[2] As indeed they were to Milton: 'Mombasa and Quiloa and Melind'. On the other hand, Garcia de Resende in one of the *decimas* of his *Miscellania* has twenty-six names: *Tem Ceita, Tanger, Arzilla*, &c., ordered rather for the rhyme than for harmony.

families, the malicious *catalogue raisonné* of courtiers in the *Cortes de Jupiter*, Branca Gil's comical litany in *O Velho da Horta*, the sixty-four puzzle verses of the *Auto das Fadas*. But Vicente frequently had a deeper purpose than to enliven a fashionable gathering. The abuse of indulgences, the corruption of the clergy,[1] the subjection of married women, the danger of appointing ignorant men to the responsible position of pilot, the mingling of the classes—it was not so, he remarks, in Germany or Flanders, France or Venice—the increasing tendency to shun honest labour in order to occupy a position however humble at Court,[2] the ignorance and presumption of the peasants, the false display and false ambitions, the thousand new lies and deceits, the decay of piety, the growth of luxury and corresponding diminution in gaiety—these were matters which he sought not only to portray but to correct, with much earnestness in his *iocis levibus*. But to the end of his life he was never able to learn that religion and virtue must be melancholy. In the introduction to the *Triunfo do Inverno* (1529) he complains of the loss of the joyous dances and songs of Portugal and the disappearance in the last twenty years of the *gaiteiro* and his cheerful piping. He himself drew his inspiration from the people, from Nature, and from the Scriptures, with which he had no superficial acquaintance. In his love of Nature and his wide curiosity he studied children and birds, plants and flowers, astronomy and witchcraft—those myriad forms of sorcery in Portugal, some of which have fortunately survived in the prohibitory decrees of the Church. He included in his plays or alluded to many of the traditions, the songs and dances of old Portugal—the ancient *cossantes*, the *bailes de terreiro*, *bailos vilãos*,[3] *bailes da Beira*, *chacotas*, *folias*, *alvoradas*,

[1] He does not attack them without exception. There is much good sense in the *clerigo* of Beira, and true charity in the *frade* of the *Comedia do Viuvo*.
[2]   os lavradores
  Fazem os filhos paços,
  Cedo não ha de haver villãos:
  Todos d' El Rei, todos d' El Rei (*Farsa dos Almocreves*).
[3] Cf. the *balho vylam ou mourisco* which cost Abul his gold chain in the *Cancioneiro Geral*, and Lopo de Almeida's third letter, from Naples: *Mandaram bailar meu sobrinho com Beatriz Lopez o baylo mourisco e despois o vilão*. A century after Vicente the shepherds' dances are but a memory: *as danças e bailios antigamente tão usados entre os pastores* (Faria e Sousa, *Europa Portuguesa*, vol. iii, pt. 4).

janeiras, lampas de S. João.[1] For he stood at the parting of the ways. Desirous and capable of playing many parts, tinged unawares by the new spirit of the Renaissance, but at the same time keenly national, he linked the Middle Ages with the new learning and the old traditions of Portugal with her ever-widening dominions, for which he showed the wise enthusiasm of a true imperialist. But behind the new glitter and luxury of Lisbon he constantly saw the growing misery of the people of Portugal for which all the splendour of King Manuel's reign had been but a terrible storm[2]; and his latter sadness was perhaps less personal than patriotic. He had done what he could, far more than had been required of him. He had been expected to delight a Court audience, and had mingled warning and instruction with amusement; and when, having lived and laughed and loved, he went his way, he was not only spared by a crowning grace from the wrath that was to come but left to his countrymen an heirloom more enduring than brass, more precious than all the gold of India, with a breath of that true Portugal in its simplicity, its mirth and jollity, the disappearance of which he had deplored. Portuguese literature was never so national again. A period of splendid achievement followed, but alike in subject and language it was too often a honeyed sweetness containing in itself the seeds of decay, and if for the time it swept away all memory of Gil Vicente, for us it only emphasizes his qualities by the contrast. In his directness, his close contact with the people,[3] his humanity, his quick observation, keen satire, love of laughter and malicious humour, in his unsurpassed lyrical gift and his natural delight in words, to be used not at haphazard but weighed and set cunningly as precious stones in the hands of an *ourives*, this great lyrical poet and charmingly incorrect playwright clearly foreshadowed dramatists so different as Calderón, Lope de Vega, Shakespeare,

---

[1] Cf. *Ulysippo*, iii. 6: *aquellas mayas que punhão, aquellas lampas, aquellas alvoradas*, and D. Francisco de Portugal, *Prisoens e Solturas de hũa Alma*: *Ines* [of Almada] *moça de cantaro, a gabadinha dos ganhões do lugar, requestada da velanao dos barbeiros, a cuja porta nunca faltou Mayo florido em dia de Santiago nem ramos verdes com perinhas no de S. João a que os praticos daquella noute chamão lampas.*

[2] *A morte d'El Rei D. Manoel.*

[3] His occasional coarseness is popular, rustic, and as a rule contrasts favourably with that of the *Cancioneiro Geral*.

and Molière. Yet we look in vain for a Vicentian school of great dramatists in Portugal. His fame had reached Brussels and thence Rome, and Erasmus is credited with having wished to learn Portuguese in order to read Vicente's plays. Shakespeare, who was twenty-two when the second edition of Vicente's plays appeared and who almost certainly read Spanish, may also have been tempted. It would have been strange if Erasmus had not heard of Vicente through his friend André de Resende, who in his Latin poem *Genethliacon* declared that had not the comic poet Gil Vicente, actor and author, written in the vulgar tongue he would have rivalled Menander and excelled Plautus and Terence. In Portugal the number of plays written in the sixteenth century was large,[1] but none can be placed on a level with those of Vicente. One cannot say that he influenced Camões or Ferreira de Vasconcellos deeply, although they had evidently read him. In Spain Cervantes, who read everything, *aunque sean los papeles rotos de las calles*, had read his plays (the *Farsa dos Fisicos*, *O Juiz da Beira*, the *Comedia de Rubena* among others), Lope de Vega likewise, Calderón possibly. Lope de Rueda probably derived the idea of his *paso Las Aceitunas* from the *Auto da Mofina Mendes*. Yet it is almost with amazement, if we forget the crowded history of Portugal and Portuguese literature in the sixteenth century, the introduction of the Inquisition, and the great changes in the language, that we find a Portuguese, Sousa de Macedo, a century after Vicente's death, speaking of him as one 'whose style was celebrated of old',[2] and a Spaniard, Nicolás Antonio, declaring that his works were written in prose and knowing nothing of a collected edition.[3] It was with reasonable mis-

---

[1] For a list containing about a hundred see T. Braga, *Eschola de Gil Vicente*, p. 545, or the *Diccionario Universal*, vol. i (1882), p. 1884, s.v. *Auto*.

[2] *Flores de España*, cap. 5.

[3] *Bib. Nova*, ii. 158. Elsewhere he speaks of him as *poetae comoediarum suo tempore celebratissimi*, and in the Appendix says: *cuius comoedias Lusitani admodum celebrant*. But after the sixteenth century Vicente was little more than a name. Faria e Sousa could say that his plays had been esteemed [*con*] *poquisima causa* (the accidental omission of the *con* led to the invention *poquisima cosa*); and a learned Coimbra professor, Frei Luis de Sotomaior, caught reading *as semsaborias de Gil Vicente, que em seus tempos foi mui celebrado*, felt bound to be apologetic: *Aurum colligo ex stercore* (Francisco Soares Toscano, *Parallelos de Principes* (Evora, 1623), f. 159).

givings that Vicente just before his death wrote : *Livro meu, que esperas tu ?* ; 'my book, what is in store for you ? ' We know that it remained in manuscript for a quarter of a century, that a second edition in 1586 was so handled by the Censorship that it contains but thirty-five mutilated plays, and that for two and a half centuries no new edition was printed.

§ 2
Lyric and Bucolic Poetry

THE romantic story of Macias had not been given literary form, but it exercised a wide influence over the Portuguese poets of the sixteenth century. Together perhaps with Diego de San Pedro's *Carcel de Amor*, the Spanish version of Boccaccio's *Fiammetta*, and especially Rodriguez de la Cámara's *El siervo libre de Amor* (containing the *Estoria de los dos amadores Ardanlier e Liesa*), it must have been in the mind of BERNARDIM RIBEIRO (1482–1552) when he wrote that 'gentle tale of love and languishment' the book of *Saudades*, which is always known (like the first farce of Gil Vicente) from its first three words as *Menina e moça*. Yet it is not really an imitative work, being, indeed, remarkable for its unaffected sincerity, as the expression of a personal experience. Its passionate truth continues to delight many readers.[1] Almost all our information about Ribeiro's life is derived from his writings, which are in part evidently autobiographical, and it shrinks or expands according to the degree of the critic's wariness or ingenuity. His birthplace is declared to have been the quaint Alentejan village of Torrão. A passage in the eclogue *Jano e Franco* says that Jano fled thence at the time of the great famine. The unhappy frequency of famines makes the date doubtful, but if the year of Ribeiro's birth be correctly stated in an official document of May 6, 1642, as 1482, we may suppose—since Jano was twenty-one—that he left his native Alentejo for Lisbon in 1503. It is possible that he studied law and took his degree at the University (at Lisbon) a few years later (1507–11 ?),[2] and became secretary to King João III in 1524. As a *cavalleiro fidalgo* he had his place at Court, as poet he con-

---

[1] Cf. H. Lopes de Mendonça, *O Salto Mortal*, Act iii : *Tanto gostaes d'este livro ? É por ser triste ?—É por ser verdadeiro.*

[2] Eclogue 5 (*a qual dizem ser do mesmo autor*), which is undoubtedly by Ribeiro, refers to Coimbra in the lines : *É lembrarme os sinceiraes De Coimbra que me mata.*

tributed to the *Cancioneiro Geral* (1516). A hopeless passion drove him from the Court, drove him perhaps to Italy, and finally deprived him of his reason, so that his last years were spent in the Lisbon Hospital de Todos os Santos.[1] Successive generations have busied themselves over the object of his passion. The romantic tradition that it was the Princess Beatriz, twenty-two years his junior, the daughter of King Manuel for whose marriage to the Duke of Savoy in 1521 Gil Vicente wrote the *Cortes de Jupiter*, is now definitely discarded. That it was Queen Juana la Loca of Castille no one except Varnhagen has ever imagined. But literary critics continue to be tempted by the transparent anagrams of Ribeiro's novel (adopted evidently in order to make the story unintelligible to all except the inner circle of the Court). Dr. Theophilo Braga has an ingeniously fabricated theory that Aonia was Ribeiro's cousin, Joana Tavares Zagalo. Lamentor at least can scarcely have been King Manuel, since he sends his daughter to the king's Court. The scenery appears to be a combination of that of the Serra de Sintra near Lisbon with that of Alentejo. The story opens with an introductory chapter in which a young girl (*menina e moça*), who has taken refuge in the *serra* far from all human society, announces her intention of writing down what she had seen and heard in a small book (*livrinho*), not for the happy to read but for the sad, or rather for none at all, seeing that of him for whom alone it is intended she has had no news since his and her misfortune bore him away to far-distant lands. Thus we have the thirteenth-century *amiga* mourning for her lover. *Ai Deus! e u é?* Presently, as she shelters from the noonday *calma* beneath trees that overhang a gently flowing stream, a nightingale pours forth its song, and then dying with its song falls with a shower of leaves and is borne away songless by the silent stream.[2] She is still bewailing its fate when another, older but equally sad, lady (*dona*) appears, and the *menina* becomes an almost silent listener to the end of the

---

[1] As in the case of Gil Vicente, we are vexed with homonyms—a notary, an admiral, &c. Dr. Theophilo Braga, skilfully dovetailing hypotheses, develops his biography fully. *Casi todo lo que de él se ha escrito son fábulas sin fundamento alguno*, wrote Menéndez y Pelayo in 1905.

[2] Fray Luis de Leon may have remembered this passage in *De los Nombres de Cristo*, Bk. 3 (1917 ed., t. 1, p. 198; *Bib. Aut. Esp.*, t. 37, p. 182).

book while the *dona* unfolds the tale which is its true subject, the history of two friends Narbindel and Bastião. But it begins with the love adventure of Lamentor and Belisa. It is only in the ninth chapter that the knight Narbindel arrives and falls in love with Belisa's sister Aonia, adopting a shepherd's life in order to be near her palace. It is in fact a romance of chivalry in pastoral garb. But Ribeiro might have introduced the pastoral romance without changing the fantastic features. It is in his singular combination of passion and realism that his true originality consists. His power of giving vivid expression to tranquil scenes—the whole of the first part has something of the quiet intensity of a background by Correggio, as well as his 'softer outline', and although there is no explicit indication of colour it is clearly felt by the reader—and his gentle love of Nature, or rather his love of Nature in its gentler aspects, cast over the book a strange charm. The softly flowing streams, the trees and birds and delicious shade, beautiful dawns, the birds seeking their nests at evening, the flowers *que a seu prazer se estendem*, the *mateiros* going out to cut brushwood, the shepherds asleep round their fire at night, are described with great naturalness and truth, often with familiar words and colloquial phrases. The reason of the extreme intricacy of the plot was not the wish to conceal the author's love story in a labyrinthine maze [1] in order to exercise the ingenuity of nineteenth-century professors, but to be true to life. In life events are not rounded and distinct but merge into and react on one another in an endless ravelled skein : *Das tristezas não se pode contar nada ordenadamente porque desordenadamente acontecem ellas* (cap. 1). Ribeiro thus anticipates by four centuries the theory enunciated in Spain by Azorín that a novel, like life, should have no plot,[2] and his book has a certain modernity. We may refuse him the name of novelist, but many a novelist might envy his lifelike portrayal of scenes and sentiments. It has been doubted whether he wrote the second part of the story. It consists of fifty-eight short chapters, and opens with a new episode, the love of Avalor for Arima, daughter of Lamentor (cap. 1–24),

---

[1] *Nossos amores contados por um modo que os não entenderá ninguem*, Garrett, *Um Auto de Gil Vicente*.
[2] *La Voluntad*, Barcelona, 1902. Camillo Castello Branco held similar views.

and it is even more bewildering in its confusion than is Part I. The scenes are less idyllic, the tone more that of a conventional romance of chivalry, yet the realism is maintained. It is on no hippogriff that Avalor goes to the rescue of the distressed maiden : in fact, he had set out on his adventure in a rowing-boat and his hands blistered. If later there are mortal combats with wicked knights, with a bear, with giants, there are also scenes, as in chapters 9, 12, 23—of an impassioned *saudade*,[1] of dove and nightingale—which could only have been written by the author of Part I.[2] His own story, still related by the *dona*, is only resumed in chapter 26, or rather 32, since the intervening chapters deal with events prior to those with which Part I begins. Bimnarder, now again Narbindel—the name Bernardim was also spelt Bernaldim—after Aonia's marriage lives with an old hermit and his nephew, Godivo, and passes his time in tears and contemplation, as in Part I. But he is discovered by his faithful squire, and meets Aonia, and the lovers are killed by the jealous husband (cap. 48). The last chapters are concerned with the happier love story of Romabisa and Tasbião.

Narbindel, the second of the two knights, the two friends *de que é a nossa historia*,[3] dies : therefore Bernardim Ribeiro cannot have written the second part. But it is rather a nice point; one may imagine that Ribeiro's delight in so tragic an episode would compensate him amply for the obvious anachronism, and after all it is the *dona* who tells the story.[4] The inconsistencies of detail need not concern us overmuch. That Belisa has a mother in Part I and is 'brought up without a mother' in Part II, that the Castle of Lamentor exists in Part II at a time when, according to Part I, it was not yet begun, that the name of Aonia's husband is in Part I Fileno, and in Part II Orphileno, are just such contradictions as an alien

---

[1] The word cannot be translated exactly, but corresponds to the Greek πόθος, Latin *desiderium*, Catalan *anyoranza*, Galician *morriña*, German *Sehnsucht*, Russian тоска (pron. *taská*). It is the 'passion for which I can find no name' (Gissing, *The Private Papers of Henry Ryecroft*).
[2] Menéndez y Pelayo's strict division between the 'subjective' pt. 1 and pt. 2 as *externa y de aventuras* is thus somewhat arbitrary.
[3] Pt. 1, cap. 9 ; pt. 2, cap. 25.
[4] In pt. 2, cap. 9, this is forgotten : *outras [cousas] que não são escritas neste livro*, a slip which throws no light on the authorship.

continuer would most studiously have avoided, and we all know what happened to Sancho's ass in a far less intricate story. Or they may be explained by the fact that Ribeiro had not revised his tale before it was printed, or by corrections made in copies of the original manuscript.[1] Perhaps on the whole we may conclude that Ribeiro, like Cervantes, by an exception wrote a valuable second part, but, unlike Cervantes, was unable to maintain it altogether on a level with the first. The mingling of rapt passion and colloquialisms is with Ribeiro not the inability of a poet to express himself but a deliberate mannerism, and is present in the five eclogues with which he introduced pastoral poetry. By his quiet resolution to be natural he thus became doubly an innovator, in poetry and prose. That he was a true poet is proved by the *romances* in his novel : *Pensando vos estou, filha* (Pt. I, cap. 21) and *Pola ribeira de um rio* (Pt. II, cap. 11).[2] The eclogues may not excel those poems, but in their directness, primitive freshness, and grace they form a group apart, entirely distinct from their numerous eclogue progeny. One eclogue only, the celebrated *Trovas de Crisfal*, resembles them. The resemblance is remarkable and cannot fail to strike the most careless reader. Before Snr. Delfim Guimarães began his spirited campaign in favour of identification, the similarity had been recorded by D. Carolina Michaëlis de Vasconcellos in the *Grundriss*[3] : the extraordinary

[1] It was characteristic of the hot-house air in which Portuguese literature existed that the first publication of a book often consisted in its circulation (*correr*) in manuscript from courtier to courtier, a special licence being obtained for this apart from the licence to print. Those to whom it appealed made copies. The earliest known edition of *Menina e moça* is of 1557–8 : *Primeira & segũda parte do liuro chamado as Saudades de Bernaldim Ribeiro com todas suas obras. Treladado de seu proprio original. Nouamente impresso.* 1557 (Euora. The date of the colophon is January 30, 1558). An introductory note *Aos lectores* says : *Foram tantos os traduzidores deste liuro & os pareceres em elle tam diuersos que nam he de marauilhar que na primeira impressam desta historia se achassem tantas cousas em contrario de como foram pello auctor delle escriptas . . . foy causa de andar este liuro tam vicioso . . . conueo tirarse a limpo do proprio original*, &c., &c.). The edition of 1554, quoted by Brunet, was probably the first in spite of the words *com summa diligencia emendada* (i. e. corrections of the manuscript). The phrase *de nouo* tells more against than in favour of an earlier edition (= rather 'new' than 'anew').

[2] Ribeiro, so far as we know, wrote no line of Spanish. Boscán's *romance Justa fué mi perdición* and the *romance Ó Belerma* have been wrongly ascribed to him.

[3] p. 287 : . . . *so ganz persönlichem Stil, dass sie mit keinem anderen Dichter vor oder nach ihnen, wohl aber untereinander zu verwechseln wären*; and p. 292 :

similarity of these *Trovas* to the poetry of Ribeiro and to nothing else in Portuguese literature. In this poem of some 900 lines written in octosyllabic *decimas*, like Ribeiro's eclogues, we have that romantic, passionate *saudade* and sentimental grief, the mystic visions, the simplicity, the ingenuous conceits, wistfully humorous, the sententious reflections, the elliptical concision, the real shepherds, the familiar language, the love of Nature which are peculiarly Ribeiro's. Tradition assigns the *Trovas* to Cristovam Falcão (*c.* 1512-53 ?),[1] who was born at Portalegre, in Alentejo, was made a *moço fidalgo* in 1527, and is supposed to have fallen in love with and secretly married D. Maria Brandão (i. e. the Maria of the *Trovas*), whom her parents confined as a punishment in the convent of Lorvão. At the risk of being dubbed incorrigibly *simplicista* one must confess that the simultaneous appearance of these two poets from Alentejo, not *fertil en poetas*, taxes one's belief to the utmost. May not the secret marriage deduced from the *Trovas* have been described by Ribeiro in his keen sympathy for his friend's position, so like his own? The contention is not that Cristovam Falcão did not exist— there were several—or did not fall in love with Maria Brandão— *a do Crisfal*—or did not marry her, but that he did not write verses in the style familiar to us as that of Ribeiro.[2] It is remarkable that the very critics who represent Ribeiro in his *novela* as hiding like a cuttle-fish in his own ink change their method when

Bernardim Ribeiro writes *ganz im Stile des Falcão*. Cf. F. Bouterwek, *History of Spanish and Portuguese Literature*, Eng. tr. 1823, ii. 39 : ' A long eclogue by this writer, which forms an appendix to the works of Ribeyro, so completely partakes of the character of the poems which it accompanies that were it not for the separate title it might be mistaken for the production of Ribeyro himself. It therefore proves that Ribeyro's poetic fancies, his romantic mysticism not excepted, were by no means individual.'

[1] According to Dr. Theophilo Braga, he was born in 1515 ; married in 1529 Maria Brandão (aged eleven) ; was profoundly influenced by Ribeiro's *Trovas de dous pastores* (1536) but did not plagiarize it in the *Trovas de Crisfal* (1536-41), similar passages being due to the *situação quasi similar* (i. e. *quasi identica*) of the two friends ; went to Italy on a diplomatic mission in 1541 ; spent the year 1543 in Rome and returned to Portugal in the winter of 1543-4 ; was factor of the fortress of Arguim from 1545 to 1548 ; and died in 1577.

[2] The whole question at issue is whether the *de* of *Trovas de Crisfal* = ' by ' or ' about ' (cf. *O Livro das Trovas d'El Rei* = rather ' belonging to ' than ' by ' the king), and protests against *a illusão de pretender identificar em um mesmo poeta o apaixonado de Aonia e o de Maria* (*Obras*, 1915 ed., p. 10) or *o intuito de converterem Christovam Falcão em um mytho* (ibid., p. 42) are beside the point.

they come to the eclogues and accept every name and allusion with the greatest literalness, as though it were a poet's duty to wear his heart in his verses. It is idle to adduce the fact that Cristovam Falcão wrote ungrammatical letters (so did Keats), or to devise far-fetched interpretations (such as *Crisma falso*) for the word Crisfal. What more probable than that Ribeiro and Falcão, born in the same province, became friends at Court, and that Ribeiro introduced his friend in one of his poems as he is supposed to have introduced Sá de Miranda in another, and as Miranda introduces Ribeiro (*Canta Ribero los males de amor*) ? If in his favourite manner he added a little mystification in the word Crisfal, what more characteristic ? The very form of the poem, in which first the *Autor* and then Crisfal speaks (*Falla Crisfal*) suggests this, as does the title : *Trovas de um pastor per nome Crisfal*, compared with the definite *Trovas de dous pastores . . . Feitas por Bernaldim Ribeiro*.[1] It is not difficult to explain the printing of the *Trovas* together with the works of Ribeiro and the hesitancy of the early editions in ascribing them, on hearsay, to Cristovam Falcão; but the word Crisfal caught the fancy, and those who learnt that it stood for Cristovam Falcão would inevitably confuse the explanation of the anagram with the authorship of the poem. One of those who did so was Gaspar Fructuoso (or Antonio Cordeiro), and the tradition which had begun so shakily with a *dizem ser* gained strength with the years. Presumably the editor of the 1559 edition knew what was to be known on the subject, yet he speaks with a quavering uncertainty: it is only much later that the ascription to Cristovam Falcão becomes a fixed belief.[2] The eighth *Decada* of Diogo do Couto was not published till 1673, i.e. over half a century after the death of its author. The explanatory sentence *aquelle que fez aquellas antigas e nomeadas* (or *namoradas*) *trovas de Crisfal*[3] may well be, and probably is, a later interpolation. But although a few

[1] That one of the figures is identical in the woodcuts of these two *folhas volantes* is not significant : it appears also in an anonymous edition of the *Pranto de Maria Parda*.
[2] In the 1559 ed. the words *hũa muy nomeada e agradauel Egloga chamada Crisfal . . . que dizem ser de Cristouam Falcam, ho que parece alludir ho nome da mesma Egloga* may legitimately be held to imply merely that some persons, misled by the anagram, attributed the poem to Falcão.
[3] *Decada* 8, cap. 34 (1786 ed., p. 322).

scholars definitely hold that Ribeiro wrote this poem, *grammatici certant* and, should tradition prove too strong, we have to accept a second writer who claims an undying place in Portuguese literature owing to the marvellous success with which, divesting his muse of any qualities of its own, he identified himself with a poet who is the most characteristically Portuguese, but also the most individual of impassioned singers : Bernardim Ribeiro.

A kind of continuation of the story of *Crisfal* (who is now enchanted within the fountain of his own tears) appeared at the end of the century in a small collection of poems entitled *Sylvia de Lisardo* (1597). It contains forty-one sonnets (of which one only is in Spanish), three eclogues in *tercetos* and *oitavas*, and various *romances* (in Spanish) and shorter poems, and has been ascribed, without sufficient reason, to the historian Frei Bernardo de Brito. These poems must remain anonymous, and they throw no light on the *Crisfal* problem, but in their true poetical feeling and power of expression they deserved their popularity [1] in the first half of the seventeenth century.

It is not certain but it is probable that Ribeiro went to Italy, and his Italian travels may have coincided with those of his life-long friend, the champion of humanism in Portugal, FRANCISCO DE SÁ DE MIRANDA (*c.* 1485–1558), the most famous of all the Portuguese poets with the exception of Camões and Gil Vicente. As a lyric poet far inferior to either of them, his great influence was due partly to his character, partly to his introduction of the new school of poetry, the *versos de medida nova*, or *de arte maior*, replacing the national *trovas de medida velha* (octosyllabic *redondilhas*) by the Italian hendecasyllabics : Petrarca's sonnets and *canzoni*, Dante's *terza rima* (*tercetos*), and the *octava rima* of Poliziano and Ariosto. The exact date of Miranda's birth is still uncertain, but if he was the eldest of five sons of the Coimbra Canon, Gonçalo Mendez de Sá, who were legitimized in 1490, he must have been born about the year 1485. Yet one would willingly make him younger. His life in Minho certainly sounds too active for a man of fifty : perhaps *c.* 1490 would be nearer the mark. He studied at the University at Lisbon and

---

[1] The *licença* of the 1632 edition says, *Este livrinho ... muitas vezes se imprimio.*

early frequented the Court. He soon won distinction as a scholar and was a Doctor of Law when he contributed several poems to Garcia de Resende's *Cancioneiro* (1516). His journey to Italy a few years later, in 1521, may have been due merely to the natural desire of a scholar to see Rome or there may have been other motives, a love affair of his own or his friendship with Bernardim Ribeiro. He was distantly related to the great Italian family of Colonna (as he was to Garci Lasso) and in Italy perhaps met the celebrated Vittoria Colonna (1492–1547), Marchesa di Pescara, besides probably most of the other distinguished Italians of the time, Lattanzio Tolomei, Sannazzaro, Cardinal Bembo, Giovanni Rucellai, Ariosto. During five years he saw the principal cities of Italy and Sicily and returned to Portugal in 1526 (or earlier, possibly after three years, in 1524) with a deep knowledge of Italian literature and the firm resolve to acclimatize in his country the metres in which the Italians had written things so divine. If he had seen at Rome the *Cancioneiro* of thirteenth-century Portuguese poets [1] he must have realized that the metres were not so foreign as many might think; if he met Boscán on his homeward journey his determination to become innovator or restorer [2] would be strengthened. King João III was on the throne, and we are told in Miranda's earliest biography (1614), which is attributed with some probability to D. Gonçalo Coutinho, that he became 'one of the most esteemed courtiers of his time'. He was an enthusiastic believer in monarchy and in the divinity that doth hedge a king, but was less enamoured of the growing corruption and luxury at Court: probably he was himself more esteemed by the king than by the courtiers, and after the poetry

---

[1] Cf. 1885 ed., No. 109:
    Eu digo os Provençais que inda se sente
    O som das brandas rimas que entoaram.

Cf. Boscán ap. Menéndez y Pelayo, *Antología*, tom. xiii (*Juan Boscán*), p. 165: *En tiempo de Dante y un poco antes florecieron los Proenzales, cuyas obras por culpa de los tiempos andan en pocas manos.* Menéndez y Pelayo also (ibid., p. 174) gives a reference by Faria e Sousa to King Dinis: *El rey don Dionis de Portugal nació primero que el Dante tres ó quatro años y escrivió mucho deste propio género endecasílabo, como consta de los manuscritos.*

[2] Cf. 1885 ed., No. 112:
    ¿ Como se perdieron
    Entre nos el cantar, como el tañer
    Que tanto nombre a los pasados dieron ?

of Italy he could scarcely share their taste for the trivial verses of the *Cancioneiro Geral* nor could they see how a compliment could be turned more neatly than in the old *esparsas* and *vilancetes*. During these years he wrote his first play, *Os Estranjeiros*, the eclogue *Alexo* with *oitavas* in Portuguese, and the *Fabula do Mondego*, perhaps in order to show his superiority over Gil Vicente.

There was an obvious antagonism between the laughing and the weeping reformer (for both protested vigorously in their different ways against the growing materialism of the day), between the learned, philosophical and the natural, human poet, and Vicente's humour probably appeared to Sá de Miranda as unintelligible and undignified as Miranda's hendecasyllabic poems may have appeared melancholy-thin and artificial to Vicente : *et ce n'est point ainsi que parle la Nature*. But the line in the introduction of the *Fabula do Mondego* in which Miranda speaks of the king's condescension,

Al canto pastoril ya hecho osado,

probably refers to some previous effort of his own rather than to the work of Vicente, and Miranda was in Italy when Gil Vicente was taunted by certain *homems de bom saber* and turned the tables on them in the *Farsa de Inés Pereira*. The *Fabula do Mondego* is a cold, stilted production of 600 lines in Petrarcan stanzas, the subject of which was partly derived from Angelo Ambrogini (Poliziano). In 1532 the King gave Miranda a *commenda* (benefice) of the Order of Christ on the banks of the Neiva in Minho, and having acquired the neighbouring estate of Tapada (*quinta da Tapada*) he left the Court and retired to it not many months later. Miranda's love of Nature was very deep, from his boyhood at Coimbra he had preferred the country to life in cities, and probably no other incentive was required, although it is thought that he may have been too zealous in support of Bernardim Ribeiro and that a passage in *Alexo* (1532 ?) offended the powerful favourite, the Conde da Castanheira. Whatever the cause of his withdrawal, literature must call it blessed, for his new life in the country suited his temperament; the independence of character shown in his fine letter (one of the most famous poems in the Portuguese language) addressed to King João III developed, and close contact with the country and the peasants gave his poetry that indigenous flavour and peculiar charm which have fascinated all readers of the eclogue *Basto*, that individual stamp in which the Court poetry was infallibly lacking. He had already written his best work—for this eclogue and the letters show the real Miranda, pointed, original, racy of the soil—and written it in *quintilhas*, when in 1536 he married Briolanja, the sister of his old friend, now his neighbour at Crasto, Manuel Machado de Azevedo. Some miles away, at the straggling little village of Cabeceiras de Basto, he had other intimate friends, the Pereiras, and the gift, by one of these two brothers, Antonio Nunalvarez Pereira, of a manuscript of Garci Lasso de la Vega's poems shortly before Miranda's marriage revived his enthusiasm for the alien metres. He turned again to the hendecasyllable and wrote the eclogues *Andrés* (1535), *Celia*, and *Nemoroso* (1537), the latter in memory of the tragic death of Garci Lasso in the preceding year. He returned to the *quintilha* later, employing it with flowing ease in *A Egipciaca Santa Maria* (or *Santa Maria Egipciaca*), which was probably written between 1544 and 1554, when he was educating his two sons with *amor encoberto e moderado* (*A Egipciaca*, p. 3), and nearer the former than the latter date. Its vigour and the promise of more [1] after 721 *quintilhas* preclude the date (1556-8) assigned to it by its first editor, even without the statement of the 1614 biographer that Miranda wrote scarcely anything after his wife's death in 1555; but it may have been written even earlier, before 1544. And still through all these various poems, despite their undeniable value and incidental beauties, it is the man, his life and character, that interest us. The wild yet green and peaceful scenery of Minho accorded well with his *alma soberana*, at once active and contemplative, disciplined and independent. At first hunting the wolf and boar occupied his leisure—we see him out with his dogs Hunter, Swallowfoot, &c., in crimson dawn and breathless noonday—and gave him a hundred opportunities for quiet observation of Nature, the streams, especially the birds, and the peasants. The poems written soon after his arrival still retain the freshness of these

[1] Adeus leitor a mais ver,
Porque ainda haveis de ver mais (*A Egipciaca*, p. 181).

impressions. His evenings were spent with his friends at Cabeceiras—true *noctes cenaeque deum*—or in the more formal society at Crasto or with music—he played the viola—or his favourite authors, Homer in Greek, or Horace, the Bible, the Italians, or Garci Lasso and Boscán. Later gardening [1] and the education of his sons and entertainment of visitors took the place of his favourite wolf-hunting. As his fame and influence spread, Diogo Bernardez (whose recollections of Miranda were recorded in the 1614 life) was not the only disciple who came to see him in his retreat, and he corresponded in verse with most of the poets of the time, Andrade Caminha, Montemôr, Ferreira, D. Manuel de Portugal, Bernardez. Cardinal Henrique was a steadfast admirer of his work, and the young Prince João asked for a copy: *lhas mandou pedir*. This wide recognition after the first coldness [2] was some measure of comfort for the many sorrows of his last years, the death of his eldest son Gonçalo, killed in his teens in Africa (1553), of his wife (1555), of that promising precocious Prince João (1537-54) to whom he had thrice sent a collection of his poems, the departure of his brother, Mem, to become one of the most notable Governors of Brazil (1557). In the latter year King João died, leaving an infant heir to a distracted kingdom, and Miranda's death followed a few months later. In a sense this philosopher was the most un-Portuguese of poets, for he had no facility in verse. He went on hammering his lines, altering, erasing, compressing in a divine discontent. He had a lofty conception of the poet's art—to express the noblest sentiment in the best and fewest words—five versions of *Alexo*, twelve of *Basto*, attest his untiring zeal and his 'art to blot'. The elliptical abruptness of his native *quintilhas*, by which they have something in common with those of Ribeiro, are not their least charm, and gives an effective emphasis to his sententious philo-

---

[1] He must often have repeated Nuno Pereira's lines, which may have influenced him when he read them in the *Cancioneiro Geral* : *Privar em cas da Rainha Deos vollo deixe fazer, E a mi hũa vinha E regar hũa almoinha Em que tenho mor prazer ... Lavro, cavo quanto posso ... O gingrar de meu caseiro*, &c.

[2] His complaint in the second elegy (1885 ed., No. 147, l. 17) shows how far he was in advance of his age in Portugal : *Um vilancete brando ou seja um chiste, Letras ds invenções, motes ds damas, Hũa pregunta escura, esparsa triste, Tudo bom, quem o nega ? Mas porque, Se alguem descobre mais, se lhe resiste ?*

sophy. In introducing the new measures[1] he used the Castilian language as being the most natural and suitable until, but only until, they should be thoroughly acclimatized. He wrote Castilian not fluently—that was not his gift—but correctly, with only occasional *lusitanismos*. His best work, however, was written in Portuguese: in the new poetry with which his name is for ever associated he is only the forerunner of the work of Diogo Bernardez and Camões,[2] the founder of a school to which Portuguese literature owes some of its chief glories. In Portuguese he wrote his comedies and, about half a century before Samuel Daniel's *Cleopatra* (1592), a tragedy *Cleopatra*, of which we only possess a few lines.[3] The poem on the life and conversion of St. Mary of Egypt[4] (a favourite theme a few centuries earlier, as in the Spanish *Vida de Santa Maria Egipciaqua* (13th c.?), the fourteenth-century *Vida de Maria Egipcia*, and the French *Vie de Sainte Marie l'Égyptienne*) is stamped with the author's sententious wisdom and love of discipline. It contains quaint plays on words (*Ide ao mar que por amar*, p. 169), *tours de force* such as the three *quintilhas* of *esdruxulos* (pp. 179–80), and rises to wonderful lyric beauty in the saint's farewell to Earth (*Vou para um jardim de flores*, pp. 166–9). He intended the poem to be 'rare, unique and excellent' and to some extent he achieved his aim. In much of his work the diction is rough and halting, but the greatness of the man nevertheless extends to his poetry. Perhaps the best example of this is the melancholy grandeur of the sonnet, technically so imperfect, *O sol é grande*. Force of character made him not only a laborious but a successful craftsman. When he died, honoured and admired by all the best intellects in the country, the position of the new school was assured and he had been able

---

[1] Often he combines several in the same poem. Thus the long (533 lines) eclogue on the death of Garci Lasso (*Nemoroso*) begins in *tercetos*, proceeds with *rima encadeada* (internal rhyme), and ends with Petrarcan stanzas.

[2] Cf. the sonnet (1885 ed., No. 126) *Esprito que voaste* with *Alma minha gentil*.

[3] The autograph manuscript of this and of other poems, discovered in the Lisbon Biblioteca Nacional by Snr. Delfim Guimarães in 1908, has been reproduced in facsimile by D. Carolina Michaëlis de Vasconcellos in the *Boletim* of the Lisbon *Ac. das Sciencias*, vol. v (1912), pp. 187–220. See *infra*, p. 164.

[4] Leonel da Costa, the translator of Virgil and Terence, later wrote a poem in seven cantos of *redondilhas* on the same subject: *A Conversão miraculosa da felice egypcia penitente Santa Maria* (1627).

to hail with joy the support of younger writers: *Venid buenos zagales!* Foremost in time among these poets of *el verso largo* was D. MANUEL DE PORTUGAL [1] (1520 ?–1606), son of the first Conde de Vimioso and of D. Joana de Vilhena, cousin of King Manuel. He outlived all his fellow-poets, welcomed the appearance of *Os Lusiadas*, and in 1580 took the side of the Prior D. Antonio. His *Obras* (1605) consist of seventeen books of poems, mostly of a religious character and written in Spanish—books 9 and 15 contain some Portuguese poems, and among them the fine mystic sonnet *Apetece minha alma* (Bk. ix, f. 199 v.).

Among those who welcomed and acclimatized the new style none was a more talented or truer poet than DIOGO BERNARDEZ (*c*. 1530–*c*. 1600),[2] who confessed that he owed everything to Sá de Miranda and Antonio Ferreira.[3] Born of a distinguished family [4] at Ponte da Barca on the river Lima, he would ride over to visit Sá de Miranda or send him letters in verse, and he mourned his death in sonnet, letter, and eclogue with unaffected grief. He himself continued to sing by the banks of his beloved Lima, endeared to him all the more by disillusion at Lisbon and captivity in Africa. In a letter to Miranda he alludes to an apparently unhappy love affair at Lisbon. Later the retirement of his poet brother, Frei Agostinho, into a convent, the deaths of Miranda and Ferreira, the great plague of 1569, and the misfortunes of his country were all deeply felt by his affectionate nature. In 1576 he went as secretary of Embassy to Madrid, but otherwise he seems to have been disappointed in hopes of lucrative employment, and he

---

[1] Faria e Sousa even makes him the first Portuguese poet to write hendecasyllabics, setting aside those of Sá de Miranda as unreadable: *son incapaces de ser leidos!* (*Varias Rimas*, pt. ii, p. 162).

[2] He was *Moço da camara* in 1566. He was appointed a knight of the Order of Christ in 1582. He married apparently after his return from Africa in 1581. He was alive in 1596 (although in one of his poems he refers to a premature old age) and dead in 1605. On the other hand, he was apparently over twenty-five in 1558. It is thought that the right of passing on his official posts to his children (*sobrevivencia*), granted to his father in 1532, may indicate the date of the birth of the eldest of his eleven children: Diogo Bernardez (who did not, like some of his brothers, use his father's second name, Pimenta).

[3] *Carta* 12: *Confesso dever tudo áquella rara Doutrina tua.*

[4] The succeeding generation was also distinguished, one of the poet's nephews becoming Bishop of Angra, another Governor of Angola, a third Professor at Coimbra University.

was always ready to exchange the mud of the streets and the 'bought meals' of Lisbon, with its penurious, importunate *moços*,[1] for the dewy golden dawns, the hills and streams of Minho, *entre simples e humildes lavradores* (*Carta* 27). In 1578, however, he who had lamented that no Maecenas encouraged those eager to sing the deeds of Portuguese heroes was chosen to accompany as official poet[2] the Portuguese expedition which ended disastrously in *aquelle funeral e turvo dia*—the battle of Alcacer Kebir. It was not till 1581 that Bernardez returned from captivity. Whether he was ransomed by King Philip, or by the Trinitarians or Jesuits, or by himself or his friends, is not known. After his return and his marriage he frequently laments his poverty: not, he says, that he wishes to be the Pope in Rome, but merely to have enough to eat (*Carta* 31). Yet apparently he had no cause to regret the change of dynasty so far as his personal fortunes were concerned. Whereas he had merely held the post of *servidor de toalha* at the palace under King Sebastian, he was now (1582) appointed a knight of the Order of Christ with a pension of 20,000 *réis* and was granted 500 *cruzados* ('in property and goods') in the same year. In 1593 his yearly pension was 40,000 *réis*, of which one-half was to revert to his wife and children. Either these moneys remained unpaid or the new *cavaleiro fidalgo's* ideas had changed greatly since he had sung of the joys of rustic poverty and the vanity of riches. Bernardez found his inspiration in the Portuguese and Spanish poets of the new school (*cantigas strangeiras, strañas*),[3] and through them in the great Italians. Dante's name does not occur in his letters, written in *tercetos*,[4] but Tasso—*o meu Tasso*—Ariosto, Petrarca, and others are mentioned.[5] In form and sound some of his *canções* are not unworthy of Petrarca, but they are more homely and bucolic,

[1] Bernardez' letters in verse contain many such references to everyday life, e.g. the Lisbon negress selling fried fish in the *Betesga*.
[2] A confident sonnet by him in this capacity is extant: *Pois armarse por Christo não duvida Sebastião*.
[3] *O doce estillo teu tomo por guia* and *Escrevo, leio e risco* he writes to Miranda, but his muse was far more spontaneous than Miranda's, and it appears from another passage (in *Elegia* 5) that his alterations were less of style than of matter.
[4] *Carta* 32 is an exception, and consists of seventy-two *oitavas*.
[5] He introduces Italian lines (*Cartas* 23, 27, 30) and wrote a sonnet in Italian.

LYRIC AND BUCOLIC POETRY

have more *saudade* and less definite images, no concrete pictures like that of *la stanca vecchierella pellegrina* of the fourth *Canzone*. His second source of inspiration was his native Minho and the transparent waters and *fresca praia* of the Lima. He was never happier than when wandering *lungo l'amate rive*, and this gives a pleasant reality to his eclogues. His muse, *a bosques dada e a fontes cristalinas*, sings not only of the conventional 'roses and lilies' but of honeysuckle, of cherries red in May, grapes heavy with dew, golden apples, nuts, acorns, the trout so plentiful that they can be caught with the hand, hares, partridges, doves, the thrush and the nightingale, and mentions oak, ash, elm, poplar, beech, hazel, chestnut, and arbutus. These eclogues, written in various metres, sometimes with *leixapren* or internal rhyme, are collected in *O Lima* (1596), which also contains his letters. His other works are sonnets, elegies, odes in *Rimas Varias, Flores do Lima* (1596), and a third small volume *Varias Rimas ao Bom Jesus* (1594) which includes elegies and odes to the Virgin written during his captivity, a long *Historia de Santa Ursula* in octaves, and other devotional verse of much fervour and his wonted perfection of technique. If, read in the mass, his poems produce the impression of a cloying sweetness, it must be remembered that never before had Portuguese poetry risen to so harmonious a music. Faria e Sousa accused him of plagiarizing Camões, but in the case of a writer whose accepted poems, the *dulcissima carmina Limae*, are of such excellence the accusation cannot be seriously entertained. Neither he nor Camões was a great original poet, but in both the command of the new style was such that their poems were often confused by collectors. A passage in one of Bernardez' letters (5, l. 6) seems to imply that his poetry was not appreciated at Lisbon. It was too genuine and clear to suit the clever Court rhymesters. But he had his followers, who would send him their poems to be corrected, or rather, praised, and later Lope de Vega recognized him as his master in the eclogue in preference to Garci Lasso.

Francisco Galvão (*c.* 1563–1635 ?), equerry to the Duke of Braganza, was a true poet if he wrote the sonnet *A Nosso Senhor* ascribed to him by his editor, Antonio Lourenço Caminha, in *Poesias ineditas dos nossos insignes poetas Pedro da Costa Peres-*

trello, coevo do grande Luis de Camões, e Francisco Galvão (1791) : *Ó tu de puro amor Deos fonte pura.* Innocencio da Silva vigorously doubts the authenticity of these poems, which are mostly of a religious character or concerned with Horace's theme of the golden mean, as that of the *Obras ineditas de Aires Telles de Meneses* (1792) published by the same editor, who professed to have faithfully copied them from the *antigos originaes* of the time of João II. Bernardez' brother Frei AGOSTINHO DA CRUZ (1540–1619), born at Ponte da Barca, entered as a novice the Convent of Santa Cruz in the Serra de Sintra in 1560, and took the vows a year later. In 1605 he obtained permission to live as a hermit in the Serra da Arrabida, where he cultivated *saudade* and the muses, although his poems were no longer profane, as when in his youth as Agostinho Pimenta he haunted with his brother Diogo the banks of the Lima. These early verses he burnt: *Queimei, como vergonha me pedia, Chorando por haver tão mal cantado.* The eclogues, elegies, letters, sonnets, and odes that survive prove that *mal* is here a moral, not an aesthetic adverb, and that he shared his brother's love of Nature and in no mean degree his power of expressing it in soft, harmonious verse.

That gift was denied to ANTONIO FERREIRA (1528–69), who combined enthusiasm for the new style—*a lira nova*—and for classical antiquity with a rooted antipathy against the use of a foreign language or foreign subjects. His uneventful life as judge, courtier, and poet was cut short by the plague of 1569. His poetry is not that of a poet but of the Coimbra law student who had become a busy magistrate.[1] It is thus at its best when it does not attempt to be lyrical, for instance in his excellent letters in *tercetos*. His odes are closely modelled on those of Horace (*o meu Horacio*). Nor did he claim originality: indeed, his plan of introducing certain new forms was a little too deliberate for a great poet,[2] and his best sonnet is a translation from Petrarca. For bucolic poetry neither the grave doctor's

[1] Cf. *Carta* 4 : *Foge inda o dia ao muito diligente*, although whether this is due to his work or to the number of his friends is not clear.

[2] *Com cujo* [Miranda's] *exemplo meu pai, que entam estaua nos estudos, pretendeo com a variedade destes seus manifestar como a lingua Portugueza assi em copia de palauras como em grauidade de estylo a nenhuma he inferior* (Miguel Leite Ferreira, Preface to *Poemas Lvsitanos*, 1598).

style nor his inclinations were well suited. Not only is the smooth flow of the verse which charms us in Diogo Bernardez here absent but the metre often actually halts,[1] and throughout his work we have sincerity, lofty aims, a stiff unbending severity, but not poetical genius. Ferreira was a true patriot, and it was his boast and is his enduring fame that he devoted himself to exalt the Portuguese language.[2] It was most fortunate for Portuguese literature that at this time of changing taste a poet of Ferreira's great influence should have forsworn foreign intrusions in the language with the exception of Latin (in the introduction of which, however, his characteristic restraint forbade excess), and left both in prose and verse abiding monuments of pure Portuguese. This was the more remarkable in a poet who disdained the old popular metres (*a antiga trova deixo ao povo*) and had no thought apparently for popular customs or traditions. His *Poemas Lusitanos*, published posthumously, contain over a hundred sonnets, besides his odes, eclogues, elegies, epigrams (which are but fragments of sonnets), and letters, and he also wrote a *Historia de Santa Comba* in fifty-seven *oitavas*.

The work of PERO DE ANDRADE CAMINHA (1520?–89), an industrious writer of verse rather than a poet, is as cold and unmusically artificial as Ferreira's in its form, while it lacks Ferreira's high thought and ideals and his love for his native language. One may imagine that it was through friendship with Ferreira—who scolds him for writing in Spanish—that he became one of the set of Miranda and Bernardez. Camões he must have known,[3] and indeed refers to him satirically in his epigrams : he seems to have actively disliked so wayward a genius, a man so unfitted to be a Court official. Caminha himself was the son of João Caminha, Chamberlain of the Duchess Isabel of

---

[1] To take an example not from the eclogues but from one of his sonnets, the words
da guerra
Nossa livres viveis em paz e em gloria
correspond but ill to their peaceful sense.

[2] Cf. *Carta* 2. Bernardez (in an elegy on Ferreira's death addressed to Andrade Caminha) records that among all Ferreira's verses not a line was written in a foreign tongue : *um só nunca lhe deu em lingua alhea.*

[3] Thirteen times the same subject is treated by Camões and Caminha, sometimes exclusively by them (C. Michaëlis de Vasconcellos, *Pero de Andrade Caminha* (1901), p. 55).

Braganza, and of Philippa de Sousa of Oporto, where (or at Lisbon) the poet may have been born. After studying at the University, either at Lisbon, or after its transference to Coimbra in 1537, he entered the household of the Infante Duarte. In 1576 the poet retired to the palace of the Braganzas at Villa Viçosa and died there thirteen years later. During the last ten years of his life he held a *tença* of two hundred milreis besides other sources of income (he was Alcaide Môr of Celorico de Basto, as his father had been of Villa Viçosa), so that his lot compares handsomely with that of Camões. He had planned an edition of his works in nine books, but only a few occasional poems were published during his lifetime. He wrote short poems in all the usual kinds, but, although trusted and honoured by the princes he served, he entirely lacked Camões' divine *furia* and had no compensating sympathy or insight or lyrical charm. What would not Camões have made of his chanty, *cantiga para çalamear*![1]

In perfect contrast to the laboured verses of Andrade Caminha is the spontaneous flow of the lines to the river Leça beginning *Ó rio Leça*, by which the Conde de Mattosinhos, FRANCISCO DE SÁ DE MENESES (1515?-84), is chiefly remembered. They place him at once among the principal poets of the century. He succeeded the Conde de Vimioso as Camareiro Môr of Prince João, held the same post in the first years of King Sebastian's reign, and subsequently under King Henrique, who created him Count of Mattosinhos in return for his services as Governor of Portugal (during the absence of King Sebastian) and on other occasions. After the death of the Portuguese king he retired to Oporto, and no doubt spent the remaining summers at Mattosinhos near the gentle stream which he had immortalized.

The Portuguese poems of ANDRÉ FALCÃO DE RESENDE (1527?-98), born at Evora, nephew of the antiquarian André and of the poet Garcia de Resende, were first published at Coimbra in an incomplete volume *Poesias* [1865], and consist of the *Microcosmographia* and some spirited anti-Drake ballads and good sonnets (e.g. *Ó fragil bem, Ó breve gosto humano*) and

[1] *Obras*, ed. Priebsch, p. 361.

LYRIC AND BUCOLIC POETRY

satires. BALTHASAR DE ESTAÇO (born in 1570), Canon of Viseu, and his brother the antiquarian GASPAR DE ESTAÇO, Canon of Guimarães and author of *Varias Antiguidades de Portugal* (1625), were both born at Evora. The former's *Sonetos, Eglogas e ovtras rimas* (1604), published, according to the preface, in the author's mature age but written in the green, contain some religious sonnets of high merit.

A far more celebrated writer than these minor poets was JORGE DE MONTEMÔR (*c.* 1520–61), or *hispanice* Montemayor, who was early driven by poverty from Montemôr o Velho (where he was born between 1518 and 1528) a few years after Mendez Pinto. Fortunately the latter did not relate his travels in Chinese, but Montemôr, with the exception of a few brief passages[1] in his *Diana*, wrote exclusively in Spanish. In Spain his musical talent gave him a livelihood, and as musician and singer of the Royal Chapel he remained at the Court till 1552, when he accompanied the Infanta Juana as *aposentador* on the occasion of her marriage with that promising patron of letters, the Infante João. But even before the prince's death in 1554 Montemôr returned to Spain. In 1555 he may have gone in the train of Philip II to England, and subsequently served as a soldier in Holland and Italy till a duel, perhaps in a love affair, at Turin ended his days in 1561.[2] Despite his brief and restless life Montemôr, who showed in *Las obras de George de Montemayor* (1554) that he was no mean poet, found time to write one of the most famous books in literature. The date of its publication—it was dedicated to Prince João and Princess Juana—is uncertain, but it was probably an early work. In spirit, since not in the letter, it belongs to Portugal. Its gentle, easy style (Menéndez y Pelayo calls it *tersa, suave, melódica, expresiva*), the sentimental love and melancholy, the introduction of bucolic scenes, the references to Portugal—*cristalino* applied to the Mondego is no conventional epithet, as only those who have seen its transparent waters can fully

---

[1] All that he wrote in Portuguese is contained in two pages (389–91) of Garcia Peres' *Catálogo* (1890).

[2] Fray Bartolomé Ponce, *Primera Parte de la Clara Diana a lo divino* (1582 ?): *Me dijeron como un muy amigo suyo le habia muerto por ciertos zelos ó amores* (quoted by Ticknor, iii. 536, and by T. Braga (omitting *ciertos*), *Bernardim Ribeiro* (1872), p. 80).

realize—mark the *Diana* as the work of a Portuguese. Its fame soon overleapt the borders of the Peninsula. In Spain it had a numerous progeny, to which Cervantes refused the grace somewhat grudgingly given to Montemôr's work as ' the first in its kind '. In Portugal this, the eldest child of Bernardim Ribeiro's *Menina e moça*, had to wait over half a century before it found a worthy successor in the *Lusitania Transformada*.

Little certain is known of the life of FERNAM ALVAREZ DO ORIENTE (*c.* 1540–*c.* 1595 ?). Born at Goa, he served in the East, and may have fought in the battle of Alcacer Kebir. His resemblance to Moraes in temperament and adventures perhaps gave rise to the assertion that he wrote the fifth and sixth parts of *Palmeirim de Inglaterra*. The scene of his *Lvsitania Transformada* (1617) is partly in Portugal (the banks of the river Nabão and the seven hills of Thomar) and partly in India (*no nosso Oriente*). Like Montemôr's *Diana*, it is divided into *prosas* and poems, and it is modelled on the *Arcadia* of Jacopo Sannazzaro (1458–1530)—the mountains of Arcadia transformed into Lusitania [1]—which, however, each of its three books equals in length. The prose setting, although devoid of thought, is mellifluous and clear, and the poems, which contain reminiscences of Camões, rival in the harmony and transparent flow of the verse that ' prince of the poets of our time ', as Alvarez calls him. Some critics have even ventured to attribute the work to Camões, as though his genius were so poor that he must needs fall to quoting himself in whole lines, as is here the case. But Alvarez had certainly caught some measure of Camões' skill and of *il soave stilo e 'l dolce canto* of Sannazzaro and Petrarca. He is, moreover, less vague [2] than many writers of eclogues, and in singing his own love story describes what his eyes have seen. It was, however, an aberration to favour the *verso esdruxulo* (Ariosto's *sdruccioli*) (cf. Sannazzaro's *Arcadia*, Ecl. 1, 6, 8, 9, 12), a truly Manueline adornment which other Portuguese poets unfortunately copied as a new artifice.[3]

---

[1] *Argumento desta obra.*
[2] e.g.　　　No mato o rosmaninho, a branca esteva,
　　　　　　No campo o lirio azul que o chão cubria.
[3] *Que estes se chamem poetas !* rightly exclaims Frei Lucas de Santa Catharina (*Seram Politico* (1704), p. 146) of those who revel in the use of *esdruxulos*.

As a poet Manuel de Faria e Sousa, who was something more than a pedant of pedants, deserves a place among the multitude of Portuguese writers of eclogues, since of the twenty long eclogues contained in his *Fvente de Aganipe y Rimas Varias* (7 pts., 1624-7) the first twelve are in his native tongue. They show no originality but have occasional passages of quiet beauty. Nos. 7 and 8 are both entitled 'rustic' and purpose to represent peasants of Minho. They are so overcharged with archaisms and rustic words and expressions (*samicas* and *namja* of course occur, and *grolea* (glory), *marmolea* (memory), the form *suidade*, &c.) that they would probably have been Greek to the peasants. As a critic Lope de Vega called Faria the prince of commentators, on the strength of his learned and copious editions of the Lusiads and lyrics of Camões, for whom he had a genuine devotion. Time has lent an interest, if not validity, to his literary criticisms. In poetry he was as prolific as in prose: he boasted, in the age of Lope de Vega, that he had written more blank verse than any other poet and that his printed sonnets exceeded those of Lope by 300.

ELOI DE SÁ SOTTOMAIOR (or Souto Maior), the author of *Jardim do Ceo* (1607) and *Ribeiras do Mondego* (1623), is generally perhaps more familiar with the Saints than with the Muses, but some of his poems are not without merit. The latter work, in prose and verse, has no originality, although the author was careful to state that he had composed it before the *Primavera* of FRANCISCO RODRIGUEZ LOBO (*c.* 1580-1622), who in strains not less sweetly harmonious than the Lima poems of Bernardez sang the little stream of Lis that runs so gaily through his native Leiria. He went to study at Coimbra in 1593, took his degree there in 1602, returned to Leiria and before 1604 was in the service of Theodosio, Duke of Braganza, at Villa Viçosa. He was drowned in his prime in the Tagus coming from Santarem to Lisbon. He was alive in 1621, but, as Dr. Ricardo Jorge has shown in his able biography, died before the end of 1622. The fact of his drowning is well established, otherwise the tradition might have been attributed to passages in his works in which he seems to foretell such a fate. An extraordinarily prolific writer, his fame rests chiefly on his three pastoral works of mingled prose and verse: *A Primavera* (1601) and its second and third parts *O Pastor Peregrino* (1608) and *O Desenganado* (1614). Rodriguez Lobo somewhere speaks disparagingly of books 'long as leagues in Alentejo', but length and monotony are not absent from his own pastorals. Look into them where you will, beautiful descriptions, showing deep love of Nature, will present themselves, and delightful verse and harmonious prose, excellent in its component parts although allowed to trail in the construction of the sentences. But the reader who attempts more than a desultory acquaintance is soon overcome by a feeling of satiety, for the *Primavera* in its *brandura sem fim* and the complete absence of thought is like a stream choked by water-lilies: lovely, but tiring to the swimmer.

Through all these love-lorn shepherd scenes runs a vague thread of autobiography. The passion of Bernardim Ribeiro is replaced by a suaver melancholy. The poet leaves the Lis for Coimbra and then goes to Lisbon and thence to distant lands, where he wanders as a pilgrim till he is shipwrecked at the mouth of the Lis and returns to his home to find Lisea given to another. It is divided into *florestas*. In the opening *florestas* the quiet streams, the green woods and pastures, are charmingly described; later the scene is transferred to the *campos do Mondego* and the *praias do Tejo*. A breath of the sea is welcome in *O Desenganado*, but the story soon returns to shepherd life and its series of natural but rather insipid incidents.

Had Rodriguez Lobo written not better but less, his pastoral romances would probably be far more widely read. But his finest work is of a different kind, a long dialogue, *Corte na Aldea e Noites de Inverno* (1619), between a *fidalgo*, D. Julio, and four friends in the long winter evenings near Lisbon. Suggested by Baldassare Castiglione's famous *Il Cortigiano*, which had been popularized in Spain by Boscán's excellent translation (1534), this work, for which Gracián prophesied immortality, is full of the most varied interest. The prose, excellent as is all that of this champion of the Portuguese language, *jardineiro da lingua portuguesa* (which his countrymen, he complained, patch and patch like a beggar's cloak), is here more vigorous and compact in its construction without losing its harmonious rhythm, attractive as the conversations which it records. Besides the beautiful

LYRIC AND BUCOLIC POETRY

verses lavishly scattered through his prose works, Rodriguez Lobo wrote a long epic on Nun' Alvarez in twenty cantos of *oitavas*: *O Condestabre de Portugal D. Nuno Alvarez Pereira* (1610),[1] a volume of *Eglogas* (1605), in which he is a recognized master, a volume of *Romances* (1596) written, with two exceptions, in Spanish,[2] and, perhaps, a Christmas play entitled *Auto del Nascimiento de Christo y Edicto del Emperador Avgvsto Cesar*, published in 1676. It is written in *redondilhas* in Spanish and Portuguese.[3] This *auto* is followed by an *Entremes do Poeta* in Portuguese. A poet, an obdurate Gongorist (*Do Gongora tive sempre opinadas preferencias*), recites a sonnet to a lady: *Celicola substancia procreada*, which she does not understand, and a *ratinho*, also at a loss (*he para mim cousa grega*), advises him to give over his jargon for a more natural language:

> Gerigonças no fallar,
> Que amor nam he contrafeito.

But Rodriguez Lobo has no need of such attributions to justify his great and enduring fame.

---

[1] The whole of Canto XIV is given to a vigorous account of the battle of Aljubarrota, already described more vividly in fewer stanzas by Camões. Another poem in *oitavas* by Rodriguez Lobo, *Historia da Arvore Triste*, was published in *Fenix Renascida*, vol. iv.

[2] In Spanish also are the fifty-six *romances* which make up the poem *La Jornada*, &c. (1623), written on the coming of Philip III to Portugal in 1619. In the eclogues, written chiefly in *redondilhas*, he sings with spontaneous charm *as praticas humildes e os cuidados Não por arte fingidos e enfeitados* of the *rusticos vaqueiros*, as he says in the prefatory sonnet. Many of the words are pleasantly indigenous: *milho, boroa, salgueiraes, rafeiro, charneca, chocalho, abegões, ovelheiros*.

[3] For instance, when the Angel has announced in Spanish *las alegres nuevas*, the goatherd, *ratinho*, Mendo, says: *A din Rey, a din Rey ay! Que estou amorrinhentado, Acudame algum Cristom ou Sancristom*. Laureano, the shepherd, speaks Portuguese and Spanish, and Silvia says: *Porque o que sinto quisera Dizelo em bom Portugues*. An *Auto e Colloquio do Nascimento de Christo* (1646) attributed to Francisco Lopes was reprinted in 1676.

§ 3
The Drama

AFTER Gil Vicente's death the *autos* continued to flourish in number if not in excellence, and evidently answered to a very real popular demand. It was in vain that the Jesuits produced their Latin plays and that serious poets of high reputation sought to wean the affections of the people from the *auto* to the classical drama.[1] This opposition of the educated did, however, conduce to the swift deterioration of the *auto*, although some of those of a religious character, chiefly the Nativity plays, still succeeded in reflecting a part of the charm that characterized the Vicentian drama. To Gil Vicente's lifetime probably belongs the *Obra famosissima tirada da Sancta Escriptura chamada da Geração humana, onde se representam sentenças muy catolicas & proueitosas pera todo christã : Feita por huũ famoso autor* (1536?). Indeed, the verse runs so easily, the peasants are so natural, that one might almost suspect him of having had a hand in its composition. But the metre (8 8 4 8 8 4) is more monotonous than he would have used throughout. The *dramatis personae* are angels, peasants,[2] Adam, Justice, Reason, Malice, two devils, a priest, four saints and doctors of the Church, a Levite, the Church, the Heavenly Samaritan. Adam in a scene closely resembling that of the *Auto da Alma* is tempted by Malice. Justice intervenes, and finally the Samaritan leads him to the *estalagem* of Holy Mother Church. The *Auto de ds [Deus] padre & justiça & mia [Misericordia]*

---

[1] The disapproval of the popular drama is frequent in religious writers. In the seventeenth century Antonio Vieira declared that *uma das felicidades que se contava entre as do tempo presente era acabarem-se as comedias em Portugal*. Feo earlier, in common with many others, had similarly denounced the romances of chivalry *pelos quaes o Demonio comvosco fala ; livraria do diabo* (*Tratt. Qvad.* (1619), ff. 156, 157).

[2] One of them, João, *lavrador*, says : *Vimos ver se he assi ou nam De hũa arremedaçam Que s'a ca d'arremedar . . . Ora nos dizei se he assi Que fazem ho ayto cá*.

belongs to the same period. It is written in octosyllabic verse and contains a similar medley of peasants, prophets, and abstract virtues. In the first part the angels in Portuguese announce to the Virgin the birth of Christ, and in the second part the peasants, who speak Spanish, go to offer rustic gifts to *el muy chiquito donzel*. Another early and anonymous play is the *Auto do Dia do Juizo*, included in the *Index* of 1559, which for its subject closely follows Gil Vicente's *Auto da Barca do Inferno*. A peasant, a false and lying notary, a market-woman who had offered weekly bread and wax to Santa Catharina but had 'robbed the poor people', a butcher, a miller who had mixed bran in his sacks of flour, are introduced in turn and duly consigned by Lucifer to Hell.

If we only knew the quondam Franciscan monk ANTONIO RIBEIRO CHIADO (*c.* 1520?-91) and his contemporary and rival, the mulatto servant of the Bishop of Evora, by their mutual abuse, we could form no very high opinion of their character or their wit. In bitter *quintilhas* Chiado reviles the latter for his dark complexion; AFONSO ALVAREZ answers by upbraiding *nonno Chiado* as the son of a cobbler and a market-woman and for the habits which had made the cloister seem so dismal a place to Frei Antonio do Espirito Santo. Fortunately some of the plays of both of them survive, and we are better able to judge of their merits. The mulatto, who was a valued member of his master's household and prides himself that Chiado has nothing worse to throw in his face than the colour of his skin, was certainly Chiado's inferior in wit and talent. Both imitate Gil Vicente without having a vestige of his lyrical genius or greater skill in devising a plot. Alvarez preferred religious subjects. In his *Auto de Santo Antonio* St. Anthony restores to life the drowned son of two peasants, who are imitated from Vicente's *Auto da Feira*.[1] The only other of his plays that we have is the *Auto de Santa Barbara*, but we know that he also wrote an *Auto de S. Vicente Martyr* and an *Auto de Santiago Apostolo*.

---

[1] e.g. Branca Janes says of her husband:
  He hum grão comedor,
  Destruidor da fazenda, &c.

Chiado's plays and witty sayings, *avisos para guardar* and *parvoices*, appear to have made him extremely popular in Lisbon, Camões recognized his talent, and Lisbon's most famous street still bears his name in common speech. His boisterous life at Lisbon after leaving his convent may have given him his name Chiado (cf. the *chiar* of ox-carts), but it existed as a surname earlier. His *Pratica de Oito Figuras* (1543?), *Auto das Regateiras* (1568 or 1569), and *Pratica dos Compadres* (1572), are the work of an accomplished wit who was intimately acquainted with the farces of Gil Vicente and, in the last two, with the prose plays of Jorge Ferreira. Many of Vicente's types are present, but all in a town atmosphere, in which cards take the place of the rustic dances and lyric yields to epigram, the natural genius of Vicente to a laboured smartness. We have the *clerigo de vintem*, the *ratinho* from Beira, the vain *pação*, the poor *fidalgo* or *escudeiro*, the negro with his pidgin Portuguese, the witch, the ill-tempered *velha*, the *trovador* chaplain, the ambitious priest, the corrupt judge. The scenes are even more disconnected and less dramatic, and the ingenious *redondilhas* necessarily seem artificial because their author so often challenges comparison with the more genuine skill of his master, Gil Vicente. Chiado's *Auto de Gonçalo Chambão* was reprinted several times in the seventeenth century, but is now unknown. Of his *Auto da Natural Invençam* (*c*. 1550) a single copy survives, in the library of the Conde de Sabugosa, whose edition (1917) is of exceptional interest. The play, as reminiscent of Vicente as are the other plays of Chiado, describes the acting of an *auto* in a private house in the reign of João III, and bears witness to the frequency of such representations at Lisbon and to their extraordinary popularity.

BALTHASAR DIAZ, a blind poet (or *jogral*) of Madeira, in the first half of the sixteenth century wrote plays which have retained their popularity. He versified at great length traditions of chivalry and of mediaeval saints. We do not possess his *Trovas* written on the death of D. João de Castro (1548), and many of his plays, *Auto da Paixam de Christo*, *Auto de El Rei Salomão*, *Auto da Feira da Ladra*, have become rare or unknown. One of the best of them, the *Auto de Santo Aleixo*, perhaps owes its survival to its subject, akin to the popular theme of a prince in disguise. The rich and noble Aleixo wanders in rags to the Holy Land. The Devil, who tempts him in the form of a wayfarer, declares that now—the eternal querulous 'now' of the poets—only the rich are honoured and learning is neglected. Later the Devil becomes a courtier and again tempts St. Aleixo, who is defended by an angel. The *Auto de Santa Catherina* is a long devout play of which the persons are St. Catherine, her mother, her page, the Emperor Maxentius, a hermit, three *doutores*, Christ, the Virgin, angels. The saint, who receives news of her mother's death with admirable equanimity, suffers martyrdom at the end of the play with equal fortitude. Diaz also dramatized the story of the Marques de Mantua. Although devoid of dramatic or lyric talent, he is sometimes interesting. Women, whose dresses and fashions are contrasted in the *Auto de Santo Aleixo* with the hard toil of the men, are represented in the *Auto da Malicia das Mulheres* as treating their husbands 'like negroes'. We do not know whether Diaz spoke from experience, his life is very obscure; but he may have spent his last years in Beira if the passage in his *O Conselho para bem casar* :

> estou nesta Beira
> tão remoto de trovar (1680 ed., p. 2)

be not merely a reference to Boeotia, any place far from Lisbon.

Traces of Vicente and the *Celestina*[1] are apparent in Anrique Lopez' *Cena Policiana* or *O Estvdante*, in which a *fidalgo* and a student[2] figure. The poor *escudeiro* and his fasting *moço* are prominent in Jorge Pinto's *Auto de Rodrigo e Mendo*. Spanish romances are quoted with great frequency, and Vicente's *En el mes era de Abril* is parodied by the *moços*.[3] Indeed, their knowledge of literature was become embarrassing since, when his master's guest, invited to a dinner which did not exist,

---
[1] Cf. *este leo ja Celestina* (*Primeira Parte dos Avtos*, &c. (1587), f. 44).
[2] The student's song on f. 44 v. and f. 46, *Polifema mi postema Grande mal he querer bem*, parodies Lobeira's *Leonoreta fin roseta*.
[3] Ibid., f. 49.

recites some verses that he has made, Rodrigo has already read them in Boscán and heard them sung in the street.[1]

The exact dates of ANTONIO PRESTES, of Torres Novas, are unknown, but seven of his plays, after having been acted at Lisbon and published in *folhas volantes*, were first collected by Afonso Lopez half a century after Gil Vicente's death in the *Primeira Parte dos Avtos e Comedias Portuguesas*, &c. (1588). The *Auto da Ave Maria*, written between 1563 and 1587, is an allegorical play in which Reason is vanquished by Sensuality; Heraclitus mourns over her fall while Democritus laughs. A knight in league with the Devil[2] robs in turn an almoner, a *ratinho*, and Fast, but his pious habit of saying an *Ave Maria* causes St. Michael to rescue him from the Devil and reconcile him with Reason. Of the profane plays, that with the most definite plot is the *Auto dos Dous Irmãos*, in which an old man, after refusing to see his sons who have married without his permission, divides all his money between them and is then neglected by both: he is sent from one to the other like King Lear. But the story is feebly worked out here as in the other plays. Their action is mostly that of a puppet show. Sometimes the *moço*, who always plays a prominent part, seems to be the only link in the plot, as Duarte in the *Autos dos Cantarinhos*. These *moços*, who show the author's acquaintance with Gil Vicente[3] and *Lazarillo de Tormes*,[4]

[1] *Primeira Parte dos Avtos*, f. 57:
    Ro. Senhor, se me dá licença,
    Ja eu aquela trova li.
    Os. Qual trova leste? *Ro.* Essa sua,
    Como a disse nua e crua.
    Os. E onde a leste, vilão?
    Ro. Cuido, señor, que em Boscão,
    E canta-se pela rua.

[2] The Devil speaks both Portuguese and Spanish. All the other characters in Prestes' plays, with the exception of an enchanted Moor, speak Portuguese. On the other hand, there are frequent Spanish words and quotations. The word *algorrem* occurs twice in these plays, but the attempt to retain the old style of peasant conversation is but half-hearted.

[3] Duarte in the *Auto dos Cantarinhos* sleeps on an *arca* (chest) like the *moço* in *O Juiz da Beira*. There are other echoes of Vicente, as the words *quem tem farelos?* (1871 ed., p. 65), the reference to *Flerida e Dom Duardos* (p. 485), the line *Que má cousa são vilãos* (p. 420), the peasant who, like Mofina Mendes, builds up his future on the strength of an apple of gold, which proves to be a coal (pp. 407–8).

[4] *Auto do Mouro Encantado* (p. 347). Unless there was an earlier edition of *Lazarillo de Tormes*, this play must therefore have been written after 1554. Prestes' *Auto do Procurador* was written before 1557.

are quite unlike either Lazarillo or Apariço. They are certainly hungry, but they combine starvation with laziness, presumption and abundant learning. The names of Petrarca and Seneca are on their lips; they read *Palmeirim* and quote romances of chivalry and Spanish *romances* glibly.[1] Indeed, the chief interest of these artificial plays is the light thrown on the times: the position of women, the bribery of judges and lawyers, the aping of foreign manners, the mixed styles of architecture. They contain no poetry, little drama, and their wit is seldom natural. Like Prestes, JERONIMO RIBEIRO, perhaps a brother of Chiado, was born apparently at Torres Novas. Only one of his plays was published: the *Auto do Fisico*, written in the last third of the sixteenth century. It has some farcical Vicentian scenes, the inevitable hits against the doctors and lawyers—the *moço* dresses up as a *doutor* to receive a simple fisherman from Alfama —and is generally more popular and natural than Prestes' plays.

SIMÃO MACHADO (*c.* 1570–*c.* 1640), who as a Franciscan monk— Frei Boaventura—ended his life at Barcelona, was also born at Torres Novas. His plays—*Comedias portvgvesas* (1601?)— are two: *Comedia de Dio* and *Comedia da Pastora Alfea*. They are written in Spanish and Portuguese indiscriminately despite Gonçalo's admonition *palrar como Pertigues*.[2] The author explains that, well aware of his countrymen's love of what is foreign, he uses Castilian to save his plays from the neglect often bestowed in Portugal upon works written in Portuguese. His verse is ordinarily the *redondilha*, although Nuno da Cunha in the first part of *O Cerco de Dio* makes a speech in *oitavas*. He has lyrical facility and his peasant scenes are full of life, for instance, the dialogue between the cowherd Gil Cabaço and Tomé the goatherd in *Alfea*.

The Gospel story was dramatized by FREI FRANCISCO VAZ of Guimarães in a long *Auto da Paixão*. The oldest edition we have is dated 1559, and it has been often reprinted, with

---

[1] p. 262. For a corresponding knowledge of *Amadis de Gaula*, &c., among English servants see Dr. Henry Thomas, *The Palmerin Romances*, London, 1916, pp. 38–40.

[2] *Alfea* (ed. 1631), p. 59. The wonderful spelling is due to the printer (e. g. *sesse* = cease) as well as to the peasants (e. g. *monteplica* = multiply, *pialdrade* = piety).

thirty rough woodcuts. Some of these are very spirited, as that of the cock crowing after St. Peter's denial, or that of Judas hanging himself. After a long introductory speech in *versos de arte maior* the play proceeds in *redondilhas* (over 2,000 lines). Religious subjects have always been favourites with the Portuguese, especially those affording scope for lavish scenic display, not only those of martyred saints, as the *Auto de Santa Genoveva*, but those based on the New Testament, as the later play *Acto figurado da degolação dos Innocentes* (1784) in seven scenes.[1]

Two plays, the *Auto da Donzella da Torre* and *Auto de Dom André*, are attributed to Gil Vicente's grandson, GIL VICENTE DE ALMEIDA. The latter, written before 1559, in which a peasant brings his unlettered son (*nem nunca falei Gramatica*) to Court, and a *ratinho*, on becoming a page, promises himself to learn to sing and play on the guitar within a month, has a Vicentian character.

To the beginning of the seventeenth century also belongs the *Pratica de Tres Pastores* (1626), a Christmas play by FREI ANTONIO DA ESTRELLA, who may perhaps be identified with Frei Antonio de Lisboa, author of the lost *Auto dos Dous Ladrões* (1603). The three shepherds, Rodrigo, Loirenço, and Sylvestre, are awakened by an angel singing *cousas de preço*. They agree that the song echoing over the hills is no earth-born music but *algum Charubim ou Anjo ou Charafim*, and presently they go to Bethlehem to offer their rustic gifts. The author has caught the charm and spontaneity of the earlier Christmas *autos*. Another seventeenth-century *auto* of the same kind is the *Colloquio do Nascimento do Menino Jesus* by the Lisbon bookseller, FRANCISCO LOPEZ. The scene and conversation of the three shepherds, Gil, Silvestre, and Paschoal, with their *assorda ou migas de alho* in the cold night—*mas como queima o rocio*, says Gil—are very naturally drawn. An echo of the satirical side of Gil Vicente's genius is to be found in the *Auto das Padeiras chamado da Fome* (1638),[2] in which the various frauds

[1] *Composto por A. D. S. R.* There is an earlier *Acto Sacramental da Jornada do Menino Deus para o Egypto* (1746).
[2] It contains a dispute between Maize and Rye, after the very popular fashion of the contention between Winter and Spring in Vicente's *Auto dos Quatro Tempos*, and the poetical contrasts common in the Middle Ages and

of the bakeresses, sardine-sellers, market-women, pastry-cooks, and tavern-keepers of Lisbon are shown up by the devils Palurdam and Calcamar, as in the *Barca do Purgatorio*. There is nothing of Vicente in the *Auto novo da Barca da Morte* (1732) by a Lisbon author who wrote under the name of Diogo da Costa (Innocencio da Silva, ii. 153, believed that his real name was André da Luz). It consists of a single scene crowded with classical allusions. Death has deprived Midas of his gold, Alexander of his victories, Aristotle of his learning. The actors here are a rich miser, a poor man, a youth, an old man, and Death, whose boat Time steers. The title of the *Auto novo e curioso da Forneira de Aljubarrota* (1815), also attributed to Diogo da Costa, is misleading, since it is a prose narrative of the experiences of that *valorosa matrona*, who, dressed as an *almocreve*, comes to Lisbon with her two *bestinhas* laden with wine.

Of the twenty-five plays contained in the *Musa entretenida de varios entremeses* (1658) edited by Manuel Coelho Rebello, No. 17 (*Castigos de vn Castelhano*) is in Spanish and Portuguese, six are in Portuguese,[1] all the rest in Spanish. Popular plays continued to be written long after the introduction of the classical drama and in spite of the antagonism of the priests. They were often composed in a variety of metres, as the *Acto de Sta Genoveva, Princesa de Barbante* (1735) by Balthasar Luis da Fonseca, if its verse can be called metre,[2] or the *Comedia famosa intitulada A Melhor Dita de Amor* (1745) by Rodrigo Antonio de Almeida,[3] which opens with a sonnet and proceeds in *redondilhas*, hendecasyllables, and prose.

---

in the East, and still in vogue among the *improvisatori* of Basque villages, between wine and water, boots and sandals, &c.

[1] i.e. No. 3 : *De hvm almotacel borracho*; No. 5 : *Dos conselhos de hvm letrado* (a *ratinho* figures in this, as a *ratiño* figures in No. 17) ; No. 6 : *Do negro mais bem mandado* (the *escudeiro's moço* is here a negro who speaks in broken Portuguese, e.g. Zesu) ; No. 11 : *Dous cegos enganados*; No. 13 : *Das padeiras de Lisboa* (besides the bakeresses there is a *meleiro* (honey-seller), an *alheiro* with his *braços* of leeks, an *azeiteiro*, &c.), and No. 25. The titles of these plays sufficiently show their homely character.

[2] Of its author we only know that he was *Ulysbonense*. The play had many editions : 1747, 1758, 1789, 1853.

[3] A priest of the same name wrote political and religious pamphlets in the middle of the nineteenth century.

In the Christmas plays and peasant scenes some of Gil Vicente's poetry had lingered; the plays of more fashionable authors caught no gleam of his lyrism, but sketched types and satirized manners successfully, none more so than Mello's *Auto do Fidalgo Aprendiz*, written, it must be remembered, before *Le Bourgeois Gentilhomme* (1670). Both kinds, consciously or unconsciously, were derived from Vicente's genius as manifested in his plays for the Court and of the people.

During Gil Vicente's lifetime, perhaps, Sá de Miranda had written the two plays, *Os Estrangeiros* (*c*. 1528) and *Os Vilhalpandos* (1538 ?),[1] with which he introduced classical comedy into Portugal (nearly a quarter of a century before its introduction into France and England). *Os Estrangeiros* was a novelty[2] in more ways than one, for it was written in prose. Both plays were, as the author admitted, imitated from Plautus and Terence and also from Ariosto, whose comedies were composed in the first third of the century. *Os Estrangeiros* was, he further observed in a brief introductory letter to the Cardinal Henrique, rustic and clumsy.[3] Its only claim to be called rustic, in character as apart from treatment, consists in a few allusions to popular customs. We would have had it more indigenous. The scene is Palermo, the plot, *à la* Plautus, consists of the difficulties and differences between father and son, and there is the *aio*, the vainglorious soldier Briobris, *nas armas um Roldão*, and the *truão* who plays the part of *gracioso*. The action advances in long soliloquies to the final reconciliation between father and son. The character of *Os Vilhalpandos*, which Mello called ' a mirror of courtly wit ', is similar, with the difference that Fame instead of Comedy speaks the prologue and the action between son, father, and courtesan is placed in Rome. Both the plays were acted before Cardinal Henrique and printed by his command. As if to mark his initiative in every field, Miranda also composed a classical tragedy entitled *Cleopatra* (*c*. 1550), the title of which is of interest as preceding the plays of Shakespeare and Samuel

---

[1] The *affronta de Dio* is mentioned. It may have been written in the same year as Ferreira de Vasconcellos' *Eufrosina*.
[2] In a letter sent with *Os Vilhalpandos* to the Infante Duarte he says that *ninguem que eu saiba* had so written in Portuguese.
[3] *A comedia qual he tal va, aldeaã e mal atauiada.*

Daniel (1562–1619). The twelve octosyllabic lines (*abcabcdefdef*) that survive (from a chorus ?) give no idea of its character, but it probably followed closely the *Sofonisba* (1515) of Gian Giorgio Trissino (1478–1550). A Spanish version of Sophocles' *Electra* by Hernan Perez de Oliva appeared in 1528, and in 1536 Anrique Ayres Victoria had translated this into Portuguese octosyllabic verse : *A Vingança de Agamemnon*. The date of the first edition is unknown ; the second appeared in 1555. Nor do we know when *Cleopatra* was written,[1] although it must have been prior to Antonio Ferreira's classical tragedy acted at Coimbra, *Inés de Castro* (c. 1557), which has hitherto been considered the first of its kind in Portugal. Written when the author was about thirty, that is, about the time of Miranda's death, it copied the form of Greek tragedies and, the better to acclimatize this, a thoroughly national subject was chosen—the death of Inés— whereas Miranda had gone to Rome and Egypt. As might be expected from Ferreira's other work the conception was executed with the careful skill of a conscientious craftsman. The drama has unity, the style is purest Portuguese, the chorus sometimes soars into poetry, as in the celebrated passage *Quando amor naceo*. That the same high language is spoken throughout, that, as has often been observed, scenes of dramatic opportunity —a meeting between D. Pedro and his father or Inés—are omitted, merely shows that Ferreira had no dramatic instinct. Perhaps the only dramatic passage—and even so it is of more psychological than dramatic interest—is that in Act III : *Inés*. ' Ah, woe is me ! what ill, what fearful ill dost thou announce ? ' *Chorus*. ' It is thy death.' *Inés*. ' Is my lord dead ? ' Nevertheless, the play was a remarkable achievement, carried out without faltering and with a sustained loftiness worthy of its subject. No one any longer believes that Ferreira copied from the *Nise lastimosa* by Geronimo Bermudez, published under the pseudonym Antonio da Silva eight years after Ferreira's death. This is a slightly expanded Spanish translation, closely following the 1587 edition[2] of *Inés de Castro*, which differs considerably from

---

[1] A passage in *Aulegrafia* (1555 ?) describes the dramatic death of Antony as a new thing : *parece-me que o estou vendo* (f. 129).
[2] *Tragedia mvy sentida e elegante de Dona Inés de Castro . . . Agora*

that of 1598. The *Nise laureada* which accompanied it is perfectly insignificant. Like Miranda, Ferreira wrote, besides one tragedy, two comedies, *Bristo* and *O Cioso*. There are indications that he had in mind Ferreira de Vasconcellos' *Eufrosina* as well as Miranda's comedies. Bristo soliloquizing is the counterpart of Philtra, and in his dedication of *Bristo* to Prince João he acknowledges his debt to previous plays.[1] In this comedy, written during some vacation days at Coimbra University, the action is very primitive, but the braggart Annibal and the charlatan Montalvão account for some farcical scenes. His later play, *O Cioso* (the jealous husband is also handled by Gil Vicente and Prestes), belongs to a higher plane, i. e. to comedy rather than farce, although *Bristo* is not entirely devoid of character-drawing. *Bristo* was 'made public' (*publicada*) before 1554, but neither play was published till 1622. Both are remarkable for the correctness and concise vigour of their prose.

The three plays of Camões, written perhaps between the years 1544 and 1549 during his first stay at Lisbon, belong entirely neither to the classical drama nor to the more ancient *autos*, but combine elements of both. They are written in *redondilhas*, mostly *quintilhas*. The third, *El Rei Seleuco* (1549?), is slighter even than a Vicentian farce. It has a curious prologue scene (*Vorspiel auf dem Theater*) in prose. The versification is easy, but its chief interest is the important part it may have played in its author's life. The earliest in date, *Filodemo*, although it lacks Vicente's savour of the soil, has a graceful charm and faintly recalls the *Comedia do Viuvo*. Filodemo, orphan son of a Danish princess and a Portuguese *fidalgo*, is in love with Dionysa, daughter of his father's brother, whose son Venadoro is in love with Filodemo's sister Florimena. Their relationship is unknown, but the discovery of their true birth smoothes the path of love and ends the play. *Os Amphitriões*,

---

nouamente acrescentada (31 ff. unnumbered). The one who published *first* was the most likely to be the thief. *Saudade* is translated *soledad*.

[1] *Nesta Universidade . . . onde pouco antes se viram outras que a todas as dos antigas ou levam ou não dam ventagem. Bristo* was written *por só seu desenfadamento em certos dias de ferias e ainda esses furtados ao estudo.* It is a *comedia mixta, a mor parte della motoria.*

in Portuguese and Spanish,[1] is based on the *Amphitruo* of Plautus. The predicaments resulting from the appearance of Jupiter as Amphitrião's double and Mercury as the double of Sosia are deftly and humorously worked out in delightfully spontaneous verse.

For those so fastidious as to be satisfied neither by the popular *autos* nor the staid classical plays, yet another kind was provided in the shape of Celestina comedies in prose. Of the life of their author we know scarcely more than that he was very well known in his day. Judging by literary merit only, one might assign the verses written by Jorge de Vasconcellos in the *Cancioneiro Geral* to JORGE FERREIRA DE VASCONCELLOS (*c.* 1515–63?), since the poems, alike in the new and the old style, interspersed in his works do not prove him to have possessed high poetical talent. It is as a dramatist and still more as a writer of Portuguese prose that the distinguished courtier of King João III's reign [2] deserves a higher place in Portuguese literature than his ungrateful countrymen have habitually accorded him. But the dates forbid the identification of the dramatist with the earlier poet, who was also a notable courtier since he is specially mentioned in Vicente's *Cortes de Jupiter* (ii. 404). One of the few definite facts known to us concerning Jorge Ferreira is that affirmed in the preface of his *Eufrosina* : that this play was the firstfruit of his genius, written in his youth.[3] The exact date of *Eufrosina* is unknown, but it was written after the University had been finally established at Coimbra in 1537—the date of the letter from India (December 20, 1526 [4]) is clearly a misprint since mention is made of the siege of Diu (1538). Ferreira de Vasconcellos evidently studied law at the University. If he was born, not at Coimbra but at Lisbon, he may have begun his studies in the capital. At the time of Prince Duarte's death (1540) he was in his service, as *moço da camara*, and he

---

[1] In *El Rei Seleuco* the doctor and in *Filodemo* the shepherd and *bobo* speak Spanish.

[2] *Homem fidalgo m^{to} cortezão & discretto* (Rangel Macedo, manuscript *Nobiliario*, in Lisbon *Bib. Nac.*) ; *aquelle galante e elegante cortesão Portugues* (*licença* of 1618 ed. of *Ulysippo*).

[3] *As primicias do meu rustico engenho, que he a Comedia Eufrosina, e foi ho primeiro fruito que delle colhi, inda bem tenrro.*

[4] *Eufrosina*, ii. 5.

continued as a Court official, first, perhaps, in the service of the heir to the throne, Prince João, who died on January 2, 1554, and then in that of King Sebastião. In 1563 he was succeeded as Secretary (*escrivão do Tesouro*) by Luis Vicente, probably son of the poet Gil. The document[1] which nominates his successor by no means implies his death, since, as Menéndez y Pelayo[2] observed, his name is unaccompanied by the formula *que Deus perdoe* or *aja*. But it is strange, if he did not die till 1585, the date given by Barbosa Machado, that nothing more is heard of him after 1563 (we are told that his son died at the battle of Alcacer Kebir), and that his son-in-law called *Aulegrafia*, written before the death of Prince Luis (1555), his swan-song.[3] Apart from manuscript treatises which were never published, Jorge Ferreira is the author of four works in prose, the three plays, *Eufrosina, Ulysippo, Aulegrafia,* and the *Memorial da Segunda Tavola Redonda*. The latter is an involved romance of chivalry[4] which describes the adventures of the Knight of the Crystal Arms, emulator of the Knights of the Round Table and Amadis of Gaul. Each chapter commences with a brief sententious reflection, from which the reader is plunged into mortal combats of knights, centaurs, giants, and dragons. It begins by giving an account of King Arthur, his disappearance, and the prosperous reign of Sagramor. It ends with a vivid description of the tournament (August 5, 1552) at Enxobregas (= Xabregas) in which the ill-fated Prince João was the principal figure. Barbosa Machado included among Ferreira de Vasconcellos' works *Triunfos de Sagramor em que se tratão os feitos dos Cavalleiros da Segunda Tavola Redonda* (Coimbra, 1554). A passage in the *Memorial*[5] may have led to the belief that this was a second part of the

---

[1] Discovered by General Brito Rebello in the Torre do Tombo and printed in his *Gil Vicente* (1902), p. 114.

[2] *Orígenes de la Novela*, vol. iii, p. ccxxx.

[3] Sousa de Macedo, in *Eva e Ave* (1676 ed., p. 131), says that he lived in the reign of King João and in the beginning of that of King Sebastian, which confirms the date 1563 as that of his death.

[4] Some of its heroes have geographical names, as King Tenarife of the Canary Islands and the Spanish Moor Juzquibel, who now survives in the name of the mountain that falls to the sea above Fuenterrabía. The author shows considerable knowledge of the Basque country, and we may perhaps infer that he was at the French Court and studied the Basque provinces on the way.

[5] 1867 ed., p. 21 : *como se vee ao diante no triumpho del rey Sagramor*.

Memorial, of which the first known edition is that of Coimbra, 1567, but from the preface[1] it appears that the *Memorial is* the *Triunfos*. The title *Triunfos de Sagramor* may have been given to an earlier edition,[2] or it may have been the title of the second half of the work. The author himself declares that his story had been 'presented' to Prince João.[3] The editor of *Ulysippo* in 1618 says that the *Memorial* had been printed at least twice during the author's lifetime.[4] Yet it is difficult not to suspect that the date 1554 was a confusion with the year of the death of the prince to whom the work was dedicated. The same uncertainty, as we have seen, prevails as to the date of the first edition of the author's masterpiece *Eufrosina*. (He published his plays anonymously, partly perhaps for the same reason that made him insist that his characters represented no definite persons but types.) The earliest edition that we have is that of Evora, 1561, that of Coimbra, 1560, having disappeared, if it ever existed.[5] The words on the title-page, *de nouo reuista & em partes acrecentada*, need not imply more than that, as we know, the manuscript had circulated among his friends: *por muitas mãos deuassa e falsa*. As a novelty, *invençam noua nesta terra, Eufrosina* with its proverbs and its ingenious thoughts and phrases was appreciated in Portugal, whose inhabitants were justifiably proud now to possess a *Celestina* of their own, a *Celestina* with less action and rhetoric but more thought and sentiment.[6] Quevedo was loud in its praises, Lope de Vega

---

[1] *Nesta trasladação do triumpho del Rey Sagramor*, ibid., p. viii.
[2] A vague tradition placed the 1554 edition in the Lisbon Torre do Tombo, but inquiries in 1916 proved that nothing is known of it there.
[3] *Ao esclarecido Principe ja apresentada*, ibid., p. vii.
[4] *A primeira parte da Tabola redonda que pera a terceira impressão emendou o Autor em sua vida* (*Aduertencia ao leitor*).
[5] Nicolás Antonio, whose information as to Portuguese books was often far from accurate, says that there were several editions before that of 1616, probably an erroneous deduction from the 1561 title-page. The late Menéndez y Pelayo, who also made many slips in dealing with Portuguese literature, declared that the 1560 edition was in the British Museum, which, however, only possesses a (mutilated) copy of the edition of Evora, 1561 (lacking the colophon with the date). Of the 1561 edition several copies exist, that of the Torre do Tombo, that in the library of the late Snr. Francisco Van Zeller at Lisbon, and that of the British Museum.
[6] João de Barros, *Dialogo em lovvor da nossa lingvagem* (1540), wrote that the Portuguese language *parece nam consintir em si hũa tal obra como Celestina* (1785 ed., p. 222).

perhaps quoted it,[1] its influence on the style of Mello and other Portuguese writers is clear. It was a legitimate success and its modern neglect is all the more deplorable because in this play the Portuguese language, the richness, concision, and grace of which are exalted in the preface, appears in its purest, raciest form. The author's vocabulary is immense, his sentences admirably vigorous and clear. After heading the E's in the *Index* of 1581 (*Evphrosina* simply, without author) it was reprinted by the poet Rodriguez Lobo in 1616, in a slightly modified form, shorn, that is, of some of the coarser passages and of all reference to the Scriptures.[2] The style is not the only merit of *Eufrosina*. Despite the lack of proportion in some of the scenes, in which Jorge Ferreira proves himself to have been, like Richardson, 'a sorry pruner' (four scenes out of the thirty-nine constitute a quarter of the play), there is a certain unity in this story of the love of the poor courtier Zelotipo de Abreu for Eufrosina, proud and beautiful daughter of the rich *fidalgo* D. Carlos, Senhor das Povoas, in the little ancient university town above the green waters and willows of Mondego. The numerous other persons are strictly subordinate, and both scenes and characters are skilfully drawn. The artificial construction, the convention by which emotion finds vent in a string of classical allusions, scarcely mar the exceedingly natural presentment of many of the scenes. Charming, for instance, is that in which Eufrosina and her companion and friend Silvia de Sousa, Zelotipo's cousin, watch from the terrace of their house the river's gentle flow and along its bank the citizens and students taking the air in the cool of the evening. The play contains as many characters as a modern novel. There is Cariofilo, a gay good-hearted Don Juan; his friend, the more serious Zelotipo, type of the Portuguese lover, the *galante contemplativo*; D. Carlos, quick to anger but easily appeased; the

---

[1] *La Filomena*, 1621 ed., p. 188. The quotation, if direct, was from the 1561 edition, not that of 1616, in which part of the sentence quoted is omitted, as in the Spanish translation first published ten years later, in 1631.

[2] They were considered out of place in a comedy. The Catalogue of 1581 condemns *todos os mais tratados onde se aplicam, vsurpam & torcem as autoridades & sentenças da sancta escriptura a sentidos profanos, graças, escarnios, fabulas, vaidades, lisonjarias, detracções, superstições, encantações & semelhantes cousas.* The rules were carried out most mechanically.

pedantic, unscrupulous Dr. Carrasco, whose conversation with D. Carlos gives scope for a vigorous attack on the legal profession; Silvia, who sacrifices her love and gives up to Eufrosina her cousin's verses that she had so carefully kept; the *moços* Andrade and Cotrim, greedy, timid, and talkative; the gentleman of Coimbra, Philotimo, a wise and kindly man of the world. Other phases of Coimbra life are shown in the *moças de rio* and *de cantaro*, who fetch water or wash clothes in the Mondego and metaphorically toss in a blanket Galindo, the rich D. Tristão's agent from Lisbon; in the love-lorn student with his Latin, the morose and jealous workman Duarte, proud of his position as *official*, the resolute goldsmith and his languid daughter Polinia, the old servant Andresa and the merry servant girl Vitoria, and, most prominent of all, Philtra the *alcoviteira*, deploring the wickedness and degeneracy of the world and full of wise saws—the play contains many hundreds. Eufrosina herself is first described by the lover—brow of Diana, lips of Venus, limbs of Pallas, clear green eyes [1] of Juno, quietly mirthful; then by his servant Andrade—the fairest thing that ever he thought to see, fan in hand, the sleeves of her dress like a ship at full sail [2]—so that we have an effective impression of her beauty. Besides Coimbra life we obtain glimpses of that of the Court at Lisbon and Almeirim in a letter from the courtier Crisandor, of India in a very real and interesting letter from Silvia's brother, even of Cotrim's native village. That the unity was not sacrificed to these many by-scenes says much for the author's skill. This praise cannot be given to his second play written some ten years after the first, *Ulysippo* (1547?), for here the reader loses his way among the many courses of true love. There are twenty-one *dramatis personae*, but the principal interest is in the sketch of Constança d'Ornellas, the hypocritical *beata*,[3] or, rather, that is the most original

---

[1] Green eyes are beloved by Portuguese writers for their rarity or from an early mistaken rendering of the French *vair* (e.g. Sylvia in the sixteenth, Joaninha in the nineteenth century). The *glosadores* inclined to them on account of the second person of the infinitive 'to see': *verdes*.

[2] In Arraez, *Dialogos* (1604), f. 311 v. fashionable women *parecem . . . velas de nao inchadas*.

[3] In the first edition she had been called a *beata*. In that of 1618 she became merely a widow woman, *dona viuva*, but the editor defeated the

part, since in the play as a whole there is a certain monotony after *Eufrosina*, and many of the proverbs are the same.[1] Excellent as the earlier play in its terse and idiomatic prose,[2] full of interest in the insight it gives into the customs and life of the people, its chief fault is the intricacy, or absence, of plot which makes it difficult reading, and of course it would naturally please less on its first appearance as being no longer a new thing. The author, who knew how the Portuguese prized *novidades*, appears to have been conscious of this, since his third play, *Aulegrafia*, written perhaps in 1555,[3] and first published in 1619, was developed on somewhat different lines. It is concerned, as its name implies, exclusively with the Court, and the people and popular proverbs are in abeyance. In its fifty scenes we are introduced to typical Court ladies, noble *fidalgos*, poor gentlemen and their servants, one of whom considers it *mais fidalgo nam saber ler*. The play is by its author termed 'a long treatise on Court manners',[4] and as such it is admirable and full of interest, however negligible it may be as drama. Its style, moreover, even excels in atticism Ferreira's other works. The most remarkable character is that of the young (*menina e moça*) and very wily aunt of Filomela. She is twice described in detail (f. 46 and f. 153 v.), and we perceive that Philtra of the people, the middle-class Constança d'Ornellas, and the aristocratic Aulegrafia are really three persons and one spirit. In *Ulysippo* one of the lesser personages was the Spanish *Sevilhana* (mentioned also in *Eufrosina*), and here a boastful Spanish adventurer is introduced in the person of Agrimonte de Guzman, who disdains to speak Portuguese. The scene of both the later plays is Lisbon. The author drew from his experience here, as previously

---

censor's intentions by noting the change in the preface and declaring that but for this she remained exactly the same as before.

[1] Here the doctors, not the lawyers, are *conjurados contra o mundo*.
[2] Cf. the brief but eloquent praises of wine and of love.
[3] One might be inclined to place it later were not the Infante Luis (†November 27, 1555) still alive.
[4] *Um largo discurso da cortesania vulgar*, f. 178 v. Cf. f. 5: *pretende mostraruos ao olho o rascunho da vida cortesaã*. On f. 5 v. it is called *esta selada Portuguesa*. The courtiers spend all the time they can spare from the pursuit of love in discussing the rival merits of the *romance velho* and new-fangled sonnet, of Boscán and Garci Lasso, of Spanish and Portuguese, a line of a Latin poet, &c.

at Coimbra, and often describes to the life the persons that he had met. Scarcely any other writer gives us so intimate an idea of the times—of this the latter heyday of Portugal's greatness—or of the gallant, lovesick, dreaming Portuguese, who considers love as much a monopoly of his country as the ivory and spices of India.[1]

[1] *O amor é portugues* (*Aulegrafia*, f. 38 v.).

§ 4
Luis de Camões

THE plays of LUIS DE CAMÕES (1524?–80) are in a sense typical of his genius, for they show him combining two great currents of poetry, the old indigenous and the classic new. A generation had sprung up accustomed to wide horizons and heroic deeds, and poets and historians regretted that there was no Homer or Virgil to describe them adequately. Camões was not a Homer nor a Virgil, but he was a more universal poet than Portugal had yet produced, and by reason of his marvellous power of expression he triumphantly completed the revolution which Sá de Miranda had tentatively begun. In a sense he was not a great original poet, but in his style he was excelled by no Latin poet of the Renaissance. The eager researches of modern scholars have succeeded in piercing the obscurity that enveloped his life, although many gaps and doubtful points remain. Four or five generations had gone by since his ancestor Vasco Perez had passed out of the pages of history,[1] and some of the intervening members of the family had also won distinction, but Camões' father, Simão Vaz de Camões, was a poor captain of good position (*cavaleiro fidalgo*) who was shipwrecked near Goa and died there soon after the poet was born in 1524. Through his grandmother, Guiomar Vaz da Gama, he was distantly related to the celebrated Gamas of Algarve. His mother, Anna de Sá e Macedo, belonged to a well-known family of Santarem.[2] Whether he was born at Lisbon or Coimbra

[1] *Seu quarto avô foi um Gallego nobre* (Diogo Camacho, *Jornada ás Cortes do Parnaso*).
[2] Dr. Wilhelm Storck, the author of the most elaborate life of Camões in existence, considered that the words *quando vim da materna sepultura* in one of Camões' poems could only mean that his mother (Anna de Macedo) died at his birth, and that he was survived by Anna de Sá, his stepmother. It may have been so, but there is not a scrap of evidence in favour of the theory nor were the words *materna sepultura* anything more than a conventional phrase. Cf. Antonio Feo, *Trattados Quadragesimais* (1609), pt. 1, f. 2 : *Como Nazianzeno diz... e tumulo prosiliens ad tumulum iterum contendo, em nacendo saimos de hũa sepultura que foi as entranhas da mãi e morrendo entramos noutra.* So Pinto, *Imagem*, pt. 2, 1593 ed., f. 342 v.: *tornar nu ao ventre*

is still uncertain. His great-grandfather had settled at Coimbra. That Camões studied there scarcely admits of doubt. He alludes to it in his poems, and nowhere else in Portugal could he have received his thorough classical education. In the year 1542 or 1543 he went to Lisbon. The exact dates of events in his life during the next ten years are difficult to determine, but the events themselves are clear enough. His birth and talents assured him a ready welcome in the capital. Whether he became tutor to D. Antonio de Noronha, son of the Conde de Linhares (the Portuguese ambassador whom Moraes accompanied to Paris), or not, he soon had many friends and was probably received at Court. Referring later to this time he is said to have spoken of himself as *cheo de muitos favores*, and in this popularity he wrote a large number of his exquisite *redondilhas* and also sonnets, odes, eclogues, and the three *autos*. But Camões had fallen passionately in love with a lady-in-waiting of the queen, Catherina de Athaide.[1] Tradition has it that he first saw her in church on a Good Friday (1544?). We may surmise that Natercia's parents objected to the suit of the penniless *cavaleiro fidalgo*, and that Camões pressed his suit on them with more vehemence than discretion. He was banished from Court, and spent six months in the Ribatejo (Santarem) and two years in military service in North Africa (Ceuta). He admits that he had been in the wrong, but not seriously so, and hints that envy had played its part in his downfall. It is probable that his play *El Rei Seleuco* had given a handle to the enemies that his growing reputation as a poet had made. It must be confessed that its subject was tactless, for in the play the king gives up his bride to his son, which could easily be interpreted as a reflection on the conduct of the late King Manuel, who had married his son's bride. The two years in Africa passed slowly. In a letter (*Esta vae com a candea na mão*) he describes sadness eating away his heart as a moth a garment, and it was with his thoughts in Lisbon that he took part from time to time in skirmishes against the Moors, in one

de sua mãi, o qual é a sepultura da terra, and Bernardes, *Nov. Flor.* i. 122 : *A terra é nossa mãe, de cujo tenebroso ventre que é a sepultura*, &c.

[1] She may have been a distant relation of the poet's : the name was a common one, but Camões was connected with the Gamas, and the wife and granddaughter of the first Conde de Vidigueira were both named Catherina de Athaide.

of which he lost his right eye. Hard blows, scanty provisions, and no chance of enriching oneself as in India were the features of military service in North Africa, and when Camões returned to Lisbon his prospects contrasted sharply with those which had been his when he first came from the University a few years before. He was now nearly thirty,[1] disfigured by the loss of an eye and embittered by the turn his fortunes had taken. He no longer looked on life from the inside, gazing contentedly at the show from the windows of privilege, but was himself in the arena. For the school of Sá de Miranda he had probably never felt much sympathy, considering it too severe and artificial. He wished to live and enjoy, and although the patronage of literary Prince João may have encouraged him to hope for better times, he meanwhile set himself to sample life as best he might, associating with rowdy companions (*valentões*), who brought out the Cariofilo side of his character at the expense of the contemplative Zelotipo. Whether he had intended to embark for India in 1550, or this be a pure invention on the part of Faria e Sousa, it is certain that he was still in Lisbon on June 16, 1552. On that day the Corpus Christi procession passed through the principal streets. In the crowded Rocio Camões was drawn into a quarrel with a Court official, Gonçalo Borges, and wounded him with a sword-cut on the head. For nearly nine months Camões lay in prison, and then, Borges having recovered and bearing no malice, he was pardoned[2] (March 7, 1553) and released, but only on the understanding that he would leave Portugal to serve the king in India. Before the end of the month he had embarked in the ship *S. Bento*. Hitherto he had hoped against hope for an improvement in his lot; now he went, he says, as one who leaves this world for the next, and with the words *Ingrata patria, non possidebis ossa mea*,[3]

[1] According to Dr. Storck he was banished in 1549, and in the same year, after the sentence of banishment had been commuted to service in Africa, left Portugal, returning to Lisbon in the autumn of 1551. Others believe that he was in Lisbon again in 1550 and that his two years in Africa must be placed between 1546 and 1549.
[2] The important document containing his pardon is printed in Juromenha's edition of his works, i. 166–7.
[3] This quotation is assigned to various other persons, as to Nuno da Cunha when arranging that he should be buried at sea.

turned his back on the calumnies and intrigues of Lisbon. In one of his finest elegies[1] he described the voyage, a storm off the Cape of Good Hope, and the arrival at Goa in September 1553. The voyage was full of interest to him, and he made good use of it, becoming what Humboldt called him—a great painter of the sea[2]—but so far as comfort was concerned he fared probably much as would a modern emigrant. His disillusion at Goa is poignantly described in a letter[3] written soon after his arrival. He found it ' the stepmother of all honest men ', money the only god and passport, and he sends a note of warning to *aventureiros* in Portugal eager to make their fortune in India. We know from the bitter pages of Couto and Corrêa how difficult it was for a private soldier to thrive there, and the position of a *reinol* newly arrived from Portugal was precarious. Camões joined a few weeks later (November 1553) in a punitive expedition along the coast of Malabar against the King of Chembe, and in 1554 probably accompanied D. Fernando de Meneses in a second expedition to Monte Felix or Guardafui (Ras ef Fil), the Red Sea and the Persian Gulf. After his three years' service (1553–6) he continued to live at Goa. He had found time to write poetry, and sent home a sonnet and an eclogue on the death of his friend D. Antonio de Noronha. His play *Filodemo* was acted, probably in the winter of 1555, before the popular Governor Francisco Barreto, who provided him with the post of *Provedor Môr dos Defuntos e Ausentes* (i.e. trustee for the property of dead or absent Portuguese) at Macao. Whether his satiric verses had anything to do with the appointment we do not know—some have maintained that the Portuguese of Goa appreciated his poetical powers best at a distance—but it is more probable that his appointment was a favour, since every post in India was eagerly coveted, and it was a kinder action to give him a comparatively humble one at once than the reversion to a more lucrative office, filled thrice or even ten times over by the deplorable system of 'successions'.[4] He set sail in the

---

[1] *O poeta Simonides fallando.*
[2] Cf. *Lus.* i. 19, 43 ; ii. 20, 67 ; v. 19–22 ; vi. 70–9.   [3] *Desejei tanto.*
[4] Couto, in the *Dialogo do Soldado Pratico*, remarks that if a man is given a post at the age of twenty he only receives it at the age of sixty (p. 99). The soldier, who wishes *ter logo em tres annos vinte mil cruzados*, suggests,

spring of 1556, and after touching at Malacca, arrived at the Molucca Islands, the most lawless region in India. Camões himself, according to Storck, was wounded about this time, but in a fight at sea, not in one of the chronic broils at Ternate or Tidore. In 1557 or 1558 he reached Macao, but two years later he was relieved of his post owing to a quarrel with the settlers, whose part was taken by the captain of the silver and silk ship passing from Goa to China. On his authority Camões was sent to Goa, protesting against *o injusto mando*, which was a common fate of officials in India. He was shipwrecked off the coast of Tongking, lost all his possessions, and arrived penniless and perhaps in debt at Goa in 1560 or 1561. To these four or five chequered years are ascribed the wonderful *quintilhas*, the most beautiful in the language, *Sobolos rios que vam*, which may owe something to Vicente's admirable paraphrase of Psalm l, the *canção Com força desusada*, the *oitavas Como nos vossos*, and the completion of the first six books of the *Lusiads*. Soon after his return he was probably imprisoned for debt, but was released, probably at the instance of the Viceroy, D. Francisco Coutinho, Conde de Redondo, to whom Camões addressed his first printed poem, the ode in Orta's *Coloquios* (1563). Camões' thoughts must have now more than ever turned homeward. Fortune had danced tantalizingly before him, holding out hopes which broke as glass in his hands whenever he attempted to seize them.[1] Of his life between 1564 and 1567 we know nothing. He did not occupy the post of factor of Chaul, the reversion to which indeed he may perhaps only have received after his return to Portugal. He was eager to get home. In 1567 he accompanied Pedro Barreto to Mozambique, glad to get even so far on the return voyage. There poverty and illness delayed him till 1569, when through the generosity and in the company of some friends, among whom was the historian Couto, he was able to embark for Portugal. They reached Lisbon in April, 1570.[2] Sixteen

among other posts for himself, that of *Provedor dos Defuntos : porque com qualquer destes ficarei mui bem remediado*. To which the *Desembargador* objects: *he necessario que quem houver de servir esses cargos seja letrado e visto em ambos os Direitos*.

[1] *Vinde cá*. It is advisable to give the first words of his poems without the number until there is a definitive edition of his works.

[2] It is uncertain whether Camões' ship was the *Santa Clara* or the *Fe*.

years had passed. The popular, impulsive, talented youth returned middle-aged, poverty-stricken, and unknown. Antonio de Noronha and many others of his friends were dead. Catherina de Athaide had died in 1556 (although she may have continued to receive Camões' rapt devotion as the dead Beatrice that of Dante), Prince João, hope and patron of poets, two years earlier. The plague, to which nearly half the city's population had succumbed, had only recently abated, and Camões may have witnessed the thanksgiving procession in Lisbon on April 20, 1570. Modern critics have even denied him the only consolation which probably remained to him in the *patria esquiva a quem se mal aproveitou*[1], but there seems no reason to reject the tradition that his mother was alive; in fact she survived him and continued to receive the pension of 15,000 *réis*[2] granted him from 1572 till his death on Friday, June 10, 1580. It was a sum barely sufficient to support life, and it was not always regularly paid, so that he is reported to have been in the habit of saying that he would prefer to his pension a whip for the responsible officials (*almoxarifes*). Tradition, to the indignation of reasonable historians, loves to represent a faithful Javanese slave, who had accompanied Camões to Europe, begging for his master in the streets of Lisbon. Camões did not go with King Sebastian to Africa. He may have been already ill when the expedition set out in June 1578—the plague soon began again to ravage Lisbon, and long years of suffering and disappointment must have sapped his strength. Two years later his life of heroic endurance, in patience of the *juizos incognitos de Deos*,[3] ended. He was perhaps buried in a common grave with other victims of the plague.[4] Long absence had served to strengthen his love for his *patria ditosa amada*, and the news from Africa left him no heart to battle against disease, content, as he wrote to the

---

[1] Barros, *Decada*, III. ix. 1.
[2] It is about the sum (apart from any grant of *pimenta*) which a common soldier on active service might earn in India (see Barros, I. viii. 3: 1,200 × 12 = 14,400); *environ huit cents livres de notre monnoie d'aujourd'hui* (Voltaire). It would scarcely correspond to more than £50 of to-day.
[3] *Lus.* v. 45.
[4] Prophetically he had echoed (*Lus.* x. 23) the complaint of the historians of India: *Morrer nos hospitaes em pobres leitos Os que ao Rei e á lei servem de muro.*

Captain-General of Lamego, to die with his country, with which his name has ever since been intimately linked. Couto and Mariz agree that he brought *Os Lusiadas* with him virtually complete on his return to Portugal. It was published through the influence of the poet D. Manuel de Portugal in 1572. Camões has often been called the prince of heroic poets, but it is noteworthy that Faria e Sousa in 1685 says that ' all have hitherto, especially in Spain, considered him greater as a lyric than as an heroic poet '.[1] *Os Lusiadas* rather than an epic is a great lyrical hymn in praise of Portugal, with splendid episodes such as the descriptions of the death of Inés, the battle of Aljubarrota, the storm, Adamastor, the Island of Venus. Apart from the style, its originality consists in the skill with which in a poem but half the length of Tasso's *Gerusalemme Liberata* and a fifth of Ariosto's *Orlando Furioso* the poet works in the entire history of his country. It is this which gives unity to his ten cantos of *oitavas*, this and the wonderfully transparent flow of the verse, which carries the reader over many weaknesses and inequalities of detail. It is a nobler poem than the crowded garden of flowers in a high wind that is the *Orlando Furioso*, and at once more human and intense than the *Gerusalemme Liberata*. Camões, with a wonderful memory and intimate knowledge of the legends of Greece and Rome, read everything, and we find him gathering his material from all sides[2] like a bird in spring, from a Latin treatise of the antiquarian Resende, from the historians Duarte Galvão, Pina, Lopez, Barros, or Castanheda, or literally translat-

[1] *Todos hasta oy, y principalmente en Castilla, tuvieron siempre a mi Maestre por mayor en estes Poemas que en el Heroyco* (*Varias Rimas*, Prólogo, 2 vols., 1685, 1689). Cf. the praise of his *versos pequenos* in Severim de Faria, *Vida*, p. 121.

[2] See the important work by Dr. Rodrigues : *As Fontes dos Lusiadas* (1904–1913). Cf. Camões' *Vão os annos decendo* (x. 9) and *Leal Conselheiro* (cap. 1, p. 18), where the words are used in the same connexion. With Virgil he was obviously acquainted at first hand, with Homer perhaps in the translation of the Florentine scholar Lorenzo Valla (1405–57). In *As Fontes dos Lusiadas* is also discussed the origin of the word Lusiads, as by D. Carolina Michaëlis de Vasconcellos in *O Instituto*, vol. lii (1905), pp. 241–50 : *Lucius Andreas Resendius Inventor da palavra Lusiadas*. It was one of the Latin words acclimatized by Camões. It occurs in a Latin poem by André de Resende, *Vicentius Levita et Martyr* (1545), and in his *Encomium Erasmi* written, but not published, in 1531 ; in a Latin poem by Jorge Coelho, perhaps written in 1526 but touched up before its publication in 1536; and is twice used by Manuel da Costa (in and about 1537).

ing lines of Virgil, as in his shorter poems he imitated Petrarca, Garci Lasso, and Boscán. Tasso used the *mot juste* when in a sonnet addressed to Camões he called him *dotto e buon Luigi*.[1] If, as seems probable, he had early wished to sing the deeds of the Portuguese, the first volumes of Castanheda and Barros must have been an incentive as powerful as the destiny which made him personally acquainted with the scenes of Gama's voyage and of the Portuguese victories in the East. It seems probable that cantos iii and iv, containing the early history of Portugal, were already written, and that around them he wove the epic grandeur revealed in the histories of the discovery of India. The poem opens with an invocation to the nymphs of the Tagus and to King Sebastian, and then, in a wonderful stanza of the sea (*Já no largo oceano navegavam*, i. 19), Gama's ships are shown in mid-voyage. The gods of Olympus take sides, and Venus protects the daring adventurers in seas never crossed before, while Mars stirs up the natives of Mozambique and of Mombaça to treachery (i–ii). In contrast to the natives farther south, the King of Melinde receives them with loyal friendship, and Gama rewards him by relating the history of Portugal (iii–iv). He then continues his voyage, and after weathering a terrible storm brewed by Bacchus, arrives at Calicut (v–vi). After a visit to the Samori (the King of Calicut), the Catual (the Governor) accompanies Gama on board, and Paulo da Gama explains to him the warlike deeds of the Portuguese embroidered on the silken banners of the ships (vii–viii). On the return voyage they are entertained by Tethys and her nymphs in the island of Venus, supposed to be one of the Azores (ix–x), and the poem ends with a second invocation to King Sebastian (x. 145–56). Thus the time of the poem occupies a little over two years (July 1497–September 1499). Into this the previous four centuries had been ingeniously worked, but in order to include the sixteenth century fresh devices were adopted, by which

---

[1] The word is undoubtedly *dotto* in the facsimile of the text given in Antonio de Portugal de Faria, *Torquato Tasso a Luiz de Camões* (Leorne, 1898) although there, as always, it has been transcribed as *colto*. Diogo Bernardez calls Tasso *culto*, perhaps mistaking the reference in Garci Lasso, whose *culto Taso* is not Torquato but Bernardo. Lope de Vega called Camões *divino* and reserved *docto* for Corte Real.

Jupiter (canto ii), Adamastor (v), and Tethys (x) foretell the future. Almost every land and city connected with Portuguese history finds a place in the poem. Small wonder that it was well received by the Portuguese, combining as it did intense patriotism with hundreds of exotic names. The extraordinary number of 12,000 copies is said to have been printed within a quarter of a century of Camões' death,[1] and by 1624 the sale had increased to 20,000 and his fame had spread throughout the world. It would have been still stranger if the *murmuradores maldizentes* had been silent. As early as 1641 we find a critic, João Soares de Brito (1611–64), defending Camões against the charges of plagiarizing Virgil and of improbabilities of time and place.[2] Not every one apparently was of the opinion of the Conde de Idanha, who considered that the only fault of the *Lusiads* was that it was too long to learn by heart and too short to be able to go on reading it for ever. Montesquieu found in it something of ' the fascination of the Odyssey and the magnificence of the Aeneid ', and Voltaire, while objecting to its *merveilleux absurde*, adds : ' Mais la poésie du style et l'imagination dans l'expression l'ont soutenu, de même que les beautés de l'exécution ont placé Paul Véronèse parmi les grands peintres.'

In 1820 appeared José Agostinho de Macedo's *Censura dos Lusiadas*, in which he noted with some asperity Camões' *erros crassissimos*. Prosaic lines, hyperbole, the use of the supernatural, lack of proportion,[3] absence of unity, and historical improbabilities are the main heads of his indictment, and he quotes Racine as to Camões' ' icy style '. He also has much petty detailed criticism, for he finds in Camões a *notavel falta de grammatica*. And Macedo was certainly right. Most of the faults he attributes to Camões do exist in the *Lusiads*. Macedo himself could write more correctly. When he says that the line *Somos hum dos da ilha, lhe tornou* (i. 53) is unpoetical (*não tem tintura de poesia*), we agree ; it is sheer prose. We can add other instances : the line *as que elle para si na cruz tomou* (i. 7) is as

---

[1] His works are *ja muitas vezes impressas* in 1594. In 1631 Alvaro Ferreira de Vera speaks of twelve Portuguese editions (*Breves Lovvores*, f. 87).

[2] *Apologia em qve defende*, &c. (1641).

[3] The instance he gives is the long story of *Magriço e os Doze de Inglaterra* (vi), which he admits is in itself very fine.

unmusical as the rhyming of *Heliogabalo, Sardanapalo* (iii. 92), or *impossibil, terribil* (iv. 54). Only Macedo forgot that genius is justified of its children, and that these details are all merged in the incomparable style, imaginative power, and lofty theme of the poem. If a man is unable to feel the heat of the sun for its spots, we will vainly try to warm or enlighten him, but it is not pedantic grammarians such as Macedo [1] who could obscure the fame of Camões. That could only be done by those whom Macedo calls *os idolatras camoneanos*. Lope de Vega [2] effusively professed to place the *Lusiads* above the *Aeneid* and the *Iliad*, and Camões' fellow-countrymen have eagerly followed suit. He has also suffered much at the hands of translators. Since the *Lusiads* is clearly not the equal of the *Iliad* or the *Odyssey*, it may be worth while to consider by what reasons Camões really is one of the world's greatest poets. There is celestial music in much that he wrote, in incidents of the *Lusiads* such as the death of Inés de Castro,[3] in his eclogues and *canções* and elegies, in many of the sonnets, and in the *redondilhas*, most of all perhaps in the seventy-three heavenly *quintilhas* beginning *Sobolos rios que vam*. But other Portuguese poets have been musical; Diogo Bernardez in this respect vies with Camões: Camões excels them all in the vigour and transparent clearness that accompany his music. But his principal excellence is that, still without losing the music of his *versos deleitosos*, he can think in verse [4]—the thought in some of his elegies and *oitavas* is remarkable—and describe with scientific precision, as in the account of the *tromba* (*Lus.* v.

[1] One of the best instances of his pedantry is his comment on the lines *E tu, nobre Lisboa, que no mundo Facilmente das outras es princesa.* The ordinary reader is content to understand ' cities ' after *outras*. But no, says Macedo, you can only understand Lisbons. Princess of all the other Lisbons !

[2] *Laurel de Apolo*: *Postrando Eneidas y venciendo Iliadas.*

[3] Even here some of the lines are a literal translation of Virgil, but if we compare
>   Para o ceo crystallino alevantando
>   Com lagrimas os olhos piadosos,
>   Os olhos, porque as mãos, &c.,

with the passage
>   Ad coelum tendens, &c.,

it is not at all clear that the picture of the older poet is more beautiful than that of *il lusiade Maro*.

[4] He is thus an exception to Macedo's axiom in the *Motim Literario* that Portuguese poets (most of whom, it must be admitted, are, like Byron, children in thought) either have *versos sem cousas* or *cousas sem versos*.

19-22). Like Milton, he could transform an atlas into a fair harmony of names. His influence on the Portuguese language has been very great. Whether it was wholly for good may be open to doubt—a doubt mentioned by one of his earliest biographers, Severim de Faria, in 1624. The *Lusiads*, he says, ' greatly enriched the Portuguese language by ingeniously introducing many new words and expressions which then came into common use, although some severe critics have censured him for this, considering the use of latinized forms a defect in his poem '.[1] An inch farther than he went in this direction, or in that of *furia grande e sonorosa*, and *estilo grandiloquo*, would have been an inch too far, and subsequent writers did not always observe his restraint, the sobriety due to his classical education. But his poem certainly helped to fix the language, and he cannot be blamed for the excesses of his followers, or for a change which had begun before his time.[2]

Couto records the theft of the *Parnaso* in which Camões was collecting his lyrics with a view to publishing them. He must have written many more lyrics than we possess, but even so the number existing is not small. Successive editors have added to them from time to time, and often clumsily. Faria e Sousa, a century after Camões' death, declared that he had added 200, and, while upbraiding Diogo Bernardez for his *robos*, was himself the thief. Camões might have been somewhat surprised to find in the first edition of his lyrics (1595) two poems which had been in print in the *Cancioneiro de Resende* eight years before he was born. This 1595 edition contained but 65 sonnets, but their number grew to 108 (1598), 140 (1616), 229 (1668), 296 (1685), 352 (1860), 354 (1873). D. Carolina Michaëlis de Vasconcellos has already contributed much towards a critical edition, and it is to be hoped that before long it may be possible

---

[1] *Discvrsos politicos varios* (1624), f. 117 : *& com esta obra ficou enriquecida grandemente a lingua Portuguesa; porque lhe deu muitos termos nouos & palauras bem achadas que depois ficárão perfeitamente introducidas. Posto que nesta parte não deixárão algûs escrupulosos de o condenar, julgandolhe por defeito as palauras alatinadas que vsou no seu poema.*

[2] Cf. Fr. Manuel do Sepulchro, *Reflexão Espiritual* (1669) : *Não ha duvida que maior mudança fez a lingua Portuguesa nos primeiros vinte annos do reinado de D. Manuel que em cento e cincoenta annos dahi para ca.* Barros, however, in his *Dialogo em lovvor* (1540), says latinization had not yet begun : *se o nos usáramos*.

to read the genuine lyrics of Camões in a complete edition by themselves.[1] That would certainly cause him to be more widely read abroad. It is perhaps inevitable that a comparison should arise between Camões and Petrarca (although it must be remembered that they are separated by two centuries), yet he would be an extremely bold or extremely ignorant critic who should place the one of them above the other. In genius they were equal, but a different atmosphere acted on their genius, the artistic atmosphere of Italy and the natural atmosphere of Portugal. Petrarca was the more scholarly writer, so that if he perhaps never attains to the rapturous heights occasionally reached by Camões, he also keeps himself from the blemishes which sometimes disfigure Camões' work. Camões' life was far more varied, many-coloured as an Alentejan *manta*,[2] and this is reflected in his poems. Intensely human, he is swayed by many moods, while Petrarca is merged in the narrower flame of his love. Petrarca excels him in the sonnet, for although many of those by Camões are beautiful, and nearly all contain some beautiful passage, he was not really at his ease in this scanty plot of ground. His genius required a larger canvas for its expression. The following lines from his long and magnificent *canção Vinde cá* are worth quoting because they triumphantly display many of the noblest characteristics of his poetry:

> No mais, canção, no mais, que irei fallando,
> Sem o sentir, mil annos; e se acaso
> Te culparem de larga e de pesada,
> Não pode ser, lhe dize, limitada
> A agoa do mar em tão pequeno vaso.
> Nem eu delicadezas vou cantando
> Co' gosto do louvor, mas explicando
> Puras verdades ja por mi passadas:
> Oxalá foram fabulas sonhadas!

Here we see the force and precision, the amazing ease and rapidity, the crystalline transparency, the sad *saudade*, and above all the deep sincerity that mark so much of his work. Both

[1] The authorship of the fine sonnets *Horas breves do meu contentamento* (attributed to Camões, Bernardez, the Infante Luis, &c.) and *Formoso Tejo meu, quam differente* (attributed to Camões, Rodriguez Lobo, &c.) is still under dispute.
[2] *Filodemo*, v. 3.

Petrarca and Camões are representative of their country, the latter not only in his poems, in which almost every Portuguese hero is included, but in his character and his life. In his wit and melancholy, his love of Nature, his passionate devotion, his persistency and endurance, his independence and sensitive pride, in his lyrical gift and power of expression, in his courage and ardent patriotism, he is the personification and ideal of the Portuguese nation.

Many of Camões' friends were also lyric poets, but their poems have mostly vanished. One of them, Luis Franco Corrêa, compiled a *cancioneiro* of contemporary poems which still exists in manuscript. A few later poets, chiefly pastoral, have already been mentioned, but after Camões' death the star of lyric poetry waned and set, and the only compensation was a brilliant noonday in the realm of prose. Camões was a learned poet, but he also plunged both hands in the songs and traditions of the people. The later poets withdrew themselves more and more from this perennial spring of poetical images and expression, till at last in the ripeness of time Almeida Garrett turned to it again for inspiration, even Bocage, devoted admirer of Camões though he was, having neglected this side of his genius, as was inevitable in the eighteenth century.

Epic poetry scarcely fared better than the lyric, despite a hundred honest efforts to eclipse the *Lusiads*. A favourite legend of Portuguese and other folk-lore tells how the stepdaughter comes from the fairies' dwelling speaking flowers for words or with a star on her forehead, but her envious half-sister, who then visits the fairies, returns uttering mud and toads or with an ass's head. If the epic poems of those who emulated the fame of Camões are something better than mud they nevertheless fail for the most part lamentably in that inspiration which Portuguese history might have been expected to give.

>   Alguns (misera gente) inutilmente
>   Compõem grandes Iliadas,

wrote Diniz da Cruz (*O Hyssope*, canto 1). The epic-fever had not abated even in the beginning of the nineteenth century. The Madeira poet Francisco de Paula Medina e Vasconcellos

(c. 1770-1824) alone wrote two: *Zargueida* (1806), *Georgeida* (1819); and José Agostinho de Macedo in his *Motim Literario* imagines himself at the mercy of a poet with an epic in sixty cantos entitled *Napoleada*, and himself became the mock-hero of one in nine: *Agostinheida* (Londres, 1817), written by his unfortunate opponent Nuno Alvares Pereira Pato Moniz (1781-1827). The strange poet of Setubal, Thomaz Antonio de Santos e Silva (1751-1816), published a *Braziliada* in twelve cantos in 1815. Of the earlier epics Camillo Castello Branco wrote sarcastically: 'They contain impenetrable mysteries of dullness and inspire a sacred awe, but they are the conventional glory of our literary history, untouched and intangible.'[1]

Of the two long epic poems of JERONIMO CORTE REAL (c. 1530-1590?): *Svcesso do Segvndo Cerco de Div* (1574) and *Naufragio, e Lastimoso Svcesso da Perdiçam de Manoel de Sousa de Sepulveda*, &c. (1594), we may perhaps say that they are excellent prose. He dwells more than once upon the inconstancy of fortune, and this may be something more than a platitude. Of his life little is known. He is by some believed to have been born in the Azores in 1533. A document in the possession of the Visconde de Esperança shows that he died before May 12, 1590. He may have been a musician as well as a poet and a painter. It is probable, but not certain, that he accompanied King Sebastian to Alcacer Kebir and was taken prisoner. Faria e Sousa says that he was too old to go. After varied service by land and sea he wrote these poems when living in retirement on his estate near Evora, and his own experiences stood him in good stead for his descriptions, which are often not without life and vigour, as the account of the battle in canto 18 of the *Segundo Cerco de Diu*, or of the storm in canto 7 of the *Naufragio*. The former poem records the famous defence of Diu by D. João de Mascarenhas and its relief by D. João de Castro (1546), in whose mouth is placed a long and tedious speech. The last two cantos (21, 22) are tacked on to the main theme and occupy more than a quarter of the whole. They tell from paintings the deeds of past captains and prophesy future events and the 'golden reign' of King Sebastian. The prophetic vision, although it

[1] *Os Ratos da Inquisição*, Preface, p. 97.

included a generation beyond the nominal date of the poem (1546), did not extend to the battle of Alcacer Kebir (1578). The hendecasyllables of the blank verse have an exceedingly monotonous fall and the lines merge prosaically into one another.[1] The use of adjectives is excessive, and generally there is an inclination to multiply words without adding to the force of the picture.[2] The same plethora of epithets, elaborate similes, and slow awkward development of the story mark the seventeen cantos—some 10,000 lines of blank verse, with some tercets and *oitavas*—which constitute the *Naufragio*. In cantos 13 and 14 a learned man tells from sculptures the history of the Portuguese kings, from Afonso I to Sebastian. The remaining cantos have a more lively interest, ending with the death of D. Lianor in canto 17, but the poet could not resist the temptation to round off with an anticlimax, in which Phoebus, Proteus, and Pan make lamentation. His short *Auto dos Quatro Novissimos do Homem* (1768) in blank verse is written with some intensity, but the style is the same.[3] His *Austriada*, composed to commemorate Don John of Austria's *felicissima victoria* [4] of Lepanto, consists of fifteen cantos in Spanish blank verse.

Luis Pereira Brandão, born at Oporto about 1540, was present at Alcacer Kebir, and after his release from captivity is said to have worn mourning for the rest of his life. That later generations might also suffer, his epic *Elegiada* (1588)—in spite of his professed *temor de ser prolixo*—was published in eighteen cantos. Beginning with the early years of King Sebastian, it recounts the king's dreams and ambitions, his first expedition to Africa, and the later disastrous adventure. Not even the story of D. Lianor de Sousa (canto 6) nor the excessively detailed description of the battle of Alcacer Kebir (canto 17) rouses the poet from his implacable dullness. The defects of his style have

[1] e. g. *D. Alvaro de Castro e D. Francisco De Meneses*, or *hum grave Prudente capitam.*
[2] e. g. *valor, esforço e valentia; mar sereno e calmo; abundosa e larga vea; a dura defensa rigurosa; açoutando e batendo.* The line often consists of three adjectives and a noun.
[3] Between Corte Real's *cruel molesto duro mortal frio* and Dante's *eterna maladetta fredda e greve* (*Inf.* vi) is all the difference between a heap of loose stones and a shrine. The conception of the *Auto*, especially the third *novissimo, que he o Inferno*, was no doubt derived from Dante.
[4] These are the first words of the original title of the poem (1578).

perhaps been exaggerated, but it is certainly inferior to that of Andrade, with whom he shares the inability to distinguish a poem from a history. The introduction of contemporary events in India (cantos 6, 10, 14), however legitimate in a history, is singularly out of place in an epic.

If the author of the history of King João III's reign, FRANCISCO DE ANDRADE (*c.* 1535–1614), brother of the great Frei Thomé de Jesus, regarded his epic *O Primeiro Cerco . . . de Diu* (1589) merely as a supplementary chapter of that history, we can only regret that he did not write it in prose. It is a straightforward account, in excellent Portuguese, of the first siege of Diu (1538), but *oitava* follows prosaic *oitava* with a relentless wooden tread, maintaining the same level of mediocrity throughout and rendering it unreadable as poetry. The author begins by imploring divine favour that his song may be adequate to his subject (i. 1–3). It is only when he has passed his two-thousandth stanza that he expresses some diffidence as to whether his 'fragile bark' was well equipped for so long a voyage, but he consoles himself, if not his reader, with the sincere conviction that his rude verse cannot detract from the greatness of the deeds which he describes (xx. 1–6).

§ 5
The Historians

It was a proud saying of a Portuguese *seiscentista* that the Portuguese discoveries silenced all other histories.[1] Certainly this was so in the case of the history of Portugal, which was neglected while writer after writer recorded the history of the Portuguese in India. Nor need we quarrel with a vogue which has preserved for us so many striking pictures in which East and West clash without meeting, new countries are continually opening to our view, and heroism and adventure go hand in hand. Sometimes the pages of these historians seem all aglow with precious stones, emeralds from Peru, turquoises from Persia, rubies, cat's-eyes, chrysolites, amethysts, beryls, and sapphires from Ceylon, or scented with the opium of Cairo, the saffron of Cannanore, the camphor of Borneo, sandalwood from Timor, pepper from Malabar, cloves from the Moluccas. Blood and sea-spray mingle with the silks from China and ivory from Sofala, and among the crowd of rapacious governors and unscrupulous adventurers move a few figures of a simple austerity and devotion to duty, Albuquerque, Galvão, Castro, St. Francis Xavier.

Little is known of Alvaro Velho except that he was one of the immortals (unless he was the *degredado* (convict) from whose *caderno* Couto derived his account of the discovery) who accompanied Vasco da Gama on his first voyage. To him is attributed the simple, clear narrative contained in the log or *Roteiro da Viagem de Vasco da Gama em 1497*, filled with a primitive wonder, which pointed the way to the historians of India. Indeed, it provided material for the first book of a writer who may perhaps be called the first [2] historian of the discoveries ' enterprised by the

[1] Antonio Vieira, *Historia do Futuro* (1718), p. 24: *esta historia era o silencio de todas as historias.*
[2] *O primeiro Portugues que na nossa lingoa as [façanhas] resuscitei.* João de Barros, in his preface, makes a similar claim: *foi o primeiro.*

Portingales '. FERNAM LOPEZ DE CASTANHEDA (*c.* 1500–59) was born at Santarem, and in 1528 accompanied his father, appointed Judge at Goa, to India. For the next ten years he diligently and not without many risks and discomforts consulted documents and inscriptions in various parts of the country with a view to writing a history of the discovery and conquest of India, making himself personally acquainted with the ground and with many of those who had played a part in the half-century (1498–1548) under review. After his return to Portugal he continued his life-work with the same devotion for twenty years, during which poverty constrained him to accept the post of bedel at Coimbra University. When he died, worn out by his *continuas vigilias*, his history was complete, but only seven books had been published: *Historia do Descobrimento e Conqvista da India* (1551–4). He had at least the satisfaction to know that a part had already been translated into French and Italian. The eighth book, bringing the history down to 1538, was published by his children in 1561, but books nine and ten never appeared. This history of forty years, which has less regard to style than to sincerity and the truth of the facts, is written in great detail. It is a scrupulous and trustworthy record of high interest describing not only the deeds of the Portuguese, ' of much greater price than gold or silver ', ' more valiant than those of Greek or Roman ', but the many lands in which they occurred. The narrative can rise to great pathos, as in the account of Afonso de Albuquerque's death (iii. 154), and is often extremely vivid.[1] The interest necessarily diminishes after 1515, and the seventh book is largely concerned with dismal contentions between Portuguese officials. But the great events and persons, the capture of Goa or Diu, the characters of Gama or Albuquerque, Duarte Pacheco Pereira or Antonio Galvão, stand out the more clearly from the deliberate absence of rhetoric.

LOURENÇO DE CACERES, in his *Doutrina* addressed to the Infante Luis in twenty short chapters on the parts of a good prince, showed that he could write excellent prose. His death in 1531 prevented him from undertaking a more ambitious work,

---

[1] Cf. vi. 37, 38; vii. 77, 78; or vi. 100, where the ships bristling with the enemy's arrows are likened to porcupines.

which was accordingly entrusted to his nephew João de Barros (1496?–1570).[1] But much earlier and a generation before Lopez de Castanheda's work began to appear, the most famous of the Portuguese historians had resolved to chronicle the discovery of India. Born probably at Viseu, the son of Lopo de Barros, he came of ancient Minhoto stock and was brought up in the palace of King Manuel. When the Infante João received a separate establishment Barros became his page (*moço da guardaroupa*). It was in this capacity, *por cima das arcas da vossa guardaroupa*, that with the active encouragement of the prince he wrote his first work, *Cronica do Emperador Clarimundo* (1520). It is a long romance of chivalry crowded with actors and events, and contains affecting, even passionate episodes. But the most remarkable feature of this work, written in eight months when the author was little over twenty, is its inexhaustible flow of clear, smooth, vigorous prose, entirely free from awkwardness or hesitation. One may also note that he regarded it merely as a parergon, a preparation for his history, *afim de apurar o estilo*, that despite its length he assures his readers that he omits all details in order to avoid prolixity, that much of its geography is real—all his works prove the truth of Couto's assertion that he was *doutissimo na geografia*—and that each chapter ends with a brief moral. King Manuel, to whom he read some chapters, encouraged him to persevere in his intention to write the history of India, but the king's death in 1521 delayed the project. In the following year Barros, who meanwhile had married Maria, daughter of Diogo de Almeida of Leiria, is said to have gone out as Captain of the Fortress of S. Jorge da Mina (although probably he never left Portugal) and later became Treasurer of the *Casa da India* (1525–8), and its Factor in 1532, a post which he retained for thirty-five years. Although he lost a large sum of money in an unfortunate venture in Brazil, this was partly made good by the king's munificence, and when in 1568, the year after his resignation, he retired to his *quinta* near Pombal *sibi ut viveret* he went as a *fidalgo* of the king's household

---

[1] 1496, the generally accepted year of his birth, is the calculation of Severim de Faria, followed by Barbosa Machado, Nicolás Antonio, &c. As he retired at the end of 1567 it is difficult not to suspect (from his love of method and the decimal system) that he was born in 1497—the year of Vasco da Gama's expedition.

and with a pension over twenty-five times as large as that of Camões.[1] In old age he is described as of a fine presence, although thin and not tall, with pale complexion, keen eyes, aquiline nose, long white beard, grave, pleasant, and fluent in conversation. Before beginning his history he wrote several brief treatises of great interest and importance, *Ropica Pnefma* (1532), a dialogue written at his country house in 1531 in which Time, Understanding, Will, and Reason discuss their spiritual wares (*mercadoria espiritual*), and incidentally the new heresies; three short works on the Portuguese language, a *Dialogo da Viçiosa Vergonha* (1540), and a *Dialogo sobre preceptos moraes* (1540) in which he reduced Aristotle's *Ethics* to a game for the benefit of two of his ten children and of the Infanta Maria. He also wrote two excellent *Panegyricos* (of the Infanta Maria and King João III) which were first published by Severim de Faria in his *Noticias de Portugal* in 1655. As a historian he chose Livy for his pattern both in style and system. The first *Decada* of his *Asia* appeared in 1552, the second in 1553, and the third ten years later (1563). Their success was immediate, especially abroad—in Portugal, like other historians of recent events, he was accused of partiality and unfairness [2]—copies soon became extremely rare, the first two Decads were translated into Italian before the third appeared, and Pope Pius IV is said to have placed Barros' portrait (or bust) next to the statue of Ptolemy.[3] Barros had prepared himself very thoroughly for his task. His work as Factor seems to have been exacting—he says that it was only by giving up holidays and half the night and all the time spent by other men in sleeping the *sesta*, or walking about the city, or going into the country, playing, shooting, fishing, dining, that he was able to attend to his literary labours. Yet he read everything, pored over maps and chronicles and documents from the East, and even bought

---

[1] 400,000 *réis*. He also obtained the privilege of trading with India free from all taxes so as to clear a profit of 1,600,000 *réis*. Innocencio da Silva adds 'yearly' to this sum, mentioned by Severim de Faria. In any case Barros' complaints of his poverty seem misplaced.

[2] Faria e Sousa (*Varias Rimas*, pt. 2 (1689), p. 165), says that neither Lopez de Castanheda nor Barros was widely read, one of the reasons being the length of their histories.

[3] According to Pero de Magalhães de Gandavo (*Dialogo em defensam da lingua portvgvesa*) Barros 'is in Venice preferred to Ptolemy'.

a Chinese slave to translate for him. With this enthusiasm, his unfailing sense of order and proportion, and his clear and copious style he necessarily produced a work of permanent value. His manner is lofty, even pompous, worthy of the great events described. If his history is less vivid and interesting than Castanheda's, that is because he wrote not as an eyewitness[1] or actor in them but as Court historian. He was a true Augustan, and the great edifice that this Portuguese Livy planned and partly built was of eighteenth-century architecture. He was fond of comparing his work to a building in which each stone has its appointed place. The material to his hand must be moulded to suit the symmetry of the whole—Albuquerque had never in his life used so many relative sentences as are attributed to him by Barros (II. v. 9)—and with a pedantic love of definitions and systematic subdivisions we find him measuring out the proportions of his stately structure, while picturesque details are deliberately omitted.[2] The merits of his style have been exaggerated. It is never confused or slovenly, but is for use rather than beauty; its ingredients are pure and energetic but the construction is inartistic and monotonous.[3] It is rather in the forcible, crisp sentences of his shorter treatises than in the *Asia* that Barros displays his mastery of style. His great narrative of epic deeds is interrupted by interesting special chapters or digressions on trade, geography, Eastern cities and customs, locusts, chess, the Mohammedan religion, sword-fish, palm-trees, and monsoons. It was planned in four *Decadas* and forty books, to embrace 120 years to 1539, but the fourth was not written and the third

[1] His account of the fleet leaving Lisbon (I. v. 1) *is* that of an eyewitness.
[2] *Mais trabalhamos no substancial da historia que no ampliar as miudezas que enfadam e não deleitam* (I. vii. 8). Cf. I. v. 10 (1778 ed., p. 465) ; III. ix. 9 (p. 426); III. x. 5 (p. 489). Yet the vivid light thrown by the details recorded in other writers, such as the 'bushel of sapphires' sent to Albuquerque by one of the native kings, or the open boat drifting with a few Portuguese long dead and a heap of silver beside them, is of undeniable value. Goes inserts details, but is too late a writer to do so without apology, like Corrêa and Lopez de Castanheda : *pode parecer a algũa pessoa* [e. g. his friend Barros] *que em historia grave nam eram necessarias estas miudezas* (*Cron. do Pr. D. Joam*, cap. cii).
[3] e. g. the following mortar of conjunctions between the stones on p. 335 of *Decada* II (1777 ed.) opened at hazard : *nas quaes ... que ... que ... qual ... que ... como ... que ... que ... o qual ... cujos ... que ... que ... que ... posto que ... como ... porque ... que.*

ends with the death of D. Henrique de Meneses (1526). Probably he did not find the dispute as to the Governorship of India a very congenial subject, especially as the feud was resumed in Portugal. Material and notes were however ready, and these were worked up into a lengthy fourth *Decada* by João Baptista Lavanha (†1625) in 1615, which covers the same ground as, but is quite distinct from, the fourth Decad of Couto. The *Asia* was only a block of a vaster whole. *Europa*, *Africa*, and *Santa Cruz* were to treat respectively of Portugal from the Roman Conquest and Portuguese history in North Africa and Brazil, while Geography and Commerce were to be the subjects of separate works, the first of which (in Latin) was partly written.

Inseparably connected with the name of Barros is that of DIOGO DO COUTO (1542–1616), who continued his *Asia*, writing *Decadas* 4–12. He was born at Lisbon, and at the age of ten entered the service (*guardaroupa*) of the Infante Luis, who sent him to study at the College of the Jesuits and then with his son, D. Antonio, under Frei Bartholomeu dos Martyres, afterwards Archbishop of Braga, at S. Domingos, Bemfica. When thirteen he was present at the death of his talented patron Prince Luis, and remained in the palace as page to the king till the king's death two years later.[1] Couto then went to seek his fortune in India, and there as soldier, trader, official (in 1571 he was in charge of the stores at Goa),[2] and historian he spent the best part of the following half-century, his last visit to Portugal being in 1569–71. At the bidding of Philip II (I of Portugal), who appointed him *Cronista Môr* of India, he undertook the completion of Barros' *Asia*. Probably he needed little inducement—his was the pen of a ready writer, and the composition of his history was, he tells us, a pleasure to him in spite of frequent discouragement. He had received a classical education; as a boy in the palace he had listened to stories of India[3] and had been no doubt deeply im-

---

[1] *E sendo eu moço servindo a El Rey D. João na guardaroupa* (*Dec.* IV. iii. 8). In *Dec.* VII. viii. 1 he speaks of having served João III for two years as *moço da camara* (1555–7). In the same passage he embarks for India in 1559 aged *fifteen*. In *Dec.* VII. ix. 12 (1783 ed. p. 396) he is eighteen (April 1560).

[2] According to the Governor, Francisco Barreto, he was more at home with arms than with prices (*Dec.* IX. 20, 1786 ed., p. 160). Another passage in the *Decadas* proves him to have been an excellent horseman.

[3] Cf. *Dec.* IV. iii. 8 (1778 ed. p. 234).

pressed by the vivid account of the Sepulveda shipwreck.[1] In India he won general respect. At Goa he married the sister of Frei Adeodato da Trindade (1565-1605), who in Lisbon saw some of his *Decadas* through the press ; he became Keeper of the Indian Archives (Torre do Tombo) and more than once made a speech on behalf of the City Councillors, as at the inauguration of the portrait of Vasco da Gama in the Town Hall in the centenary year of the discovery of India, before Gama's grandson, then Viceroy, and a gathering of noblemen and captains. Couto knew every one—we find him conversing with Viceroy, Archbishop, natives, Moorish prisoners, rich merchants from Cambay or the Ambassador of the Grand Mogul. This personal acquaintance with the scenes, events, and persons gives a lively dramatic air to his work. The sententious generalities of the majestic Barros are replaced by bitter protests and practical suggestions. He is a critic of abuses rather than of persons.[2] He writes from the point of view of the common soldier, as one who had seen both sides of the tapestry of which Barros smoothly ignored the snarls and thread-ends. He displays a hatred of *semjustiças*, treachery, and 'the insatiable greed of men', with a fine zest in descriptions of battles, but he has not Barros' skill in proportion and the grand style.[3] He can, however, write excellent prose, and he gives more of graphic detail [4] and individual sayings and anecdotes than his predecessor. Nor is he by any means an

[1] He himself describes with great detail and pathos the wrecks of the ships *N. Senhora da Barca* (VII. viii. 1), *Garça* (VII. viii. 12), *S. Paulo* (VII. ix. 16), *Santiago* (X. vii. 1), as well as that of Sepulveda (*Dec.* VI. ix. 21, 22). In his account of the loss of the *S. Thomé* (which was printed in the *Historia Tragico-Maritima*, in the *Vida de D. Paulo de Lima*, and no doubt in the lost eleventh *Decada*), the separation of D. Joana de Mendoça from her child is one of the most tantalizing and touching incidents ever penned.

[2] *Não particularizo ninguem* (*Dec.* XII. i. 7).

[3] What he lacks in *gravidade* (cf. *Dec.* X. x. 14)—he is quite ready to admit that he writes *toscamente* (VII. iii. 3), *singelamente, sem ornamento de palavras* (VI. ii. 3), *simplesmente, sem ornamento nem artificio de palavras* (v. v. 6)—he makes good by directness as an eyewitness, *de mais perto* (IV. i. 7 ; cf. IV. x. 4 *ad init.*). When he had not himself been present he preferred the accounts of those who had, as Sousa Coutinho's description of the siege of Diu (*Commentarios*) *em estilo excellente e grave, e foi o melhor de todos, porque escreveo como testemunha de vista*, v. iii. 2) or Miguel de Castanhoso's *copioso tratado* (V. viii. 7). Among the traces of his close touch with reality are the popular *romances, cantigas, adagios*, which Barros would have deemed beneath the dignity of history.

[4] As the fleets grew, long catalogues of the captains' names were perhaps

ignorant chronicler. A poet[1] and the friend of poets, he read Dante and Petrarca and Ariosto, was old-fashioned enough to admire Juan de Mena, consulted the works of ancient and modern historians, travellers, and geographers, and was deeply interested in the customs and religions of the East. The inequality of his *Decadas* is in part explained by their history, which constitutes a curious chapter in the *fata* of manuscripts. He first wrote *Decada* x, which is the longest and most resembles those of Barros: this was only sent to Portugal in 1600 and was not immediately published, apparently because the period, 1580–8, was too recent. It remained in manuscript till 1788. Meanwhile Couto, working with extraordinary speed, sent home the fourth and fifth *Decadas* in 1597, the sixth in 1599, and the seventh in 1601. Noting the fact that the last two books (9 and 10) of Castanheda's history had been suppressed by royal order as being excessively fond of truth (*porque fallava nelles verdades*), he remarks that, should this happen to a volume of his, another would be forthcoming to take its place. Friends and enemies, indeed the very elements, took up the challenge, but fortunately Couto's spirit and independence continued to the year of his death. The fourth *Decada* was at once printed, but the text of the fifth was tampered with and its publication delayed, the sixth was destroyed by fire when ready for publication and recast by Frei Adeodato, the seventh was captured at sea by the English and re-written in 1603 by Couto and sent home in the same year, the eighth and ninth, finished in 1614, were stolen from him in manuscript during a severe illness. This was a crushing blow, but he partially reconstructed them *a modo de epilogo* and, writing in old age from memory, dwelt, to our gain, on personal recollections: his literary bent appears—his friend Camões, Cristovam Falcão,

inevitable. They are certainly out of place in a biography, but Couto's *Vida de D. Paulo de Lima Pereira* (1765) is really a collection of those passages from the *Decadas* which bear on the life of Couto's old friend, a *fidalgo muito pera tudo*. As far as chapter 32 it is told in words similar to or identical with those of *Decada* x. Chapter 32 corresponds with the beginning of the lost *Decada* xi.

[1] His biographer, Manuel Severim de Faria, says that he left (in manuscript) 'a large volume of elegies, eclogues, songs, sonnets and glosses' (Barbosa Machado calls them *Poesias Varias*), and that he wrote a commentary on the first five books of the *Lusiads*. *Carminibus quoque pangendis non infeliciter vacavit*, says N. Antonio.

and Garcia de Resende are mentioned. Finally *Decada* xi (1588–97), which, writing to King Philip III in January 1616, he says ' survived this shipwreck', has disappeared and *Decada* xii is incomplete, although the first five books bring the history to the end of the century (1599). His successor in the Goa Archives, Antonio Bocarro, took up the history at the year 1612, in a work which was published in 1876: *Decada 13ª da Historia da India*. The manuscript of his *Dialogo do Soldado Pratico na India* (written before the fourth *Decada*) was also stolen. The indomitable Couto re-wrote it and both versions have survived. They were not published till 1790, the title given to the earlier version being *Dialogo do soldado pratico portugues*. With its *verdades chans*, this dialogue between an old soldier of India, an ex-Governor, and a judge forms a most valuable and interesting indictment of the decadence of Portuguese rule in India, where the thief and rogue escaped scot-free, while the occasional honest man was liable to suffer for their sins, and the sleek soldier in velvet with gold ribbons on his hat had taken the place of the bearded *conquistadores* (*Dialogo*, pp. 91–2).

GASPAR CORRÊA (*c*. 1495–*c*. 1565) claims, like Fernam Lopez de Castanheda and Barros, to have been the first historian of the Portuguese in the East.[1] He went to India sixteen years before Lopez de Castanheda and no doubt soon began[2] to take notes and collect material, but he was still working at his history in 1561 and 1563, and his *Lendas da India* were not published till the nineteenth century. In the year 1506 Corrêa entered the king's service as *moço da camara*,[3] and six years later went to India, where he became one of the six or seven secretaries of Afonso de Albuquerque.[4] They were young men carefully chosen by the Governor from among those who had been brought

[1] *Lendas*, iii. 7 : *nom ouve alguem que tomasse por gloria escrever e cronizar o descobrimento da India*. In an earlier passage (i. 3) he refers to narratives of travellers such as that of Duarte Barbosa.
[2] He says (*Lendas*, ii. 5) : *quando comecei esta ocupação de escrever as cousas da India erão ellas tão gostosas, per suas bondades, que dava muito contentamento ouvilas recontar*.
[3] *Lenda*, iii. 438.
[4] *Fui hum dos seus escrivães que com elle andei tres annos* (ii. 46). Elsewhere (i. 2) he says that he went to India *moço de pouca idade* sixteen years after the discovery of India. 1512 was fourteen years after the actual discovery (1498), but might be counted the sixteenth year from 1497.

up in the palace and to whom he felt he could entrust his secrets.[1] Theirs was no humdrum or sedentary post, for they had to accompany the Governor on foot or on horseback, in peace and war, ever ready with ink and paper. Thus Corrêa had occasion vividly to describe Aden in 1513, and helped with his own hands to build the fortress of Ormuz in 1515. After Albuquerque's death Corrêa seems to have continued to fight and write. In 1526 he was appointed to the factory of Sofala,[2] and in the following year the *moço da camara* has become a *cavaleiro* and is employed at the customs house at Cochin.[3] He cannot have remained much longer at Cochin than at Sofala, since he signed his name in the book of *moradias* at Lisbon in 1529, and in 1530–1, in a ship provided by himself (*em um meu catur*), went with the Governor of India's fleet to the attack of Diu. Later he was commissioned by the Viceroy, D. João de Castro, to furnish lifesize drawings[4] of all the Governors of India, so that he must then have been living at Goa. The ever-growing abuses in India and the scanty reward given to his fifty years of service and honourable wounds[5] embittered his last years, and if his spoken comments were as incisive as the indictment of the Governors and Captains contained in the *Lendas*[6] he must have made enemies in high positions : it seems, at least, that his murder one night at Malacca went unpunished, as if to prove the truth of his frequent complaint that no one ever was punished in India. At the time of his death he may still have been at work, as in 1561 and 1563, on the revision of his *Lendas* or *Coronica dos Feytos da India*,[7] originally completed in 1551.[8]

---

[1] *Homens da criação d'El Rei*, says Corrêa with some pride, *de que confiasse seus segredos* (ii. 46).

[2] Lima Felner, *Noticia preliminar* (*Lendas*, i, p. xi).

[3] Ibid. ; but Corrêa says (*Lendas*, ii. 891) that he held this post at Cochin (*almoxarife do almazem da Ribeira*) in 1525.

[4] *Por ter entendimento em debuxar*. The portraits, drawn by Corrêa and painted by ' a native painter ' so cleverly that you could recognize the originals (iv. 597), as well as Corrêa's very curious drawings of Aden and other cities, are reproduced in the 1858–66 edition of the *Lendas*.

[5] *Passa de cincoenta annos* [i.e. 1512–63] *que ando no rodizio d'este serviço, aleijado de feridas com que irei á cova sem satisfação*.

[6] Cf. ii. 608, 752 ; iii. 437 ; iv. 338, 537–8, 567–8, 665, 669, 730–1.

[7] He so styles his work in the preface of *Lenda* iv.

[8] He is writing, he says, in 1561 (*Lendas*, i. 265) ; 1561 again (i. 995 : *não cessando este trabalho até este anno*) ; 1563 (iii. 438) ; 1550 (iv. 25) ; 1551 (iv. 732).

The first three books relate the events from 1497 to 1538; the last carries the history down to 1550. The account of the discovery is based on the narrative of one, and the recollections of others, of Vasco da Gama's companions, and the subsequent events are drawn largely from Corrêa's own experience. He spared no trouble to obtain first-hand information, from aged officials, Moors, natives, captives, a Christian galley-slave, or a woman from Malabar, distrusting mere hearsay. He lays frequent stress on his personal evidence.[1] Without necessarily establishing the trustworthiness of his work on every point, this method had the advantage of rendering it singularly vivid, and it contains many a brilliantly coloured picture of the East. In many respects he is the most remarkable of the historians of India. It was not for nothing that he had written down some of Albuquerque's letters to King Manuel.[2] If Albuquerque's words are still striking when read after four centuries, we may imagine their effect on the boy still in his teens to whom he dictated them. *Tinha grande oratoria*, says Corrêa, and many years afterwards some of the phrases remained in his memory.[3] He no doubt learnt from Albuquerque his direct, vigorous style, his love of concrete details, his regard for truth. His account of the sack of Malacca—the rifled chests of gold coins and brocades of Mecca and cloth of gold, the narrow dusty streets in shadow in the midday *calma*—must, one thinks, be that of an eyewitness; yet Corrêa was not in India at the time. The explanation is that it was largely the account of Albuquerque.[4]

Corrêa writes in even greater detail than Lopez de Castanheda. There is no trace of literary leanings in his work; he is sparing of descriptions as interrupting the story.[5] Whole pages have scarcely an adjective, and this gives his narrative clearness and

[1] The value of that evidence varies. For instance, he assures us (iii. 689) that he saw with his own eyes a native 300 years old and his son of 200; yet there is something suspicious in the roundness of the figures.

[2] *Escrevia com elle as cartas pera El Rei* (ii. 172).

[3] Albuquerque in one of his letters (No. 95) says that in Portugal a man is hanged for stealing Alentejan *mantas*. Corrêa repeats this phrase twice (*Lendas*, ii. 752; iv. 731).

[4] Cf. ii. 247: *Eu ouvi dizer a Afonso d'Albuquerque.*

[5] *Neste meu trabalho não tomei sentido senão escrever os feitos dos Portugueses e nada das terras* (iii. 66). Cf. i. 651, 815; ii. 222.

rapidity, yet he is careless of style. It has been called redundant and verbose, but that is true mainly of the prefaces, which show that Corrêa in a library might have developed into a rhetorical Zurara of *boas oratorias*. It is, however, no longer the fashion to sneer at this 'simple and half barbarous chronicler', this 'soldier adventurer in whose artless words appears his lack of culture'.[1] His *Lendas* are infinitely preferable to the sleek periods of Barros and often as reliable, being legendary in little beyond their title, as understood by the ignorant (for the word *lenda* meant not legend but record or log). They have a harsh flavour of religious fervour and of lust for gold [2] and an intense atmosphere of the East—*sangre e incenso, cravo e escravaria*, St. James fighting for the Christians, St. Thomas transformed into a peacock, all in a region of horror and enchantment. Corrêa was aware that it was dangerous to write history in India (iii. 9)—*periculosae plenum opus aleae*—but although he had no intention of immediately publishing it [3] he evidently expected some recognition of his work. The appearance of Lopez de Castanheda's *Historia* and Barros' *Decadas* must have been a blow almost as cruel as the daggers of his assassins a few years later.

The events of India from 1506–15, chronicled by Castanheda and Barros, necessarily centred round the great figure of Afonso de Albuquerque, and they were recorded afresh by his illegitimate son BRAS DE ALBUQUERQUE (1500–80), whom the dying Governor recommended to the king in his last letter. King Manuel in belated gratitude bestowed his favour on this son and bade him assume the name of Afonso in memory of his father. His *Commentarios de Afonso de Alboquerque* (1557) were revised by the author in a second edition (1576) four years before his death. They are written in unassuming but straightforward style and furnish a very clear and moderate account based on letters

---

[1] Latino Coelho, *Fernão de Magalhães* in *Archivo Pittoresco*, vi (1863), p. 170 et seq.
[2] Corrêa himself seems to have been rather unsuccessful than scrupulous in amassing money. He tells without a hint of embarrassment (ii. 432) how he took the white and gold scarf (*rumal*) of the murdered Resnordim (or Rais Ahmad) and sold it for 20 *xarafins* (about £7), and (iii. 281) helped to dispose of stolen goods in 1528 at Cochin.
[3] *Protestando d'em meus dias esta lenda nom mostrar a nenhum* (i. 3).

written by Albuquerque to King Manuel.[1] The author seems to have realized that Albuquerque's words and deeds speak sufficiently for themselves, but the reflection produced is somewhat pale.

The gallant and chivalrous apostle of the Moluccas, ANTONIO GALVAM (c. 1490?–1557), 'as rich in valour and knowledge as poor in fortune ',[2] printed nothing in his lifetime but his manuscripts were handed over after his death to Damião de Goes as *Cronista Môr*.[3] We have only a brief treatise by him published posthumously. Copious in matter rather than in length, for it has but eighty small folios in spite of its lengthy title, this *Tratado* (1563), or, if we adopt the briefer title from the colophon, this *Lyvro dos Descobrimentos das Antilhas & India*, is remarkable for the curious observation shown and its vivid, concise style of a man of action. Written in the form of annals, it begins with the Flood, and on f. 12 we are still in the age of Merlin; but the most valuable part consists in the writer's direct experience—he tells of buffaloes, cows and hens ' of flesh black as this ink ', of mocking parrots, fires made of earth ' as in Flanders '. Goes, who had certainly handled the manuscript, may have added this comparison; he evidently interpolated the account of his own travels (ff. 58 v.–59 v.). The life of Galvam gives a further interest to this rare book, for, a man of noble and disinterested character, himself a prince by election, he has always been regarded as a stock instance of the ingratitude of princes. Born in the East, the son of Albuquerque's old friend, the historian Duarte Galvam, he won fame by his courage and martial qualities, both as soldier and skilful mariner. After subduing the Molucca Islands he, as their Governor (Captain), spent his energies and income in missionary zeal and in developing agriculture. On the expiry of his term as Governor (1536–40) he refused the position of Raja of Ternate,

---

[1] *Que colligi dos proprios originaes*. The work is a history of events in India, not a biography of Albuquerque, the first forty years of whose life are represented only by half a dozen sentences (1774 ed., iv. 255).

[2] *Aquelle tão pouco venturoso como sciente & valeroso Antonio Galvão* (João Pinto Ribeyro, *Preferencia das Letras ás Armas*, 1645). In his youth in India he won the regard of that keen judge of men, Afonso de Albuquerque, who could see in him nothing to find fault with except his excessive generosity.

[3] *Tratado. Prologo* [3 ff.]. *Em este tractado con noue ou dez liuros das cousas de Maluco & da India que me o Cardeal mandou dar a Damiam de Goes.*

which the grateful natives besought him to accept. He arrived penniless in Portugal and penniless died seventeen years later in the Lisbon hospital.

Besides the general histories many briefer records of separate regions or events were written, and these are often of great value as the accounts of men who had seen and taken part in what they describe.

LOPO DE SOUSA COUTINHO (?1515–77), father of Frei Luis de Sousa and one of the captains in the heroic siege of Diu (1538)—he is said to have died by accidentally running himself through with his sword when dismounting from his horse—wrote a striking account of the siege, especially of its last incidents, in his *Livro Primeiro do Cerco de Diu* (1556). The siege of Mazagam (1562) was similarly described in clear, vigorous prose by AGOSTINHO GAVY DE MENDONÇA: *Historia do famoso cerco que o Xarife pos á fortaleza de Mazagam* (1607). JORGE DE LEMOS, of Goa, wrote a careful *Historia dos Cercos . . . de Malaca* (1585), and ANTONIO CASTILHO, the distinguished son of the celebrated architect João, published a *Commentario do Cerco de Goa e Chaul no anno MDLXX* (1572). Events in the Moluccas were briefly recorded in an *Informaçam das cousas de Maluco* (1569) by GABRIEL DE RABELLO, who went out as factor of Tidore in 1566.

The anonymous gentleman of Elvas who wrote the *Relaçam verdadeira* (1557) of Soto's discovery of Florida was a keen observer and related what he saw in direct language. His publisher, André de Burgos, in a short preface washes his hands of the style as insufficiently polished (*limado*).

The deeds of D. Cristovam da Gama, his conquest of a hundred leagues of territory in Ethiopia, his defeat, torture, and beheadal, are recounted with the vivid details of an eyewitness by MIGUEL DE CASTANHOSO, of Santarem, who accompanied him on his fatal expedition. This *Historia* (1564) was published by João da Barreira, who dedicated it to D. Cristovam's nephew, D. Francisco de Portugal.

MANUEL DE ABREU MOUSINHO wrote in Spanish a brief account of the conquest of Pegu by Salvador Ribeiro de Sousa, of which a Portuguese version appeared in the 1711 edition of Mendez Pinto's travels: *Breve discurso em que se contem a conquista do reyno de Pegu,* nearly a century after the original edition, *Breve Discvrso en qve se cventa,* &c. (1617). The *Jornada do Maranhão feita por Jeronymo de Albuquerque em 1614* is ascribed to DIOGO DE CAMPOS MORENO, who took part in that *conquista*. It was published in the *Collecção de Noticias para a Historia e Geographia das Nações Ultramarinas*.[1] The second volume of this collection contains several re-translations of *Navegações* (by Thomé Lopez and anonymous Portuguese pilots) surviving in Italian in Ramusio. It would require a separate volume to give an account of all the sixteenth- and seventeenth-century narratives of newly conquered countries written in Portuguese and often immediately translated into many European languages, e. g. the *Novo Descobrimento do Grão Cathayo* (1626) by the Jesuit ANTONIO DE ANDRADE (*c.* 1580–1634), or the *Relaçam* of the Jesuit ALVARO SEMMEDO (1585?–1658) written in Portuguese but published in the Spanish translation of Faria e Sousa: *Imperio de la China* (1642). However unliterary, they are often so vividly written as to be literature in the best sense.

PEDRO DE MAGALHÃES DE GANDAVO, of Braga, whose *Regras* (1574) ran into three editions before the end of the century, described Brazil and its discovery in two short works: *Historia da prouincia Sãcta Cruz* (1576) and *Tratado da terra do Brazil* first published in 1826 in the *Collecção de Noticias*. This collection also prints works of the following century, such as the *Fatalidade historica da Ilha de Ceilão*[2] by Captain JOÃO RIBEIRO, who had served the king as a soldier for eighteen years in the *preciosa ilha de Ceilão*. His manuscript, written in 1685, was translated and published in French (1701) 135 years before it was printed in Portuguese. Gandavo's *Historia* (48 ff.), his first work (*premicias*), was introduced by *tercetos* and a sonnet of Luis de Camões, who speaks of his *claro estilo*, and *engenho curioso*. The author himself in a prefatory letter says that he writes as an eyewitness, content with a 'plain and easy style' without seeking *epithetos exquisitos*.

The Jesuit BALTHASAR TELLEZ[3] (1595–1675) won considerable fame as an historian and prose-writer in his *Cronica da Com-*

---

[1] Vol. i, No. 4.   [2] Vol. v, No. 1 (1836).
[3] The name would seem to have been really Tillison, i.e. son of John Tilly, who married a granddaughter of Moraes, the author of *Palmeirim*.

panhia de Iesus (2 pts., 1645, 1647) in which he forswears what he calls the artifices and liberties of ordinary *seiscentista* prose. He also edited the work of the Jesuit missionary MANUEL DE ALMEIDA (1580-1646), recasting it in an abbreviated form : *Historia Geral da Ethiopia a Alta ov Preste Ioam* (1660), for which Tellez' friend, Mello, provided a prefatory letter. Almeida, born at Viseu, had gone to India in 1601 and in 1622 was sent to Ethiopia, where he became the head of the mission. He died at Goa after a life of much hard work and various adventure. In writing his history of Ethiopia he made use of the *Historia da Ethiopia* of an earlier (1603-19) head of the mission, PEDRO PAEZ (1564-1622), who had started for Ethiopia in 1595 but was captured by the Turks and only ransomed in 1602. Although a Spaniard by birth (born at Olmeda), Paez wrote in Portuguese. A third Jesuit missionary, MANUEL BARRADAS, born in 1572 at Monforte, who went to India in 1612, was also a prisoner of the Turks for over a year at Aden. In 1624 he went to *Ethiope, terre maldite*, and remained there some ten years. Of his three treatises the most important is that entitled *Do Reyno de Tygrê e seus mandos em Ethiopia*. The modern editor of these works, P. Camillo Beccari, considers that their authors' simple style caused their treatises to be regarded rather as the material of history than in themselves history,[1] but their value for us is in this very simplicity and in the detailed observation which bring the country and its inhabitants clearly before us. Scarcely less important, as material for history and as human documents, are the *Cartas* from Jesuits in China and Japan, especially the collection of 82 letters (Coimbra, 1570), and that of 206 letters (Evora, 1598). The Jesuit FERNAM CARDIM at about the same time rendered a like service to Brazil in his *Narrativa epistolar*, edited in 1847 by F. A. de Varnhagen. A more important work on Brazil was that of GABRIEL SOAREZ DE SOUSA (*c.* 1540-92)—

---

[1] He speaks of their *lingua alquanto negletta e lo stile molto semplice, naturale e piano, la qual cosa deveva apparire un' anomalia a confronto della lingua purgata con cui si scriveva allora in Portogallo* (*Contenuto della storia del Patriarca Alfonso Mendez*, p. 115). This work was written in Latin in 1651 by AFONSO MENDEZ (1579-1656), born at Moura, who became Patriarch of Ethiopia in 1623. This splendid edition (*Rerum Aethiopicarum Scriptores*) also contains three volumes of *Relationes et Epistolae Variorum* (Romae, 1910-12).

the *Tratado descriptivo do Brasil em 1587*, which its modern editor, F. A. de Varnhagen, described in a moment of enthusiasm as 'the most admirable of all the works of the Portuguese *quinhentistas*'. Two other works of interest, half history, half travels, are the *Jornada do Arcebispo de Goa Dom Frey Aleixo de Meneses* (1606) by ANTONIO DE GOUVEA, Bishop of Cyrene (*c.* 1565–1628), in three parts, describing the archbishop's life and visits in his diocese; and the *Discvrso da Iornada de D. Gonçalo Covtinho á villa de Mazagam e sev governo nella* (1629). The writer—the admirer of Camões and alleged author of the 1614 life of Sá de Miranda—who, as he says, had grown white in the council-chamber, lived on till 1634. He here relates with much directness his voyage and four years' Governorship (1623–7).

The *Saudades da Terra* (1873) of GASPAR FRUCTUOSO (1522–91), who was born at S. Miguel in the Azores, was written in 1590 and waited three centuries in manuscript for an editor. Both its title and the 'preamble', in which Truth says that she will write of nothing but sadness, are misleading, since the book is an account—in good, straightforward style after the manner of Castanheda and other historians—of the discovery and subsequent conditions of various islands, especially of Madeira and the lives of its Governors. ANTONIO CORDEIRO (1641–1722), Jesuit, of Angra, wrote at the age of seventy-six an uncritical but interesting work entitled *Historia Insulana das Ilhas a Portugal sujeitas no Oceano Occidental* (1717), based partly on Fructuoso's manuscript.

It was only as it were by an afterthought that the historians turned to consider the history of Portugal as apart from separate chronicles of the kings or episodes of Eastern conquest. The historical scheme of João de Barros was too vast to be executed by one man and the European part was never written. André de Resende likewise failed to carry out his project of a history of Portugal. PEDRO DE MARIZ (*c.* 1550–1615), son of the Coimbra printer, Antonio, in the last four of his *Dialogos de Varia Historia* (1594) between a Portuguese and an Italian, embraces the whole history of Portugal, but these dialogues, although industriously written in good plain style, were eclipsed by the appearance three years later of the first part of the *Monarchia Lusitana*

(1597). Its author, a young Cistercian monk of Alcobaça, FREI BERNARDO DE BRITO (1569–1617), in the world Balthasar de Brito de Andrade, at once became known as one of the best writers of his time, and he is still reckoned among the masters of Portuguese prose. His style, clear, restrained, copious, proved that the mantle of Barros had fallen upon worthy shoulders. But, despite his rich vein of humanity, as a historian he is far inferior to Barros and even more uncritical than Mariz. The value of evidence seems to have weighed with him little when it was a question of exalting his language, literature, religion, or country, and he used and incorporated documents entirely worthless. Whether he deliberately manufactured spurious documents to serve his purposes cannot be known, but he seems at least to have quoted authorities which had never existed.[1]

In a word he failed to make good use of the incomparable material which the library of Alcobaça afforded. His was a misdirected erudition, and we would willingly exchange the knowledge of where Adam lies buried, or on what day the world began, or how Gorgoris, King of Lusitania, who died 1227 years after the Flood, invented honey, for accurate details of more recent Portuguese history. Yet he had the diligence and enthusiasm of the true historian and made use, sometimes a skilful use,[2] of coins and inscriptions. His brief *Geographia antiga da Lusytania* also appeared in 1597, and in the same year the Cistercian Order appointed him its chronicler. Thus he interrupted his main work—the second part of the *Monarchia Lusitana* was only published in 1609—in order to write the *Primeira Parte da Cronica de Cister* (1602).[3] This, in many ways his best work, runs to nearly a thousand pages, and treats of the saints of the Order and especially of the life of the charming St. Bernard,

[1] Nicolás Antonio dwells more than once on the invisibility of Brito's authorities (*Bib. Vet.* i. 65, 453; ii. 374): *Nos de invisis hactenus censere abstinemus.* Antonio Brandão, Brito's successor, he says, *nullum horum vidit librorum quos Brittus olim historiae suae Atlantes iactaverat ; nihil autem horum librorum (quod mirum si ibi asservabantur) vidit.* Soares (*Theatrum*) remarks epigrammatically : *fama est eloquentiam minus desiderari quam fidem.*

[2] From a comparison of inscriptions he notes the similarity between the Etruscan and 'our ancient' (Iberian?) letters. The Iberians may have originally gone East from Tuscany.

[3] His *Elogios dos Reis de Portugal* appeared in 1603.

with contemporary events in Portugal.[1] It was to be followed by two other parts, but Brito's early death at his native Almeida on his way back to Alcobaça from Spain, a year after he had been appointed *Cronista Môr* (1616), left his work unfinished. He is remembered as a fine stylist, a poet who wrote history rather than as a great historian. Mariana, the Latin original of whose *Historia de España* (1592) he knew and quoted, is by comparison almost a scientific writer—at least he is not, like Brito, pseudo-scientific.

The two parts of the *Monarchia Lusitana* written by Brito ended with the beginning of the Portuguese monarchy. Parts 3 and 4, by FREI ANTONIO BRANDÃO (1584–1637), to whose sincerity and skill Herculano paid tribute, appeared in 1632 and carried it down to the year 1279. Brandão had spent nearly ten years collecting and sifting documentary evidence for his work and is a far better historian than Brito, although in style he is not his equal. His nephew FREI FRANCISCO BRANDÃO (1601–80), *vir modestus, diligens et eruditus*, succeeded Frei Antonio as *Cronista Môr* and wrote Parts 5 and 6 (1650), describing the reign of King Dinis. The style was less well maintained in Part 7 (1633) by FREI RAPHAEL DE JESUS (1614–93). Part 8 (1727), the last to be published, was added by FREI MANUEL DOS SANTOS (1672–1740) over a century after the publication of the first Part, but only brought the history to the battle of Aljubarrota (1385). Santos' Part 7 as well as Parts 9 and 10 remained in manuscript. His prose is worthy of a work which is a monument of the language, not of the history of Portugal. Perhaps the truest epitaph of this history as a whole—after allowance has been made for Brito's style and the excellent work of Antonio Brandão—is a severe sentence from the preface of the author of Part 7: 'There are histories whose tomes are tombs.'

It could hardly, perhaps, be expected that the historians of the reigns of King Manuel and King João III should pass over events in the East as already fully related, and in Damião de

[1] ff. 248 v.–249 v. give a very curious description of Ireland: *tam remota de nossa conversação e metida debaixo do Polo Arctico*. Brito had not inherited Barros' knowledge of geography and confuses Ireland with Iceland, but is far richer in fables, as these pages delightfully prove.

Goes' *Cronica do Felicissimo Rey Dom Emanvel* and Francisco de Andrade's *Cronica de Dom João III* (1613), although they lose much by compression, they still occupy a disproportionate space. Andrade wrote most correct prose, even in his poems, and the style of his history is excellent, but neither of these works gives any adequate account of the internal history of Portugal, any more than does that of Frei Luis de Sousa on João III's reign, in which there should have been more scope for originality. The same prominence is given to India in the history of JERONIMO OSORIO (1506–80), Bishop of Silves, *De Rebvs Emmanvelis Regis Lvsitaniae* (1571), written in Latin in order to spread the knowledge of these events *per omnes reipublicae Christianae regiones*.[1] Osorio, whose father, like Lopez de Castanheda's, had been a judge (*ouvidor*) in India, was born at Lisbon, but studied abroad, at Salamanca, Paris, and Bologna. After occupying the Chair of Scripture at Coimbra for a brief space, he went to Lisbon and became secretary to the Infante Luis. In 1560 he was made Archdeacon of Evora and four years later Bishop of Silves. (The see was removed to Faro three years before his death and his title is sometimes given as Bishop of Algarve.) A few remarkable letters in Portuguese, in one of which (1567) he attempted to convert Queen Elizabeth, show that he was skilled in the use of his native tongue; his countrymen delighted to call him the Portuguese Cicero. According to Sousa de Macedo ' many people came from England, Germany and other parts with the sole object of seeing him '.[2] In England certainly his book was highly prized, and both Dryden and Pope praised Gibbs' translation, although Francis Bacon noted the diffuseness of Osorio's style : *luxurians et diluta*, certainly not a just verdict on the style as a whole ; we have but to think of the concise sketches of Albuquerque (*De Rebus*, p. 380) and King Manuel (p. 478). Osorio acknowledged his ample debt to the chronicle of Goes, which he describes as written ' with incredible felicity '. FREI BERNARDO DA CRUZ, who accompanied King Sebastian to Africa in 1578 as chaplain, in his *Cronica de El Rei D. Sebastião* wrote the history of his life and reign and happily

---

[1] To Spanish readers they were presented later by Faria e Sousa in his *Asia*.
[2] *Flores de España* (1631), f. 248. Arias Montano refers to him as a close friend (*Doc. inéd.* t. xli. p. 386).

describes him as ' a young king without experience or fear '. The *Cronica do Cardeal Rei D. Henrique* (1840) completed the history of the house of Avis. It chronicles in fifty-four diminutive chapters the eighteen months' reign of the *pouco mimoso e severo* Cardinal King Henry. It was written in 1586,[1] and, although anonymous, is ascribed with some probability to the Jesuit Padre ALVARO LOBO (1551–1608).

The *Jornada de Africa* (1607) by JERONIMO DE MENDOÇA, of Oporto, is divided into three parts, describing the expedition and the battle of Alcacer Kebir, the ransoms and escapes of the captives, and the death of Christian martyrs in Africa. Its object was to refute certain statements in Conestaggio's recent work *Dell' unione del regno di Portogallo alla corona di Castiglia*, but Mendoça had fought at Alcacer Kebir and had been taken prisoner; he thus writes as an eyewitness, and his excellent style and power of description give more than a controversial value and interest to his book and make it matter for regret that this short history was apparently his only work.

MIGUEL DE MOURA (1538–1600), secretary to five kings and one of the three Governors of Portugal in 1593, set an example too rarely followed by those who have played an important part in Portuguese history by composing a brief autobiography: *Vida de Miguel de Moura*. It was written on the eve of St. Peter's Day, 1594, except a few pages which were added in the year before the author's death. Incidentally it has the distinction of containing one of the longest sentences ever written (114 lines— 1840 ed., pp. 126–9).

The painstaking and talented DUARTE NUNEZ DE LEAM (*c*. 1530–1608), born at Evora, son of the Professor of Medicine João Nunez, besides genealogical and legal works, *Leis extravagantes* (1560, 1569), wrote two valuable treatises on the Portuguese language and an interesting *Descripção do Reino de Portugal* (1610), which he finished in 1599. He also found time to spare from his duties as a magistrate to recast the chronicles of the Kings of Portugal. The *Cronicas dos Reis de Portugal* (1600) contain those from Count Henry to King Fernando, and the *Cronicas del Rey Dom Ioam de gloriosa memoria* those of Kings

See *Cronica*, p. 46.

João I, Duarte, and Afonso V. Shorn of the individuality of the early chroniclers, they yet retain much of interest, and Nunez de Leam would be accorded a higher place as historian were it not for our knowledge of the inestimable value of the originals which he edited and 'improved'. Two generations earlier Cristovam Rodriguez Azinheiro (or Acenheiro), born in 1474 (he tells us that he was sixty-one in May 1535), had treated the early chronicles in the same way, but only succeeded in retaining all that was jejune without preserving their picturesqueness in his *Cronicas dos Senhores Reis de Portugal*.[1]

More interesting personally than as historian, the humanist DAMIÃO DE GOES (1502–74[2]) was one of the most accomplished men of his time,[3] and, thanks partly to his trial before the Inquisition, partly to the not unpleasant egotism with which he chronicled autobiographical details, not only in his *Genealogia*[4] but in many of his other works, we know more of his life than we know of most contemporary writers. Traveller and diplomatist, scholar, singer, musician, he was a man of many friends during his lifetime, and the tragic circumstances of his last years have won him fresh sympathizers after his death. Born at Alenquer and brought up at the Court of King Manuel, he became page to the king in 1518, and five years later was appointed secretary at the Portuguese Factory at Antwerp. In 1529 he was sent on a diplomatic mission to Poland, and in this and the following years, on similar missions or for his own pleasure, ' saw and conversed with all the kings, princes, nobles and peoples of Christen-

---

[1] Ten chronicles from Afonso I to João III. He says (1824 ed., p. 12): *Estam em este presente vollume recopiladas, sumadas, abreviadas, todas as lembranças dos Reys de Portugal das caroniquas velhas e novas sem mudar sustancia da verdade.*

[2] *Dise q̃ hee de jdade de setenta anos, hos faz ē este feu^{ro} q̃ vē* (Examination before the Inquisition, April 19, 1571). The name appears as Goes, Gooes, Goiz, Guoes, Guoez, Guoiz, Goyos. Goes is a small village some twenty miles north-east of Coimbra. The name also occurs in the Basses-Pyrénées. See P. A. de Azevedo, *Alguns nomes do departamento dos Baixos Pirineos que teem correspondencia em Portugal* (*Boletim da Ac. das Sciencias de Lisboa*, viii (1915), pp. 280–1). It may be one more trace of the former occupation of the whole Peninsula by the Iberians (= high, on the height, as in Goyetche, &c.).

[3] See Marqués de Montebello, *Vida de Manoel Machado de Azevedo* (1660), p. 3, ap. J. de Vasconcellos, *Os Musicos Portugueses*, i. 268.

[4] ff. 269 v.–71. The original manuscript disappeared, but a copy (that of the Marqueses de Castello Rodrigo) is in the Biblioteca Nacional at Lisbon.

dom '.[1] He made the acquaintance of Montaigne's *aubergistes allemands*, '*glorieux, colères et ivrognes*', turned aside to visit Luther and Melanchthon at Wittenberg,[2] and was for several months the guest of Erasmus at Freiburg. In Italy he lived with Cardinal Sadoletto at Padua (1534-8) and met Cardinal Bembo and other celebrated men of the day. At Louvain, too, *mihi intime carum et iucundum*, as throughout Europe, he had many devoted friends. A senator of Antwerp welcomed him in Latin verse on his return from his Scythian travels,[3] Luis Vives addressed affectionate letters to *mi Damiane*, Albrecht Dürer painted his portrait, Glareanus in his *Dodecachordon* included music of his composition.[4]

In 1542 he was on his way to Holland with his Flemish wife when he heard that Louvain was threatened by a French force commanded by Longueval and *meus ille in Academiam Louvaniensem fatalis amor* took him back to share its perils. He played a principal part in the defence, and finally remained a prisoner in the enemy's hands, *quasi piacularis hostia*, as he says.[5] His imprisonment in France lasted nine months, and after paying a ransom of 6,000 ducats he went back to Louvain. The Emperor Charles V rewarded him for his services with a splendid coat of arms. In 1545, after twenty-one years of European travel, he returned with his wife and children[6] to Portugal, and three years later was entrusted with Fernam Lopez' old post, the

[1] Antonio Galvam, *Tratado*, f. 59 v. He visited the Courts of Charles V, François I, Henry VIII, and Pope Paul III. Nicolás Antonio says of him (*Bib. Nova*): *morum quippe suavitate atque elegantia, ergaque doctos liberalitate insinuabat se in cuiusque animum qui Musarum commercio frueretur, facile atque alte.*

[2] He arrived on Palm Sunday, 1531, and learning that Luther was preaching at once left the inn to hear him, but could only understand the Latin quotations. Next day he had dinner (*jantar*) with Luther and Melanchthon and afterwards returned to Luther's house, where the latter's wife regaled them with a dessert of nuts and apples. Thence he went to Melanchthon's house and found his wife spinning, shabbily dressed.

[3] Venisti nimium usque et usque et usque
Expectate tuis.

[4] Lib. III, pp. 264, 265: *Aliud Aeolij Modi exemplū authore D. Damiano à Goes Lusitano.*

[5] He had gone with others to negotiate terms and, when barely half an hour was allowed to refer the terms to the Senate, remained in the enemy's camp in order to create a delay by conversing with Longueval. Meanwhile relief had been received and the Senate refused the terms.

[6] In his trial he says that three of them became monks: *meteo tres filhos frades*.

Keepership of the Archives. He lived in the Paços d'Alcaçova with a certain magnificence, keeping open house for all foreigners, one of whom records that already in 1565 *il se faict fort vieulx*. Six years later, on April 4, 1571, he was arrested by the Inquisition and spent twenty months in prison.

It was, perhaps, inevitable that he should have incurred suspicion, nor is it necessary to explain his trial by the enmity of certain persons at Court due to passages in his works. His life had been out of keeping with the *gravedades de Hespanha*, and the charges against him were numerous and varied. He had eaten and drunken with heretics, he had read strange books, the sound of songs not understanded of the people and organ music had issued from his house at Lisbon, he had omitted to observe fasts, he had called the Pope a tyrant, he set no store by papal indulgences or auricular confession. Even the testimony of his grand-niece is recorded, to the effect that her mother had said of Goes, her husband's uncle, that he had no more belief in God than in a stone wall (she seems to have had Berkeleian tendencies). As usual it is less the proceedings of the Inquisition than the bad faith of the witnesses that arouse disgust. The poet Andrade Caminha, who apparently came forward of his own accord—we are not told that he was *chamado*—admitted that certain words of Goes which he now denounced had not seemed so serious to him before he knew that Goes was in the prison of the Inquisition. Goes had already been denounced to the Inquisition in 1545 and 1550, and his book *Fides, Religio Moresque Aethiopum* (Lovanii, 1540) had been condemned in Portugal in 1541. He was examined frequently in 1571 and 1572, was left for three months without news of his family, and complained of being old, weak, and ill, and that his body had become covered with a kind of leprosy (July 14, 1572). His sentence (October 16, 1572) pronounced him to have incurred, as a Lutheran heretic, excommunication, confiscation of all his property, and the life-long confinement of his person. He was transferred to the famous monastery of Batalha in December, but his death (January 30, 1574) occurred in his own house. His return and his death probably explain one another. He was growing very old in 1565 and we must suppose that his recent experiences had not made him younger. His last request

—to die among his family—was apparently granted, and the further explanations (that he fell forward into the fire, that he died of an apoplexy, was killed by order of the Inquisition, was beaten to death by the lackeys of the Conde da Castanheira, or murdered and robbed by his own servants) are superfluous. His works consist of several brief Latin treatises crowded with interesting facts (especially his *Hispania*); and in Portuguese the *Cronica do Principe Dom Ioam* (1567) and *Cronica do Felicissimo Rey Dom Emanvel*, 4 pt. (1566, 1567). He also found time to translate Cicero's *De Senectute* : *Livro . . . da Velhice*, (Veneza, 1534). He had not the imagination of an historian, and unless events have passed before his eyes, or happen to interest him personally, he can be bald and meagre as an annalist. But in any matter which touches him closely, as the expulsion and the cruel treatment of the Jews, or the massacre of new Christians, or the account of Ethiopia, he broadens out into moving and detailed description. The result is that this long Chronicle of King Manuel is a number of excellent separate treatises rather than a history with unity and a sense of proportion. It is the work of a scholar who likes to describe directly, from his own experience. The *Cronica do Principe* was written some months before that of King Manuel. The latter was a difficult undertaking,[1] for many persons concerned were still alive, and subjects such as the expulsion of the Jews needed delicate handling. For thirty-one years it had hung fire in the hands of previous chroniclers when in 1558 Cardinal Henrique entrusted it to Damião de Goes. After eight years the four parts were ready for press,[2] but the difficulties were not yet over, for certain chapters met with strong disapproval at Court[3] and had to be altered, so that two editions of the first part appeared in 1566 (the first being apparently submitted as a proof and not for sale), but the publication of the work as a whole was not completed before 1567.

---

[1] Cf. *Prologo*: *em que muitos, como em cousa desesperada, se nam atreveram poer a mão.* One of these 'many' was Goes' rival, the eloquent Bishop Antonio Pinheiro.

[2] The fourth part was approved on January 2, 1566.

[3] For the grounds of this disapproval see *Critica contemporanea á Chronica de D. Manuel*, 1914, ed. Edgar Prestage from a manuscript in the British Museum. Dr. Joaquim de Vasconcellos and Mr. G. J. C. Henriques have dealt very ably with many interesting points of Goes' life and works.

Scarcely less celebrated than Goes, the archaeologist LUCIO ANDRÉ DE RESENDE (1493 ?–1573),[1] friend of Goes, Clenardus, and Erasmus, left the Dominican convent of Bemfica, in which he was a novice, in order to study abroad, at Salamanca, Paris, and Louvain. 'Tall, with very large eyes, curling hair, rather dark complexion but of a cheerful, open countenance', living in his house (*as casas de Resende*) at Evora among his books and coins, statues and inscriptions—his small garden hedged with *marmores antigos* as, according to Brito, too often were peasants' vineyards—he exercised a considerable influence on the writers of his time [2] and was held in high esteem by the Emperor Charles V and by King João III. The principal of his own works were written in Latin, but besides his *De Antiquitatibus Lusitaniae* (1593), which was edited by Mendez de Vasconcellos with the addition of a fifth book from notes left by the author, he composed in Portuguese a 'brief but learned' *Historia da Antiguidade da Cidade de Evora* (1553). In his *Vida do Infante Dom Duarte* (1789)[3] he did not write the 'very copious history' which Paiva de Andrade [4] said the subject required. He did better, for this sketch of a few pages is a little masterpiece in which the vignettes, for instance, of the boatman and his figs, or the meal in the mill, must ever retain their vividness and charm. Resende had been the prince's tutor and writes of what he saw; he shows that he could decipher a person's character as keenly as a Latin inscription. Resende's legitimate successor in archaeology, MANUEL SEVERIM DE FARIA (1583–1655), scarcely belongs to the sixteenth century although he wrote verses in 1598 and 1599. He succeeded his uncle as Canon (1608) and Precentor (1609) of Evora Cathedral and resigned in favour of his nephew Manuel de Faria Severim as Canon in 1633 and Precentor in 1642. Living in ancient

---

[1] His friend Diogo Mendez de Vasconcellos (1523–99), Canon of Evora, says that he died in 1575 aet. 80 (so the *Theatrum*: *obiit octogenarius A.C.* 1575). Probably the 5 is an error or misprint for 3, and the 80 correct.

[2] Luis de Sousa (*Hist. S. Dom.*, Pt. I, Bk. i, cap. 2) praises his *juizo e curiosidade de bom antiquario*, and there are many similar passages in other writers. Resende furnished Barros, as Severim de Faria later furnished Brito, with materials and advice.

[3] In a similar though more elaborate work (88 ff.) Frei Nicolau Diaz (†1596) told the life and death of Princess Joana (†May 1490): *Vida da Serenissima Princesa Dona Joana, Filha del Rey Dom Afonso o Quinto de Portugal* (1585).

[4] *Casamento Perfeyto*, 2ª ed. (1726), p. 61.

Evora when the memory of Resende was still fresh, this antiquary of the pale face and blue eyes, 'store-house of all the treasures of the past',[1] with his medals and statues and choice library of rare books, soon rivalled Resende's fame. His most important works are *Discursos varios politicos* (1624) containing four essays and the lives of Barros, Camões, and Couto, and *Noticias de Portugal* (1655).

A less attractive personality is that of MANUEL DE FARIA E SOUSA (1590–1649), born near Pombeiro (Minho), a most accomplished, industrious, but untrustworthy author who wrote mainly in Spanish. His *Epitome de las Historias Portuguesas* was published in 1628 at Madrid, where he spent the greater part of his life, and where he died. He seems to have retained a real affection for his native country, but he was not a man of independent character and bestowed his flatteries as his interest required. After the Restoration of 1640 he stayed on at the Spanish Court, and there appears to be some doubt whether it was João IV, his nominal master, or Philip IV of Spain that he served best. His long historical works, *Europa Portuguesa*, *Asia Portuguesa*, *Africa Portuguesa*, appeared posthumously, between 1666 and 1681. He is most pleasant when he is not trying to 'make' history but is simply describing, as in his account of the various provinces of Portugal.[2] In his own not over-modest verdict in Part 4 of the same volume, *De las primazias deste Reyno*, he was *el primero que supo historiar con más acierto*. Faria e Sousa was enthusiastic but unscrupulous and he has been severely handled by the critics. With posterity he has fallen between two stools, since the Spanish are only moderately interested in his subject, Portugal, and the Portuguese consider him to belong to Spanish literature.

[1] *Monarchia Lusitana*, Pt. V, Bk. xvii, cap. 5. Bernardo de Brito also praises him, and Frei Antonio Brandão acknowledges his debt to him. Faria e Sousa says that he received from him *cantidad de papeles*.

[2] *Europa Portuguesa*, vol. iii, pt. 3. Portugal, he says, is a perpetual Spring, and he speaks of the women who earn their living by selling roses and other flowers in Lisbon, of the almonds of Algarve, the excellent honey, &c., &c. Vol. i covers the period from the Flood to the foundation of Portugal; vol. ii goes down to 1557; vol. iii to Philip II of Spain.

§ 6
Quinhentista Prose

HAD latinization and the Renaissance come to Portugal in a quiet age it is not pleasant to think what havoc they might have wrought on Portuguese prose in the unreal atmosphere of the study. Fortunately they found Portugal in turmoil. Stirring incidents and adventures were continually occurring which needed no heightening of rhetoric or Latin pomp of polysyllables. A scientific spirit of accuracy was abroad, and the missionaries and adventurers, travellers, mariners, merchants, officials, and soldiers who recorded their experiences wrote as men of action, with life and directness.

Few stories are more intense and affecting than those told by the Portuguese survivors of shipwreck in the sixteenth and seventeenth centuries. Twelve of these appeared in the original collection edited by BERNARDO GOMES DE BRITO (born in 1688) : *Historia Tragico-Maritima* (2 vols., 1735, 6).[1] The earliest and most celebrated is the *Relaçam da mui notavel perda do galeão grande S. João* [June 24, 1552], an anonymous narrative based on the account of a survivor, Alvaro Fernandez, probably the ship's mate, which tells of the death of D. Lianor de Sepulveda and her husband with a simple pathos and dramatic power unattained by the many poets who later treated the same theme. But the accounts of the wreck of the *S. Bento* (1554), the *Conceição* (1555), the *S. Paulo* (1561), of D. Jorge de Albuquerque (1565),

[1] For a full list see Innocencio da Silva, *Dicc. Bibliog.* i. 377, and *Grundriss*, p. 339. Five volumes were announced by Barbosa Machado as ready for press. The modern editors, besides eleven wrecks of the sixteenth, eight of the seventeenth, and two of the eighteenth, have included three of the nineteenth century. Some of the original chap-books survive, with a fine woodcut of a tossing galleon on the title-page : *Historia da mui notavel perda do galeam grande S. Joam* (1554 ?) ; *Relaçam do lastimozo navfragio da nao Conceiçam chamada Algaravia a Nova* (1555) ; *Naufragio da nao Santo Alberto* (1597) ; *Memoravel relaçam da perda da nao Conceiçam* (1627). The *Relaçam da viagem do galeão São Lovrenço e sua perdição* (1651) is by the Jesuit Antonio Francisco Cardim (1596–1659) ; the *Relaçam sumaria da viagem que fez Fernão d'Alvarez Cabral*, by Manuel Mesquita Perestrello, is an account of the wreck of the fine ship *S. Bento*, which had taken Camões to India.

and others, are scarcely less moving. The ships, of 1,000 tons, as the *Aguia*, 'the largest vessel that had hitherto sailed to India' (1558), and under, often with rotten rudder, or the whole ship rotten, *sepulturas dos homens*, with few boats, careless and ignorant pilots, badly careened, overloaded, overcrowded, ill-supplied with worm-eaten biscuit, 'poisonous' wine, and insufficient water, seemed to invite destruction. Between 1582 and 1602 alone thirty-eight ships were lost. The sea was not the only enemy: corsairs off the coast of Portugal, French, Dutch, and English, Lutheran heretics who threw overboard beads and missals, or a Turkish fleet 'in sight of Ericeira', exacted their toll when all other dangers had been successfully overcome. The story is told immediately after the event, sometimes almost in the form of a diary or log, or years later, by survivors or based on the account of survivors, and it varies according as the narrator is the captain of the ship, a landsman with a dislike of sailors, a plain soldier, a Jesuit priest, a Franciscan monk, a distinguished Lisbon chemist (Henrique Diaz in i. 6), or a famous historian (ii. 3 by Diogo do Couto,[1] ii. 4 by João Baptista Lavanha [2]). All or most of their accounts are masterpieces of vivid phraseology. We follow as in a novel their adventures as the sea 'breaks into flower—*quebrando em frol*', as they are stranded on a desert island, boarded in sight of home, entrapped by savages, devoured by wild beasts, tottering, *arrimados em paos*, exhausted by thirst and hunger, or prostrated by heat, in comparison with which the *calmas* of Alentejo 'are but as Norwegian cold': toils and perils borne with heroic courage, told with the simplicity of heroes, without *adorno de palavras nem linguagem floreada*.

Many books of travel were the natural consequence of the discovery of India. The historian João de Barros' passion for knowledge, especially geographical knowledge, was the first cause[3] of the learned and instructive *Chorographia* (1561) of his nephew

[1] In this *Relaçam do naufragio da nao S. Thomé*, written in 1611, twenty-two years after the event, he refers several times to his *Decadas*.
[2] *Naufragio da nao S. Alberto* (1593). It is a summary of a *largo cartapacio* of the pilot.
[3] *pedirme meu tio Ioam de Barros que lhe screuesse muito particularmente todos os lugares deste meu caminho.*

Gaspar Barreiros (†1574), a description of the places through which he passed on his way to Rome in 1545 to thank the Pope on behalf of the Infante Henrique, *Cardinalem amplissimum*, for his cardinal's hat. But this work (edited by his brother, Lopo Barreiros) was an exception. Most of the travel books were concerned with the far East.

The *Livro em que da relação do que viu e ouviu no Oriente* (1516) by DUARTE BARBOSA of Lisbon, brother-in-law of Fernam de Magalhães, exists in a Portuguese manuscript in the Public Library of Oporto, but was first published in Portuguese in 1821 as a translation from the Italian *Libro di Odoardo Barbosa Portoghese*, itself a translation from a copy at Seville. The author had spent the greater part of his youth in India, and his work contains vivid and accurate notes on Eastern lands and cities, especially Malabar.

One of the causes that most moved Portugal to curiosity and acted as an incentive to discovery were the vague rumours of the existence of a mighty Christian prince, the half-mythical Prester John, Negus of Abyssinia. The priest FRANCISCO ALVAREZ (*c.* 1470?–*c.* 1540) set out with Duarte Galvam, first Portuguese Ambassador to Abyssinia, in 1515, but Galvam's death delayed the mission, and it was not till 1520 that Alvarez and the new ambassador, D. Rodrigo de Lima, reached the Court of Prester John. They remained for six years in the country, and during this time Alvarez recorded in straightforward notes every detail of the country and its inhabitants with minuteness and accuracy. He considered himself old [1] in 1520; he was certainly active: he shoots hares and pheasants, washes unsuccessfully for gold, looks after his slaves, his nine mules, his fourteen cows, and organizes a procession against locusts. On their return, in Alvarez' friend Antonio Galvam's ship, to Lisbon, bringing 'the length of Prester John's foot', he was eagerly questioned by king, prelates, and courtiers—the whole Court trooped out along the road from Coimbra to meet them—and when he published his fascinating diary of travel, *Verdadeira Informaçam das terras do Preste Joam* (1540), it was soon translated into almost every language of

[1] *Verd. Inf.*, p. 110: *nam era pera velhos.*

Europe.[1] FREI GASPAR DA CRUZ of Evora, missionary in China, returned to Portugal in 1569, and in the same year began his *Tractado em que se cõtam muito por estêso as cousas da China* (1570). He calls it a *singella narraçam*, but it contains valuable information about China, nor did the author neglect his style. The Dominican FREI JOÃO DOS SANTOS (*c*. 1550 – *c*. 1625 ?)[2] was born at Evora about the middle of the sixteenth century, and went out to East Africa and India as a missionary in 1586. He returned to Lisbon in August 1600 and nine years later published his *Ethiopia Oriental* (1609), an attractive, curious account, written in a clear and easy style, of the natives, their land and customs. It is to be feared that some of the settlers sadly abused his credulity, as in the case of the *mercador's* tale of the native sorcerer or the man 380 years old, but this does not by any means impair the interest of his book. More individual and vivid is the *Itinerario* (1560) of ANTONIO TENREIRO, who in brief, staccato sentences describes minutely what he saw (the *rosaes* of red, white, and yellow roses in May near Damascus, the red roses of Shiraz, the fair, white Gurgis, complexioned like Englishmen) during his travels from Ormuz to the Caspian Sea and in Palestine and Egypt, and his overland journey from Ormuz to Portugal (1529) in which, alone with an Arab guide, he spent twenty-two days in crossing the desert. A similar land journey, a generation later, is described with an equal wealth of curious detail in the *Itinerario* (1565) of Mestre MARTIM AFONSO, surgeon to the Viceroy, Conde de Redondo,[3] while the Franciscan FREI PANTALEAM DE AVEIRO in his *Itinerario da Terra Santa*, &c. (1593) described his journey to the Holy Land. Not less adventurous were the travels of another

---

[1] This seems to have aroused the resentment of Barros (*Asia*, III. iv. 3). The author, he says, had no learning. In II. iii. 4 he again refers to him slightingly as 'a certain Francisco Alvarez'. Barros as grammarian similarly ignored Oliveira.

[2] Barbosa Machado says, *ultimamente em o Convento de Goa, para onde tinha passado no anno de 1622 falleceu com saudade*, &c. Innocencio da Silva read this with a comma after *passado*.

[3] Afonso de Albuquerque mentions another surgeon Mestre Afonso in India in his time, i. e. half a century earlier. The value of the *Itinerario* consists in its having been written as a diary on the journey, and its author, perhaps thinking of Mendez Pinto, says *hee hũu grande descuido de homens que fazem semelhantes viagens e as nom escreuem . . . porque a memoria nom pode ser capaz de tamanha cousa e tantas particularidades* (p. 82).

Franciscan, FREI GASPAR DE S. BERNARDINO, who related them with greater parade of erudition in a clear, elegant style in his *Itinerario da India por terra* (1611), the promised second part of which was unhappily not finished or at least not published. Half a century later the Jesuit MANUEL GODINHO (*c.* 1630– 1712),[1] in the *Relaçam do novo caminho que fez por terra e mar* (1665), gave a remarkable account, in a style not untouched by the *culteranismo* of the time, of his return journey in 1663 from Baçaim. But various and arresting as are the books of Portuguese travellers, they are all eclipsed by the wonderful *Peregrinaçam* (1614) of FERNAM MENDEZ PINTO (*c.* 1510–83). This prince of travellers and adventurers was born at Montemôr o Velho. His parents were of humble station, and at the time of King Manuel's death (1521) he was brought by an uncle to Lisbon in order to earn his living. Although he remained in Portugal for sixteen years, in the service first of a lady of Lisbon and later of D. João de Lencastre,[2] lord of Montemôr o Velho, at Setubal, he was but just in his teens when, crossing in a boat from Alfama, he was captured off Cezimbra by a French corsair as a foretaste of pleasures to come. In March 1537 he set out for India and his odyssey began in earnest. He had no sooner reached Diu than he re-embarked on an expedition to the Straits of Mecca. His hope was to make a rich prize and become *muito rico em pouco tempo*. He went next with three others on a mission to Ethiopia, and on the return voyage he was captured by the Turks, placed in a subterranean dungeon, and then sold to a Greek renegade, whom he describes as 'the most inhuman and cruel dog of an enemy ever seen'. Fortunately after three months the Greek sold him for 12,000 *réis* to a Jew, who brought him to Ormuz. After spending little over a fortnight there he embarked with a cargo of horses for Goa, and later was wounded in a fight with the Turks. He next proceeded to Malacca, and was sent thence on a mission to the King of the Batas, by whom he was made welcome 'as rain to our rice crops'. After accompanying the

[1] According to Barbosa Machado he entered the Jesuit College as a novice in 1645 and died in 1712 aet. 78. Godinho also wrote a life of Frei Antonio das Chagas.
[2] He was the son of D. Jorge, illegitimate son of João II., and was created Duke of Aveiro.

king on a campaign he returned to Malacca, losing his cargo of tin and benjamin on the way. His next mission was to the King of Aaru. He returned to Malacca a slave, as his ship was wrecked, and after fearful sufferings he, the only survivor, was bought cheap by a poor Moorish trader. A trading expedition to Pão and Lugor ended as disastrously : after a fight with Moors he succeeded in swimming wounded to land, but returned penniless to Patane. In despair he joined the freebooting Antonio de Faria, and they preyed on Chinese junks till their ship was weighed down with silver and silk, damask and porcelain. Faria and his men are represented fighting, torturing, murdering, plundering, playing at dice on deck for pieces of silk, praying a litany, and promising rich and good spoil to Our Lady of the Hill at Malacca. After being shipwrecked they joined a Chinese pirate and again built up their fortunes. They weathered a storm by throwing overboard twelve cases of silver, sacked a Chinese city, were received in honour at Liampo (Ningpo), but again inordinate greed for gold proved their ruin, and, after a daring attempt to plunder the rich tombs of the Emperors of China in the island of Calemplui, they were finally stranded in China and arrested as vagabonds. After six weeks in the crowded prison at Nanking the Portuguese were taken to Peking and thence deported to Quansi (Kansu), where they were freed by the timely attack of the King of Tartary. He sent them to Cochin-China, but on the way they entered the service of a Chinese pirate. When they reached Japan only three Portuguese survived, the first Europeans, Mendez Pinto claims, to set foot there. When he brought news of this land to Liampo a trading expedition was hastily equipped and set out in defiance of times and seasons. Few of those who embarked in the nine junks ever saw land again. Mendez Pinto eventually reached Malacca (1544). Pedro de Faria later sent him on a mission to the King of Martavão. Martavão was, however, sacked soon after his arrival, and he was carried a prisoner to Pegu. He escaped by night and after many adventures returned to Goa. He immediately set out again ' to challenge fortune in China and Japan '. After accompanying the King of Sunda on a war expedition he was again wrecked and spent thirteen days on a raft. Of the eleven survivors three were eaten by crocodiles and the rest sold as slaves. Released by the King of Calapa, Mendez Pinto served under the King of Siam and returned to Pegu and thence to Malacca. Once more he set out for Japan, and this time his voyage prospered and he came back with a fair profit. At Malacca he was eagerly questioned by St. Francis Xavier (1506–52) as to the conditions in Japan. He seems to have been infected with the saint's enthusiasm, as were most of those who met him, and after his death he perhaps gave up a considerable fortune in order to return as missionary and ambassador to Japan. Before leaving Goa (April 1554) with St. Francis Xavier's successor, Padre Belchior, he had been received into the Company of Jesus. After many hardships they landed in China in July 1556. In the spring of 1558, a few weeks after returning to Goa, Mendez Pinto sailed for home and arrived at Lisbon on September 22. The Lisbon officials dallied with his pretensions to reward for his services. During his wanderings in India, Ethiopia, China, Japan, Tartary, and Arabia he had persevered through captivities, battles, and shipwrecks, but four or five years of official evasions broke his spirit, and he retired to live in poverty at Almada. Philip II, stirred to interest in this legendary figure, granted him two bushels of wheat in January 1583, and in July of the same year he died. He had long before left the Company of Jesus, either of his own free will or expelled, perhaps on suspicion of Jewish descent.[1] His name was erased from the Company's records and letters. Of his twenty-one years of trader, envoy, pirate, and missionary in the far East he wrote for his children a narrative of breathless interest, and, speaking generally, it bears the stamp of truth. We gather that he was brave and adventurous, despite a natural timidity, of a consuming curiosity which often got the better of his fears, pious, temperate, apt to be carried away by fugitive enthusiasms, but persistent, gay, and optimistic in defeat and disappointment. He appears not to have been particularly vain. He does not disguise some of his less creditable actions, and he certainly does not exaggerate his services in

---

[1] See the important works by Colonel Cristovam Ayres, *Fernão Mendes Pinto*, 1904; *Fernão Mendes Pinto e o Japão*, 1906.

Japan.[1] He may possibly have been one of the three Portuguese who discovered it in 1542 : their names are given by Couto (V. viii. 12) as Mota, Zeimoto and Peixoto. Gifted with keen imagination, he could exaggerate [2] when expediency required, but he knew that in the account of his travels exaggeration was not expedient, and he was constantly on guard against the notorious scepticism of his fellow-countrymen.[3] He may have heightened the colour occasionally, but as a rule he writes with restraint, although with delight in a good story and skill in bringing out the dramatic side of events. It is one of the charms of his work that it is very definite in dates and figures, but this also, through inevitable errors and misprints, afforded a handle to the pedantry of critics. The fatal similarity of Mendez and mendacity gave rise to the play on his name : *Fernam, mentes? Minto* (' Fernam, do you lie?—I lie '), and Congreve, in *Love for Love*, by calling him ' a liar of the first magnitude ' clinched the matter in England. But comparatively early a reaction set in,[4] and modern travellers have unequivocally confirmed the more favourable verdict and corroborated his detailed descriptions of Eastern countries. The mystery of the East, the heavy scent of its cities, its fervent rites and immemorial customs, as well as the magic of adventure, haunt his pages. A hundred pictures refuse to fade from the memory,

[1] His work did not appear till 1614 and it is uncertain to what extent it was edited by the historian Francisco de Andrade. It is thought that the account of his services as missionary in Japan may have been excised owing to the hostility of the Jesuits.

[2] Cap. 223 : *eu respondi acrecentando em muitas cousas que me perguntava por me parecer que era assim necessario á reputação da nação portuguesa.*

[3] Cf. caps. 14, 70, 88, 114, 126, 198, 204. The complaint is echoed by almost every Portuguese traveller of the day. Bishop Osorio refers to the *fidei faciendae difficultas*; even the truthful and exact Francisco Alvarez fears his readers' disbelief.

[4] Cf. Faria e Sousa (*laudari a laudato !*) : *Yo le tengo por muy verdadero* ; A. de Sousa Macedo, *Eva e Ave,* ii. 55, 1676 ed., p. 495 : *El Rey Catholico D. Philippe II, quando veio a Portugal, gostava de ouvir a Fernão Mendes, em cujas peregrinaçoens & sucessos que dellas escreveo mostrou o tempo com a experiencia a verdade que se lhe disputava antes que ouvesse tantas noticias d'aquellas partes* ; Soares, *Theatrum* : *diu apud Lusitanos fidem non meruit donec rerum qui secuti sunt eventus et aliorum scripta nihil Ferdinandum a vero discrepasse confirmarunt* ; Manuel Bernardes, *Nova Floresta*, i (1706), p. 124 : *as Relações do nosso Fernão Mendez Pinto que não merecem tão pouco credito como alguns lhe dão*. ' Either never man had better memory or he was the most solemn liar that ever put pen to paper ' is the verdict of José Agostinho de Macedo (*Motim Literario*, 1841 ed., ii. 17).

QUINHENTISTA PROSE

whether they are of silk-laden Chinese junks or jars of gold dust, vivid descriptions of shipwreck (the hiss and swell of the waves are in his rich sea-Latin) or the awful pathos of the Queen of Martavão's death, the sketch of a supercilious Chinese mandarin or of St. Francis Xavier tramping through Japan.

Five years after Mendez Pinto's return to Portugal a book scarcely less strange than his *Peregrinaçam*, of atmosphere as oriental and of interest as absorbing although more scientific, was printed at Goa. Its author, GARCIA DA ORTA [1] (*c.* 1495–*c.* 1570), born at Elvas, the son, perhaps, of Jorge da Orta, owner of a shop (*temdeiro*) in that town, studied medicine for ten years (1515–25) at Salamanca and Alcalá, and in 1526 began to practise as a doctor at Castello de Vide. From 1532 to 1534 he was Professor at the University of Lisbon, and in March 1534 sailed with his friend and patron, the insatiable Governor Martim Afonso de Sousa,[2] to India as king's physician. The East cast its spell over his curious and inquiring mind; he remained under twelve or more Governors and died at a good old age, probably at Goa. There, on the veranda of his beautiful garden, in this land of *bellissimi giardini*,[3] served affectionately by many slaves, and with the books of his well-stocked library ready to his hand,[4] he would regale his

---

[1] In France he was known as du Jardin. Familiarly this great botanist seems to have been called Herbs. A copy of the first edition of the *Coloquios* has GRACIA DORTA O ERVAS on the back of the binding. This might be an ignorant mistake for D'ELVAS.

[2] The Governor's brother, Pero Lopez de Sousa, wrote a *Diario da Navegação* (1530–2) first published at Lisbon in 1839. The soldier in Couto's *Dialogo* says, *não vai tão mal negociado hir por Fysico môr pois todos os que este cargo serviram tiraram nos seus tres annos sete ou oito mil cruzados*.

[3] *Libro di Odoardo Barbosa Portoghese*.

[4] He must have spent many a half-hour in the corner bookshop in Goa mentioned by Couto (*Dec.* VI. v. 8, 1781 ed., p. 400): *o canto onde pousa um livreiro*—unless this is a misprint for *luveiro*, as the neighbouring *sirgueiro* seems to indicate. The growth of Portuguese literature in the East would furnish matter for a curious essay. Great folios like the *Cancioneiro de Resende* (see Lopez de Castanheda, v. 12, and Barros, *Asia*, III. iii. 4, for the strange use made of it in India) and the *Flos Sanctorum* were taken out, and it is improbable that they were brought back when every square inch was required for pepper. Thousands of precious volumes must have gone down in shipwrecks, others—profane books and *autos*—were thrown overboard at the bidding of the priests. For the fate of a case of Hebrew Bibles (*briuias*) see Corrêa, *Lendas da India*, i. 656–7. *Amadis de Gaula* was apparently in India in 1519 (Lopez de Castanheda, v. 16). A most interesting list of books ready to be sent to the Negus of Abyssinia in 1515 is given in Sousa Viterbo's *A Livraria Real* (1901), p. 8.

guests with strange fruits—all the *maneiras á gula* of India—and with still stranger knowledge His knowledge was based on personal observation, for although he respected Galen and Dioscorides as the princes of medicine and was possessed of great erudition, he was not disposed to bow blindly to the authority of any writer, Arab or Greek, least of all to Scholasticism, he went to Nature and in his *Coloquios dos Simples* (1563) recorded what he had seen and heard, the truth without rhetoric, setting aside the *mil fabulas* of Pliny and Herodotus. These fifty-nine dialogues, arranged in alphabetical order, pay more regard to facts than to style. They are full of varied information and give us a most pleasant insight into the writer's character, strong, humorous, obstinate, and into his life at Goa. From a scientific point of view they are of great importance : not only did they provide the first description of cholera [1] and of many unknown plants, but after three and a half centuries they retain their scientific interest and value. Begun many years earlier in Latin,[2] they were published in the author's old age, with an introductory ode by his friend, the poet Camões. Unhappily they became known to Europe chiefly in a garbled Latin version by Charles de l'Écluse (Clusius)—a fifth edition appeared in 1605—from which the Italian and French translations were made. It was not until the nineteenth century that the skilful and eager care of the Conde de Ficalho enabled a larger number of those who read Portuguese to appreciate Orta at his true worth.

Born at Alcacer do Sal, the celebrated scientist PEDRO NUNEZ (1492 ?–1577 ?), whose name lives in the instrument of his invention, the *nonius*,[3] was Cosmographer to Kings João III

[1] Unless Corrêa's description (*Lendas*, iv. 288-9) is earlier. Other events recorded by Corrêa which must have closely affected Orta are the fate of a bachelor of medicine strangled and burnt by the Inquisition at Goa in 1543 (iv. 292) and the outbreak of small-pox, from which 8,000 children died there in three months in 1545 (iv. 447). The *Dialogo da perfeyçam & partes que sam necessarias ao bom medico* (1562), with the exception of the dedicatory letter to King Sebastian and the title, is written in Spanish (25 ff.). Apparently AFONSO DE MIRANDA found it in Latin among the books of his son Jeronimo (who had studied at Coimbra and Salamanca) and translated it.

[2] *Composto*, he says (*Coloquios*, i. 5). Dimas Bosque (ib. i. 11) says *começado*.

[3] Thus he contributed to the fact, which he notices in the *Tratado da carta de marear*, that the Portuguese sea enterprises were based on careful preparation. The *nonius* was perfected in the following century by Vernier.

and Sebastian and Professor of Mathematics at the University of Coimbra (1544-62). Prince Luis and D. João de Castro were his pupils. He wrote indifferently in Latin, Spanish, or Portuguese, declared that as science treats of concrete things it can be expressed in any language however barbarous,[1] and, in order to secure for it a wider public, translated into Portuguese the Latin treatise (*libellus*) *De Sphaera* by John of Halifax (Joannes de Sacro Bosco): *Tratado da Sphera* (1537),[2] and into Spanish his own *Libro de Algebra en arithmetica & geometria* (1567), originally written in Portuguese and addressed to his pupil and friend the Cardinal-King Henrique. His other works, including the *De Crepusculis* (1542), were written in Latin.

The Homeric hero DUARTE PACHECO PEREIRA (1465?-1533?), about whose life, apart from the hundred days at Cochin (1504) and a fight off Finisterre (1509) with the French pirate Mondragon, singularly little is known,[3] on his return from India in 1505 wrote a work entitled *Esmeraldo de Situ Orbis* [1505-6?]. This curious and important survey of the coast of Africa, the work of one more accustomed to wield sword than pen, but sometimes as picturesque and interesting as Duarte Barbosa, was to have consisted of five books, but only three and a part of the fourth were written. It remained in manuscript for nearly four centuries.

The three *Roteiros* (logs)[4] written by the famous Viceroy

[1] *Tratado da Sphera*, Preface.
[2] This volume contains also two brief treatises by Nunez in Portuguese: *Tratado ... sobre certas duuidas da nauegação*, answering certain questions put to him by Martim Afonso de Sousa, and *Tratado ... em defensam da carta de marear*, addressed to the Infante Luis. The *De Sphaera* of Joannes de Sacro Bosco was printed with a preface by Philip Melanchthon in 1538. Arraez, in his *Dialogos*, 1604 ed., f. 56, says: *sei algo da Sphera porque quando Pero Nunez a lia a certos homens principais eu me achava presente*.
[3] He himself says that he was born in the excellent city of Lisbon (*Esmeraldo*, iv. 6), and he was one of the captains sent out by João II to continue the discovery of the West Coast of Africa. In 1520-2 he was Governor of the fortress of S. Jorge da Mina, but his last years were spent in poverty.
[4] Other works of a similar nature, *livros das rotas* or *derrotas*, are printed in *Libro de Marinharia*. *Tratado da Aguia de Marear* [1514] *de João de Lisboa* [†1526]. *Copiado e coordenado por J. I. Brito Rebello*, 1903. Cf. also G. Pereira, *Roteiros Portuguezes da viagem de Lisboa á India nos seculos xvi e xvii*, 1898; H. Lopes de Mendonça, *Estudos sobre navios portuguezes nos seculos xv e xvi*, 1892, and *O Padre Fernando Oliveira e a sua obra nautica*, 1898 (pp. 147-221 contain *O Liuro da fabrica das naos*, of which,

D. João de Castro (1500–48) on his voyages (1) from Lisbon to Goa in 1538, (2) from Goa to Diu, 1538–9, (3) from Goa to the Red Sea in 1541, are decked out with no literary graces. He wrote, he said, for seamen, not for ladies and gallants. Yet the scientific curiosity and enthusiasm of this keen-eyed, broad-minded observer give his descriptions force and truth, the same practical lucidity that marks his letters, which according to his friend Prince Luis contained *todas as cousas necessarias e nenhũas superfluas,* and they were early prized in Spain as *harto notables, muy curiosos.*[1] The third *Roteiro* would seem to have been originally written in Latin, and perhaps translated by Castro at his beloved Sintra home. The manuscript was bought by Sir Walter Raleigh, and it appeared in English in 1625, 208 years before it was published in Portuguese.

Greater historical interest attaches to the letters of an earlier Governor, Afonso de Albuquerque (1461–1515). That grim conqueror of the East might have smiled somewhat sardonically to be numbered among Portugal's writers. He merely said what he had to say, and there was an end of it, would be his comment. But it is precisely this directness—the powerful grasp of reality and the horror of useless rhetoric—which gives excellence to the prose of his *Cartas.* These incomparable reports, written to King Manuel in moments snatched from his many occupations as Governor of India (1509–15), sometimes rise to a biblical grandeur and eloquence, as in the splendid passage beginning *Goa é vossa ; Onor, o rei dele paga-vos pareas.* Perhaps, after all, he was not wholly unconscious of his art, and certainly the source of it is clear : as Osorio[2] notices, he was a devoted student of the Bible. In more familiar mood he can give a vivid sketch in a few emphatic words, as when he describes the judge, ' a little man dressed in a cloak of coarse cloth with a crooked stick

says the preface, *ninguem escreveo ateegora*) ; and Sousa Viterbo, *Trabalhos nauticos dos portuguezes nos seculos xvi e xvii* (*Historia e Memorias da Ac. das Sciencias,* tom. vii (1898), *mem.* 3 ; tom. viii (1900), *mem.* 1). Diogo de Sá's *De Navigatione* was published in Paris in 1549 ; the *Arte Practica de Navegar* (1699) by the *Cosmographo Môr* Manuel Pimentel (1650–1719) appeared a century and a half later and had several editions in the eighteenth century.

[1] Fr. Antonio de San Roman, *Historia General de la India Oriental,* Valladolid, 1603.

[2] *De Rebvs Emmanvelis* (1571), p. 380 : *Non erat alienus a literis, & cum otium erat lectione sacrarum praecipue literarum oblectabatur.*

under his arm', or the impostors who will practise 'a thousand wiles and deceits for one ruby'.

To turn to lesser men, FERNAM RODRIGUEZ LOBO SOROPITA (born c. 1560), a distinguished Lisbon advocate and the first editor of the *Rythmas* (1595) of Camões, was a poet celebrated for his wit in his day. That of his letters is perhaps a little forced, and the obscurity of the allusions now interferes with our enjoyment. The interest of the extracts from a manuscript in the British Museum written by FRANCISCO RODRIGUEZ SILVEIRA (1558–c. 1635) in 1608, published under the title *Memorias de um Soldado da India* (1877), consists both in the record of his thirteen years' service in India (1585–98) and in the account during the succeeding ten years of Portugal and especially Beira, the condition of the roads, the land, the peasants, and the sway of the local *caciques*—thief, Turk, Pasha, tyrant, he calls them—and his indignation gives a pleasant vigour to his prose. The *Arte da Caça da Altanaria* (1616) of DIOGO FERNANDEZ FERREIRA (born c. 1550), page of the Pretender D. Antonio, is a work of great interest. The writer evidently delights in his theme and has a real love of birds, the migratory habits of which he describes in Part 6; and he treats 'of swallows and of the swallow-grass which restores sight', of the food made of sugar, saffron, and almonds for nightingales, and other alluring topics. Among the rare and curious books of the time we may notice that on the prerogatives of women, *Dos priuilegios & prærogatiuas q ho genero femenino tẽ por dereito comũ & ordenações do Reyno mais que ho genero masculino* (1557), by RUY GONÇALVEZ, Professor of Law at Coimbra in 1539 and subsequently Court Advocate at Lisbon.

Two writers especially attract attention even in the feast of interest which Portuguese prose in this century offers so abundantly. The son of a distinguished Dutch illuminator and painter settled in Portugal, Antonio de Hollanda, who painted Charles V at Toledo and may have illuminated the Book of Hours of Queen Lianor, FRANCISCO DE HOLLANDA (1518–84), born in Lisbon, painter, illuminator, and architect, in his short treatises *Da fabrica que fallece á cidade de Lisboa* and *Da sciencia do desenho*, showed an enthusiasm for his subject almost out of place in the Portugal of the second half of the sixteenth century. Indeed, he nearly ran into trouble with the Inquisition by seeming to make painting ' divine ', but prudently altered the passage. His curious and celebrated treatise *Da Pintvra Antigva* (1548) is written in a style which may be rather rejoiced in than imitated, for, as he tells us, he was more at home with the brush than with the pen, but it is full of ingenious and original remarks. The first part deals in forty-four brief chapters with painting generally, and opens with a fine passage describing the work of God as the greatest of all painters. The second part contains the *Quatro dialogos*, in the first three of which he records the conversations of Vittoria Colonna, Michelangelo, Lattanzio Tolomei, and himself in the church of St. Sylvester or in a garden overlooking Rome ; conversations which, despite their Portuguese dress, bear the stamp of truth and will retain their fascination so long as interest in art endures. Francisco worked first in the household of the Infante Fernando and then in that of the Archbishop of Evora. In 1537 he set out on a journey to Rome by land (Valladolid, Barcelona, Provence), and in Italy remained from 1538 to 1547. His friendship with Michelangelo continued after his return to Portugal, as a letter from Hollanda to Michelangelo in 1553 proves. The last part of his life he spent in the country between Lisbon and Sintra among the Portuguese whom he had called *desmusicos*, and despite his comfortable circumstances—he received a pension of 100,000 *réis* from Philip II—he must often have looked back with regret to the fullness of those nine years in Italy. But his countrymen, thanks largely to the scholarly researches and studies of Dr. Joaquim de Vasconcellos, are now fully alive to his merits. And, indeed, even in the sixteenth century a passage in Frei Heitor Pinto's *Imagem da Vida Christam* sets him side by side with the great Italian.[1] PHILIPE NUNEZ, who professed as a Dominican in 1591, wrote on painting in the next century : *Arte poetica e da pintura e symmetria* (1615). A work on music by ANTONIO FERNANDEZ of about the same date, *Arte de Mvsica de canto dorgam e canto cham*

---

[1] Pt. 1, 1572 ed., f. 224 : *não feyto por mão do nosso Olãda nẽ do vosso Michaël Angelo mas por meu bayxo ingenho.*

(1626), consists of three treatises which do not profess to be original. MANUEL NUNEZ DA SILVA wrote on the same subject in his *Arte Minima* (1685).

In the preface (1570) to his *Regra Geral*, written in 1565, GONÇALO FERNANDEZ TRANCOSO[1] (*c.* 1515–*c.* 1590) professed not to have sufficient literary skill even for this simple calendar of movable feasts. Yet in the previous year (1569), in which at Lisbon he lost both wife and children in the great plague (a beloved daughter of twenty-four, a student son, and a choir-boy grandson), in order to distract his mind from these sorrows,[2] he wrote a remarkable work, unique of its kind in Portuguese literature; or at least he wrote then the first two books, which appeared under the title *Contos e historias de proveito e exemplo* (1575).[3] A third part was published posthumously in 1596. The number and kind of the editions in the seventeenth and eighteenth centuries testify to its popularity, but since the eighteenth century no new edition has been printed and the book has fallen into a strange neglect.[4] Trancoso did not claim originality: he merely collected stories from what he had heard or read.[5] The stories, only thirty-eight in number, are very various. The subjects of many of them resemble those of Franco Sacchetti's *Novelle* or Giovanni Francesco Straparola's *Le xiii Piacevoli Notti*, and some are directly imitated from Boccaccio's *Il Decamerone* or Giovanni Battista Giraldi's *Gli Ecatommiti* or from Matteo Bandello (†1565).[6] But often they are traditions so widespread that they occur in many authors and languages, as that (ii. 7) which corresponds to Straparola's third *Notte* and of which Dr. F. A. Coelho recorded twenty-one other foreign versions, besides four popular variants in Portuguese; or i. 17, in which the cunning answers to difficult questions are similar to those in Sacchetti, No. 4 (*Mestre Bernabò signor di Milano*), and Dr. Braga's *Contos tradicionaes do povo portuguez*,

[1] Or Gonçalo Fernandez of Trancoso (Beira). His name has no connexion with the phrase *contar historias a trancos* (*de coq à l'âne*).
[2] Preface addressed to the Queen in Pt. 1. His object was *prender a imaginação em ferros*.
[3] Timoneda's *El Patrañuelo* appeared in the following year.
[4] See, however, Dr. Agostinho de Campos' selections (1921).
[5] *O que aprendi, ouui ou li* (1624 ed.); *o que aprendi, vi ou li* (1734 ed.).
[6] See Menéndez y Pelayo, *Origenes de la Novela*, tom. ii (1907), p. lxxxvii et seq.

No. 71 (*Frei Joam Sem Cuidados*). Others are apparently of oriental origin, as the judge's verdict, worthy of Sancho Panza (i. 15), or the king and the barber (iii. 3). But the subject and place (Lisbon, Oporto, Evora, Coimbra, &c.) of most, although not of the longest, of these tales are Portuguese.[1] Some are trifling anecdotes which acquire a charm and vividness through their popular character and the author's simple details of description, as the picture of the peasant family near Oporto sitting round the fire after their supper of maize-bread and chestnuts (i. 10). The author is not content that we should draw our own moral, but this scarcely spoils the reader's pleasure in these malicious and ingenious tales.

Despite inroads of the exotic and all the chances and changes of life and literature in this century, the Portuguese maintained their interest in the romances of chivalry, in which indeed they saw a reflection of their own prowess in the East. Dull as *Clarimundo* may now seem, it made a great impression in its day, and was eagerly read, from Lisbon to the Moluccas.[2] Even as late as 1589 Bishop Arraez considers it necessary to say that a prince should have better ways of spending his time than *ler por Clarimundo*,[3] while Rodriguez Lobo, thirty years later, brackets it with *Amadis* and *Palmeirim*.[4] Many a young page and *escudeiro* must have aspired not only to pore over the *cronicas* but to write one of his own.[5] The facility of a Barros is, however, given to few, and both Jorge Ferreira's *Memorial* and Moraes' *Palmeirim de Inglaterra* were written later in life. FRANCISCO DE MORAES (c. 1500-72),[6] a well-known courtier in the reign of King João III, whose Treasurer he was, and a *Comendador* of the Order of Christ, in 1540 accompanied the Portuguese Ambassador, D. Francisco de Noronha, to Paris as Secretary,

[1] The alternation of the indigenous and the exotic may be seen in the spelling of the same name as Piro (= Pero, Pedro, Peter) and Pyrrho (Pyrrhus) in iii. 8.
[2] *Ropica Pnefma*, 1869 ed., p. 2.
[3] *Dialogos*, 1604 ed., f. 157. A third edition of *Clarimundo* (1601) had appeared before the second edition of the *Dialogos*.
[4] *Corte na Aldea* (1619), *Dialogo* 1 (1722 ed., p. 5).
[5] Moraes, *Dialogo* 1 (1852 ed., p. 11).
[6] Barbosa Machado seems to have considered him much under seventy at the time of his death in 1572.

and at the French Court he fell passionately in love with one of the ladies-in-waiting of Queen Leonor (sister of the Emperor Charles V and widow of King Manuel of Portugal) named Claude Blosset de Torcy. His love was not returned : there was a great discrepancy of age between them, his knowledge of French was very slight, and his passion robbed him of wit and reason. If the Duc de Châtillon was favoured, or if the English Ambassador gave Mademoiselle de Torcy his arm, Moraes would flare up in jealousy, and when in the presence of the queen the elderly lover went down on his knees *la belle Torcy* (to whom Clément Marot had addressed one of his *Étrennes* and who eventually married the Baron de Fontaines) prayed him not to continue to make her as well as himself ridiculous. Moraes, after leaving France in 1543, or early in 1544, recovered from his passion and married in Portugal. Of his subsequent life little is known; he appears to have returned to France, and in 1572 he was murdered at the entrance of the Rocio, the central square of Evora. His *Cronica de Palmeirim de Inglaterra*, written in France or Portugal or both, was probably published in 1544, but the earliest existing Portuguese edition is that of Evora, 1567, which contains the dedication to the Infanta Maria, written over twenty years earlier (1544). Chiefly remarkable for the excellence of its style, *Palmeirim* will always retain its place in Portuguese literature as a masterpiece of prose, musically soft, yet clear and vigorous. Cervantes considered it worthy to be preserved in a golden casket like the works of Homer,[1] but few of its readers will now differ from the more modern and moderate opinion of Menéndez y Pelayo that 'it requires a real effort' to read the whole of it. The effort required to read the miserable Spanish translation of 1547-8 is infinitely greater. The fact that this translation is of earlier date than any surviving Portuguese edition gave rise to the theory that Moraes had translated his work from the Spanish. No competent critic now believes this; any doubts that may have lingered were dispelled wittily and for ever in Mr. Purser's able essay (1904).

[1] The tradition, mentioned by Cervantes, that it was written by a learned and witty king of Portugal is clearly traceable to that other tradition that King João III as Infante had been joint-author of *Clarimundo*.

The Spanish version, with its painful efforts to avoid *lusitanismos* and its palpable mistranslations (such as *suavidad* or *alegria* for *saudade*), shows less knowledge of the sea, of Ireland,[1] and of Portugal. Moreover, the preference of the author of *Palmeirim* for Portugal is obvious, and the passage in which ladies of the French Court are introduced corresponds to Moraes' *Descvlpa de hvns amores*,[2] first published with the *Dialogos* in 1624. Moraes himself would probably not have been greatly troubled by the impudent claim set up for Luis Hurtado and Miguel Ferrer. To have made a masterpiece out of their book would have been an achievement as great as to have made it out of old French and English legends in Paris. *Palmeirim's* predecessors, *Palmerin de Oliva* (1511), *Primaleon* (1512), and *Platir* (1533), were probably all genuinely Spanish, although some doubts have been raised as to the first of the line, *Palmerin de Oliva* attributed to a cryptic lady, a *femina docta* called Agustobrica.[3] Its successors were as genuinely Portuguese: to Moraes' parts 1 and 2 DIOGO FERNANDEZ added parts 3 and 4 (1587), concerned with the deeds of Palmeirim's son, *Dom Duardos*,[4] and BALTHASAR GONÇALVEZ LOBATO parts 5 and 6 (1602), in which are told those of his grandson, *Dom Clarisol de Bretanha*. Three brief but very lively and natural *Dialogos* (1624) show that Moraes was not only an excellent stylist but a keen observer. The *fidalgo* and *escudeiro*, the lawyer and the love-lorn *moço*, are all clearly and wittily presented.

[1] Mount Brandon, Smerwick (and The Three Sisters) of the 'pleasant' but 'densely wooded' coast of Kerry, are Greek to the Spanish translator and become San Cebrian (Cyprian) and San Maurique.
[2] The title continues: *que tinha com hũa dama francesa da raynha dona Leanor per nome Torsi, sendo Portugues, pela quai fez a historia das damas francesas no seu Palmeirim*.
[3] It is scarcely possible that the author (Francisco Vazquez?) considered that Burgos, as his birthplace—his mother—had a part in the work.
[4] From being merely the legend above, the mounted knight on the title-page *Dom Duardos de Bretanha* became the title of the book.

§ 7.
Religious and Mystic Writers

AMADOR ARRAEZ in one of his dialogues defines mysticism thus: 'There is a theology called mystic, as being hidden and unintelligible to those who have no part in it. It is attained by much love and few books and with much meditation and purity of heart, which alone suffices for its exercise, and consists mainly in the noblest part of our will inflamed in the love of God, its full and perfect good.'[1] 'Our will inflamed': perhaps these words explain the excellence of the style, the intensity and directness, of the writers in this mystic theology. Style, so shy and elusive to Flaubert and his disciples, came unsought to the religious writers of the sixteenth century, because they wrote not with an eye on verbal artifices but out of the fullness of the heart, 'self-gathered for an outbreak'; and their works can still be read with pleasure by priest and pagan. Mysticism, inherent in the character of the Portuguese, runs through a great part of their literature; we find it, for instance, in the merry poetry of Gil Vicente or in the precious accents of Soror Violante do Ceo. Strength of character, aloofness, rapt enthusiasm, singleness of purpose: these are the qualities of mysticism at its best, and if it also manifests itself in vagueness and confusion, this was not so with the great mystic and religious writers of the golden age of Portuguese literature. To them mysticism was not a cloudy goodness or an abstract perception-dulling humanity, not a mist but a pillar of fire, in the light of which the facts and details of reality stood out the more clearly. But if the intensity of many of the mystics has its natural complement in the fervour and directness of their prose, this was not always the case, and it was not only in profane works that the Portuguese language fell into the pitfalls of *culteranismo*. All the more remarkable is the purity, the exquisite taste, the

[1] *Dial.* x. 4.

simplicity and charm of some of the later, seventeenth century, prose. The secret of this prose lay in fact in *culteranismo* itself, the points and conceits of which were based on a recognition of the value of words. All the *seiscentistas* set to playing with words as with unset stones of price. The more critical or inspired writers joined in the game but selected the genuine stones, leaving the rest to those who did not care to distinguish between gems and coloured glass.

A faint vein of mysticism is to be found in the work of FREI HEITOR PINTO (*c.* 1528–1584 ?), who was born at the high-lying little town of Covilhan and professed in the famous Convento dos Jeronimos at Belem in 1543. After taking the degree of Doctor of Theology at Siguenza he in 1567 competed for a Chair at Salamanca University, but came into collision with Fray Luis de Leon, and in a bitter contest between the Hieronymite and Augustinian Orders Pinto was defeated. He returned to Portugal, became Professor of the new Chair of Scripture at Coimbra University in 1576, Rector of the University and Provincial of his Order.[1] After the death of the Cardinal-King he appears vehemently to have espoused the cause of the Prior of Crato. King Philip accordingly invited Pinto to accompany him to Spain—he was one of the fifty excluded from the amnesty of 1581—and scandal added that the king had him poisoned there in 1584. Pinto was an eminent divine, a man of wide learning, a master of Portuguese prose, and he appears to have inspired his pupils with affection; but King Philip could scarcely have considered him worth poisoning, especially when removed from his sphere of influence. No doubt he went to Spain with extreme reluctance—on other occasions of his busy life when the affairs of his Order drove him to France and Italy he had sighed in tears (in spite of his interest in travel, his love of Nature, and especially his antiquarian curiosity [2]) for his quiet cell at Belem, 'where he had lived many years in great content'. Perhaps too he

---

[1] The dates given by Barbosa Machado are Rector 1565, Provincial 1571.
[2] He introduces himself as a theologian in his dialogues, and one may infer several facts concerning his life, e.g. that he had been in Rome (*Imagem*, Pt. 2, 1593 ed., f. 351 v.), Montserrat (f. 88), Marseilles (f. 88), Savoy (f. 295), Madrid (f. 190), that he kept a diary (f. 190), that he was *curioso de antigualhas* (f. 352).

had not forgotten his defeat at Salamanca. 'King Philip', he now said sturdily, 'may put me into Castille but never Castille into me.' Pinto wrote commentaries on various books of the Old Testament, which were published in Latin, but his principal work consists in the dialogues, *a maneira dos de Platão*, of his *Imagem da Vida Christam* (1563), followed by the *Segunda Parte dos Dialogos* (1572). The first part has six dialogues, the subjects being true philosophy, religion, justice, tribulation, the solitary life,[1] and remembrance of death. The five of the second part treat of tranquillity of life, discreet ignorance, true friendship, causes,[2] and true and spurious possessions. It is impossible to read a page of these dialogues and not be struck by the extraordinary fascination of their style. It is concise and direct without ever losing its harmony. Perhaps its best testimonial is that its magic survives the innumerable quotations, although one may regret that the work was not written, like the *Trabalhos de Jesus*, in a dungeon instead of in a well-stocked library.[3] Apart from the proof it affords of the exceptional capacity of the Portuguese language for combining softness and vigour, the work contains much ingenious thought, charming descriptions, and elaborate similes. Some twenty editions in various languages before the end of the century show how keenly it was appreciated. It was certainly not without influence on the *Dialogos* (1589) of the energetic and austere Bishop of Portalegre, AMADOR ARRAEZ (*c.* 1530–1600), who spent his boyhood at Beja and professed as a Carmelite at Lisbon a year after Frei Thomé de Jesus and two years after Frei Heitor Pinto had professed in the same city. Like the former he studied theology at Coimbra.[4]

[1] Macedo, quoted by Innocencio da Silva (iii. 176), alleged this to be a 'faithful translation' from Petrarca. Why Petrarca (1304–74) should praise Belem Convent and Coimbra University, refer to the recent death (1557) of King João III, or speak of 'our' Francisco de Hollanda we are not told. Pinto in a later dialogue, *Da Tranquillidade da Vida*, refers to Petrarca's *Vita Solitaria* (Pt. 2, 1593 ed., f. 47 v.).

[2] Since 1590 is implied as the date of this dialogue on f. 290 of the 1593 edition it must be emphasized that the *Segunda Parte* appeared originally in 1572.

[3] Pt. 2, 1593 ed., f. 366 v.: *eu revolvo os livros . . . com grandes trabalhos & vigilias.*

[4] Cf. *Dialogos*, 1604 ed., f. 346: *Coimbra, onde gastei a flor de minha adolescencia.* (This edition really has but 344 ff. since f. 29 follows f. 22.)

Cardinal Henrique, when Archbishop of Evora, chose Arraez to be his suffragan, and in 1578 appointed him to the see of Tripoli. Three years later he was made Bishop of Portalegre by Philip II. He resigned in 1596, and spent the last four years of his life in retirement, in the college of his Order at Coimbra. A few weeks before his death he wrote the prefatory letter for the revised edition of his great work.[1] It consists of ten long dialogues between the sick and dying Antiocho and doctor, priest, lawyer, or friends. The longest, over a quarter of the whole, is a mystic life of the Virgin, and of the others some are purely religious, as *Da Paciencia e Fortaleza Christam*, some historical or political (*Da Gloria e Triunfo dos Lusitanos* ; *Das Condições e Partes do Bom Principe*). That on the Jews (*Da Gente Judaica*) is marred by a spirit of bitter intolerance ; on the other hand there is an outspoken protest against slavery. The whole of this interesting miscellany, which incidentally discusses a very large number of subjects,[2] is tinged with mystic philosophy, and at the same time shows a keen sense of reality. In style as in degree of mysticism it stands midway between Pinto's *Imagem* and the *Trabalhos de Jesus*. It is evident that its composition, although less artificial than that of the *Imagem*, has been the subject of much care, and the author declares in his preface that while adopting a ' common, ordinary style ', to the exclusion of forced tricks and elegances, he has striven after clearness and harmony (the two postulates of his contemporary, Fray Luis de Leon). The result is a treasury of excellent prose, in which the harmonious flow of the sentences in nowise interferes with precision and restraint, that grave brevity which Arraez notes as one of the principal qualities of Portuguese. It can rise to great eloquence (as in the lament of Olympio) without ever becoming rhetorical or turgid.

The prose of Pinto and Arraez was a very conscious art, that of the still greater FREI THOMÉ DE JESUS (1529 ?–82) was the man, and the man merged in mysticism, without thought of

---

[1] *Dialogos de Dom Frey Amador Arraiz*, Coimbra, 1604. The idea of the work belonged to his brother, Jeronimo Arraez, who did not live to complete what he had begun.

[2] The same variety occurs in *Poderes de Amor em geral e horas de conversaçam particular* (1657), by Frei Cristovam Godinho (*c.* 1600–71) of Evora.

style. He was the son of Fernam Alvarez de Andrade, Treasurer to King João III, and of Isabel de Paiva. One of his brothers was the celebrated preacher Diogo de Paiva de Andrade (1528–75), another the historian Francisco de Andrade; a third, Frei Cosme da Presentação, distinguished himself in philosophy and theology, but died at the age of thirty-six at Bologna, while the work of a nephew (son of Francisco de Andrade), Diogo de Paiva de Andrade (1576–1660), *Casamento perfeito* (1636), is counted a classic of Portuguese prose. His sister D. Violante married the second Conde de Linhares. As a boy at the Augustinian Collegio de Nossa Senhora da Graça at Coimbra he is said to have been all but drowned while swimming in the Mondego. He professed at the Lisbon convent of the same Order in 1544, went to Coimbra to study theology, and then became master of novices at the Lisbon convent.[1] Here in 1574 he planned a reform of the Order, but when all was ready for the secession of the new *Recoletos* an intrigue put an end to the scheme, which a kindred spirit, Fray Luis de Leon, later carried into effect. Frei Thomé was permitted to retire to the convent of Penafirme by the sea, near Torres Vedras, where he might hope to indulge his love of quiet and solitude. He was, however, appointed prior of the convent and Visitor of his Order, and in 1578 was chosen by King Sebastian to accompany him to Africa. At the battle of Alcacer Kebir, as he held aloft a crucifix or tended the wounded, he was speared by a Moor and taken prisoner to Mequinez. Here he was loaded with chains and placed in a dungeon, and as the slave of a marabout received 'less bread than blows'. The Portuguese Ambassador, D. Francisco da Costa, intervened, and he was removed to Morocco. Frei Thomé had borne all his sufferings with the most heroic fortitude, and now, broken in health but not in spirit, he refused to lodge at the ambassador's and asked to be placed in the common prison. During a captivity of nearly four years, regardless of his own fate,[2] with unflagging devotion he ministered

[1] He wrote the life of the prior, Frei Luis de Montoia, whose *Vida de Christo* he completed.
[2] *Tendo elle sua mãi e irmãos muito ricos e a Condessa de Linhares sua irmãa, todos offerecidos a pagar o grosso resgate que os Mouros pediam, por saberem a qualidade de sua pessoa* (*Cronica do Cardeal Rei D. Henrique*, p. 38).

to the numerous Christian prisoners, and was occupied to the last with their needs. Costa, who shared the general respect and affection for this saint and hero, visited him as he lay dying (April 17, 1582). *Vattene in pace, alma beata e bella!* It was during his captivity that he composed the work that has given him the lasting fame earned by his life and character, writing furtively in the scant light that filtered through the cracks of the prison door.[1] These fifty *Trabalhos de Jesus* (2 pts., 1602, 9) embrace the whole life of Christ, and deserve, more than Renan's *Vie de Christ*, to be called a gracious fifth Gospel. Each *trabalho* is, moreover, followed by a spiritual exercise, and these constitute a Portuguese *De Imitatione Christi*. Rarely, if ever, has such glow and fervour been set in print: none but the very dull could be left cold by these transports of passionate devotion. The prose wrestles and throbs in an agony of grief or rapture, of mysticism carried to the extreme limit where all power of articulate expression ends.[2] Frei Thomé de Jesus is a master of Portuguese prose not by any arts or graces but through the white heat of his intensity. No book shows more clearly that style must always be a secondary consideration, that if there be a burning conviction excellence of style follows. It could evidently only have been written by one who had greatly suffered, indeed by one who still suffered, one who expressed in these fervid accents of heavenly communion an oblivion of self and an energy habitually employed in eager earthly service of his fellow men. In a prefatory letter (November 8, 1581) addressed to the Portuguese people he declared his intention of publishing as it stood this masterpiece of mystic ecstasy, which he believed to have been written by divine inspiration.[3]

Another celebrated treatise of a mystic character is the *Voz do*

---

[1] See his prefatory letter in the *Trabalhos*. Cf. Antonio, *Bib. Nova*, ii. 307. Barbosa Machado speaks of *hũa horrivel masmorra*.

[2] Cf. p. 39 (1666 ed.) : *Ó , ó, ó amor ; ó, ó, ó amor, cale a lingua e o entendimento, dilatai-vos vos por toda esta alma*, &c. ; or p. 54 : *Ah, ah, ah bondade ; ah, ah amor sem lei, sem regra, sem medida, adoro-te, louvo-te, desejo-te, por ti suspiro.*

[3] He also wrote *Oratorio sacro de soliloquios do amor divino* (1628) and various works in Latin. Manuel Godinho refers to his *Estimulo das Missões* (*Relação*, 1842 ed., p. 47).

Amado (1579) by the learned Canon D. HILARIAM BRANDÃO (†1585). The religious works of this century are very numerous. We may mention the anonymous *Regras e Cautelas de proueito espiritual* (1542), which is written in biblical prose and deals with the fifteen perfections or excellences of charity and kindred subjects; the dialogues *Desengano de Perdidos em dialogo entre dous peregrinos, hũ christão e hũ turco* (Goa, 1573) by the first Archbishop of Goa, D. GASPAR DE LEÃO (†1576), and the *Dialogo espiritual: Colloquio de um religioso com um peregrino* (1578) by FREI ALVARO DE TORRES [Vedras] (fl. 1550), who was drowned in the Tagus when on the way to his convent at Belem.

D. JOANA DA GAMA (†1568), a nun of noble birth who directed a small community founded by herself at Evora, a few miles from her native Viana, published a short collection of moral sentences in alphabetical order, followed by a few poems (*trovas*): *Ditos da Freyra* (1555). She insists, perhaps a little too emphatically for conviction, on her lack of intelligence and ability, and says that these sayings were written down for herself alone and that she purposely avoids subtleties (*ditos sotijs*), but her aphorisms contain some shrewd personal observation. Fact and legend have combined to weave an atmosphere of romance about the life of Manuel de Sousa Coutinho, better known as FREI LUIS DE SOUSA (1555 ?–1632). A descendant of the second Conde de Marialva, he early entered or was about to enter the Order of Knights Hospitallers at Malta, but was captured by the Moors in much the same way and at about the same time (1575) as was Cervantes. He was taken to Algiers, and may have known Cervantes there, or the statement that he became Cervantes' friend may have been an inference from the latter's mention of him in *Los Trabajos de Persiles y Sigismunda*; they may have met in Lisbon in 1590, or at Madrid. Sousa Coutinho returned to Portugal in 1578, and some years later married D. Magdalena de Vilhena, widow of D. João de Portugal, one of all the peerage that fell with King Sebastian at Alcacer Kebir. Sousa Coutinho, at the invitation of his brother in Panama, is said to have gone thither in the hope of making a fortune, but the date is not clear. His unbending patriotism was immortalized when as Governor of Almada in 1599 he burnt down his house rather than receive as guests the Spanish Governors of Portugal. The prospect of riches at Panama may have seemed especially alluring after this rash act. He appears to have lived quietly in Portugal for some years before 1613, when both he and his wife entered a convent. Their act has been variously explained as due to melancholy disposition or to the early death of their daughter, D. Anna de Noronha. Probably after her death the example of their friend the Conde de Vimioso and the conviction that the only abiding pleasure is the renunciation of all the rest were prevalent factors in their decision. The legend, however, related by Frei Antonio da Encarnação and dramatized two centuries later by Garrett, records that D. João de Portugal, D. Magdalena de Vilhena's first husband, had been not killed but taken prisoner in Africa, and after many years' captivity he reappears as an aged pilgrim and bitterly reveals his identity. In the convent of Bemfica, where he had professed in September 1614, Frei Luis de Sousa was consulted on various matters by the Duke of Braganza and others who valued his fine character and clear judgement, but he did not live to see the Restoration. He was entrusted by his Order with the revision of works left by another Dominican, FREI LUIS DE CACEGAS (*c.* 1540–1610). These he re-wrote, giving them a lasting value by virtue of his style. The first part of the *Historia de S. Domingos*, ' a new kind of chronicle ' as he calls it in his preface addressed to the king, appeared in 1623, but the second (1662) and third (1678) parts were not published in his lifetime. A fourth part (1733) was added by FREI LUCAS DE SANTA CATHARINA (1660–1740), who among other works wrote a curious miscellany of verse and prose, romance and literary criticism, entitled *Seram politico* (1704). In the biography of the saintly and strong-willed Archbishop of Braga, *Vida de D. Fr. Bertolomeu dos Martyres* (1619), the excellence of Sousa's style is even more apparent, for it has here no trace of rhetoric and the pictures stand out with the more effect for the economy with which they are drawn—the dearth of adjectives is noticeable. The archbishop's visits to his diocese give occasion for charming, homely glimpses of Minho. Neither of these books is the work of a critical historian (in the *Vida*, for instance, winds and waves obey the archbishop), but the

RELIGIOUS AND MYSTIC WRITERS

latter, especially, is in matter and manner one of the masterpieces of Portuguese literature, a *livro divino*, as a modern Portuguese writer called it.[1] The *Annaes de El Rei Dom João Terceiro*, written at the bidding of Philip IV, was published in 1844 by Herculano, who described the work as little more than a series of notes, except in the Indian sections, which summarize Barros. It is as a stylist, not as a historian, that Frei Luis de Sousa will always be read, and read with delight.[2] The subject of his biography, FREI BARTHOLOMEU DOS MARTYRES (1514–90), wrote in Portuguese a simple *Catecismo da Dovtrina Christam* (Braga, 1564), resembling the Portuguese work of his friend Fray Luis de Granada (1504–88) : *Compendio de Doctrina Christãa* (Lixboa, 1559).

The *Historia da Vida do Padre Francisco Xavier* (1600), by the Jesuit JOÃO DE LUCENA (1550–1600), born at Trancoso, who made his mark as an eloquent preacher and Professor of Philosophy in the University of Evora, is also one of the classics of the Portuguese language. It receives a glowing fervour from the author's evident delight in his subject—the life of the famous Basque missionary in whose arms D. João de Castro died. His command of clear, fluent, vigorous prose, his skilful use of words and abundant power of description, enable him to convey this enthusiasm to his readers. Part of the matter of his book was derived from Fernam Mendez Pinto, but the style is his own.

Like Frei Luis de Sousa, FREI MANUEL DA ESPERANÇA (1586–1670) became the historian of his Order in the *Historia Seraphica da Ordem dos Frades Menores* (2 pts., 1656, 66). We know from remarks in the second part that he paid the greatest attention to its composition, for which he had prepared himself by reading *hũa multidão notavel* of books on that and kindred subjects. Similar excellence of style marks the later work of the Jesuit

---

[1] C. Castello Branco, *Estrellas propicias*, 2ª ed., p. 204. Its only fault, artistically, is the detailed description of the commemoration festivities, which come as an anticlimax.

[2] Other works of the period are similarly read rather for their style than as history, as the *Historia Ecclesiastica da Igreja de Lisboa* (1642) and the *Historia Ecclesiastica dos Arcebispos de Braga* (2 pts., 1634, 1635) by D. RODRIGO DA CUNHA (1577–1643), the Archbishop of Lisbon who had an active share in the liberation of Portugal from the yoke of Spain in 1640.

Francisco de Sousa (1628?–1713), *O Oriente conquistado* (2 vols., 1710), in which he chronicles the history of the Company in the East.

The most celebrated Portuguese preacher of his time,[1] Frei Thomé de Jesus' brother, Diogo de Paiva de Andrade (1528–75), represented Portugal at the Council of Trent in 1561. His eloquent *Sermões* (1603, 4, 15) were published posthumously in three parts. His mantle fell upon Francisco Fernandez Galvão (1554–1610), the prose of whose *Sermões* (3 vols., 1611, 13, 16) is admirably restrained and pure. Less sonorous than the periods of Paiva de Andrade, the *Trattados* [sic] *Quadragesimais e da Paschoa* (1609) and *Tratados das Festas e Vidas dos Santos* (2 pts., 1612, 15) of the Dominican Frei Antonio Feo (1573–1627) perhaps gain rather than lose by being read, not heard. In the clearness and precision of their prose they are scarcely inferior to the remarkable *Sermões* (3 pts., 1617, 18, 25) of the Augustinian Frei Philipe da Luz (1574–1633), confessor to the Duke of Braganza (afterwards King João IV), in whose palace at Villa Viçosa he died. He, too, writes *sem grandes eloquencias*; he is as precise as Feo in his use of words, and his vocabulary is as extensive. Purity, concision, clearness, and harmony give him, together with Feo, Ceita, and Veiga, a high place in Portuguese prose.

The sermons for which the Dominican Frei Pedro Calvo (born *c.* 1550) was celebrated were published in *Homilias de Quaresma* (2 pts., 1627, 9), and at the repeated request of a friend he wrote his *Defensam das Lagrimas dos ivstos persegvidos* (1618) to prove that 'tears shed in time of trouble do not lessen merit'. The *Sermões* (1618) and *Considerações* (1619, 20, 33) of Frei Thomas da Veiga (1578–1638), like his father a Professor of Coimbra University, are written in a style of great excellence, as, although a trifle more redundant[2] and latinized, is that of his contemporary, like him a Franciscan, Frei João da Ceita

---

[1] Another renowned Court preacher was D. Antonio Pinheiro († 1582 ?), Bishop of Miranda, whose works were collected by Sousa Farinha : *Collecção das obras portuguesas do sabio Bispo de Miranda e de Leiria*, 2 vols., 1785, 6.

[2] e.g. *officio e dignidade, gritos e brados, boca e lingoa, cuidão e imaginão*. Macedo (*O Couto*, p. 82) rightly calls Ceita *um dos principaes textos em lingua portugueza*.

(1578–1633), whose prose has a natural grace and harmony, if it is less pure and indigenous than that of Luz. His best known works are the *Quadragena de Sermoens* (1619) and *Quadragena Segunda* (1625). Two more volumes of *Sermões* (1634, 5) appeared after his death. Two slightly later writers were FREI CRISTOVAM DE LISBOA (†1652), brother of Manuel Severim de Faria, and FREI CRISTOVAM DE ALMEIDA (1620–79), Bishop of Martyria. The former, author of *Jardim da Sagrada Escriptura* (1653) and *Consolaçam de Afflictos e Allivio de Lastimados* (1742), in the preface to his *Santoral de Varios Sermões* (1638) deplores the new fashion of certain preachers who hide their meaning under their eloquence. He is himself sometimes inclined to be florid. Bishop Almeida attained a reputation for great eloquence even in the days of Antonio Vieira.[1] His *Sermões* (1673, 80, 86) are simpler than those of Vieira, but for the reader their prose lacks the quiet precision of Ceita, Veiga, or Luz, whose sermons may be considered one of the sources from which a greater master of Portuguese, Manuel Bernardes, derived his magic. The Jesuit LUIS ALVAREZ (1615?–1709?), who was born a few years after Vieira, and lived on into the eighteenth century, also had a great reputation as a preacher. The fire is absent from the printed page, but his works, *Sermões da Quaresma* (3 pts., 1688, 94, 99), *Amor Sagrado* (1673), and *Ceo de graça, inferno custoso* 1692), are notable for the purity of their prose.

The religious works of the seventeenth, as of the sixteenth century are very various in subject and treatment. FREI JOÃO CARDOSO (†1655), author of *Ruth Peregrina* (2 pts., 1628, 54), also wrote a lengthy commentary on the 113th Psalm in twenty-one discourses: *Jornada Dalma Libertada* (1626). Ten years earlier a Jew, JOÃO BAPTISTA D'ESTE, had published in excellent Portuguese a translation of the Psalms: *Consolaçam Christam e Lvz para o Povo Hebreo* (1616). His title was suggested by

---

[1] Other noted preachers were the Jesuits FRANCISCO DO AMARAL (1593–1647), who published the first (and only) volume of his *Sermões* (1641) in the year in which Vieira came to Portugal, and FRANCISCO DE MENDONÇA (1573–1626), a master of clear and vigorous prose in his two volumes of *Sermões* (1636, 9); and the Trinitarian BALTASAR PAEZ (1570–1638), whose *Sermões de Quaresma* (2 pts., 1631, 3), *Sermões da Semana Santa* (1630), *Marial de Sermões* (1649), may still be read with profit.

that of a far more remarkable book by another Jew, SAMUEL USQUE (fl. 1540), *Consolaçam ás Tribulaçoens de Israel*, written probably between 1540 and 1550[1] and first printed at Ferrara by Abraham ben Usque in 1553. The author was the son of Spanish Jews who had taken refuge in Portugal, where he was born, probably at the end of the fifteenth century.[2] His famous work is an account of the sufferings of the Jewish race. In three dialogues Jacob (*Ycabo*), Nahum (*Numeo*), and Zachariah (*Zicareo*) converse as shepherds. Israel, in person, relates his sorrows down to the fall of Jerusalem, an event which is described in detail, and so on to the persecutions in European countries (*novas gentes*), and at the end of each dialogue the prophets administer their comfort. The book closes with a chorus of rapturous psalms in biblical prose, rejoicing at the coming end of Israel's tribulations and calling for vengeance on their enemies, and thus finishes on a note of joyful faith and courageous hope, without an inkling of charity. The first dialogue, which condenses Old Testament history, has a rhythmical, luxuriant style, rich in Oriental imagery, but later, where Roman history is the authority, or in the tragic account of the persecution of Jews in Portugal[3] under João II and the two succeeding kings, the style is shorn of rhetoric. Nor is there a trace of false ornament in a long passage of wonderful eloquence, Israel's final complaint and invocation to sky and earth, waters and mortal creatures. The agony and awful glow of indignation at these recent events had a restraining influence on the style, which loses nothing by this simplicity. Quieter descriptions are those of the shepherd's life and of the chase in the first, and of spring and evening in the third part.

The Jesuit DIOGO MONTEIRO (1561–1634), when towards the end of his life he published his *Arte de Orar* (1631), promised, should his 'great occupations' allow, to print very soon the

[1] *Ha poucos annos que he arribado* (the Inquisition in Portugal), Pt. 3, 1908 ed., f. xxxii.
[2] See p. 5 of *Prologo* : Portuguese is *a lingoa que mamei*, but his *passados* are from Castile.
[3] The inhabitants of the Peninsula are *astutos e maliciosos*, Spain is ' a hypocritical and cruel wolf ', the Portuguese are *fortes e quasi barbaros*, the English *maliciosos*, the Italians, since the book was to appear in their country, merely ' warlike and ungrateful '.

second volume dealing with the divine attributes. This did not appear in that generation: *Meditações dos attribvtos divinos* (Roma, 1671). The *Arte de Orar* contains twenty-nine treatises (604 ff.). Its subjects are various (of the virtue of magnificence; of the esteem in which singing is held by God, &c.), and they are presented with fervour and clear concision, and especially with a complete absence of oratorical effect. Quintilian takes part in one of the six dialogues which compose the *Peregrinaçam Christam* (1620) by TRISTÃO BARBOSA DE CARVALHO (†1632); he is on a pilgrimage from Lisbon to the tomb of Saint Isabel at Coimbra, but he expresses himself in excellent Portuguese, modelled perhaps on that of Arraez. The prose of the *Retrato de Prvdentes, Espelho de Ignorantes* (1664) by the Jesuit FRANCISCO AIRES (1597–1664) often rises to eloquence, notably in the fervent prayers. His *Theatro dos Trivmphos Divinos contra os Desprimores Hvmanos* (1658) is of a more practical character. The Franciscan FREI MANUEL DOS ANJOS (1595–1653) laid no claim to originality in his *Politica predicavel e doutrina moral do bom governo do mundo* (1693), written in a clear and correct but slightly redundant[1] style.

FREI LUIS DOS ANJOS (*c*. 1570–1625) in his *Iardim de Portugal* (1626) gathered edifying anecdotes of saintly women from various writers, and set them down in good Portuguese prose. The Franciscan FREI PEDRO DE SANTO ANTONIO (*c*. 1570–1641) in his *Iardim Spiritual, tirado dos Sanctos e Varoens spiritvaes* (1632) contented himself with translation of his authorities, adding, he modestly says, 'some things of my own of not much importance'. He carefully avoided interlarding his Portuguese with Latin, his object being *fazer prato a todos*. Even more humble is the work of the Cistercian FREI FRADIQUE ESPINOLA (*c*. 1630–1708), who compiled in his *Escola Decurial* (12 pts., 1696–1721) an encyclopaedia of themes so various as the fate of King Sebastian, the duties of women, and the habits of storks. Although it lacks the literary pretensions of the

---

[1] If, for instance, the bracketed words in the following sentence (p. 3, § 5) be omitted it gains in vigour and loses little in the sense : *Este poder se não deo aos Reys para extorsoens [& violencias] mas para amparar [& defender] os vassallos porque até o proprio Deos parece que tem as mãos atadas a rigores [& castigos] & livres a clemencias [& misericordias].*

Divertimento erudito by the Augustinian Frei João Pacheco (1677–? 1747), it contains some curious matter. A similar miscellany of anecdotes and precepts was written by João Baptista de Castro in the eighteenth century: *Hora de Recreio nas ferias de maiores estudos* (2 pts., 1742, 3).

The life of the ardent Frei Antonio das Chagas (1631–82) abounded in contrasts. Born at Vidigueira, of an old Alentejan family, Antonio da Fonseca Soares began his career as a soldier in 1650; a duel (arising out of one of his many love affairs), in which he killed his man, drove him to Brazil, and it was only after several years of distinguished service [1] that he returned to Portugal, perhaps in 1657. In 1661 he attained the rank of captain, but in the following year abandoned his military career, and in 1663 professed in the Franciscan convent at Evora, exchanging the composition of gongoric verse for a voluminous correspondence in prose, and his unregenerate days of dissipation for a glowing and saintly asceticism. (*Trocando as galas em burel e os caprichos em cilicios* are the words with which he veils the real sincerity of his conversion.) Preferring the humbler but strenuous duties of missionary in Portugal and Spain to the bishopric of Lamego, he founded the missionary convent of Varatojo, and died there twenty years after his novitiate. During those years he built up and exercised a powerful spiritual influence throughout Portugal, and it continued after his death. Few of his poems survive, since he committed the greater part of his profane verse to the flames, but some of his *romances* may still be read. It is, however, as a prose-writer, especially in his *Cartas Espirituaes* (2 pts., 1684, 7), that he holds a foremost place in Portuguese literature. There is less affectation in these more familiar letters than in his *Sermões genuinos* (1690) or his *Obras Espirituaes* (1684). The very titles of some of his shorter treatises, *Vozes do Ceo e Tremores da Terra*, *Espelho do Espelho*, show that he had not even now altogether escaped the false taste of the time, and artificial flowers of speech, plays on words, laboured metaphors and antitheses appear in his prose. But if it has not the simple severity of

---

[1] He had been fortunate, for, says Antonio Vieira in 1640, *não ha guerra no mundo onde se morra tão frequentemente como na do Brazil*.

a Bernardes, it possesses so persuasive, so passionate an energy, and is of so clear a fervour and harmony that its eloquence is felt to be genuine.

The Jesuit FREI JOÃO DA FONSECA (1632–1701), in the preface to one of his works, *Sylva Moral e Historica* (1696), which may have given Bernardes the idea of his *Nova Floresta*, rejects affected periods and new phrases, and there is no false rhetoric in his *Espelho de Penitentes* (1687), *Satisfaçam de Aggravos* (1700), which takes the form of dialogues between a hermit and a soldier, and other devotional works. Another Jesuit, ALEXANDRE DE GUSMÃO (1629–1724), although born at Lisbon, spent most (eighty-five years) of his long life in Brazil. He wrote, among other works, *Rosa de Nazareth nas Montanhas de Hebron* (1715), compiled from various histories of the Company of Jesus, and *Historia do Predestinado Peregrino e seu Irmão Precito* (1682). The latter is an allegory in six books which lacks the human interest of Bunyan's *Pilgrim's Progress*, which it preceded. It describes the journey of two brothers, Predestinado and Precito, out of Egypt to Jerusalem (Heaven) and Babylon (Hell). The style is simpler and more direct than might be inferred from the inflated title, and often has an effective if studied eloquence.[1]

Vieira dying is reported to have said that the Portuguese language was safe in the keeping of Padre Manuel Bernardes. The aged Jesuit, who maintained his interest in literature to the end, may have received Bernardes' *Luz e Calor*[2] (1696) in the last year of his life, and the *Exercicios Espirituaes* (2 vols., 1686) had appeared ten years earlier. Other works, *Sermões e Praticas* (1711),[3] *Nova Floresta* (5 vols., 1706–28), *Os Ultimos Fins do Homem* (1727), *Varios Tratados* (2 vols., 1737), were soon forthcoming to justify the prophecy. MANUEL BERNARDES (1644–1710), the son of João Antunes and Maria Bernardes, was born at Lisbon, studied law and philosophy at Coimbra

---

[1] e.g. in the following passage (p. 47), in which Calderon and João de Deus join hands: 'The world and its glory is a passing comedy, a farce that ends in laughter, a shadow that disappears, a thinning mist, a fading flower, a blinding smoke, a dream that is not true.'

[2] *Estimulos de amor divino* (1758) is an extract from this, as the *Tratado breve da oraçam mental* (5th ed., 1757) is extracted from the *Exercicios Espirituaes*.   [3] Pt. 2 appeared in 1733.

University, and at the age of thirty entered the Lisbon Oratory, where he spent thirty-six years. That was all his life, yet through his books this modest, humorous, austere priest has exercised a profound influence not only, as Barbosa Machado declares, in guiding souls to Heaven, but in moulding and protecting the Portuguese language. His style is marked in an equal degree by grace and concision, intensity and restraint, smoothness and vigour.[1] With him the florid cloak, in which many recent writers had wrapped Portuguese, falls away, leaving the pith and kernel of the language; the conceits of the *culteranos* disappear, and the most striking effects are attained without apparent artifice. In his hands the pinchbeck and tinsel are transmuted into delicate pieces of ivory. The charm of his style is difficult to analyse, but it may be remarked that his vocabulary is inexhaustible, his precision unfailing, that he is not afraid to employ the commonest words, and that the construction of his sentences is of a transparent simplicity, as bare of rhetoric as is the poetry of João de Deus. His reputation as a lord of language has survived every test. His works are not merely the *deliciae* of a few distant scholars but an acknowledged glory of the nation, praised by that literary iconoclast Macedo, and quoted as an authority in the Republican Parliament of 1915. The most popular of his works are *Luz e Calor*, and especially the *Nova Floresta*, in which moral and familiar anecdote go quaintly hand in hand, but if one must choose between excellence and excellence his masterpiece is the *Exercicios Espirituaes*, in which thought and expression often rise to sublime heights. One may perhaps compare him with Fray Juan de los Ángeles (†1609). His simple doctrines spring from the heart and, winged by shrewd knowledge of men, touch the heart of his readers. One of his more immediate followers was Padre Manuel Consciencia (*c.* 1669–1739), author of a large number of works on moral and religious subjects, the best known of which is *A Mocidade enganada e desenganada* (6 vols., 1729–38).

[1] He often deliberately links a soft and a hard word, as *caça e cão, candores da celestial graça, licita a guerra*. Thus his style becomes *crespo sem aspereza*.

IV

1580–1706

The Seiscentistas

Philip II entered his new capital under triumphal arches on June 29, 1581, and the subjection of Portugal to Spain during the next sixty years in part accounts for the fact that nowhere was the decadence of literature in the seventeenth century more marked than at Lisbon. For Spain in her sturdy independence and reaction from rigid classicism had led the way in those precious affectations which invaded the literatures of Europe, and the universal malady, gongorism with its Lylyan conceits and cultured style, now found a ready welcome in Portugal. The literary style which corresponded to the Churriguerresque in architecture naturally proved congenial to the land of the *estilo manuelino*. King Philip was glad to conciliate and provide for Portuguese men of letters,[1] but if in the preceding centuries many of them wrote in Spanish, that tendency was now necessarily strengthened. Another cause of decadence was no doubt the Inquisition, although its influence in this respect has been greatly exaggerated. It required no immense tact on the part of an author to prevent his works from being placed on the Index. An examination, for instance, of the differences between the 1616 edition of *Eufrosina* and the condemned 1561 edition shows that the parts excised were chiefly coarse passages or unsuitable references to the Bible (this was also the charge against the letters of Clenardus). That remarkable mathematician, Pedro Nunez, pays a tribute to the enlightened patronage of letters by Cardinal Henrique, the most ardent promoter of the Inquisition in Portugal: *qui cum nullum*

---

[1] Bernardo de Brito, no lover of Spain, bears witness to *o favor e benevolencia com que trata os homens doutos*.

tempus intermittat quin semper aut animarum saluti prospiciat aut optimos quosque auctores evolvat aut literatorum hominum colloquia audiat.[1]

No literary figure in Portugal of the seventeenth century, few in the Peninsula,[2] can rank with D. FRANCISCO MANUEL DE MELLO (1608–66). Born at Lisbon,[3] he belonged to the highest Portuguese nobility and began both his military and literary career in his seventeenth year. He wrote in Spanish, although, in verse at least, he felt it to be a hindrance,[4] and it was not till he was over forty that he published a work in Portuguese: *Carta de Guia de Casados* (1651).[5] Few men have accomplished more, and towards the end of his life he could say with pride that it would be difficult to find an idle hour in it. He was shipwrecked near St. Jean de Luz in 1627 and fought in the battle of the Downs in 1639. He was sent with the Conde de Linhares to quell the Evora insurrection in 1637, and took part in the campaign against revolted Catalonia (1640), which he described in his *Guerra de Cataluña*[6] (1645), written *em varias fortunas* and recognized as a classic of Spanish literature. A man frankly outspoken like Mello must have made many enemies, enemies dangerous in a time of natural distrust. During the Catalan campaign he was sent under arrest to Madrid, apparently on suspicion of favouring the cause of an independent Portugal,[7] and a little later, when he was in the service of the King of Portugal, the suspicion as to his loyalty recurred. On November 19, 1644, he was arrested at Lisbon on a different charge. It appears that a servant dismissed by Mello revenged himself by implicating his former master in a murder that he had committed

---

[1] *De Crepusculis*, Preface. Martim Afonso de Miranda later (*Tempo de Agora, prologo* to Pt. 2, 1624) writes of *a pouca curiosidade que hoje ha acerca da lição dos liuros, como tambem o risco a que se expõem os que escreuem.*

[2] Menéndez y Pelayo set Mello above all except his friend Quevedo.

[3] Mr. Edgar Prestage discovered his baptismal certificate and established the date (1608) beyond doubt, though it is still often given as 1611. On his mother's side Mello was great-grandson of the historian Duarte Nunez de Leam.

[4] Prefatory letter to *Las tres Mvsas del Melodino* (1649): *el lenguaje estrangero tan poco es favorable al que compone.*

[5] He was writing it in January 1650.

[6] *Historia de los movimientos y separacion de Cataluña y de la guerra*, &c. Lisboa, 1645.

[7] On his release after four months of imprisonment the Count-Duke Olivares said to him: *Ea, caballero, ha sido un erro, pero erro con causa.*

THE SEISCENTISTAS

(of a man as obscure as himself). Whether he did this of his own initiative or at the bidding of Mello's enemies is uncertain, but they saw to it that Mello once in prison should not be soon released. They might, probably did, assure the king that this was the best place for one ' devoted to the cause of Castile '. There are other theories to account for Mello's long imprisonment, the most romantic of which—that he and the king were rivals in the affections of the Condessa de Villa Nova, and, meeting disguised and by accident at the entrance of her house, drew their swords, the king recognizing Mello by his voice—is now generally abandoned. Although no evidence of Mello's participation in the murder was forthcoming, he was condemned to be deported for life to Africa, for which Brazil was later substituted. It was only in 1655, after eleven years of more or less[1] strict confinement, that he sailed for Brazil. João IV died in 1656 and two years later Mello returned to Portugal: he was formally pardoned[2] and spent the last years of his life in important diplomatic missions to London, Rome, and Paris. The unfaltering courage and gaiety with which he faced his adventures and misfortunes win our admiration, but his life can strike no one as literary. Yet it is probable that but for his long imprisonment he would never have found leisure to write many of his best works, and prosperity might have dimmed his insight and dulled his style—that style (influenced no doubt by Quevedo and Gracián) which is hard and clear as the glitter of steel or the silver chiming of a clock, with *concinnitas quaedam venusta et felix verborum*.[3] Even when full of points and conceits it retains its clearness and trenchancy, and in his more familiar works he is unrivalled, as the *Carta de Guia de Casados*, in which, *innuptus ipse*, he brings freshness and originality to the theme already treated in Fray Luis de Leon's *La Perfecta Casada* (1583), Diogo Paiva de Andrade's sensible but less caustic *Casamento Perfeito* (1631), and Dr. João de Barros' *Espelho de Casados*

---

[1] The first five years were, in his own words, rigorous. In 1650 he was removed from the *Torre Velha* to the Lisbon *Castello*, and thenceforth enjoyed greater liberty. He had been transferred from the Torre de Belem to the *Torre Velha* on the left bank of the Tagus in 1646.

[2] The document was discovered by Dr. Braga and published in his *Os Seiscentistas* (1916), p. 339.

[3] *Approbatio* of *Cartas*, Roma, 1664.

(1540),[1] or the pithy and delightful *Cartas Familiares*, of which five centuries—a mere fragment—were published at Rome in 1664, with a rapier-thrust of his wit and a maxim of good sense on every page, preserving for us some vestige of what Frei Manuel Godinho described as his 'admirable conversation' when he met him at Marseilles in 1633.[2] The *Epanaphoras de varia Historia Portugueza* (1660) are unequal and often excessively detailed.[3] Three of the five are, however, the accounts of an eyewitness and as such are full of interest: the *Alteraçoens de Evora* (i), the *Naufragio da Armada Portuguesa em França* (ii), and the *Conflito do Canal de Inglaterra* (iv).[4]

Mello's knowledge of men was as wide as his knowledge of books, and both appear to great advantage in his *Apologos Dialogaes* (1721). An individualist in religion[5] and politics,[6] an acute thinker and a keen student of men and manners, he found no dullness in life even at its worst and no solitude, for, if alone, his fancy instilled wit and wisdom into clocks[7] and coins[8] and fountains.[9] The first three *Apologos* contain incisive portraits in which types and persons are sharply etched in a few lines: the poor *escudeiro*, the *beata*, the Lisbon market-woman, the litigious *ratinho*, the *fidalgo* from the provinces,[10] the ambitious priest, the shabby grammarian, the worldly monk, political place-hunter, *miles gloriosus*, or melancholy author, a tinselled nobody boiling down the good sayings of

[1] A copy of this rare and curious work exists in the Lisbon Biblioteca Nacional (*Res.* 264 v.). It contains 71 ff. divided into four parts. The author, in his apophthegms on the character of women, quotes the classics widely, and refers to the Uthopia [so] of Sir Thomas More and to *Celestina*.
[2] *Relaçam*, 1842 ed., p. 233.
[3] His digressions are methodical: *por este modo de historiar (que é aquelle que eu desejo ler) pretendo escrever sempre* (*Epan.* ii). In *Epan.* i he says: *Refiro, pode ser com demasia, todos os accidentes deste negocio*.
[4] He re-wrote this *Epanaphora* twice, the first two versions having been lost.
[5] Cf. *Visita das Fontes* (*Ap. Dial.* 3), 1900 ed., p. 89: *cada qual desde o logar em que está acha uma linha muito junto de si que é o caminho por onde pode ir a Deus*.
[6] Cf. *Hospital das Lettras* (*Ap. Dial.* 4), 1900 ed., p. 114: *por falta de cuidar cada um em se aproveitar deste mundo o que delle lhe toca, o lançam todos a perder todos juntos do modo que vemos*.
[7] *Relogios Fallantes* (*Ap. Dial.* 1).
[8] *Escriptorio Avarento* (*Ap. Dial.* 2).
[9] *Visita das Fontes* (*Ap. Dial.* 3).
[10] Cf. the backwoodsman described by Couto as *algum fidalgo criado ld na Beira que nunca vio o Rei* (*Dialogo do Sold. Prat.*, p. 31).

past writers. The fourth *Apologo* entitled *Hospital das Lettras* (1657) is devoted more especially to literary criticism; Mello with Quevedo, Justus Lipsius, and Traiano Boccalini (who died when Mello was five) makes a notable scrutiny of Spanish and Portuguese literature. As a literary critic Mello is excellent within limits. Himself an artificial writer, although as it were naturally artificial, bred at Court, versed in social and political affairs, he considered that the proper study of mankind was man, and, like Henry Fielding a century later, admired ' the wondrous power of art in improving Nature '.[1] For him the country and Nature, the bucolic poetry and prose of Fernam Alvarez do Oriente, the ingenuous narratives of the early chroniclers, had no charm; he preferred Rodrigo Mendez Silva's *Vida y hechos del gran Condestable* (Madrid, 1640) to the *Cronica do Condestabre*.[2] But all that was vernacular and indigenous attracted him, as is proved in his letters, in his lively farce *Auto do Fidalgo Aprendiz* (1676), and in the *Feira dos Anexins*, which is a long string of popular maxims and of those plays upon words in which Mello delighted. His poetry—*Las Tres Musas del Melodino* (1649), *Obras Metricas* (1665)—is marred by the conceits which in his prose often serve effectively to point a moral or drive home an argument. It is far too clever. When in a poem ' On the death of a great lady ' we find the line *contigo o sepultara a sepultura* we do not know whether to laugh or weep, but we suspect the sincerity of the author's grief, and although he wrote some excellent *quintilhas*, most of his poems, which are, as might be expected, always vigorous, are too sharp and thin, stalks without flowers, the very skeletons of poetry. It is to his prose in its wit and grace, its shrewd thought, its revelation of a sincere and lofty but unassuming character, its directness,[3] its *bom portugues velho e relho*, that he owes his place among the greatest writers of the Peninsula.

The taste in poetry in the seventeenth and eighteenth cen-

---

[1] Cf. *Aulegrafia* (1619), f. 85 v. : *emendar a Natureza*.
[2] Edgar Prestage, *Esboço*, pp. 128–9.
[3] Like another equally brilliant soldier historian, Napier, he rarely spells a foreign word aright. Cf. *Epanaphoras*, p. 204 : *A este nome* Milord *corresponde no estado feminil o nome* Léde. Falmouth, where he had actually been, becomes Valmud, the Isle of Wight Huyt, Whitehall Huythal, the Earl of Northumberland Notaborlan (Brito has Northũbria).

turies is seen in two collections, partly Spanish, partly Portuguese: *Fenix Renascida* (5 vols., 1716–28) and *Eccos que o Clarim da Fama dá* (2 vols., 1761, 2). The latter is sufficiently characterized by its title, too long to quote in full. As to the former the Phoenix seems to have given real pleasure to contemporary readers, but for us the bird and song are flown and only the ashes remain, from which a sixteenth-century poem such as the sonnet *Horas breves* stands out conspicuously. The subjects are often as trivial as those of the *Cancioneiro* published two centuries earlier and more domestic: to a cousin sewing, to an overdressed man, to a large mouth, a sonnet to two market-women fighting, another to the prancing horse of the Conde de Sabugal, on a present of roses, two long *romances* on a goldfinch killed by a cat, verses sent with a gift of handkerchiefs or eggs or melons, or to thank for sugar-plums—the *Fenix* rarely soars above such themes. The magistrate ANTONIO BARBOSA BACELLAR (1610–63) figures largely, with glosses on poems by Camões, a *romance A umas saudades*, a satirical poem *A umas beatas*. His *romances varios* are mostly in Spanish, but a few of his sonnets in Portuguese have some merit. The fifth volume opens (pp. 1–37) with a far more elaborate satire by DIOGO CAMACHO (or Diogo de Sousa): *Jornada que Diogo Camacho fez ás Cortes do Parnaso*, the best burlesque poem of the century, in which the author did not spare contemporary Lisbon poets.[1] The poems of JERONIMO BAHIA likewise cover many pages. He it is who bewails at length the sad fate of a goldfinch. In *oitavas* he wrote a *Fabula de Polyfemo a Galatea*,[2] and in octosyllabic *redondilhas* jocular accounts of journeys from Lisbon to Coimbra and from Lisbon into Alentejo (on a very lean mule) which are sometimes amusing. His sonnet *Fallando com Deos* shows a deeper nature, and the collection contains other religious verse, notably that of Violante Montesino, better known as SOROR VIOLANTE DO CEO (1601–93). Here,[3] as in her *Rythmas varias* (Rouen, 1646) and *Parnaso*

[1] A more personal and picaresque satirist was D. THOMAS DE NORONHA († 1651), whose works were collected by Dr. Mendes dos Remedios in his *Subsidios*, vol. ii: *Poesias Ineditas de D. Thomás de Noronha* (Coimbra, 1899). The satiric poem *Os Ratos da Inquisição* by ANTONIO SERRÃO DE CASTRO (1610–85) was first published by Castello Branco in 1883.

[2] Vol. iii contains a poem by Jacinto Freire de Andrade with the same title.

[3] *Fenix Ren.* ii. 406; iii. 225; v. 376.

Lusitano de divinos e humanos versos (2 vols., 1733), this nun, who spent over sixty years in the Dominican Convento da Rosa at Lisbon, and who from an early age was known for her skill upon the harp and in poetry—admiring contemporaries called her the tenth Muse—showed that she could write with simple fervour, as in the Portuguese *deprecações devotas* of the *Meditações da Missa* (1689) or her Spanish *villancicos*. But she could also be the most gongorical of writers, her very real native talent being too often spoilt by the taste of the time.[1] BERNARDA FERREIRA DE LACERDA (1595–1644), another *femina incomparabilis*, like Soror Violante and Dercylis considered the tenth Muse and fourth Grace, wrote almost exclusively in Spanish, nor can her *Soledades de Buçaco* (1634) or her epic *Hespaña Libertada* (2 pts., 1618, 73) be considered a heavy loss to Portuguese literature. SOROR MARIA MAGDALENA EUPHEMIA DA GLORIA (1672–? *c.* 1760), in the world Leonarda Gil da Gama, in *Brados do Desengano* (1739), *Orbe Celeste* (1742), and *Reino de Babylonia* (1749), rarely descends from the high-flown style indicated in these titles. On the other hand, the Franciscan nun of Lisbon, SOROR MARIA DO CEO (1658–1753), or Maria de Eça, in *A Preciosa* (2 pts., 1731, 3) and *Enganos do Bosque, Desenganos do Rio* (1741), among much verse of the same kind has some poems of real charm and an almost rustic simplicity.

By reason of a certain intensity and a vigorous style D. FRANCISCO CHILD ROLIM DE MOURA (1572–1640), Lord of the towns of Azambuja and Montargil, although more versed in arms than in letters, wrote in *Os Novissimos do Homem* (1623) a poem quite as readable as the longer epics of his contemporaries, despite its duller subject (man's first disobedience and all our woe). The four cantos in *oitavas* are headed Death, Judgement, Hell, Paradise.[2]

---

[1] Hers is the deplorable pun of a superior superior :
Que se Prior sois agora
Sempre fostes suprior.

[2] The real title of the first (1623) edition is *Dos Novissimos de Dom Francisco Rolim de Moura*. Adam is conducted by his son Abel through Hell and comforted by a vision of Paradise. As he is the first man and only Abel has died, he must forgo Dante's pleasure in meeting his personal enemies there, but there is something perhaps even more awful in the thought of the emptiness of these *infinitos logares* (iii. 48). Virgil's *Facilis descensus*, &c., is translated in two lines of great badness : Onde descer he cousa tão factivel Quanto tornar atraz tem de impossivel (iii. 36).

Of the life of Manuel da Veiga Tagarro we know little or nothing, but his volume of eclogues and odes, *Lavra de Anfriso* (1627), stands conspicuous in the seventeenth century for its simplicity and true lyrical vein. There is nothing original in these four eclogues, but the verse is of a harmonious softness. In the odes he succeeds in combining fervent thought with a classical restraint of expression. He aimed high; Horace, Lope de Vega, and Luis de Leon seem to have been his models. Some measure of the latter's deliberate tranquillity he occasionally attained. The works of the 'discreet and accomplished', keen-eyed and graceful D. Francisco de Portugal (1585–1632) appeared posthumously[1]: *Divinos e humanos versos* (1652) and (without separate title-page) *Prisões e solturas de hũa alma*, consisting of mystic poems mostly in Spanish in a setting of Portuguese prose, and, in Spanish, *Arte de Galanteria* (1670), of which a second edition was published in 1682. Lope de Vega praised the 'elegant verses' of the *Gigantomachia* (1628) written by Manuel de Galhegos (1597–1665). That he could write good Portuguese poetry the author showed in the 732 verses of his *Templo da Memoria* (1635), in the preface of which he declares that it had become a rash act to publish poems written in Portuguese but quotes the example of Pereira de Castro and of Góngora as having used the language of everyday life and plebeian words without indignity.

The later epics testified to the perseverance of their authors rather than to their poetical talent. They are perhaps less guilty than the critics, who should have discouraged the kind and recognized that the *Lusiads* were only an accident in Portuguese literature, the accident of the genius of Camões. As a rule the epic spirit of the Portuguese expressed itself better in prose. Gabriel Pereira de Castro (1571?–1632) forestalled Sousa de Macedo in his choice of a subject. His *Vlyssea, ov Lysboa Edificada, Poema heroyco* (1636) was published posthumously by his brother Luis, and perhaps the most remarkable thing about it is that it should have run through six editions. The structure of the poem, in ten cantos of *oitavas*, is closely

---

[1] *Nihil tamen eo vivente excussum nisi Solitudines* (*hoc est Saudades*), says the *Theatrum*.

modelled on that of the *Lusiads*, and the gods of Olympus duly take a part in the story. He sings, he says boldly, to his country, to the world and to eternity, but his sails flap sadly for lack of inspiration and enthusiasm, and his daring *enjambements* [1] do not compensate for the dullness of theme and treatment. If, for instance, we compare his storm [2] with that of the *Lusiads* (vi. 70–91) it must be confessed that the former has much the air of a commotion in a duckpond. Ulysses on his way to Lisbon visits (canto 4) the infernal regions, is astonished to meet kings there, and (canto 6) relates the siege and fall of Troy.

The life of BRAS GARCIA DE MASCARENHAS (1596–1656) was more interesting than his verses. He was born at Avó, near the Serra da Estrella, and his adventures began early, for he was arrested on account of a love affair (1616) and made a daring escape from Coimbra prison after wounding his jailer. His careful biographer, Dr. Antonio de Vasconcellos, has shown that there is no record of his having studied at Coimbra University. Subsequently he travelled and fought in Brazil (1623–32), Italy, France, Flanders, and Spain, and in 1641, as captain, raised and commanded a body of horse known as the Company of Lions. As Governor of Alfaiates, the 'key of Beira', he was wrongfully accused of having a treasonable understanding with Spain and imprisoned at Sabugal, some ten miles from Alfaiates (1642). He obtained a book (the *Flos Sanctorum*), flour, and scissors and cut out a letter in verse to King João IV, who restored him to his governorship and gave him the habit of Avis. His long epic *Viriato Tragico* (1699) contains some forcible descriptions and has a pleasantly patriotic and indigenous atmosphere—one feels that he is singing *os patrios montes* as much as the hero—but in style it differs little from prose. Tedious geographical descriptions, dry catalogues of names, a whole stanza (vii. 39) composed exclusively of nouns, another (iv. 63) of proper names, incline the reader less to praise than sleep,

---

[1] e.g. (x. 126):
    Hũa montanha e serra inhabitada
    Se erguia ao ar, em cuja corpulenta
    Espalda. . . .

[2] ii. 30–49:
    Do undoso leito, donde repousava
    O mar, &c.

from which he is only gently stirred when the sun is called *a solar embaixadora*. In the prevailing fashion of the time the author works in lines of Camões, Sá de Miranda, Garci Lasso, Ariosto, and other poets. While the work was still in manuscript another poet, and perhaps a relation, André da Silva Mascarenhas, helped himself liberally to its stanzas (they number 2,287) for his epic *A Destruição de Hespanha* (1671). He could have given no better proof of the poverty of his genius. FRANCISCO DE SÁ DE MENESES (*c.* 1600–1664?), although less true a poet than his cousin and namesake the Conde de Mattosinhos, won a far wider fame by his epic poem *Malaca Conqvistada* (1634), in which he recounts *a heroica historia dos feitos de Albuquerque*. The reader who accompanies his frail bark[1] through twelve cantos of *oitavas* feels that he has well earned the fall of Malacca at the end. For although the author is not incapable of vigorous and succinct description he too often decks out the pure gold of Camões' style [2] with periphrases and Manueline ornaments which delay the action. The sun is ' the lover of Clytie ' or ' the rubicund son of Latona '. He stops to tell us that a diamond won by Albuquerque had been ' cut by skilled hand in Milan ', and some of his more elaborate similes are not without charm. Canto 7 tells of the future deeds of the Portuguese in India. The gods interfere less than in the *Lusiads* (Asmodeus plays a part in canto 6), but the general effect is that of a great theme badly handled. After the death of his wife, the author spent the last twenty years of his life (from 1641) in the Dominican convent of Bemfica as Frei Francisco de Jesus.

ANTONIO DE SOUSA DE MACEDO (1606–82), *moço fidalgo* of Philip IV and later Secretary of Embassy and Minister (*Residente*) in London (1642–6) and Secretary of State to the weak and unlettered Afonso VI, wrote at the age of twenty-two *Flores de España, Excelencias de Portugal* (1631). This historical work of considerable interest and importance was written in Spanish *por ser mais universal*, but he returned to Portuguese presently in

---

[1] xii. 79: *Sou fragil lenho*.
[2] In the storm in canto 2 (*Eis que o ceo de improuiso se escurece*) he seems to have realized that Camões' description could not be improved upon.

a curious prose miscellany, *Eva e Ave* (1676), and in the epic poem *Vlyssippo* (1640) in fourteen cantos of *oitavas*. He seems to have felt that interest could not easily be sustained by the subject, the foundation of Lisbon by Ulysses. Accordingly, following the example of Camões, he inset various episodes. Canto 6 summarizes the events of the *Iliad* and the *Odyssey*, canto 10 describes a tapestry adorned with future Portuguese victories, in canto 11 the Delphic Sibyl foretells the deeds of Portugal's kings, down to Sebastian, in canto 12 the wise Chiron prophesies of her *famosos varões*. The style is correct, but the poem as a whole is commonplace. VASCO MOUSINHO DE QUEVEDO, of Setubal, although no records of his life remain, won high fame by his epic poem in *oitavas* (twelve cantos) *Afonso Africano* (1611), in which 'the marvellous prowess of King Afonso V in Africa' is described. The poem, admired by Almeida Garrett, is particularly wearisome because it is largely allegorical. The king conquering Arzila represents the strong man subduing the city of his own soul, the Moors are the spirits of the damned, and seven of their knights representing the seven deadly sins are defeated by seven Christian knights who stand for the virtues.

The poverty of profane prose, compared with its flourishing condition in the preceding century, is also remarkable. A few historians of the seventeenth century have already been mentioned. The literary academies, of which the most famous were the *Academia dos Generosos* (1649-68) and the *Academia dos Singulares* (1663-5),[1] existed rather for the interchange of wit and complimentary or satiric verses than for the encouragement of historical and scientific research. The Conde da Ericeira's *Portugal Restaurado* and Freire de Andrade's Life bear no comparison with works of the *Quinhentistas*. Yet it was the second golden age of Portuguese prose, as the names of Manuel Bernardes and Vieira prove. The latter's letters, with those of Frei Antonio das Chagas and Mello, are in three different kinds—the political, religious, and familiar—the most notable written in the century.

---

[1] Numerous other academies of the same kind came into being in this and the first half of the next century. Most of their members now belong to the (Brazilian) *Academia dos Esquecidos*—the Forgotten.

Gaspar Pires de Rebello in the preface to his *Infortvnios tragicos da Constante Florinda* (1625) excuses himself for its publication on the ground that ' not spiritual and divine books only benefit our intelligence '. The book, which records the love of Arnaldo and Florinda, of Zaragoza, shows the modern novel growing through *Don Quixote* out of the *Celestina* plays and the romances of chivalry, but has little other interest. A second part was published in 1633, and *Novellas Exemplares*, six stories by the same author, in 1650. Numerous other works appeared with more or less alluring or sensational titles but contents disappointingly dull. Mattheus de Ribeiro (c. 1620-95), in his *Alivio de Tristes e Consolação de Queixosos* (1672, 4), shows greater skill than Pires de Rebello in the invention of the story, but it is marred by the diffuse and pedantic style—April becomes an ' academy in which Flora was opening the doors for the study of flowers '. The pastoral novel ended in sad contortions with the *Desmayos de Mayo em sombras de Mondego* (1635) by Diogo Ferreira de Figueiroa (1604-74). Its title and the three involved sentences which cover the first three pages (ff. 10, 11) convey an adequate idea of its character and contents.

Of several prose works written by Martim Afonso de Miranda, of Lisbon, in the first third of the century, the most important is *Tempo de Agora* (2 pts., 1622, 4). It contains seven dialogues dealing with truth and falsehood, the evils of idleness, temperance, friendship, justice, the evils of dice and cards, and precepts for princes. Much of their matter is interesting and the comments incisive, especially as to the prevailing luxury in food and dress. They tell of the infinite number of curiously bound books at Lisbon, of the soldiers unpaid, ' eating at the doors of convents ', of the delight in foreign fashions, and the craze for ' diabolical ' books from Italy to the exclusion of *livros de historias* and books in Portuguese. The anonymous *Primor e honra da vida soldadesca no Estado da India* (1630), edited by the Augustinian Frei Antonio Freire (c. 1570-1634), is a different work from Geronimo Ximenez de Urrea's *Diálogo de la verdadera honra militar* (1566), which it resembles slightly in title. It is divided into four parts and contains various episodes of the Portuguese in the East and some curious information. MIGUEL LEITÃO DE ANDRADE (1555–1632) went straight from Coimbra University to Africa with King Sebastian. After the battle of Alcacer Kebir he succeeded in escaping from captivity, followed the cause of the Prior of Crato, and was imprisoned under Philip II. In his book, in twenty dialogues, *Miscellanea do Sitio de N. S^a da Lvz do Pedrogão Grande* (1629), he disclaims any purpose of writing history. It reveals an inquiring and observant but uncritical mind, interested in fossils, inscriptions, astrology, the early history of Portugal, etymology, heraldry, and the 'infinite wonderful secrets of Nature daily being revealed'. It contains a graphic account of his escape from Fez, but on the whole, in spite of attractive passages and interesting details, scarcely merits its great reputation. *Do Sitio de Lisboa* (1608), which Mello praises as *aquelle elegantissimo livro*, by the author of *Arte Militar* (1612), LUIS MENDES DE VASCONCELLOS, is written in the form of a dialogue between a philosopher, a soldier, and a politician, and deserves its place among the minor classics of Portuguese literature.

The famous love letters of the Portuguese nun MARIANNA ALCOFORADO (1640–1723), which bring a breath of life and nature into the stilted writing of that day, only belong to Portuguese literature in the sense that Osorio's history belongs to it—by translation. They first appeared in indifferent French (*Lettres Portvgaises*, Paris, 1669) and were not retranslated, or, if we accept the theory that the nun originally wrote them in French[1]—French *suranné et dénué d'élégance*—translated into Portuguese for a century and a half: *Cartas de uma Religiosa Portugueza* (1819).[2] Meanwhile, even before their obscure author died in the remote

[1] The slip in the second letter by which in the French version not the Beja Mertola Gate but Mertola itself is seen from the convent, does not favour this theory, which recently has been sustained by the Conde de Sabugosa. This passage is held to be a convincing proof, were such proof needed, of the genuineness of the letters. It is rather a proof of the reality of the love intrigue than of the nun's authorship. If Chamilly, for the edification of his vanity, were fabricating such a letter, what more likely than that he should wish to add his note of local colour and remembered vaguely the word Mertola in connexion with the view from the convent terrace? What he could scarcely have invented or expressed is the real depth of feeling.

[2] Seven spurious letters, and subsequently others, were added in many of the editions. Filinto Elysio translated the twelve.

and beautiful city of Beja, they had been translated into English
and Italian and had received over fifty French editions. Colonel
(later Marshal) Noël Bouton, Comte de Saint-Léger, afterwards
Marquis de Chamilly (1636–1715), accompanied the French
troops sent to help Portugal against Spain, and was in Portugal
from 1665 to 1667. Marianna Alcoforado, belonging to an old
Alentejan family, was a nun in the convent of Nossa Senhora
da Conceição at Beja. Her five letters, written between the end
of 1667 and the middle of 1668 after her desertion, in their art-
lessness, contradictions, and disorder, vibrate with emotion.
They are a succession of intense cries like the popular quatrain:

> Por te amar deixei a Deus:
> Ve lá que gloria perdi!
> E agora vejo-me só,
> Sem Deus, sem gloria, sem ti.

Sometimes, it is true, a trace of French reason seems to mingle
with the ingenuous Portuguese sentiment, and it is almost
incredible, although of course not impossible, since *omnia vincit
amor*, that the nun should have written certain passages. From
these and not on the amazing assumption of Rousseau that
a mere woman could not write so passionately—he was ready
to wager that the letters were the work of a man[1]—one may
suspect that the lover, who did not scruple to hand over the
letters to a publisher (unless he was merely guilty of showing
them to his friends), sank a little lower and edited them, adding
a phrase here and there more peculiarly pleasing to his vanity.[2]
In that case the nun actually wrote these letters, full of passion
and despair, and perhaps in French, to her French lover; but
we only read them as they were touched up for publication by
another hand.

A work which has nothing in common with these fervent
love letters except an enigmatic origin is the *Arte de Furtar*,
which in part at least probably belongs to the seventeenth

---

[1] *Je parierais tout au monde que les Lettres portugaises ont été écrites par un homme.*

[2] e.g. 'You told me frankly that you were in love with a lady in your own country' (letter 2). 'Were you not ever the first to leave for the front, the last to return?' (5). 'My passion increases every instant' (4). 'I do not repent having adored you. I am glad that you betrayed me' (3).

century. It is a curious and amusing treatise on the noble art of thieving in all kinds, private and official, civil and military. Its anecdotes are racy if not original. Two of the happiest incidents (in caps. 6 and 41) are copied without acknowledgement from *Lazarillo de Tormes*.[1] The author seems to have had misgivings that he had presented his subject in too favourable a light, for he ends by assuring his reader thieves that many tons of worldly glory are not worth an ounce of eternal blessedness, and promises them before long another 'more liberal treatise on the art of acquiring true glory'. These tardy qualms did not save his book from the Index. The first edition, purporting to be printed at Amsterdam, bears the date 1652[2] and attributes the work to Antonio Vieira. That attribution may be set aside. Were there no other reasons for its rejection it would suffice to read the book or even its title in order to be convinced that it is not from the *veneravel penna* of that great statesman and preacher. He might dabble in Bandarra prophecies, but would scarcely have sunk to the picaresque familiarities of the *Arte de Furtar* or occupy himself with the sad habits of innkeepers, the long stitches of tailors, or the price of straw. It has also been attributed, without adequate ground, to Thomé Pinheiro da Veiga (1570?-1656), the author of a lively account of the festivities at the Spanish Court and description of Valladolid in 1605, entitled *Fastigimia* (it mentions Don Quixote and Sancho (p. 119) but says nothing of Cervantes), and to João Pinto Ribeiro (c. 1590-1649), the magistrate who played a notable part in the Restoration of 1640 and wrote various short treatises such as *Preferencia das Letras ás Armas* (1645); and even less plausibly to DUARTE RIBEIRO DE MACEDO (1618?-80), statesman and diplomatist, an indifferent poet but an excellent writer of prose and a careful although not

---

[1] Ed. H. Butler Clarke (1897), pp. 17-18 and 65-7.
[2] The 1652 edition speaks of *coroneis* (p. 277) who, it has been argued, were called *mestres de campo* till 1708 (Goes, however, in his *Cron. de D. Manuel*, 1619 ed., f. 213, has *os fez todos quatro coroneis de mil homens*; cf. Gil Vicente, i. 234: *Corregedor, coronel*); it refers (p. 393) to João IV as still alive (†1656): *Que Deos guarde e prospere*. It would appear to have been written at two periods, in the seventeenth and eighteenth centuries, unless the passages implying the earlier date are as deliberately misleading as the 1652 title-page.

original historian. His halting verses and his treatises were collected in his *Obras* (2 vols., 1743). Of the latter the *Summa Politica* has been shown by Snr. Solidonio Leite[1] to be copied almost word for word from the work of identical title by D. SEBASTIÃO CESAR DE MENESES (†1672), Bishop of Oporto and Archbishop of Braga. Both author and book were too well known for Ribeiro de Macedo to claim it as his own. He seems merely to have translated it from the original Latin published at Amsterdam in 1650, a year after the first Portuguese edition. The work is remarkable for acute thought and clear and concise expression. A work of a similar character is the well-written *Arte de Reinar* (1643) by P. ANTONIO CARVALHO DE PARADA (1595-1655). The *Tratado Analytico* (1715), by MANUEL RODRIGUEZ LEITÃO (*c*. 1620-91), a controversial treatise written to prove the right of Portugal to appoint bishops, is also the work of a good stylist. Some would say the same of one of the best-known books of the seventeenth century, the *Vida de Dom João de Castro* (1651), by JACINTO FREIRE DE ANDRADE (1597-1657). The author, born at Beja, was suspected at Madrid of nationalist inclinations, and retired to his cure in the diocese of Viseu; after the Restoration he refused the bishopric of Viseu. His book has often been regarded as a model of Portuguese prose. Pompous and emphatic,[2] it may be described as inflated Tacitus, or rather a mixture of Tacitean phrases, conceits, and rhetorical affectation. But if as a whole it is more akin to Castro's garish triumph at Goa than to the scientific spirit of his letters, it scarcely deserves the severe strictures which followed excessive praise[3]: it might even become excellent if judiciously pruned of antitheses and artifice.[4] The second Conde da Ericeira,

[1] *Classicos Esquecidos* (Rio de Janeiro, 1915). Duarte de Macedo in his dedicatory letter says: 'I have taken this *Summa Politica* from the Latin and Italian languages.' 'I do not offer it as my own, because I restore it to your Highness as yours', so that he had armed himself against such charges of plagiarism.
[2] It loses nothing in Sir Peter Wyche's translation. Cf. the account of Castro's first arrival at Goa: 'When the entry was to be, the two Governours were in a Faluque with gilded Oars, and an awning of divers-coloured silks; the Castles and Ships entertain'd 'em with the horrour of reiterated shootings, the Vivas and expectation of the common people did without any cunning flatter the new Government, &c.'
[3] *Cada clausula he filha da eloquencia mais sublime*, &c. (Barbosa Machado).
[4] e.g. 1759 ed., p. 342: *cujas ruinas serião de sua fama os elogios maiores*

D. Fernando de Meneses (1614–99), wrote a *Historia de Tangere* (1732) and the *Vida e Acçoens d'El Rei D. João I* (1677), which ends with an elaborate parallel between Julius Caesar and the Master of Avis. Equally clear but far more artificial is the style of the third Count, D. Luis de Meneses (1632–90), in the best-known historical work of the century in Portuguese: *Historia de Portugal Restaurado* (2 pts., 1679, 98). Its author ended his life by leaping from an upper window into the garden of his palace on a May morning in a fit of melancholy.

The great prose-writer of the century, Antonio Vieira (1608–97), was born in the same year and city as D. Francisco Manuel de Mello and spent a life as unquiet. He was not literary in the same sense as Mello, but he has always been considered one of the great classics of the Portuguese language. He was the son of Cristovam Vieira Ravasco, *escrivão das devassas* at Lisbon, but at the age of seven he accompanied his parents to Brazil (1615) and began his education in the Jesuit college at Bahia. In 1623, by his own ardent wish, long opposed by his parents, he became a Jesuit novice and professed in the following year. Before he was thirty he was Professor of Theology in the Bahia college and a celebrated preacher, the sermons in which he encouraged the citizens of Bahia in the war against the Dutch being especially eloquent. In 1641 he was chosen with Padre Simão de Vasconcellos to accompany D. Fernando de Mascarenhas, son of the viceroy, to Europe in order to congratulate King João IV on his accession. Vieira preached in the Royal Chapel on New Year's Day, 1642. Both his sermons and his conversation greatly impressed the king, and from 1641 to the end of the reign (1656) his influence was great although not unchallenged. They were critical years in Portugal's foreign policy, and Vieira, who refused a bishopric but was appointed Court preacher, was entrusted with several important missions—to Paris and The Hague (February–July 1646), London, Paris, and The Hague (1647–8), and Rome (1650). In 1652 he returned to Brazil as a missionary in Maranhão, and during two years roused the bitter hostility of the settlers by his protection of the slaves

---

would be straightened out from Latin into Portuguese: *serião os maiores elogios de sua fama.*

or rather by his opposition to slavery. In 1655 he again left Lisbon for Maranhão,[1] and during five arduous years showed unfailing courage and energy in dealing with natives and settlers. The latter in 1661 attacked the mission-house and arrested and expelled the Jesuits. At home King João, Vieira's friend, was dead. Differences arose between the Queen Regent supported by Vieira, and her son, and one of the first acts of the latter on taking power into his own hands was to banish Vieira to Oporto and later to Coimbra. Here in the spring of 1665[2] he wrote that curious work *Historia do Futuro* (1718), which was to interpret Portugal's destiny by the light of old prophecies, but of which only the introduction (*livro anteprimeiro*) was printed. An even stranger book, in which he had paid serious attention politically to the prophecies of Bandarra, was denounced in 1663, and in October 1665 Vieira was consigned to the prison of the Inquisition at Coimbra. His sentence was not read till 1667 (December 24), and it condemned him to seclusion in a college or convent of his Order and to perpetual silence in matters of religion. The deposition of King Afonso VI (1667) and the accession of his brother Pedro II altered Vieira's prospects, and his eloquent voice was again heard in the pulpit. After preaching before the Court in Lent 1669 he proceeded to Rome on business of the Company and spent six years there. He preached several times in Italian, and Queen Christina of Sweden, who had settled in Rome in 1655, offered him the post of preacher and confessor, which he refused. In August 1675 he returned to Lisbon, where he was coldly received by the Prince Regent, and in 1681 retired to Brazil. In the same year he was burnt in effigy by the mob at Coimbra. A special brief given to him by the Pope secured his person from the attacks of the Inquisition. But even at Bahia he was not free from troubles and intrigues. His activity continued to the end of his long life. In 1688 he preached in Bahia Cathedral, and was Visitor of the Province of Brazil from 1688 to 1691. Even in 1695 we find him, although feeble and

[1] On his homeward voyage in 1654 he had suffered from a violent storm, and was only saved by a Dutch pirate who landed the passengers of the Portuguese ship at the Ilha Graciosa without their belongings.
[2] *Historia do Futuro* (1718), p. 93.

broken, writing letters and eager to finish his *Clavis Prophetica*[1] (or *Prophetarum*), which now lies in manuscript in the Bibliothèque Nationale at Paris and elsewhere. Seventy years earlier he had been entrusted by the Jesuits with the composition of the annual Latin letters of the Company. Vieira's vein of caustic satire no doubt made him numerous enemies and increased the difficulties which his advocacy of the Jews and slaves and his fearless stand against injustice and oppression were certain to produce. Ambitious and fond of power, he could devote himself to causes which entailed a life of toil and poverty. An energetic if unsuccessful diplomatist, an ingenious thinker, a statesman of far-reaching views, he was also a fantastic dreamer, but his dreams and restlessness rarely affected the sanity of his judgement. The works of this great writer and extraordinary man are an inexhaustible mine of pure and vigorous prose, at its best in his numerous *Cartas*, written in *selecta et propria dictio, nusquam verbis indulgens sed rebus inhaerens*. A Portuguese critic, Dias Gomes, notes his ' sustained elegance ', and we may sometimes sigh for an interval of Mello's familiarity or Frei Luis de Sousa's charm. In his famous *Sermões* he bowed intermittently to the taste of the time for conceit and artifice. He condemned the practice in a celebrated sermon, but indeed a certain humorous quaintness was not foreign to his temperament, and in the obscurity, at least, of the *cultos* he never indulged. When inspired by patriotism or indignation his words soar beyond cold reason and colder conceits to a fiery eloquence. Among writers whom he influenced was the Benedictine FREI JOÃO DOS PRAZERES (1648–1709), of whose principal work, *O Principe dos Patriarchas S. Bento*, or *Empresas de S. Bento*, only the first two volumes were published. Closer imitators of Vieira were FREI FRANCISCO DE SANTA MARIA (1653–1713), author of *O Ceo Aberto na Terra* (1697) and many sermons, and the Jesuit preacher ANTONIO DE SÁ (1620–78), whose *Sermões Varios* appeared in 1750.

See letters from Bahia, July 22, 1695.

V

1706–1816

The Eighteenth Century

THE eighteenth century did not kill literature in Portugal any more than in other countries, but poetry had lost its lyrism, and under the influence of French and English writers assumed a scientific, philosophical, or utilitarian character. No mighty genius arose in Portuguese literature at the bidding of João V (1706–50), but the king's lavish patronage gave an impulse, and he founded the *Academia Real de Historia* in 1720. A crop of scholars and poets followed in the second half of the century, so that it was not without some unfairness that Giuseppe Baretti wrote of the Portuguese in 1760 that *di letteratura non hanno punto fama d'essere soverchio ghiotti . . . quel poco que scrivono, sia in prosa sia in verso, è tutto panciuto e pettoruto*.[1] It was the age of Arcadias: the famous *Arcadia Ulyssiponense*[2] (1756–74) and the *Nova Arcadia* founded in 1790 (i. e. precisely a century after the Italian *Arcadia*). All the poets of the century belonged to one or other of these societies or made their mark as *dissidentes* from them. One of the founders of the *Nova Arcadia*, FRANCISCO JOAQUIM BINGRE (1763–1856), lived on into the middle of the nineteenth century, and a few of his poems were collected under the title *O Moribundo Cysne do Vouga* (1850). A typical eighteenth-century poet is D. FRANCISCO XAVIER DE MENESES (1673–1743), fourth Conde da Ericeira, who in turning to literature was but following the traditions of his family. A staunch defender of pure Portuguese against those who, he said, disfigure and corrupt the language by the introduction of foreign words and phrases, he wrote a large

[1] *Lettere Familiari*, No. 30.
[2] Or *Arcadia Lusitana*. For a list of its members see T. Braga, *A Arcadia Lusitana* (1899), pp. 210–29 ; for its statutes, ibid., pp. 189–205.

number of works in prose and in verse. The best known of them is his *Henriqueida* (1741), a heroic poem on the conquest of Portugal by Count Henry in twelve long cantos of prosaic *oitavas*. It may contain lines more inspiring than these:

> E a contramina fabricou Roberto,
> Da mina conhecendo o lugar certo,

but they do not really differ greatly from the rest of the poem. The large quantity of poetry still written at the beginning of the century had met with severe criticism in Frei Lucas de Santa Catharina's *Seram Politico*. He slyly calls the *egloga campestre* '*poesia ervada*'. The objects of the *Arcadia* of 1756 were to free Portuguese literature from foreign influences and restore the purity of the language. If to some extent it merely substituted French or Italian influence for Spanish, its cry was also back to the classics and to the Portuguese *quinhentistas*. As to the language its services were invaluable, for at a time when French influence was great in Portugal and in the rest of Europe it checked the use of gallicisms; as to literature the attempt to write poetry on an ordered plan was perhaps foredoomed to failure: it plodded along in an artificial atmosphere of Roman gods and antiquities, and became hidebound in imitation of the Horatian ode.

PEDRO ANTONIO CORRÊA GARÇÃO (1724–72), one of the first members and most prominent poets of the *Arcadia*, did good service in his determined efforts to deliver his country's literature from foreign imitations and the false affectation of the time, and to revert to the classics, Greek, Roman, and Portuguese. He even prophesied that Gil Vicente's day would come. His master was Horace, *grande Horacio*, and his Horatian odes, if they show no remarkable lyrical gift, have a dry native flavour in the purity of their language. He was also successful in reviving the cultivation of blank verse. There is a fine sound in some of the sonnets in which he sings Marilia, Lydia, Belisa, Maria, Nise, writes to a friend to ask for a doubloon or for Spanish tobacco, sends birthday congratulations or laughs at a bald priest: the themes are mostly of this level. His satirical vein is marked in his two short comedies in blank verse, *Theatro*

Novo, a skit on the drama then in vogue, and *Assembléa ou Partida*, in which certain Lisbon types are ridiculed and which contains the famous and much overpraised *Cantata de Dido*. Corrêa Garção's days ended tragically in prison. The motive of his arrest is not clear. Tradition wavers between a love intrigue and political reasons,[1] and declares that the Marques de Pombal, whom he had offended, signed the order for his release on the very day of the poet's death after eighteen months of imprisonment.

Pombal was effusively praised by DOMINGOS DOS REIS QUITA (1728-70), a Lisbon hairdresser who wrote bucolic poetry melodiously, but with perhaps even less originality than we have learnt to expect in that kind since the time when Virgil mistranslated Theocritus. The influence of Bernardez and Camões is clear,[2] in many passages too clear, and he had undoubtedly caught something of their skill and harmony in technique. But his poems leave the impression that he had no real feeling for the rustic life which they describe; no doubt he was more at home with the scissors than with the faithful Melampus or the nymphs and shepherd's pipe. When he is relating an event, such as the earthquake of 1755, which touched him nearly, his ready flow of verse deserts him, in spite of his skill in improvisation,[3] although the sonnet written on the same occasion, *Por castigar, Senhor*, stands out with a certain majesty from most of his other sonnets, which are mere slices of eclogue. If his mellifluous idylls show no individuality, his return to the classic poets of Portugal was, as with other Arcadian poets, a welcome change from the Spanish influence, the *mao uso*, as he calls it, of ' rude strangers from the Manzanares ' (Eclogue 6). His tragedies and pastoral drama *Licore* are not more original.

[1] Debt might seem a more probable cause, were it not for the apparent rigour of his confinement.
[2] *A sua alma conversava com Bernardes e Ferreira*, says his friend Tolentino, who advises another *cabelleireiro* poet to cease writing verses, since *vale mais que cem sonetos a peior penteadura*. The *Arte de Furtar* mentions a barber who sank still lower, since he left his profession in order to cut purses. The modern writer Antonio Francisco Barata (1836-1910) likewise began life as a poor hairdresser at Coimbra.
[3] Cf. *Ecloga* 1. Dorindo to Alcino (*Alcino Mycenio* was Quita's Arcadian name) :

E tu és dos pastores mais famosos
No cantar de improviso o verso brando.

THE EIGHTEENTH CENTURY

One of his tragedies, *Inés de Castro*, suggested that of João Baptista Gomes (†1803), *Nova Castro*, which had a great vogue in its day but is now scarcely more remembered than *Osmia* (1788), a tragedy of which the blank verse has vigour, although it is often scarcely distinguishable from prose. This play, published anonymously, was long attributed to Antonio de Araujo de Azevedo (1754-1817), but its real author was D. Theresa de Mello Breyner, Condessa de Vimieiro, who married her cousin, the fourth Count, in 1767.

It was a cruel kindness to edit the works of ANTONIO DINIZ DA CRUZ E SILVA (1731-99) in six volumes, for, despite the fame of his high-flown Pindaric odes, his three centuries of sonnets and his other lyrics are not of conspicuous merit and are often imitative. Having nothing to say, *Elpino Nonacriense*, like too many of the Arcadian poets, said it at inordinate length. *Que enorme confusão!* he exclaims in an elegy on the Lisbon earthquake, and most of his poems are on a like plane of thought and expression. The son of a *Sargento Môr*,[1] he was born at Lisbon, and after studying law at Coimbra was appointed a judge at Castello de Vide. With Manuel Nicolau Esteves Negrão (†1824) and Theotonio Gomes de Carvalho (†1800) he founded the *Arcadia Ulyssiponense*, of which he drew up the statutes in September 1756. The first aim of these early Arcadians was, as we have noticed, to break the shackles of Spanish influence and *gongorismo*, which was, indeed, on the wane in the land of its birth. Diniz da Cruz' own poems were written in good idiomatic Portuguese. In *O Hyssope* he satirizes with telling vigour the use of gallicisms, and his comedy *O Falso Heroismo* is thoroughly Portuguese in subject and treatment. From 1764 to 1774 he was stationed at Elvas, and here a quarrel between the bishop, D. Lourenço de Lancastre, and the dean, D. José Carlos de Lara, furnished him with the subject of his celebrated mock-heroic poem *O Hyssope*. The legend runs that he was summoned to read his satire to the all-powerful Pombal in the presence of the infuriated bishop, and that the poem proved too much for the gravity of the minister, who appointed him a judge at Rio de

---

[1] i.e. the military governor of a district, with rank next to that of *Capitão Môr*.

Janeiro (1776). Thence he was transferred to Oporto (1787), but in 1790 was again appointed to Rio de Janeiro, and showed himself merciless in sentencing the Brazilian poets Claudio Manuel da Costa, Gonzaga, and Ignacio José de Alvarengo Peixoto (1748–93), accused of conspiring to secure the independence of their country. *O Hyssope* was first published in 1802, three years after the author's death. The idea of the poem was derived from Boileau's *Le Lutrin*. Boileau would have been horrified by its eight cantos of slovenly and monotonous blank verse, which often scarcely rises above prose; but as a satire on the times and in its grotesque portraiture of prelate and lawyer and notary it is sometimes irresistibly comic. The mock-heroic *Benteida*, written by ALEXANDRE ANTONIO DE LIMA of Lisbon (1699–c. 1760?) and published fifty years before *O Hyssope*, consisted of three cantos of *oitavas*. Two editions appeared in 1752, published at 'Constantinople' as written by 'Andronio Meliante Laxaed'. Pedro de Azevedo Tojal (†1742) had used the same metre for his *Foguetario* (1729). The burlesque poem *O Reino da Estupidez* (1819), written in four cantos of easily-flowing blank verse by the Brazilians Francisco de Mello Franco (1757–1823) and José Bonifacio de Andrade e Silva (1763–1838), is professedly an imitation of *aquelle activo e discreto Diniz na Hyssopaïda*, only the butt here is not the Chapter of Elvas but the professors of Coimbra University.

Like the less celebrated poet son of an Alentejan painter, JOSÉ ANASTASIO DA CUNHA (1744–87), artillery officer, mathematician, Professor of Geometry at Coimbra, who translated Pope and Voltaire and had milk in his tea and buttered toast on a fast-day, FRANCISCO MANUEL DO NASCIMENTO (1734–1819), better known as *Filinto Elysio*,[1] was denounced to the Inquisition. His thrilling escape in the year of Cunha's condemnation for apostasy and heresy (1778) brought him almost as much fame as his poems. The son of a Lisbon lighterman and a humble *varina*,[2] he was accused of not believing

---

[1] This Arcadian name was given to him by the Marquesa de Alorna, although he did not properly belong to the *Arcadia*, being, like Tolentino, one of the *dissidentes*.
[2] = fishwife; literally 'woman of Ovar', a small sea-town between Aveiro and Oporto.

THE EIGHTEENTH CENTURY 275

in the Flood and of throwing ridicule on the doctrine of original sin, and by another witness of being simply an atheist. He succeeded in locking up in his own rooms the official sent to arrest him early on the 4th of July, hid for eleven days in Lisbon, and then, disguised as a poor man carrying a load of oranges, escaped on a boat bound for Havre. Had this persecution come earlier, the disquieting atmosphere of Paris, into which he was now transplanted and where, except for a few years at The Hague, he lived for the rest of his life, might have given some originality to his talent. But his mind and poetic style were already fixed, and through every political disturbance he continued his steady flow of Horatian odes and similar artificial verse. He wrote for seventy years (Lamartine notes the *précoces faveurs* of his muse), and at the age of sixty-four calculated that he had already composed 730,000 lines, probably too modest an estimate. He received by royal decree an amnesty and the restoration of his property, but never returned to Portugal. His influence on younger Portuguese poets was nevertheless great. Bocage, when his verses were praised by the older poet, exclaimed:

> Filinto, o gran cantor, prezou meus versos
> . . . Posteridade, és minha!

His influence was bad and good. It encouraged a dry and artificial classicism, but also careful versification in pure Portuguese. Although the poems of Lamartine's *divin Manuel* are no longer even by his countrymen held to be divine, they may be read with satisfaction by virtue of their indigenous expressions and a hundred and one allusions to popular traditions. It was by these characteristics that he expressed his revolt from the *Arcadia*. Half a long life spent in Paris was unable to imbue Filinto with the *mimo de fallar luso-gallico*, against which he vigorously protested to the end. This purity of style gives excellence to the many translations which he was obliged to write for a bare livelihood, and his native land is present even in his closest imitations of Horace (Falernian becomes *louro Carcavellos*). Unfortunately his contemporaries and successors were not always so discreet.

The genial satirist NICOLAU TOLENTINO (1741–1811), son of a Lisbon advocate, after studying law at Coimbra spent some years teaching rhetoric to the raw youth (*bisonhos rapazes*) of Lisbon. He was perpetually discontented with his lot or ready to profess himself so. 'Long years have I already spent in begging,' he says candidly, 'and shall perhaps pass my whole life in the same way.' He harps on his poverty; the kitchen, he complains, is the coolest room in his house. In 1781 he obtained a comfortable post in the civil service, his poems were printed for him in two volumes twenty years later, he would receive a pheasant from one friend, a Sunday dinner of turkey from another, he acknowledges a thousand benefits, and still begs on. Before he had had time to grow rich the habit had become incurable. His was no lyrical gift, but he imitated with success the *quintilhas* of Sá de Miranda,[1] in which much of his work is composed (*O Bilhar* is in *oitavas*). He writes naturally; his style is thoroughly Portuguese, often prosaic. His satire, repressed for personal reasons rather than from any failure of wit or talent, reducible to silence by the gift of a pheasant, lacks independence and thought, but sheds a gentle light on the manners of the time—on the travelled coxcomb who returns to Portugal affecting almost to have forgotten Portuguese, or the rich nun who knows by heart whole volumes of the *Fenix Renascida*—and one or two of his entertaining sonnets are likely to endure. The *Obras Poeticas* of the MARQUESA DE ALORNA (1750–1839), in Arcadia *Alcippe*, are now more often praised than read, but her poetry is scarcely inferior to that of many even more celebrated writers of the time. As a child she defied the anger of the Marques de Pombal. She was detained with her sister Maria and her mother D. Leonor de Almeida in the convent of Chellas from the age of eight till the death of King José (1777). Two years later she married the Count of Oeynhausen, who became minister at Vienna in 1780. After his death in 1793 she lived partly in England, but spent the last twenty-five years of her life in the neighbourhood of Lisbon, and exercised con-

---

[1] Sá de Miranda, he says, *em quem das doces quintilhas Sómente a rima aprendí. . . . Falta-me arte e natureza, Mas pude delle imitar A verdadeira singeleza.*

siderable influence on young writers—not Garrett but Bocage, and especially Herculano—and thus with Macedo formed a link between the poets of the *Arcadia* and the nineteenth century. Her works contain over 2,000 pages of verse. There are sonnets and odes, eclogues, elegies, epistles, translations or paraphrases of Homer, Horace, Claudian (*De raptu Proserpinae*), Pope (*Essay on Criticism*), Wieland, Thomson's *Seasons*, Goldsmith, Gray, Lamartine, and the Psalms. There is a long poem on botany which notices more than a hundred kinds of scented geranium, and indeed the range of her subjects is very wide, from May fireflies to the 'barbarous climate' of England, from Leibniz to the ascent of Robertson in a balloon. Classical allusions are everywhere; she even drags in Cocytus in a sonnet on the death of her infant son. At the same time we have a constant sense of high ideals and love of liberty.

The compositions of the 'pale, limber, odd-looking young man', which 'thrilled and agitated' William Beckford in 1787, now scarcely move us, vanished the fire and glow which BOCAGE (1765-1805) brought to his improvisations. For the reader they are for the most part *carboni spenti*. His parents were a Portuguese judge and the daughter of a French vice-admiral in the Portuguese Navy, and he enlisted in an infantry regiment in the town of his birth, Setubal, in 1779. Ten years later he deserted at Damão, and after wandering in China reached Macao and thence Goa, which he still found a stepmother to poets, and Lisbon. Here he continued to live a dissipated life, till in 1797 his revolutionary opinions and his poem *A Pavorosa Illusão da Eternidade* brought him first to the Limoeiro and then for a few months to the prison of the Inquisition. His unstable romantic spirit was influenced as much by the French Revolution during the latter years of his life as by the wish in his youth to become a second Camões, but he wrote an elegy on the execution of Queen Marie Antoinette, which he described as 'a crime from Hell'. He supported life during his last years principally by translation. He was himself his chief enemy, and he was also the victim of the critics who applauded his improvisations until he no longer distinguished between poetry and prose, sense and absurdity. No better Portuguese pendant to the celebrated line of blank verse 'A Mr. Wilkinson, a clergyman' will be found than that in one of Bocage's elegies: *Carpido objecto meu, carpido objecto.* The undoubted talent of *Elmano Sadino*, as he was in Arcadia, was thus frittered away in occasional verse in which his fecund gift of satire found expression, and a great poet was lost to Portuguese literature. His impromptu sallies against rival poets, such as Macedo, brought him contemporary fame, but in some of his poems, especially the sonnets, we have proof of a possibility of greater things. No doubt his work is disfigured by pompous phrases [1] and hollow classical allusions. He did not always rise above the bad taste of the period; he was unable to concentrate his talent or separate prosaic from poetical subjects. Thus he sang of an ascent in a *balão aerostatico* in 1794, and saw in the *vil mosquito* a proof of the existence of God. But his was nevertheless a very real and above all a very Portuguese inspiration,[2] and some of his sonnets have force and grandeur and hover on the fringes of beauty, especially when they voice his unaffected enthusiasm for Portugal's past greatness and heroes.

One of the foremost poets of the *Nova Arcadia* was BELCHIOR MANUEL CURVO SEMEDO (1766-1838), two volumes of whose *Composições Poeticas* appeared in 1803. A crowd of secondary lights revolved round the great planets of the two *Arcadias*. The poems of *Alfeno Cynthio*, DOMINGOS MAXIMIANO TORRES (1748-1810), are not without vigour (*Versos*, 1791). Their unfortunate author died a political prisoner at Trafaria. The gay and lively Abbade of Jazente, PAULINO ANTONIO CABRAL [3] (1719-89), was the son of an Oporto doctor, and was parish priest at Jazente (near Amarante) from 1753 to 1784. His poems are still read for their pleasant satire, but he was careless of literary fame. Some of the sonnets of both these writers deserve not to be forgotten. JOÃO XAVIER DE MATTOS (†1789), a fourth edition of whose *Rimas*

[1] The sky is *a estellifera morada* (the starry abode), birds *o plumoso aereo bando*, bees *mordazes enxames voadores*, &c.

[2] Menéndez y Pelayo (*Antologia*, tom. xiii (1908), p. 377) calls him *el poeta de más condiciones nativas que ha producido Portugal después de Camoens*, 'the most indigenous Portuguese poet since Camões', and elsewhere gives the highest praise to his sonnets.

[3] His modern editor, Visconde (Julio) de Castilho, has shown that the additional surname de Vasconcellos was bestowed on him gratuitously.

appeared in the year after his death, is now remembered chiefly for some of his sonnets, as that beginning *Poz-se o sol*, with its melancholy charm. He was a true but not a great or original poet. Born at Oporto, the son of a Brazilian father and a Portuguese mother, THOMAS ANTONIO GONZAGA (1744–1807 ?) was a judge at Bahia when he was accused of taking part in the Republican conspiracy of Minas Geraes (1789), and after three years' imprisonment was deported (1792) to Mozambique, where he died several years after his sentence had expired. Some of his Horatian and Anacreontic *lyras* in many metres, addressed to Marilia and collected under the title *A Marilia de Dirceo* (*Dirceo* being his Arcadian name), are graceful lyrics of an idyllic character. Of the other poets implicated in the conspiracy, CLAUDIO MANUEL DA COSTA (1729–69), who was found dead in his prison cell, was an Arcadian poet of the Italian school, and shows a gentle love of Nature in his sonnets. Of the hundred sonnets printed in his *Obras* (1768) some are in Italian. The eclogues number twenty. In Brazil at this time, as earlier in Portugal, patriotism if not poetry suggested epics. JOSÉ BASILIO DA GAMA (1740–95), who spent the greater part of his life in Portugal and died at Lisbon, wrote *O Uraguay* (1769) in five cantos of prosaic blank verse—an account of the struggle between Portuguese and Indians. JOSÉ DE SANTA RITA DURÃO (*c.* 1720–84), Doctor in Theology (Coimbra), composed an epic entitled *Caramurú* (1781) on the discovery of Bahia in the sixteenth century by Diogo Alvarez Corrêa. This poem in ten cantos of *oitavas* is inferior to *O Uraguay*, but it contains some interesting notes on the country and the customs of Brazil.[1]

If a great poet lurked in Bocage, he had certainly never existed in Bocage's contemporary and rival in Arcadia, JOSÉ AGOSTINHO DE MACEDO (1761–1831), who lived to be confronted by an even more formidable adversary in his old age, Almeida Garrett. (In one of his fierce political letters he prays that either he or Garrett may be sent to the galleys.) Born at Beja, he took the vows as an Augustinian monk at Lisbon in 1778.

---

[1] The *Couvade* (ii. 62) is also described by Henrique Diaz, *Naufragio da Nao S. Paulo*, 1904 ed., p. 25, and Pero de Magalhães Gandavo, *Historia da Provincia Sancta Cruz* (1576), cap. 10.

The future champion of law and order provoked the displeasure of his superiors at Lisbon, Evora, Coimbra, Braga, Torres Vedras, by his pranks and mutinies, his boisterous and dissipated life. Methodical theft of books was one of his minor failings. At last after fourteen years, his Order, tired of transferring and imprisoning, formally expelled the delinquent in 1792. He, however, obtained recognition as a secular priest, won fame as a preacher, and for the next forty years wrote in verse and prose with an amazing copiousness.[1] He is said to have composed a hundred Anacreontic odes in three days: *Lyra Anacreontica* (1819). During the last three years of his life, after he had, as he said, capitulated to the doctors, he continued to write, although in great pain. His financial circumstances did not require this effort. His works had brought him considerable sums, he had become Court preacher and chronicler, and had many friends in high places, including Dom Miguel himself. His vanity was soothed, the unfrocked Augustinian had won the regard of princes. But to this learned [2] and splenetic priest virulent denunciation of his literary and political opponents had become a necessity, and he was at work on the twenty-seventh number of his periodical *O Desengano* a fortnight before his death. He was spared the mortification of seeing his enemies triumph in 1832. His character was not amiable, and a large part of his life was unedifying, but there is something fine in his unfailing energy, for by sheer energy he imposed himself, and his self-conceit was so colossal as to be virtually innocuous, while his real horror of revolution, a horror based on experience, was expressed with persistency and courage. He seems to have been quite honest in the belief that the poems of Homer, which he could not read in the original, were worthless,[3] and that his own *O Oriente* was a great epic. His utilitarian

---

[1] His works in the *Dicc. Bibliog.* go from J. 2163 to J. 2475. Many are, however, single odes, sermons, &c. Other eighteenth-century sermons worth reading are those of the learned Franciscan Frei Sebastião de Santo Antonio: *Sermões*, 2 vols. (1779, 84).

[2] Superficially, at least, more than Manuel Caetano de Sousa (1658-1734) he deserves to be called a *varão encyclopedico*.

[3] He admires Cicero—not only as philosopher and orator but as a 'sublime poet'! (*O Homem* (1815), p. 98)—and Seneca, calls Petrarca immortal, Tasso incomparable, and is generous in his appreciation of English writers. At

conception of literature was inevitably fatal to his verse. He wished to extend the boundaries of poetry.[1] He wrote a long poem—four cantos of blank verse—on *Newton* (1813), recast and increased to 3,560 lines under the title *Viagem Extatica ao Templo da Sabedoria* (1830), because Newton had conferred greater benefits on humanity than many a great conqueror (yet so may a dentist). He composed a long poem, *Gama* (1811), re-written as *O Oriente* (1814),[2] to show how Camões should have written *Os Lusiadas*. His poem is no doubt more correct; it observes all the rules, but unfortunately it lacks genius and is as dull and turgid as Macedo's other verse. A good word for the sea in Portuguese is *mar*; the poets often call it *oceano*, Camões had ventured to name it *o falso argento, o liquido estanho, o fundo aquoso, o humido elemento*; with Macedo it becomes *o tumido elemento* (or perhaps he adopted the phrase from *Caramurú*, in which it occurs). We can scarcely blame Bocage for labelling him *tumido versista*.[3] Among his other philosophical poems are *Contemplação da Natureza* (1801), *A Meditação* (1813), *A Natureza* (1846), and *A Creação* (1865), now not more often read than his many odes and other verse. The most scandalous of his satires is *Os Burros* (1827), in blank verse, in which he lavishly and outrageously insults nearly all the writers of the time, and which may have been suggested by Juan Pablo Forner's *El Asno Erudito* (1782). Like his poems, his dramatic works usually have some ulterior object; their purpose is not less practical than his pamphlets against *Os Sebastianistas* (1810) or *Os Jesuitas* (1830) : behind Ezelino and Beatriz in his tragedy *Branca de Rossi* (1819) loom Napoleon and Joséphine, and the prose comedy *A Impostura Castigada* (1822) is an attack upon the doctors. The fact is that Macedo was essentially not a poet or a dramatist or a philosopher, but a forcible and eloquent pamphleteer. His philosophical letters and treatises, *A Verdade*

---

about the same time John Keats, as Petrarca five centuries earlier, was also reading Homer in translation, but in a somewhat different spirit.

[1] *Newton, Proemio*.
[2] In the second edition (1827) he says that this poem, in twelve cantos and about 1,000 *oitavas*, written with ' more fire and a purer light ' than those of Camões, had cost him ' nine years of assiduous application '.
[3] Macedo called Bocage *fanfarrão glosador,* and much abuse of the same kind varied the monotony of *elogio mutuo*.

(1814), *O Homem* (1815), *Demonstração da Existencia de Deos* (1816), *Cartas filosoficas a Attico* (1815), are at their best not when he is developing a train of scientific thought but when he is arguing *ad hominem*; and his literary criticism in *Motim Literario* (1811) is primarily personal. As a critic militant he has his merits, and he is pleasantly patriotic in denouncing the glamour of *missangas estranjeiras*. But it is in his political periodicals, pamphlets, and letters, *Cartas* (1821), *Cartas* (1827), *Tripa virada* (1823), *Tripa por uma vez* (1823), *A Besta Esfolhada* (1828–31), *O Desengano* (September 1830–September 1831), that he puts forth all his spice and venom. Ponderous and angry like a lesser Samuel Johnson, he bullies and crushes his opponents in the raciest vernacular. He may be unscrupulous in argument, but his idiomatic and vigorous prose will always be read with pleasure.

Macedo's dramatic works were neither better nor worse than those of other playwrights of the time. It was the professed object of MANUEL DE FIGUEIREDO (1725–1801) to 'write plays morally and dramatically correct'. The effect of this didacticism in the fourteen volumes of his *Theatro* (1804–15) is disastrous. He wrote in prose and verse, but the plays in ordinary prose are to be preferred, since in the others, like M. Jourdain, he made *de la prose sans le savoir*. He wrote comedies, and tragedies in which he is involuntarily comic. Even in *Ignez* he keeps the even tenor of his dullness, and he warns the reader in a preface that his Inés is not to be considered beautiful since she was probably over thirty, and that her and Pedro's passion had had time to cool.[1] There is more life in the plays written in a medley of prose and verse by ANTONIO JOSÉ DA SILVA (1705–39), whom Southey considered 'the best of their dramatic writers', but it is doubtful whether they would have received any attention in the nineteenth and twentieth centuries had it not been for the tragedy of their author's life. He was born at

---

[1] Such woodenness was unlikely to appreciate El Greco's pictures. In the preface to his *Agriparia* (*Theatro*, vol. v, 1804) he speaks of *a extravagancia do vaidoso Domenico*, herein following Faria e Sousa, who calls Theotocopuli the Góngora of painters and adds: *Pero vale más una llaneza del Ticiano que todas sus extravagancias juntas por más que ingeniosas* (*Fuente de Aganipe Prólogo*, § 37).

Rio de Janeiro, the son of Portuguese Jews, his mother had been arrested by order of the Inquisition as early as 1712, and the whole family came to Lisbon, where the father practised successfully as a lawyer. In 1726 his mother was re-arrested, and this time Antonio José with her. He was released after suffering torture and publicly abjuring Jewish doctrines in an *auto da fé*. Eleven years later, after studying at Coimbra and following his father's profession in Lisbon, he was again arrested, with his wife—he had married his cousin despite the dangerous fact that her mother had been burnt and she herself imprisoned by the Inquisition—and on October 18, 1739, he was first strangled and then burnt in an *auto da fé* at Lisbon. For some years (1733-8) before his death the people of Lisbon had admired the plays of 'the Jew', as they called him, at the *Theatro do Bairro Alto*. Of the eight plays that have survived in print it must be said that they are for the most part very purposeless and ineffective. He attracted his audience sometimes by wit, more often by sheer farcical absurdity; the constant plays on words, the meaningless snatches of verse interpolated, do not increase the interest, which flags on every page because the author has not the slightest power of concentration. The action at least is quick and varied; it shows Silva's inventive talent and explains the popularity of his *galhofeiras comedias*,[1] however much it may weary the reader. His plays with classical subjects are especially cold and dull, *A Ninfa Syringa ou Amores de Pan e Syringa*,[2] *Os Encantos de Medea*,[3] *Esopaida*,[3] *Amphitrião*,[3] *As Variedades de Proteo*,[4] *Laberinto de Creta*.[4] His best play, *Guerras do Alecrim e Mangerona* (1737), contains some elements of character-drawing and describes the devices of the starving gentlemen D. Gilvaz and D. Fuas to obtain rich wives at the expense of miserly father and country cousin. The action consists in a bewildering succession of disguises, the scene (Pt. ii, Sc. 5) in which Gilvaz and Fuas doctor their stolid rival and ridicule the medical profession has humour but shows the usual inability to end before the reader's patience has been long exhausted.

---

[1] Arnaldo Gama, *Um motim ha cem annos*, 3ª ed. (1896), p. 35.
[2] *Theatro Comico Portuguez*, 4 vols. (1759-90), vol. iii.
[3] Ibid., vol. i. [4] Ibid., vol. ii.

In the *Vida do Grande D. Quixote de la Mancha* (1733) Silva made bold to dramatize *Don Quixote* in a series of scenes not over-skilfully connected. Of his own invention there is a comical scene (Pt. i, Sc. 8), in which Don Quixote is harassed by doubts as to whether the enchanters have not transformed Dulcinea into Sancho Panza: he begins to see a certain likeness; but most of the scenes are directly copied and here become signally insipid, as that of Sancho's judgements (ii. 4), or that of the lion (i. 5), which is as far removed from Cervantes as the sorry lions of the Alhambra at Granada from those in Trafalgar Square. The drama of NICOLAU LUIS, whose life is obscure but whose name was possibly Nicolau Luis da Silva, belongs to the *literatura de cordel*, popular plays imitated and often directly translated from the Spanish and Italian and acted with great applause in the eighteenth century at Lisbon. Most of them were published without the author's name, and although it is believed that he wrote over one-third of the numerous *comedias de cordel* of the century [1] only a few, as *O Capitão Belisario* (1781) and *O Conde Alarcos* (1788), can be definitely assigned to him, a fact which incidentally bears witness to his lack of individuality. His best-known tragedy is *D. Ignez de Castro* (1772), an imitation of *Reinar después de morir* by Luis Velez de Guevara (1579–1644).

In prose it was not an age of great writers, but of research and learning. The Lisbon *Academia Real das Sciencias*,[2] founded by the Duque de Lafões, met for the first time in 1780, and was not slow in inaugurating the work which has won for it the gratitude of all who care for the language or literature of Portugal. D. ANTONIO CAETANO DE SOUSA (1674–1759) had published his valuable *Provas da Historia Genealogica* (1739–48) in seven volumes, and the learned *curé* of Santo Adrião de Sever, DIOGO BARBOSA MACHADO (1682–1772), had spent a long life in bibliographical study and compiled his indispensable and magnificent *Bibliotheca Lusitana* (1741–59) with a generous inaccuracy which is attractive in the minute pedantry of a later age. The scarcely less famous *Vocabulario Portuguez* of RAPHAEL

[1] Innocencio da Silva, *Dicc. Bibliog.* vi. 275–85; xvii. 91–3, gives 217 titles.
[2] Now *Academia das Sciencias de Lisboa*, but it is found convenient to retain the original title in order to distinguish it from a more recent (private) institution, the *Academia das Sciencias de Portugal*.

BLUTEAU (1638-1734), who was born of French parents in London but spent over fifty years in Portugal, began to appear in 1712. The work of research was now carried on, among others by FRANCISCO JOSÉ FREIRE (1719-73); FREI JOAQUIM DE SANTA ROSA DE VITERBO (1744-1822); the librarian ANTONIO RIBEIRO DOS SANTOS (1745-1818); D. FRANCISCO ALEXANDRE LOBO (1763-1844), Bishop of Viseu; CARDINAL SARAIVA (1766-1845), Patriarch of Lisbon; and FREI FORTUNATO DE S. BOAVENTURA (1778-1844). Critics of poetry were LUIS ANTONIO VERNEY (1713-92), Archdeacon of Evora, 'El Barbadiño', whose criticisms in his *Verdadeiro Methodo de Estudar* (2 vols., 1746) are severe, even harsh; FRANCISCO DIAS GOMES (1745-95), whom Herculano called *o nosso celebre critico*, and who was indeed a better critic than poet, as may be seen in the notes and poems of his *Obras Poeticas* (1799); and MIGUEL DE COUTO GUERREIRO (*c.* 1720-93), who showed good sense in the twenty-six rhymed rules of his *Tratado da Versificaçam Portugueza* (1784).

The best-known work of the learned son of a Lisbon blacksmith who became the first Bishop of Beja and Archbishop of Evora, MANUEL DO CENACULO VILLAS-BOAS (1724-1814), is his *Cuidados Litterarios* (1791). THEODORO DE ALMEIDA (1722-1804), an erudite and voluminous writer, one of the original members of the Academy of Sciences, was more ambitious. In *O Feliz Independente do Mundo e da Fortuna* in twenty-four books (3 vols., 1779), he took Fénelon's *Télémaque* for his model and sought to combine the gall of instruction with the honey of entertainment. He wrote it first (*uma boa parte*) in rhyme, then turned to blank verse, but, still dissatisfied, finally adopted prose, taking care, however, he says, that it should not degenerate into a novel. The book had a wide vogue, but is quite unreadable. One may be thankful that it was not written in verse like that of his *Lisboa Destruida* (1803), an account of the earthquake of 1755, with sundry moralizings in six cantos of *oitavas*, of which a Portuguese critic has said that the author, in an excess of Christian humility, resolved to mortify his pride of learning by making himself ridiculous to posterity in verse. A flickering interest enlivens the *Cartas Familiares* (1741, 2) of FRANCISCO XAVIER DE OLIVEIRA (1702-83). Their subjects are various : love, literature, witchcraft, and even the relation of a man's character to the ribbon on his hat. The author gave up a diplomatic career, perhaps on account of his Protestant tendencies, and went to Holland (1740) and England (1744), where he publicly abjured Roman Catholicism (1746). After the Lisbon earthquake of 1755 he addressed a pamphlet in French to the King of Portugal, exhorting him to mend his ways; to become Protestant with all his subjects and abolish the Inquisition. He was duly burnt in effigy at Lisbon (1761), but died quietly at Hackney twenty-two years later. The letters of ALEXANDRE DE GUSMÃO (1695–1753), born at Santos in Brazil, have not been collected; those of the remarkable Portuguese Jew of Penamacor, ANTONIO NUNES RIBEIRO SANCHES (1699–1783), physician to the Empress Catherine II of Russia, *Cartas sobre a Educação da Mocidade*, appeared in 1760 at Cologne. The *Cartas Curiosas* (1878) of the Abbade ANTONIO DA COSTA (1714–*c*. 1780) consist of thirteen letters written from Rome and Vienna from 1750 to 1780, mainly on the subject of music. The century was not rich in memoirs. The *Miscellaneas* of D. JOÃO DE S. JOSEPH QUEIROZ (1711–64) contain some interesting and amusing anecdotes. He speaks of the *Memorias Genealogicas* of Alão de Moraes and of the general discredit of genealogists, and attributes Mello's imprisonment to his polite acquiescence in the suggestions of the Condessa de Villa Nova, made at the instigation of King João IV : *para lisongea-la disse que seguiria o partido de Castella*. But without seeing the manuscript it is impossible not to suspect that there is as much of Camillo Castello Branco as of the Bishop of Grão-Para in the *Memorias* (1868), which he was the first to publish.

VI
1816–1910

§ 1

The Romantic School

IN Portugal the first quarter of the nineteenth century was filled with violence and unrest. The French invasion and years of fighting on Portuguese soil were followed by a series of revolutions and civil wars. It seemed as if a more general earthquake had come to complete the ruin of 1755, against which Lisbon had so finely re-acted. The historian who attempts to record the conflicts between Miguelists and Constitutionalists, and the miserable political intrigues which accompanied the ultimate victory of the latter, must waver disconsolately between tragedy and farce. But horrible and pitiful as were many of these events, they succeeded in awakening what had seemed a dead nation to a new life. The introduction of the parliamentary system called into being eloquent orators, and, more valuable than much eloquence, the conviction sprang up, partly under foreign influence, partly through love of the soil, deepened by persecution and banishment, that literature might have a closer relation to earth and life than a philological Filintian ode. Returning exiles brought fresh ideas into the country, and the two men who dominated Portuguese literature in the first half of the century had both learnt much from their enforced sojourn abroad. ALMEIDA GARRETT (1799–1854), one of the strangest and most picturesque figures in literature, was born at Oporto, but spent his boyhood in the Azores (Ilha Terceira), where his uncles, especially the Bishop of Angra, gave him a classical education and destined him for the priesthood. He, however, preferred to study law at Coimbra (1816–21). Here politics were in the air and he soon made himself conspicuous as a Liberal. The fall of the Constitution drove him into exile (1823) in

England (near Edgbaston and in London), and France (Havre and Paris), and for the next thirty years politics remained one of his ruling passions. His first great opportunity for rhetorical display was his defence in the law-courts against the charge of impiety incurred by the publication of his poem *O Retrato de Venus* (1821), although even before going to Coimbra he is said to have preached to a church full of people. He was able to return to Portugal in 1826, and edited *O Chronista* and *O Portuguez*, which evoked Macedo's wrath and ended in Garrett's imprisonment. When Dom Miguel returned from Brazil and, instead of 'signing the paper' (the famous *Carta* of 1826), had himself declared absolute king (1828) Garrett again became an exile, chiefly in London, and did not return to his country till July 1832, when he landed as a private soldier at Mindello, one of the famous 7,500 who fought for King Pedro and his daughter, Maria da Gloria. His zeal and outspokenness rendering him an uncomfortable colleague at Lisbon, he fared rather badly in the ignoble scramble for office which followed the triumph of the cause. He was sent first on a mission to London and then as *chargé d'affaires* to Brussels (1834–6). The diplomatic service was in many ways congenial to his character, but his enemies made the mistake of slighting and neglecting him, and, refusing the post of Minister at Copenhagen, he returned to Portugal and helped to bring about the Revolution of September 1836. But his life is the whole history of the time: enough to say that for the next fifteen years his activities in politics and literature were unceasing. In a hundred ways he showed his versatility and energy. He served on many commissions, was appointed Inspector of Theatres (1836), *Cronista Môr* (1838), elected deputy (1837), raised to the House of Peers (1852). As journalist, founder and editor of several short-lived newspapers, as a stylist and master of prose, his country's chief lyric poet in the first half of the nineteenth century (coming as a fire to light the dry sticks of the eighteenth-century poetry) and greatest dramatist since the sixteenth; as politician and one of the most eloquent of all Portugal's orators, an enthusiastic if unscientific folk-lorist,[1]

---

[1] His *Romanceiro* published in 3 vols. (1843, 51) contains poems of national themes drawn from popular songs and traditions, written by himself (as

THE ROMANTIC SCHOOL

a novelist, critic, diplomatist, soldier, jurist and judge, Garrett played many parts and with success. This patriot who did not despair of his country, this marvellous dandy who seemed to bestow as much thought on the cut of a coat as on the fashioning of a constitution, and who refused to grow old, preferring to incur ridicule as a *velho namorado* (his love intrigues ended only with his life and he wrote his most passionate lyrics when he was over fifty), this artist in life and literature, lover of old furniture and old traditions, this lovable, ridiculous, human Garrett, whom his countrymen called divine, can still alternately charm and repel us as he scandalized and fascinated his contemporaries. His motives were often curiously mixed. His immeasurable peacock vanity as well as his generosity prompted him to champion weak causes and assist obscure persons. A man of high ideals and an essential honesty, he only rarely deviated into truth in matters concerning himself. When past fifty he was still ' forty-six ' and he wrote an anonymous autobiography and filled it with his own praise. He often gave his time and talent ungrudgingly to the service of the State and then cried out that his disinterestedness went unrewarded. Fond of money but fonder of show and honours, he died almost poor but a viscount. Although of scarcely more than plebeian birth he liked to believe that the name Garrett, which he only assumed in 1818, was the Irish for Gerald and that he was descended from Garrt, first Earl of Desmond,[1] and through the Geraldines from Troy.[2] At the mercy of many moods, easily angered but never vindictive, capable occasionally of half-unconscious duplicity but never of hypocrisy, he remained to the last changing and sensitive as a child. His faults were mostly on the surface and injured principally himself, offering

---

Adozinda, based on the *romance Sylvaninha* and originally published in London in 1828 and reviewed in the *Foreign Quarterly Review*, October 1832) or by others, e. g. Balthasar Diaz' *O Marques de Mantua*, or popular *romances* revised and polished by their collector. His own compositions (vol. i) often have great charm, as *Miragaia, Rosalinda, Bernal Francez*.

[1] The name of the first Earl of Desmond (cr. 1328) was Maurice fitzThomas (†1356) not Gerald, Gerod, Gerott, Garrett, or Garrt (see Lord Walter FitzGerald, *Notes on the FitzGeralds of Ireland*). The forms Garret and Gareth existed in Catalonia in the fifteenth and sixteenth centuries, e. g. the Catalan poet Bernardo Garret, born at Barcelona, who wrote in Italian and became known as Chariteo (*c*. 1450–*c*. 1512).

[2] Amorim, *Memorias*, i. 28.

a hundred points of attack to critics incapable of understanding his greatness. That he did not play a more fruitfully effective part in politics was less his fault than that of the politics of the day; but the twofold incentive of serving his country by useful legislation and of a personal triumph in the Chamber prevented this ingenuous victim of political intrigue from ever devoting himself exclusively to literature. In politics he was an opportunist in the best sense of the word and a Liberal who detested the art of the demagogue. His few months as Minister in 1852 gave no scope for his real power of organization and of stimulating others. In the life and literature of his country he was a great civilizing and renovating force. He taught his countrymen to read and what to read, and, having freed them from the trammels of pseudo-classicism, did his utmost to prevent them from merely exchanging pedantry for insipidity.

His early verses, many of the poems published or reprinted in *Lyrica de João Minimo* (1829), *Flores sem Fructo* (1845), and *Fabulas e Contos* (1853), were written under the influence of Filinto Elysio and the eighteenth century, but, fired by romanticism during his first exile in France, he introduced it into Portugal in his epic poems *Camões* (1825) and *Dona Branca* (1826),[1] in which prosaic passages alternate with others of fervent poetic beauty and glimpses of popular customs which in themselves spell poetry in Portugal. But Garrett was no super-romantic, in fact he deprecated 'the extravagances and exaggerations of the ephemeral romanticism which is now coming to an end in Europe'.[2] At Brussels he learnt German, and the poetry, and especially the plays, of Goethe cast a steadying influence over his work. Garrett had early been attracted towards the theatre. His *Merope*, in its subject derived from Alfieri, and *Catão* (1821) were both written in his student days. Neither of them can be called dramatic. In vain a glow of liberty[3] and rhetoric strives

---

[1] Of *O Magriço*, a still longer epic, only fragments remain; it went down in manuscript in the *Amelia*, sunk by the Miguelists off the Portuguese coast.

[2] Preface to 4th ed. (1845) of *Catão*.

[3] The 'tyranny' of the day was that of General Beresford. Some scenes of *Catão* (derived from the *Cato* (1713) of Addison), of which a Portuguese version by Manuel de Figueiredo (*Theatro*, vol. viii) had appeared in Garrett's boyhood, were directed against this English despot. A few years later Garrett learned to enjoy English society, as his Anglophobe biographer, Amorim, admits.

to melt the ice of *Catão* : its parliamentary debates still leave the reader cold. When fifteen years later, in the tercentenary year of Vicente's last comedy, he was able definitely to undertake his favourite scheme of providing Portugal with a national drama, he found difficulties. He had to provide not only theatre, actors, and audience, but also the plays. He succeeded in instilling his keenness into some of his more lethargic countrymen, but, not content with translating from the French, Italian, or Spanish, himself wrote a series of plays to pave the way. His themes, unlike those of his earlier efforts, were now entirely national : the legendary love of the poet Bernardim Ribeiro for the daughter of King Manuel in *Um Auto de Gil Vicente* (1838);[1] the patriotism of the Condessa de Athouguia in arming her two sons on the morning of December 1, 1640, to throw off the Spanish yoke, in *Dona Philippa de Vilhena* (1840) ; an early incident in the life of one of the most chivalrous soldiers that the world has seen, the Constable Nun' Alvarez, in *O Alfageme de Santarem* (1842); the fall of Pombal in *A Sobrinha do Marquez* (1848);[2] two famous episodes in the life of Manuel de Sousá Coutinho, the first of which, the setting fire to his palace rather than entertain the Spanish Governors, preserves the national atmosphere, in *Frei Luiz de Sousa* (1844). These plays, with the exception perhaps of the hastily improvised *D. Philippa de Vilhena*, are all remarkable, although their merit is unequal. The characters, and especially the epoch in which they are presented, lend their chief interest to the first and third. The fifth, overpraised by some critics but praised by all—Menéndez y Pelayo called it ' incomparable '— *Frei Luiz de Sousa*, far excels the others by reason of the concentration of interest and the really dramatic character of the plot (or at least of the anagnorisis of Act II) and by its intensity and deliberately simple execution. The intensity may be almost too unrelieved, but the conception of the play showed a fine dramatic instinct. Like most of Garrett's work it was composed in a white heat, and the effect is enhanced by its excellently clear and restrained style, which brings out every shade and symptom of tragedy without distracting the attention by any extraneous ornaments. But all these plays are written in admirable prose.

[1] Published in 1841.   [2] Written ten years earlier.

Indeed, a value is given even to Garrett's slighter pieces—*Tio Simplicio* (1844), *Fallar Verdade a Mentir* (1845)[1]—apart from their indigenous character, by his pliant, transparent, glowing prose, to which perhaps even more than to his poetry he owes his foremost place in Portuguese literature. Although essentially a poet, his poems of enduring worth are a mere handful of beautiful episodes and graceful lyrics—in *Folhas Cahidas* (1853) and vol. 1 (1843) of his *Romanceiro*—but his prose stamps with individuality works so diverse as his historical novel *O Arco de Santa Anna* (2 vols., 1845, 51),[2] his charming miscellaneous *Viagens na minha terra* (1846) with its famous episode of Joaninha of the nightingales, his treatises *Da Educação* (1829), *Portugal na balança da Europa* (1830), *Bosquejo da Litteratura Portugueza* (1826), as well as his plays. All his work was thoroughly national, and when he died a group of younger writers was at hand ready to continue it.

Garrett intended as *Cronista Môr* to write the history of his own time. More serious historians existed in the Canon of Evora, ANTONIO CAETANO DO AMARAL (1747–1819); his fellow-academician the Canon JOÃO PEDRO RIBEIRO (†1839); LUZ SORIANO (1802–99), author of a *Historia da Guerra Civil* (1866–90) in seventeen volumes; the VISCONDE DE SANTAREM (1791–1856), whose able and persistent researches were of inestimable service to the history and incidentally to the literature of his country; and the patient investigator CUNHA RIVARA (1809–79).

While scientific research work was accumulating the bones of history a creator arose in the person of ALEXANDRE HERCULANO (1810–77). He had emigrated to France and England in 1831, lived for a time at Rennes, and from the Azores in 1832 with Garrett accompanied the Liberal army to Oporto as a private soldier. In the following year he obtained work as a librarian. His *A Voz do Propheta* (1836) (Castilho in this year translated Lamennais' *Paroles d'un Croyant*), written in the impressive style of a Hebrew prophet, although it appeared anonymously, brought its author fame, and in 1839 the King Consort D. Fernando appointed him librarian of the Royal Library of Ajuda. The salary was not

---

[1] These two plays were published in vol. vii of his *Obras* (1847) with *D. Philippa de Vilhena*.

[2] A contemporary novel, *Helena* (1871), remained unfinished at his death.

large, under £200 a year, but the post gave him the two necessaries of literary work, quiet and books. From that year to 1867 his life was taken up with his work, with which politics only occasionally interfered. He edited *O Panorama* from 1837 to 1844 and joined in founding *O Paiz*. Although he was elected deputy to the Cortes in 1840 he rarely attended the sittings. His friendship with D. Fernando and King Pedro V continued unbroken till their death. In 1867 with characteristic abruptness he left Lisbon and literature and gave his last ten years almost entirely to agriculture on the estate of Val de Lobos, near Santarem.[1] The call of the land was combined with disgust at the politics of the capital and probably a natural disinclination to a sedentary mode of life. His retirement was greeted as a betrayal, and attacks formerly directed against his historical work were now directed against him for abandoning it. But since he had no intention of continuing his history, his literary work was really ended. It has three main aspects, poetry, the historical novel, and history. From the prosaic height of forty-six he informed Soares de Passos in a letter that he had been a poet till he was twenty-five. Some of the poems of *A Harpa do Crente* (1838),[2] especially *A Tempestade* and *A Cruz Mutilada*, rise to noble heights by reason of a fine conviction and a rugged grandeur, as of blocks of granite. Herculano had returned to Portugal imbued with profound admiration for the historical novels of Sir Walter Scott, 'immortal Scott' as he called him, and Victor Hugo, and in his remarkable stories and sketches contributed to *O Panorama* and published as *Lendas e Narrativas* (1851), as well as in the more elaborate *O Monasticon*, consisting of two separate parts *Eurico o Presbytero* (1844) and *O Monge de Cister* (1848), he wrote romance based upon scrupulous historical research. A slight leaning towards melodrama is as a rule successfully withstood, and his intense and powerful style enchains the attention. *Eurico* is really a splendid prose poem,[3] in which the eighth-

[1] It was, however, no sudden decision. As early as 1851 he wrote, in a letter to Garrett, '... *me ver entre quatro serras com algumas geiras de terra proprias, umas botas grossas e um chapeu de Braga, bello ideal de todas as minhas ambições mundanas*'.
[2] The second edition with additional poems was entitled *Poesias* (1850).
[3] *Cronica, poema, lenda ou o que quer que seja*, he says.

century priest Eurico is Herculano brooding over the degeneracy of Portugal in the nineteenth century. His glowing patriotism unifies the action and raises the style to an impassioned eloquence. The Middle Ages were well suited to him in their mixture of passion and ingenuousness and their scope for violent contrasts of evil and virtue, light and shadow. Most of the *Lendas e Narrativas* and *O Bobo* belong to that period, and his *Historia de Portugal* (4 vols., 1846-53) ends with the year 1279. That he should have stopped there when the character and achievements of King Dinis must have offered him a powerful incentive to proceed shows how deeply he had felt the controversial attacks levelled at his work; but with the Renaissance and the subsequent history of Portugal he was too intensely national to have great sympathy. As a historian he has been compared with Hallam, Thierry, and Niebuhr, and he stands any such comparison well. A passion for truth drove him to the original sources and documents, and, since *alle Gelehrsamkeit ist noch kein Urteil*, he brought the same patience and impartial sincerity to their interpretation. The results obtained he imposed on thousands of readers by his impressive and living style.[1] In his case the style was the man. Beneath coldness or roughness he concealed an affectionate, impetuous nature, a hatred of meanness and injustice. In his personal relations austere and difficult, sometimes no doubt unfair and undiscerning in the severity of his judgements, he was a perfect contrast to Almeida Garrett, compared with whom he was as granite to chalk or as the rock to the stream that flows past it. His strong will was fortunately directed by the Marquesa de Alorna in his youth to the thoroughness of German writers. Thoroughness marked all his work. When the Academy of Sciences entrusted him with the task of collecting documents on the early history of Portugal he threw himself into the labour with a fervour which produced the splendid *Portvgaliae Monvmenta Historica*, a series of historical works and documents of the first importance which began to appear in 1856. From 1867 to 1877 he undertook agriculture not as an amateur's pastime but as

---

[1] The late Dr. Gonçalvez Viana considered Herculano 'the most vernacular, scrupulous and perfect writer of the nineteenth century' (*Palestras Filolójicas*, 1910, p. 116).

the work of his life, with the result that he achieved another great success scarcely inferior to his success as a writer. The same thoroughness is evident in the Cyclopean fragment of his history and in his shorter writings, the *Opusculos* (1873–76). His *Da Origem e Estabelecimento da Inquisição em Portugal* (3 vols., 1854–9), a deeply interesting account of the negotiations and intrigues at the Vatican, in ceasing to be dispassionate may suffer as a purely historical work, but its vigour brooks no denial and its literary excellence is acknowledged even by those who dispute its fairness. Great as scholar and man, too great to be always understood during his life, his memory received a tribute from men so different as Döllinger and Núñez del Arce, and it is probable that his reputation will only increase with time.

In the historical novel Herculano had many followers. ANTONIO DE OLIVEIRA MARRECA (1805–89) wrote two laborious fragments in *O Panorama*: *Manoel Sousa de Sepulveda* (1843) and *O Conde Soberano de Castella* (1844, 53). JOÃO DE ANDRADE CORVO (1824–90), poet and dramatist,[1] author of a novel of contemporary politics, *O Sentimentalismo* (1871), which contains excellent descriptions of Bussaco, wrote a long historical novel, *Um Anno na Corte* (1850), in which interest in the actors at the Court of Afonso VI, in incidents such as a bullfight or a boarhunt, in witchcraft or the Inquisition, is skilfully maintained. His style in its sober restraint is superior to that of ARNALDO DA GAMA (1828–69), whose historical episodes of the French invasion of 1809 (*O Sargento Môr de Villar* and *O Segredo do Abbade*), or of Oporto in the fifteenth century in *A Ultima Dona de S. Nicolau*, or in the eighteenth in *Um Motim ha cem annos* (1861), are of considerable interest despite their author's excessive fondness for Latin quotations. Perhaps the influence of Camillo Castello Branco may be traced in his novel *O Genio do Mal* (4 vols., 1857). GUILHERMINO AUGUSTO DE BARROS (1835–1900) is the author of a novel of the fifteenth century, *O Castello de Monsanto* (2 vols., 1879), of great length and dullness. Its chief interest is for the student of the Portuguese language, owing to its large vocabulary. BERNARDINO PEREIRA PINHEIRO (born in 1837) in *Sombras e Luz* (1863) described scenes from the reign of King Manuel, and drew a strange portrait

---

[1] *O Alliciador* (1859), *O Astrologo* (1860).

of King João III in *Amores de um Visionario* (2 vols., 1874). But the mantle of Herculano, as historical novelist, fell especially upon Luiz Augusto Rebello da Silva (1822-71), politician and journalist. His *Rausso por Homizio*, a short novel of the time of King Sancho II, written with the exaggeration of extreme youth, appeared in the *Revista Universal Lisbonense* (1842-3), followed by *Odio Velho não cansa* (reign of Sancho I), with similar defects, in 1848. In the same (the first) volume of *A Epocha* appeared his short *conto* entitled *A Ultima Corrida de Touros em Salvaterra*, which won and has retained popularity by its skilful presentment of a stirring and pathetic episode in the reign of José I (1750-77). Four years later Rebello da Silva published his principal novel, *A Mocidade de D. João V* (1852). In its somewhat tedious descriptions the reader soon loses the thread of the story, but is entertained by the quick dialogue and almost clownish humour of the separate scenes. *Lagrimas e Thesouros*[1] (1863) may interest English readers from the fact that its principal character is William Beckford, but it has not the great merits of the preceding novel. The author was already at work on his unfinished *Historia de Portugal nos seculos XVII e XVIII* (5 vols., 1860-71). In this, as in his *Fastos da Igreja* (1854-5) and *Varões Illustres* (1870), his defects fall away, while his real skill as a historian, his intensity, and his excellent style remain; indeed, an added intensity gives his style a new vigour and simplicity. His *Historia*, although less rigorously scientific and far less methodically ordered than that of his master Herculano, has value as history as well as literature. Rebello da Silva wrote too much, but his work generally improved with the years and might have resulted in a real masterpiece had he not died before attaining the age of fifty.

Meanwhile the novel had entered on a new and intensely modern phase in the hands of a slightly younger contemporary. The life of Camillo Castello Branco (1825-90), whose numerous novels have been and still are read enthusiastically in Portugal, had about it an element of improbability which is reflected in his works and made it possible to combine their

---

[1] The last novel to appear in Rebello da Silva's lifetime was *A Casa dos Phantasmas* (1865). *De Noite todos os gatos são pardos* was published posthumously.

apparent sincerity with a peculiar unreality. Born at Lisbon but left an orphan at the age of eight, and brought up by a sister, wife of a doctor, in a small village of Tras-os-Montes,[1] a widower in his teens, then a boisterous Oporto medical student, twice imprisoned for love affairs and finally guilty of abducting an heiress as a bride for his son, his whole life was spent in a whirlwind, actual or imaginary, a tragicomedy which, stricken with blindness, he ended by suicide. He read and wrote in the same tempestuous fashion. The sentimental atmosphere of his novels is relieved systematically by outbursts of cynicism and sarcasm. When he began to write romanticism was in full swing, but his last twenty years were spent under what was to him the vexing and tantalizing shadow of the new realism. His first story, *Maria não me mates, que sou tua mãe!* (1848),[2] was sentimental and sensational, and something of these qualities remained in the greater part of his work. His first more elaborate novel *Anathema* (1851), in which the story is interrupted by lengthy musings and moralizings, he himself described as ' a kind of literary crab ', and most of his novels are somewhat lop-sided : he confessed that his discursiveness was incurable. It is the more hysterical among his works, such as *Amor de Perdição* (1862)—its character is well described by the title of the Italian version, *Amor sfrenato* —or *Amor de Salvação* (1864) and those which combine this character with a chain of amazing coincidences, as *Os Mysterios de Lisboa* (1854) and *O Livro Negro do Padre Diniz* (1855), which were read most avidly in Portugal. He himself favoured the quieter *Romance de um Homem Rico* (1861) and *Livro de Consolação* (1872). We may prefer the attic flavour of the humorous sketch of a country gentleman (born in the year of Waterloo) at Lisbon, in *A Queda d'um Anjo* (1866), which somehow recalls the best work of Pedro Antonio de Alarcón. Castello Branco had a true vein of comedy, and although a great part of the work of this specialist in hysterics has an air of unreality, he is many-sided and yields frequent surprises. The true Camillo appears only intermittently

---

[1] After Camillo, as he is always called in Portugal, had been created Visconde de Corrêa Botelho in 1885, his descent was traced back to Fruela, son of Pelayo.
[2] That is, a year before the novel *Memorias de um Doudo* (1849) by Antonio Pedro Lopes de Mendonça (1826–65).

in his novels, and charms with a simplicity of style and description worthy of Frei Luis de Sousa, as in some of his *Novellas do Minho* (12 vols., 1875–7), the country-house in *Coração, Cabeça e Estomago* (1862), the Tras-os-Montes *fidalgo*'s house in *Os Mysterios de Lisboa*, the village priest in *A Sereia* (1865), Padre João in *Doze Casamentos Felizes* (1861), the farrier in *Amor de Perdição*, the charcoal-burners in *O Santo da Montanha* (1865). Then (as if with the question : what will the Chiado, what will the Lisbon critics say ?) he pulls himself up, lashes himself with sarcasms, and plunges into his improbabilities and passions. A poet and a learned and ingenious if unscholarly critic, he saw and described the charm of the villages of North Portugal, but he satirized with peculiar venom the *bourgeois* life and the enriched *brazileiros* of Oporto, as in *A Filha do Arcediago* (1855), *A Neta do Arcediago* (1856), *A Douda do Candal* (1867), *Os Brilhantes do Brazileiro* (1869), *Memorias de Guilherme do Amaral* (1863), and *Um Homem de Brios* (1856),[1] the last two being continuations of *Onde está a Felicidade?* (1856). This last work has a broader historical setting, and many of his novels are really historical episodes,[2] some of which bear a strong resemblance to Pérez Galdós' *Episodios Nacionales*. Especially is this the case with the latter part of *As Tres Irmãs* (1862) and with *A Bruxa de Monte Cordova* (1867), both written before the appearance of the first *Episodio Nacional*. In *Eusebio Macario* and *A Corja* he set his hand to the naturalistic novel, and in *A Brazileira de Prazins* (1882) modified this method to suit his favourite phantasy of extremes, in which the angel and martyr are contrasted with the romantic Don Juan or vulgar *brazileiro* or narrow-minded Minho noble. Apart from their historical interest and occasional charming glimpses of life and literature, his books are invaluable for their style, and he is the author of many masterly passages rather than of any masterpiece. He sometimes—here, as in all else, leaving moderation to the *bourgeois*

[1] Cf. also *Carlota Angela* (1858), *O que fazem mulheres* (1858), *Annos de Prosa* (1863), *O Sangue* (1868), *Estrellas Propicias* (1863), *Estrellas Funestas* (1869).
[2] e.g. *Lagrimas Abençoadas* (1857), *Carlota Angela* (1858), *O Santo da Montanha* (1865), *A Engeitada* (1866), *O Judeu* (2 vols., 1866), *O Regicida* (1874), *A Filha do Regicida* (1875).

épaté—allows himself to be carried away by his immense vocabulary, but often, indeed usually, his language is a flawless marble, a rich quarry of the purest, most vernacular Portuguese, derived from the Portuguese religious and mystic writers of the sixteenth and seventeenth centuries.[1] Absorbed in his work night after night till the first songs of birds announced the dawn, writing in or after a paroxysm of grief or excitement in his own life, he first lived, then swiftly set on paper, the incidents of his novels—*Amor de Perdição* was written in a fortnight. Their plot may be ill constructed, the delineation of characters shallow, Balzac *manqué*, the episodes far-fetched and melodramatic, but they corresponded, if not to life, to the life of their author and thereby attained intensity of style and a certain unity of action. Yet he was always greatly concerned with schools and tendencies (he imitated Émile Zola in *Eusebio Macario*, although he declared the realistic school to be the perversion of Nature, Émile Souvestre in *As Tres Irmãs*, Octave Feuillet in *Romance de um Homem Rico*), sure of his genius but not of the channels into which he should direct it, at his best perhaps in brief essays and sketches from which his high-flown romanticism is absent, as in the studies of the lives of criminals in *Memorias do Carcere* (2 vols., 1862) and his many scattered reminiscences of life in Minho, the valley of the Tamega, and Oporto. With his sensitive restless temperament, his imagination, his satire and sadness (of tears rather than *saudade*, for which the action in his stories is too rapid), his intolerant hatred of tyranny and intolerance, his essential interest not in things nor even characters but in life and passion, and his unfailing power of expression, he may well be called 'the [modern] Portuguese genius personified'.[2] His life is a strange contrast to the almost idyllic serenity of that of Antonio Feliciano de Castilho (1800–75), whose admirable persistency as poet and translator during a period of nearly sixty years—he had been blind from the age of six—enabled him to attain an extraordinary pre-eminence in Portuguese poetry after Garrett and other poets had been broken like crystals while he remained

---

[1] That it is not impeccable such a phrase as *confortar o palacio* (*O Livro Negro do Padre Diniz*, 1896 ed., p. 135) well shows.
[2] M. A. Vaz de Carvalho, *Serões no Campo* (1877), p. 171.

as a tile upon the housetop. A romantic with a natural leaning to perfection of form, he always retained something of the Arcadian school, and like the Arcadians sought his inspiration in Bernardim Ribeiro and other bucolic *quinhentistas*. Unsympathetic critics incapable of appreciating Castilho's masterly style may feel that in the twenty-one letters of the *Cartas de Echo e Narciso* (1821), in *A Primavera* (1822)[1] and *Amor e Melancholia ou a Novissima Heloisa* (1828) he combined the classical school's dearth of thought with the diffuseness of the romantics. But his *quadras* (*A Visão, O São João, A Noite do Cemiterio*) and his blank verse are alike so easy and natural, his style so harmonious and pure that, despite the lack of observation and originality in these long poems, they have not even to-day lost their place in Portuguese literature. In their soft, vague melancholy and gentle grace they were even more popular than his romantic poems, *A Noite do Castello* (1836)[2] and *Os Ciumes do Bardo* (1838), and influenced many younger writers. Like Garrett he taught them to seek the subjects of their verse in the popular traditions of their own land. Indeed, so great was his bent for the national in literature that his numerous translations (from the French and English, Latin and Greek, to which, with an occasional aftermath of poems such as *Outono* (1862), his later years were devoted) are often remarkable rather for their excellent Portuguese versification than for faithfulness to the originals, and the *Faust* of Goethe, whose powerful directness was unintelligible to his translator, especially as he only read the poem in a French version, became translated indeed.

The most prominent or the least insipid of the numerous group of romantic and ultra-romantic poets, a generation younger than Garrett and Castilho, who published their verses in *O Trovador* (1848)[3] and *O Novo Trovador* (1856), were LUIZ AUGUSTO PAL-

---

[1] Part 2 is entitled *A Festa de Maio* (two cantos).
[2] Written in 1830.
[3] This 'collection of contemporary poems' contains verses of considerable merit. Of some 200 poems by twenty-one poets twenty-eight are by João de Lemos, thirty by José Freire de Serpa Pimentel (1814–70), second Visconde de Gouvêa, author of *Solaos* (1839), thirty-four by Antonio Xavier Rodrigues Cordeiro (1819–1900), and thirty-six by Augusto José Gonçalves Lima (1823–67), who reprinted his contributions in *Murmurios* (1851). A similar collection of verse was *A Grinalda* (Porto, 1857).

MEIRIM (1825-93), whose *Poesias* appeared in 1851, and JOÃO DE LEMOS (1819-89), some of whose poems (one of the best known is *A Lua de Londres*) in *Flores e Amores* (1858), *Religião e Patria* (1859), and especially *Canções da Tarde* (1875), have a delicacy of rhythm and are more scholarly than those of most of the romantic poets. The three volumes form the *Cancioneiro de João de Lemos*. JOSÉ DA SILVA MENDES LEAL (1818-86), author of *Historia da Guerra no Oriente* (1855), and, like Palmeirim, a successful dramatist, in *Os Dois Renegados* (1839) and *O Homem da Mascara Negra* (1843), and also a novelist (*O que foram os Portugueses*), as a poet is at his best in patriotic, military, or funeral odes: *O Pavilhão Negro* (1859), *Ave Cesar, Gloria e Martyrio* (perhaps suggested by Tennyson's *Ode on the Death of the Duke of Wellington*), *Napoleão no Kremlin* (1865), *Indiannas*, in which his sonorous verse has a certain grandeur. His *Canticos* (1858) contain among others a good translation of *El Pirata* of Espronceda, whose influence is evident in the ode to Vasco da Gama, which forms the first part of *Indiannas*. ANTONIO AUGUSTO SOARES DE PASSOS (1826-60), son of an Oporto chemist, studied at Coimbra and published a volume of sentimental romantic poems in 1856 (*Poesias*). The most remarkable is the noble if a little too grandiloquent ode entitled *O Firmamento*, which far excels the poems of death, pale moonlight, autumn regrets, and vanished dreams of this excellent translator of Ossian. After his death a fellow-student, Dr. Lourenço de Almeida e Medeiros, accused him of having stolen *O Firmamento* and other poems. He had himself, he said, written the melancholy ballad *O Noivado do Sepulchro* in February 1853, but unfortunately for his contention it had appeared over Soares de Passos' signature eight months earlier in *O Bardo*. A miscellaneous writer, like so many of his contemporaries, FRANCISCO GOMES DE AMORIM (1827-92) achieved popularity with his plays, published two volumes of sentimental poems, *Cantos Matutinos* (1858) and *Ephemeros* (1866), of which perhaps *O Desterrado* is now alone remembered, and several pleasantly indigenous stories of his native Avelomar (Minho) collected in *Fruitos de Vario Sabor* (1876), with an attractive sketch of the priest, Padre Manuel, *Muita parra e pouca uva* (1878), and *As Duas Fiandeiras* (1881).

He played the sedulous Boswell to Almeida Garrett during the last three years of the latter's life, and the result was one of the few interesting biographies in the modern literature of the Peninsula : *Garrett, Memorias Biographicas* (3 vols., 1881–8). Among the host of pale moon-singers following in the wake of Castilho it is a relief to find a satirist, FAUSTINO XAVIER DE NOVAES (1822–64), who in his *Poesias* (1855), *Novas Poesias* (1858), and *Poesias Postumas* (1877), preferred to take Tolentino for his model. He ridiculed the *janota com pouco dinheiro, com fumos de grande* and other types of his native Oporto, where for some time he worked as a goldsmith. Later he emigrated to Rio de Janeiro, but there found 'everything except literature well paid'.

Two of the romantic poets lived on into the twentieth century, one even survived the Monarchy. THOMAZ RIBEIRO (1831–1901), born at Parada de Gonta in the district of Tondella (Beira), advocate, journalist, playwright, historian, politician, deputy, minister, peer of the realm, won enduring fame with his long romantic poem *D. Jayme* (1862), which opens with fifteen striking stanzas addressed to Portugal. In this introductory ode he rises on the wings of ardent patriotism and sturdy faith in Portugal to a fine achievement in verse. Less rhetorical, the rest of the poem (or series of poems in varying metre) would have gained by reduction to half its length, but is sometimes not without charm in its meanderings. Yet it is a kind of inspired rhetoric and natural grandiloquence that best characterize Ribeiro, and when his inspiration falters it leaves but a hollow and metallic shell of verse. We will expect no delicate shades from a lyric poet who calls the sky *o celico espectaculo*. Subsequent volumes—*Sons que passam* (1867), which contains poems written as early as 1854, *A Delfina do Mal* (1868), *Vesperas* (1880), *Dissonancias* (1890), *O Mensageiro de Fez* (1899)—maintained, but did not increase, his reputation as a poet. The chief work of RAIMUNDO ANTONIO DE BULHÃO PATO (1829–1912), a Portuguese born at Bilbao, was *Paquita*, which he began to publish in 1866, and to the completion of which he devoted nearly forty years of loving care. It is a facetious romantic poem of sixteen cantos, mostly in verses of six lines (*ababcb* or *ababca*), intended to be in the manner of Byron but more akin to Antonio de Trueba, whose

THE ROMANTIC SCHOOL 303

verses are imitated in *Flores Agrestes* (1870). The modern reader, after readily agreeing with Herculano that the poem has its faults, will perhaps be disposed to inquire further if it has any merits; but, although its subject is often unpoetical and trivial, the versification is easy and occasionally excellent. Bulhão Pato published other volumes of gentle album poetry, as *Poesias* (1850), *Versos* (1862), *Canções da Tarde* (1866), and *Hoje: Satyras, Canções e Idyllios* (1888), besides sketches and recollections in prose. Nearly fifty years before his death the romantic school in Portugal had received a severe shock, and the fact that long romantic poems continued to appear is proof how deep its roots had penetrated.

§ 2

The Reaction and After

It was in 1865 that Castilho, the acknowledged high-priest of literary aspirants, wrote a long letter which was published as introduction (pp. 181–243) to Pinheiro Chagas' *O Poema da Mocidade* (1865), in which he deprecated the pretentious affectations of the younger poets. For while Castilho was dispensing his patronage to the acolytes of romanticism a new school of writers had grown up at Coimbra, who refused to know Joseph. They turned to Germany as well as to France, professed to replace sentiment by science, and in the name of philosophy chafed unphilosophically at the old commonplaces and unrealities. Castilho stood not only for romanticism but for the classical style of the eighteenth century, and in some respects the secession from his school may be described as the revolt of the Philistine against Filinto. Anthero de Quental now voiced the cause against the aged Castilho's preface in an article entitled *Bom Senso e Bom Gosto* (1865). For the next few months it rained pamphlets.[1] Snr. Julio de Castilho, subsequently second Visconde de Castilho (1840–1919), and author of many well-known works, including the drama *D. Ignez de Castro* (1875) and the eight volumes of *Lisboa Antiga* (1879–90), took up the cudgels on behalf of his father. The high principles at stake, good sense and good taste, were sometimes forgotten in personal bitterness; a duel was even fought between Quental and Ramalho Ortigão, in which both the poet and his critic were happily spared to literature.

But romanticism in Portugal has nine lives, and raised its head at intervals during the second half of the century. In the domain of

[1] The incomplete list in the *Dicc. Bibliog.*, vol. viii, records forty-four published in 1865 and 1866. These include Julio de Castilho's *O Senhor Antonio Feliciano de Castilho e o Senhor Anthero de Quental* (1865, 2ª ed., 1866), R. Ortigão's *Litteratura d'Hoje* (1866), Snr. Braga's *As Theocracias Litterarias* (1865), Quental's *A Dignidade das Lettras* (1865), and C. Castello Branco's *Vaidades irritadas e irritantes* (1866).

THE REACTION AND AFTER

history JOAQUIM PEDRO DE OLIVEIRA MARTINS (1845-94) always remained more than half a romantic. His life explains the character of his historical writings. Born at Lisbon, obliged to work for a living when he was barely fifteen, he succeeded at the same time in educating himself, supported his mother and her younger children, married before he was twenty-five, had published a dozen works before he was forty, was elected deputy for Viana do Castello in 1886, became Minister of Finance in 1892, and died in his fiftieth year. A career so meteoric could scarcely give scope for that scrupulous research, that careful sifting of evidence which modern ideas associate with the work of the historian; and Oliveira Martins as historian embraced not only the whole of Portuguese but the whole of Iberian history, and that of Greece and Rome to boot. But even had he had more time, the result would only have been more subjects treated, not a different treatment. His whole idea of history was coloured with romance, his work impetuous and personal as that of a lyric poet. His first book, the historical novel *Phebus Moniz* (1867), passed almost unnoticed. After several pamphlets, appeared his first historical work, *O Hellenismo e a Civilisação Christã* (1878), and then in marvellous rapidity the *Historia da Civilisação Iberica* (1879), *Historia de Portugal* (1879), *Elementos de Anthropologia* (1880), *Portugal Contemporaneo* (1881), and a further succession of historical works ending with the *Historia da Republica Romana* (1885). Although politics now occupied much of his time he continued to publish, and wisely emphasized the biographical side of his work, of which *Os Filhos de D. João I* (1891) and *A Vida de Nun' Alvares* (1893) are not the least valuable part. *O Principe Perfeito* (1896), dealing with King João II, appeared posthumously and incomplete. A master of psychology and impressionistic character-sketching, all his work is a gallery of pictures—and especially of portraits—from Afonso Henriquez to Herculano, which reveal the artist as well as his subjects. His style, nervous, coloured, insinuating, is a swift and supple implement for his exceptional power of skilfully summarizing a person or a period. He is capable of vulgarity (as in the account of Queen Philippa and the frequent use of colloquialisms perfectly unbefitting the dignity of history) but not of dullness. He uses and abuses epigram and metaphor, and is not free from the pompous rhetorical antitheses of Victor Hugo (e. g. *De Cid transformou-se em Wallenstein*), till the reader suspects him of being ready at all times to sacrifice truth to a phrase. Yet it is surprising, considering the circumstances of his life and the extent of his work, how often he bases his history, if not on documents, on the work of reliable earlier historians, Portuguese and foreign. If he fills in the gaps with pure romance or an uncritical use of texts (for instance, in *A Vida de Nun' Alvares* he incorporates as authentic those charming 'letters of Nun' Alvarez' which a mere glance at their style shows to be apocryphal) these are but the poet's arabesques, the main structure is often sound enough. Were there no other history of Portugal it might be necessary to consider his work not only fascinating but dangerous, nor would *Portugal Contemporaneo* alone convey an impartial or complete idea of Portuguese history in the first two-thirds of the nineteenth century. We may deny him the title of great historian, we cannot deny him a foremost place in the literature of the century as a writer of brilliant intellect and feverish energy and a powerful re-constructor of characters and scenes in their picturesqueness and their passions.

The work of Manuel Pinheiro Chagas (1842–95), poet, playwright, critic, novelist, historian, was even more abundant and for the most part of a more popular character and more commonplace. He is also more Portuguese, and his works deserve to be read if only for their pure and easily flowing style. Many of his novels are historical. *A Corte de D. João V* (1867) has an account of an *outeiro*[1] in which figures the *Camões do Rocio* as the poet Caetano José da Silva Souto-Maior (*c.* 1695–1739) was called. The subject of the earlier novel *Tristezas á beira-mar* (1866) is that which Amorim in his *A Abnegação* derived from an English novel, but is here more naturally treated. *A Mascara Velha* (continued in *O Juramento da Duqueza*) appeared in 1873. *As Duas Flores de Sangue* (1875) is concerned with revolution in France and at Naples. *A Flor Secca* (1866) treats of more everyday scenes and

---

[1] The *outeiro* (lit. 'hill') was an assembly of poets to *glosar motes*. Often the gathering-place was outside a convent, from the windows of which the nuns gave the *motes* for the poets to gloss.

contains some amusing if rather obvious character-sketches, as the old servant Maria do Rosario (a rustic Juliana), or the devout and vixenish old maid D. Antonia. His *Novelas Historicas* (1869) contains six historical tales dealing with Afonso I, Nun' Alvarez, Prince Henry the Navigator, King Sebastian, Pombal, and the French Revolution. His *Historia de Portugal* (8 vols., 1867), begun on a plan originally laid down by Ferdinand Denis, contains lengthy and frequent quotations from previous historians but is coloured by later political ideas. The two shorter works *Historia alegre de Portugal* (1880) and *Portugueses illustres* (1869) are admirably suited for their purpose—to interest the people in the history and heroes of their country.

The chief work of the able and industrious critic and historian JOSÉ MARIA LATINO COELHO (1825–91) was his *Historia Politica e Militar de Portugal desde os fins do seculo XVIII até 1814* (3 vols., 1874–91). ANTONIO COSTA LOBO (1840–1913), editor of the instructive *Memorias de um Soldado da India*, in his *Historia da Sociedade em Portugal no seculo XV* (1904) began a meticulous and well thought-out study of an earlier period of Portuguese history. JOSÉ RAMOS COELHO (1832–1914) is chiefly known for his elaborate romantic biography of the brother of King João V: *Historia do Infante D. Duarte* (2 vols., 1889, 90). Dr. HENRIQUE DA GAMA BARROS (born in 1833) in the invaluable *Historia da Administração Publica em Portugal nos seculos XII a XV* (3 vols., 1885, 96, 1914) has collected an abundance of concrete, carefully verified details, and thrown a searching light on the early history of Portugal.[1]

In literary criticism as well as in historical research the nineteenth century worthily continued the traditions of the eighteenth. FRANCISCO MARQUES DE SOUSA VITERBO (1845–1910) after first appearing in print as a poet in *O Anjo do Pudor* (1870) rendered excellent service in both those fields; the best-known work of LUCIANO CORDEIRO (1844–1900) is his study *Soror Marianna* (1890); ZOPHIMO CONSIGLIERI PEDROSO (1851–1910) and ANTONIO THOMAZ PIRES (†1913) were celebrated for their

[1] Historical research and compilation are carried on by Snr. Fortunato de Almeida in his *Historia da Igreja em Portugal* (1910, &c.), and by Snr. Afonso de Dornellas (*Historia e Genealogia*, 1913, &c.). Snr. Lucio de Azevedo, well known for his studies of Pombal (*O Marquez de Pombal e a sua epoca*, 1909) and Antonio Vieira (*Historia de Antonio Vieira*, 2 vols., 1918, 21), is a Brazilian.

studies in folk-lore[1]; the Visconde de Juromenha (1807–87) for his edition of the works of Camões; the Conde de Ficalho (1837–1903) for several remarkable studies and his edition of Garcia da Orta; Annibal Fernandes Thomaz (1840–1912) as a bibliographer; Augusto Epiphanio da Silva Dias (1841–1916) as scholar and critic; José Pereira de Sampaio (1857–1915), who used the pseudonym *Bruno*, as a critic; Aniceto dos Reis Gonçalvez Viana (1840–1914) and Julio Moreira (1854–1911) as philologists; Luiz Garrido (1841–82) as critic and classical scholar in his *Ensaios historicos e criticos* (1871) and *Estudos de historia e litteratura* (1879). After the death of the diligent and enthusiastic but sadly unmethodical bibliographer Innocencio da Silva (1810–76), his celebrated *Diccionario Bibliographico Portuguez* was carried on by Brito Aranha (1833–1914), and the task of continuing it is now entrusted to Snr. Gomes de Brito. To the eminent folk-lorist Francisco Adolpho Coelho (1847–1919) the language, literature, and folk-lore are indebted for many works of permanent value. Notable among living scholars, apart from D. Carolina Michaëlis de Vasconcellos and Mr. Edgar Prestage, who both write in Portuguese, are Colonel Francisco Maria Esteves Pereira, whose editions of early works are invaluable; Dr. José Joaquim Nunes, who has devoted his careful scholarship to the early poetry and prose; the Camões scholar, Dr. José Maria Rodrigues; Snr. Pedro de Azevedo, archaeologist and historian; Snr. David Lopes, a scholar equally versed in literature and history; Snr. Candido de Figueiredo (born in 1846), enthusiastic student and exponent of the Portuguese language; while Dr. Fidelino de Figueiredo has a wide and growing reputation as critic and as editor of the *Revista de Historia*. Snr. Anselmo Braamcamp Freire (born in 1849), founder and editor of the *Archivo Historico Portugues* and a most sagacious critic and keen investigator, is the author of attractive and important historical studies and editions, which have become more frequent since he has been able to spare more time from public affairs. Dr. José Leite de Vasconcellos (born in 1858) has a European reputa-

[1] For the works of these and other authors here mentioned consult the Bibliography.

THE REACTION AND AFTER

tion as archaeologist, folk-lorist, philologist, and founder and editor of the *Revista Lusitana*. Ethnology, numismatics, and poetry are among his other subjects, and he maintains the renown of the Portuguese as polyglots, since he writes in Portuguese, Spanish, French, Latin, and Galician. His untiring enthusiasm for all that is popular or genuinely Portuguese is reflected in his numerous books and pamphlets, and he happily infects younger scholars. The gift and training of exact scholarship were denied to Dr. THEOPHILO BRAGA (born in 1843), but his exceptional ardour, industry, and ingenuity have been of inestimable value to Portuguese literature, which will always venerate his name even though his works perish. More than thirty years ago they numbered over sixty, and that was, as it were, only a beginning. His volumes of verse, *Folhas Verdes* (1859), *Visão dos Tempos* (1864), *Tempestades Sonoras* (1864), *Ondina do Lago* (1866), *Torrentes* (1869), *Miragens Seculares* (1884), which was intended to succeed where Victor Hugo's *Légende des Siècles* had failed through lack of a *plano fundamental*, have been variously judged, some regarding them as real works of genius, others as a step removed from the sublime; his works on the Portuguese people are always full of interesting matter. His important *Historia da Litteratura Portuguesa* was to have been completed in thirty-two volumes, but his energies have been spent in many directions, and he has further written works of history, including that of Coimbra University in four volumes, positivist philosophy, and sociology, as well as short stories and plays.

The Portuguese novelists in the nineteenth century showed an increasing tendency to write plays, while authors whose reputation belonged more exclusively to the drama rarely rose above mediocrity. The success of Garrett's plays was bound to fire a crowd of dramatists. Gomes de Amorim's *Ghigi* (1852), on a fifteenth-century theme, was followed by plays with a thesis, such as *A Viuva* (1852), *Odio de Raça* (1854), written on the slavery question at Garrett's request, and *Figados de Tigre* (1857), which entitles itself a parody of melodramas. Having emigrated as a boy to Brazil, he was able to use his knowledge of South America, sometimes with more zeal than discretion, as in *O Cedro Vermelho*, an exotic play in five acts and seventy-nine scenes, which the unfamiliar dresses and hybrid dialogue helped to make popular at Lisbon.[1]

The notable success of more recent playwrights has perhaps developed in proportion as the drama has ceased to be drama in order to become a series of isolated scenes, a novel or *conto* in green-room attire. They are at their happiest when they abandon formal drama for the lighter *revista*. Pathos is theirs and a deft handling of social themes; they can reproduce the peasant or *bourgeois* or noble as a class in thought and action and external conditions. Some of them possess technical skill, choose indigenous subjects and an atmosphere of chastened romanticism. But individual psychology and dramatic action are scarcely to be found. A reader with the patience to peruse the hundreds of plays acted and published in Lisbon during the last fifty years would be rewarded by many delicate half-tones, polished and impeccable verse, excellent prose, admirable sentiments, and poignant scenes, but could with difficulty afterwards recall a striking character or situation. FERNANDO CALDEIRA (1841-94) was a poet, and his plays, *O Sapatinho de Setim*, *A Mantilha de Renda* (1880), *Nadadoras*, *A Madrugada* (1894), are read less for the plot than for his carefully limned verse. His volume of poems, *Mocidades*, appeared in 1882. ANTONIO ENNES (1848-1901), journalist, librarian, politician, diplomatist, Minister of Marine, showed command of pathos and humour as well as of style in his plays *O Saltimbanco* (1885), the tragedy of the noble devotion of a mountebank, Falla-Só, descendant of Jean Valjean, for his daughter, who has been brought up in ignorance of her birth, *Os Lazaristas* (1875), and *Os Engeitados* (1876), which insists throughout on its thesis, the wickedness and cruelty of exposing children, but has some good scenes and living characters, and the notable one-act piece *Um Divorcio* (1877). The principal play of MAXIMILIANO DE AZEVEDO (1850-1911), author of many light and commonplace comedies, as *Por Força* (1900), was the drama *Ignez de Castro* (1894). The scene in which Inés, full of foreboding, takes leave of Pedro before he goes hunting, and that at the end of Act IV, in which Pedro returns to find Inés, in the words of their little son, *ali a dormir*,

[1] It was published, with the necessary explanations, in two volumes (1874).

GREAT PORTUGUESE

ANTÓNIO ENES

António José Enes was born in Lisbon on August 14th 1858. After his early studies in the College of Lazarist Fathers he entered the Higher Course of Letters, now Faculty of Letters, in Lisbon and took his degree, an infrequent achievement at that period.

His literary talent had already become manifest and it was prophesied that he would have a brilliant career. He abandoned the career in trade which he had at first taken up and turned himself with energy to journalism.

At that time the atmosphere was tense amongst opposing parties, characterized by the violent polemics and campaigns caused in the press by political or social incidents. In the midst of this the calm but firm mind of António Enes, his vigorous powers of argument, his simple, clear mode of expression soon won him a name, by the side of other journalists whose names had long been household words.

He was brilliantly successful in political journalism and soon he was to add to his laurels with his growing fame as a dramatist. A series of his plays was staged in Portugal and Brazil, and while they cannot be considered to be masterpieces of Portuguese literature, they are interesting specimens of the romantic theatre of the close of the last century. Such works as «Os Lazaristas» (The Lazarist Fathers), «Eugénia», «Os Engeitados» (The Luckless), «O Saltimbanco» (The Strolling Player), «O Luxo» (Luxury) and «A Emigração» (Emigration) were enthusiastically received by theatre audiences on both sides of the Atlantic and brought their author deserved fame and popularity.

Meanwhile he continued his career as a polemical writer but he maintained, what was rare at that time, his independence of all parties. Yet, even so, he was elected to Parliament in 1880. His parliamentary career was not, however, a brilliant one, as he was more at home with the written than the spoken word.

Two years after his mandate ended he was appointed Chief Librarian of the Lisbon National Library. He was happy in his new post, which seemed to suit to perfection the trends of his mind. He himself

hoped to have found a definite course to follow and to be able calmly
go on with his already multiple activities to the benefit of culture a
the public life of his country.

But an unexpected twist of fate was to lead him into a complete
different enterprise, and bring him into the first rank of those wh
fought for the political restoration of Portugal.

*

In the 19th century Portugal found herself faced with a viole
political crisis. Her historical traditions had made of her an essential
overseas nation and her economic and political structure had been s
up on that basis. In the 17th century she had seen her Eastern Empi
crumble, and was only not tragically affected thereby because in th
meantime the colonization and development of Brazil brought her a ne
source of incalculable wealth. For a century Portugal's economic life ha
become stronger and more prosperous, largely thanks to that gre
overseas province. It can thus be understood that the independence
Brazil in 1820 should have dealt a powerful blow to the integrity
the nation. This small country on the shores of the Atlantic was le
to develop the resources of her vast territories in Africa, almost comple
domination over which was hers by the right of discovery.

Now this principle also guided other European nations with ove
seas interests which had undergone similar vicissitudes. Among the
Great Britain, which held tremendous military and economic powe
had launched out on a policy of imperialistic expansion which threatene
to cover India and a large part of Africa. So that Portugal was no
finding in her oldest and most faithful ally an indomitable rival.

At all bilateral conferences between the two countries Portugues
diplomats sought to make the voice of historical rights heard. The
invoked for Portugal possession of the territories comprised between th
west and east coasts of Africa, from Angola to Mozambique.

When the Berlin Conference was held, Portugal once more expounde
her reasons and rights, which became connected with a famous map o
which the zone in question was marked in pink. By a strange twist o
irony, the «pink» map was a mere dream which could never become fac
Indeed, as the Berlin Conference established the principle of the effectiv
occupation of the territories, it would be difficult for a small countr
like Portugal, poorly armed and scantily populated, to carry out the rapi
occupation of so vast a zone, so difficult to penetrate.

All the efforts made on this basis came up against the presenc
of the British who in their turn desired to occupy the interior of Africa
Their resources were enormous and with them they soon moved from
North to South, so as to unite the Sudan to the Cape Colony.

The situation was serious, but this did not discourage the Portuguese. The efforts made in every sector were multiplied so as to effect geographical exploration and the topographical survey of regions till then unknown to the white man. The aim was to carry the Portuguese flag to the remotest regions of the interior and thus fulfil the «effective occupation» prescribed at the Berlin Conference. Many men played noteworthy parts in this hard task of pioneering and exploring. These pacific missions were on occasions attacked by British military forces or by native tribes stirred up by the British. For years the Portuguese army fought most honourably in a harsh war and against the opposition of nature herself, seeking by all means to protect settlers and pioneers against the attacks and the illicit ambitions of British imperialist capitalism, led by Cecil Rhodes and his South Africa Company.

In view of the unexpected Portuguese resistance, the British Government decided to take more radical measures. In 1890 the British representative in Lisbon delivered to the Portuguese Government an ultimatum on the immediate withdrawal of our troops from Central Africa. Throughout Portugal an immense wave of pain and indignation rose up, all the deeper because we knew that it was quite impossible for us to attempt any resistance.

The crisis even engulfed the Government and internal security. Panic was felt in official circles. Our troops retired in obedience of the ultimatum. Threats continued to hover over the frontier zones of Mozambique, which had to be kept in a permanent state of alert, always defending itself against the British and the natives. The government resigned and a serious financial crisis, worsened by the war overseas, raged. In this predicament, some suggested extreme solutions and remedies, dictated rather by passion and a temporary aberration than by a lucid, realistic vision of events. Why not abandon Mozambique, that gulf into which men and money were being poured, and devote the money and men thus freed to improving the financial situation of Portugal herself?

In this climate of weakness and abandonment of principles, the practical consequences of which could only be disastrous, António Enes came into the limelight of national politics. Until then he had kept aloof from such problems but he possessed to a high degree those qualities of lucidity, realism, rapid understanding and capacity for leadership that were most necessary to face the situation. The new ministry was entirely formed of men who were more notable for their dignity and competence than for their party affiliations; António Enes accepted appointment as Minister of the Navy and the Overseas Territories. His work in Mozambique was most intensive. He sought to raise morale among the settlers there, as well as the armed forces, and to make possible the first measures of economic development and utilization of resources. He instituted the military medal for services overseas, granted privileges to priests who served in missions in the interior, created the Overseas Institute to protect the families of officials, officers and soldiers who died doing their duty in Africa and, finally, gave the already existing but ineffective Mozambique Company the means to act.

A few months later he resigned his post after having managed to effect a transformation in minds which made it possible to sign a new treaty with Great Britain, on conditions providing greater security and dignity for the Portuguese cause in the overseas territories.

The Portuguese Government next asked him to go to Mozambique to demarcate frontiers and at the same time gave him the mission of collecting material for the administrative re-organization of that province. The reports and studies he later published on this, his first, experience of African territories can be considered models of their kind. Not only do they give a faithful and informative picture, pessimistic but realistic, but they also provide most shrewd suggestions on all sectors of overseas life. When António Enes returned to Lisbon he had already definite ideas on a policy of economic exploitation, the betterment of the native through work, financial and administrative organization and military defence.

His fundamental thesis was that there should be an administrative authority served by officials of proven honesty and dedication to the cause of Africa, an increase in the emigration of settlers, together with capital and supported by a legislation providing protection and technical aid, and a decided, firm policy as regards the natives, who should be encouraged to work, without their freedom being thereby endangered. To conquer the native's resistance in this instance would be, in fact, to solve the manpower problem, and with it the question of economic development and the creation of a population conscious and worthy of the freedoms it enjoyed. Furthermore, to promote the civic rise of that population would be to transform Mozambique into a «province» equal in rights and duties with those of European Portugal, in fact and not merely in law.

But other problems, concerning the security of the region, arose in greater urgency and importance. The rebelliousness of the natives, incited by foreign agents, was gaining disturbing proportions. The Vatua people, led by the famous Gungunhana, did not recognize Portuguese sovereignty and was daring enough to advance as far as the coastal regions to incite other native peoples to rebel against the weak Portuguese outposts and strongholds. António Enes already had his views on this problem. He thought it was possible to make Portuguese sovereignty respected throughout Mozambique, and at the same time to grant a certain measure of autonomy to the native kings and chiefs. But before an administrative system of this nature could be set up, it was first necessary to dominate completely and firmly, without further delay the focal points of revolt, which were all in fact the reflection of the activity of Gungunhana.

In 1894 the Portuguese Government received the first alarming telegrams from Mozambique and in this emergency decided to appoint António Enes Royal Commissioner in the province of Mozambique. This was a post with wide executive duties, and to fulfil it he carried out remarkable activity to save Portuguese East Africa.

Accompanied by a noteworthy group of officers, such as Caldas Xavier, Paiva Couceiro, Aires de Ornelas and Mouzinho de Albuquerque, he launched an intelligent campaign in Mozambique. Slowly, prudently, our troops surrounded the enemy; raising outposts at various points, always progressing, gaining victory after victory, some remarkable, the glorious echoes of which reached Portugal, others which passed almost unnoticed, but were no less important in their consequences. They represented two years of hard marches through the jungle, the sacrifice of countless lives cut short by the war and illness, betrayals and unexpected ambush, fighting against man and hostile nature, but the result was very positive, the victories of Marracuene, Cossine, Magul and Manjacaze, in short, the virtual pacification of the whole province.

What part was played amidst these military successes by Antonio Enes, then and always a man of letters, politician and administrator? He was the directing brain, the co-ordinator of the various campaigns, even the stategist who laid down plans, ordered the movement of troops, timely advances and halts, the holding of negotiations.

In 1896 António Enes and the greater part of our troops in Africa were able to return home. The whole Gaza region had been pacified and Gungunhana had taken refuge in far-off Chimomo, having lost all his prestige and authority. There, at Chaimite, he was taken prisoner by Mouzinho de Albuquerque, whom Enes had appointed as military governor of the Gaza region. In him he had sensed those qualities of daring, decision and bravery which made him, with this last blow, the greatest hero of the African campaigns.

The public life of António Enes was almost at a close. For some time he served as Portuguese diplomatic representative in Brazil, and then returned to Portugal once and for all, to set down on paper his recollections of that heroic period. «A guerra em África» (The African War) and the series of articles «De Lisboa a Mozambique» (From Lisbon to Mozambique) were thus the last echoes of an untiring existence, a versatile talent and an indomitable energy, which ceased for ever on July 6th 1901, after they had served Portugal for so long.

Tip. da E. N. P. (Secção Anuário Comercial de Portugal)

are effective. A fifth act six years later [1361] comes as an anti-climax. *O Auto dos Esquecidos* (1898) is the work not of a dramatist but of a poet, José de Sousa Monteiro (1846-1909), whose poems were published under the title *Poemas: Mysticos, Antigos, Modernos* (1883). The *auto*, written in the old *redondilhas* of which another modern poet has sung the praises, necessarily suffers by comparison with plays in which Gil Vicente touched upon the subject—the humbler forgotten heroes of the Portuguese discoveries—but it has its own charm and pathos.

But the most noteworthy of the dramatists of the latter part of the century was D. João da Camara (1852-1908), son of the first Marques and eighth Conde da Ribeira Grande and grandson of the third Duque de Lafões. He early began writing for the stage one-act pieces such as *Nobreza* (1873). His work is various, for it includes elaborate historical dramas in heroic couplets, as *Affonso VI* (1890), in which the king is treated with a sympathy denied to Cardinal Henrique in *Alcacer-Kibir* (1891), slight pieces in verse, as *O Poeta e a Saudade* or the *Auto do Menino Jesus* (1903); and prose plays of contemporary Lisbon society: *O Pantano* (a series of scenes of madness and murder), *A Rosa Engeitada, A Toutinegra Real, A Triste Viuvinha, Casamento e Mortalha*. In these he is lifelike and natural, but many may prefer him in his more fanciful pieces, portraying the old Canon who lives up under the roof of Lisbon Cathedral, in *Meia Noite* (1900), or the *prior* and other rustic worthies of Alentejo, in *Os Velhos* (1893), or the ancient mariner of *O Beijo do Infante* (1898). The mad José of *O Pantano*, the scatterbrained Clytemnestra in *A Toutinegra Real*, the *parvenu* Arroiolos and select Dona Placida in *A Rosa Engeitada* give little idea of the essential mellow humanity of his work, enhanced by a prose style carefully chosen and at times slightly archaic. Snr. Abel Botelho is more peculiarly concerned with the novel, and his plays *Germano* (1886), *Os Vencidos da Vida* (1892), *Jucunda* (1895) derive their interest from the description of certain phases of Lisbon life which could have been presented equally well in novel form. Marcellino Mesquita (1856-1919), doctor and deputy, wrote historical dramas, *O Regente* [1440] in prose, *Leonor Telles* (1889, published in 1893) in verse, *O Sonho da India* (1898) (scenes from the discoveries of Gama and ten other famous Portuguese navigators), and *Pedro O Cruel* (1916). If these historical tragedies are somewhat ponderous, he has a lighter touch in the *redondilhas* of *Margarida do Monte* (1910) and in the charming sketch *Peraltas e Secias*, and displays psychological insight in prose plays dealing with more modern problems : the comedy *Perola* (1889), *Os Castros* (1893), *O Velho Thema* (1896), *Sempre Noiva* (1900), *Almas Doentes* (1905), which treats of hereditary madness and suicide, and in the moving tragedy *Envelhecer* (1909), although it is perhaps out of keeping with the finely portrayed character of Eduardo de Mello that he should so end who had endured so nobly. His prose style has great merit (a few words require excision, e. g. *restaurante, rewolver, desconforto*), and he wrote many shorter problem pieces or episodes in prose: *Fim de Penitencia* (1895), *O Auto do Busto* (1899), *O Tio Pedro* (1902), *A Noite do Calvario, A Mentira* (in which a wife lies to her husband by the life of their child, who dies). The monotony of the rhymed couplets in *Leonor Telles* is intensified in the work of Snr. HENRIQUE LOPES DE MENDONÇA (born in 1856). His verse is more declamatory, the use of strained *esdruxulo* endings is carried so far that it becomes a mannerism and the verse often resembles a hurdle-race, the line running on smoothly to the obstacle at its end (*thalamo—cala-m'o; silencio—recompense-o ; phantasma—faz-m'a*). This no doubt helps to increase the effect of hollow resonance. Nor is there a compensating skill in psychology. There is nothing subtle, for instance, in the characters of *O Duque de Vizeu* (1886) : the cruel João II, the timid Manuel, the high-minded Duke, and self-sacrificing Margarida. *A Morta* (1891) deals with Pedro I's justice and *saudade* for the dead Inés. *Affonso d'Albuquerque* (1898) has a tempting subject (handled previously by Costa Lobo in his play—also in verse—*Affonso d'Albuquerque*, 1886), but it is embarrassing to find the most unrhetorical of heroes, will of iron but not as here tongue of gold, solemnly haranguing in couplet after couplet, (although here, as in the other plays, the atmosphere of Portugal's spacious days is well maintained) :

> E em psalmos de christão se ha de mudar o cantico
> De Brahma, confundindo o Indico no Atlantico.

It is perhaps a relief to turn to the prose plays, *O Azebre* (1909,

THE REACTION AND AFTER 313

written in 1904), the interest of which centres in the artist Fidelio, *Nó Cego* (1904), dealing with divorce, and especially to *O Salto Mortal*, which treats of more homely peasant affairs, and to the admirably natural fishermen's scenes and dialogues enacted at Ericeira in the second half of the nineteenth century, in *Amor Louco* (1899). The author succeeds in giving a more definite picture of a whole community here than of any of his individual heroes in high places. *A Herança* (1913) also has the lives of fishermen for its subject. An equally slight but charming one-act piece in verse is *Saudade* (1916), while the dramatist's power of evoking past scenes is shown in the glowing historical tales of *Sangue Português* (1920), *Gente Namorada* (1921), and *Lanças n'Africa* (1921).

The most conspicuous among slightly younger dramatists is Snr. JULIO DANTAS (born in 1876), who published a first volume of poems, *Nada*, in 1896. He is gifted with wit, lightness of touch, an excellent style, and a sense of atmosphere, which enables him to bring a pleasant archaic flavour to reconstructions of the past and observe the true spirit of history in periods the most diverse. His malleable talent is equally at its ease in *O que morreu de amor* (1899) and *Viriato Tragico* (1900); in Spain of the seventeenth century: *Don Ramón de Capichuela* (1911); contemporary Lisbon: *Crucificados* (1902), *Mater Dolorosa* (1908), *O Reposteiro Verde* (1912); the Inquisition-clouded Portugal of the seventeenth century: *Santa Inquisição* (1910), or its lighter side, with the bonbon marquis: *D. Beltrão de Figueiroa* (1902); the gentle, romantic Portugal of the middle of the nineteenth century: *Um Serão nas Laranjeiras* (1904), or the bull-fighting Portugal of the same period: *A Severa* (1901) with the gallant Marques de Marialva and the beautiful and magnanimous gipsy of the Mouraria. The filigree of his elaborate stage directions is skilfully used to enhance the effect,[1] and some of his scenes are exquisite, especially the simple, very charming, and tragic one-act comedy *Rosas de todo o anno* (1907). If the characters are usually sacrificed to their setting, here and there a slight sketch stands out, as that of the cynical old cardinal who delights in the mental torture of others, in *Santa Inquisição*, the attractive bishop of *Soror Mariana* (1915), or the characters in *A Ceia dos Cardeais* (1902).

[1] In this most delicate upholstery, if Wedgwood and Baedeker (as well as Maple and Mappin) are introduced, they should surely be spelt correctly.

ERNESTO BIESTER (1829-80) in the middle of last century wrote lively comedies of contemporary Lisbon life. The comedies of GERVASIO LOBATO (1850-95), as *Os Grotescos*, *A Condessa Heloïsa* (1878), *O Festim de Balthazar* (1892), *O Commissario de Policia*, *Sua Excellencia*, and many others, are natural, farcical scenes of high spirits and real good humour and good feeling. More literary and charming is the work of Snr. EDUARDO SCHWALBACH, whose *O Dia de Juizo* (1915) and *Poema de Amor* (1916) came to crown a long series of plays and *revistas*. There are touches of real comedy in the lightly sketched scenes and characters of Snr. AUGUSTO DE CASTRO's *Caminho perdido* (1906), *Amor á Antiga* (1907), *As nossas amantes* (1912), *A Culpa* (1918), as in his slight, attractive essays *Fumo do Meu Cigarro* (1916), *Fantoches e Manequins* (1917), and *Conversar* (1920); thought and character in Snr. AUGUSTO LACERDA's *O Vicio* (1888), *Casados Solteiros* (1893), *Terra Mater* (1904), *A Duvida* (1906), *Os Novos Apostolos* (1918). In Snr. BENTO MANTUA's *O Alcool* (1909) and *Novo Altar* (1911) the problem may be a little too much in evidence, but in his prose plays *Má Sina* (1906) and *Gente Moça* (1910) the human interest is insistent. *Má Sina*, apart from the author's weakness for strained coincidences, is a story of peasant life very naturally told. A young playwright of promise is Snr. VASCO DE MENDONÇA ALVES, author of *Promessa* (1910) and *Filhos* (1910). The subject of *Filhos* is unpleasant if not original (it is that of Eça de Queiroz' *Os Maias* and Ennes' *Os Engeitados*), but is treated with dignity and in a good prose style. Snr. JAIME CORTESÃO, hitherto known rather as a poet, has turned to the drama in *Egas Moniz* (1918).

The novelists of the second half of the century were numerous and, as a rule, too dependent upon foreign models, chiefly French. JOAQUIM GUILHERME GOMES COELHO (1839-71) neither by date nor inclination belonged to one or other of the two schools between which lies his brief ten years' activity. His talent developed early. As a medical student at his native Oporto he published poems and several stories, originally printed in the *Jornal do Porto* and later collected with the title *Serões de Provincia* (1870), and at the age of twenty-one, under the pseudonym JULIO DINIZ, he wrote the novel which brought him immediate fame and is still sometimes preferred to his later works: *Uma Familia Ingleza* (1868). In these scenes of the life of Oporto he drew with the most elaborate analysis the relations between English and Portuguese which he had had frequent opportunities of observing in that city. Portuguese critics hint that what to superficial readers has seemed the tediousness of his novels is due to the influence of Dickens and other English novelists who revel in detail, and it is interesting that Gomes Coelho's maternal grandmother was an Englishwoman, Maria, daughter of Thomas Potter. But it is a mistake to call his work tedious; the deliberate dullness of his novels has an excitement of its own, ''tis a good dullness'. The reader, tired with sensational plots and strained incidents, follows not only with relief but with growing absorption the homely daisy-chain of his stories, in which not the tiniest link in the development of the action or thought, especially the latter, is omitted. The interest never flags and never disappoints, leading gently on with carefully measured steps; the approval of virtue and disapproval of wickedness only occasionally becomes obtrusive and insipid. Julio Diniz confessed to a preference for *bourgeois* types, but his real interest was in the country, and *Ass Pupillas do Senhor Reitor*[1] (1866), a village chronicle suggested by Herculano's *O Parocho de Aldea*, is by many held to be his best work. The characters are delineated with the same delicate charm as that of Jenny in his earlier novel, and there is a background of curious observation— *esfolhadas* (husking the maize), *espadeladas* (braking flax), *ripadas* (dressing the flax), *fiadas* (gatherings of women to spin at the winter *lareira* in the faint light of a lamp hanging on the smoke-blackened wall), the men at cards in the tavern, the old country doctor going his rounds on horseback, the solemn greetings *Guarde-o Deus, Louvado seja nosso Senhor Jesu Christo*. If he sometimes sees the peasants as he would have them be rather than as they are, if his realism is subdued and gentle, his descrip-

---

[1] *The Athenaeum* in 1872 announced that Lord Stanley of Alderney was preparing a translation of *As Pupillas*. According to a letter of Julio Diniz (March 25, 1868), 'an Englishman, a relation of Lord Stanley, who is here [Oporto] studying the history of the Portuguese discoveries', had expressed a wish to translate it. The translation was never published. The date of the first Portuguese edition is 1867. It was dramatized at Lisbon in 1868.

tions are at least truer than those of the naturalistic school. In *A Morgadinha dos Canaviaes* (1868), another village chronicle of Minho, the winter life of the peasantry is described, the *consoada* preceding ' cock-crow mass ' on Christmas Eve, the *auto* represented on a rough stage in the village on the Day of Kings, together with the inevitable missionaries, *beata*, enriched 'Brazilian', and electioneering intrigues. Some critics have seen a falling off in his last novel, *Os Fidalgos da Casa Mourisca* (1871), written in the winter of 1869-70 at Madeira, whither he went in vain quest of health, but it is perfectly on a level with his previous work. There may be a slight tendency to exaggerate some of the characters, as there was in *A Morgadinha*, the contrast between Jorge and Mauricio may be too crude, the last scenes may be touched with melodrama, the style may have traces of the *francesismo* which Castilho noticed in his first novel, the execution may be excessively minute—these were not new defects in his works. On the other hand, the ruined *fidalgo* D. Luiz, his chaplain and agent Frei Januario, who scents a Liberal doctrine leagues away, the large-hearted peasants Anna do Vedor and Thomé da Povoa, are as interesting as Tio Vicente the herbalist or any of his previous characters, and the charming and accurate descriptions of the country that he loved so well show him at his best. This demure chronicler of quiet scenes, this specialist in the obvious, in his *romances lentos*, as he calls them—a Portuguese blend of Jane Austen, Enrique Gil, and Fernán Caballero : his delicacy is essentially feminine—achieved an originality which so often eludes those who most furiously pursue it. His *Poesias* (1873), partly consisting of poems interspersed in his novels, have a quiet, intimate charm. A curious originality had been attained earlier by a young naval lieutenant, FRANCISCO MARIA BORDALLO (1821-61). When he published *Eugenio* (1846) at Rio de Janeiro, and a second edition at Lisbon in 1854, it was claimed that this sea novel (*romance maritimo*) was the first of its kind to be written in Portuguese ; but his use of naval technical terms and descriptions of the sea is perhaps too deliberate. His *Quadros maritimos* appeared in *O Panorama* in 1854.

Few authors are more interesting to the critic (owing to the

courageous and persistent development of his art) than José
Maria de Eça de Queiroz (1843-1900), a far more robust writer
than Julio Diniz and the greatest Portuguese novelist of the
realistic school. Born at Villa do Conde, the son of a magistrate, he was duly sent to study law at Coimbra, and after taking
his degree contributed in 1866 and 1867 a series of *feuilletons*
to the *Gazeta de Portugal*. These *folhetins*, reprinted in *Prosas
Barbaras* (1903), are remarkable because they show beside a love
of the gruesome and fantastic (*O Milhafre, O Senhor Diabo,
Memorias de uma Forca*) at least one story (*Entre a neve*) of
a perfect simplicity, such as the author is sometimes supposed
to have attained only towards the end of his life. His partiality
for the exotic was fostered by travels in Egypt and Palestine
in 1869 and manifested itself in *A Morte de Jesus, Adão
e Eva no Paraiso*, and *A Perfeição*, as well as in *A Reliquia* and
in part of *A Correspondencia de Fradique Mendes*. In 1873 he
went to Havana as Portuguese Consul, and twenty-six years
as Consul at Newcastle-on-Tyne (1874-6), Bristol (1876-88),
and Paris (1888-1900), where he died, enabled him to see his
own country in a new light. His prose lost its exuberance, his
taste became more severe, his extravagant fancy, so strangely
combined with realism in many of his works, was merged
in natural descriptions of his native land. He regained his
own soul without losing that peculiar mockery with which
he veiled a kindly, sensitive temperament, and which agree-
ably stamps the greater part of his writings. But indeed the
introducer of the naturalistic novel into Portugal only played
with materialism, which in his hands was always unreal: legendary and romantic, as in *Frei Genebro, S. Christovam, O Tesoiro*;
deliberately false and artificial, as *A Civilisação*; a macabre
fantasy, as *O Defunto*; or half-intentional caricature, as *O Primo
Basilio* and *Os Maias*. What more chimerical than *A Reliquia* or
more elusive than *O Suave Milagre*, or more fanciful than *O Man-
darim* (1879), in which without himself knowing China the author
makes his readers know it! All through his life he was as it were
groping through Manueline for a purer Gothic; the pity was that
his education from the first should have thrown him into contact
with French models—so that his very language too often reads like

translated French—instead of directing him to a truer realism (such as that of his nearer neighbour Pereda), to which he turned in his last works, and in which he might have written regional masterpieces had he not died at a moment when his art apparently had lost nothing of its vigour. More probably, however, his still unsatisfied craving for perfection would have sought relief in mysticism. His first novel was a sensational story written in collaboration with Ramalho Ortigão: *O Mysterio da Estrada de Cintra* (1870), originally published in the *Diario de Noticias* (July 24–September 27, 1870). It was, however, *O Crime do Padre Amaro* (1876), in which he grafted the naturalistic novel on the quiet little town of Leiria, and the two notable if unpleasant Lisbon stories *O Primo Basilio* (1878) and *Os Maias* (1880), that marked him out as the most powerful writer of the time in Portugal. But he was still feeling his way. *A Reliquia* (1887) is as different from *Os Maias* as it is from the remarkable and charming letters of *A Correspondencia de Fradique Mendes* (1891) and his last two novels, *A Illustre Casa de Ramires* (1900), most Portuguese of his works, and *A Cidade e as Serras* (1901). The three fragments in *Ultimas Paginas* (1912) were probably written earlier. There are samples of all his phases in his *Contos* (1902), and the short story gave scope for his powers of observation and insight without calling for an elaborate plot, in which he often failed. *A Cidade e as Serras*, after developing the earlier story *A Civilisação*, is but a fascinating succession of country scenes. All Eça de Queiroz' characters are caricatures, some more so, others less, but they are nevertheless true to a certain degree, that is to say, they are good caricatures, and living, and this is so especially in these later novels, which show how great a regionalist writer was lost in him through the influence of French schools. Yet no one can deny that his works have an originality of their own as well as power and personal charm, and all contain some striking character-sketches or delightful descriptions that are not easily forgotten.

The dullness of the naturalistic novels of JULIO LOURENÇO PINTO (1842–1907) is not relieved by Eça de Queiroz' pleasant irony and definite characterization. These 'scenes of contemporary life', while they display a praiseworthy restraint, give the idea rather of exercises in imitation of a French exemplar or of

THE REACTION AND AFTER 319

one of Eça de Queiroz' early novels than of living stories. Their style is slovenly, the development of the plot prolix and monotonous. A certain interest attaches to *Margarida* (1879)—although even here the author is too methodical in detailing the past lives of the four protagonists, the nonentity Luiz, the aspiring Adelina (a Portuguese Madame Bovary), Fernando, and Margarida, after they have been duly presented in the opening pages—and to the descriptions of a fair, a bull-fight, a flood, or provincial politics in *Vida Atribulada* (1880), *O Senhor Deputado* (1882), *Esboços do Natural* (1882), and *O Homem Indispensavel* (1884). Snr. JAIME DE MAGALHÃES LIMA (born in 1857) in *O Transviado* (1899), *Na Paz do Senhor* (1903), *O* and *Reino da Saudade* (1904), has written novels *à thèse* which are quite as interesting as naturalistic novels and more natural, but his art, especially in the presentation of contemporary politics, is a little too photographic. Snr. LUIZ DE MAGALHÃES (born in 1859), author of several volumes of verse, wrote a single novel, *O Brasileiro Soares* (1886). It would offer little new in theme or treatment to distinguish it from other naturalistic novels were it not for the author's success in drawing in Joaquim Soares a natural and attractive portrait of the Portuguese returned rich from Brazil (the *Brasileiro*). None of these novelists can rival the reputation of FRANCISCO TEIXEIRA DE QUEIROZ (1848-1919). He became prominent as a novelist of the realistic school over forty years ago when under the pseudonym of BENTO MORENO he inaugurated the series of his *Comedia do Campo* (8 vols.), of which the last volume is *Ao Sol e á Chuva* (1916), followed by a second series: *Comedia Burgueza* (7 vols.), which began with *Os Noivos* (1879). The obvious defects of his work—its laborious realism, its insistence on medical or physical details, its vain load of pedantry [1]—need not obscure its real merits. The careful style has occasional lapses, the psychology is thin, the conversations commonplace. His art, like a winter sunshine, fails to penetrate. Yet even in the *Comedia Burgueza*, where the interest must depend on the psychology, he succeeds in *D. Agostinho* and

---

[1] e.g. a girl, Rosario, in *Amor Divino*, is described—annihilated—with the assistance of Cybele, Goya, the Venus of Milo, Reynolds, Shakespeare. Cf. the names, from Descartes to Darwin, in *O Conto do Gallo*.

A Morte de D. Agostinho (1895) in giving individuality to that strange rickety figure of the old *fidalgo* in his ruined Lisbon *palacio*. And in the Minho scenes of the *Comedia do Campo* his scrupulous descriptions obtain their full effects. In the *romaria* (pilgrimage), the *cantadeira* (improvisator), the *diligencia* with its load of priests (in *Amor Divino*), the girl shepherdess, the *abbade* fond of hunting wolves and boars, the old women spinning, the lawsuit of centuries over the fruit of an orange-tree, the sexton Coruja and his dog Coisa (in *Vingança do morto* and *O Enterro de um Cão*), and especially some old familiar country-house, with Dona Maria and her preserves and *receios infernaes*, in *Amor Divino* and *Amores, Amores* (1897), Minho and the Minhotos are presented with naturalness and skill. Many of these scenes are from the short stories of *Contos, Novos Contos* (1887), *A Nossa Gente* (1900),[1] and *A Cantadeira* (1913),[2] some of which have been collected in an attractive volume, *Arvoredos* (1895).

Snr. MANUEL DA SILVA GAYO (born in 1860), poet and novelist, wrote in *Peccado Antigo* (1893) a short *novela* as it calls itself, or rather a *conto*, remarkable for its combination of colour and restraint. It describes country scenes and customs in a style that may not be spontaneous but is well subservient to the matter in hand, and has a vigour, purity, and concision too often lacking in modern Portuguese prose. Some of his early stories were collected in *A Dama de Ribadalva* (1904). In his later novels this style is not maintained. We will not quarrel with its abruptness in *Ultimos Crentes* (1904), a remarkable story of nineteenth-century *Sebastianistas* in a fishing village to the extreme north of Estremadura, but it is more slovenly in *Os Torturados* (1911), in which a certain originality of thought seems to have damaged the form in which it was expressed. There is a welcome Spanish directness in the work of the able journalist Snr. CARLOS MALHEIRO DIAS (deputy for Vianna do Castello in 1903–5) in his novels *O Filho das Hervas* (1900), *Os Telles de Albergaria* (1901), and *A Paixão de Maria do Ceo* (1902). Frankly sensational in *O Grande Cagliostro* (1905), he displays his gift for the short story in *A Vencida* (1907), a volume of dramatic tales, of which *A Consoada* is especially effective.

[1] *Comedia do Campo*, vol. vi.   [2] Vol. vii.

Snr. João Grave (born in 1872) carefully elaborates his prose in *A Eterna Mentira* (1904) and *Jornada Romantica* (1913). It turns to marble in the musings of the marble faun in *O Ultimo Fauno* (1906), but loses this unreality in studies of the poor in country, *Gente Pobre* (1912), and town, *Os Famintos* (1903), a tragic story of a workman's family at Oporto. More recently he has treated historical themes with success in *Parsifal* (1919) and *A Vida e Paixão da Infanta* (1921). In the historical novel Snr. Francisco de Rocha Martins has won a special place by picturesque works such as *Os Tavoras* (1917). He has an eye for dramatic episodes and has composed many a living picture of the past.

Abel Botelho (1856–1917), a colonel in the Army, and for some years Minister of the Portuguese Republic at Buenos Aires, author of a volume of verse, *Lyra Insubmissa* (1885), showed an intermittent power of description in seven stories of his native Beira, collected under the title *Mulheres da Beira* (1898). In his series of novels published under the heading *Pathologia Social*: *O Barão de Lavos* (1891), *O Livro de Alda* (1898), *Fatal Dilemma* (1907), *Prospera Fortuna* (1910), he would seem to have laboured under a misapprehension, believing apparently that the introduction of physiology into literature might prove him an original writer.[1] Sainte-Beuve may speak of the *saletés splendides* of Rabelais, a great stylist like Signor Gabriele d'Annunzio, except when his art fails, may redeem if he does not justify any theme. But Abel Botelho's style in these wearisome novels can only be described as worthy of their matter. They are a welter of shapeless sentences, long abstract terms, French words, gallicisms, expressions such as *pathognomonico, autopsiação, neuro-arthritico, a etiologia dos hystero-traumatismos*. This may be magnificent pathology, but it is not art or literature. *As Farpas* had come to an end some years before these novels began to appear, otherwise

[1] Pathology, religious and social, crops up in the later novels of Snr. Vieira da Costa, *Irmã Celeste* (1904), *A Familia Maldonado* (1908); yet his earlier work, *Entre Montanhas* (1903), a story of contemporary life in the highlying vine-lands of Douro written in 1899, was more original. The modern Portuguese novelists are nearly, although not quite, as numerous as the poets. José de Caldas is the author of *Os Humildes* (1900) and *Cartas de um Vencido* (1910), D. João de Castro of *Os Malditos* (1894) and *A Deshonra*, in which a strange situation is too long drawn out.

their defects might have been pilloried by an adept in ridicule who in contemporary literature occupies a place apart. As critic José Duarte Ramalho Ortigão (1836–1915) took his share in the controversy of 1865, as a traveller he wrote a vivid, witty, and charming account of Holland, with malicious side-reflections on Portugal: *A Hollanda* (1883). Between these two dates a series of papers, *As Farpas* (1871–87), originally suggested by Alphonse Karr's *Les Guêpes* and begun in collaboration with his friend Eça de Queiroz, had made him famous. His clear and pointed style was an excellent instrument for the barbed shafts of his satire and irony and, having discovered how powerful a weapon he possessed, he wielded it to right purpose. With abundant good sense he ridiculed and undermined the foibles and follies of Lisbon life, obstinately determined to bring health to the minds and the bodies of his fellow-countrymen and succeeding by his wit where a more sedate reformer might have failed. The range of subjects covered was very wide—the interest of many of them necessarily ephemeral—and his skill in brief character-sketches is remarkable. But although Ramalho Ortigão will always be remembered as the author of *As Farpas* it is perhaps *A Hollanda* that will be read. The former work was imitated by Fialho de Almeida in *Os Gatos* (1889–94), which achieved popularity in Lisbon. His is a more lumbering wit: the rapier of Ramalho Ortigão is exchanged for bludgeon or umbrella. But *Os Gatos*, despite much that is vulgar and much that is dull, contains some good literary criticism and successful descriptions, of places rather than of persons. A battling critic was Manuel José da Silva Pinto (1848–1911) in *Combates e Criticas* (1882), *Frente a frente* (1909), and *Na procella* (1909). Equally vigorous and pure was the style of Joaquim de Senna Freitas (1840–1913) in *Per agoa e terra* (1903) and *A Voz do Semeador* (1908), as likewise that of Francisco Silveira da Mota in *Viagens na Galliza* (1889). The literature of travel is not extensive. Oliveira Martins published in the *Jornal do Commercio* of Rio de Janeiro in 1892 his *A Inglaterra de hoje* (1893); Eça de Queiroz showed a deeper acquaintance with England in his *Cartas de Inglaterra* (1905). Snr. Wenceslau José de Sousa Moraes (born in 1854), sometimes called the Portuguese

GREAT PORTUGUESE

VENCESLAU JOSÉ DE SOUSA MORAIS

«Chained to this land for I don't know how many years now, I sometimes ask myself whether in my European blood there does not in fact run some Asiatic blood to explain this loving presence by natural afinities». It was thus that Venceslau de Morais sought to justify, in a letter to one of the few friends he still had in Portugal, the irresistible attraction that he felt for the legendary and mysterious land of the Rising Sun where he lived for thirty years until his death.

Indeed the life and work of this author born in Lisbon in 1854 bear eloquent witness to this predilection. The venerable figure with a patriarchal beard, whom his Japanese neighbours called Portugaru-San (Mr. Portugal), is wrapped in the mystery of the East, the spell of the adventure lived by the voluntary exile from his country, who suffered the bitterness of nostalgia, the story of the disappointments in love that he took pleasure in provoking «in order to make sorrow his companion», the romantic dream of the man who sought in his adaptation to Japanese life the peace he never encountered in life.

From his youth Venceslau de Morais felt that irremediable boredom which would go with him until his death and that to some extent fatalistically determined the course of his life.

When he was 17 he chose a military career and enlisted as a volunteer in the 5th Rifleman Regiment but two years later he left the army. He decided to attend the Polytechnic preparatory to entering the Navy. He later attended the Naval College and completed his course in 1875. His career was a rapid one: he was promoted to midshipman in

Hunting is carried on for few months in the year, with the restrictions called for by the biological demands of the victims, and seems to be going through a period of difficulties, due not to any lessening of interest but the scarcity of game.

Basket-ball has recently attracted public attention on a large scale and will certainly become associated in the popular taste with rink hockey, a sport in which Portugal has already gained the title of World Champion on several occasions, in contests sometimes held in Portugal. In the overseas provinces of Mozambique and Macau rink hockey possesses some of its most important nuclei of good players, as is true in Portugal of Sintra and Paço d'Arcos, near to Lisbon.

In Portugal ping-pong is also greatly appreciated, together with billiards, both divulged in large and small sporting clubs, as well as hand-ball, fencing, rugby, cross-country running, badmington, judo, etc.

All these sports usually have their military teams, for this chapter of sports culture has been attentively borne in mind in the pre-military or army barracks and schools.

Wrestling and boxing in our country are spectacles rather than sports practised by amateurs.

As for motor-cycling and motoring as competitive sports, and we should here point out the great preference in their touristic opportunities, with the exception of yearly speed trials with foreign competitors taking part held in Lisbon and Oporto, and the presence of some amateur aces of the wheel in foreign contests, their activity is limited to the holding of *rallies* and trips round the country, which always enjoy very considerable participation of competitors and spectators.

The panorama of Sport in Portugal is at the present moment one of brilliant emphasis and frank colourfulness, and to these agreeable qualities has greatly contributed, as we have said, the political atmosphere which encourages initiative and takes a wide interest in their difficulties, solving them with excellent common sense and fully satisfying sportsmen and the public in general.

If homelands are the best judges of the men who direct them, in this brief report of ours on the general activities of sport in Portugal the view of Portuguese sportsmen as to the work of their Government has been implicitly and clearly enunciated. This is enough to warrant our work in writing this report.

the year he finished the course, and sixteen years later he became lieutenant-commander.

His naval career made it necessary for him to spend periods abroad, but when in 1881 he was ordered to sail for Mozambique for the first time the young lieutenant was very disappointed because the call of duty was taking him away from the woman with whom he had fallen in love. Their separation was sad. His return strengthened their love, but the long periods of absence, the writer's unfounded jealousy, violent scenes tired the fair Isabel, who broke off with her young lover. The hyper-excitable soul of Venceslau de Morais bled. He was cruelly wounded and set out again on his travels. In 1891 he was appointed second in command in the Captaincy of the port of Macau, where he also worked as Lecturer in Portuguese at the Seminary-High School of S. José.

If the road to the East had been taken by the writer as a refuge from the scourge of violent jealousy, from the troubles brought upon him by others' lack of understanding, from the conflicts that his temperament with its impetuosity and sickly romanticism created for him, the disappointments he suffered in Macau were strong enough to worsen the state of depression of his morale. In that Portuguese territory he had a passionate love-affair with a young Chinese woman, who bore him two children. But the misunderstandings between the two caused by the writer's complexes finally caused the submissive Atchan to rebel against the seclusion to which she was subjected. One day he returned from a journey to the Chinese coast to find the house empty. Atchan had run away from the tyranny of a great love.

The extraordinary circumstances of his life, together with the innate qualities of the author, created the conditions which at this time, 1897, led him to produce «Dai-Nippon», as a result of a rapid visit to Japan. It was Venceslau's first great work and was to mark him out as one of the foreign writers who have best known how to understand the Japanese soul.

With a view to leaving Macau, which now only brought back the remembrance of an unhappy love, and alleging that from the point of view of hierarchy his situation as second-in-command was untenable, as the commander of the port was now an officer of lower rank than he, Venceslau de Morais asked permission to resign from the post. The government considered the request a just one and in 1898 he was appointed acting consul in Hiogo and Osaka, and soon after a decree made him consul, placing him in Kobe and Osaka.

A new life was beginning for him in the country that had always fascinated him and was to bring about in him a progressive separation from his homeland.

During his years in Kobe the writer worked actively on his books He created a genre that was clearly Japanese in its inspiration, describing his personal reflections on the Nature and people he saw about him, with a sense of pure impressionism. He described habits, dress and environments, defined characteristic types and emphasised the dazzling landscape of exoticism that blinded him, and wrapped all this in a halo of admiration that served to gild misery and make misfortune poetic.

On one of the regular excursions that the consul-writer made in the surroundings of Kobe, he one day made the aquaintance of a pretty maid who worked in a typical restaurant in Tokushima and fell in love with her. His love was returned and in 1900 they got married according to the Japanese ritual and went to live in a comfortable house in Kobe, which greatly pleased the gentle Ó-Yoné. But her home became a prison for her. The considerable difference in age between them aggravated the writer's jealousy and he guarded the wife he had chosen like a miser guards his gold. Ó-Yoné was grateful to her husband for the affection he showered on her and suffered in resigned silence until death took her away from him after twelve years of married life.

The high social position to which Venceslau de Morais attained when he became doyen of the consular corps, as the official of highest rank there, could not soothe the unhappiness which took hold of the writer when his great love was taken from him. He was deeply moved by this event, sold the books in his fine library by weight, left the house where they had lived together and obeyed the morbid voice of his will, which told him to leave the living, go to Tokushima near the tomb which recalled the name of the loved one and gave shape to his nostalgic longing. He decided then to break once and for all the ties which bound him to the west. He resigned as consul and as commander in the navy and he set off for Tokushima accompanied by the niece of Ó-Yoné, who had served as maid in the writer's house, and began to live in a humble cottage. There he spent his life like a hermit, isolated, unhappy and his only affection was now the little maid, Ko-Haro. But one day she went away, lured by a dream of love that proved to be fleeting. When she returned she was ill and asked to go to hospital. Venceslau de Morais looked after her with affection, untiringly until she died.

The death of the only person he loved had a frightening effect on the writer's nervous system. His daily walk to the grave where the ashes of Ó-Yoné and Ko-Haro were at rest became an obsession of his hypochondriacal mind. Soon he would even have to abandon these walks when a slight paralysis chained him more and more to his old chair, where he spent hour after hour lost in his memories of the past. In spite of all he had suffered he would never regret the decision he had taken of staying forever in his favourite land, and in this respect the declaration he wrote in Japanese, Portuguese and English on the wall of his room is very significant: «When I die I wish my body to be cremated at Tokushima».

In July 1929 Venceslau de Morais died as a result of a fall on the stairs leading to the tiny garden by his cottage.

The writer had devoted all his literary activity to the legendary land of the Rising Sun, which had always fascinated his imagination, as the titles of his works clearly show: «Outline of the Far East — Siam, China and Japan» (1895); «Dai Nippon» (1897); «Tea Cultivation» (1905); «Japanese Life» (1907); «Fernão Mendes Pinto in Japan» (1920); «Outline of the History of Japan» (1926); «View of the Japanese Soul» (1926) and «Bon-odori in Tokushima» (1928). Japan was grateful to the author and paid him a just tribute by placing his bust in a public garden and opening a national subscription to provide funds to build and maintain in Tokushima a museum destined to perpetuate the memory of the writer who takes his rightful place as one of the great naturalists of our century.

THE INAUGURATION OF THE PRESS ROOM

The first important initiative taken by the new National Secretary was the opening of a Press Room in the National Office of Information with the aim of making possible closer collaboration between the Press and sources of information.

Both Portuguese and foreign Press circles received the news with natural enthusiasm and were present at the inauguration to lend their support to this very promising initiative.

The words of Dr. Moreira Baptista and the enthusiasm with which those present participated in the gathering with their manifold questions and suggestions and expressing their agreement revealed that the Press Room will very quickly become the centre of contact between two worlds: that of information and that of public opinion, through the conscious, co-ordinated effort of journalism.

On the morning of March 26th a simple opening ceremony was held, which became more an open and profitable exchange of opinions. Those present included the directors of newspapers and news agencies, chairman and high officials of the National Broadcasting Station, of the Portuguese Radio Television Company and other stations, editors of the principal papers, foreign correspondents in Portugal, heads of information offices, etc.

The National Secretary opened the session by delivering a speech, most of which we reproduce here:

«If we thought that this National Office's mission in the sphere of information could suffer delays in the modernization of methods we consider pressing, we should postpone the inauguration of this Press Room and make it part of the cycle of commemorations marking the 25 years of this Organization's existence.

The programme we would wish to realise for these commemorations would perhaps be thereby significantly enhanced but we should lose some time in the realization of an initiative that I believe has evident utility.

Pierre Loti, has skilfully described China and Japan in *Traços do Extremo Oriente* (1905), *Paisagens da China e do Japão* (1906), and *Cartas do Japão* (three series, 1904–7). In a letter in French at the end of his *Traços* he says: *J'ai dit ce que je pensais, naïvement, au gré de mes souvenirs.*

Snr. MANUEL TEIXEIRA GOMES, versatile and gifted, traveller, diplomatist (Portuguese Minister at the Court of St. James), and author, is essentially an artist. With a clear, coloured, liquid style he excels in painting the blue seas, transparent air, and sunburnt soil of Algarve in *Agosto Azul* (1904). His pagan and unconventional art has the power of impressing incidents on the mind, as of giving sharp relief to fantastic persons such as the Canon and his three witless sisters in *Gente Singular* (1909), the Danish literary lady in *Inventario de Junho* (1899), or the avaricious Dona Maria and the inane Minister of *Sabina Freire* (1905). This 'comedy in three acts' contains sufficient shrewdness, humour, and clever characterization for a long novel instead of a short play. The tiny volumes *Tristia* (1893) and *Alem* (1895) by Snr. ANTERO DE FIGUEIREDO (born in 1867) were notable for their style, and in other works, *Partindo da Terra* (1897), the passionate letters of *Doida de Amor* (1910), the novel *Comicos* (1908), and the fascinating historical studies *D. Pedro e D. Inês* (1913) and *Leonor Teles, Flor de Altura* (1916), his prose maintains a restraint and charm which place him among the best stylists of the day. One of the noblest qualities of this prose is its precision, the scrupulous use of the right word, common or archaic. It is the more disconcerting to find good Portuguese words such as *estação, hospedaria, comodo, bondade* ousted by *gare, hôtel, confortavel, bonomia*. But these are only occasional blemishes in a style of rare distinction. It can paint a whole scene in a brief sentence, as *os milheiraes amarellecem-se caladamente*. This power of description gives excellence to his *Recordações e Viagens* (1905), whether the recollections be of Minho or of *uma aldeia espiritual* in Italy. It is really as a writer of short sketches and essays that he excels. In *Senhora do Amparo* (1920) and especially in the seventeen sketches of *Jornadas de Portugal* (1918) skill in the choice of indigenous words gives a forcible and original poetry to glowing descriptions redolent of the soil.

D. MARIA AMALIA VAZ DE CARVALHO (1847-1921) collaborated with her husband, the poet Gonçalves Crespo, in *Contos para os nossos filhos*, and in *Serões no Campo* (1877), three stories, in one of which, *A Engeitada*, one may perhaps see reminiscences of Julio Diniz' *A Casa Mourisca*, and *Contos e Phantasias* (1880) treated slight themes with a delicate charm. But she is less well known as writer of *contos* or as poet, in *Vozes do Ermo* (1876), than as the author of a notable historical biography, *Vida do Duque de Palmella* (1898–1903), and of critical essays on Portuguese and foreign literatures. In the latter the English predominates, but French, German, and Italian, as in *Arabescos* (1880), are not forgotten. The sane judgement, sympathy, and insight of *Alguns homens do meu tempo* (1889), *Figuras de Hoje e de Hontem* (1902), *Cerebros e Corações* (1903), *No Meu Cantinho* (1909), *Coisas de Agora* (1913), and other volumes have been appreciated by countless readers in Portugal and Brazil. A writer who likewise combines literary and historical criticism with original work in verse (*Poemetos*, 1882) and prose is the CONDE DE SABUGOSA (born in 1854), skilful and delicate reconstructor of the past in *Embrechados* (1908), *Donas de Tempos Idos* (1912), *Gente d'Algo* (1915), *Neves de Antanho* (1919), and *A Rainha D. Leonor* (1921), who collaborated with another stylist, the CONDE DE ARNOSO[1] (1856–1911), author of *Azulejos* (1886), in the volume of *contos* entitled *De braço dado* (1894). His historical portraits are full of life and charm, painted in the warm colours of knowledge and emotion.

If we except D. Maria Amalia Vaz de Carvalho, the literary achievement of women in Portugal in recent years has not been remarkable. Like D. CLAUDIA DE CAMPOS, author of the novels *Elle* (1898) and *A Esfinge* and short stories, D. ALICE PESTANA (*Caiel*) has cultivated with success both the novel, as in *Desgarrada* (1902), and the *conto*, as in *De Longe* (1904), which contains stories of familiar life written with sincerity and truth. If D. ANNA DE CASTRO OSORIO's *Ambições* (1903) gives the impression rather of a series of scenes than of a long novel, in her short stories *Infelizes* (1898)—especially *A Terra*—and *Quatro Novelas* (1908) she ably describes common family life in town

[1] He wrote under the name Bernardo de Pindella or Bernardo Pinheiro.

THE REACTION AND AFTER

or country, or (in *A Sacrificada*) the lives, past and present, of aged nuns in a dwindling convent. D. VIRGINIA DE CASTRO E ALMEIDA has written two novels concerning the development of the soil in Alentejo : *Terra Bemdita* (1907) and *Trabalho Bemdito* (1908).[1] They are frankly novels with a thesis to prove, but contain so much vigour and zest of living that they stand out from other more futile or anaemic novels of contemporary Portugal.

The growing prominence of the *conto* is felt in the work of Castello Branco, Eça de Queiroz, Teixeira de Queiroz, Snr. Jaime de Magalhães Lima (*Via Redemptora*, 1905, *Apostolos da Terra*, 1906, *Vozes do Meu Lar*, 1912), and many other novelists. JULIO CESAR MACHADO (1835–90) showed talent in *Contos ao luar* (1861), *Scenas da minha terra* (1862), *Quadros do campo e da cidade* (1868), *A' Lareira* (1872). His skill in the description of rustic scenes would have been more convincing had he not thought it necessary to introduce touches of extraneous elegance and humour into his very real love of the country, so that the patent leather boot is ever appearing among the *tamancos* in these light humorous sketches and romantic tales. As slight but perhaps more natural are the *Contos do Tio Joaquim* (1861) by RODRIGO PAGANINO (1835–63); the pleasant stories of village life, *Contos* (1874) and *Serões de Inverno* (1880), written by CARLOS LOPES (born in 1842) under the pseudonym PEDRO IVO; and *Contos* (1894) and *Azul e Negro*[2] (1897) by Afonso Botelho. The poet AUGUSTO SARMENTO (born in 1835) also wrote stories of village life, *Contos do Soalheiro* (1876), but stories à *thèse*, treating of emigration and other *minhoto* evils, among which he includes *beatas*, witches, and *brasileiros de torna-viagem*. A writer of *contos* as disappointing as Machado is ALBERTO BRAGA (1851–1911). He has a sense of style and technique, and some of his tales, especially *O Engeitado*, are pathetic, but after reading his *Contos da minha lavra* (1879), *Contos de aldeia*, *Contos Escolhidos* (1892), *Novos Contos*, one has the perhaps

---

[1] In novels intimately connected with the Portuguese soil such expressions as *colorido gritante* (*criard*), *lunchar* (to partake of luncheon), *endomingado* (*endimanché*) are more than ever out of place. The authoress has written other stories: *Capital Bemdito* (1910), *Fé* (a Socialist novel), *Inocente* (1916), *A Praga* (1917).

[2] A *conto* written by Snr. Julio de Lemos in 1905 bears the same title.

somewhat unfair impression that they are mainly concerned with *viscondessas* and canaries. The learned Conde de Ficalho in *Uma Eleição Perdida* (1888) evidently relates his own experiences, and this and the five accompanying *contos* contain some charming descriptions of Alentejo, of the *reisinho cacique* Lopes, Paschoal the *passarinheiro*, the gossips of the village *botica*, the girls carrying *bilhas*, the scent of rosemary in morning dew. The same province supplies the background of the work of JOSÉ VALENTIM FIALHO DE ALMEIDA (1857–1912). Born at Villa de Frades, the son of a village schoolmaster, he spent seven years sadly against the grain as chemist's assistant before he was able to turn more exclusively to literature. No recent writer has had a greater vogue in Portugal. One must account for this by the fact that in the somewhat nerveless literature of the day he showed a virile and often brutal colour and energy. A few descriptions of Alentejo gave interest to his *Contos* (1881) and *A Cidade do Vicio* (1882), an interest strengthened in *O Paiz das Uvas* (1893). This collection of naturalistic stories of great variety and very unequal merit is, indeed, redeemed by the author's love for his native province. He sometimes obtains powerful effects when his subject is the wide spaces, the night silences, or the summer drought and midday zinc-coloured sky of Alentejo. The shepherdess with her distaff, the village crier, the small proprietor, the harvesters with their week's provision of coarse bread, goat's cheese, and olives, toiling in a temperature of 122 degrees, appear in his stories. His art is wholly external. One need not have complained of his lack of psychology had he been able to express what he saw in good Portuguese prose. But if we turn to his style we find uncouth constructions, the constant use of French words, and worse still, French words disguised as Portuguese: *deboche, coquettemente, crayonar*. This is the more pity because, had he written in Portuguese, he might have left robust pictures of the Alentejan peasant's life in its grim reality which would have been read with pleasure. A sober and fastidious style, sometimes recalling that of the Spanish essayist Azorín, marks the *Contos* (1900) of the dramatist D. João da Camara. The clear etching of the blind man and his grandson going through the streets on Christmas Eve in *As Estrellas do Cego* and, especially, the poignant sketch of the ruined old scholar *fidalgo* in *O Paquete* show admirably what a skilful craftsman can make of the slightest of themes. This is true to an even greater degree of the best of all the Portuguese *contistas*, JOSÉ FRANCISCO DE TRINDADE COELHO (1861-1908). His *contos* collected under the title *Os Meus Amores* (1891), natural and deeply felt scenes of peasant life, are all marked by an exceptional delicacy of style and by a most alluring freshness and simplicity. The tinkling of the bells of flocks, the thin blue smoke above the roofs, the evening mists, the flight of doves are in these pages. And the peasants are treated with the same sympathetic insight as their surroundings, the women singing at their work in the fields, the olive-gatherers at supper in the great farm kitchen; vintage and harvest, tragedy and idyll. The sympathy is extended to the animals, donkey (*Sultão*), goat (*Mãe*), and hen (*A Choca*). The *saudade* of peasant soldiers for the land in *Terra-Mater* gives an opportunity for describing the life of the peasants with its hardy toil and many simple pleasures. In *A' Lareira*, the longest of these stories, a rustic *serão* of peasants *ao borralho* is pleasantly drawn out with quatrains, riddles, anecdotes, fairy-tales, only interrupted by the ringing of the angelus for the saying of prayer on prayer. Two little masterpieces stand somewhat apart from the rest : *Abyssus Abyssum*, the tragic story of two small boys, brothers, rowing to overtake the evening star, and *Idyllio Rustico*, which with its two ingenuous little shepherds and their flocks of sheep in the lonely places might almost be a chapter from Don Ramón María del Valle Inclán's *Flor de Santidad* (1904). *Os Meus Amores* shows realism at its best, that is to say, hand in hand with idealism. The author is not so enamoured of his delightful style that he does not make the peasants speak their natural language, and although he realizes keenly and expresses the poetry of their life, he never sacrifices truth to this perception any more than to the strange and essentially false propensities of the naturalistic school, nor refines his descriptions to a rose-colour insipidity. A good scent of the earth and of wild flowers pervades these realistic descriptions. On such lines, if this book influences younger writers, it might lead the way to many a delightful novel of the *parfum du terroir* of Portugal. Snr. JULIO

Brandão (born in 1870), equally distinguished in prose and verse, is the author of *Maria do Ceo* (1902), mystic love letters in a chiselled style, only with the mystic writers of old the style flowed naturally from an inner fervour, here it has evidently been the chief consideration. If the effort is apparent it is sometimes very successful, and in *Perfis Suaves* (1903) and *Figuras de Barro* (1910), fantastic stories and fascinating fairy-tales, he occasionally achieves simplicity. Equally studied is the prose of Snr. Justino de Montalvão's *Os Destinos* (1904), twelve stories, of which *Conto dos Reis* relates the death of a peasant child as voices outside sing *São chegados os tres Reis*. The Visconde de Villa-Moura (born in 1877) has shown in the five *contos* of *Doentes da Belleza* (1913), as in *Bohemios* (1914), that his sensitive plastic style is excellently suited to the short story. Snr. Antonio Patricio's *Serão Inquieto* (1910) contains two poignant *contos*: *O Precoce* and *O Veiga*. *Os Pobres* by Snr. Raul Brandão (born in 1869) is a succession of scenes, a striking analysis of suffering as exhibited in various strange types of the poor and of its beauty and necessity in the philosophy of Gabiru. Snr. Severo Portela displays a tortured style in *Os Condemnados* (1906) and *Agua Corrente* (1909); smoother but equally artificial is that of Snr. Henrique de Vasconcellos in *Contos Novos* (1903) and *Circe* (1908), the former of which contains the slight sketch *O Caminheiro*. *Excentricos* is the title of a volume containing some notable stories by Snr. Alberto de Sousa Costa. The large number of *contos* is a sign of the times, corresponding to the favour shown towards the brief *revista* in the drama and the host of sonnets which now replace the long romantic poems of the past.

Anthero de Quental [1] (1842–91), the Coimbra student who waved the banner of revolt against a too complacent romanticism in 1865, was that rare thing in Portuguese literature, a poet who thinks. Powerfully influenced by German philosophy and literature, his was a tortured spirit, and when in his sincerity he attempted to translate his philosophy into action the result was too often failure. Born at Ponta Delgada in the Azores, he

---

[1] de Quental or do Quental. See J. Leite de Vasconcellos, *Lições de Philologia Portuguesa* (1911), p. 125 *ad fin*.

studied law at Coimbra from 1858 to 1864, became a socialist, worked for some time as a compositor in Paris, in spite of his independent means; then, after a visit to the United States of America, settled at Lisbon for some years and figured as an active socialist. Weary and ill, he retired in 1882 to the quieter town in the north, Villa do Conde, but he could not escape from his own turbulent thoughts and nine years later he shot himself in a square of his native town. If his life was ineffectual in its series of broken, noble impulses, there is nothing vague or uncertain about the splendid sonnets of *Odes Modernas* (1865) and *Sonetos* (1881). They are the effect, often perfectly tranquil, of a previous agony of thought, like brimmed furrows reflecting clear skies after rain. His search was for truth, not for words to express it, far less for words to describe his own sensations. Indeed, he was far from considering poetry as an end in itself and destroyed more of his poems than his friends published. In his autobiographical letter addressed to Dr. Storck in 1887 he states that his poetry was written *involuntariamente*. That is to say, after much thought on the great problems of existence verse came to him unrhetorical and spontaneous, as it did to João de Deus without any thought whatever:

> Já sossega depois de tanta luta,
> Já me descansa em paz o coraçam.

Quental's poems owe their strength and intensity to the fact that they had passed through the fire of *tanta luta*.

Totally different from Quental's was the genius of JOÃO DE DEUS (1830–96), the most natural Portuguese poet of the nineteenth century. Born at Messines in Algarve, he studied law at Coimbra, became a journalist, but did not come to live permanently at Lisbon until he was elected to represent Silves in the Chamber of Deputies in 1868. It is significant that many of his most perfect lyrics were contributed to provincial journals. They are written in the simple language of a peasant composing a quatrain. He sought his inspiration not in books or any of the rival schools of poetry but in his native soil and popular speech, and through him Portuguese poetry was renovated. His first published work, *A Lata* (Coimbra, 1860), in *oitavas*, gives no measure of his genius, but some of his best poems, such as *A Vida*, were widely known before *Flores do Campo* (1868) appeared, followed by *Ramo de Flores* (1875), *Folhas Soltas* (1876), and finally the collected edition, *Campo de Flores* (1893). His last years were spent in advertising and perfecting his special method for teaching children to read. If ever poet was born, not made, it was João de Deus. He is at his best when he does not attempt thought or philosophy or even give rein to his satire. His verse, clear and light as a leaf, a cloud, a stream—its favourite metaphors—and entirely free from rhetorical effects, has a most spontaneous charm. Despite occasional defects, the use of lukewarm or unpoetical words, *objectos, chaile, affavel, bussola*, or such rhymes as *gotta—dou-t-a*, his work, which lacks the fire that more spacious times might have elicited, abounds in exquisite love lyrics. The popular inspiration is also evident in the *Peninsulares* (1870) of JOSÉ SIMÕES DIAS (1844–99), many of whose poems are a mere string of *quadras*.

GUILHERME BRAGA (1843–76), who wrote vigorous political verse against 'Jesuit reactionaries' and the like in *Os Falsos Apostolos* (1871) and *O Bispo* (1874), proved himself a talented poet in *Heras e Violetas* (1869), although even here are to be found words and expressions frequently out of tune. Like ALEXANDRE DA CONCEIÇÃO (1842–89), whose best-known volume of verses, *Alvoradas* (1866), belongs to the romantic school, GUILHERME DE AZEVEDO (1846–82) began with romantic verse in imitation of Garrett in *Apparições* (1861), wavered in *Raçõdiaes da Noite* (1871), and succumbed to the new school in *A Alma Nova* (1874). JOÃO PENHA (1839–1919) in *Rimas* (1882) and *Novas Rimas* (1905) shows a command of metre and harmony worthy of something better than his commonplace themes. Gonçalves Crespo heard in his verse 'the plaining music of a guitar of Andalucía', but Penha never cared to be serious. CESARIO VERDE (1855–86) was a Lisbon poet who in verse written between 1873 and 1883, *O Livro de Cesario Verde* (1886), showed a most promising gift of presenting reality in phrases limpidly clear without straining after effect. Another poet who died almost as young left a far more definite achievement, although his poems are scarcely more numerous than those of Verde. Few Portuguese

writers have, indeed, published less than ANTONIO CANDIDO
GONÇALVES CRESPO (1846-83), a Portuguese born at Rio de
Janeiro. He studied at Coimbra University, and became a distinguished journalist and a colonial member of the Portuguese
Parliament from 1879 to 1881. Two tiny volumes of lyrics, *Miniaturas* (1870) and *Nocturnos* (1882), comprise his whole work, but
his restraint and his fastidiously chiselled verse place him at the
head of the Portuguese Parnassians. Portuguese in his hands
becomes a pliant medium crystallizing round an emotion, *longes
de saudade*, or, more frequently, round a concrete image, a parting
at sunset (*Mater dolorosa*) or a village in a summer noontide (*Na
Aldeia*). The latter sonnet recalls a few lines of Leopardi's
Il Sabato del Villaggio, and in one respect, the perfection of form
with which he describes quite ordinary scenes, the Portuguese
poet need not fear the comparison. An old woman spinning,
children at play, a peasant's song in the fields, an orange-grove
at dawn musical with birds—these are incidental pictures in his
poems, and by his combination of a vague dreaming temperament
with a delicate, definite artistic sense they receive a new significance. An earlier Brazilian poet, ANTONIO GONÇALVES DIAS
(1823–64), author of *Primeiros Cantos* (1846), *Segundos Cantos
e Sextilhas de Frei Antão* (1848), and *Ultimos Cantos* (1851),
made a name for himself by his *sextilhas*.

It might be said of that marvellous poet Victor Hugo that he
is not for exportation : the tendency has been for those who lack
his genius to take shelter in his defects. Since one of his earliest
followers, CLAUDIO JOSÉ NUNES (1831-75), published *Scenas Contemporaneas* (1873) his influence has been very marked in Portugal
and manifests itself in the grandiloquence, over-emphasis, and
love of antithesis of much of Snr. ABILIO MANUEL GUERRA JUNQUEIRO's work. The greatest of Portugal's living poets was born
at Freixo de Espada á Cinta in 1850 and was thus a small child
when Hugo's poems *Les Contemplations* (1856) and *La Légende des
Siècles* (1859) appeared. After studying law at Coimbra he was
returned to Parliament in 1878. Enthusiastically revolutionary
until 1910, he became Portuguese Minister at Berne in the following
year, but retired from the service of the Republic in 1914. His first
verses were published at the age of fourteen, *Duas paginas dos*

quatorze annos (1864), and before he was twenty he had written *Mysticae Nuptiae* (1866), *Vozes sem Echo* (1867), and *Baptismo do Amor* (1868), with a preface by Camillo Castello Branco. But it was *A Morte de Dom João* (1874), a poem or series of poems in which Don Juan and Jehovah are attacked impartially, that brought him resounding success, a success followed up and increased by *A Velhice do Padre Eterno* (1885) and, under the influence of the political crisis of 1890, *Finis Patriae* (1890) and the play *Patria*, in which his eager and vigorous patriotism found vent. In all these, as in the quieter volume *A Musa em Ferias* (1879), there is true poetry (as well as unfailing sincerity and passionate sympathy for the oppressed), but it has to be looked for. A weird ghostliness in *Finis Patriae* and in the *doido's* part in *Patria* is accompanied by a strange and impressive lilt in the rhythm[1] which corresponds to the haunting refrains of some of the shorter poems. But there seemed a danger that on the wings of applause, in political invective, and turgid rhetoric the poet might allow his genius to be totally misdirected, and it is his most remarkable achievement that in *Os Simples* (1892) he laid all that aside and returned to the simpler themes of peasant life which cast a spell over some of the lyrics in *Finis Patriae* : harvesters, the *linda boeirinha* guiding her great oxen, the old shepherd with his flute and crook on the scented hills, the *cavador* going to his work at cockcrow beneath the red morning star. *A Caminho*, the inimitable opening poem, has a delicate inspiration which is masterly in its restraint and ingenuous charm. It was well to rest on such laurels. In two subsequent odes, *Oração ao Pão* (1902) and *Oração á Luz* (1904), filled with a vague music, Snr. Guerra Junqueiro's poetry merges into a mystic philosophy which he intends to express in prose. Some early poems appeared in *Poesias Dispersas* (1921). A victim of Victor Hugo to whom it is not easy for a critic to do justice, is the Lisbon poet

[1] e.g. *Tive castellos, fortalezas pelo mundo. . . . Não tenho casa, não tenho pão.* The cadence here, as in many of Snr. Guerra Junqueiro's lines, is singularly arresting. The tendency to morbid repetition is exaggerated in *Patria* and has influenced many younger poets, as Snr. Corrêa de Oliveira and, especially, Antonio Nobre. The reader is credited with no imagination and the effect is diminished. For instance, in *Patria* : *deixa-me dormir, Dormir em paz . . . dormir!* That is excellent ; but the word *dormir* is then again thrice repeated, until the reader sleeps.

Antonio Duarte Gomes Leal (1849-1921). His capacity is felt to be so much greater than his achievement. The grandiloquence and declamatory character of the verse in his first volume, *Claridades do Sul* (1875), are accentuated in subsequent works: *A Fome de Camões* (1880), *A Historia de Jesus* (1883), *O Fim de um Mundo* (1900), *A Mulher de Luto* (1902). His satire here, as in *Satyras Modernas* (1899), or the biting sonnets of *Mefistófeles em Lisboa* (1907), is sincerely indignant but too often based on ignorance. In *O Anti-Christo* (1884) it voices the eternal revolt against false civilization and materialism. This, the most celebrated of his works, presents a strange medley of persons, from Barabbas to Tolstoi and Huysmans, who have this in common that they all declaim in hollow sonorous Alexandrines. Science, saints, Hebrew prophets, Chinese philosophers, the eleven thousand Virgins pass in a vision before the Anti-Christ and converse with him. It is as if a Goethe without genius had written the second part of *Faust*. But *Claridades do Sul* contains poems in a totally different kind, poems like *De Noute* and *Os Lobos*, which seem to have caught something of the pathos and simplicity of *Les Pauvres Gens*, satire and *humorismo* forgotten. In his descriptions of homely scenes his verse becomes quiet, natural, and effective; after reading the restrained and skilful *tercetos* of *De Noute* one is inclined to wonder whether the secret of his comparative failure is that here was an excellent Dutch genre-painter striving to be a high-flown Velazquez. But certainly he has no lack of talent, imagination, and power of expression in resonant verse.

The cult of *saudade* has been deliberately revived by a group of poets in the north who have founded the school of *Saudosismo*, and in their monthly *A Aguia* and the *Renascença* press seek to foster all that is native in Portuguese literature. Their creed is a vague pantheism, their poetry is often equally vague and lacking in individuality, but they have the advantage of being remote from Lisbon and of not concerning themselves with foreign schools, and can therefore be natural and Portuguese. At the head of these poets Snr. Joaquim Teixeira de Pascoaes (born in 1877) sings musically in an enchanted land of mists and shadows of pantheism, *saudade*, and his native Tras-os-Montes. Merging itself entirely in Nature, his poetry becomes a wavering symphony[1] woven of night and silence. The vagueness present in the lyrics of *Sempre* (1897), *Terra prohibida* (1899), *Jesus e Pan* (1903), *Vida Etherea* (1906), *As Sombras* (1907), is more marked in his longer poems *Marános* (1911), in eighteen cantos, and *Regresso ao Paraiso* (1912), in twenty-two cantos of monotonous blank verse. But Nature is justified of her child, and *Marános*, like a mountain-stream threading its transparent pools, shows abundantly that the author has also the power of condensing a picture into a single line. To this group belong Snr. MARIO BEIRÃO (born in 1891), whose verse in *O Ultimo Lusiada* (1913) and *Ausente* (1915) is strong and concrete; Snr. AFONSO DUARTE (born in 1896), Snr. AUGUSTO CASIMIRO, author of *Para a Vida* (1906), *A Victoria do Homem* (1910), and *A Evocação da Vida* (1912), and other young writers of promise.

Few if any of the younger poets have found in Portugal so ready a reception for their work as ANTONIO NOBRE (1867–1900), whether this be due to the all-pervading melancholy, *saudades de tudo*, to the metrical skill, or to the haunting intensity of his verse. In a series of poems written between 1884 and 1894 he combined the dreams of a student at Coimbra, *a lendaria Coimbra*, the home-sickness of a Portuguese in Paris, and a real sympathy for the poor and miserable. In these poems of suffering and disillusion, published under the title *Só* (1892), a strange alternation of ingenuousness and satanism, fantastic visions and serene simplicity, genuine poetry and sheer prose, refrains of rustic gaiety and of morbid sentiment, produces a certain measure of originality. He can fit his pliant metres to his will, mould them like wax, and if the book contains no perfect poems this is partly due to a deliberate intention to reflect his own incoherent moods and to an evident pleasure in incongruous effects. A second volume, of poems written between 1895 and 1899, *Despedidas* (1902), appeared posthumously.

The permanent Secretary of the Lisbon Academy of Sciences, Colonel CRISTOVAM AYRES (born in 1853), has won distinction in many fields. Well known as an historian of the army (*Historia Organica e Politica do Exercito Portuguez*, 8 vols., 1896–1908) and

[1] In details his ear is not faultless. Cf. the unscannable line *E que na corda do remorso enforcou Judas* (unless this is deliberately onomatopoeic).

as a critic, he has also written short stories and volumes of verse which have placed him in the front rank of the living Parnassian poets of Portugal. In *Indianas* (1878), *Intimas* (1884), *Anoitecer* (1914), and *Cinzas ao Vento* (1921), he displays great technical skill, especially in the reproduction of still scenes as in the sonnets *Paizagem, Aguarella*, or *Ao luar*. The Parnassian verse of JOAQUIM DE ARAUJO (1858–1917) in *Lyra Intima* (1881) *Occidentaes* (1888), and *Flores da Noite* (1894) has a narcotic spell, a slow lulling music. And there is real opium in the pliant melodies of ANTONIO FEIJÓ (1862–1917), during sixteen years Portuguese Minister at Stockholm, in *Lyricas e Bucolicas* (1884) and *Ilha dos Amores* (1897). The words are heavy with sleep like cistus flowers: *Astros das noites limpidas velae-vos* or *A neve cae na terra lentamente* (*les lourds flocons des neigeuses années*). This perfection of metre is seen at its highest in his *Cancioneiro Chinez* (1890), translations from the French *Livre de Jade* (1867), itself a translation by Judith Gautier from various Chinese poets. The poems of JOÃO DINIZ, in *Aquarellas* (1889); MANUEL DUARTE DE ALMEIDA (1844–1914), in *Estancias ao Infante Henrique* (1889), *Ramo de Lilazes* (1887), and *Terra e Azul*; Snr. Manuel da Silva Gayo, in *Novos Poemas* (1906); Snr. Julio Brandão, in *Saudades* (1893), in which he weaves the *linho luarento das saudades*, *O Jardim da Morte* (1898) and *Nuvem de Oiro* (1912); Snr. FAUSTO GUEDES TEIXEIRA (born in 1872), in his remarkable *O Meu Livro, 1896–1906* (1908); Snr. LUIZ OSORIO, in *Neblinas* (1884), *Poemas Portuguezes* (1890), and *Alma lyrica* (1891); Snr. GUILHERME DE SANTA RITA in *Vacillantes* (1884) and *O Poema de um Morto* (1897), and indeed of a great *caterva vatum*,[1] belong to this school. The chiselling of faultless sonnets has become a mannerism, but the critic who recalls the vague and often slipshod diffuseness of earlier romantic poems pauses before condemning. Perhaps it may be possible in time to combine the cunning artifice of the verse-cutter with thought and a breath of life and Nature.

The CONDE DE MONSARAZ (1852–1913) wrote some pleasant

---

[1] Without counting those of Brazil, which had an exquisite word-chiseller in the poet OLAVO BILAC (1865–1918), author of *Panoplias* and other verse published in *Poesias* (1888, Nova ed. 1904).

regional verse in *Musa Alemtejana* (1908), in which he describes life in the *charnecas* (moors) and *herdades* (estates) of Alentejo : the sound of the well-wheel among orange-trees, the ringing of *trindades*, the long lines of women hoeing, the old herdsman singing melancholy *fados*, the smoking *açorda* of the workmen's meals, the storks fleeing from the July heat, the processions to pray for rain. The same out-of-door air and fullness of treatment pervade the work of Snr. AUGUSTO GIL, with a more popular strain, in *Musa Cerula* (1894), *Versos* (1901), *Luar de Janeiro* (1909), *Sombra de Juno* (1915), *Alba Plena* (1916), Snr. JOSÉ COELHO DA CUNHA's *Terra do Sol* (1911) and *Vilancetes* (1915),[1] and D. BRANCA DE GONTA COLLAÇO's *Canções do Meio Dia* (1912). A more vigorous talent, also, is that of Snr. JOÃO DE BARROS in *Algas* (1899), *Entre a Multidão* (1902), *Dentro da Vida* (1904), *Terra Florida* (1909), and *Anteu* (1912). At the head of the Portuguese Symbolists (their symbolism has been rather external than philosophic) stands Snr. EUGENIO DE CASTRO (born in 1869). He wished, while retaining perfection of form, to fill it with a new imagery and colour, and that his verse in describing Nature through his sensations should remain detached and impersonal : the poet is *uma sombra saudosa d'outras sombras*. The success achieved in *Oaristos* (1890) was strikingly maintained in *Sagramor* (1895), *O Rei Galaor* (1897), *Constança* (1900), *Depois da Ceifa* (1901), *A Sombra do Quadrante* (1906), *O Annel de Polycrates* (1907), *O Filho Prodigo* (1910), and the twenty-one sonnets of *Camafeus Romanos* (1921). His versification is not sufficiently varied (a defect naturally less apparent in the shorter poems), his rare words and rhymes often have a cumbrous air, but a real fire occasionally runs through the cold monotony of his verse, lighting up its heavy jewels with a glow almost of life. If it is sometimes an echo of Baudelaire, it is a Baudelaire thoroughly acclimatized.[2] His debt was not wholly to French Parnassian or Symbolist, for he had also drunk deep of Greek and

---

[1] He is the son of Snr. ALFREDO CARNEIRO DA CUNHA (born in 1863), whose *Versos* (1900) contains the poignant lines *A uma creança morta*, which recall Coventry Patmore and the pathos of Dr. Robert Bridges' *On a Dead Child*. The earlier edition, *Endeixas e Madrigaes*, appeared in 1891.

[2] The word *Nephelibatas* (= Cloud-treaders), formerly applied to poets of the decadent school in Portugal, is now seldom heard.

GREAT PORTUGUESE

ANTÓNIO CORREIA DE OLIVEIRA

On February 20th last the poet António Correia de Oliveira died at the age of eighty after a long and painful illness.

He was a remarkable figure in Portuguese letters. Through his long life his genius was dedicated to the praise of the land where he was born, the simple things surrounding him, the people he so well knew, and God.

He was a simple, good soul readily corresponding to all spontaneous feelings, and humble. He lived in close contact with the common people and from them got the finest themes that inspired him. In return he offered them real simple jewels of moving lyricism.

His spirit was mystical, with a candid, pure, almost linear, mysticism. He remained faithful to the Christian tradition of our people and paid sincere and moving testimony to its highest virtues.

His poems are usually very simple in form, but they are most adequate to a sensibility touched by the infiniteness of little things, the most tender feelings, humble respect for persons, for his neighbour, for *revealed* truths. He feels himself in the universe and communicates with it. It might be said that a mingling of pantheism enlivens and feeds his pure but exalted spirituality:

Ao sopro do meu amor	By the breath of my love
De tal forma me confundo	I so mingle
Com a vida em derredor,	With life about me
Que eu não sou eu: sou o mundo.	That I am not I, but the world

The fact that he lived from a very early age in a village in direct contact with nature and the ancient habits and customs of the Port-

«St. Peter», «Christ's Baptism», «Whitsuntide», and «The Martyrdom of St. Sebastian».

In the organization of these rooms, an attempt has been made to meet the need to give them an arrangement which would allow of a well-made selection as well as enhancing those items which call for emphasis.

At no point in the layout of the various genres has it been forgotten that it would have to be based on the items themselves, to the exclusion as far as possible of the use of secondary objects which would only serve to distract the visitor's attention.

The presentation of the various collections has been subordinated to the criterion of quality and not the number of items displayed.

Furthermore, preference has been given to a free rhythmical presentation instead of the severe symmetry which is still to be found in many museums. At the same time, of course, a due balance has been maintained.

The possessions of this Museum include the most representative works of Portuguese painting of the 16th century, the retables by Vasco Fernandes, a well as many other works by his pupils and successors.

A visit to the Grão Vasco Museum is indispensable for anyone who is interested in studying Portuguese painting of the 16th century, since its collections comprise the greatest number of Portuguese-Flemish 16th century painting outside Lisbon.

uguese people had a very great influence on his work. In it we clearly see a sense of the expression of the immediate, of others' experience, that could only be attained by an almost complete aloofness from the complex, dizzy life and bustle of the refined and highly developed cultures of great towns. This does not mean that António Correia de Oliveira was not a cultured man or that he could not have followed, had he chosen, more novel paths, for contact with personalities rich in sensitivity and erudition was not denied him. It does mean that he preferred to stand alone before his spontaneity, the natural, unwearying flow of his poetic Muse. He neither sought nor retained any of the European currents that influenced so many and which at the outset of his career were the masters of Portuguese letters, such as symbolism. Neither did he take his sustenance from a bookish culture, so often rootless. He dug down to the origins, meditated on the immediate world surrounding him, the world of natural beings and the world of men, with their beliefs, their simple love, the tenderest emotions, nostalgia, that is, the whole galaxy that characterizes the feelings of Portuguese country folk.

He did this in the most suitable manner, in themes and forms as simple as those feelings, following the oldest and most direct line of our great tradition of lyric poetry, from the «cantigas de amigo» in the 12th and 13th centuries down through Gil Vicente in the 16th and João de Deus in the 19th, in simple, unpretentious lines, popular in tone:

Sino, coração da aldeia.	The church bell is the heart of the village
Coração, sino da gente.	Our heart is our bell
Uma a sentir quando bate.	The bell feels when it rings
Outro a bater quando sente.	Our heart rings with joy when it feels.

* * *

António Correia de Oliveira was born at São Pedro do Sul on July 30th 1879. He was the son of Dr. José Correia de Oliveira, an outstanding figure in the district, which he represented in Parliament for many years, and Joaquina de Figueiredo de Almeida Correia. He soon revealed the vocation that was to occupy his mind for the rest of his life.

At the age of twelve he already wrote verses with a certain facility. From that time dates a small collection of poems, now lost, which the young poet specially composed for Queen Amélia, who was to pass through his birthplace. The Queen's words of thanks were the first signs of apreciation of his talent.

At 18, in 1897, with the title «Ladaínha» («Litany»), the young poet presented his first fruits of poetry. Perhaps even he did not foresee that this book was to take him into the sphere of literature. The great short-story writer Trindade Coelho welcomed the poet's first book with so enthusiastic an article that it had a great influence on the poet's perseverance. Later Correia de Oliveira was to call this article and its importance for his life and work «a miracle».

Soon after, in 1898, he brought out «Eiradas» («Rural Entertainments») and, in 1900, published his «Auto do Fim do Dia» («Poem of Nightfall»). He had now made his reputation as a first-class lyric poet.

At the dawn of the twentieth century he came to Lisbon, tempted by other rhythms and other manners of contemplating the world. He experimented with journalism, but, it would seem, without success. He had begun to work for the «Diário Ilustrado», but left after six months. That profession did not match his personality, which was above all contemplative, and he abandoned it once and for all.

In the meantime he had published his «Alívio dos Tristes» («To Console the Sad»), making a total of four works so far. Thanks to his great friend António Cândido, he obtained the post of clerk in the Crown Legal Department, where he remained until the advent of the Republic.

Between 1902 and 1911 he published «Cantigas» («Songs»), «Romance do Berço» («Cradle Tales»), «Raiz» («Roots»), «Ara» («Altar»), «Parábolas» («Parabolas»), «Tentações de São Frei Gil» («Temptations of St. Friar Gil»), «O Pinheiro Exilado» («The Banished Pine»), «Elogio dos Sentidos» («In Praise of the Senses»), «Alma Religiosa» («Religious Soul») and «Cravos» («Carnations»). This amazingly prolific creative vein was to remain one of his most outstanding characteristics until almost the end of his life, although it was not always an unmixed blessing for a qualititative view of his genius, since it included less valid aspects of his work, some poetic dross we might easily dispense with.

His fame was of value to him in the cultured society of the time. He frequented the salon of the writer Maria Amália Vaz de Carvalho, which grouped some of the greatest figures of Portuguese letters, such as Eça de Queiroz, Ramalho Ortigão, Oliveira Martins, Sousa Martins and many others. He was the friend of Guerra Junqueiro, who supported him at the crucial moments of his life like an elder brother.

In 1908 he was elected a member of the Lisbon Academy of Sciences, and his personality and work were praised by Henrique Lopes de Mendonça. One year later he was elected to the Brazilian Academy of Letters, to the place left vacant by Zola.

These facts rather correspond to a first phase of his life in which he stated his message, when his work abounds in simple themes, intimate contact with the land, stones, plants, animals, the pulsing of a

centuries-old tradition of spontaneous lyricism, the loving manner of seeing and feeling the little signs of everyday life, the communion of man with the soil. His work was inspired by a kind of popular Christianity. We may say that in his work we find above all a profession of acceptances of faith, the opposite of the rather dramatic, almost heretical, critical spirit of the Catholicity of Teixeira de Pascoais, the recently deceased poet, with whom he did have things in common, but more in life than in their work.

This phase of simplicity of themes is then gradually outstripped and gives place, at some finer moments, to the flowering of deeper poems, connected by unusual density, because an essentially religious series of problems comes to the surface.

This development began with an important event in his life, his marriage in 1912 to Adelaide da Cunha Sottomayor de Abreu Correia, who belonged to a distinguished family of the Minho province. On his marriage he settled down at Belinho, a village in the Esposende district. This had a great influence on all his later work.

In contact with nature, country life, his words were decisively touched by the shades and rhythms of the landscape he saw about him. It is also that *climate* which gives rise to those rare moments of reflection and discreet fantasy to be found in some of his books.

He published the following works: «Auto das Quatro Estações» («Poem of the Four Seasons»), «Dizeres do Povo» («The People Say»), «Romarias» («Pilgrimages»), «A Criação — Vida e História das Árvores» («Creation, the Life and History of Trees»), «Os Teus Sonetos» («Your Sonnets»), «Menino» («Boy»), «A Minha Terra» («My Land»), «Estas Mal Notadas Regras» («These Neglected Rules»), «Na Hora Incerta ou a Nossa Pátria» («In the Hour of Perplexity, or Our Homeland»), and «Pão Nosso, Alegre Vinho, Alegre de Candeia» («Our Daily Bread, Happy Wine, Happiness by Lamplight»). This period extends from 1912 to 1922 and here again we note a constant, not always sufficiently exacting, fertility. The typical themes are more widely developed and include what we might call, perhaps too facilely, the author's pantheism. The basis of his poetry is always the expression of the Christian, traditionalist and popular feature that is predominant in his work and also a quite noteworthy fidelity to all the forms and traditions that characterize Portuguese tradition.

Then, from 1926 to 1930, comes what might be called, with all the reserves due to all the more or less didactic divisions of an author's work, his zenith and most deeply theological period. He goes deeper into topics that he had already touched on, as in the «Tentações de São Frei Gil». Unexpectedly we hear the echoes of a deep meditation, rich in meaning, worked out in a language quite different from his usual and specific style. It is thought rich in substance, expressed above all in his notable «Verbo Ser e Verbo Amar» («The Word to be and the Word to love»), in which we may discover unsuspected heights of metaphysical speculation, as we see in this sonnet, entitled «Antes» («Before»);

Deus era Deus. Só Deus preexistia. Deus sempre foi (A vida, argila obscura, alma celeste: dúplice escultura) Não acordara na algidez sombria.	God was God. Only He pre-existed God has always been. Life — that obscure clay, a heavenly soul, a double sculpture — had not yet woken in the icy dark.
Não se medira a luz, à noite e ao dia, A eternidade ao Tempo, o espaço à altura — Fluida em névoa, criação futura Qual no silêncio, o corpo da harmonia.	Light had not been measured by night and day; eternity by Time; space by height. The future Creation was a fluid in haze, like the body of harmony in silence;
Mar e não onda que na praia, à solta Se espraia, a onda e logo às ondas volta O verbo enchia a imensidão calada	As a sea, no wave, that spreads at will upon the shore, covers and so returns to the waves, thus the word filled that silent deep.
Sem onde ou quando, nem depois nem antes Ele era... — As mais palavras conjungantes Não lhas ouvira ainda o frio Nada.	Without where or when, no after or before, He was. No other words of conjugation had the cold Nothing heard.

This was the road that the poet in the greater part of his work did not choose to follow, as his fellow-poet Teixeira de Pascoais had. We are almost tempted to say that it was a pity. By so doing he would have given a new life to his work at a level within his grasp. It would have lost nothing of its poetical quality from the change and would have gained in depth and complexity. Moreover, it would have allowed him to keep closer company with the expressionist forms of modern aesthetics.

Some of the oblivion and some of the incomprehension that characterized the poet's last years, although his work was now and again exalted, was largely due to this fact, that he kept true to himself, not only to his own kind of sensivity but even to the moulds into which, from the very outset, he had poured his lyricism. Considerable ambiguous applause inspired by certain interests, and on the other hand much unjust, no less «interested» criticism created about the figure of Correia de Oliveira a climate that made it difficult to arrive at any objective, cool judgement of his merits.

But let us return to his life and work. During this period, when metaphysical speculation kept company with a genuine religious preoccupation, he published, in 1926, the «Verbo Ser e Verbo Amar» we have already mentioned, the highest point of his lyricism, in 1929 his «Teresinha» and in 1930 «Cartas em Verso» («Letters in Verse») and «Job». It was an unequalled phase in his artistic career.

uguese people had a very great influence on his work. In it we clearly see a sense of the expression of the immediate, of others' experience, that could only be attained by an almost complete aloofness from the complex, dizzy life and bustle of the refined and highly developed cultures of great towns. This does not mean that António Correia de Oliveira was not a cultured man or that he could not have followed, had he chosen, more novel paths, for contact with personalities rich in sensitivity and erudition was not denied him. It does mean that he preferred to stand alone before his spontaneity, the natural, unwearying flow of his poetic Muse. He neither sought nor retained any of the European currents that influenced so many and which at the outset of his career were the masters of Portuguese letters, such as symbolism. Neither did he take his sustenance from a bookish culture, so often rootless. He dug down to the origins, meditated on the immediate world surrounding him, the world of natural beings and the world of men, with their beliefs, their simple love, the tenderest emotions, nostalgia, that is, the whole galaxy that characterizes the feelings of Portuguese country folk.

He did this in the most suitable manner, in themes and forms as simple as those feelings, following the oldest and most direct line of our great tradition of lyric poetry, from the «cantigas de amigo» in the 12th and 13th centuries down through Gil Vicente in the 16th and João de Deus in the 19th, in simple, unpretentious lines, popular in tone:

Sino, coração da aldeia.	The church bell is the heart of the village
Coração, sino da gente.	Our heart is our bell
Uma a sentir quando bate.	The bell feels when it rings
Outro a bater quando sente.	Our heart rings with joy when it feels.

* * *

António Correia de Oliveira was born at São Pedro do Sul on July 30th 1879. He was the son of Dr. José Correia de Oliveira, an outstanding figure in the district, which he represented in Parliament for many years, and Joaquina de Figueiredo de Almeida Correia. He soon revealed the vocation that was to occupy his mind for the rest of his life.

At the age of twelve he already wrote verses with a certain facility. From that time dates a small collection of poems, now lost, which the young poet specially composed for Queen Amélia, who was to pass through his birthplace. The Queen's words of thanks were the first signs of apreciation of his talent.

At 18, in 1897, with the title «Ladaínha» («Litany»), the young poet presented his first fruits of poetry. Perhaps even he did not foresee that this book was to take him into the sphere of literature. The great short-story writer Trindade Coelho welcomed the poet's first book with so enthusiastic an article that it had a great influence on the poet's perseverance. Later Correia de Oliveira was to call this article and its importance for his life and work «a miracle».

Soon after, in 1898, he brought out «Eiradas» («Rural Entertainments») and, in 1900, published his «Auto do Fim do Dia» («Poem of Nightfall»). He had now made his reputation as a first-class lyric poet.

At the dawn of the twentieth century he came to Lisbon, tempted by other rhythms and other manners of contemplating the world. He experimented with journalism, but, it would seem, without success. He had begun to work for the «Diário Ilustrado», but left after six months. That profession did not match his personality, which was above all contemplative, and he abandoned it once and for all.

In the meantime he had published his «Alívio dos Tristes» («To Console the Sad»), making a total of four works so far. Thanks to his great friend António Cândido, he obtained the post of clerk in the Crown Legal Department, where he remained until the advent of the Republic.

Between 1902 and 1911 he published «Cantigas» («Songs»), «Romance do Berço» («Cradle Tales»), «Raiz» («Roots»), «Ara» («Altar»), «Parábolas» («Parabolas»), «Tentações de São Frei Gil» («Temptations of St. Friar Gil»), «O Pinheiro Exilado» («The Banished Pine»), «Elogio dos Sentidos» («In Praise of the Senses»), «Alma Religiosa» («Religious Soul») and «Cravos» («Carnations»). This amazingly prolific creative vein was to remain one of his most outstanding characteristics until almost the end of his life, although it was not always an unmixed blessing for a qualititative view of his genius, since it included less valid aspects of his work, some poetic dross we might easily dispense with.

His fame was of value to him in the cultured society of the time. He frequented the salon of the writer Maria Amália Vaz de Carvalho, which grouped some of the greatest figures of Portuguese letters, such as Eça de Queiroz, Ramalho Ortigão, Oliveira Martins, Sousa Martins and many others. He was the friend of Guerra Junqueiro, who supported him at the crucial moments of his life like an elder brother.

In 1908 he was elected a member of the Lisbon Academy of Sciences, and his personality and work were praised by Henrique Lopes de Mendonça. One year later he was elected to the Brazilian Academy of Letters, to the place left vacant by Zola.

These facts rather correspond to a first phase of his life in which he stated his message, when his work abounds in simple themes, intimate contact with the land, stones, plants, animals, the pulsing of a

In the period from 1935 to 1954 he published «Pátria Nostra» («Our Homeland»), «Roteiro da Gente Moça» («Young People's Guide-Book»), «Pátria Nossa, Pátria Vossa» («Our Homeland, Your Homeland»), «História Pequenina do Portugal Gigante» («A Little History of Great Portugal»), «Elogio da Monarquia» («In Praise of Monarchy»), «Saudade Nossa» («Our Nostalgia»), «Redondilha», «Antologia» («Anthology», in two volumes) and «Azinheira em Flor» («The Flowering Oak»). Although they include the whole range of his already customary topics, the subjects and forms he had already cultivated, we here find a certain kind of philosophical, or rather political, theme bursting out with a new force, in which he explains and expounds his own ideas with uncontrolled enthusiasm. This is poetry of an aplogetic type, where ideological aspects predominate.

Amid this outpouring of poems some important events took place in his life. In 1936 the poet was made a honorary member of the Coimbra Academy and on this occasion he was paid many warm tributes throughout the country. A year before his name had been proposed for the Nobel Prize for Literature by a group of Portuguese intellectuals. In 1937 he visited Brazil and at a session held in his honour in the Brazilian Academy of Letters the Brazilian poet Olegário Mariano spoke in praise of his work.

In 1945 he was elected a full member of the Lisbon Academy of Sciences, which paid public and official tribute to him in 1951. In 1947 he celebrated the fiftieth anniversary of his beginning his literary career and he received further tributes of admiration and praise. On his eightieth birthday, at Belinho, there was a very impressive session of celebration in his home.

* * *

In a very rapid sketch we can say that the life of António Correia de Oliveira was entirely devoted to his poetic work, which was the irresistible expression of a natural impulse towards fine words and the poetic art.

His privileged emotions and feelings were expressed, most admirably, in lines of the highest quality. We can say of him, without fear of exaggeration, that he was one of the few who dedicate themselves entirely to their vocation. While he did not always defend sufficiently strongly the economy of his work, a characteristic which fundamentally derived from his untrammelled spontaneity, he has left us fine examples of high artistry to bear witness to his poetic genius. If we explore the paths he followed, his works, his poems, we shall easily take the measure of his stature, his unusual power, the guaranteed immortality of his words in the noble history of Portuguese poetry.

GENERAL INFORMATION FOR VISITORS TO PORTUGAL

I

GENERAL PASSPORT REGULATIONS

Citizens of the countries listed below require no visa when visiting Portugal as tourists:	Entry and visit not exceeding 60 days (entitling French and Spanish citizens to 90 days)	Transit (entitling bearer to a stay of 30 days)	Exit
Austria Belgium Canada Denmark France German Federal Republic Greece Ireland Italy Liechtenstein Luxemburg Monaco Netherlands Norway Spain Sweden Switzerland United Kingdom U. S. A.	Presentation of valid passport NOTE: Citizens of Belgium, Luxemburg, U. S. A. and Canada require entry or transit visas, when visiting the Azores Islands.		Presentation of valid passport
Countries with which Portugal does not maintain diplomatic or consular relations	Visas may be granted in certain cases, after consultation of the competent Portuguese authorities, and obtention of their agreement.		Presentation of valid passport
All other countries	1) Presentation of valid passport; 2) Entry or transit visa. NOTE: Brazilian citizens are entitled to free entry and/or transit visas, when using a diplomatic or special passport in the course of duty, or when entering the country as tourists.		Presentation of valid passport

NOTE: Amongst the countries with which Portugal does not maintain diplomatic or consular relations are the following:
Albania, Bulgaria, Czechoslovakia, German Democratic Republic, Hungary, Indian Union, Poland, People's Republic of China, Roumania, U. S. S. R., Yugoslavia.

PERSONALITIES OF PORTUGUESE LIFE

DR. JOSÉ GONÇALO DA CUNHA CORRÊA DE OLIVEIRA

Dr. José Gonçalo da Cunha Sottomayor Corrêa de Oliveira was appointed to the newly instituted post of Secretary of State for Trade in August 1958. His dynamism, his intelligence, his deep knowledge of the economic problems of the country and his practical spirit have brought him to high office. He heads a department of State which is of ever-increasing importance in national life, because of internal economic development and the extraordinary intensification that is taking place in international trade. Dr. Corrêa de Oliveira has fully justified his appointment to these functions. Quite apart from his other activities, the negotiations for the laying down of the Stockholm Convention in 1959, in which, as the able negotiator and diplomat that he is, he brilliantly defended Portugal's position in the Market of the Seven Powers, as well as the negotiations carried out during an economic conference of the West in February 1960 which brought about Portugal's participation in the committee of nine members that makes up the D. A. G. (Development Assistance Group), would be enough to assure him an outstanding position in the Nation and give him a right to its gratitude.

Dr. Corrêa de Oliveira is one of the youngest members of the Government. He was born at São Paio de Antas, Esposende in 1921. He is the son of the poet António Corrêa de Oliveira, a famous name in Portuguese letters.

In 1944 he concluded the law course at Lisbon University with a very good degree. He was appointed technical adviser to the Corporative Technical Council and became, in succession, head of a department, Head of the Study Department, and vice-chairman. He was appointed to this last office as a reward for proven merit in 1949. The Corporative Technical Council underwent a thorough reform in 1950 and became known as the Committee for Economic Co-ordination.

which arise from the existence of the European Economic Community and the European Free Trade Association.

On the occasion of his stay in Paris Minister Marcello Mathias attended the laying of the first stone of the Portugal Hostel in the University City. He was also present at the inauguration of the Exhibition of the Gulbenkian Collection in the Palace on the Avenue d'Iéna, where the Portuguese-French Cultural Institute is to be installed. These innovations, which we owe to the Gulbenkian Foundation, bear witness to the spirit of friendship and community of interests that unite the two countries.

The visit took place in an atmosphere of the greatest cordiality and it strengthened the close ties already existing between France and Portugal».

Dr. Marcello Mathias stayed on in Paris privately until October 11. He also attended the dinner party given by the Committee of French Friendship and the Jacques Bainville Circle, which formed part of the ceremonies held in France to celebrate Prince Henry the Navigator. At the end of the dinner party the chairman of the two associations, M. Pierre Detaillère-Chanteraine, delivered a speech in which he evoked the nautical enterprise of Prince Henry the Navigator. Dr. Marcello Mathias later gave a lecture on the Discoveries and the Overseas Policy of Portugal which roused the greatest interest in view of the manner in which, in France, the relations between European Portugal and the Overseas Provinces are viewed.

As regards this visit paid by Dr. Marcello Mathias to France we should also stress the fact that on October 11 he took up the functions of honorary chairman of the Council of the North Atlantic, a post he will fill for one year as is laid down by the North Atlantic Treaty Organization system of rotation.

The chairmanship of the new organization was given the ample and essential mission of carrying out the home and external economic policy laid down by the Government, superintending for this purpose the activity of the nation's economic co-ordination bodies. The post was then filled by Dr. Corrêa de Oliveira, who served for five years with the greatest competence.

In 1955 his career took a new road with his inclusion in the Government as Under-Secretary of State for the Budget. Three years later he became Secretary of State for Trade, a position which he has occupied with distinction and the sureness of a mind matured in contact with those economic problems that are of vital interest for Portugal.

For several years Dr. Corrêa de Oliveira was a collaborator in the Prime Minister's Department for economic matters. As such he took part in several conferences leading to economic agreements, having played an especially active part in the Agreements signed between Portugal and Great Britain, Italy, France and Egypt.

As the Portuguese delegate he has attended all the meetings of the OEEC organization. As a personal honour he was elected to sit on its Trade Committee.

He has also served as a member of the Corporative Chamber. He drew up the report on the Law of Means for 1955, the alterations to the Law ruling the Development Plan, as well as a report on the organization of the Fish-Canning Industry.

INTERNATIONAL CONGRESS ON THE HISTORY OF THE DISCOVERIES

The most important cultural event in the Commemorations of Prince Henry was undoubtedly the International Congress on the History of the Discoveries. The Congress amply rewarded the feeling of expectation not only of the scholars who contributed valuable papers but also of a large section of the general public, anxious to hear sensational revelations. This was because, in the first place, the quality of the work done reached the high level that was to be expected of the eminent Portuguese and foreign scholars who took part. In the second place very careful organization made it possible to gain the greatest yield from the study sessions and to guarantee the results obtained the widest repercussion. Although the topic seems to be a restricted one, in actual fact it is very wide and has attracted an interest that far outstrips the sphere of historiography and encroaches on the fields of ethnology, sociology and politics. In its purely historical aspect the theme still offers a most uncommon richness. The discovery of hitherto unknown sources has raised numerous problems or has revived others, and this in its turn has created a constant need for critical revision, explanatory syntheses, theories and hypotheses. The sociological and ethnological aspects of the subjects are only now beginning to be analysed and thus possess a novel interest. Finally, the present significance of the Discoveries and European Colonization raises thorny political problems which some specialists have not shunned dealing with in a straightforward manner.

The Organizing Committee of the Congress was fully aware of these countless implications of the subject. It decided not to exclude any of them arbitrarily but to allow the debate to be carried to its utmost consequences.

In accordance with this point of view the programme was divided into two sections; the «History of the Discoveries» and «Overseas Expansion». These were also divided, into three and four sub-sections respectively, as follows: «Cartography», «Nautical Science», «Voyages of Discovery» and «The Causes and Consequences of the Discoveries» for the first section, and «The Expansion until the end of the 16th century», «Expansion in the 17th and 18th centuries», and «Civilizing activity in the 19th and 20th centuries» for the second section.

German literature. His originality in modern Portuguese poetry is a very real one. Yet it is a pleasure to pass from verse often so perfect, always so artificial, to the more natural poems of two younger writers. Snr. ANTONIO CORRÊA DE OLIVEIRA (born in 1880) in his *Auto do Fim do Dia* (1900), *Raiz* (1903), and *Auto de Junho* (1904) shows a true lyrical gift, an inspiration of the soil, of the quatrains of popular poetry :

> Passou Maio taful, Maio magano,
> E por onde passou nasceram rosas.

In his later works, *Alma Religiosa* (1910), *Auto das Quatro Estações* (1911), *Os Teus Sonetos* (1914), *A Minha Terra* (1916), the effect is sometimes strained or marred by an almost morbid iteration. Snr. AFONSO LOPES VIEIRA (born in 1878) displays a genuine talent in *O Naufrago* (1898), *O Encoberto* (1905), *Ar Livre* (1906), and *O Pão e as Rosas* (1908). *Ilhas de Bruma* (1918) is filled with the rhythm of the sea and with the traditions and native poetry of Portugal. There is a certain strength as well as a subtle music about his verse which is of good promise for the future. Whatever that future may be for Portuguese literature, Portugal will join the more worthily in the great literary age which will eventually spring from years of terrific upheaval if she studies and utilizes her full heritage of prose and verse. There is the less excuse now for its neglect since the devoted labour of many Portuguese scholars is rendering it yearly more accessible.

APPENDIX

§ 1

Literature of the People

SIDE by side with literature proper there has always existed in Portugal a literature of the people. Indeed, before Portuguese poetry was written it flourished on the lips of the people, in the songs of the women. Sometimes this popular literature almost coalesced with written literature, as in the case of the *cossantes* in the thirteenth century. Its poetry lent a glow and magic to the work of Gil Vicente and later to some of the lyrics of Camões; its proverbial lore was reproduced in Jorge Ferreira de Vasconcellos' prose plays and later by D. Francisco Manuel de Mello; in indigenous folk-tales Trancoso found part of his material. Eighteenth-century writers neglected it, but Filinto Elysio returned to popular sources, and in the nineteenth century they inspired two great poets, Almeida Garrett and João de Deus. Literature and illiteracy have often gone hand in hand. In Ferreira de Vasconcellos' *Eufrosina* (Act III, sc. ii) we read of the workwoman (*lavrandeira*) who 'sings *de solao*, composes songs, loves to learn *trovas* by heart, gives a schoolboy farthings to buy cherries in return for reading *autos* to her'; and the *Pratica de Tres Pastores* gives us a picture of an old peasant reading out from the Bible[1] of an evening to the whole village:

> Esse velhinho
> Tinha hum cartapolinho
> Feito de letra de mão
> Em papel de pergaminho,
> E chamava-se o feitinho
> Do livro da creação.

[1] The whole Bible in Portuguese was not translated until the eighteenth century, by JOÃO FERREIRA DE ALMEIDA, *O Novo Testamento* (Amsterdam, 1681), *Do Velho Testamento*, 2 vols. (Batavia, 1748, 53). This is the version still commonly in use. Another translation, entitled *Biblia Sagrada*, was made from the Vulgate at the end of the eighteenth century by ANTONIO PEREIRA DE FIGUEIREDO (1725–97), author of some fifty theological and historical works in Latin and Portuguese, and a paraphrase (*Historia Evangelica*, 1777, 78, *Historia Biblica*, 1778–82) by Frei FRANCISCO DE JESUS MARIA SARMENTO (1713–90). See C. Michaëlis de Vasconcellos et S. Berger, *Les Bibles Portugaises* in *Romania*, xxviii (1899), pp. 543–8 : *La littérature portugaise est en matière de traductions bibliques d'une pauvreté désespérante*. The *Parocho Perfeito* (1675) speaks of *os parochos que não tiverem Biblias* (p. 19). See also G. L. Santos Ferreira, *A Biblia em Portugal, 1495-1850* (L. 1906).

E então
Que sempre cada serão
Á noyte depois da cea
Com oculos á candea
O lia por devoção
A toda a gente d'aldea.

The popular appetite for *autos*, simple Christmas plays, legends of saints, and for long vague *romances* never flagged, and some of the literature written to satisfy it, by Balthasar Diaz and others, is reprinted and hawked about the country in *folhas volantes* at the present day, as Diaz' *Historia da Imperatriz Porcina* (Porto, 1906)—a *romance* of some 1,500 octosyllables in *-ia*—and his *Tragedia do Marques de Mantua*. The prose *Verdadeira Historia do Imperador Carlos Magno* (Porto, 1906) is the last descendant of Nicolas Piamonte's Spanish translation (from the French original) *Carlomagno*, printed at Seville in 1525 and at Alcalá in 1570, or rather of Jeronimo Moreira de Carvalho's Portuguese version (2 pts., 1728, 37). It is an instance of the Portuguese delight in strange, even fantastic, but in any case foreign, themes. The *Verdadeira Historia da Donzella Theodora* (Porto, 1911), daughter of a merchant of Babylon, was introduced from the East and was translated by Carlos Ferreira from the Spanish (1524) and published at Lisbon in 1735. The *Verdadeira Historia do Grande Roberto Duque de Normandia e Imperador de Roma* (Porto, 1912) is a belated echo of the French story of Robert le Diable, which also came to Portugal through Spain (Burgos, 1509). The *Verdadeira Historia da Princeza Magalona* (Porto, 1912) has a similar derivation from France (14th or 15th c.) through Spain (Sevilla, 1519), and retains its popularity as a record of unswerving constancy *na fe e na virtude*. The *Verdadeira Historia de João de Calais*, reprinted at Oporto in 1914, is also undisguisedly foreign. The story of *Flores e Branca Fror*, last offshoot (a 'vile extract' Menéndez y Pelayo called it) of the charming Greek tale which came originally from the East,[1] was mentioned by several poets (King Dinis, Joan de Guilhade, the Archpriest of Hita) in the thirteenth and fourteenth centuries[2] and in the *Gran Conquista*

---

[1] See *Floire et Blancheflor. Poèmes du xiiie siècle. Publiés d'après les manuscrits ... par E. du Méril*, Paris, 1856. In the original story Flores in a basket of roses enters the tower where Brancaflor is imprisoned. Señor Bonilla y San Martín (*La Historia de los dos Enamorados Flores y Blancaflor*, Madrid, 1916) attributes an Italian origin to the Spanish prose story. The Spanish translation probably dates from the fifteenth century.

[2] For its popularity with the Provençal troubadours see Raynouard, *Choix*, e.g. ii. 297, 304, 305.

de Ultramar (13th c.), and was condemned by Luis Vives. The prose story copied by Boccaccio in his *Filocolo* is still popular in Portugal and Galicia. There is an edition printed at Oporto in 1912: *Historia de Flores e Branca-Flor, seus amores e perigos que passaram por Flores ser mouro e Branca-Flor christã*. García Ferreiro refers to *a historia de Branca Fror* as recited at a Galician *escasula*.[1] Most of these popular threepenny leaflets are very quaintly illustrated on the title-page. The woodcut on the 1912 edition of *Flores e Branca-Flor* is worth many an epic.[2] The portrait of Robert le Diable (1912 ed.) represents no less a person than Napoleon III, and the ' true likeness of the beautiful Princess Magalona '[3] (1912 ed.) is Queen Alexandra. These *folhas volantes* of the *literatura de cordel* with many *farsas*, such as *Manoel Mendes* by Antonio Xavier Ferreira de Azevedo (1784–1814), reprinted at Oporto in 1878, and various progeny of the ingenious Bertoldo, as *Astucias de Mengoto, Industrias de Malandrino* (both Porto, 1879), *Astucias de Zanguizarra* (Porto, 1878), *Vida de Cacasseno* (Porto, 1904), contain little of the real people and less of literature. More indigenous, but still attracting by virtue of its foreign episodes, is the *Auto, Livro* (1554?), *Historia* or *Tratado do Infante D. Pedro que andou as quatro (sete) partidas do mundo*, which is attributed to Gomez de Santo Estevam, one of the prince's attendants in his long travels, and of which the first known edition (1547) is in Spanish. It has been constantly reprinted and, with romances of chivalry, formed the education of the notary in *O Hyssope*.[4] Nor do the *Trovas do Bandarra* belong to literature, although these verses of the cobbler prophet of Trancoso, GONÇALO ANNEZ BANDARRA (†1556?), which caused him to figure in one of the earliest trials before the Inquisition (1541) and were subsequently interpreted as referring to the return of King Sebastian, exercised the fancy of the people and even the wits of the educated for some three centuries. Forbidden in Portugal, they were printed abroad, probably at Paris in 1603, at Nantes in 1644, Barcelona 1809, London 1810 and 1815. It was not until 1852 (Porto) that an *Explicação* of them could be published in Portugal. Their interest was then much diminished, since the thirty scissors of the verse,

[1] *A historia de Branca Fror Outra saca a relocer* (*Chorimas* (1890), p. 148).
[2] It has been reproduced, from an earlier edition, in T. Braga, *Os Livros Populares Portuguezes* (*Era Nova*, vol. i, 1881).
[3] At either side explanatory verses, the only verse in the leaflet, tell us that 'Magalona was the most beautiful of all contemporary princesses, beloved daughter of the King of Naples, and her heart full of goodness. She was a model of virtues, of pure beliefs and a loving heart, married with Pierres, Pedro of Provence, a noble knight and virtuous man.'
[4] One of the Elvas Chapter was *homem versado Na lição de Florinda e Carlo Magno*.

Augurai gentes vindouras
Que o Rey que de vos ha de hir
Vos ha de tornar a vir
Passadas trinta tesouras,

had been thought to signify the year 1808, i.e. thirty closed scissors = 30 × 8 : 240 years after King Sebastian began to reign (1568). A more reasonable computation would have been from Alcacer Kebir (*de vos ha de hir*) = 1818, or, if the scissors were open : ✂ (10), = 1878. Many sought to connect with Bandarra's prophecies the sayings of Simão Gomez (1516–76), the 'Holy Cobbler', and his biography, written by the Jesuit MANUEL DA VEIGA (1567–1647), *Tratado da Vida, Virtudes e Doutrina Admiravel de Simão Gomes, vulgarmente chamado o Çapateiro Santo* (1625), a book in more than one respect singular and charming, was burnt by the public hangman at Lisbon in 1768 in 'Black Horse Square'. The 1759 edition had received the ordinary *licenças*. But farther afield, deeper in the heart of the people and far more ancient, exists another literature. Writers who have gone to this source have never come away unrewarded. Their work has gained a freshness and a charm [1] which the most successful disciples of imported learning and latinity have in vain attempted to rival, and gives the reader the impression that if he is not plucking the bough of gold he is not far from the tree on which it grows. And the reason is, perhaps, that the Portuguese people still retains an element pre-Christian, even pre-Roman, an element which goes back to solar myths and pagan beliefs, and about which hangs a primaeval mystery and wonder, a glamour and enchantment born of direct contact with the forces of Nature, and the worship, fear, and propitiation of many unseen powers and divinities. A great part of the people still inhabits a region of fiery dragons and apples of gold, and with ready imagination peoples streams and woods, sea and air with spirits. December and June are connected with the birth and supremacy of the sun's power, and paganism, thinly disguised, survives in several of the ceremonies of the Christian Church, and serves to increase the Church's hold on the minds of the people. Both the songs and the dancing with which it was accompanied were no doubt originally religious.

---

[1] This charm hangs over many anonymous lyrics of popular inspiration, as the *Trovas da Menina Fermosa*, seventeenth or eighteenth century variations of a sixteenth century song : *Menina fermosa Dizei do que vem Que sejais irosa A quem vos quer bem ; Porque se concerta Rosto e condiçam Dais por galardam A pena mui certa. Sendo tam fermosa Dizei*, &c. Even less genuinely popular are the *Trovas do Moleiro* (1602), written by an obscure native of Tangier, Luis Brochado, and others.

APPENDIX

The movements of the dance seem to have influenced the song, so that its metre was divided by real feet. When the Archbishop of Braga, Frei Bartholomeu dos Martyres, was visiting his diocese in the sixteenth century he was met by Minhoto peasants with *danças e folias* and with *cantigas que entoavam entre as voltas e saltos dos bailes*,[1] songs evidently similar to those in the works of Gil Vicente, with *leixapren* and refrain (*aaxbbx*[2] or *abxbcx*).[3] The *volta* would correspond in action to the *leixapren*[4] of the song, the *salto* to the refrain. The origin of the refrain was perhaps the pause (preceded by a final leap into the air) made by the breathless dancers, as in the words *no penedo* of this version of 'The House that Jack Built': *Quaes foram os perros que mataram os lobos que comeram as cabras que roeram o bacello que posera João preto no penedo.*[5] The phrase *ver cantar*, 'to see these songs sung', might be defended.[6]

In modern times the refrain has not been entirely lost, it occurs occasionally, e.g. *Valhame Deus*, or *Valhame Deus e a Virgem Maria*, but the usual song is a refrainless quatrain rhyming in the second and fourth lines, perhaps originally a distich broken up into four lines like the sixteen-syllable lines of the old *romances*, and from which the refrain has disappeared. It is essentially a love song: instead of the song of the people, sung to the tread of dancing feet, the song of the love-lorn individual, sung to the strumming of his guitar or of the professional *cantadeira* at a rustic pilgrimage. But they are also sung by the people generally, often by women[7] who can neither read nor write but have a large stock of these *cantigas*, which, indeed, are almost innumerable. They may be read in their thousands in Antonio Thomaz Pires' *Cantos Populares Portuguezes* (4 vols., Elvas, 1902–10), Dr. Theophilo Braga's *Cancioneiro Popular Portuguez* (2 vols., Lisboa, 1911, 1913), Snr. Jaime Cortesão's

---

[1] Luis de Sousa, *Vida*, 1763 ed., i. 462.

[2] e.g. *Em Belem vila do amor* (i. 183).

[3] e.g. *Que no quiero estar en casa* (i. 73) (which is *como laa cantaes co' gado*, essentially a peasant's song).

[4] The *leixapren* occurs in most of the songs accompanied by dance in Gil Vicente: e.g. *Quem é a desposada* (*chacota*, i. 147), *Pardeus bem andou Castella* (*em folia*) (ii. 389), *Ja não quer minha senhora* (ii. 439, *Esta cantiga cantarão e bailarão de terreiro os foliões*). *Não me firaes madre* (ii. 440, *em chacota*), *Mor Gonçalves* (ii. 509, *bailão ao som desta cantiga*), *Por Mayo era, por Mayo* (ii. 525, *a vozes bailarão e cantarão a cantiga seguinte*: i.e. a *romance* with *leixapren* and refrain). They are thus a combination of glee and dance.

[5] Gil Vicente, *Obras* (ii. 448).

[6] *Não nas quero ver cantar* (Gil Vicente) is, however, probably a misprint, for which D. Carolina Michaëlis de Vasconcellos suggests *quer' eu*.

[7] Cf. J. Leite de Vasconcellos, *Ensaios Ethnographicos*, ii. 264: *O povo (principalmente as mulheres) canta-as [cantigas soltas] em qualquer occasião.*

LITERATURE OF THE PEOPLE

Cancioneiro Popular (Porto, 1914), and in other collections, and hundreds of thousands die uncollected and unknown. Although it is perhaps a pity that all the popular poetical talent should tend to adapt itself to one mould—the quatrain—their brevity is excellent in that it imposes concision. Their thought has to be expressed in some twenty words, although they are rarely epigrammatic in the sense of the modern epigram. Some are geographical, or local, in praise of some town or village, river or fountain. Many are religious, that is, they combine love and religion in honour of the Lady of the Hills, the Star, the Snows, the Rosary, the Sands, Pity, Affliction, Health, Hope, or in honour of saints, and especially of the three popular saints of June : St. Anthony, St. John, and St. Peter. Others are devoted to special festivals : Christmas (*Natal*), the New Year (*Anno Bom*), the Epiphany (*Os Reis*), the Resurrection.[1] The majority are concerned with Nature, either generally or in detail. Sometimes they are frankly pantheistic, more often they content themselves with singing the praises of a favourite flower, rosemary, myrtle, the rose, and especially the carnation—the red *cravos* which glow in doorway or window-ledge of countless houses and cottages in June. Among the birds the swallow,[2] 'the bird of the Lord', as the peasants call it, is rare—perhaps its rhyme is disdained as too easy—the parrot, the dove, and the nightingale are far commoner. Numerous *cantigas* are concerned with the sea, fewer with the sun, the stars, superstitions, witches, sirens ; many with dancing and various occupations—the herdsman (*ganadeiro*), yokel (*ganhão*), shepherd (*pastor*), harvesters (*ceifeiros, ratinhos, malteses, mondadeiras*). But of course the principal subject is love, jealousy, separation, constancy, *saudade*, satire. The occasional presence of a French word, e.g. *négligé* or *cache-nez*, is not necessarily a proof that the *cantiga* in question is not of popular origin, but merely that it is urban. Of many *cantigas* the first line consists simply of a long-drawn *Ailé* (αἴλινον, αἴλινον εἰπέ, τὸ δ' εὖ νικάτω) or *Ai lari lari lolé* (where the fanatic of Basque can find *il* (= dead) as easily

---

[1] *Já os campos reverdecem, Já o alecrim tem flor,
Já cantam os passarinhos A resurreição do Senhor.*
(Now to the fields returns the green and the rosemary's in flower, and the little birds are singing the Lord's Resurrection hour).

[2] *Ó triste da minha vida, Ó triste da vida minha,
Quem me dera ir contigo Onde tu vaes, andorinha.*
(O how sad my life is, O how sad my plight !
Would I might go with thee, swallow, in thy flight !)
recalls the French *Si j'étais hirondelle Que je pusse voler, Sur votre sein, ma belle, J'irais me reposer* (A swallow I Would be to fly And take my rest Upon thy breast).

as in the refrain of C. V. 415), so that they really consist of three lines, the *ailé* being introductory.

Some of the quatrains rise to real poetical beauty, and most of them are charmingly spontaneous, forming in their unpremeditated art the natural song-book of a nation of poets. The number in print already approaches fifty thousand. In the mass they perhaps produce a monotonous effect, being mostly of the one pattern, despite the variety of their contents:

> Tudo o que é verde se seca Em vindo o pino do verão:
> Só meu amor reverdece Dentro do meu coração.[1]

> Inda que o lume se apague Na cinza fica o calor:
> Inda que o amor se ausente No coração fica a dor.[2]

> Os tres reis foram guiados Por uma estrella do ceu:
> Tambem teus olhos guiaram Meu coração para o teu.[3]

A few links in these modern *cantigas* carry us back to the songs in Gil Vicente's plays and beyond: a dialogue between mother and daughter, a reference to dancing *de terreiro, balho,* dance and song, to the *casada, mas mal casada,* or *i-a* sequence, as *Filho da Virgem Maria* (*Sagrada*). Other links in the popular literature throughout the ages are the riddles (*adivinhas*) at which Gil Vicente's shepherds played in the *Auto Pastoril Castelhano* (the example given in João de Barros' *Grammatica* (1540) is:

> Ainda o pae não é nado
> Já o filho anda pelo telhado (1785 ed., p. 176)

—the father is still unborn and the son is on the roof: a fire and its smoke; modern instances are printed in Dr. Theophilo Braga's *Cancioneiro Popular Portuguez,* vol. i (1913), pp. 363-70); the lullabies (cf. the modern *Ró ró, meu menino, Dorme e descansa, Tu es meu alivio E a minha esperança* with Gil Vicente's *Ro, ro, ro, Nuestro Dios y Redentor, No lloreis,* &c., i. 57); the *cantigas de Anno Bom*; the 'pagan *janeiras*', as Filinto Elysio called them; the *cantigas dos Reis,* the *alvoradas,* the *maios.* The *alva* or *alvorada* should properly contain the word *alva* in the refrain, as in C. V. 172, or Guiraut de Bornelh's

> Qu'el jorn es apropchatz,
> Qu'en Orien vey l'estela creguda
> Qu'adutz lo jorn, qu'ieu l'ai ben conoguda,
> Et ades sera l'alba.

[1] All green things in summer Their freshness lose: Only my heart Its love renews.
[2] When the light of the fire is dead The ashes its heat retain: When love is over and fled In the heart abides the pain.
[3] To the three kings was given A star in heaven for sign: And thy eyes have guided My heart unto thine.

(For day is near, and high in the East appears the star that brings in the day : I know it well, and soon it will be dawn.) The theme is the parting of lovers at dawn :

>Wilt thou be gone ? it is not yet near day. . . .

A Catalan *alba-cossante* is given in Milá y Fontanals' *Romancerillo Catalán* [1] :

>Marieta lleva't lleva't de mati
>Que l'aygua es clara, el sol vol sortir.
>Como m'en llevaré si gipo no tinch?
>Marieta lleva't, de mati lleva't,
>Que el sol vol sortir, que l'aygua es clara.
>Como, &c.

An example of a Galician *mayo*, that is, a song introducing the *Mayo* or May-boy (corresponding to our Queen of the May), is given in Milá's article in vol. vi of *Romania*. It closely resembles that of Gil Vicente (*Este é o Mayo, o Mayo é este*) in the *Auto da Lusitania* :

>Este é o Mayo que Mahiño é,
>Este é o Mayo que anda d'o pé.
>O noso Mayo anque pequeniño
>Da de comer á Virxen d'o Camiño.
>Velay o Mayo cargado de rosas,
>Velay o Mayo que las trae más hermosas.

It then breaks into a *muiñeira* (in Castilian) :

>Ángeles somos, del cielo venimos (bajamos),
>Si nos dais licencia a la Reina le pedimos (la cantamos).

To the *janeiras* more than one classical author alludes. Mello (*Epan.* i) thus notices them at Evora on New Year's Eve, 1638, before the house in which the Conde de Linhares was lodged : *a fim de se lhe cantarem certas Bençoens & Rogatiuas (costume de nossos anciãos que com nome de Janeiras entoavam placidamente pelas portas dos mais caros amigos) se congregou grande numero de pouo.*[2] Some *romances* (also *xacara, xacra,* and in the Azores *arabia*) have been printed direct from the lips of the people

---

[1] Reprinted in his article in *Romania*, vol. vi, and by Dr. Braga. *Aygua* in the second line is probably a corruption from *alua* (dawn) to *agua* (water).

[2] Fernam Rodriguez Lobo Soropita, speaking of the *noites privilegiadas*—the eves of New Year and Epiphany—refers to *os villões ruins que essas noutes vos perseguem* and to their *pandeirinhos, musica de agua-pé que toda a noute vos zune nos ouvidos como bizouro, e sobre tudo isto haveis de lhe offertar os vossos quatro vintens, e quando lh'os entregais a candeia vos descobre o feitio dos ditos musicos ı um mocho com sombreiro com mais chocas que um corredor de folhas.* They thus resembled Christmas 'waits'.

by Dr. Leite de Vasconcellos in his *Romanceiro Portuguez* (1886). The degenerate, more modern, and subjective form of the *romance* is the *fado*, a ballad (melancholy as the old *solao*[1]), composed by the professional *fadistas* of the towns. The *fado* is even more modern than the *modinha* (end of eighteenth and beginning of the nineteenth century). It dates from the first third of the nineteenth century, and has not even now penetrated to the south, being indeed largely a Lisbon product. It may be composed in verses of four (*quadras*), five (*quintilhas*), or ten (*decimas*) lines.

The individual in the favourite *quadras* expresses his personal sorrow and his love; the immemorial lore of the Portuguese people as a whole survives less in them than in the no less numerous proverbs—*um bosque de muitas e varias maneiras de adagios*. There is scarcely a Portuguese writer whose works do not furnish a goodly crop of these proverbs, often in evidently popular form, sometimes betraying their Spanish origin in the rhyme. They have been collected in Antonio Delicado's *Adagios Portugueses* (1651), in *Adagios* (1841), *Philosophia Proverbial* (1882), and elsewhere. The language is full of proverbial phrases, and most Portuguese could at will conceal their meaning from a foreigner in a maze of idiomatic expressions. The variety of their names is sufficient proof of the extraordinary number of the proverbs. They are crystallizations of some forgotten fable or event (*adagios*)[2] or of a more personal anecdote (*anexins*), or the refrain of a long-lost song (*rifões*).[3] Or they are moral (*maximas* and *sentenças*), biblical (*proverbios*), satirical (*dictados* or *ditados, ditos*). Many of them embody the wisdom of the ages in a form admirably concise and forcible, e. g. *Quem muito abarca pouco abraça* (which is the very reverse of Portuguese history: *e nulla stringe e tutto 'l mondo abbraccia*), or *Até ao lavar das cestas é vindima*. Many of course correspond more or less closely to those of other countries, e. g. *Muitos enfeitadores estragão a noiva* (Too many cooks spoil the broth), *Gato escaldado de agua fria ha medo* (The burnt child fears the fire); *Manhan ruiva, ou vento ou chuva* (= *Alba gorri, hegoa edo uri*);

---

[1] The Spanish translator of *Eufrosina* apparently derived this name from musical notes (= a sung *romance*), since he translates *un romance de sol la*, *Eufr.* i. 3; iii. 2 (*Orig. de la Novela*, iii. 77 and 110), but even he would not derive it from the *selah* of the Psalms (T. Braga, *Hist. da Litt. Port.* i (1914), p. 205). In the Spanish *solao* in *Obras de Dom Manoel de Portvgal* (1605), Bk. XII, pp. 282–7, each singer takes three lines, of which the last two rhyme together.

[2] Formerly *verbos* (e. g. in the *Canc. da Vat.*) and *exemplos* (*enxempros*).

[3] The word *rifão* does not now mean the refrain or burden (*estribilho*) of a song but proverb, like the Spanish *refrán*.

Pedra movediça não cria bolor (= *Pierre qui roule n'amasse pas mousse*).[1] Many of these saws as well as the *contos* (folk-tales) have their birth at *fiandões* as the women sit spinning, or as *nossas velhas* sit at their cottage doors and gossip in the sun (*soalheiro*), or as all gather round the spacious *lareira*. After the day's work on the farm, in field and granary, to the sound of singing, legend and tradition come into their own of an evening round the great fire of logs and scented brushwood. The *contos* have been collected by Z. Consiglieri Pedroso, *Portuguese Folk Tales* (London, 1882); F. Adolpho Coelho, *Contos Populares Portuguezes* (Lisboa, 1879); Dr. Theophilo Braga, *Contos Tradicionaes do Povo Portuguez* (2 vols., Porto, 1883); F. X. de Athaide Oliveira, *Contos Tradicionaes do Algarve* (2 vols., Tavira, 1900, 5). As was to be expected, they have their equivalents in the folklore of other nations, a fact which does not prevent them from possessing an indigenous character, a charm and flavour of their own. The glowing imagination of the peasants spins out fairy and allegorical tales with marvellous facility. Thus old Mother Poverty (*Tia Miseria*) owned a pear-tree in front of her cottage, and had obtained the privilege that whoever went up it to steal her pears should be unable to come down. When Death comes she asks him to fetch her one more pear. Once up the tree all the priests and lawyers cannot bring him down, and only when he agrees to the bargain that Poverty shall never die is she willing to release him.

A great part of the popular literature has been set down in cold print during the last half-century. Much remains ungarnered. In every province there are peculiar words, phrases, traditions, heirlooms of times prehistoric, waiting to be gathered in, and both the Portuguese literature and the Portuguese language of the future will owe a debt of gratitude to their collectors, and find rich material in the pages of the *Revista Lusitana*.

§ 2

The Galician Revival

For over four hundred years—with the exception of a few poems by Padres José Sanchez Feijoo and Martín Sarmiento[2] in the eighteenth century—the Galician language held aloof from literature. It was peculiarly fitting that at a time when

[1] There is another proverb *Mentras a pedra vae e vem Deus dará de seu bem* (While the [mill?] stone doth come and go God his blessing shall bestow).
[2] See Antolín López Peláez, *Poesías Inéditas del P. Feijoo . . . seguidas de las poesías gallegas* ' Dialogo de 24 Rusticos ' y 'O Tio Marcos da Portela ' *por el P. Sarmiento*, Tuy, 1901.

Portugal was recovering for her own literature the early Galician lyrics, which are now one of its most precious possessions, a new company of poets should have sprung up in the region now, as of old, *fertil de poetas* [1]—Galicia. They were no doubt multiplied and encouraged by the discovery of the *Cancioneiros*, but began independently of these, in the wake of that regionalism which manifested itself so vigorously in the second half of the nineteenth century, for instance in Provence, Catalonia, and Valencia. Besides their general character—the mingling of irony and sentimental melancholy—and a few conscious imitations, the new poets and the ancient *Cancioneiros* present several striking similarities. It is now some three-quarters of a century since regionalism in Galicia assumed its first literary pretensions. In 1861 the poets had become sufficiently numerous and distinguished to warrant the holding of *Juegos Florales* (*xogos froraes*) at La Coruña. JUAN MANUEL PINTOS (1811-76) had published eight years earlier a small volume of verses, *A Gaita Gallega* (Pontevedra, 1853), and FRANCISCO AÑON (1817-78) had contributed poems to various local newspapers. Añon led the life of a wandering *jogral* of old, and his occasional verses soon won him popularity, so that he came to be regarded as the father of modern Galician poetry. He could express his love for his native province in the tender and melancholy stanzas (*abbcdeec*) *A Galicia*, and in his other poems, at once ingenuous and satirical; he is also thoroughly Galician and foreshadowed the poetry that was to follow. A leaflet of his verses appeared in the year after his death, *Poesías* (Noya, 1879), and a more satisfactory collection ten years later: *Poesías Castellanas y Gallegas* (1889). JOSÉ MARÍA POSADA Y PEREIRA (1817-86), born at Vigo, the son of a Vigo advocate, published his first volume of verses in 1865 and others were collected in *Poesías Selectas* (1888). The second part of this collection (pp. 111-250) is written in Spanish, but the Galician poems include a series of letters in octosyllabic verse, the wistful humour of which is attractive. Born in the same year as Añon, he survived Rosalía de Castro, twenty years his junior. He survived in disillusion, for he had been one of the pioneers and now felt himself neglected in the changed conditions. When the first floral games were celebrated the most talented of these early poets, ALBERTO CAMINO (1821-61), had but a few months to live. Another generation passed before his poems were published: *Poesías Gallegas* (1896). Camino was not a prolific writer, and this tiny book contains but twelve of his poems; but there is not one of them that we would

---

[1] Cf. A. Ribeiro dos Santos, *Obras* (MS.), vol. xix, f. 21 : *Galicia ... muito affeita desde alta antiguidade ao exercicio de trovas e cantares.*

willingly miss, whether he is giving harmonious form to a poignant theme, as in *Nai Chorosa* and *O Desconsolo*, or in lighter verses describing with a contagious glow and spirit some scene of village merriment, as in *A Foliada de San Joan* or *Repique*.

Galician patriots, indignant at the neglect or contempt habitually meted out to their region, might persevere in their belief that the language which had produced the *cantigas* of King Alfonso X, the Portuguese *Cancioneiros*, and the poems of Macías was capable of revival as an instrument of poetry; but it was for the most part by scattered poems, manuscript or printed in periodicals (especially the Coruña paper *Galicia*, 1860–6), that they justified their faith, until in 1863 appeared *Cantares Gallegos* by ROSALÍA DE CASTRO [1] (1837–85). The authoress, born at Santiago, was but twenty-six when this collection of poems gave her a wider celebrity than has been granted to any Galician writer since Macías Emilio Castelar wrote a preface for her second volume, *Follas Novas* (1880), and hailed her as 'a star of the first order'. Indeed, so great was her fame as a Galician singer that until recently it obscured her Spanish poems, *En las orillas del Sar* (1884). It was an unsought fame. Rosalía de Castro wrote much more than she published and destroyed much that was worth publishing. She sank herself in Galicia; her voice is that of the Galician *gaita* in all its varying moods. In her preface to *Cantares Gallegos* she wrote : ' I have taken much care to reproduce the true spirit of our people.' That she succeeded in this all critics are agreed. A favourite method in the *Cantares Gallegos* is to take a popular quatrain and develop it at some length, as, for instance, in the beautiful variations on the lines *Airiños, airiños, aires, Airiños da miña terra, Airiños, airiños, aires, Airiños, levaime á ela*.[2] Here, as throughout the book, there is such yearning passionate sadness that we may say, in her own words, *non canta que chora*. The sadness is of *soedade* and brooding over her country's plight. She has felt all the peasants' sorrows, the longing of the emigrant for his country, the fate of the women at home who find no rest from toil but in the grave,[3] above all the neglect and poverty in which those sorrows centre—with the result of sons torn from their families and scattered abroad to Castile

---

[1] Or Rosalía Castro de (or y) Murguía. Her husband, Don MANUEL DE MURGUÍA (born in 1833), author of *Los Precursores* (1886), *Diccionario de Escritores Gallegos* (1862), and other works devoted to the study of Galicia, its ethnology and history, is still alive.

[2] O winds of my country blowing softly together, Winds, winds, gentle winds, O carry me thither ! (1909 ed., pp. 95–8).

[3] *Follas Novas : Duas palabras d'a autora*, 1910 ed., p. 31.

and Portugal and across the seas in search of bread. Her themes are thus often homely ; their treatment is always plaintive and musical. The metres used are very various. The book opens with a chain of *muiñeiras* singing *Galicia frorida*, and the rhythmical beat of the *muiñeira* constantly recurs throughout. Nothing could serve better to express, as she so marvellously expresses, the very soul of the Galician peasantry in its gentle, dreaming wistfulness and tearful humour. Her style is so thin and delicate, yet so flowing and natural, that it is more akin, almost, to music than to language. Few writers have attained such perfection without a trace of artifice. It is Galician—*esta fala mimosa* [1]—seen at its best, clear, soft, and pliant, rising in protest or reproach to a silvery eloquence. In *Follas Novas* the melancholy note is accentuated, without becoming morbid : the new leaves are autumnal. The music of her sad and exquisite poetry had been forged in the crucible of her own not imaginary suffering and grief, and in these lyrics she utters her *inmortales deseios* (immortal longings) as well as the woes of the peasant women of Galicia, 'widows of the living and widows of the dead'. New metres are introduced, the old skill and perfection of form is maintained. A few poems in the second half even succeed in repeating that identification between the poet and the genius of the people which makes much of *Cantares Gallegos* almost anonymous and assures its immortality.

Midway between the publication of *Cantares Gallegos* and *Follas Novas* appeared the first volume of Galician verse by the blind poet of Orense, VALENTÍN LAMAS CARVAJAL (1849–1906). This book, *Espiñas, Follas e Frores* (1871), has remained the most popular of his works.[2] He is a true poet of the soil (*poeta del terruño*), the soil of Galicia which he sings with melancholy charm, and his verse is filled with *soedades*. He complains of the peasant's lot, protests against its injustice and the tyranny of the *caciques*, laments the drain on Galicia's best forces through emigration and military service, and his later work especially betrays a rustic cynicism and disillusion. But the value both of his first book and of *Saudades Gallegas* (1889) and *A Musa d'as Aldeas* (1890) is that in them speak the voices of the peasants. Only occasionally does Aesop or Macías intrude to dispel the charm, and even sophisticated touches—as when he speaks of 'this century of enlightenment', of Galicia as 'a poetical garden', or of the *tamborileiro* as 'the inseparable companion'

---

[1] *Follas Novas* (1910 ed.), p. 254.
[2] A sixth edition appeared in 1909, whereas most books of Galician verse cling to the obscurity of their first edition or at best obtain a second in the hospitable *Biblioteca Gallega*.

of the *gaiteiro*—are not out of keeping, since the peasant, to whom a long word is a sign of education, will in ambitious moments use such phrases. The Galician peasants are shown in their sadness and superstitions, at their common tasks and *festas*. When Lamas Carvajal is describing an *escasula*[1] or a *fiadeiro*,[2] a dance in the beaten space before the doors (*baile de turreiro*), a *foliada*[3] in honour of some saint, a *ruada* or *rueiro* (street courting), a summer *romaxe* or *romaria* (pilgrimage), or autumn *magosto* (feast of chestnuts), his melancholy almost deserts him, and he can sing, in his own phrase,

Algun ledo cantar d'a sua terriña.

The toil often becomes a *festa*, in which, he says, there is more mirth than in all the city's joys. In *Ey, boy, ey* he admirably reproduces the thoughts of the slow-footed, slow-reasoning peasant as he trudges along to market in front of his droning and shrieking ox-cart. And, generally, all the life of the province of Orense is in his poems: witches, exorcisers, *beatas*, *curandeiros* (to whom the peasants turn in place of the doctor), pilgrims, blind singers, *santeiros* selling images of saints, the wailing *alalaa*, the evening litany or *rosario*, the angelus (*Ave Maria* or *as animas*, or *tocar ás oraciós*). The *gaiteiro*, of course, is a prominent figure, for without his bagpipe (the *gaita gallega*) and the accompanying drum (*tamboril*), cymbals (*ferriñas, conchas*), tambourine (*pandeiro, pandeireta*), and castanets (*castañolas*),[4] no village *fête* would be welcome or complete, and his *alborada* or his rhythmical dance-song, the *muiñeira*, is the emblem of all the peasant's pleasures. Melancholy pervades the *Rimas* (1891) of D. JUAN BÁRCIA CABALLERO (born in 1852), but it is no longer the melancholy of the peasant, but of the poet. His verse is more artificial and subjective, and expressions such as the 'bed of Aurora', 'Olympic disdain', 'the Nereids', carry us far away from the peasant scenes so pleasantly described by Lamas Carvajal. Yet in his lyrics lives a faint music which raises them above the commonplace. He writes of moonlight, the fall of the leaves, a flowing stream, tears, death, and admires Heine and Leopardi; but in his slight fancies, often built into a single brief sentence, he has a natural charm of his own.

[1] *Esfolhada* or *desfolla*: gathering to husk the maize.
[2] *Fiada, fiandon*: a rustic *tertulia* (evening party) of women to spin.
[3] *Fuliada, afuliada, folion*.
[4] In Tras-os-Montes potatoes are called *castanholas*, i.e. large chestnuts, which recalls the fact that Andrea Navagero, eating potatoes for the first time at Seville in 1526, considered them to taste like chestnuts. In parts of Galicia they are called *castañas d'a terra*.

APPENDIX

BENITO LOSADA (1824–91) gained great popularity in Galicia with his *Contiños* (1888), epigrammatic and often far from edifying stories in verse which mostly do not exceed ten lines. He is said to have had them printed on matchboxes *ad maiorem gloriam*, but for this he was probably not responsible. More interesting and equally racy of the soil are the poems of his *Soaces d'un Vello* (1886), of which the *contiños d'a terra* form only Part 3. The first part consists of a long legend in octosyllabic verse, and in the second some thirty poems give a coloured, homely, delightful picture of peasant life in Galicia:

> En fias e espadelas,
> En festas, en foliadas[1]

—song and dance, the pot of chestnuts (*zonchos*) over the *lareira* fire on the night of All Saints' Day, the ox-girl quietly singing, the girl with spindle and distaff keeping the cows, the sorrowful, hard-working peasant women, the priests exorcising those possessed by the Devil. The gay notes of the *gaita* with its plaintive undertone sound from his pages. The language, *a garrida lengua nosa*, has rarely been written more idiomatically or with a surer instinct for the force and fascination of the native word used in its rightful place. To turn from Losada to EDUARDO PONDAL (1835–1917), the poet of Ponteceso, a small village in the district of Coruña, is to go from a village *praça* to a high mountain-top. He stands quite apart from the other Galician poets.[2] Their irony and scepticism, sorrows and mirth, are mostly of the peasant. But here we have no dance or rustic merriment. The pipe and the drum give place to the wind blowing through an Aeolian harp. The poet

> soña antr'as uces hirtas
> Na gentil arpa apoyado
> En donde o vento suspira.[3]

He is a lonely, martial spirit, disdainful but never arrogant, hating all servitude and looking upon a comfortable inertness as a kind of servitude. There is no pettiness in him, although details of Nature he may notice and love. The most learned of Galician poets, and not sparing of classical allusions, he is yet entirely merged in the forces of Nature and becomes a voice, a mystery. Some of his poems are a single sentence of perhaps twenty words, a musical cry borne slowly away on the wings

---

[1] *Soaces*, p. 156. The *espadela* is the task of braking flax.
[2] Perhaps the only poem that might have been written by Pondal is that on p. 177 (the first verse) of Rosalía de Castro's *Follas Novas* (1910 ed.).
[3] *Queixumes dos Pinos* (1886), p. 101.

of the wind. He sings of mists (the Gallegan *brétoma*) and pregnant silences, the whispering of the pines, the great chestnut-trees and Celtic oaks, of the swift daughter of the mists and the ' intrepid daughter of the noble Celts ', of old forgotten far-off things, battles long ago. One must go to Ireland for a parallel. It has been noticed of him that he is entirely pre-Christian ; he is almost prehistoric. His long epic on the discovery of America, in twenty-seven cantos, *Os Eoas*, remained unpublished at his death. Nor would it be easy to account for his popularity were it not for the poem by which he won early fame: *A Campana d'Anllons*. It is full of music and melancholy, a plaintive farewell addressed to his native village by a Galician peasant imprisoned at Oran. His subsequent verses, collected in *Rumores de los Pinos* (1879) and *Queixumes dos Pinos* (1886), if they could not increase his popularity, brought him a wide recognition among all lovers of poetry. The undefinable fascination of many of these poems is due to their aloofness, tenderness, and sorrowful music. He is a genuine Celtic bard, child of the wind and the rain, with Rosalía de Castro the truest poet produced by modern Galicia.

The most prominent of the later Galician poets was MANUEL CURROS ENRIQUEZ (1851–1908), whose work *Aires d'a miña terra* (1880) was condemned by the Bishop of Orense and republished in the following year. Born at Celanova in the middle of the nineteenth century, he studied law at Santiago de Compostela and became a journalist. His advanced opinions caused him to emigrate, first to London, then to South America. His anticlericalism was pronounced in *Aires d'a miña terra*, and even more so in a forcible satire describing a pilgrimage to Rome, written in *triadas*[1] and entitled *O Divino Sainete* (1888). He writes of dogma assassinating liberty, heaps abuse on Ignacio de Loyola, hails the advent of the railway to Galicia as bringing not priests but progress. All this has caused his poems to be widely read. But the reader has the agreeable surprise to find that many of them deal quite simply with the legends (*A Virxe d'o Cristal*) or customs (*Unha Boda en Einibó, O Gueiteiro*, &c.) of his native country, and show a true poetic power and a quiet and accurate observation of Nature. We forget all about anticlericalism and the Pope in reading of spring in Galicia, of the *xentis anduriñas*, the *anemas* ringing, and the children who come singing a *mayo* and asking for chestnuts. Curros Enriquez would not be a Galician were not his work of a melancholy cast, and the charm of some of his poems is also indigenous. The

---

[1] For an earlier example of the same kind of tercets (*abacdcefe*) see R. de Castro, *Follas Novas*, 1910 ed., p. 158.

torch of Galician poetry burnt on after Curros Enriquez had ceased to write. D. EVARISTO MARTELO PAUMAN (born *c.* 1853) in his *Líricas Gallegas* (1891) showed that he possessed the traditional charm and satire of Galician verse, but a charm and satire that in his case had become all individual and subjective. AURELIANO J. PEREIRA (†1906), author of *Cousas d'a Aldea* (1891), displayed a rustic humour in sketching with many a gay note the life of the Galician peasantry, and, in his more subjective poems, a very real and delicate lyrical gift. A sly humour also marks the work of ALBERTO GARCÍA FERREIRO (1862–1902) in *Volvoretas* (1887) and *Chorimas* (1890). It is sometimes marred by the bitterness of his anticlerical and anti-Spanish feeling. In the stream's voice he hears a murmur against the mayor and the judge, the *cacique* is 'dragon, tiger and snake', the monks and priests are greedy and ignorant. On the other hand, when they describe a fair (*N'a feira*) or a pilgrimage or the woes of the Galician emigrant, his poems are moving, vivid, and full of local colour. In a slight volume of poems, *Salayos* (1895), MANUEL NÚÑEZ GONZÁLEZ (1865–1917) shows true lyrical power. They are poems in Galician rather than of Galicia, telling in a plaintive music of night, autumn, *morriña, soedades*. For all the author's love of his smaller country, it is Galicia seen from without,[1] or sung from memory. The 'vintage songs and the gay din of chestnut gatherings' are no longer, as with Losada and Lamas, a part of life, but 'a dream in the ideal realm of thought',[2] a subject of disillusion and regret. *Folerpas*[3] (1894) by D. ELADIO RODRÍGUEZ GONZÁLEZ (born in 1864) is also essentially not of the people. In its less elaborate poems it often describes, attractively and with much colour, popular customs and dances, the night of St. John, *as festas d'a miña terra*. Yet after recording the pleasant superstition that on St. John's Day the sun rises dancing, the author must needs pause to say 'away with these fanatical beliefs, unworthy of a civilized region', to which the answer is that such reflections may be sincere but are unworthy of poetry, and should be expressed in prose. But the author of these verses can, when he wishes, identify himself with the peasants whose life he depicts,[4] and is capable of writing poems

---

[1] The very word *morriña* is more common (in the sense of *saudade*) at Madrid than in Galicia.

[2] *Salayos*, p. 65.

[3] Also *flepa, folepa, folepiña*, Portuguese *folheca—floço, froco, copo* (= 'flake').

[4] The passage (*Folerpas*, p. 182) in which a peasant, refusing alms to an old woman, bids her beg of the rich, is scarcely drawn from life.

of great delicacy. The general impression is that he has not grown up among these scenes but is observing them keenly as might a stranger. The edict of the Archbishop of Santiago (June 26, 1909), which made it a deadly sin to read *Fume de Palla* (1909), by ' ALFREDO NUN DE ALLARIZ ', as containing impious, blasphemous, and heretical propositions, gave these poems a wider publicity than they might otherwise have attained, and they received a second edition in the same year. It certainly savours of blasphemy and is bad criticism to call Curros Enriquez the Galician Christ, but it is to be feared that the excommunication of the author will only encourage him to abandon ' simple verses written without art ', as in his preface he describes these, for more studied poems with a thesis to prove. It is perhaps disquieting to find that three poets in most respects so different, agree in this, that between them and popular poetry a gulf is fixed, owing to the sensitive aloofness of a true poet (for Núñez González was undoubtedly the most talented of the younger Galicians), or owing to the adoption of the superior standpoint of the rationalist or the anticlerical. Younger poets of remarkable promise and achievement are D. GONZALO LÓPEZ ABENTE (born in 1878), a relative of Eduardo Pondal, whom he sometimes recalls in the original inspiration of *Escumas da Ribeira* (1914) and *Alento da Raza* (1917) ; D. ANTONIO NORIEGA VARELA (born in 1869), whose deep love for his native moors and mountains gives an eternal magic to *Montañesas* (1904) and *D'O Ermo* (1920) ; D. RAMÓN CABANILLAS, who voices the sorrows and aspirations of Galicia in *Vento Mareiro* and *Da Terra Asoballada* (1917) ; and D. ANTONIO REY SOTO, who, however, writes chiefly in Castilian. D. XAVIER PRADO expresses the very soul of the peasantry in *A Caron do Lume* (1918). The poets of the last half-century have unquestionably justified the literary revival of the Galician language, and even if in the future no poetry of the highest order be written in Galicia, it is unthinkable that so musical an instrument should be allowed to perish. Galician poetry may be a thin, an elfin music, a scrannel voice, as of a wind blowing through tamarisks, but it has a natural charm, a raciness, a native atmosphere which give it a peculiar flavour and attraction. Literary contests, *veladas*, *certames*, *xogos froraes*, keep the flame of poetry alive in Galicia, but in its anonymous form it is a very vigorous growth which needs no fostering, and flourishes now as it flourished in the twelfth and thirteenth centuries, as it flourished in the time of the Romans. Hundreds of anonymous *quadras* (*cantiga, cantar, cantariño, cantilena, cantiguela, cantiguiña, copra,* or *canció*) have been collected in the *Cancionero Popular Gallego* (Madrid, 3 vols.,

1886) by José Pérez Ballesteros (†1918). The peasant women compose and sing their songs to-day[1] as when Fray Martín Sarmiento (1695–1772) noticed that *en Galicia las mujeres no solo son poetisas sino tambien músicas naturales*,[2] or the Marqués de Montebello listened to *los tonos que a coros cantan con fugas y repeticiones las mozuelas*, or the Archpriest of Hita watched the *cantaderas* dancing (as well as singing) in neighbouring Asturias.[3]

The ancient *muiñeira* rhythm continues, and the parallel-strophed songs of the early *Cancioneiros* have their echoes in the anonymous poetry of to-day. It is, indeed, of interest to note how the poets of the revival fall quite naturally into the same parallelism and the same repetition.[4] Besides these *muiñeiras* the popular poetry consists principally of *quadras*.[5] Traditional *romances* are nearly non-existent. This popular poetry (soft, musical, malicious, satirical) connects by a thread of anonymous song the Galicia of to-day with the whole of its past life, and the revivalists are likely to prosper in proportion as they seek their inspiration in popular sources, as did Rosalía de Castro. For the Galician peasants, living in a land of mists and streams, inlet arms of sea, dark pinewoods, deep-valleyed mountains, green maize-fields, and grey mysterious rocks, a land of spirits and fairies and witches, of legends and ruins, have the Celt's instinct and love of poetry. Poetry is their natural expression. For prose in Galician literature there is less genius, and perhaps less incentive, since the country has been described with intimate knowledge and charm in the Castilian novels of Doña Emilia Pardo Bazán (1851–1921) and Don Ramón María del Valle-Inclán (born in 1870), and more recently by Don Jaime Solá (born in 1877). But the value and possibilities of Galician prose have been shown by D. Aurelio Ribalta (born in 1864) in

---

[1] Cf. *Cancionero*, i. 50 : *Cantade, nenas, cantade* ; G. Ferreiro, *Chorimas*, p. 76, *as cantiguiñas das moças* ; R. de Castro, *Cant. Gall.*, p. 102, *As meniñas cantan, cantan.* Cf. also E. Pardo Bazán, *De mi tierra* (1888), p. 122 : *las [coplas] gallegas de las cuales buena parte debe ser obra de hembras*.

[2] *Memorias para la historia de la poesia y poetas españoles* (*Obras Postumas*, vol. i, Madrid, 1775, p. 238, § 538).

[3] See *C. da Ajuda*, ed. C. Michaëlis de Vasconcellos (1904), ii. 902.

[4] Cf. R. de Castro, *Cantares Gallegos* (1909 ed.), p. 18 (*mantelo, refaixo*), p. 19 (*mar, río*), pp. 20–1 (*e–a*), p. 27 (*terras, vilas*), p. 29 (*pousaban, vivian*), p. 85 (*vestira, calzara*) ; *Follas Novas* (1910 ed.), p. 229 (*a–e*) ; *Aires d'a miña terra* (ed. 1911), p. 35 (*quería, pensaba*), p. 139 (*i–a*), p. 249 (*á miles, á centos*) ; *Chorimas*, p. 36 (*estrevidos, ousados*) ; A. Camino, *Poesías Gallegas*, p. 19 : *Qué noite aquela en que eu a vin gemindo ! (chorar !)*.

[5] Quatrains of which lines 2 and 4 are in rhyme or assonance, e.g. *Ruliña que vas volando Sin facer caso á ninguen, Vai e dille á aquela nena Que sempre a quixen ben.* *Tercetos* are rarer (*aba*). Sometimes the *quadra* is really a tercet with line 1 repeated (*aaba*).

Ferruxe (1894) and by D. MANUEL LUGRIS Y FREIRE (born in 1863) in *Contos de Asieumedre* (1909). It is, indeed, in the *conto* that especial success has been won, and HERACLIO PÉREZ PLACER, whose novel *Predicción* appeared in 1887, is widely known for his *Contos, Leendas e Tradiciós de Galicia* (1891), *Contos da Terriña* (1895), and *Veira do Lar* (1901). *Contos da Terriña*, thirty-four stories in some two hundred brief pages, are various and unequal in value. Most of them are sad, even the harmless St. Martin *magosto* ends in a death. They contain many intimate descriptions of Galicia and the life of the villages about Orense. There is much pathos in *Velliña, miña velliña!*, in *Rapañota de Xasmís*, and especially in *Follas Secas*, an exquisite picture of an old peasant dying alone in a dark room—its walls are black with smoke, yellow maize-cobs hang from the ceiling—while through the open door come all the gay sounds and colours of a Galician vintage. The poetess FRANCISCA HERRERA, author of *Almas de Muller* (1915) and *Sorrisas e Bágoas* (1918), has recently turned to prose with remarkable success in *Néveda* (1920). Few Galician poets have published volumes of prose, although many have contributed as journalists to the local press, but it would be difficult to find a prose-writer who is not also a poet.[1] And it is by its poetry that Galicia has won for itself a notable place in modern literature and added another leaf to the literary laurels of the Peninsula.

[1] D. Aurelio Ribalta is author in verse of *Os meus votos* (1903) and *Libro de Konsagrazión* (1910); D. Manuel Lugris of *Soidades* (1894), *Noitebras* (1910); Snr. Pérez Placer of *Cantares Gallegos* (1891). D. FLORENCIO VAAMONDE (born in 1860), author of a *Resume da Historia de Galicia* (1898), also wrote, in verse, *Os Calaicos* (1894). Recently Galician literature has found a keen historian in D. EUGENIO CARRÉ ALDAO, whose *Literatura Gallega* (2nd ed., 1911) also contains an anthology.

INDEX

A

Aboim (D. Joan de), 46, 52.
Abranches, Conde de, 88.
Abreu Mousinho (Manuel de), 203.
Academia das Sciencias de Portugal, 284.
Academia dos Esquecidos, 261.
Academia dos Generosos, 261.
Academia dos Singulares, 261.
Academia Real da Historia, 270.
Academia Real das Sciencias de Lisboa, 14, 15, 284, 294.
Acenheiro. *See* Rodriguez Azinheiro.
Actos dos Apostolos, 59.
Adagios, 346.
Addison (Joseph), 290.
Aesop, 60, 350.
Afonso I, 188, 211, 305, 307.
Afonso III, 38, 42, 46, 52.
Afonso IV, 38, 87.
Afonso V, 82, 86, 87, 88, 89, 92, 93, 100, 111, 211, 261.
Afonso VI, 260, 268, 295, 311.
Afonso, Infante [xiii c.], 67.
Afonso, Infante [xiv c.], 67, 70.
Afonso, Infante [xv c.], 88, 100, 101, 103.
Afonso, Mestre, 220.
Afonso (Gregorio), 124.
Afonso (Martim), Mestre, 220.
Aguia, A, 333.
Agustobrica, 234.
Airas (Joan), 52.
Aires (Francisco), 247.
Alarcón (Pedro Antonio de), 297.
Alarte (Vicente) *pseud. See* Gomez de Moraes.
Albuquerque (Afonso de), 57, 88, 99, 107, 108, 116, 127, 190, 191, 194, 198, 199, 200, 201, 202, 209, 220, 228-9, 260, 312.
Albuquerque (Bras de), 201-2.
Albuquerque (Jeronymo de), 204.
Albuquerque (D. Jorge de), 218.
Alcobaça (Bernardo de), 59, 95.
Alcoforado (Marianna), 263-4, 307.
Aleandro, Cardinal, 126.
Aleixo, Vida de Santo, 60.
Alexandra, Queen, 340.
Alfieri (Vittorio), 290.
Alfonso X, 13, 26, 28, 30, 37, 40, 41-6, 53, 54, 55, 56, 59, 61, 69, 91, 98, 103, 124, 126, 349.
Alfonso XI, 38, 42, 90.
Alfonso Onceno, Poema de, 73.
Almeida (Cristovam de), 245.
Almeida (Diogo de), 192.
Almeida (Fortunato de), 307.
Almeida (D. Francisco de), 92, 98.
Almeida (D. Leonor de), 276.
Almeida (Lopo de), 92, 128.
Almeida (Manuel de), 205.
Almeida (Rodrigo Antonio de), 163.
Almeida (Theodoro de), 285.
Almeida e Medeiros (Lourenço de), 301.
Almeida Garrett (João Baptista da Silva Leitão), Visconde de, 21, 33, 74, 186, 242, 261, 277, 279, 287–92, 293, 294, 299, 300, 302, 309, 338.
Alorna, Marqueza de [D. Leonor de Almeida Portugal Lorena e Lencastre, Condessa de Assumar, Condessa de Oeynhausen], 274, 276-7, 294.
Alvarengo Peixoto (Ignacio José de), 274.
Alvarez (Afonso), 157.
Alvarez (Francisco), 33, 219-20, 224.
Alvarez (João), 89.
Alvarez (Luis), 245.
Alvarez de Andrade (Fernam), 239.
Alvarez de Lousada Machado (Gaspar), 62.
Alvarez de Villasandino (Alfonso), 77, 79, 125.
Alvarez do Oriente (Fernam), 152, 253, 255.
Alvarez Pereira (Nuno), 50, 62, 81, 84, 86, 92, 155, 291, 306, 307.
Amadis de Gaula, 64, 65-71, 119, 225.
Amaral (Antonio Caetano do), 292.
Amaral (Francisco do), 245.
Amaro, Vida de Santo, 60.
Ambrogini (Angelo). *See* Poliziano.
Amigo (Pedro) de Sevilha, 51.
Amorim. *See* Gomes de Amorim.
Andrade (Antonio de), 204.
Andrade (Francisco de), 189, 209, 224, 239.
Andrade (Thomé de). *See* Jesus (Thomé de).
Andrade Caminha (Pero de), 143, 149-50, 213.

INDEX

Andrade Corvo (João de), 295.
Andrade e Silva (José Bonifacio de), 274.
Anez Solaz (Pedro), 29.
Angeles (Juan de los), 250.
Angra, Bishop of, 287.
Anjos (Luis dos), 247.
Anjos (Manuel dos), 247.
Annunzio (Gabriele d'), 321.
Añon (Francisco), 348.
Anrique. *See* Henrique.
Anriquez (Luis), 100, 102–3.
Antonio, Mestre, 125.
Antonio, D., Prior of Crato, 145, 195, 229, 236, 263.
Antonio (Nicolás), 68, 93, 130, 169, 192, 197, 207, 212.
Antunes (João), 249.
Aquinas (Thomas). *See* Thomas.
Araujo (Joaquim de), 335.
Araujo de Azevedo (Antonio de), 273.
Arcadia, A Nova, 270.
Arcadia Ulyssiponense, 270, 271, 272, 273.
Archivo Historico Portuguez, 308.
Argote de Molina (Gonzalo), 77.
Arias Montano (Benito), 209.
Ariosto (Lodovico), 139, 140, 146, 152, 164, 180, 197, 260.
Aristotle, 85, 90, 92, 119, 163, 193.
Arnoso, Bernardo Pinheiro Corrêa de Mello, Conde de, 324.
Arquivo. See *Archivo.*
Arquivo Historico Português. See *Archivo Historico Portuguez.*
Arraez (Jeronimo), 238.
Arraez de Mendoça (Amador), 16, 227, 232, 235, 237–8.
Arte de Furtar, 125, 264–5, 272.
Asenjo Barbieri (Francisco), 36, 123.
Athaide (Catherina de), 175, 179.
Athaide Oliveira (Francisco Xavier de), 347.
Augustine, Saint, 26, 56, 101, 115.
Austen (Jane), 316.
Auto da Fome, 162.
Auto da Forneira de Aljubarrota, 163.
Auto da Geração Humana, 156.
Auto das Padeiras, 162.
Auto de Deus Padre, 156–7.
Auto del Nascimiento de Christo, 155.
Auto de Santa Genoveva, 162.
Auto do Dia de Juizo, 157.
Auto do Escudeiro Surdo, 125.
Auto Figurado da Degolação dos Inocentes, 162.
Aveiro, D. João de Lencastre, Duque de, 221.
Aveiro, Dukes of, 71.
Aveiro (Pantaleam de), 220.

Avellar Brotero (Felix de), 17.
Avicenna, 85.
Avis, Mestre de. *See* João I.
Ayres de Magalhães Sepulveda (Cristovam), 223, 334–5.
Ayres Victoria (Anrique), 165.
Azevedo (Briolanja de), 142.
Azevedo (Guilherme de). *See* Azevedo Chaves.
Azevedo (João Lucio de), 307.
Azevedo (Luis de), 100.
Azevedo (Manuel de), 17.
Azevedo (Maximiliano Eugenio de), 310.
Azevedo (Pedro A. de), 13, 81, 211, 308.
Azevedo Chaves (Guilherme Avelino de), 330.
Azevedo Tojal (Pedro de), 274.
Azinheiro. *See* Rodriguez Azinheiro.
Azorín *pseud.* [Don José Martínez Ruiz], 134, 326.
Azurara. *See* Zurara.

B

Bacellar (Antonio Barbosa). *See* Barbosa Bacellar.
Bacon (Francis), 209.
Bahia (Jeronimo), 256.
Baião (Antonio), 13.
Baist (Gottfried), 65, 70.
Balzac (Honoré de), 299.
Bandarra (Gonçalo Annez), 265, 268, 340–1.
Bandello (Matteo), 231.
Barata (Antonio Francisco), 272.
Barbieri (Francisco Asenjo). *See* Asenjo Barbieri.
Barbosa (Ayres), 106.
Barbosa (Duarte), 198, 219, 227.
Barbosa Bacellar (Antonio), 256.
Barbosa de Carvalho (Tristão), 247.
Barbosa Machado (Diogo), 87, 168, 192, 197, 217, 220, 232, 236, 240, 250, 284.
Barcellos, Conde de. *See* Pedro Afonso.
Bárcia Caballero (Juan), 351.
Baretti (Giuseppe), 270.
Barlaam e Josaphat, Lenda dos Santos, 59.
Barradas (Manuel), 205.
Barreira (João da), 203.
Barreiros (Gaspar), 219.
Barreiros (Lopo), 219.
Barreto (Francisco), 177, 178, 195.
Barreto (Pedro), 178.
Barros (Bras de), 95.
Barros (Guilherme Augusto de), 295.
Barros (João de), 20, 69, 75, 86, 88,

INDEX

95, 113, 169, 180, 181, 184, 190, 192-5, 196, 197, 198, 201, 206, 207, 208, 215, 216, 218, 220, 232, 233, 243, 344.
Barros (João de), of Oporto, 68, 125, 253.
Barros (João de), poet, 336.
Barros (Lopo de), 192.
Baudelaire (Charles), 336.
Beatriz, Infanta, mother of King Manuel, 111.
Beatriz, Infanta, daughter of King Manuel, 120, 133, 291.
Beauvais (Vincent de), 44.
Beccari (Camillo), 205.
Beckford (William), 111, 277, 296.
Beirão (Mario), 334.
Beja, Bishop of. *See* Villas-Boas.
Belchior, Padre, 223.
Bembo (Pietro), 39, 140, 212.
Bento, Regra de S., 59.
Berceo (Gonzalo de), 43.
Beresford (William Carr), Viscount, 290.
Berger (S.), 338.
Bermudez (Geronimo), 165.
Bernard, St., 94, 207.
Bernardes (Manuel), 14, 16, 20, 224, 245, 249-50, 261.
Bernardes (Maria), 249.
Bernardez (Diogo), 14, 143, 145-7, 148, 149, 153, 181, 183, 184, 185, 272.
Bezerra (Branca), 110.
Bible, The, 59, 94, 95, 113, 128, 170, 246, 251, 338.
Biester (Ernesto), 314.
Bilac (Olavo), 335.
Bingre (Francisco Joaquim), 270.
Bluteau (Raphael), 284-5.
Bocage (Manuel Maria de Barbosa du), 186, 275, 277-8, 281.
Bocarro (Antonio), 198.
Boccaccio (Giovanni), 132, 231, 340.
Boccalini (Traiano), 255.
Boileau (Nicolas), 274.
Bonamis, 122.
Bonaval (Bernaldo de), 28, 29.
Bonifazio II, 41.
Bonilla y San Martín (Adolfo), 339.
Boosco Delleytoso, 93-4.
Bordallo (Francisco Maria), 316.
Borges (Gonçalo), 176.
Bornelh (Guiraut de), 48, 344.
Boron [=Borron] (Robert de), 64.
Boscán Almogaver (Juan), 58, 136, 140, 143, 154, 160, 172, 181.
Bosco Deleitoso. See *Boosco Delleytoso*.
Bosque (Dimas), 226.
Boswell (James), 302.

Botelho (Abel Acacio de Almeida), 311, 321-2.
Botelho (Afonso), 325.
Bouterwek (Friedrich), 14, 137.
Braamcamp Freire (Anselmo), 14, 15, 81, 84, 112, 115, 308.
Braga (Alberto Leal Barradas Monteiro), 325-6.
Braga (Guilherme), 330.
Braga (Joaquim Theophilo Fernandes), 14, 15, 23, 24, 37, 65, 70, 74, 75, 76, 90, 111, 112, 133, 137, 142, 231, 253, 304, 309, 342, 344, 345, 347.
Braganza, Ferdinand, Duke of, 97.
Braganza, Isabella, Duchess of, 149.
Braganza, James, Duke of, 103, 120.
Braganza, John, Duke of. *See* João IV.
Braganza, Theodosio, Duke of, 147, 153.
Brancuti, di Cagli, Paolo Antonio, Conte, 37.
Brandão (Antonio), 73, 207, 208, 216.
Brandão (Diogo), 102, 103-4.
Brandão (Francisco), 62, 208.
Brandão (Hilario), 241.
Brandão (Julio), 327-8, 335.
Brandão (Maria), 137.
Brandão (Raul), 328.
Braunfels (Ludwig von), 65.
Bridges (Robert), 336.
Brito (Bernardo de), 18, 72, 139, 206-8, 215, 216, 251.
Brito (Duarte de), 104, 118, 124, 127.
Brito Aranha (Pedro Wenceslau de), 308.
Brito de Andrade (Balthasar de), 207.
Brito Pestana (Alvaro de), 100, 101, 127.
Brito Rebello (Jacinto Ignacio de), 112, 168.
Brochado (Luis), 341.
Brulé (Gace), 48.
Bruno *pseud. See* Pereira de Sampaio.
Buchanan (George), 106.
Bulhão Pato (Raimundo Antonio), 302-3.
Bunyan (John), 249.
Buonarroti (Michelangelo), 230.
Burgos (André de), 18, 203.
Bussinac (Peire de), 47.
Byron, George Gordon Noel, Lord, 183, 302.

C

Caamoões. *See* Camões.
Caballero (Fernán) *pseud.* [Cecilia Böhl de Faber], 316.

INDEX

Cabanillas (Ramón), 355.
Cabedo de Vasconcellos (José de), 109.
Cabral (Paulo Antonio), 278.
Cabral (Pedro Alvarez), 107.
Cacegas (Luis de), 242.
Caceres (Lourenço de), 191, 192.
Caiel *pseud.* See Pestana (Alice).
Cairel (Elias), 112.
Caldas (José de), 321.
Caldeira (Fernando Afonso Geraldes), 310.
Calderón de la Barca (Pedro), 129, 130, 249.
Calvo (Pedro), 244.
Camacho (Diogo), 256.
Camara (D. João Gonçalves Zarco da), 311, 326, 327.
Caminha (Antonio Lourenço), 147.
Caminha (João), 149, 150.
Camino (Alberto), 348–9.
Camões (Luis de), 14, 16, 20, 77, 130, 139, 147, 148, 149, 150, 152, 153, 155, 158, 166, 167, 174–86, 193, 197, 204, 206, 216, 217, 226, 229, 256, 258, 259, 260, 261, 272, 277, 278, 281, 338.
Campancho (Airas). See Carpancho.
Campos (Agostinho de), 231.
Campos (Claudia de), 324.
Campos Moreno (Diogode), 204.
Cancioneirinho de Trovas Antigas, 36, 37, 39.
Cancioneiro Colocci-Brancuti, 27, 36, 37, 38, 63, 66, 69, 70, 140.
Cancioneiro da Ajuda, 36, 37, 38, 39, 56, 61.
Cancioneiro da Vaticana, 13, 36, 37, 38, 50, 73, 96, 98, 125, 344.
Cancioneiro del Rei D. Dinis, 36, 37.
Cancioneiro de Resende. See *Cancioneiro Geral*.
Cancioneiro Gallego-Castelhano, 36, 67, 76, 77.
Cancioneiro Geral, 13, 33, 36, 79, 96–105, 118, 122, 123, 124, 125, 128, 129, 140, 141, 167, 184, 225, 256.
Cancionero de Baena, 36, 66, 77, 79, 96.
Cancionero General, 36, 98, 104.
Cancionero Musical. See Asenjo Barbieri.
Cancionero Popular Gallego, 36, 355–6.
Cantanhede, Conde de, 101.
Canzoniere Portoghese Colocci-Brancuti. See *Cancioneiro Colocci-Brancuti*.
Canzoniere Portoghese della Biblioteca Vaticana. See *Cancioneiro da Vaticana*.
Cardim (Antonio Francisco), 217.
Cardim (Fernam), 205.

Cardoso (João), 245.
Cardoso (Jorge), 71.
Carlos Magno, Verdadeira Historia do Imperador, 339.
Carneiro da Cunha (Alfredo), 336.
Carpancho (Airas), 29.
Carré Aldao (Eugenio), 357.
Cartagena (Alonso de), Bishop of Burgos, 91.
Cartas que os Padres . . . escreveram, 205.
Carvalho de Parada (Antonio), 266.
Casimiro (Augusto), 334.
Casquicio (Fernam), 77, 78.
Castanheda (Fernam Lopez de). See Lopez de Castanheda.
Castanheira, Conde de [*or* da], 141, 214.
Castanhoso (Miguel de), 196, 203.
Castelar (Emilio), 349.
Castello Branco (Camillo), Visconde de Corrêa Botelho, 109, 134, 187, 243, 256, 286, 295, 297–9, 304, 325, 332.
Castello Rodrigo, Marqueses de, 211.
Castiglione (Baldassare), 154.
Castilho (Antonio de), 203.
Castilho (Antonio Feliciano), Visconde de, 292, 299–300, 302, 304, 316.
Castilho (João de), 203.
Castilho (Julio), second Visconde de, 278, 304.
Castillejo (Cristobal de), 33.
Castro (Augusto de), 314.
Castro (Eugenio de), 336–7.
Castro (Inés de), 75, 84, 97, 165, 273, 282, 284, 304, 310, 312.
Castro (D. João de), 158, 187, 190, 199, 227–8, 243, 266.
Castro (D. João de), novelist, 321.
Castro (João Baptista de), 248.
Castro (Publia Hortensia de), 107.
Castro de Murguía (Rosalía de), 348, 349–50, 352, 353, 356.
Castro e Almeida (Virginia de), 325.
Castro Osorio (Anna de), 324–5.
Catherina, Queen, 120.
Catherine II, Empress of Russia, 286.
Cava, Poema da, 72.
Caxton (William), 60.
Ceita (João da), 17, 244–5.
Celestina, La, 65, 124, 159, 167, 169, 254, 262.
Ceo (Maria do) [Maria de Eça], 257.
Ceo (Violante do) [Violante Montesino], 35, 235, 256–7.
Cervantes (Miguel de), 78, 116, 130, 152, 233, 241, 262, 265, 284.
Cerveira (Afonso), 86.
Chagas (Antonio das), 221, 248–9, 261.

INDEX

Chamilly, Noël Bouton, Marquis de, 263, 264.
Chariño (Pai Gomez). See Gomez Chariño.
Charles V, Emperor, 121, 212, 215, 229.
Châtillon, Duc de, 233.
Chiado. See Ribeiro Chiado.
Child Rolim de Moura (Francisco), 257.
Chrisfal, Trovas de. See Crisfal.
Christina, Queen of Sweden, 268.
Chronica. See Cronica.
Cicero, 86, 87, 90, 91, 92, 94, 209, 214, 280.
Cid, Poema del, 23, 46, 63.
Claro (João), 59.
Claudian, 277.
Clenardus (Nicolaus), 106, 125, 215, 251.
Cleynarts (Nicholas). See Clenardus.
Clusius. See Écluse.
Codax (Martin), 29.
Coelho (Estevam), 30, 52.
Coelho (Francisco Adolpho), 15, 112, 231, 308, 347.
Coelho (Jorge), 180.
Coelho da Cunha (José), 336.
Coelho Rebello (Manuel), 163.
Coimbra (Leonardo de), 20.
Coincy (Gautier de), 43, 44.
Colocci (Angelo), 37, 39.
Colonna (Egidio), 66.
Colonna (Vittoria), 140, 230.
Conceição (Alexandre da), 330.
Conestaggio (Girolamo Franchi di), 210.
Congreve (William), 224.
Conquista de Ultramar, Gran, 339.
Consciencia (Manuel), 250.
Consiglieri Pedroso (Zophimo), 307, 347.
Cordeiro (Antonio), 138, 206.
Cordeiro (Luciano), 307.
Cornu (Jules), 59.
Corpancho (Airas). See Carpancho.
Corpancho (Manuel Nicolás), 29.
Corpus Illustrium Poetarum Lusitanorum, 18.
Coronica do Condestabre de Purtugal. See Cronica.
Corrêa (Gaspar), 14, 20, 88, 177, 194, 198–201, 226.
Corrêa (Jeronimo), 112.
Corrêa (Luis Franco), 186.
Corrêa de Oliveira (Antonio), 332, 337.
Corrêa Garção (Pedro Antonio Joaquim), 271–2.
Corrêa Pinto (Roberto), 85.

Correggio (Antonio Allegri da), 134.
Correia. See Corrêa.
Corte Imperial, 94, 113.
Corte Real (Jeronimo), 181, 187–8.
Cortesão (Jaime), 314, 342.
Costa (Antonio da), 286.
Costa (Bras da), 99.
Costa (Claudio Manuel da), 274, 279.
Costa (Diogo da), 163.
Costa (D. Francisco da), 239, 240.
Costa (Leonel da), 144.
Costa (Manuel da), 180.
Costa Lobo (Antonio de Sousa da Silva), 307, 312.
Costa Perestrello (Pedro da), 147–8.
Cota (Rodrigo), 23.
Coudel Môr, O. See Silveira (Fernam de).
Coutinho (Fernando de), 99.
Coutinho (D. Francisco), Conde de Redondo, 178, 220.
Coutinho (D. Gonçalo), 140, 206.
Couto (Diogo do), 138, 177, 178, 184, 190, 192, 195–8, 216, 218, 225, 254.
Couto Guerreiro (Miguel de), 285.
Craveiro (Tiburcio Antonio), 54.
Crisfal, Trovas de, 136–9.
Cristoforus, Dr., 82.
Cronica Breve do Archivo Nacional, 60.
Cronica da Conquista do Algarve, 61.
Cronica da Fundaçam do Mosteiro de S. Vicente, 61.
Cronica da Ordem dos Frades Menores, 60.
Cronica do Cardeal Rei D. Henrique, 210.
Cronica do Condestabre de Portugal, 84–5.
Cronica dos Vicentes. See Cronica da Fundaçam.
Cronica Troyana, 61.
Cronicas Breves, 60.
Cruz (Agostinho da), 145, 148.
Cruz (Bernardo da), 209.
Cruz (Gaspar da), 220.
Cunha (João Lourenço da), 31.
Cunha (José Anastasio da), 274.
Cunha (Nuno da), 161, 176, 199.
Cunha (D. Rodrigo da), 243.
Cunha (Tristão da), 97, 116.
Cunha Rivara (Joaquim Heliodoro da), 292.
Curros Enriquez (Manuel), 353–4, 355.
Curvo Semedo Torres Sequeira (Belchior Manuel), 278.

INDEX

D

Daniel (Samuel), 164.
Danse macabre, 123.
Dantas (Julio), 313.
Dante Alighieri, 19, 54, 123, 139, 146, 179, 188, 197, 257.
Danza de la Muerte, 123.
De Imitatione Christi, 240.
Delicado (Antonio), 346.
Demanda do Santo Graall, 63, 64, 67, 71.
Denis, King. *See* Dinis.
Denis (Jean Ferdinand), 19, 307.
Deslandes (Venancio), 231.
Desmond, Maurice, first Earl of, 289.
Destroyçam de Jerusalem. *See* Vespeseano, Estorea de.
Destruction de Jérusalem, 64.
Deus (João de). *See* Nogueira Ramos.
Dias (Epiphanio). *See* Silva Dias.
Dias Gomes (Francisco), 20, 21, 269, 285.
Diaz (Balthasar), 158-9, 289, 339.
Diaz (Bartholomeu), 98.
Diaz (Henrique), 218, 279.
Diaz (D. Lopo), 51.
Diaz (Nicolau), 215.
Diaz (Ruy), El Cid, 92.
Diaz de Landim (Gaspar), 88.
Dickens (Charles), 315.
Dinis, King, 13, 14, 28, 30, 37, 38, 39, 48, 51, 52, 53, 54-7, 58, 59, 60, 61, 67, 69, 70, 105, 140, 208, 294, 339.
Diniz, King. *See* Dinis.
Diniz (João), 335.
Diniz (Julio) *pseud*. *See* Gomes Coelho.
Diniz da Cruz e Silva (Antonio), 186, 273-4, 340.
Dioscorides, 226.
Ditos da Freira. *See* Gama (D. Joana da).
Döllinger (Johann Joseph Ignaz von), 295.
Dornellas (Afonso de), 307.
Dozy (Reinhart), 22.
Drake (Sir Francis), 150.
Dryden (John), 209.
Duarte, Infante [†1576], 150.
Duarte, Infante [†1540], brother of João III, 164, 167, 215.
Duarte, Infante, brother of João V, 307.
Duarte, King, 13, 38, 46, 55, 59, 63, 79, 81, 82, 83, 86, 87, 88, 90-2, 93, 124, 211.
Duarte (Afonso), 334.
Duarte de Almeida (Manuel), 335.
Dürer (Albrecht), 212.

E

Eanez (Rodrigo). *See* Yannez.
Eanez de Vasconcellos (D. Rodrigo), 54.
Eanez de Zurara (Gomez). *See* Zurara.
Eannez. *See* Eanez.
Eannez (Rodrigo). *See* Yannez.
Ébrard (Ayméric d'), 54.
Eça (Maria de). *See* Ceo (Maria do).
Eça de Queiroz (José Maria de), 97, 314, 316-18, 322, 325.
Eccos que o Clarim da Fama dá, 256.
Écluse (Charles de l'), 226.
Edward I, of England, 41.
Egas Moniz. *See* Moniz Coelho.
Elizabeth, Queen of England, 209.
Eloy, Lenda de Santo, 60.
Elysio (Filinto). *See* Nascimento.
Encarnação (Antonio da), 242.
Ennes (Antonio), 18, 310, 314.
Enzina (Juan del), 19, 109, 113, 122, 123, 124.
Erasmus (Desiderius), 130, 212, 215.
Ericeira, Conde da. *See* Meneses.
Esguio (Fernando), 29.
Esopo, Livro de, 60.
Espelho de Prefeyçam, 95.
Espelho de Christina. *See* Pisan (Christine de).
Esperança, Visconde de, 187.
Esperança (Manuel da), 243.
Espinola (Fradique), 247-8.
Espirito Santo (Antonio do). *See* Ribeiro Chiado.
Esplandian. *See* Sergas.
Espronceda (José de), 301.
Esquio (Fernando). *See* Esguio.
Estaço (Achilles), 106.
Estaço (Balthasar), 151.
Estaço (Gaspar), 151.
Este (João Baptista d'), 245.
Esteves Negrão (Manuel Nicolau), 273.
Esteves Pereira (Francisco Maria), 14, 60, 64, 84, 90, 308.
Estorea de Vespeseano. *See* Vespeseano.
Estrella (Antonio da), 162, 338.
Eufrosina, Vida de, 59.

F

Falcão (Cristovam de Sousa), 105, 137-9, 197.
Falcão de Resende (André), 21, 150-1.
Faria (Antonio de), 222.
Faria (Pedro de), 222.

INDEX 365

Faria e Sousa (Manuel de), 18, 20, 68, 130, 140, 145, 147, 153, 176, 180, 184, 187, 204, 209, 216, 224, 282.
Faria Severim (Manuel de), 215.
Feijó (Antonio Joaquim de Castro), 335.
Feijoo (José Sanchez), 347.
Felipe, Infante, 120.
Fénelon (François de), 285.
Fenix Renascida, 155, 256, 276.
Feo (Antonio), 17, 156, 244.
Ferdinand, King. *See* Fernando.
Fernandes Thomaz Pippa (Annibal), 308.
Fernandez (Alvaro), 217.
Fernandez (Antonio), 230.
Fernandez (Diogo) [xv c.], 92.
Fernandez (Diogo) [xv c. poet], 112.
Fernandez (Diogo) [xvi c.], 234.
Fernandez (Lucas), 124.
Fernandez (Roy), 30.
Fernandez Alemão (Valentim), 95.
Fernandez de Lucena (Vasco), 87, 88.
Fernandez Ferreira (Diogo), 89, 229.
Fernandez Galvão (Francisco), 244.
Fernandez Torneol (Nuno), 28, 31.
Fernandez Trancoso (Gonçalo), 231-2, 338.
Fernando, Infante [son of João I], 81, 89.
Fernando, Infante [son of King Manuel], 230.
Fernando, King Consort, 292, 293.
Fernando I, of Portugal, 84, 210.
Fernando III, of Castile, 40, 41, 51.
Ferrandez de Gerena (Garci), 78-9.
Ferreira (Antonio), 13, 67, 103, 145, 148-9, 165, 166, 272.
Ferreira (Carlos), 339.
Ferreira de Almeida (João), 338.
Ferreira de Azevedo (Antonio Xavier), 340.
Ferreira de Figueiroa (Diogo), 262.
Ferreira de Lacerda (Bernarda), 18, 257.
Ferreira de Vasconcellos (Jorge), 14, 16, 74, 101, 130, 155, 164, 166, 167-73, 232, 251, 338, 346.
Ferreira de Vera (Alvaro), 182.
Ferrer (Miguel), 234.
Ferrus (Pero), 66, 67.
Feuillet (Octave), 299.
Fialho de Almeida (José Valentim), 322, 326.
Ficalho, Francisco Manuel Carlos de Mello, third Conde de, 226, 308, 326.
Fielding (Henry), 255.
Figueira (Guilherme), 32.
Figueiredo (Antero de), 323.

Figueiredo (Antonio Candido de), 308.
Figueiredo (Fidelino de Sousa), 16, 308.
Figueiredo (Manuel de), 282, 290.
Fitzmaurice-Kelly (James), 16.
Flaubert (Gustave), 235, 319.
Flores e Branca Flor, Historia de, 65, 339, 340.
Florida. *See Relaçam Verdadeira dos trabalhos*.
Flos Sanctorum, 94, 225, 259.
Fonseca (Balthasar Luis da), 163.
Fonseca (João da), 249.
Fonseca Soares (Antonio da), 248.
Fontaines, Baron de, 233.
Forner (Juan Pablo), 281.
Fradique, Infante, 83.
Franco (Luis). *See* Corrêa (Luis Franco).
François I, 212.
Frederick III, Emperor, 93.
Freire (Antonio), 262.
Freire (Francisco José), 285.
Freire de Andrade (Jacinto), 256, 261, 266-7.
Froissart (Jean), 81, 83.
Fructuoso (Gaspar), 138, 206.
Furtado de Mendoza (Diego), 22.

G

Galaaz, O Livro de, 63.
Galen, 226.
Galhegos (Manuel de), 58, 74, 258.
Galvam (Antonio), 190, 191, 202-3, 219.
Galvam (Duarte), 88, 180, 202, 219.
Galvam (Francisco), 147-8.
Galvam de Andrade (Antonio), 17.
Gama (Arnaldo de Sousa Dantas da), 295.
Gama (D. Cristovam da), 203.
Gama (D. Estevam da), 196.
Gama (D. Joana da), 241.
Gama (José Basilio da), 279.
Gama (Leonarda Gil da). *See* Gloria (Maria Magdalena Euphemia da).
Gama (D. Vasco da), Conde de Vidigueira, 99, 107, 175, 190, 191, 192, 196, 200, 301, 312.
Gama Barros (Henrique), 307.
Gandavo. *See* Magalhães de Gandavo.
Garcia (Fernan), Esgaravunha, 52.
Garcia (Pero) de Burgos, 51.
Garcia de Castrogeriz (Johan), 66.
Garcia de Guilhade (D. Joan), 51.
Garcia de Mascarenhas (Bras), 259-60.
García Ferreiro (Alberto), 340, 354.
Garcia Peres (Domingo), 18, 151.
Garret (B.), Chariteo, 289.
Garrett. *See* Almeida Garrett.
Garrido (Luiz Guedes Coutinho), 308.

INDEX

Gautier (Judith), 335.
Gavaudan, 40.
Gavy de Mendonça (Agostinho de), 203.
Gayangos y Arce (Pascual de), 65.
Gibbs (James), 209.
Gil (Augusto), 336.
Gil y Carrasco (Enrique), 316.
Ginzo (Martin de), 29.
Giraldez (Afonso), 73.
Giraldi (Giambattista), 231.
Giraldo, Mestre, 17.
Glareanus (Henricus), 212.
Gloria (Maria Magdalena Euphemia da) [Leonarda Gil da Gama], 257.
Godinho (Cristovam), 238.
Godinho (Manuel), 221, 240, 254.
Goes (Damião de), 14, 15, 39, 83, 86, 88, 92, 113, 194, 202, 209, 211–14, 215, 265.
Goethe (Johann Wolfgang von), 290, 300, 333.
Goldsmith (Oliver), 277.
Gomes (João Baptista), 273.
Gomes Coelho (Joaquim Guilherme) [Julio Diniz], 314–16, 317, 324.
Gomes de Amorim (Francisco), 290, 301–2, 306, 309, 310.
Gomes de Brito (José Joaquim), 308.
Gomes de Carvalho (Theotonio), 273.
Gomes Leal (Antonio Duarte), 332–3.
Gomez (Simão), 341.
Gomez Chariño (Pai), 29–30.
Gomez de Briteiros (Rui), 46.
Gomez de Brito (Bernardo), 217.
Gomez de Moraes (Silvestre), 17.
Gonçalves Crespo (Antonio Candido), 324, 330–1.
Gonçalves Dias (Antonio), 331.
Gonçalves Lima (Augusto José), 300.
Gonçalves Vianna. *See* Gonçalvez Viana.
Gonçalvez (Ruy), 229.
Gonçalvez de Seabra (Fernan), 47, 48.
Gonçalvez Lobato (Balthasar), 234.
Gonçalvez Viana (Aniceto dos Reis), 18, 294, 308.
Góngora (Luis de), 74, 155, 258.
Gonta Collaço (Branca de), 336.
Gonzaga (Thomaz Antonio), 274, 279.
Gonzalez de Sanabria (Ferrant). *See* Gonçalvez de Seabra.
Gouvêa (André de), 106.
Gouvêa (Antonio de), 106, 206.
Gouveia. *See* Gouvêa.
Gower (John), 89, 90.
Gracián (Baltasar), 19, 154, 253.
Granada (Luis de), 243.

Grão Para, Bishop of. *See* S. Joseph Queiroz.
Grave (João), 321.
Gray (Thomas), 277.
Gregory, St., 90.
Grinalda, A, 300.
Guarda (Stevam), 51.
Guarda, Foros da, 17.
Guedes Teixeira (Fausto), 335.
Guerra Junqueiro (Abilio Manuel), 331–2.
Guilhade (Joan de), 28, 51, 339.
Guilherme (Manuel), 13.
Guimarães (Delfim), 136.
Gusmão (Alexandre de), 286.
Gusmão (Alexandre de), Jesuit, 249.

H

Halifax (John of), 227.
Hallam (Henry), 294.
Heine (Heinrich), 351.
Henrique, Cardinal, King, 106, 150, 164, 210, 214, 219, 227, 238, 250, 251, 311.
Henrique, Infante, 18, 86, 88, 89, 90, 92, 307.
Henriques (Guilherme J. C.), 214.
Henry VIII, of England, 212.
Henry the Navigator, Prince. *See* Henrique Infante.
Henry, of Burgundy, Count, 210, 271.
Henryson (Robert), 60.
Herberay des Essarts (Nicholas), 71.
Herculano de Carvalho e Araujo (Alexandre), 61, 87, 97, 127, 208, 243, 277, 285, 287, 292–5, 296, 303, 305, 315.
Herodotus, 226.
Herrera y Garrido (Francisca), 357.
Historia dos Cavalleiros da Mesa Redonda. *See Demanda do Santo Graall*.
Historia Tragico-Maritima, 196, 217–8.
Historia Tristani, 63.
Historias abreviadas do Testamento Velho, 59.
Hita, Archpriest of. *See* Ruiz.
Hollanda (Antonio de), 229.
Hollanda (Francisco de), 229–30, 237.
Homem (Pedro), 105.
Homer, 19, 143, 174, 180, 182, 183, 233, 277, 280, 281.
Horace, 72, 143, 148, 258, 272, 275, 277.
Horta. *See* Orta.
Hugo (Victor), 293, 306, 308, 310, 331, 332, 333

INDEX

Humboldt (Alexander von), 177.
Hurtado (Luis), 234.
Huysmans (J. K.), 333.

I

Ichoa (Martim), 89.
Idanha (Pedro de Alcaçova Carneiro), Conde de, 182.
Ignacio de Loyola, San, 353.
Isabel, Empress, 121.
Isabel, Infanta, 121.
Isabel, Queen Consort of Afonso V, 80, 95.
Isabel, Queen Consort of Dinis, 54, 60, 247.
Isabel, Queen of Spain, 127.
Isabel, Vida de Santa, 60.
Ivo (Pedro) *pseud. See* Lopes (Carlos).

J

Jardin (G. du). *See* Orta.
Jeanroy (Alfred), 29.
Jerome, St., 85.
Jesus (Francisco de). *See* Sá de Meneses (F. de).
Jesus (Raphael de), 208.
Jesus (Thomé de), 14, 20, 189, 237, 238-40.
Joana, Infanta, 215.
João I, 14, 68, 81, 82, 84, 89-90, 94, 110, 211.
João II, 88, 89, 93, 96, 100, 102, 103, 108, 125, 148, 221, 227, 246, 305, 312.
João III, 98, 103, 106, 107, 110, 117, 119, 132, 140, 141, 158, 167, 175, 189, 192, 193, 195, 208, 209, 211, 215, 226, 232, 233, 237, 296.
João IV, 216, 242, 244, 253, 259, 265, 267, 268, 286.
João V, 270.
João, Infante [xvi c.], 106, 143, 150, 151, 166, 168, 169, 176, 179.
João de Calais, Verdadeira Historia de, 339.
João Manuel (D.). *See* Manuel (D. João).
John, Prester, 219, 225.
Johnson (Samuel), 282.
Jorge, D., 221.
Jorge (Ricardo), 153.
José I, 276, 296.
Josep ab Arimatia, Livro de, 64.
Joséphine, Empress, 281.
Juan I, 78, 84.
Juan de Austria, Don, 188.
Juan Manuel, Infante Don, 91, 94.
Juana, Infanta, 151.
Juana, la Loca, Queen, 133.
Juromenha, João Antonio de Lemos Pereira de Lacerda, Visconde de, 176, 308.
Justinianus (Laurentius), 94.

K

Karr (Alphonse), 322.
Keats (John), 138, 281.

L

La Bruyère (Jean de), 91.
Lacerda (Augusto), 314.
Lafões, Duque de, 284.
Lafões, third Duque de, 311.
La Fontaine (Jean de), 117.
Lamartine (Alphonse de), 275, 277.
Lamas Carvajal (Valentín), 350-1.
Lamennais (Hugues Félicité Robert de), 292.
Lancastre (D. Lourenço de), 273.
Lang (Henry Roseman), 23, 24, 37, 76, 79, 123.
Lara (João Carlos de), 273.
Lasso de la Vega (Garci), 140, 141, 143, 147, 172, 181, 260.
Latino Coelho (José Maria), 201, 307.
Lavanha (João Baptista), 195, 218.
Lazarillo de Tormes, 115, 125, 160, 265.
Leam (Gaspar de), 241.
Lear, King, 62.
Leitão de Andrade (Miguel), 72, 73, 263.
Leite (Solidonio), 266.
Leite de Vasconcellos Cardoso Pereira de Melo (José), 15, 33, 34, 60, 308-9, 342, 346.
Leite Ferreira (Miguel), 67, 68, 69, 71, 148.
Lemos (Jorge de), 203.
Lemos (Julio de), 325.
Lemos Seixas Castello Branco (João de), 300, 301.
Lencastre (D. Philippa de), 80, 94.
Leo X, 97.
Leon (Luis de), 133, 236, 238, 239, 253, 258.
Leonor. *See* Lianor.
Leonor, successively Queen of Portugal and France, 233.
Leopardi (Giacomo), Count, 331, 351.
Lettres Portugaises. See Alcoforado.
Levi (Juda), 94.
Lianor, Empress, 93.
Lianor, Queen Consort of Duarte, 90.
Lianor, Queen Consort of João II, 93, 95, 111, 112, 113, 114, 119, 120, 229.
Lima (Alexandre Antonio de), 274.
Lima (D. Rodrigo de), 219.
Lima Pereira (Paulo de), 197.

INDEX

Linhares, second Conde de. *See* Noronha (D. Francisco de).
Linhares, Conde de [xvii c.], 252, 345.
Linhares, Violante, Condessa de, 239.
Lipsius (Justus), 255.
Lisboa (Antonio de), 162.
Lisboa (Cristovam de), 245.
Lisboa (João de), 227.
Livro da Noa, 60.
Livro das Aves, 90.
Livro das Heras, 60.
Livro de Josep ab Arimatia. See Josep.
Livro Velho, 61.
Livro Vermelho, 17.
Livros de Linhagens, 61.
Livy, 193, 194.
Lobato (Gervasio), 314.
Lobeira (Gonçalo de), 70.
Lobeira (Joan de), 68, 69, 70, 159.
Lobeira (Pedro de), 68, 70, 71.
Lobeira (Vasco de), 67, 68, 69, 70.
Lobo (Alvaro), 210.
Lobo (D. Francisco Alexandre), Bishop of Viseu, 285.
Lobo (Francisco Rodriguez). *See* Rodriguez Lobo.
Lollis (Cesare de), 45.
Lopes (Carlos), 325.
Lopes (David de Melo), 308.
Lopes (Francisco), 155, 162.
Lopes de Mendonça (Antonio Pedro), 297.
Lopes de Mendonça (Henrique), 312–13.
Lopes de Moura (Caetano), 37.
Lopes Vieira (Afonso), 337.
Lopez (Afonso), 160.
Lopez (Anrique), 159.
Lopez (Diogo), 84.
Lopez (Fernam), 14, 19, 61, 62, 68, 77, 81–5, 87, 88, 89, 97, 117, 180, 212, 255.
Lopez (Martinho), 81.
Lopez (Thomé), 204.
López Abente (Gonzalo), 355.
Lopez de Ayala (Pero), 66, 67.
Lopez de Bayan (D. Afonso), 53.
Lopez de Camões (Vasco), 77.
Lopez de Castanheda (Fernam), 180, 181, 190–1, 192, 193, 194, 197, 198, 200, 201, 206, 209.
Lopez de Sousa (Pero), 225.
Lopez de Ulhoa (D. Joan), 52.
Lopo, jogral, 29.
Losada (Benito), 352.
Loti (Pierre) *pseud.* [Julien Viaud], 89, 323.
Louis XI, 89.
Lourenço, jogral, 29.

Lucan, 99.
Lucena (João de), 16, 75, 243.
Lucena (Vasco Fernandez de). *See* Fernandez Lucena.
Lucian, 99.
Ludolph of Saxony. *See* Sachsen.
Lugris y Freire (Manuel), 357.
Luis, Infante, 106–7, 168, 170, 185, 191, 195, 209, 227, 228.
Luis (Nicolau), 284.
Lull (Ramón), 94.
Luther (Martin), 126, 212.
Luz (André da), 163.
Luz (Philipe da), 17, 244, 245.
Luz Soriano (Simão José da), 292.

M

Macedo (Anna de). *See* Sá e Macedo.
Macedo (José Agostinho de), 17, 99, 182, 183, 187, 224, 237, 244, 250, 277, 278, 279–82, 288.
Machado (Julio Cesar), 325.
Machado (Simão), 18, 161.
Machado de Azevedo (Manuel), 77, 142.
Macias, 76–77, 78, 98, 104, 132, 349, 350.
Magalhães (Fernam de), 219.
Magalhães (Luiz Cypriano Coelho de), 319.
Magalhães de Gandavo (Pedro de), 193, 204, 279.
Magalhães Lima (Jaime de), 319, 325.
Magalona, Verdadeira Historia da Princeza, 65, 339, 340.
Malheiro Dias (Carlos), 320.
Mallarmé (Stéphane), 86.
Malory (Sir Thomas), 85.
Mangancha (Diogo Afonso), 90.
Manrique (Gomez), 76, 100, 104.
Manrique (Jorge), 76, 100, 102, 104.
Mantua (Bento), 314.
Manuel I, 88, 89, 96, 101, 103, 107, 110, 111, 112, 115, 117, 118, 120, 121, 126, 129, 133, 145, 175, 192, 200, 201, 202, 208, 209, 211, 214, 221, 228, 295, 312.
Manuel, Infante, 116, 121.
Manuel (D. João), 98, 101.
Maranhão, Jornada do, 204.
Marcabrun, 39.
Marcos, Frei, 59.
Maria, Infanta, 15, 107, 110, 121, 193, 233.
Maria, Consort of King Manuel, 118.
Maria da Gloria, Queen, 288.
Maria Egipcia, Vida de, 59.
Marialva, second Conde de, 241.
Marialva, Marques de, 313.

INDEX

Mariana (Juan de), 208.
Marie Antoinette, Queen, 277.
Marinho de Azevedo (Luis), 18.
Mariz (Antonio de), 206.
Mariz (Pedro de), 206, 207.
Marot (Clément), 233.
Martelo Pauman (Evaristo), 354.
Martial, 125.
Martim Afonso, Méstre. *See* Afonso (Martim).
Martinez de Resende (Vasco), 13.
Martínez Salazar (Andrés), 61.
Martinho, de Alcobaça, 98.
Martorell (Pedro Juan), 65.
Martyres (Bartholomeu dos), 195, 242, 243, 342.
Marueil (Arnaut de), 35.
Mascarenhas (D. Fernando de), 267.
Mascarenhas (D. João de), 187.
Mascarenhas (D. Pedro de), 126.
Mattos (João Xavier de), 278–9.
Medina e Vasconcellos (Francisco de Paula), 186.
Meendinho, 29, 52.
Melanchthon (Philip), 212, 227.
Mello (Carlos de). *See* Ficalho.
Mello (D. Francisco Manuel de), 14, 74, 108, 164, 170, 205, 252–5, 261, 263, 267, 269, 338, 345.
Mello (Garcia de), 101.
Mello (Martim Afonso de), 82.
Mello Breyner (D. Theresa de), Condessa de Vimieiro, 273.
Mello Franco (Francisco de), 274.
Mena (Juan de), 77, 104, 197.
Menander, 130.
Mendes de Vasconcellos (Luis), 263.
Mendes dos Remedios (Joaquim), 16, 256.
Mendes Leal (José da Silva), 301.
Mendez (Afonso), 205.
Mendez (Manuel), 60.
Mendez de Sá (Gonçalo), 139.
Mendez de Vasconcellos (Diogo), 215.
Mendez Pinto (Fernam), 151, 203, 220, 221–5, 243.
Mendez Silva (Rodrigo), 255.
Mendoça (Jeronimo de), 210.
Mendoça (Joana de), 196.
Mendonça (Francisco de), 245.
Mendonça (Jeronimo). *See* Mendoça.
Mendonça Alves (Vasco de), 314.
Menéndez Pidal (Ramón), 73.
Menéndez y Pelayo (Marcelino), 19, 65, 83, 112, 133, 135, 140, 151, 168, 169, 233, 252, 278, 291, 339.
Meneses (D. Aleixo de), 206.
Meneses (D. Duarte de), 86.
Meneses (D. Fernando de), 177.

Meneses (D. Fernando de), second Conde da Ericeira, 266–7.
Meneses (D. Francisco Xavier de), fourth Conde da Ericeira, 270–1.
Meneses (D. Henrique de), 195.
Meneses (D. João de), 101, 103, 104.
Meneses (D. Luis de), third Conde da Ericeira, 69, 261, 267.
Meneses (D. Pedro de), 86.
Meneses (D. Sebastião Cesar de), 266.
Menina Fermosa, Trovas da, 341.
Menino (Pero), 17, 78.
Meogo (Pero), 29.
Merlim, 63.
Mesquita (Marcellino Antonio da Silva), 311–12.
Mesquita Perestrello (Manuel de), 217.
Meyer (Paul), 44.
Michaëlis (Gustav), 15.
Michaëlis de Vasconcellos (Carolina), 14, 15, 22, 23, 29, 31, 32, 33, 34, 37, 39, 50, 53, 62, 65, 75, 76, 80, 104, 112, 136, 180, 184, 308, 338, 342.
Michelangelo. *See* Buonarroti.
Mickle (William Julius), 14.
Miguel I, 280, 288.
Milá y Fontanals (Manuel), 41, 345.
Milton (John), 127, 184.
Miranda (Afonso de), 226.
Miranda (Jeronimo de), 226.
Miranda (Martim Afonso de), 252, 262.
Misterio de los Reyes Magos, 123.
Moleiro, Trovas do, 341.
Molière (Jean-Baptiste Poquelin), 116, 130, 164.
Molteni (Enrico Gasi), 38.
Monaci (Ernesto), 13, 37.
Moniz Barreto (Guilherme), 21.
Moniz Coelho (Egas), 72.
Mons (Nat de), 42.
Monsaraz, Antonio de Macedo Papança, Conde de, 335–6.
Montaigne (Michel de), 83, 106, 212.
Montalvão (Justino de), 328.
Montalvo. *See* Rodriguez de Montalvo.
Montebello, Marques de, 356.
Monteiro (Diogo), 246–7.
Montemayor (George de). *See* Montemôr (Jorge de).
Montemôr (Jorge de), 17, 151–2.
Montesino (Violante). *See* Ceo (Violante do).
Montesquieu (Charles Louis de Secondat), 182.
Montoia (Luis de), 239.
Montoro (Anton de), 23, 127.
Moogo (Pero). *See* Meogo.

INDEX

Moraes (Cristovam Alão de), 109, 286.
Moraes Cabral (Francisco de), 65, 76, 152, 161, 204, 232–4.
More (Sir Thomas), 254.
Moreira (Julio), 308.
Moreira Camello (Antonio), 338.
Moreira de Carvalho (Jeronimo), 339.
Moreno (Bento) *pseud.* *See* Teixeira de Queiroz.
Moura (Miguel de), 210.
Mousinho de Quevedo (Vasco), 261.
Murguía (Manuel de), 349.

N

Napier (Sir William), 255.
Napoleon I, 281.
Napoleon III, 340.
Nascimento (Francisco Manuel do), 263, 274–5, 290, 304, 338, 344.
Navagero (Andrea), 351.
Newton (Sir Isaac), 281.
Niebuhr (Barthold Georg), 294.
No figueiral figueiredo, 72.
Nobiliario do Collegio dos Nobres, 61.
Nobiliario do Conde. *See* Pedro Afonso, Conde de Barcellos.
Nobre (Antonio), 332, 334.
Nobrega, Padre, 45.
Nogueira Ramos (João de Deus), 249, 250, 329–30, 338.
Noriega Varela (Antonio), 355.
Noronha (D. Anna de), 242.
Noronha (D. Antonio de), 175, 177, 179.
Noronha (D. Francisco de), second Conde de Linhares, 175, 232, 239.
Noronha (D. Lianor de), 107.
Noronha (D. Thomas de), 256.
Novaes (Francisco Xavier de), 112, 302.
Nun' Alvarez. *See* Alvarez Pereira (Nuno).
Nun de Allariz (Alfredo) *pseud.*, 355.
Nunes (Claudio José), 331.
Nunes (José Joaquim), 26, 60, 308.
Nunes Ribeiro Sanches (Antonio), 286.
Nunez (Airas), 23, 31, 47, 52–3.
Nunez (João), 210.
Nunez (Pedro), 18, 107, 226–7, 251.
Nunez (Philipe), 230.
Nunez da Silva (Manuel), 231.
Nunez de Leam (Duarte), 39, 55, 56, 68, 210–11, 252.
Nuñez del Arce (Gaspar Esteban), 295.
Nuñez González (Manuel), 354, 355.

O

Oeynhausen, Count of, 276.
Olanda (Francisco de). *See* Hollanda.
Olivares, Conde-Duque de, 252.
Oliveira (Fernam de), 109, 220, 227.
Oliveira (Francisco Xavier de), Cavalheiro de Oliveira, 74, 285–6.
Oliveira Marreca (Antonio de), 295.
Oliveira Martins (Pedro Joaquim de), 305–6, 322.
Orta (Garcia da), 178, 225–6, 308.
Orta (Jorge da), 225.
Ortigão (Ramalho). *See* Ramalho Ortigão.
Osborne (Dorothy), 20.
Osmia. *See* Mello Breyner.
Osorio (Luiz), 335.
Osorio da Fonseca (Jeronimo), 18, 209, 224, 228, 263.
Ossian, 301.
Ovid, 85.

P

Pacheco (João), 248.
Pacheco Pereira (Duarte), 191, 227.
Paez (Balthasar), 245.
Paez (D. Maria), 22.
Paez (Pedro), 205.
Paganino (Rodrigo), 325.
Paiva (Isabel de), 239.
Paiva de Andrade (Diogo de) [xvi c.], 239, 244.
Paiva de Andrade (Diogo de) [xvii c.], 215, 239, 253.
Palmeirim (Luiz Augusto), 300–1.
Palmeirim de Inglaterra. *See* Moraes (F. de).
Palmerín de Oliva, 234.
Pardo Bazán (Emilia), Condesa de, 356.
Patmore (Coventry), 336.
Pato Moniz (Nuno Alvares). *See* Pereira Pato Moniz.
Patricio (Antonio), 328.
Paixam de Jesu Christo, A, 94, 95.
Paul III, Pope, 212, 219.
Paulo (Marco). *See* Polo.
Payne (Robert), 90.
Pedro I, of Portugal, 80, 84, 312.
Pedro II, of Portugal, 268, 288.
Pedro V, of Portugal, 293.
Pedro Afonso, Conde de Barcellos, 38, 57, 61–2.
Pedro, Duque de Coimbra, 71, 79, 80, 86, 88, 90, 92, 94, 100.
Pedro, O Condestavel D., 38, 77, 79–80, 86, 92, 95, 100.
Pedro, King of Aragon. *See* Pedro, O Condestavel D.

INDEX

Pedro, Tratado do Infante D., 340.
Pelagia, Vida de Santa, 60.
Penha Fortuna (João de Oliveira), 330.
Pereda (José María de), 318.
Pereira (Antonio Nunalvarez), 141.
Pereira (Aureliano J.), 354.
Pereira (Nuno), 98, 102, 143.
Pereira Brandão (Luis), 188–9.
Pereira de Castro (Gabriel), 258–9.
Pereira de Castro (Luis), 258.
Pereira de Figueiredo (Antonio), 338.
Pereira de Novaes (Manuel), 20.
Pereira de Sampaio (José) [Bruno], 308.
Pereira Pato Moniz (Nuno Alvarez), 187.
Pereira Pinheiro (Bernardino), 295–6.
Pereira Teixeira de Vasconcellos (Joaquim). *See* Teixeira de Pascoaes.
Pérez Ballesteros (José), 356.
Pérez Galdós (Benito), 298.
Pérez Placer (Heraclio), 357.
Perez de Camões (Vasco), 77, 78, 174.
Perez de Oliva (Hernan), 165.
Pestana (Alice), 324.
Petrarca (Francesco), 139, 146, 147, 148, 152, 161, 181, 185, 186, 197, 237, 280, 281.
Philip II, of Spain, 146, 151, 195, 216, 223, 224, 230, 236, 237, 238, 250, 263.
Philip III, of Spain, 155.
Philip IV, of Spain, 216, 243.
Philippa, Queen Consort of João I, 84, 85, 89, 305.
Piamonte (Nicolas), 339.
Picaud (Aimeric), 25.
Pierres de Provence, 65.
Pimenta (Agostinho). *See* Cruz (Agostinho da).
Pimentel (Manuel), 228.
Pina (Fernam de), 87.
Pina (Ruy de), 87–9, 97, 110, 125, 180.
Pindella (Bernardo de). *See* Arnoso.
Pinheiro (D. Antonio), 214, 244.
Pinheiro (Bernardino). *See* Pereira Pinheiro.
Pinheiro (Bernardo). *See* Arnoso.
Pinheiro Chagas (Manuel), 304, 306–7.
Pinheiro da Veiga (Thomé), 265.
Pinto (Heitor), 14, 16, 101, 230, 236–7, 238.
Pinto (João Lourenço), 318–19.
Pinto (Jorge), 159.
Pinto Ribeiro (João), 265.
Pintos (Juan Manuel), 348.
Pires (Antonio Thomaz), 69, 308, 342.
Pires de Rebello (Gaspar), 262.
Pirez Lobeira (Joan). *See* Lobeira (Joan de).

Pisan (Christine de), 85, 95.
Pisano (Mattheus de), 85.
Pius IV, Pope, 193.
Platir, 234.
Plato, 119, 237.
Plautus, 108, 130, 164, 167.
Pliny, 226.
Poema da Perda de Espanha. *See* Cava.
Poema del Cid. *See* Cid.
Poetica, 48, 49, 58, 66.
Poitou, Guillaume, Comte de, 39.
Poliziano (Angelo [Ambrogini]), 103, 139, 141.
Polo (Marco), 95.
Pombal, Sebastião José de Carvalho e Mello, Marques de, 272, 273, 276, 291, 307.
Ponce (Bartolomé), 151.
Pondal y Abente (Eduardo), 352–3, 355.
Ponte (Pero da), 28, 51.
Pope (Alexander), 50, 209, 274, 277.
Portela (Severo), 328.
Porto Carreiro (Lope de), 78.
Portugal (D. Anrique de), 103.
Portugal (D. Francisco de) [xvi c.], 203.
Portugal (D. Francisco de) [xvii c.], 18, 70, 129, 258.
Portugal (D. Francisco de), Conde de Vimioso, 100, 103–4, 122, 126, 145, 150.
Portugal (D. João de), 241, 242.
Portugal (D. Manuel de), 145, 180, 346.
Portugaliae Monumenta Historica. *See* Herculano (Alexandre).
Posada y Pereira (José María), 348.
Potter (Maria), 315.
Potter (Thomas), 315.
Poyares (Pedro de), 109.
Prado (Xavier), 355.
Prazeres (João dos), 269.
Presentaçam (Cosme da), 239.
Prestage (Edgar), 14, 15, 214, 252, 308.
Prestes (Antonio), 19, 160–1, 166.
Primaleon, 119, 234.
Primor e honra da vida soldadesca, 262.
Ptolemy, 193.
Purificaçam (Antonio da), 18.
Purser (William Edward), 233.

Q

Queimado (Roy), 52.
Quental (Anthero Tarquinio de), 304, 328–9.

INDEX

Quevedo y Villegas (Francisco Gomez de), 169, 252, 253, 255.
Quinet (Edgar), 19.
Quintilian, 247.
Quita (Domingos dos Reis), 272–3.

R

Rabelais (François), 321.
Rabello (Gabriel de), 203.
Racine (Jean), 182.
Raleigh (Sir Walter), 228.
Ramalho Ortigão (José Duarte), 304, 318, 321–2.
Ramos Coelho (José), 307.
Ramusio (Giovanni Battista), 204.
Rebello da Silva (Luiz Augusto), 296.
Redondo, Conde de. *See* Coutinho (D. Francisco).
Regras e Cautelas, 241.
Relaçam verdadeira dos trabalhos, &c., 203.
Renan (Ernest), 240.
Resende (Garcia de), 75, 88, 89, 96–8, 99, 100, 110, 113, 123, 124, 127, 140, 150, 199.
Resende (Lucio André de), 13, 39, 130, 150, 180, 206, 215, 216.
Revista de Historia, 308.
Revista Lusitana, 309, 347.
Rey Soto (Antonio), 355.
Ribalta (Aurelio), 356–7.
Ribeira Grande, Conde da, 311.
Ribeiro (Bernardim), 14, 19, 105, 132–9, 141, 152, 154, 291, 300.
Ribeiro (Jeronimo), 161.
Ribeiro (João), 204.
Ribeiro (João Pedro), 292.
Ribeiro (Mattheus de), 261.
Ribeiro Chiado (Antonio), 157–8, 161.
Ribeiro de Macedo (Duarte), 265–6.
Ribeiro de Sousa (Salvador), 203.
Ribeiro dos Santos (Antonio), 285.
Ribeiro Ferreira (Thomaz Antonio), 302.
Ribeiro Sanches (Antonio Nunes). *See* Nunes Ribeiro Sanches.
Ribeiro Soarez (Jeronimo). *See* Ribeiro (Jeronimo).
Richardson (Samuel), 170.
Riquier (Guiraut), 42, 55.
Roberto, Verdadeira Historia do Grande, 339.
Rocha Martins (Francisco de), 321.
Rodrigues (José Maria), 180.
Rodrigues Cordeiro (Antonio Xavier), 300.
Rodriguez (Fernan), 78.
Rodriguez (Gonzalo), Archdeacon of Almazan, 78.
Rodriguez (Gonzalo), Archdeacon of Toro, 78, 123.
Rodriguez (Melicia), 110.
Rodriguez Azinheiro (Cristovam), 211.
Rodriguez de Calheiros (Fernan), 52.
Rodriguez de Escobar (Gonçalo), 78.
Rodriguez de la Cámara (Juan), 63, 77, 104, 132.
Rodriguez de Montalvo (Garci), 65, 66, 67, 69, 119.
Rodriguez de Sá e Meneses (João), 103.
Rodriguez de Sousa (Gonçalo), 78.
Rodriguez del Padrón (Juan). *See* Rodriguez de la Cámara.
Rodríguez González (Eladio), 354–5.
Rodriguez Leitão (Manuel), 266.
Rodriguez Lobo (Francisco), 74, 153–5, 170, 185, 232.
Rodriguez Lobo Soropita (Fernam), 229, 345.
Rodriguez Silveira (Francisco), 229, 307.
Roiz. *See* Rodriguez.
Roland, Chanson de, 53.
Rolim de Moura. *See* Child Rolim.
Romances, 74–6, 124, 161, 172.
Romero (Sylvio), 17.
Roquette (José Ignacio), 91.
Rousseau (Jean-Jacques), 264.
Rucellai (Giovanni), 140.
Rudel (Jaufre), 47.
Rueda (Lope de), 112, 130.
Ruiz (Juan), Archpriest of Hita, 23, 38, 53, 90, 113, 124, 125, 339, 356.
Ruiz de Toro (Alvar), 78.

S

Sá (Antonio de), 269.
Sá (Diogo de), 228.
Sá (Gonçalo de), 143.
Sá (Mem de), 143.
Sá de Meneses (Francisco de), epic poet, 260.
Sá de Meneses (Francisco de), Conde de Mattosinhos, 13, 150, 260.
Sá de Miranda (Francisco de), 13, 19, 39, 53, 77, 104, 105, 117, 120, 138, 139–45, 146, 149, 164, 165, 166, 174, 176, 206, 260, 263, 276.
Sá e Macedo (Anna de), 174, 179.
Sá Sottomaior (Eloi de), 153.
Sabugal, Conde de, 256.
Sabugosa (Antonio Maria José de Mello Silva Cesar e Meneses), Conde de, 121, 158, 324.
Sacchetti (Franco), 231.
Sachsen (Ludolph von), 90, 95.

INDEX

Sacramental. *See* Sanchez de Vercial.
Sacro Bosco (Joannes de). *See* Halifax (John of).
Sadoletto (Jacopo), Cardinal, 212.
Sainte-Beuve (Charles-Augustin), 91, 321.
Saint-More (Benoît de), 61.
Saint Victor (Adam de), 24.
San Pedro (Diego de), 124, 132.
Sanches de Baena Farinha Augusto Romano, Visconde, 111.
Sanchez (D. Afonso), 30, 57.
Sanchez (Francisco), 20.
Sanchez de Badajoz (Garci), 104.
Sanchez de Vercial (Clemente), 95.
Sancho I, of Portugal, 22, 27, 34, 39, 87, 122.
Sancho II, of Portugal, 17, 53, 296.
Sannazzaro (Jacopo), 140, 152.
Santa Catharina (Lucas de), 152, 242, 271.
Santa Maria (Francisco de), 269.
Santa Rita (Guilherme de), 335.
Santa Rita Durão (José de), 279.
Santa Rosa de Viterbo (Joaquim de), 285.
Santarem (Manuel Francisco de Barros e Sousa de Mesquita Leitão e Carvalhosa), Visconde de, 292.
Santarem, Foros de, 17.
Santillana, Iñigo Lopez de Mendoza, Marqués de, 22, 32, 38, 41, 48, 49, 77, 79, 80, 104.
Santo Antonio (Pedro de), 247.
Santo Antonio (Sebastião de), 280.
Santo Estevam (Gomez de), 340.
Santos (João dos), 220.
Santos (Manuel dos), 208.
Santos e Silva (Thomaz Antonio de), 187.
S. Bernardino (Gaspar de), 221.
S. Boaventura (Fortunato de), 285.
S. Joseph Queiroz (D. João de), 286.
S. Luis (D. Francisco de), Cardinal Saraiva, 285.
Saraiva, Cardinal. *See* S. Luis.
Sarmento (Augusto Cesar Rodrigues), 325.
Sarmento (Francisco de Jesus Maria), 338.
Sarmiento (Martín), 347, 356.
Savoy, Duke of, 120, 133.
Schwalbach Lucci (Eduardo), 314.
Scott (Sir Walter), 293.
Sebastian, King, 146, 150, 168, 179, 181, 187, 188, 209, 210, 226, 227, 239, 241, 247, 261, 263, 307, 340, 341.
Semmedo (Alvaro), 204.
Semmedo (Curvo). *See* Curvo Semedo.

Seneca, 92, 94, 161, 280.
Senna Freitas (Joaquim de), 322.
Sepulveda (D. Lianor de). *See* Sousa (D. Lianor de).
Sergas de Esplandian, Las, 65, 68.
Serpa Pimentel (José Freire de), 300.
Serrão de Castro (Antonio), 256.
Servando (Joan), 29.
Severim de Faria (Manuel), 107, 180, 184, 192, 193, 197, 215–16, 245.
Sevilha (Pedro Amigo de). *See* Amigo.
Shakespeare (William), 19, 108, 118, 129, 130, 160, 164.
Sigea (Angela), 107.
Sigea (Luisa), 107.
Siglar (Pierres de), 43.
Silius Italicus, 41.
Silva (Antonio José da), 282–4.
Silva (Innocencio Francisco da), 61, 148, 163, 192, 193, 220, 237, 308.
Silva (Nicolau Luis da). *See* Luis (Nicolau).
Silva Dias (Augusto Epiphanio da), 308.
Silva Gayo (Manuel da), 320.
Silva Mascarenhas (André da), 260.
Silva Pinto (Manuel José da), 322.
Silva Souto-Maior (Caetano José da), 306.
Silveira (Fernam da) [†1489], 101.
Silveira (Fernam da), O Coudel Môr, 100–1, 102.
Silveira (Franciso Rodriguez). *See* Rodriguez Silveira.
Silveira (Jorge da), 102.
Silveira da Motta (Francisco), 322.
Simões Dias (José), 330.
Soares de Brito (João), 52, 68, 182, 207, 224, 258.
Soares de Passos (Antonio Augusto), 293, 301.
Soarez (Martin), 52.
Soarez Coelho (D. Joan), 52.
Soarez de Paiva (D. Joan), 48, 76.
Soarez de Sousa (Gabriel), 205.
Soarez de Taveiroos (Pai), 22.
Solá (Jaime), 356.
Sophocles, 165.
Soropita. *See* Rodriguez Lobo Soropita.
Soto (Hernando de), 203.
Sotomaior (Luis de), 130.
Sousa (D. Antonio Caetano de), 284.
Sousa (Diogo de), 256.
Sousa (Francisco de) [xvi c.], 98, 105.
Sousa (Francisco de) [xvii c.], 244.
Sousa (D. Lianor de), 188, 217.
Sousa (Luis de), 14, 16, 203, 209, 215, 241–3, 269, 291, 298.

INDEX

Sousa (Manuel Caetano de), 280.
Sousa (Martim Afonso de), 225, 227.
Sousa (Philippa de), 150.
Sousa (Rui de), 122.
Sousa Costa (Alberto de), 328.
Sousa Coutinho (Lopo de), 196, 203.
Sousa Coutinho (Manuel de). See Sousa (Luis de).
Sousa de Macedo (Antonio), 56, 68, 74, 130, 209, 224, 258, 260–1.
Sousa Falcão (Cristovam de). See Falcão.
Sousa Farinha (Bento José de), 244.
Sousa Monteiro (José de), 311.
Sousa Moraes (Wenceslau José de), 322–3.
Sousa Sepulveda (Manuel de), 187, 196, 217.
Sousa Viterbo (Francisco Marques de), 13, 307.
Southey (Robert), 15, 19, 282.
Souto-Maior (Caetano José da Silva). See Silva Souto-Maior.
Souto Maior (Eloi de Sá). See Sá Sottomaior.
Souvestre (Émile), 299.
Spinoza (B.), 20.
Stanley of Alderney, Lord, 315.
Storck (Wilhelm), 174, 176, 178, 329.
Straparola (Giovanni Francesco), 231.
Stuart (Charles), Lord Stuart of Rothesay, 37.
Sylvia de Lisardo, 139.

T

Tacitus, 266.
Tancos (Hermenegildo de), 90.
Tasso (Bernardo), 71, 181.
Tasso (Torquato), 146, 180, 181, 280.
Tavares (Manuel), 110.
Tavares Zagalo (Joana), 133.
Teive (Diogo de), 106.
Teixeira de Pascoaes (Joaquim), 333–4.
Teixeira de Quieroz (Francisco), 319–20, 325.
Teixeira Gomes (Manuel), 323.
Tellez (Balthasar), 204–5.
Tellez (Lianor), Queen Consort of Fernando I, 84.
Tellez (Maria), 84.
Tellez de Meneses (Aires), 148.
Tello, Vida de D., 60.
Tennyson (Alfred), Lord, 64, 301.
Tenreiro (Antonio), 220.
Terence, 130, 164.
Testament de Pathelin, 123.
Theocritus, 272.

Theodora, Verdadeira Historia da Donzella, 339.
Theotocopuli (Domenico), El Greco, 114, 282.
Thierry (Augustin), 294.
Thomas (Henry), 65.
Thomas Aquinas, St., 86, 90, 92, 94.
Thomson (James), 277.
Tilly (John), 204.
Timoneda (Juan de), 231.
Tinherabos nam tinherabos, 72.
Tirant lo Blanch, 65.
Tolentino de Almeida (Nicolau), 272, 274, 276.
Tolstoi (Leo), Count, 333.
Tolomei (Lattanzio), 140, 230.
Torcy (Claude Blosset de), 233.
Toro, Archdeacon of. See Rodriguez (Gonzalo).
Torres (Alvaro de), 241.
Torres (Domingos Maximiano), 278.
Torres Naharro (Bartolomé de), 124.
Trancoso (Gonçalo Fernandez). See Fernandez Trancoso.
Trindade (Adeodato da), 196, 197.
Trindade Coelho (José Francisco de), 327.
Trissino (Giangiorgio), 165.
Tristam, O Livro de, 63.
Tristan, 65, 69, 70.
Trovador, O, 300.
Trovador, O Novo, 300.
Trueba (Antonio de), 302, 303.
Tundalo, Visão de, 59.

U

Usque (Abraham ben), 246.
Usque (Samuel), 245–6.

V

Vaamonde (Florencio), 357.
Valcacer. See Valcarcel.
Valcarcel (Pedro de), 78.
Valdés (Juan de), 65.
Valente (Afonso), 112.
Valera (Juan), 19.
Valla (Lorenzo), 180.
Valle Inclán (Ramón María del), 327, 356.
Van Zeller (Francisco), 169.
Vaqueiras (Raimbaut de), 41.
Varnhagen (Francisco Adolpho de), 37, 133, 205, 206.
Vasconcellos (Antonio de), 39, 259.
Vasconcellos (Henrique de), 328.
Vasconcellos (Joaquim de), 15, 214, 230.
Vasconcellos (Jorge de), 167.

INDEX

Vasconcellos (Jorge Ferreira de). See Ferreira.
Vasconcellos (Simão de), 267.
Vaz (Francisco), de Guimarães, 161-2.
Vaz (Joana), 107.
Vaz da Gama (Guiomar), 174.
Vaz de Camões (Luis). See Camões.
Vaz de Camões (Simão), 174.
Vaz de Carvalho (Maria Amalia), 324.
Vazquez (Francisco), 234.
Veer (Pero de), 29.
Vega (Garci Lasso de la). See Lasso de la Vega.
Vega Carpio (Lope Felix de), 76, 129, 130, 147, 153, 169, 181, 183, 258.
Veiga (Manuel da), 340.
Veiga (Thomas da), 17, 244, 245.
Veiga Tagarro (Manuel da), 258.
Velázquez (Diego), 333.
Velez de Guevara (Luis), 284.
Velez de Guevara (Pero), 79.
Velho (Alvaro), 190.
Verba (João), 92.
Verde (José Joaquim Cesario), 330.
Vernier (P.), 226.
Verney (Luis Antonio), 285.
Veronese (Paolo), 182.
Vespasian, Emperor, 64.
Vespeseano, Estorea de, 64.
Vespesiano, Estoria del noble, 64.
Vicente (Belchior), 110.
Vicente (Gil), 13, 16, 19, 31, 32, 33, 34, 35, 62, 74, 75, 97, 102, 105, 106-31, 132, 133, 138, 139, 141, 156, 157, 158, 159, 160, 162, 163, 164, 166, 167, 178, 235, 271, 291, 311, 338, 342, 344, 345.
Vicente (Luis), 109.
Vicente (Luis), son of Gil Vicente, 110, 168.
Vicente (Martim), 109.
Vicente (Paula), 110.
Vicente de Almeida (Gil), 162.
Vicentes, Cronica dos. See *Cronica da Fundaçam.*
Vieira (Antonio), 14, 16, 156, 190, 245, 248, 249, 261, 265, 267-9, 307.
Vieira (Nicolao), 59.
Vieira da Costa (J.), 321.
Vieira Ravasco (Cristovam), 267.
Vilhena (D. Joana de), 145.
Vilhena (D. Magdalena de), 241, 242.

Vilhena (D. Philippa de), Condessa de Athouguia, 291.
Villa-Moura, Visconde de, 328.
Villa Nova, Condessa de, 253, 286.
Villani (Giovanni), 83.
Villareal, Fernando, Marques de, 107.
Villas-Boas (D. Manuel do Cenaculo), Bishop of Beja, 285.
Villena (D. Enrique de), 77.
Vimieiro, Counts of, 71.
Vimieiro, fourth Conde de, 273.
Vimioso, first Conde de [*or* do]. See Portugal (D. Francisco de).
Vimioso, third Conde de, 242.
Virgil, 174, 180, 181, 182, 183, 257, 272.
Visão de Tundalo. See *Tundalo.*
Viseu, Diogo, Duke of, 102.
Viseu, Henry, Duke of. See Henrique, Infante.
Visio Tundali, 59.
Vita Christi. See Sachsen (Ludolph von).
Vives (Juan Luis), 65, 212, 340.
Voltaire (François Arouet), 179, 182, 274.
Vyvyães (Pero), 52.

W

Wieland (Christoph Martin), 277.
Wyche (Sir Peter), 266.

X

Xavier, St. Francis, 190, 223, 225, 243.
Xavier de Mattos. See Mattos.
Xavier de Novaes. See Novaes.
Xenophon, 85.
Ximenez de Urrea (Geronimo), 262.

Y

Yannez (Rodrigo), 73.
Ychoa (João de), 89.

Z

Zamora (Gil de), 42.
Zola (Émile), 299.
Zorro (Joan), 29, 31, 53.
Zurara (Gomez Eanez de), 14, 15, 68, 69, 81, 82, 85-7, 88, 201.

PRINTED IN ENGLAND
AT THE OXFORD UNIVERSITY PRESS